GIMP: The Official Handbook

The Gimp User's Manual version 1.0.1

Karin Kylander & Olof S. Kylander

Gimp: The Official Handbook

Limits Of Liability And Disclaimer Of Warranty

Trademarks

The Coriolis Group, LLC
14455 N. Hayden Road, Suite 220
Scottsdale, Arizona 85260

480/483-0192
FAX 480/483-0193
http://www.coriolis.com

Library of Congress Cataloging-in-Publication Data
Kylander, Olof.
GIMP: The Official Handbook by Olof and Karin Kylander.
p. cm.
ISBN 1-57610-520-2
1. Computer graphics. 2. GIMP (computer file) I. Kylander, Karin. II. Title.
T385.K866 1999
006.6'869--dc21
99-38515
CIP

Printed in the United States of America
10 9 8 7 6 5 4 3 2 1

President, CEO
Keith Weiskamp

Publisher
Steve Sayre

Acquisitions Editor
Mariann Hansen Barsolo

Marketing Specialist
Beth Kohler

Project Editor
Toni Zuccarini

Production Coordinators
Jon Gabriel
April Nielsen

Production Artist
Christine Foley

Cover Design
Jody Winkler

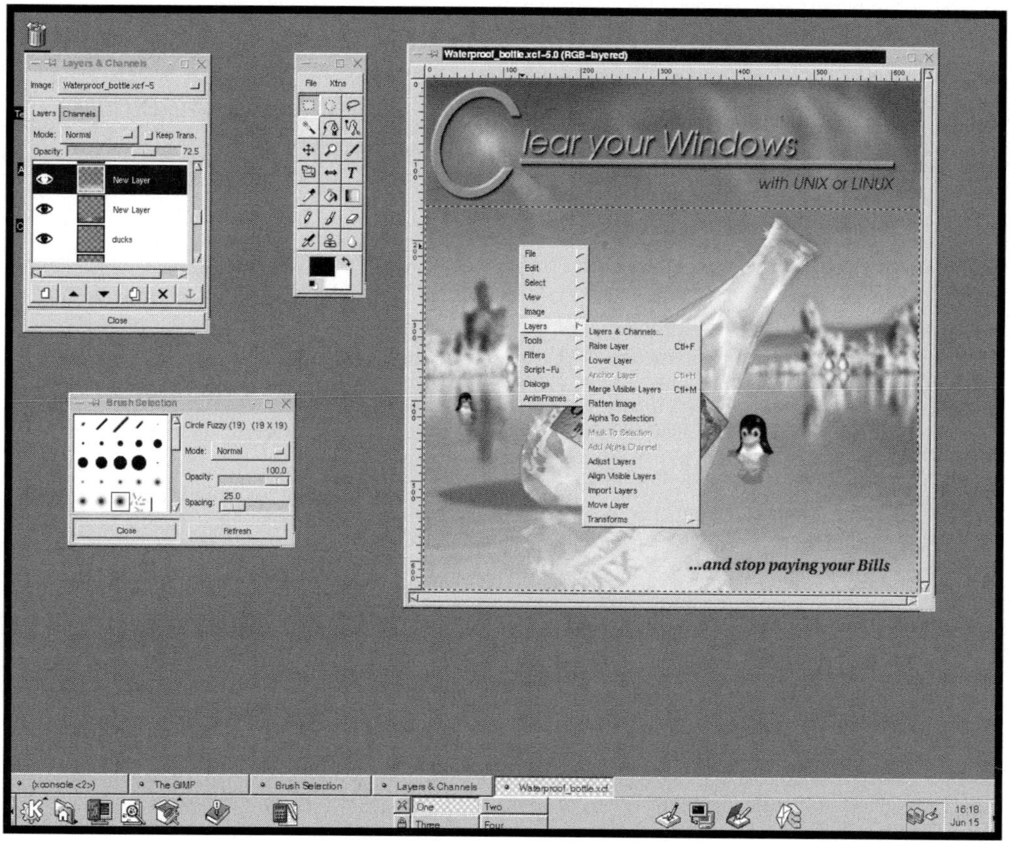
Layers & Channels
Image: Waterproof_bottle.xcf-5
Layers
Channels
Mode: Normal
Keep Trans.
Opacity: 72.5
New Layer
New Layer
ducks
Close
File
Xtns
Waterproof_bottle.xcf-5.0 (RGB-layered)
Clear your Windows
with UNIX or LINUX
...and stop paying your Bills
File
Edit
Select
View
Image
Layers
Tools
Filters
Script-Fu
Dialogs
AnimFrames
Layers & Channels...
Raise Layer Ctl+F
Lower Layer
Anchor Layer Ctl+H
Merge Visible Layers Ctl+M
Flatten Image
Alpha To Selection
Mask To Selection
Add Alpha Channel
Adjust Layers
Align Visible Layers
Import Layers
Move Layer
Transforms
Brush Selection
Circle Fuzzy (19) (19 X 19)
Mode: Normal
Opacity: 100.0
Spacing: 25.0
Close
Refresh
(xconsole <2>)
The GIMP
Brush Selection
Layers & Channels
Waterproof_bottle.xcf
One
Two
Three
Four
16:18
Jun 15

TABLE OF CONTENTS

DIGITAL design

Frozenriver

About This Book

Authors

Karin Kylander

Karin is a designer and illustrator, and also an architect with a Master's degree in Architecture from the Chalmers University of Technology. She has been working with graphic design and art since 1985. Computer aided design caught her interest in the late 1980s. At first, she worked with Macs and PCs using programs like Photoshop, PageMaker, Corel DRAW and Illustrator. In 1996, she entered the UNIX arena, and in 1997, she started using Gimp for image manipulation and graphic design. She now uses Gimp on a daily basis.

Most of Karin's work focuses on publications, posters and exhibition displays. If you'd like to see samples of her work, you have only to leaf through the Gallery chapter in this book.

Olof S. Kylander

Olof is a UNIX and network system administrator. He received his formal computer education at the Chalmers University of Technology. He has been into computers since the early 1980s. UNIX caught his attention in 1993, and he has been configuring various UNIX systems and networks ever since.

Olof currently works for the UNIX/Network consulting company Sigma-nbit in Gothenburg, and is presently occupied with configuring Solaris servers for Ericsson. He also has experience with other systems such as Mac, Windows, NT, Citrix and Novell. His specialties are thin clients and X Window System configuration, as well as Internet technologies. He is the author of the more technical parts of this book.

Frozenriver

Frozenriver, Karin's company, deals with digital design in various fields as well as providing training in digital image manipulation. The company specializes in different kinds of informational material, such as technical documentation/reports, brochures, magazines and exhibitions. Web design is also an up-and-coming service. Frozenriver can provide the entire range from a full advertisement concept to a leaflet at the local mall. Frozenriver can also provide support for Gimp users (along with other image manipulating programs such as Photoshop) in the form of training courses and advice by email.

If you wish to contact Frozenriver, please visit our website at `http://www.frozenriver.nu` or mail us at `karin@frozenriver.com`.

Or even better, contact us directly:

Frozenriver
Karin Kylander
N.Dragspelsg 12
S-421 43 V.FRÖLUNDA
SWEDEN
Phone: +46 (0)31 47 43 56
Fax: +46 (0)31 49 48 33

Gimp Contributions

First, we'd like to thank the many Gimp developers:

Spencer Kimball, Peter Mattis, Federico Mena, Zach Beane, Adrian Linkns, Miguel de Icaza, Tom Bech, Sven Neumann, Albert Cahalan, Adam D. Moss, Torsten Martinsen, Tristan Tarrant, Andreas Beck, David Mosberger, Gordon Matzigkeit, Peter Kirchgessner, Eric L. Hernes, Francisco Bustamante, Thorsten Schnier, Jochen Friedrich, Tim Newsome, Christoph Hoegl, Xavier Bouchoux, Owen Taylor, Andy Thomas, Ray Lehtiniemi, Marcelo Malheiros, Miles O'Neal, Chris Laas, Daniel Risacher, Gerd Knorr, Michel Taylor, Ole Steinfatt, Michael Sweet, Eiichi Takamori, Tracy Scott, Gordon Matzigkeit, Andrew Kieschnick, Alexander Schulz, Thomas Noel, Robert L.Cross, Kevin Turner, Sean Cier, Nick Lamb, Kim-Minh Kaplan, Matthias Cramer, Lauri Alanko, Tim Newsome, Bucky LaDieu, Scott Goehring, Morten Eriksen, Raphael Quinet, Daniel Skarda, Daniel Dunbar, Jens Ch. Restemeier, Marc Lehmann, Scott Draves, Alessandro Baldoni, Michael Schubart, Dan Risache, Josh MacDonald, Eduardo Perez, Daniel Cotting, Nathan Summers, John Beale, Marc Bless, John Breen, Brent Burton, Jim Geuther, Pavel Grinfeld, Matthias Greim, Jan Hubicka, Shuji Narazaki, Stephen Robert Norris, Tim Rowley, Christoph Hoegl, Wolfgang Hofer, Shawn Amundson, Edward Blevins, Roberto Boyd, Simon Budig, Seth Burgess, Ed Connell, Jay Cox, Andreas Dilger, Austin Donnelly, Misha Dynin, Larry Ewing, Nick Fetchak, David Forsyth, Heilco Goller, Michael Hammel, Simon Jones, Tim Janik, Tuomas Kuosmanen, Karl LaRocca, Jens Lautenbacher, Laramie Leavitt, Elliott Lee, Ralph Levien, Adrian Likins, Tor Lillqvist, Ingo Luetkebohle, Ed Mackey, Vidar Madsen, Ian Main, Michael Natterer, Erik Nygren, Tomas Ogren, Jay Painter, Asbjorn Pettersen, Mike Phillips, Mike Schaeffer, James Robinson, Manish Singh, Ian Tester, James Wang, Kris Wehner, Matthew Wilson and all of you we have forgotten (if we've forgotten you, please write to `karin@frozenriver.com` to let us know).

Contributors To This Book

We'd also like to give credit to everyone that came up with suggestions, tips, constructive criticism, contributions, etc:

- Dov Grobgeld (Author of "A Tutorial For Perl Gimp Users")
- Mike Terry (Author of "Black Belt School Of Script-Fu")
- John Sigerson (PDF file format of GUM version 0.5 to 0.9)
- Aristidi Yannick (French translation)
- Yasuhiro Shirasaki (Leader of the Japanese translation team)
- Mark Probst (Documentation)
- Peter Uray (Documentation)
- Petri Alanko (Documentation)
- Ole Steinfatt (Documentation)
- Michal Gomulinski (Documentation)
- George J. Carret (Documentation)
- PhotoDisc (For their kind donation of high-quality images for this book project)
- Thom van Os (Images in Selective Gaussian Blur)
- Eric Galluzzo and Christopher Macgowan (Proofreading)
- Nicholas Lamb (Tip about selections)
- Michael Kaiser (Correction layers)
- Cristoph Hogeld (Contrib correction)
- Marco Schmidt
- Adrian Links
- Adam D. Moss (Tips about animation filters and psd)
- Tom Bech (Tips & lesson about light effects and map objects)
- Nathan Carl Summers (Tips & lesson about scissors)
- Wolfgang Hofer (Tips about animframe)
- Markku Verkkoniemi (Tip in Pre-Press about image delivery)
- Matt Chisholm (Found a bug in the font install chapter)
- and anyone that we've forgotten (please write to `karin@frozenriver.com` and let us know!)

How To Read This Book

GIMP: The Official Handbook is the complete Gimp user's manual. It is the most comprehensive source of Gimp information available, covering nearly all aspects of this complex application. It's a user manual, so it will not cover "nuts and bolts" topics such as how to write Gimp plug-ins; however, some basic scripting tutorials have been included. All images in this manual have been created or manipulated using Gimp — no other software has been used.

GIMP: The Official Handbook is divided into several parts. If you are an experienced graphics artist, you can read the first parts quickly in order to pick up the main differences between Gimp and the programs you are used to working with.

This book also covers features that aren't part of the standard Gimp distribution. These features can be found in the developer's version, or at the Plug-in Registry. We have covered all available Gimp features up to August 1999, with the exception of how to use pressure-sensitive drawing tablets, Gimp Perl scripting extensions, Dumpwindow, xmorph (a Gimpified version of the xmorph program) and HaruspexX (a SQL Gimp extension).

Part I

- What is Gimp; a brief *history* of Gimp and GTK+
- Gimp's default *shortcuts* (accelerator keys) and how to reassign them
- A gallery showing what you can achieve with the powerful resources of Gimp and providing some insight into *advanced image manipulation.*

Part II

- How to *get* and *install* Gimp for your system and *troubleshooting*
- Migrating from *Photoshop* to *Gimp*

Part III

- What *file formats* Gimp supports and how to use them; how to *open* and *save* files in Gimp
- Personal *adjustments*
- How to use the different *paint tools*
- How you can use the different *edit* functions
- *Transformation* functions
- How to work with *text*
- How to use the *Gradient Editor* as well as information about *brushes*, *palettes* and *patterns*

Part IV

- A general discussion about *color models* (to understand how different *modes* work in Gimp, you need the information in this chapter)
- How to prepare your Gimp image for *pre-press*
- *Calibration* discussion and a simple calibration of your system

- Scanning, discussion of scanner types and what to buy.
- Installation of Sane (Gimp's scanner interface) and usage of Sane within Gimp

Part V

- In-depth discussion about the *image menu*, which includes *color*, *brightness*, *curves* and other image adjustments (also covers image *conversions* like RGB to Indexed, as well as image *transformations*)
- How to use different *selection* methods
- How *modes* work in Gimp
- In-depth discussion on how to use *layers* — the key factor to advanced image manipulation
- *Channels*: What they are and how to use them

Part VI

- The *filter* plug-ins available for Gimp; a glimpse of what they're all about
- Different *color exchange* filters
- How to use the *lighting effects*
- How to *render* fantastic patterns and images

Part VII

- *Animations*, or how *AnimFrames* can make it easy to create advanced web animations
- Xinput, usage and installation of Wacom tablets in Linux (XFree86)

Part VIII

- Discussion about the *Script-Fus* that come with Gimp
- Two different angles/tutorials on how to write *Script-Fus* and how they can help you *automate* Gimp tasks

Part IX

- Discussion about the *Perl-Fus* that come with Gimp
- Two different angles/tutorials on how to write *Perl-Fus* and how they can help you *automate* Gimp tasks

Part X

- How *fonts* works in Gimp and the X Window System; how to install more fonts
- How to *compile* plug-ins, make your own *make file* and use the *configure script*

Part XI

- *Man* pages in the Gimp distribution
- *Initiation* file descriptions as well as description of *command* line flags
- *SIOD* reference for those who write Script-Fu scripts
- *Links* and *books* that can be useful

Conventions

You'll find four different typing styles besides the normal text in the GUM.

Bold is used the first time important concepts, items or topics are introduced. This can, for example, be words you'll see onscreen in Gimp — pull-down menu titles, dialog titles, options — but it can also be used in more general terms such as: **color theory**, **font manager** or **halftone pattern**.

Italics to emphasize important points. ***Bold italics for warnings.***

`Courier` for describing the path to Gimp menu commands, programs you'll need to execute within a terminal window, file names and code.

Symbols

This is the Swedish version of the crossing traffic sign. In this case, it means that you have a crossroads in front of you; either you install the documented feature, or you ignore the passage in question.

Not A Standard Part Of The Gimp Distribution

This symbol will appear when a function or filter is not part of the standard distribution of Gimp. This means that you have to download it and probably compile it yourself. The primary source of extra functions and plug-ins are `http://registry.gimp.org` or `ftp://ftp.gimp.org/pub/gimp`. If you bought the printed version of this book, the non-standard plug-ins and functions, as well as the standard ones, have been included both as binaries and source code on the enclosed CD.

You had better look out when you see this warning sign!

Warning!

Look out for this symbol. Its purpose is to catch your attention, so you won't miss passages of vital importance or essential warnings. For example, don't do this or your system will crash, or some other unpleasantness will happen!

Install at your own risk, you may be in for a bumpy ride.

Beware Of Bugs!

This sign indicates that a filter or function is still in development stage, and that it may suffer from bug problems. Install or use functions marked with this symbol at your own risk.

We lead the way. Follow us for a guided tour.

Tutorial

Next to this sign, you'll find an example or a tutorial, helping you to understand the described function.

Read the information carefully; this is stuff you need to know!

Tip

This sign indicates useful tips or advice on how to use a certain function, or that a passage describing important subjects will follow.

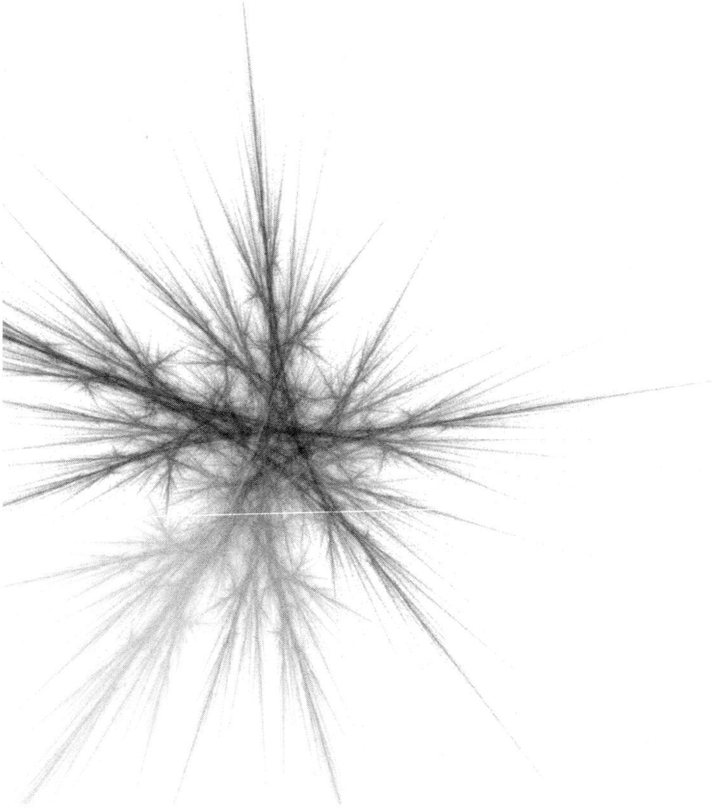

PART

About Gimp

- *About Gimp And Gimp History*
- *Shortcuts And Dynamic Key Bindings*

GIMP Startup
(gimp-selection-none temp
(gimp-image-resize temp-img
(gimp-selection-all temp-img)
The Gimp
The GNU Image Manipulation Program
Plug-ins
/opt/gtk1/lib/gimp/1.0/plug-ins/hfg

CHAPTER 1

What Is Gimp?

A quick description of Gimp.

About The Gimp

From the "About the Gimp" website at `http://www.gimp.org/`, we quote the following:

Gimp is an acronym for **G**NU **I**mage **M**anipulation **P**rogram. Gimp is a freely distributed piece of software suitable for such tasks as photo retouching, image composition and image authoring.

It is an extremely capable piece of software with many capabilities. It can be used as a simple paint program, an expert quality photo retouching program, an online batch processing system, a mass production image renderer, an image format converter and more.

Gimp is expandable and extensible. It is designed to be augmented with plug-ins and extensions to do just about anything. The advanced scripting interface allows everything to be easily scripted, from the simplest task to the most complex image manipulation procedures.

Features And Capabilities

This is only a brief list of Gimp features:

- Full suite of painting tools including brushes, a pencil, an airbrush, cloning, etc.
- Tile-based memory management so image size is limited only by available disk space
- Sub-pixel sampling for all paint tools for high-quality anti-aliasing
- Full Alpha channel support
- Layers and channels
- A procedural database for calling internal Gimp functions from external programs, such as Script-Fu
- Advanced scripting capabilities
- Multiple undo/redo (limited only by disk space)
- Transformation tools including rotate, scale, shear and flip
- File formats supported include GIF, JPEG, PNG, XPM, TIFF, TGA, MPEG, PS, PDF, PCX, BMP and many others
- Load, display, convert and save to many file formats
- Selection tools including rectangle, ellipse, free, fuzzy, bezier and intelligent
- Plug-ins that allow for the easy addition of new file formats and new effect filters

Authors

The Gimp was written by Peter Mattis and Spencer Kimball. Many other developers have contributed plug-ins and thousands have provided support and testing. Gimp releases are currently being orchestrated by Manish Singh.

End quote (we couldn't have said it better ourselves).

What We Can Say About Gimp

First, we want to congratulate Peter Mattis, Spencer Kimball and all of the other developers of this lovely program. The "About The Gimp" section is only the tip of the iceberg. Gimp is capable of everything from advanced image manipulation to basic drawing. Many of its features are inspired by Photoshop and other image manipulation programs.

Karin, who is an architect and designer and a former Photoshop user in both Mac and Windows environments, can only say this:

> *Compared to Photoshop, Gimp has it all (and even more if you don't buy third-party Photoshop plug-ins). Most of the features in Gimp are more flexible and powerful once you get to know them. The great thing is that Gimp supports the PSD file format and Filter Factory files, so you can easily switch from Photoshop to Gimp. Simply, it's a heck of a program and it comes loaded with a sack of plug-ins. So GO AND GET IT!! You will not be disappointed, and, well, it's not wrong that it is free.*

Karin Kylander & Olof S. Kylander

Gimp History

0.54

We'll quote a bit more, this time from Peter Mattis and Spencer Kimball, the original creators of Gimp, in their announcement of Gimp 0.54:

> *The Gimp arose from the ashes of a hideously crafted cs164 (compilers) class project. The setting: early morning. We were both weary from lack of sleep and the terrible strain of programming a compiler in LISP. The limits of our patience had long been exceeded, and yet still the dam held.*
>
> *And then it happened. Common LISP messily dumped core when it could not allocate the 17 MB it needed to generate a parser for a simple grammar using yacc. An unbelieving moment passed, there was one shared look of disgust, and then our project was vapor. We had to write something...ANYTHING...useful. Something in C. Something that did not rely on nested lists to represent a bitmap. Thus, the Gimp was born.*

Like the phoenix, glorious, new life sprung out of the burnt remnants of LISP and yacc. Ideas went flying, decisions were made, the Gimp began to take form.

An image manipulation program was the consensus. A program that would at the very least lessen the necessity of using commercial software under 'Windoze' or on the 'Macintoy.' A program that would provide the features missing from the other X painting and imaging tools. A program that would help maintain the long tradition of excellent and free UNIX applications.

Six months later, we've reached an early beta stage. We want to release now to start working on compatibility issues and cross-platform stability. Also, we feel now that the program is actually usable and would like to see other interested programmers developing plug-ins and various file format support.

Version 0.54 was released in February 1996, and had a major impact as the first truly professional free image manipulation program. This was the first free program that could compete with the big commercial image manipulation programs.

Version 0.54 featured:

- Support for 8, 15, 16 and 24 bit color
- Ordered and Floyd-Steinberg dithering for 8 bit displays
- Viewing images as RGB color, grayscale or indexed color
- Simultaneous editing for multiple images
- Zooming and panning in real-time
- GIF, JPEG, PNG, TIFF and XPM support
- Selection tools including rectangle, ellipse, free, fuzzy, bezier and intelligent scissors
- Transformation tools including rotate, scale, shear and flip
- Painting tools including bucket, brush, airbrush, clone, convolve, blend and text
- Effects filters (such as blur and edge detect)
- Channel and color operations (such as add, composite and decompose)
- Plug-ins that allowed for the easy addition of new file formats and new effect filters
- Multiple undo/redo (note that this is a new feature in Photoshop 5)

Version 0.54 was a beta release, but it was so stable that you could use it for daily work. However, one of the major drawbacks of 0.54 was that the toolkit (the slidebars, menus, dialog boxes, etc.) was built on Motif, a commercial toolkit. This was a big drawback for systems like Linux, because you had to buy Motif if you wanted to use the faster, dynamically linked Gimp. Many developers were also students running Linux, who could not afford to buy Motif.

VERSION 0.60

When 0.60 was released in July 1996, it had been under S&P (Spencer & Peter) development for four months. Main programming advantages were the new toolkits, GTK (Gimp Toolkit) and gdk (Gimp Drawing Kit), which eliminated the reliance on Motif. For the graphic artist, 0.60 was full of new features like:

- Basic layers
- Improved painting tools (sub-pixel sampling, brush spacing)
- A better airbrush
- Cloning between all image types
- A pattern selection dialog and a clone tool making it possible to clone from the active pattern
- Paint modes
- Border and feather selection commands
- Selection by color
- Better palette handling

Version 0.60 was only a developer's release, and was not intended for widespread use. It served as a workbench for 0.99 and the final 1.0 version, so functions and enhancement could be tested and dropped or changed. You can look at 0.60 as the alpha version of 0.99.

VERSION 0.99

In February 1997, 0.99 came on the scene. Together with other developers, S&P had made several changes to Gimp and added even more features. The main difference was the new API and the PDB, which made it possible to write scripts; Script-Fus (or macros) could now automate things that you would normally do by hand. GTK/gdk had also changed and was now called GTK+. In addition, 0.99 used a new form of tile-based memory handling that made it possible to load huge images into Gimp (loading a 100 MB image into Gimp is no problem). Version 0.99 also introduced a new native Gimp file format called XCF.

The new API made it really easy to write extensions and plug-ins for Gimp. Several new plug-ins and extensions emerged to make Gimp even more useful (such as SANE, which enables scanning directly into Gimp). At the time we're writing this, Gimp has more than 150 plug-ins, covering everything from file formats to fractal tracers.

In the summer of 1997, Gimp had reached version 0.99.10, and S&P had to drop most of their support since they had graduated and begun jobs. However, the other developers of Gimp continued under the orchestration of Federico Mena to make Gimp ready for primetime.

GTK+ was separated from Gimp in September 1997. GTK+ had been recognized as an excellent toolkit, and other developers began using it to build their own applications.

Gimp went into feature freeze in October 1997. This meant that no new features would be added to the Gimp core libraries and program. GUM version 0.5 was also released early in October 1997. The developing work continued to make Gimp stable and ready for version 1.0.

Version 1.0

Gimp version 1.0 was released on June 5, 1998. Finally, Gimp was considered stable enough to warrant a worldwide announcement and professional use.

The Future Of Gimp

Gimp will naturally continue to evolve. The future is bright, and we will see new versions of Gimp with new features and functions. The version naming convention of Gimp is the same as for Linux, meaning that stable versions will have even point release numbers (such as 1.0.X), whereas the development version will have odd point release numbers (like 1.1.X). This makes it possible for normal users to grab the stable version and use it for a primetime job, while the developers work on a bleeding-edge version without introducing new bugs into the stable version.

If you want to, you can always download the development version and test it to check out new features and give the developers feedback about bugs and enhancements. But be aware, it *will* be unstable, so don't use it for daily work, and don't flood the developers with unnecessary bug reports.

CHAPTER 2

Default Shortcuts And Dynamic Key Bindings

Gimp has many accelerator keys that make image manipulation quicker and easier. Gimp also lets you assign shortcut keys on the fly.

DYNAMIC KEY BINDINGS

Gimp has a very nice way of dealing with **shortcuts** (sometimes known as **hotkeys**). If you don't like a default shortcut, or if your favorite command hasn't been assigned to a default hotkey, just bring up the menu holding the command (for example, `right-click|File|Preference`) and press the desired key sequence — say, Ctrl+U. From now on, the Preference dialog will pop up when you press Ctrl+U (remember to keep Caps Lock off). If the Ctrl+U key sequence was originally assigned to (for example) `right-click|File|Print`, the original shortcut will not be available. All of this happens on the fly — there is no need to restart Gimp.

Changes to key bindings can also be done by editing your **personal menurc file** in your personal gimp directory. This makes it possible to share your shortcuts with your friends. If you are a former Photoshop user, you can even re-bind your keys so Gimp will use the same hotkeys as Photoshop.

We suggest that you stick to the default shortcuts; otherwise, it may be difficult to follow our instructions. (For instance, you could run into some problems when we write Ctrl+N to get a new image, and you accidentally quit Gimp because you have reassigned the shortcut.) If you want to remove all your personal shortcuts, just type `"rm .gimp/menurc"` in an xterm shell.

The next few pages list the default key bindings in Gimp.

CONVENTIONS

- The left column lists options available for a certain tool (clicking different mouse buttons and/or pressing hotkeys). The right column describes the result.
- The headings list the different tools in the left column and the hotkeys for calling up each tool in the right column.
- `{1}` represents left mouse button
- `{2}` represents the middle mouse button
- `{3}` represents the right mouse button
- Shift + {1} - Shift + Shift + Ctrl means the following:
  First press Shift, then press the left mouse button. Release Shift then press Shift again. Press Ctrl and drag the mouse while holding Shift and Ctrl. When you are finished, first release the mouse button, then release Shift and Ctrl.

DEFAULT SHORTCUTS IN GIMP

Selection Tools	
{1}	Draw selection
{1} + {3} - {1}	Cancel selection
On existing selections	
Shift + {1} - Shift	Add to selection
Ctrl + {1} - Ctrl	Subtract from selection
Shift + Ctrl + {1} - Shift - Ctrl	Union of selection
Alt + {1}	Move selection
Rectangular and ellipse	**Shortcut: R/E**
{1} + Shift	Circle/square only
{1} + Ctrl	Start from center
{1} + Shift + Ctrl	Start circle/square from center
Shift + {1} - Shift + Shift	Add circle/square to selection
Shift + {1} - Shift + Ctrl	Add rect/ellipse to selection starting from center
Shift + {1} - Shift + Shift + Ctrl	Add circle/square to selection starting from center
Ctrl + {1} - Ctrl + Shift	Subtract circle/ square from selection
Ctrl + {1} - Ctrl + Ctrl	Subtract ellipse/ square from selection starting from center
Ctrl + {1} - Ctrl + Shift +Ctrl	Subtract circle/ square from selection starting from center
Shift + Ctrl + {1} - Shift - Ctrl + Shift	Circle/square union of selection
Shift + Ctrl + {1} - Shift - Ctrl + Ctrl	Ellipse/rectangle union of selection starting from center
Shift + Ctrl + {1} - Shift - Ctrl + Shift + Ctrl	Circle/square union of selection starting from center
Bezier	**Shortcut: B**
{1} (inside bezier)	Convert to selection
{1}	Move both control handles
Shift + {1}	Move one control handle
Ctrl + {1}	Move control point
Remaining selection tools	
Fuzzy select	Z
Free	F
Intelligent scissors	I

Move tool	Shortcut: M
{1}	Move current layer
{1} + Shift	Move current even if 100% transparent
Ctrl + [arrow key]	Move layer 1 pixel
Shift + [arrow key]	Move layer 25 pixels
Alt + [arrow key]	Move selection 1 pixel
Alt + Shift + [arrow key]	Move selection 25 pixels

Magnify tool	Shortcut: Shift + M
{1} or =	Zoom in
Shift + {1} or -	Zoom out
{2}	Pan image

Crop tool	Shortcut: Shift + C
{1}	Make crop selection
{1} + {3} -{1}	Cancel crop
{1} inside crop	Perform crop

Text tool	Shortcut: T
{1}	Set top left of text

Color picker tool	Shortcut: O
{1}	Get color

Transform tool	Shortcut: Shift + T
Rotation mode	
{1}	Rotate with 1° increments
Ctrl + {1}	Rotate with 15° increments
Scaling mode	
{1}	Free scaling
Shift + {1}	Scale in X direction only
Ctrl + {1}	Scale in Y direction only
Shift + Ctrl + {1}	Scale with fixed ratio
Shearing mode	
{1}	Free shearing
Perspective mode	
{1}	Move point
All	
{1} + {3} - {3}	Preview

Bucket fill tool	**Shortcut: Shift + M**
With no selection	
{1}	Fill with FG color
Shift + {1}	Fill with BG color
With selection	
{1}	Fill selection with FG color
Shift + {1}	Fill selection with BG color

Color picker tool	**Shortcut: O**
{1}	Set active color with cursor
X	Swap BG FG color
D	Set default colors

Blend tool	**Shortcut: L**
{1} + drag - {1}	Set start => end of gradient
{1} + {2} - {1}	Cancel gradient

Paint tools	
Blend tool	**Shortcut: L**
Pencil tool	**Shortcut: Shift + P**
Airbrush tool	**Shortcut: A**
{1}	Paint
Alt + {1}	Quick draw
Shift +/- {1} + distance +/- {1}	Line draw

Eraser tool	**Shortcut: Shift + E**
{1}	Set to BG and Clear
Alt + {1}	Quick erase
Shift +/- {1} + distance +/- {1}	Line erase

Clone tool	**Shortcut: C**
{1}	Clone
Ctrl + {1}	Set clone source point
Alt + {1}	Quick clone
Shift +/- {1} + distance +/-! {1}	Line clone

Convolver tool	**Shortcut: V**
{1}	Blur/Sharpen with brush

File	
New	Ctrl + N
Open	Ctrl + O
Close	Ctrl + W
Quit	Ctrl + Q

Dialogs	
Brushes	Shift + Ctrl + B
Patterns	Shift + Ctrl + P
Palette	Ctrl + P
Gradient editor	Ctrl + G
Tool options	Shift + Ctrl + T
Layers & Channels	Ctrl + L

Edit	
Cut	Ctrl + X
Copy	Ctrl + C
Paste	Ctrl + V
Clear	Ctrl + K
Fill	Ctrl + .
Undo	Ctrl + Z
Redo	Ctrl + R
Cut Named	Shift + Ctrl + X
Copy Named	Shift + Ctrl + C
Paste Named	Shift + Ctrl + V

Filters	
Repeat Last	Alt + F
Re-show Last	Shift + Alt + F

Select	
Toggle	Ctrl + T
Invert	Ctrl + I
All	Ctrl + A
None	Shift + Ctrl + A
Float	Shift + Ctrl + L
Sharpen	Shift + Ctrl + H
Feather	Shift + Ctrl + F

View	
Zoom in	=
Zoom out	-
Zoom 1:1	1
Window info	Shift + Ctrl + I
Toggle rulers	Shift + Ctrl + R
Toggle guides	Shift + Ctrl + T
Shrink wrap	Ctrl + E

Image	
Channel Ops Dupli	Ctrl + D
Channel Ops Offset	Shift + Ctrl + O

Layers	
Dialog	Ctrl + L
Raise Layer	Ctrl + F
Lower Layer	Ctrl + B
Merge Visible Layers	Ctrl + M

Tools	
Rect Select	R
Ellipse Select	E
Fuzzy Select	Z
Bezier Select	B
Intelligent Scissors	I
Move	M
Magnify	Shift + M
Crop	Shift + C
Transform	Shift + T
Flip	Shift + F
Text	T
Color Picker	O
Bucket Fill	Shift + B
Blend	L
Paintbrush	P
Pencil	Shift + P
Eraser	Shift + E
Airbrush	A
Clone	C
Convolve	V

Layers & Channels dialog	
Layers ops menu	
New layer	Ctrl + N
Raise layer	Ctrl + F
Lower layer	Ctrl + B
Duplicate layer	Ctrl + C
Delete layer	Ctrl + X
Scale layer	Ctrl + S
Resize layer	Ctrl + R
Merge visible layers	Ctrl + M
{1}	Select layer (visible and anchor)
Shift + {1}	View current layer only
Alt + {1} Green layer mask	View layer mask (or remove green mask)
Alt + {1} Green layer mask	View layer mask (or remove green mask)
Alt + {1} Green layer mask	View layer mask (or remove green mask)
Channels ops menu	
New channel	Ctrl + N
Raise channel	Ctrl + F
Lower channel	Ctrl + B
Duplicate channel	Ctrl + C
Delete channel	Ctrl + X
Channel to selection	Ctrl + S

Gradient Editor dialog: Ops menu	
Left endpoint color	L
Load from left neighbor's right endpoint	Ctrl + L
Load from right endpoint	Alt + L
Load from FG color	Ctrl +
Right endpoint color	R
Load from right neighbor's right endpoint	Ctrl + R
Load from left endpoint	Alt + R
Load from FG color	Alt + F
Segments	
Split segment at midpoint	S
Split segment uniformly	U
Delete segment	D
Recenter segment's midpoint	C
Redistribute handles in segment	Ctrl + C

Selection operands	
Flip segments	F
Replicate segment	M
Blend endpoints' colors	B
Blend endpoints' opacity	Ctrl + B

Clear your Windows
with UNIX or LINUX
UNIX
Waterproof solutions
...and stop paying your Bills

CHAPTER 3

Don't Underestimate The Power Of Gimp...

This manual describes the many functions, plug-ins and options Gimp has to offer, but it doesn't describe how to create great digital art or designs. There are probably as many Gimp tricks and tips as there are Gimp users, and even if we wanted to, we couldn't include them all in this book.

We also can't teach you how to be an artist, but we've included a few examples that will hopefully inspire you to try new things and help you get the most out of Gimp. This is more a gallery than a tutorial, and the object of this chapter is not to give detailed instructions, but rather to demonstrate the great versatility and power of Gimp to beginners (and maybe to give more experienced users insights on new ways of using Gimp).

So let's unleash the power of Gimp!

In some of the following examples, color will be mentioned. Because the images in this chapter are printed in black and white, we recommend that you look them up in the Color Section starting on page 379 to be able to follow the discussion.

CREATING IMAGE OBJECTS

You don't always need to import a photo, drawing or 3-D image of an object. There are many ways to create astonishingly convincing images directly in Gimp.

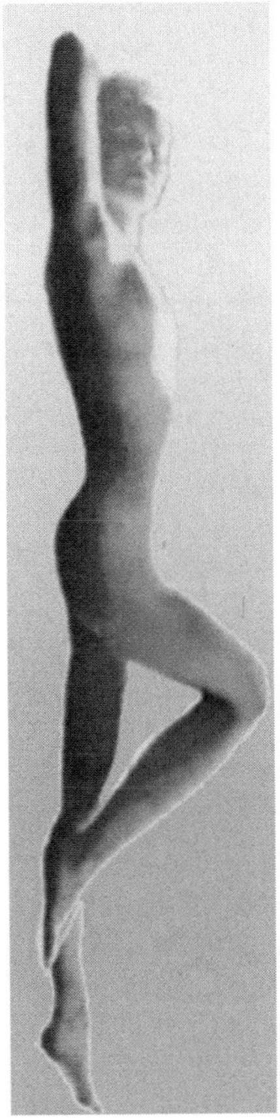

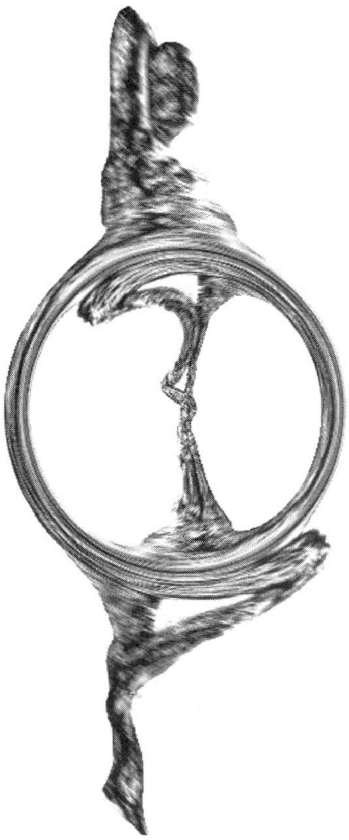

A Twisted Personality

To create the statue emblem I started out with a black-and-white photo. The background was isolated with the **Bezier tool**, removed and replaced with a **gradient** fill. The image was rotated vertically and tinted yellow with **Image/ Hue-Saturation**. I reopened the selection used to change the background, inverted it and used it again to isolate the figure, which was copied to a white layer. The figure was further adapted to supply an interesting surface for the **Distorts/Twist** plug-in to work on. Finally, the yellow layer was applied in **Difference Mode** on top of the twisted layer.

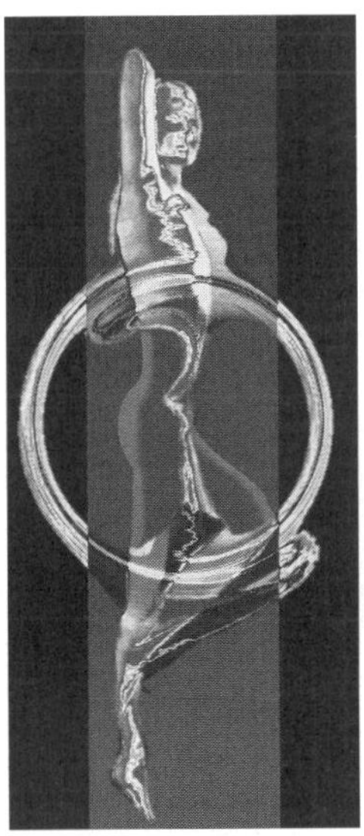

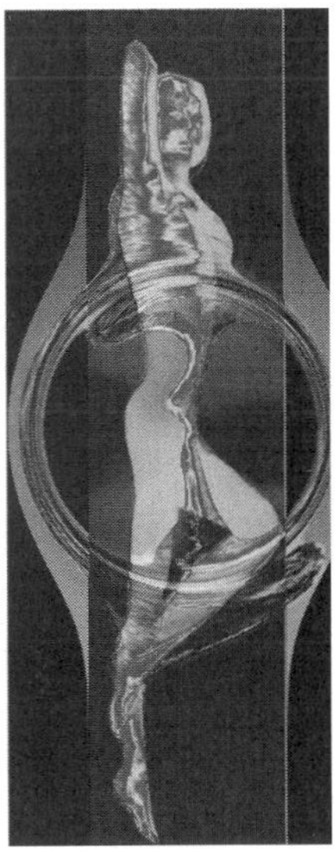

Variations — Gold And Water Spirits

The gold emblem was created by running the **Gradient Map** filter on the twisted figure (using the custom Golden gradient). The pale outline of the non-twisted parts was painted with a low opacity **airbrush** and blurred within a sharp-edged selection.

The blue ghost emblem was made using three copies of the original yellow-tint image. The middle copy was twisted, trimmed and set to **Saturation Mode**, and the top layer was set in **Difference Mode**. To accentuate the water or ghostlike appearance, the original twisted shape was added to a layer, desaturated and set to **Overlay**. The side parts needed to be more visible, so they were pasted separately in **Multiply Mode**. Finally, a pale fluorescent shape of the figure was added to enhance the shape of the woman inside the waterwheel.

CREATING A SIMPLE PEN AND INK STAIN

The pen was made by filling selection shapes with different gradients. In this case, I used **Bilinear FG to BG** with medium opacity, and also a number of **FG to Transparent** gradients on several cylinder-shaped selections.

The metal pen tip was adjusted with **Brightness-Contrast** to achieve the metallic look. The pen shadow (as well as the engraved emblem shadow) was made with the **Perspective Shadow Script-Fu**, cleared of color and filled with an **FG to transparent** linear gradient.

The Technicolor Ink Spot

To make the multi-color splash, I started by drawing a simple black sun shape on a white background, using a medium pencil tip. I then applied the **Distort/Value Propagate** plug-in, choosing **more white**. The result was **blurred** and **bumpmapped** and the background was cut away. A copy of the splash was then pasted to a transparent layer, filled with a colorful pattern and set to **Lighten Only Mode**.

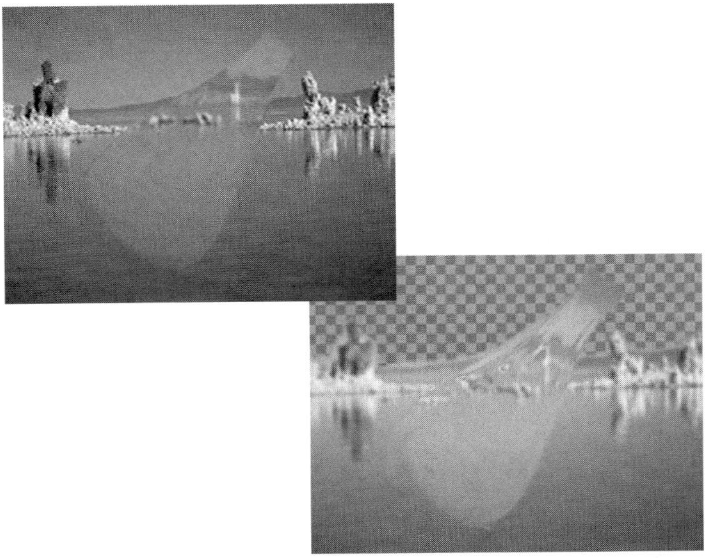

Glass Distortion

The background, a photo of a lake, was blurred to create the illusion of distance, and to keep the focus on the bottle. The highlight bottle was used twice as a **displacement map** on the background. This would make the rocks in the background appear to be distorted by the bottle's curved glass.

Rectifying Banding

Because the lake image was originally **indexed**, the sky looked banded and ugly. This was rectified by **feather** selecting the sky, and replacing it with a **linear gradient**. I also added the sun (complete with lens flare) and a few clouds.

Reflections

The water reflection was made by flipping the image of the merged bottle to a copy of the lower part of the lake, blurring it, adding some ripples with **Distort/Ripple** and lowering the **opacity** level. The waterline (where bottle meets water) was a little trickier and had to be painted by hand in a couple of **Overlay** layers. Finally, some glittering highlights were created with the **Sparkle** filter.

A white haze was added to the foreground, and, of course, so were some of Larry Ewing's adorable Linux penguins.

Transforming A Photograph To A Drawing

Because black is transparent in **Screen Mode** (also **Addition** and **Lighten Only**), black pencil strokes drawn on a white layer will reveal the image underneath, just as if you had sketched it by hand. This is an easy way of creating convincing pencil/ink "drawings" from a scanned photo.

Managing Without Artistic Plug-ins

Several commercial plug-ins, with names like *Charcoal*, *Crayon* or *Ink Drawing,* can produce similar artistic output, but they never come close to the results you can get using the following method. Naturally, the quality of the final image depends a lot on the drawing in the screen layer, so this isn't an "instant artist" trick. One way of improving coarse computer drawings is to use the **Value Propagate** filter and set it to **more white**. You can also create a crayon or charcoal look to an image by **displacing** or **warping** the pen strokes with a suitable displacement map, or just by using unusual **brushes**. We also recommend that you reduce the number of shades in the background; otherwise, too much of the underlaying image will show, spoiling the illusion.

Instant Cartoon Pictures

Of course, a very simple way of creating drawings from scanned photos is to use one of the **Edge-Detect** filters. Running **Sobel** on a duplicate results in a transparent layer with a black outline of the image object. Having done this, it's easy to paint the underlying layer in large, clean areas, and you'll get something very similar to a picture in a comic book.

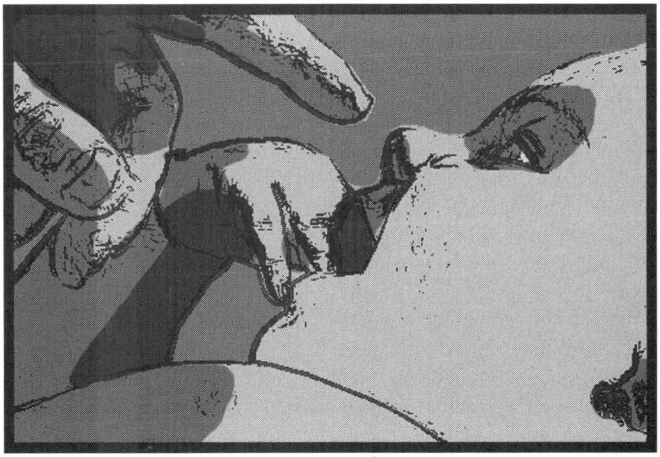

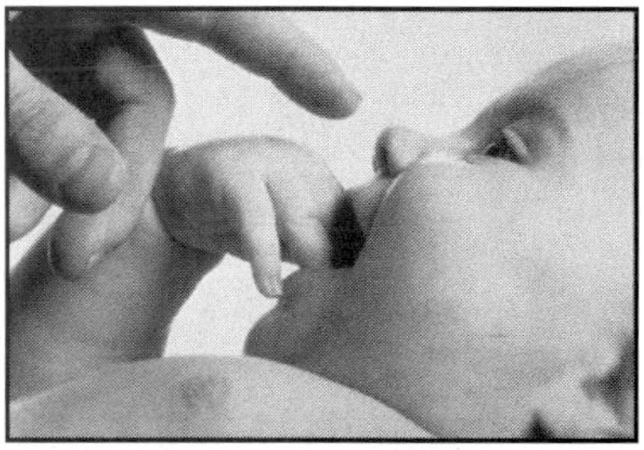

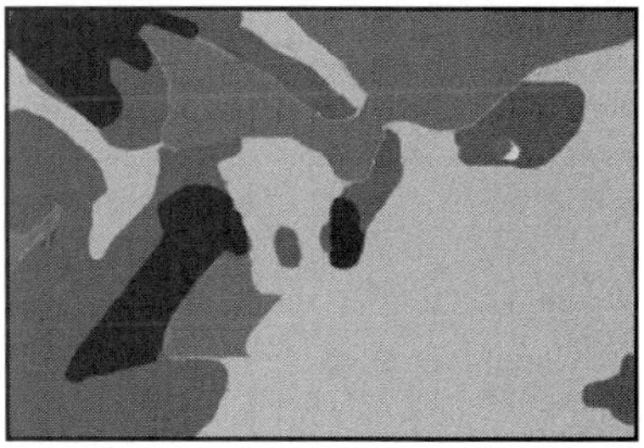

Top right: Original image
Middle right: Transparent Sobel output
Bottom right: Handpainted background

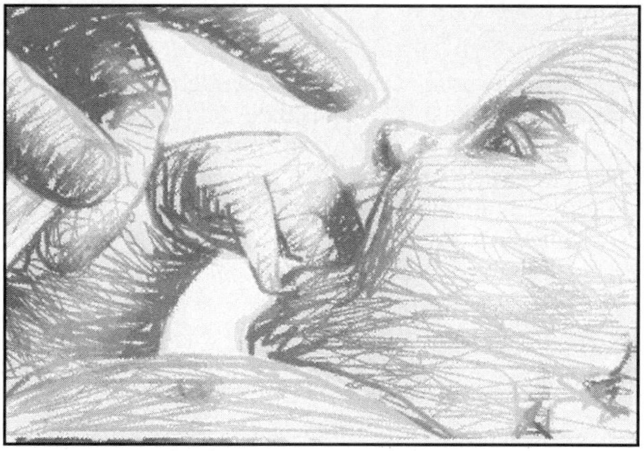

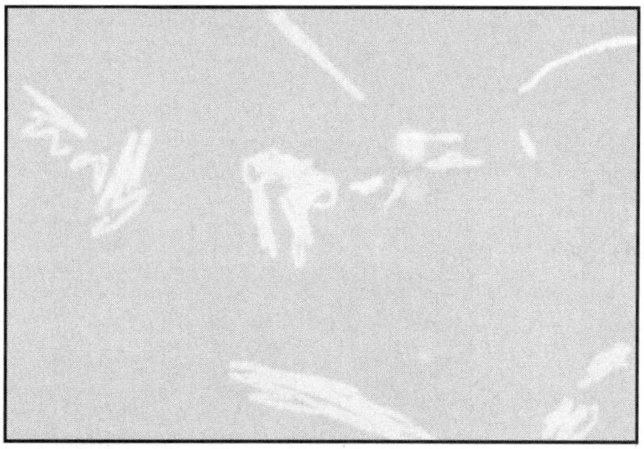

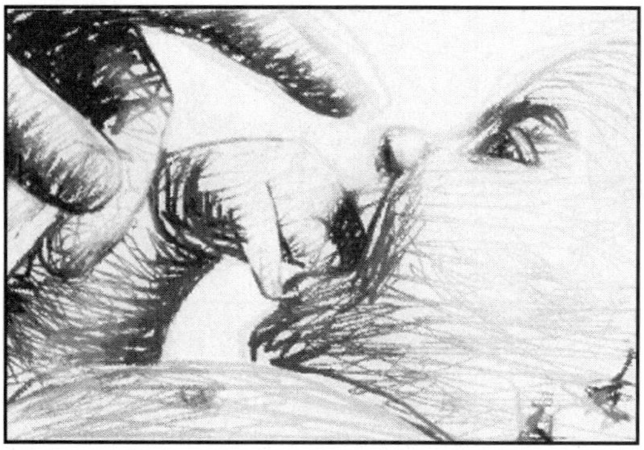

Making A Pencil Drawing

To make the pencil drawing, a white layer was placed over a black-and-white photograph in the background layer. The white layer was set to **Screen Mode**, and the **opacity** was temporarily reduced, so that the background would be visible.

The sketch was drawn with a small, sharp pencil tip, and made to follow the contours and shapes in the photo. The photo's tonal range was limited by using the **Image/Posterize** filter, and the sketch layer was displaced slightly with a canvas structure as a map. The image was flattened and adjusted with **Brightness-Contrast** to get the gray value of a pencil drawing.

From Pencil To Ink

The sepia ink drawing was created from the pencil drawing. The color was adjusted with **Hue-Saturation** and **Brightness-Contrast** to a sepia-like quality, and a beige "sketch paper" layer was added in **Multiply Mode**. The "white crayon" in the sketch paper layer was painted with the **airbrush** and several soft-edged **brushes**.

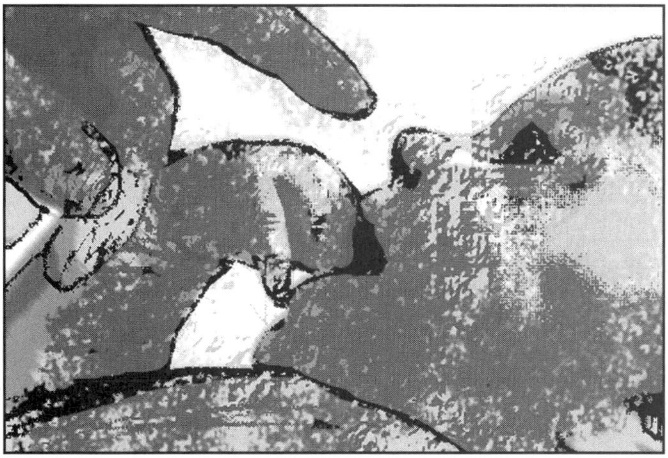

Digital Crayons

For the crayon drawing, I used coarser, rugged **brushes**. I also **displaced** the sketch layer twice to get the right scratchy crayon or charcoal look. The image was flattened and the contrast was increased with **Levels**.

I made a duplicate layer and used the **Dark 1 gradient** in the **Gradient Editor** to map to the image (**Colors/Gradient Map**). I put the old layer on top, set it to **Multiply** and erased everything except the contours and parts that I wanted to keep dark (like the baby's eye and ear).

In the top layer I placed the posterized photo as **Darken Only**, changed the color to violet and applied some motion blur. The result looks a bit like watercolor, but only if it's used in small areas of a composite image.

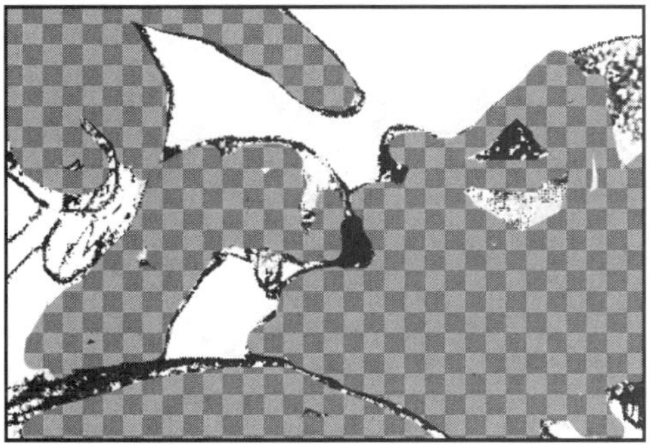

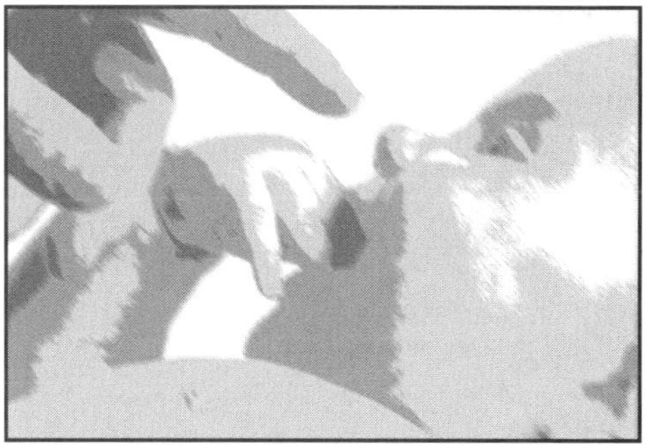

Light, Motion And Texture Transformation

These special effects can provide that extra "something" to make a good image great.

AN ELECTRIC HORSEMAN

To create the Electric Horseman, I started out with a photo of a rodeo rider. The horse and rider were selected with the **Bezier select tool** and pasted to a transparent layer in a new image. The horse's halter, mane and tail were either **cloned** away or erased, and the rider was selected separately (using a little feather) and saved as a copy in another layer. The horse and rider layer was duplicated twice, and those copies were desaturated and adjusted with **Levels** to create highlight/ shadow layers.

Shadow layer

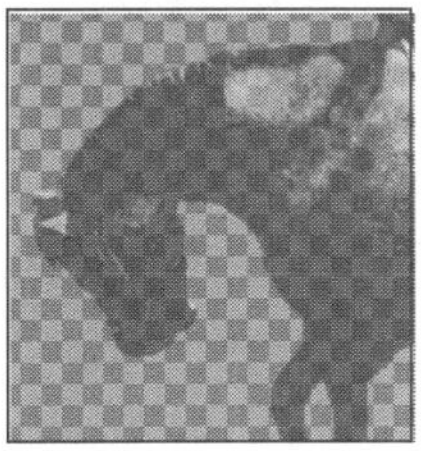

Highlight layer

Using A Cow To Make A Leopard Of A Horse...

To create the leopard skin, two more copies were made. In the first copy, the entire horse shape was filled with the Leopard pattern from the **Patterns** dialog box. Since this pattern isn't entirely seamless, it was adjusted by painting yellow and black spots along the visible joints. The leopard layer was set in **Darken Only Mode** over the second copy, which was filled with a yellow-orange gradient to add color depth to the leopard skin. To add some extra glow to the "leopard horse," one more texture layer was added. This time I used the black-and-white cow pattern, and set it to **Overlay**. Note that this does not make the horse look like a cow (!). In **Overlay**, the large dark spots on a white background give the illusion of powerful muscles under a shiny coat. Now I turned to the layer with the rider, and changed saturation, brightness and contrast to make it fit the new "horse."

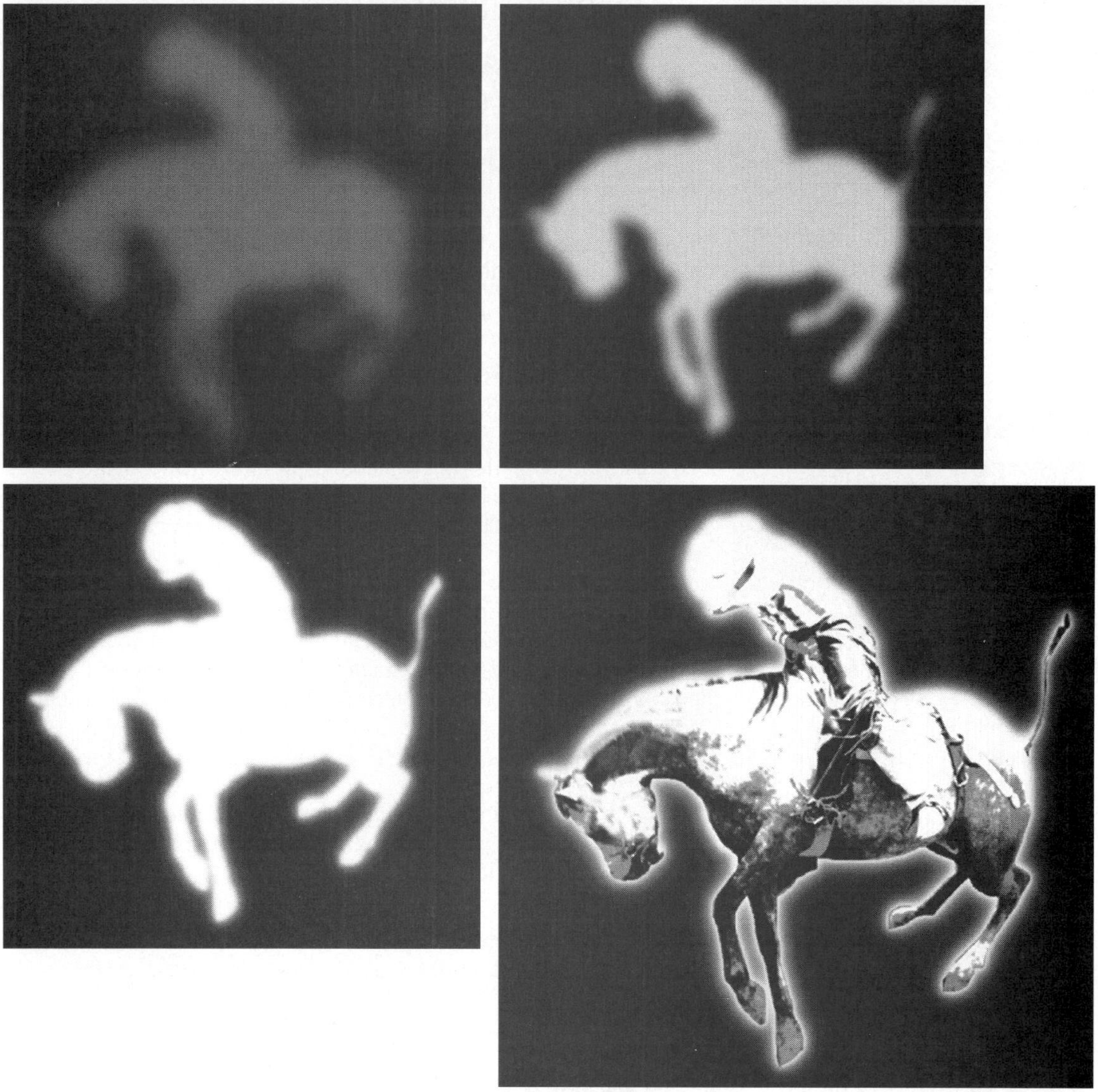

Making Things Glow

The glow layer was made by filling a feathered horse and rider selection with red, yellow and white, each time with lower **feather** values, and setting the layer to **Screen Mode**.

Dark movement layer

Light movement layer

Adding Motion

The illusion of movement was more complicated, because just adding some motion blur wouldn't suffice to create the subtle effect I wanted. I had to create two different motion layers — one dark and one light. For the dark movement layer, **Blur/Motion Blur** was applied to a copy of the cow glow layer. I then did the same for a copy of the orange gradient layer, but this time I inverted the selection, and only the blurred parts outside of the horse were used. These layers were merged after adjusting the **opacity**. The dark movement was still a bit too strong in some parts, so a **layer mask** was used to tone down or remove motion glow where it wasn't wanted. This layer was set to **Darken Only**. For the light movement layer, I blurred the shadow layer and the leopard layer (as with the orange gradient layer before), merged it and adjusted it to darker. To protect the rider figure from too much blur, a layer mask was used here as well. This layer was set to **Screen Mode**.

Adding Scenery

The background was made of a photo of a blue sky, a city panorama by night and a yellow evening sky. The blue sky image was transformed to dark clouds with **Image/Hue-Saturation**, and the yellow sky was merged to the city panorama. The flash of lightning was a bit harder, because the only lightning image I had was the Lightning pattern in the **Pattern** dialog, and that was too repetitive to be used directly. The problem was solved by scaling an image with the lightning pattern and using the **Map/Fractal Trace** plug-in. From that image I could **feather** select a suitable part, and adjust it with **Transform/Perspective** and **Screen Mode** to look the way I wanted.

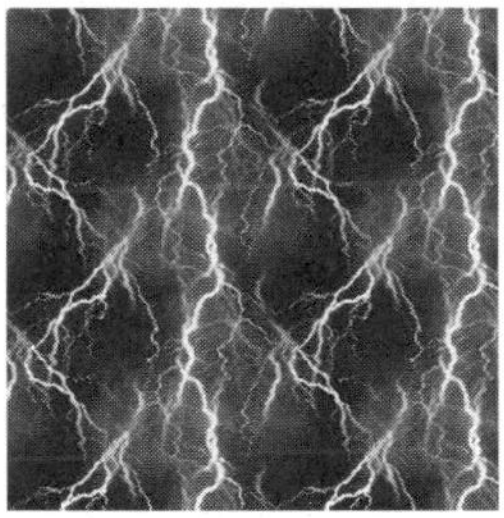

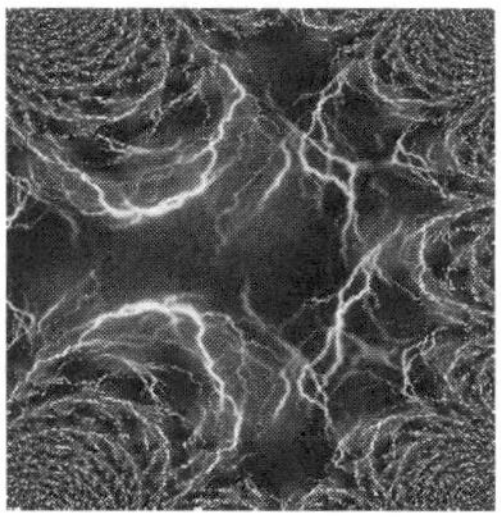

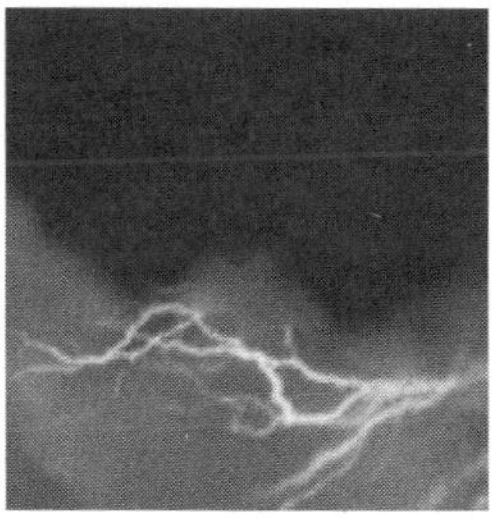

MAKING A MONTAGE

There are many ways of blending images, but for advanced montages, the most versatile method is to use different layer masks.

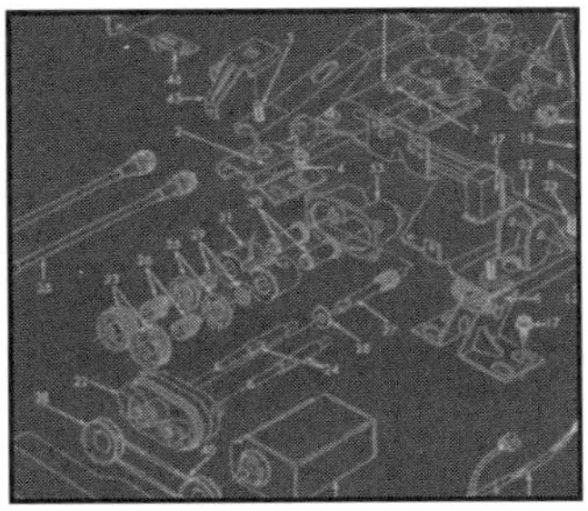

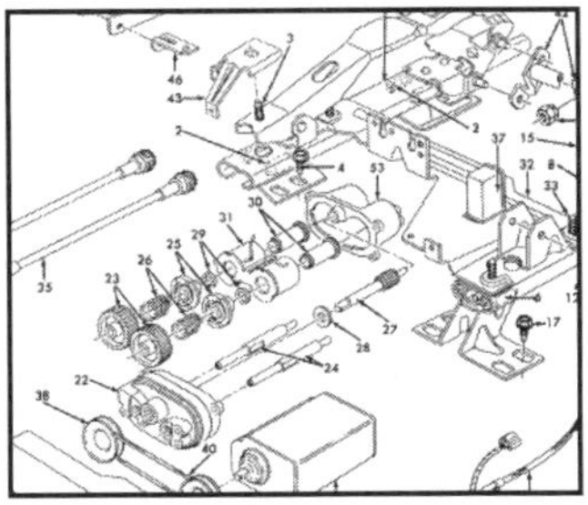

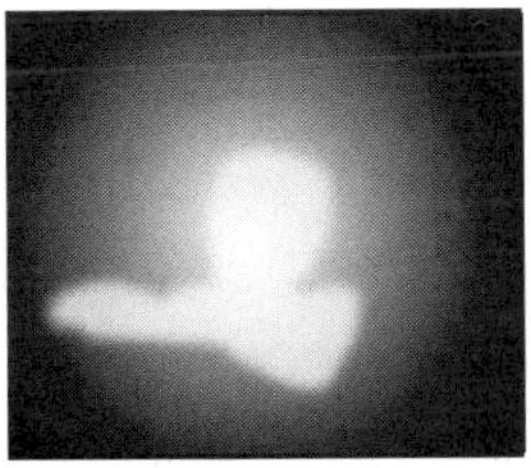

The Background

For the Chevelle montage, I used a drawing from the 1966 Chevrolet Chassis Service Manual for background. To make it less dominant, it was **inverted**, **blurred** and **noise** was added. The color and brightness were changed to a soft "old looking" sepia tone.

The Vignette

The main collage element was a snapshot of me and our Chevelle. This image was blended to the background with the help of a **layer mask**. I started by making a round vignette shape with a **radial gradient**. This masked out nice and soft, but it also meant that the gradual transparency was evenly distributed. To put an emphasis on the person rather than the car (I like to keep it that way) some of the mask was painted white to protect the face and especially the arms from transparency.

The vignette was still a little weak, and too smooth at the edges, so I made a duplicate where the layer mask was brightened up with **Levels**, and noise was added to the mask (not the image). This made the top layer blend well with the spotted background, as well as with the smooth copy underneath.

Adding Noise

The next element in the montage was a picture of the fuel pump assembly. Here, **noise** was added to *both mask and image*. The **glow mask** was made with a feathered lasso selection which was filled with black and heavily blurred before applying the noise. Finally, the image was tinted with the same tone as the background.

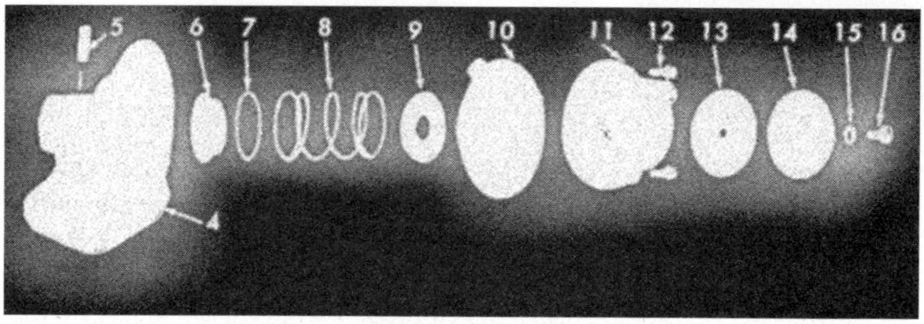

Making An Element Stand Out In A Composition

The steering wheel was treated in a similar manner, only this image was taken from an old magazine, so no noise was added (it was already quite noisy).

The picture of the car (from a 1966 Chevrolet dealer catalog) was desaturated and tinted. To create the illusion of speed, **linear motion blur** was applied to an inverted selection of the car, then a simple **layer mask** was added to blend the car with the background. To make the car stand out more in the overall composition, **contrast** and **brightness** values were increased.

Two photographs from the service manual were then pasted to a layer with low **opacity**.

Adding Depth To Text Layers

To make the Chevelle Malibu SS text, I used three different layers. The "Chevelle" layer is supposed to be sharp and look close to the observer, whereas the "Malibu" layer is further away from focus. This was accomplished by placing the Malibu layer very close to (almost under) the Chevelle layer, tinting and blurring it and placing a very soft shadow on top of it.

PART II

Gimp Installation

- *Obtaining And Installing Gimp*
- *Migrating From Photoshop*

CHAPTER 4

Obtaining And Installing Gimp

In this chapter, we will tell you how to obtain a copy of Gimp, and how to install it.

How To Install Gimp Personal Files

Most Linux distributions include Gimp. But if Gimp isn't already installed, it can most likely be installed by your Linux distribution application's installation tool. However, if you are working on, for example, an SGI workstation, Gimp will probably not be installed. Please read "Obtaining Gimp" on page 48 to get a full explanation on how to install Gimp both as a binary and as a source on your system.

At the **command prompt**, type "`gimp`" and press Enter. If you've never used Gimp before, it will display the **Gimp Installation** dialog (as shown), which tells you that it will install some personal Gimp files in your home directory.

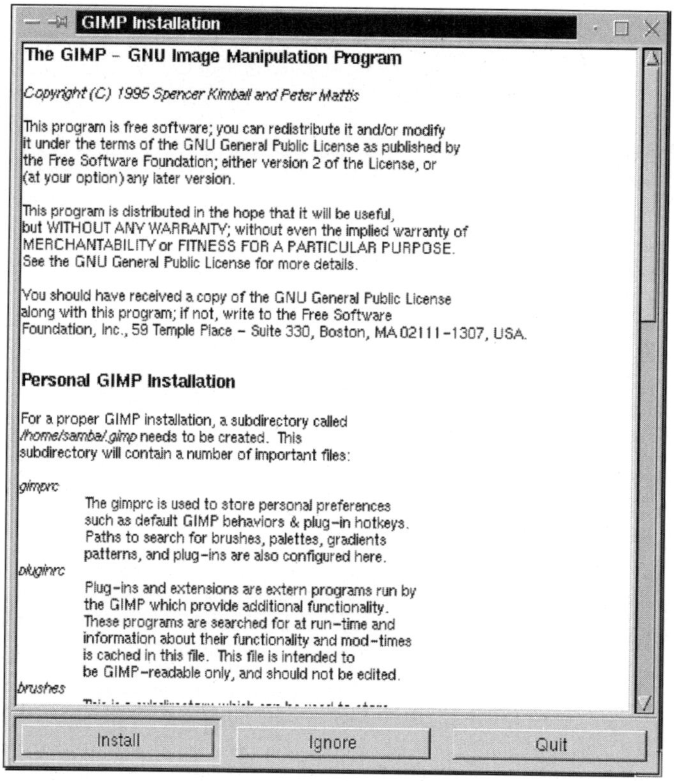

Figure 4.1 *The Gimp Installation dialog*

The dialog box also describes the Gimp license and what kinds of files Gimp will install. It's advisable to read it, but we will discuss these topics later in this chapter. If you want to run Gimp, press the **Install** button now!

After a short delay, you will see the **Installation Log** dialog box, informing you that all files were successfully installed.

Figure 4.2 *The Gimp Installation Log dialog*

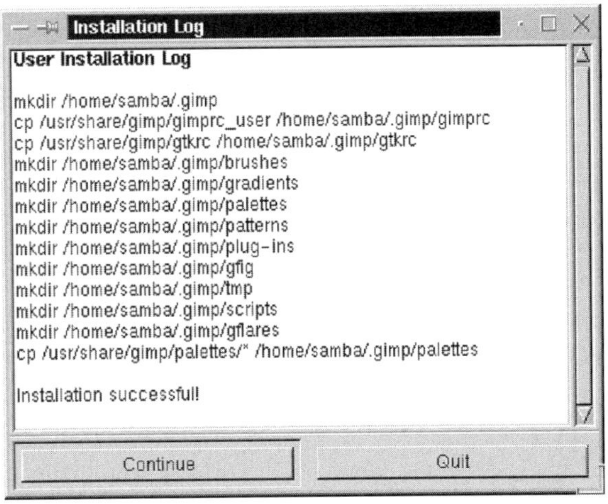

A nice feature of UNIX is that programs often store personal initialization files and modules in your home directory. Then, you can change and add features to an application without having to modify the application at a system level. Gimp is no exception.

Unfortunately, most UNIX programs do not have a GUI for making adjustments to these files and modules. Here, thankfully, Gimp *is* an exception, because it includes a GUI for adjusting **user-defined** functions. However, there are some special functions (i.e., plug-ins) that you'll have to edit using a regular text editor.

After the file installation, you'll see a splash screen, along with a progress bar. The progress bar shows Gimp loading all its extensions, data and certain plug-ins.

Gimp In 256 Colors (Using An 8 Bit Display)

Does your 8 bit X11 system cause Gimp to crash just after displaying the splash screen? If it does, you'll need to configure Gimp to use a **private color map**. Using a private color map, you'll see color flashing as you move from window to window, but at least all possible colors will be available to Gimp.

To make Gimp use a private color map, you need to edit the `gimprc` file by hand (since Gimp won't start, you can't use Gimp's GUI). You'll have to do it in an xterm window (a terminal, console, etc.). Type in the command:

```
vi ~/.gimp/gimprc
```

This command starts the vi editor (however, you're welcome to use whatever editor you prefer). Move to the line # `(install-colormap)` by pressing the j key several times. When your cursor is placed over the # sign at the beginning of the line, press the x key and the # sign will be erased. Now type:

```
:wq!
```

This command will both save and exit the file. Gimp is now configured to work in an 8 bit display environment, and will not crash.

We would like to point out that if your system can only display 256 colors, you will never be able to access the full power of Gimp. Gimp will simply not display the colors as they would appear with 16 bit (or higher) color resolution. We therefore strongly suggest that you upgrade your graphic device to at least 16 bit.

Advice On System Resources

Since we only use Intel and SPARC hardware platforms running Linux and Solaris, we can only give advice on these platforms and operating systems. Our advice is also subjective, because it is what *we* consider to be the minimum or the recommended hardware for running Gimp.

On a Linux Intel platform:

- Minimum: Pentium 75, 32 MB RAM
- Recommended: Pentium 200, 64 MB RAM

Solaris Sparc platform:

- Minimum: SparcClassic, 32 MB RAM
- Recommended: Sparcstation 5 110 MHz, 96 MB RAM

Graphic device:

- Minimum: Frame buffer capable of 16 bit color at 800x600
- Recommended: Frame buffer capable of 24 bit color at 1024x768

What Are All These Files Used For?

Now, let's examine the files and directories that Gimp installed in your home directory. Gimp created the `.gimp` directory for its files.The dot indicates that `.gimp` is a hidden directory, and you have to use the `ls -a` command (as opposed to just `ls`) in a terminal window to see it. In this directory, Gimp created three files: `gimprc`, `gtkrc` and `pluginrc`, along with subdirectories called `brushes`, `gradients`, `palettes`, `patterns`, `plug-ins`, `scripts`, `gfig`, `gflares` and `tmp`. So, what are all these files for?

- `gimprc` and `gtkrc` are your personal settings files for Gimp and GTK+, respectively (GTK+ is Gimp's GUI toolkit). Most of the settings in these files are adjustable via the **Preferences** dialog box in Gimp, but some of them are not and must be edited by hand. The Preferences dialog box is discussed in "Gimp Preferences" on page 100.
- `pluginrc` is a file that Gimp needs to store settings about plug-ins, scripts and other external programs. *You should not edit or change this file,* but you may erase it if Gimp starts complaining about it.

- The `brushes` subdirectory is where you can store your own personally created brushes. You will learn how to create and install brushes in "Brushes" on page 172. Once you've installed one or more brushes (and have refreshed the **Brushes** dialog box) your personal brushes will show up in Gimp alongside the system-wide brushes.
- The `patterns` subdirectory is where you can store your own personal patterns. You will learn more about how to create and install patterns in "Patterns" on page 173. Like personal brushes, personal patterns will appear alongside the system-wide patterns after you've installed them, and have refreshed the **Patterns** dialog box.
- The `gradients` subdirectory is for storing your own personal gradients. You will learn more about how to create and install gradients in "The Gradient Editor" on page 177. Your personal gradients will show up in the **Gradient Editor** after refreshing the **Gradients** dialog box.
- The `palettes` subdirectory holds your own personal palettes as well as system palettes that you have edited. If you want your system default palette back, you have to rename or erase the copy in your personal palette directory. You will learn about creating, editing and installing palettes in "Palettes" on page 176. The new palettes will show up in the **Palettes** dialog *after you quit and restart Gimp.*
- The `swap` subdirectory stores the cache of the images you are working on. Gimp needs this cache in order to support the **Undo** capability, and to make it possible to edit large images without consuming too much memory. If Gimp crashes, or something else happens, you may be able to find a copy of your image in this subdirectory.
- The `plug-ins` subdirectory holds any plug-ins that you have created or downloaded off the Internet. New plug-ins show up the *next time you start Gimp*. You will learn more about plug-ins in Chapters 23 through 39, and in "Compiling Plug-ins" on page 769, we provide a few tips on compiling plug-ins.
- The `scripts` subdirectory holds any personal Script-Fus that you have created or downloaded off the Internet. The scripts will show up after an `Xtns|Script-Fu|Refresh` command. You will learn about Script-Fus in "Script-Fu: Description And Function" on page 687, and in "Mike Terry's Black Belt School Of Script-Fu" on page 697, you will find some tips on making your own Script-Fus.
- The `gfig` subdirectory holds your personal Gfig drawings (created with the **Gfig** plug-in). You will learn about Gfig in "Gfig" on page 600.
- The `gflare` subdirectory holds your personal Gflares (created with the **Gflare** plug-in). You will learn more about Gflare in "Gflare" on page 519.

The nice thing about all this is that if you find any new plug-ins, scripts and so on, you can easily install them in your personal Gimp directories, and don't have to beg your system administrator to install them for you.

We encourage you to create your own brushes, palettes, gradients, plug-ins and Script-Fus, and to share them with the whole Gimp community. Don't be shy; even small contributions are welcome.

You can upload them to `ftp.gimp.org` or to the `Plug-in Registry` at `http://registry.gimp.org`. May the spirit of free software be with you!

OBTAINING GIMP

Gimp version 1.0 was released as a **source distribution**, but for some popular systems there may be **binary distributions**. To get the source code, FTP to `ftp.gimp.org`. The source code is in the directory `/pub/gimp/v1.x/v1.0.X`. `1.0.X` indicates the version, and *you should always get the latest version.*

The directory `/pub/gimp/fonts` includes some nice free fonts that you can use with Gimp (see "How To Get Fonts To Gimp" on page 759 for instructions on how to install them). The directory `/pub/gimp/libs` includes some of the libraries that enable some of Gimp's optional features, such as the ability to load and save JPEG images. The directory `/pub/gimp/contrib` contains some nice palettes, gradients, etc. If a binary distribution of Gimp exists, you'll find it under `/pub/gimp/binary`.

If you are not familiar with FTP, you can use your Web browser to download Gimp, just type the URL `ftp://ftp.gimp.org/pub/gimp` and go on from there. Realize that the Gimp FTP site is often heavily trafficked, and if `ftp.gimp.org` isn't near you, we suggest that you use a mirror site (see "FTP" on page 880 or `http://www.gimp.org` for the nearest mirror sites).

INSTALLING A SOURCE DISTRIBUTION

If you downloaded a source distribution, you should now have a file called `gimp-1.0.X.tar.gz` or a file called `gimp-1.0.x.tar.bz2`. (For binary distributions, see the next section.) If you want to, you can always get the extra data distribution as well as the unstable plug-in distribution (in the old Gimp distribution directory). The **data distribution** includes optional palettes, patterns, gradients and brushes that you may find useful. The **unstable plug-in** distribution contains some plug-ins that weren't considered stable enough to be released with Gimp 1.0, so remember that they may be unstable and difficult to compile. (However, we have used many of them with success here at Frozenriver, and they have also been documented in the manual.) You will find the unstable plug-ins under `ftp.gimp.org/pub/gimp/v1.0/old/v1.0.0`.

To unpack the archive, move to the directory containing the Gimp file you downloaded and type in the following command:

```
zcat gimp-1.0.X.tar.gz | tar -xvf
```

This command creates a subdirectory in your current directory called `gimp`. Change to the `gimp` directory by typing `cd gimp`.

Which Libraries Does Gimp Need?

If you don't have them already, you need to get the following libraries or programs:

- **GTK+** (1.0.x), to *compile* Gimp. You need this library because all of Gimp's GUI and functions are built on top of it.
- **GNU GhostScript**, to enable PostScript file viewing and editing. Type `gs -v` to output the current version of your GhostScript distribution. If you receive an error message, either you have not installed GhostScript or it is not in your path.
- **Aladdin GhostScript** (version 5.50 or higher), to enable good PDF (also known as Acrobat) file viewing and editing. Type `gs -v` to output the current version of your GhostScript distribution. If you receive an error message, either you have not installed GhostScript or it is not in your path. (Aladdin is an earlier version of the GNU GhostScript.)
- **GNU wget**, for downloading files off the Internet directly into Gimp. To check whether you have wget, type `wget` into a terminal window. If you receive an error message, either you have not installed wget or it is not in your path.
- **xv**, if you want to use **Guash**. Guash is a Gimp plug-in with a GUI interface for browsing and opening images. Guash uses xv to create its thumbnail images.
- **gzip**, to enable extra file compression/decompression of any image format. To check whether you have gzip, type `gzip -h`. If you get an error message, either you have not installed gzip or it is not in your path.
- **bzip**, to enable extra file compression/decompression of any image format. To check whether you have bzip, type `bzip -h`. If you receive an error message, either you have not installed bzip or it is not in your path.
- **SANE**, if you want to *scan* images directly into Gimp.
- **libtiff**, to enable reading and writing of TIFF images.
- **libz**, to enable PNG compression.
- **libpng**, to enable reading and writing of PNG images.
- **libjpeg**, to enable reading and writing of JPEG images.
- **libmpeg**, to enable reading of MPEG movies.

To determine whether you have these libraries, look in `/usr/lib` or `/usr/local/lib`, or contact your system administrator. Most of the programs and libraries come as standard with most Linux distributions, with the possible exceptions of GTK+, Aladdin GhostScript, SANE, wget and bzip.

Remember that even if you have the libraries you must also have the header files to compile Gimp. It's very common to divide, say, a libtiff package into a library package and a header package (development package). So please make sure that you have the header (development) package installed.

Let's Begin To Build Gimp

First of all, fire up a **new xterm** window using your window manager or via the command:

```
xterm -sl 200 -sb &
```

In the new xterm window, move to the directory where you put the Gimp files. Then, type in the command:

```
./configure
```

This command will try to locate the files that Gimp needs in order to compile. Now, scroll up and find out if the configure program could find all of the files. If not, you will have to tell the configure program where to find the missing files. For example, if your system couldn't locate the `libtiff` and `libjpeg` files, you can do this by adding the following **additions to the command-line**:

```
--with-libtiff=<path to your tiff library>
--with-libjpeg=<path to your jpeg library>
--disable-debug
```

(If you are a user and not a developer, you want to turn off debugging. Debugging is turned off by default).

So, the command line might look something like this:

```
./configure --disable-debug --with-libtif=/usr/local/
lib/tiff/
```

After the `configure` command has properly executed, you'll need to type in the command:

```
make
```

make will build your Gimp application. (If you're having problems, you will find more information on compiling in "Compiling Plug-ins" on page 769.)

If there were no errors, Gimp built successfully, and you can install it. To install Gimp, enter the command:

```
make install
```

make install will, by default, install Gimp in `/usr/local/bin`, the Gimp plug-ins in `/usr/local/lib/gimp/1.0` and shared data like scripts, brushes and configurations in the `/usr/local/share/gimp/` directory.

You are allowed to install Gimp in directories other than the ones mentioned above. To do so, read the `INSTALL` file and use the specified command-line options for the configuration program (in particular, `--prefix`).

Once you're done, go back to the first section in this chapter and read about how to install your *personal Gimp files*.

Installing A Binary Distribution

First of all, get the latest **binary distribution** for your system — download it from the Gimp FTP site or a mirror site. If you are working on a **Red Hat Linux** or **Debian** system, download the packages appropriate for your system (`.rpm` and `.deb` respectively); otherwise, download an ordinary `tar.gz` archive and unpack it into the correct directory (usually /) using the command:

```
gzip -dc xxxx.tar.gz | tar xvf
```

Make sure that Gimp is in your path and execute it (type in `gimp` and see if it works). Then, go back to the beginning of the chapter, to where personal Gimp files are discussed.

If you have bought the printed version of this book, you will find an enclosed Gimp CD-ROM compiled for Linux and Solaris systems.

Installing Extra Packages To Extend Gimp

To install the **extra data distribution** you only have to download it. Unpack it, run the configure script and do a `make install`.

You may also consider downloading and installing the contrib archive, to install more brushes, gradients, etc. You only have to download it, unpack it and install the contents in the right directory. You can install new brushes either in your personal brush directory (`~/.gimp/brushes`) or in the system-wide directory (`usr/local/share/gimp/brushes`). Some of the contribution archives come with configure scripts; if that is the case, you install them as you installed Gimp. Since it is only data, it should be quite simple. Just type:

```
./configure && make install
```

Most of the time this will install the data distributions correctly.

It's a good idea to download the `freefont` and `sharefont` archives, so you can get some more fonts for Gimp. Read about how to install them in "How To Get Fonts To Gimp" on page 759.

Extra Plug-ins

Many of the plug-ins described in GUM are not found in the standard Gimp distribution. They are either in the `gimp-plug-ins-unstable` distribution or at the plug-in registry (`http://registry.gimp.org`).

We don't want to recommend that you download all of the extra plug-ins available for Gimp (they are quite numerous). If you don't, you will most probably lack some of the filters described in the manual, or have an older version of the plug-in. Most of the time you have to compile these plug-ins by hand; no binary distribution or configure scripts are available. But if you find an interesting plug-in in this book that you don't have, don't hesitate to download it and install it.

On the other hand, when you installed Gimp, a second program called **gimptool** was also installed. Gimptool makes it easy for you to compile plug-ins for Gimp.

Read more about gimptool in "Compiling Plug-ins" on page 769 and "The gimptool Man Page" on page 804. So, if you don't have a plug-in (or a filter) that is described in the GUM and you would like to get it, you'll need to download and compile it.

Note that many of the plug-ins are beta software and can be considered unstable, but most of them are (as usual in the UNIX world) of very high quality, and we have encountered very few problems (compared to the bugs in commercial alternatives).

Gimp Airlines

CHAPTER 5

Gimp For Photoshop Users

This chapter is for experienced graphic artists and Photoshop users who want to learn how to use Gimp without having to go through the basics of image manipulation. We'll explain why you want Gimp when you have Photoshop. We'll also try to point out the differences between Gimp and Photoshop so that you can get started right away.

WHY SHOULD I USE GIMP WHEN I HAVE PHOTOSHOP?

Perhaps you reckon that you already have the best of the best when it comes to image editing programs. In our view, you don't have the best of the best, simply because there is no single image editing program that is "the" best. There are several reasons why you should migrate to Gimp, and there are also some reasons why you shouldn't. First, we'll describe Gimp's strengths.

Gimp has nearly all the functionality that Photoshop has. In certain areas, Gimp has more capacity, and in some areas less. Contrary to what many people believe, Gimp is not just another Photoshop clone. Even if there are likenesses between Gimp and Photoshop, many other programs such as Paintshop Pro, X-res, Picture Publisher and Photo Paint also have their fair share of such similarities. This is not surprising, because Photoshop and its user interface is more or less a de facto standard when it comes to image editing programs.

Of all the image manipulation programs for advanced users that we have worked with, we have found Gimp to be one of the most versatile and powerful instruments available.

GIMP IS FREE

Gimp is a free program, and it can be downloaded from the Internet. But even more importantly, it's not freeware. Gimp is an **OSS** (**Open Source Software**) program covered by the GPL license, which gives you the freedom to access and also to change the source code that makes up the program. This is how and why Gimp is constantly being developed and improved.

GIMP HAS A LOT OF GREAT PLUG-INS AND SPECIAL FUNCTIONS

- Gimp comes with more than 220 plug-ins, some with very advanced functions. Practically all of the usual plug-ins that you can purchase as accessories to Photoshop are already there in Gimp, or they can be downloaded from `http://registry.gimp.org` at no cost.
- Gimp's plug-ins are often much more powerful than Photoshop's. We are not saying that all Gimp filters will produce better results. But if you compare them to plug-ins that are supposed to do the same thing, then a Gimp filter is usually a more fine-tuned instrument that will supply the user with a large number of parameters.

  This is for better or for worse, depending on what kind of user you are. Photoshop filters are often of the *"press OK and get an instant effect"* type. They are more static, and provide the artist with less choices. Still, Photoshop filter effects are generally very well chosen. Settings are mindful, and the effect they yield is extremely useful for many standard assignments in graphic design. In short, it is hard to fail with a Photoshop filter. Gimp filters on the other hand are more unpredictable in the hands of an inexperienced artist just because they offer such a wide range of parameters and settings. However, for an advanced user, they provide an incomparable artistic freedom.

- Gimp has predominantly been targeting web design, and comes with a variety of tools designed for creating electronically distributed graphics. Most of these tools are not available with Photoshop, which means that you have to invest in a number of additional programs to be able to access these features.

Gimp Has An Innovative And Intuitive Structure

- Gimp has a much smarter menu system that is far more efficient than the one present in Photoshop, or for that matter in all other image manipulation programs that we know of.
- Gimp has a very different outlook on layers, which is much more flexible than what you will find in Photoshop. Layers in Gimp don't come in one size only; you can create layers of different sizes, or Gimp will optimize the layer size automatically.
- Gimp has a much more intuitive way of dealing with patterns. All patterns are displayed in thumbnail format in a pattern dialog. To select a pattern, you just press one of the thumbnails, and the chosen pattern can be applied with the bucket fill or clone tool.
- Gimp is faster than Photoshop when you work with relatively small images, such as those targeting web design.

Nothing Beats Gimp Scripting

- Gimp has no less than four powerful scripting languages that can be used to create very powerful plug-ins. (Note that in the 220 plug-ins mentioned earlier, the numerous scripting plug-ins have not been included.)
- Yes, Photoshop also has certain scripting capabilities, but it doesn't compare to the power of an advanced scripting language such as Perl. When it comes to scripting, we don't think it's unfair to compare Photoshop with a little baby and Gimp with a full-grown adult with 30 years of working experience. That's how big the difference is.
- Gimp can be a backend in your web server, serving your web site with stunning graphics.
- Gimp has functions such as revision control, so you can keep track of changes made to a file. You can also connect Gimp directly to a database and create a very nice image database. Those functions are among the more exotic, but they are just some of the things that indicate that this is no ordinary image manipulation program.

If you are working with a UNIX version of Photoshop, such as version 3.01, or if you have an older Mac or Windows version of Photoshop, then we could make this list about twice as long. Let's just say that if you are working with a UNIX version of PhotoShop, then you shouldn't contemplate switching to Gimp. Just do it! You will still have Photoshop for tasks where Gimp is insufficient.

So What's The Drawback?

Gimp can't handle anything other than 8 bit RGB, grayscale and indexed images. That's the big disadvantage of Gimp. Since Gimp doesn't support CMYK or spot colors such as PANTONE, Gimp can't compete with Photoshop in the prepress field.

Photoshop has more third-party plug-ins than Gimp. Yes, even though Gimp has around 220 real plug-ins at the moment and that number is constantly growing with around one plug-in every two weeks, there are still more plug-ins that you can buy as accessories to Photoshop, and they aren't available for Gimp.

Photoshop is also more effective (faster) when it comes to big images with a lot of layers (images bigger than 500x500 pixels).

Conclusion

It is more or less impossible to tell you what you should or shouldn't do; we will always be wrong in some cases. Still, there are situations where it is relatively safe to suggest that you should migrate to Gimp:

- If you work in a UNIX environment and already have Photoshop installed on your workstation, don't hesitate for a second, switch to Gimp right away. You can still work with Photoshop when you need to deal with prepress matters.
- If you are a graphic designer working with web design, then it's a very good idea to migrate to Gimp.
- If you're interested in advanced scripting, and you need to automate certain functions for your daily work, Gimp is the program for you.

As the authors of this book, we'd like to recommend Gimp for all kinds of graphic design. Gimp is so powerful and gives you so much more freedom. There are, however, cases when you should think twice before switching to Gimp:

- If your chief occupation is prepress, then it's not a good idea to switch to Gimp. The exception to this rule is if you work with a UNIX version of Photoshop. If you work with the UNIX version, then you can create the design in Gimp and import the final outcome into Photoshop.
- If you are working with a Mac and don't want to change operating systems, you will not be able to use Gimp.

Migrating To Gimp

So, you have decided to switch to Gimp, or at least to try it out. In this section, we will try to describe the main differences between Gimp and Photoshop. We will assume that you are fairly well acquainted with a reasonably recent version of Photoshop.

We will not cover every dissimilarity between Gimp and Photoshop, because then this chapter would turn into a new book. Look at it as a quick guide that will serve as a starting point.

What's Compatible?

Gimp can read Photoshop files, so if you have a large image library of PSD files you need not worry. You can open PSD images in Gimp, but you have to remember that Gimp doesn't understand CMYK or spot color specifications. The PSD file must be 8 bit grayscale, 8 bit RGB or indexed.

If you are an Adobe Filter Factory fan, and have a lot of Filter Factory filters, we have some good news for you. By copying the FF filters to Gimp's User Filter directory, they will be available for use in Gimp. Please read "User Filter (Adobe Filter Factory Emulator)" on page 507 how to install your filters.

There's also a file that will make Photoshop shortcut commands available in Gimp, so you can control functions with the same shortcuts that you're used to in Photoshop. You are also free to assign any shortcut key to a function of your choice, simply by typing the new shortcut beside the function in the menu.

Where Are The Menus?

The first time you run Gimp, it will install some personal configuration and data files. Just answer OK to those questions (see "How To Install Gimp Personal Files" on page 44). A moment later Gimp will start by displaying the Gimp splash screen. Then the toolbox, which is quite similar to the one in Photoshop, will appear on your desktop.

The questions that every Photoshop user will ask themselves now are undoubtedly: Where are the *menus* and where is my *working area*? There is only a File menu and an Xtns menu, and there isn't much in those menus.

How To Get To The Menus

To access the menus in Gimp you have to **open** or **create** a new image. Select `File|New` to create a new image.

Select `File|Open` to open an existing image file. If your file has a well-known suffix, such as tif(f), psd, jp(e)g, etc., then the **Determine File Type** menu should be set to *Automatic*. For further information on how to open files, read "Opening Files" on page 79.

THE RIGHT MOUSE BUTTON

Press the *right mouse button* in the opened image, and voilà, there are the menus! In our opinion, this is one of the best things about Gimp, and you will probably agree with us as soon as you get used to it. In most other programs, you have to travel a long way with the mouse to access the different function menus. This results in a constant clicking, dragging and moving the mouse up and down, to perform even the simplest task (which is why remembering shortcut commands by heart tends to be so important in Photoshop). In Gimp, you simply press the right mouse button and all the menus are there, close at hand.

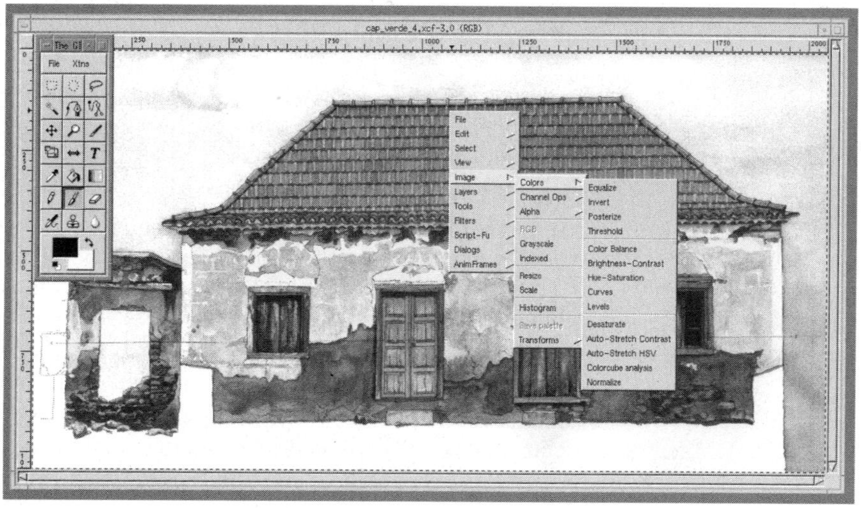

Figure 5.1 *Gimp's menu system is activated by the right mouse button. Just press the right mouse button in the image, and you have instant access to all of Gimp's features.*

WHERE DO I SET RESOLUTION AND CANVAS SIZE?

Resolution In A New Image

Let's try to make a new image in Gimp with `File|New`. In the **New Image** dialog box, you'll find that the only available size parameters for the new image are the **Width** and the **Height**, and they are measured in *pixels*. This is quite different from Photoshop, where the Width and Height parameters can be specified in *inches* or *cm*, and you are asked to set the **resolution** of the image.

Gimp only has one resolution, and that is the most common monitor resolution; 72 ppi (pixels per inch). This is also known as *web resolution*. Images created in Gimp will look the same when they're open in Gimp as when they are displayed in a browser such as Netscape, so this is no disadvantage if you design for the web.

Since Gimp only displays one resolution, it's only natural that the width and height variables are measured in pixels. Fixed units such as inches or millimeters are not relevant on a monitor and you can't make decent printouts from 72 ppi resolution, so there is no point in using them when you create your image.

Figure 5.2 *In Gimp you can only set the image size in pixels, and the resolution is always 72 ppi. If you need a higher resolution, then you'll have to make a few calculations.*

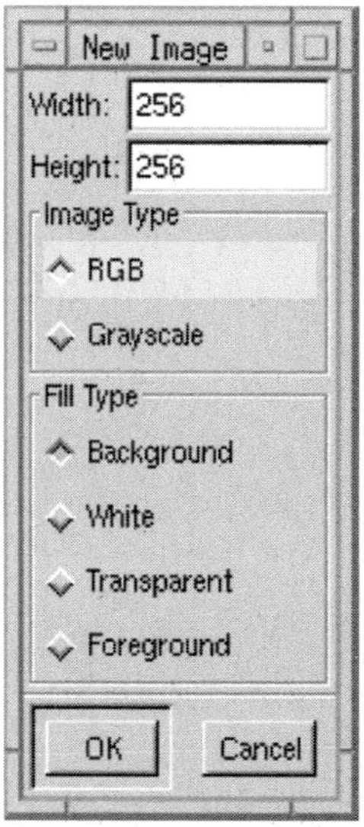

Still, you will need to set the resolution if you want to print your image, and you can do that from Gimp's **Print** dialog (or from **Save As PostScript**). However, there is some math involved. For more information, take a look at "Preparing For The Press" on page 201 for formulas that you can use.

Image Size And Image/Scale

In Photoshop, you are used to changing the resolution and print size with the **Image Size** command. As we have just explained, in Gimp you can't change the resolution and print size until you print (to paper or to file), but you can prepare your image for a certain resolution by changing the *size* (in pixels) of your image. In Gimp, this function is called **Scale** (`right-click|Image|Scale`).

Canvas Size And Image/Resize

In Photoshop, the relative size and proportions of an image can be changed with **Canvas Size**. In Gimp, this command is called **Resize** (`right-click|Image|Resize`). This has caused a lot of confusion among Photoshop users. A common mistake is to confuse the `Image|Resize` command with Photoshop's `Image Size` command, because they associate the terms *image* and *size* with resolution and not with canvas size.

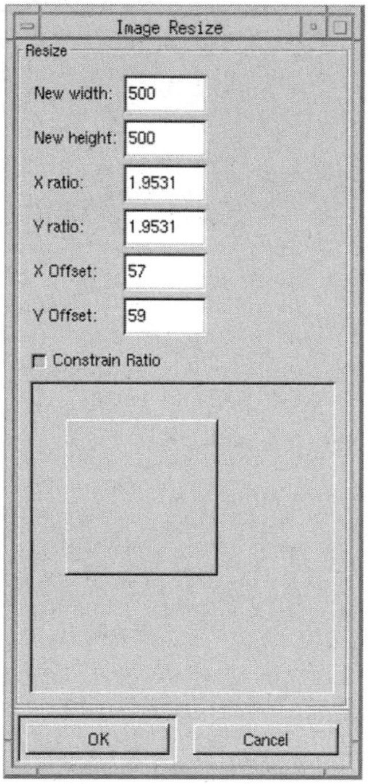

Figure 5.3 *The Image Resize dialog. Notice that you resize the canvas and not the size of the layers because Gimp layers don't have a fixed size.*

The next thing that will bewilder Photoshop users when they increase the canvas size is that the background layer (or any of the other layers for that matter) will not conform to the new size. The reason for this is that in Gimp, layers can have *different sizes*.

By changing the canvas size, you have specified the new maximal layer size (see "Layers And Channels" on page 66). If you want any of your layers to assume this layer size you must select right-click|Layers|<Layers & Channels>|Resize Layer, or invoke the shortcut command Ctrl+R. All new layers that you add to your image will assume the new size, unless you specify another size in the New Layer dialog. Also note that Gimp's `Resize` command will allow you to place your image in a more exact position on the new canvas than is possible in Photoshop (`Canvas Size`), and that you'll get a preview of the proportions to help you set the new size and position.

Dialogs

When you open Photoshop, the Palette windows will appear containing:

- Navigator, Info and Options
- Color, Swatches, Brushes and Actions
- History
- Layers, Channels and Paths.

Gimp also has such dialogs or palettes, but they aren't open when you start Gimp. They are also arranged a bit differently. Let's just say that in Gimp there are no Navigator, Path, Action or History dialogs. We will, however, discuss Actions in "Actions" on page 70.

First of all, you have to open all dialogs in Gimp yourself, because they aren't open by default. You will find them under `File|Dialogs` and `right-click|Dialogs`, and there are also other ways to bring them up. Here is a list of which is which:

- The **Color Info** dialog will pop up when you use the color picker.
- **Tool Options** is the same as Options in Photoshop.
- To access the **Color** dialog, you have to double-click on the foreground or background color swatch in the toolbox.
- **Palettes** is the same as Swatches.
- **Brushes** in Gimp equals Brushes in Photoshop.
- **Layers and Channels** are in the Layers & Channels dialog.
- In Photoshop, you set the gradient type both in the toolbox and in the option dialog of the Gradient tool. In Gimp you have the same (only more advanced) possibilities, but the **Gradient Editor** is invoked from the Dialogs menu, not from the Tool Options dialog.
- Using Gimp's **Patterns** dialog to apply a pattern is much easier than to search for pattern libraries in Photoshop.
- If your image is indexed, then you can view and edit all of the indexed colors in the **Indexed palette**.

Brushes

The Gimp Brush Selection dialog is similar to the Brushes dialog in Photoshop, but there are some differences. In Photoshop, there is a *brush editing dialog,* where you can change or create new round or calligraphic brushes. In Gimp you can also make your own brushes, but not as quickly, because there is no brush editing dialog. In both Photoshop and Gimp you are quite free to create brushes in any form, but the way brushes are handled in Gimp is much easier than in Photoshop. The biggest advantage is Gimp's Brush dialog. If you have a big brush in Photoshop, you will only see the left top corner, which may be totally white. In Gimp, if the brush doesn't fit into the thumbnail image, you can click on the Brush icon, and a life-size image of the brush will pop up. As soon as you release the mouse button, the image will disappear. Read more about brushes in "Brushes" on page 172.

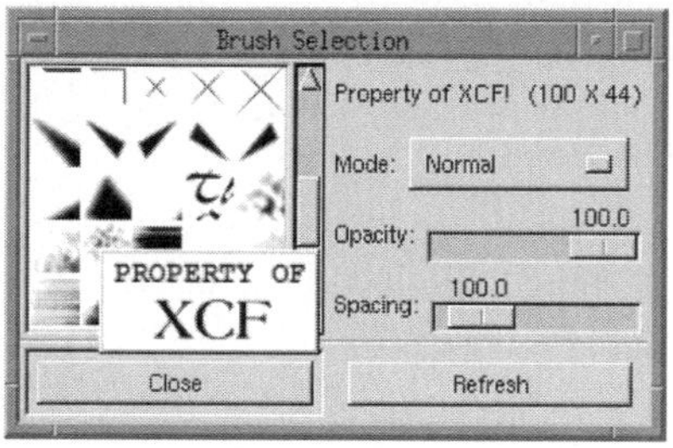

Figure 5.4 *Gimp's Brush Selection dialog. As you can see, a Gimp brush can have any shape. Notice the instant preview of the brush when you click on it.*

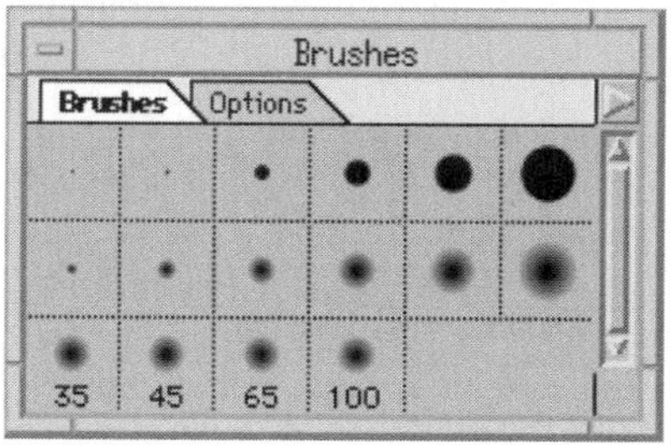

Figure 5.5 *The Photoshop brushes dialog.*

Patterns

Working with patterns is much easier under Gimp than under Photoshop. In Gimp, the currently active pattern is determined by the selected pattern in the **Pattern Selection** dialog. This pattern is available for all tools that use patterns in Gimp (the **bucket fill tool** and the **clone tool**). You can apply patterns in different opacity and modes by setting these parameters in the Bucket Fill dialog or in the Brushes dialog. You can also create and save your own patterns (Gimp has a bundle of excellent tools for making seamless tiles for patterns). When you browse the patterns in the Pattern Selection dialog, you can view the pattern in full scale by clicking on it, just as in the Brushes Selection dialog. Read "Patterns" on page 173 for more information on patterns in Gimp.

Figure 5.6 *Gimp's Pattern Selection dialog. Gimp's way of dealing with patterns is easier than in Photoshop.*

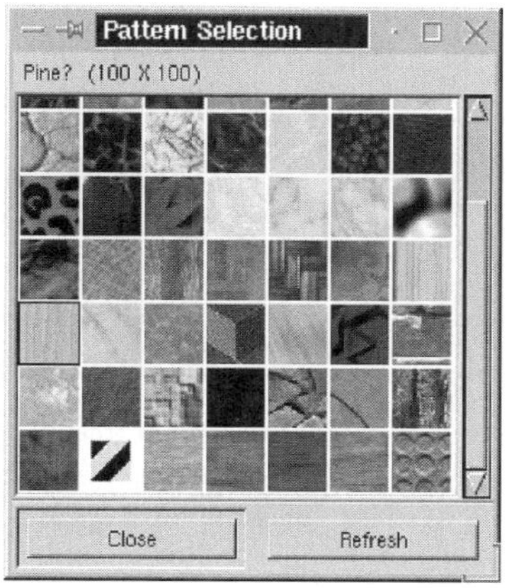

Gradients

The Gimp **Blend tool** has everything that Photoshop's five Gradient tools have, and much more. Gimp has more gradient types, notably the **Shapeburst** gradients, where the gradient follows the shape of the selection so that it looks three-dimensional. There is also an **Offset** control and a very useful **Repeat** function that creates sine- or sawtooth gradient patterns. If you set Blend type to *custom gradient*, Gimp will use the currently active gradient, which is specified in the **Gradient Editor** dialog. Gimp's Gradient Editor is far more advanced than Photoshop's. In fact, it is such a complex tool that we have dedicated an entire section to it, see "The Gradient Editor" on page 177 for more information.

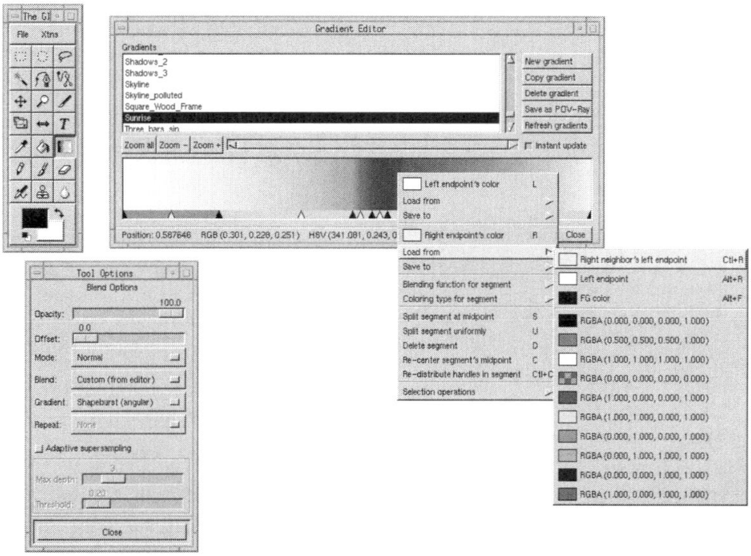

Figure 5.7 *Gimp's gradient tools in action. The menus are, as usual, accessed via the right mouse button.*

Figure 5.8 *Photoshop's Gradient Editor*

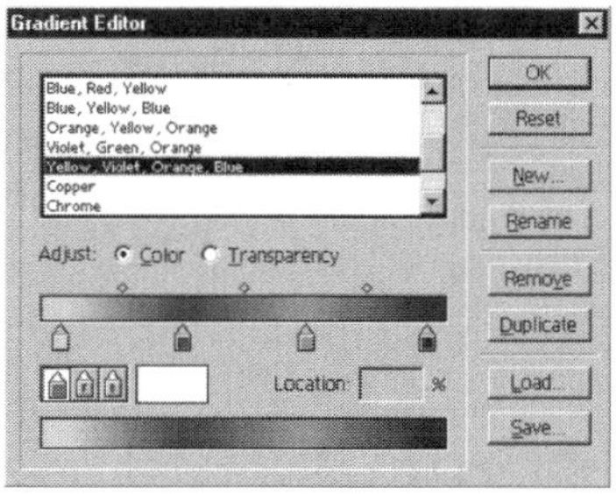

Tool Options

Tool options work just like in Photoshop. However, Gimp doesn't have multiple toolbox buttons, so you can't, for example, click on on the Gradient tool to change to another gradient type. Instead, Gimp keeps the tool controls in the **toolbox option** dialog. This means that you will have to change the gradient type in the Blend tool's option dialog instead of pressing another button in the toolbox.

Layers And Channels

The Layers & Channels dialog looks a lot like Photoshop's, but there are some big differences. We will discuss Layers and Channels further in "Layers And Layer Controls" on page 68 and "Layers And Floating Selections" starting on page 315 will give you even more information. How layers are handled is one of the major dissimilarities between Photoshop and Gimp.

First of all, there is no **Path** dialog. Gimp does support *paths* (see "Paths" on page 68) but only one at a time, and you must store it in an alpha channel to be able to save it.

Channels

- There is no support for CMYK or spot color, so only alpha channels and RGB channels are available in the channels tab.
- All RGB channels are displayed in *color* in Gimp; for example, if you select a single color channel, it won't look like the grayscale thumbnail; it will be blue, green or red.
- Split and Merge Channels functions are in `right-click|Image|Channel Ops|`**`Compose`** and **`Decompose`**.
- To load the selection from an alpha channel, right-click in that channel bar and select **Channel to Selection**.
- To save a selection in a channel, use `right-click|Select|`**`Save to Channel.`**
- Color in a channel always indicates masked areas (default color is black).
- There is no simple way of merging (add, subtract or intersect) two alpha channels to create more advanced selections. To do this you must load one of the channels into another and:
  - Fill the selection with *white* to **add**.
  - Fill with *black* to **subtract**.
  - `right-click|Select|`**`Invert`** and fill with *black* to **intersect**. Then, you may load the selection of this new channel as usual.

Layers

- Since layers can have different sizes in Gimp, you may want to change the layer's size and relative position. The commands that will do that are called **Scale Layer** and **Resize Layer**, and you'll find them in the Layers tab's right-click menu.
- To enable transparency in a solid background layer, alpha must be enabled; select `right-click|Layers|Add Alpha Channel` to do so.
- To load layer transparency, select Alpha to Selection in the menu accessed by right-clicking in the Layers tab.
- When you move layers or channels up and down the stack in Photoshop, you simply drag and drop. In Gimp, you move layers one step up or down with the *arrow buttons*. This is one of the rare occasions when Gimp's UI isn't as good as Photoshop's.

SELECTIONS

Selections in Gimp and selections in Photoshop are alike in the idea, but not in the implementation. Therefore, this is one of the areas that Photoshop users tend to say "% #% #" since they don't understand what's happening.

Moving Selections/Floating Selections

When you make a selection in Photoshop, your Selection tool will be translated to a "Move tool" and you can move the selection. The same happens in Gimp, but when you move the selection you move the *substance* of the selection, not the empty selection outline.

If you now (in desperation) use the selection tool again (within the selection) you will create a mask, not a real selection. This is because when you moved the selection the first time, you created a **floating selection**, and when you moved it the second time, you created a **subselection** (a selection in a floating selection).

To use selections as you're used to in Photoshop (v.5.0) you have to hold Alt + your mouse button when you move the selection. You may now move the selection without creating a floating selection. Does it sound complicated? Well, it both is and isn't. Please read "Moving Selections" on page 112 and everything will be clear.

Selection Control

Basic selection control is nearly the same as in Photoshop, but not exactly the same. Adding to a selection is the same in both Gimp and Photoshop. But where Photoshop uses Alt to subtract, Gimp uses Ctrl. Intersect is therefore quite logically Ctrl+Shift in Gimp.

However, Shift also controls the shape of your selection. If you press Shift it will a create a square or circular selection, depending on which tool you use. If you want a rectangular or an elliptical selection when you add or intersect, the trick is to start the selection with Shift pressed down, and then release Shift immediately after dragging the mouse. For a full understanding of all Gimp tricks with selections, please read "Selection Control" on page 110.

Quick Mask

There is no quick mask function in Gimp. But quick mask is really the same as painting a mask in a channel. The difference is that you can invoke the selection really quickly, and also switch to and from mask/selection in an instant. You can achieve the same effect in Gimp (or Photoshop) using channels. It will be a bit slower, but that's nothing a good script can't take care of.

Paths

Gimp doesn't have multiple, re-editable paths. Gimp paths can't be stored, so once you have converted a path to a selection, there is no way back. Of course, you can use channels to store the selections. For more information about paths in Gimp, i.e., Bezier selection, read "The Bezier Selection Tool" on page 120.

Magnetic Selections

Gimp's equivalent is called *Intelligent Scissors*, but we must admit that Photoshop's tool is much more effective. This is a bit strange because Gimp was first with this feature (Gimp 0.54), well ahead of Photoshop. However, when Gimp 0.99 arrived, the internal image handling was so different that the Intelligent Scissors feature no longer worked. An experimental version was used instead; it was stable but not very efficient. The current rumor is that Intelligent Scissors will be in good shape when Gimp 1.2 is released sometime in the future.

Magic Wand

Gimp's Magic Wand tool is called Fuzzy Select. In the Photoshop tool, you set the sensitivity in the Option dialog. With Fuzzy Select you do it this way:

After you position the cursor and press the mouse button, you have to drag the cursor (don't release the mouse button yet) from the upper-left corner, either to the right or straight down (that doesn't matter) to go from a small, stingy selection to a very generous one.

Layers And Layer Controls

Layers is one of the areas where Gimp differs most from Photoshop — not in the essence of basic usage, but Gimp's layers are much more powerful because they don't suffer from the "one size fit all" syndrome.

Moving Layers

When you use the **Move tool** for the first time, you will probably move the whole image, which will seem very confusing to a Photoshop user. Actually, you didn't move the image, you moved the Background layer. In Gimp, layers can be moved without restrictions, so it's no problem to move the layer outside the image canvas. This is a very handy way of moving text in a *text layer*. Please read "The Move Tool" on page 156 for more information about moving layers.

Layer Size

Since you can move layers freely, even outside the image canvas, you can naturally create layers that are bigger than the image itself. When you create a new layer (right mouse button in the Layers dialog), a dialog will appear, where you'll be asked to specify the size of the new layer. It's now up to you to make it as big or as small as you want. The fact that the layers can be bigger than the canvas is used very effectively in a plug-in called **GAP** (see "Advanced Animation With Gimp Or How To Use AnimFrames" starting on page 639) where you can use this possibility to effectively panorate the background in an animation. (Yes, Gimp has its own animation studio.) For more information about layers and layer size, please read "Resize Layer" on page 321.

Layer Optimizing

We were discussing *floating selections* in an earlier paragraph. Just as in Photoshop, when you create a floating selection you will get a special layer in the **Layers & Channel** dialog. Just double-click on the floating selection bar in the dialog, and Gimp will create an optimized layer from the floating selection. The new layer will not be bigger than the selected object that made up the floating selection. Read "Floating Selections" on page 331 for more information about floating selections.

Layer Alignment And Manipulation

Gimp's layer alignment differs from Photoshop's. Because Gimp works with optimized layer size, you align the layers and not the substance in the layers. Gimp provides several ways of layer aligning, rotating, and redistributing. It may seem confusing in the beginning, but once you get to know it you will love it. Read more about it in "Layer Align, Adjust And Move Operations" on page 326.

You can also bend and otherwise manipulate layers and the objects within them. After being manipulated, the layer will be resized on the fly to fit its new optimized size. If you want to know more about these special layer functions, read "Transforms" on page 330.

Types And Fonts

There are two ways of handling fonts in Gimp. The first one is the **Text tool** in the toolbox, which is a rather simple and restricted way to add text to an image. If you are used to Photoshop's Text tool, you will probably find this Text tool very limited. This Text tool is useful for simple texts where only a few characters are involved.

Relax, there is an advanced Gimp text tool. It is similar to the one in Photoshop 5.0, and you will find it under `right-click|Filters|Render|Dynamic Text`. Dynamic Text is a very versatile Text tool, and you can edit and replace text just as usual. If you are used to Photoshop's Text tool, you will have no trouble working with Dynamic Text.

Actions

Here is one of many areas where Gimp is a lot more powerful than Photoshop. Gimp supports Script-Fu, Perl-Fu, Tcl-Fu and Python-Fu — no less than four types of "actions" languages.

Script-Fu is the current default script language and it is based on Scheme. **Perl** is the new runner-up. Perl is the de facto standard scripting language for CGI scripts. There are literally thousands of Perl algorithms and functions that you can use for image manipulation in your scripts.

You can even use Gimp as a CGI script, delivering custom graphics on the fly. Furthermore, you can enable image editing from the web with the help of **Net-Fu** which is a way to access Gimp from a web server.

A lot of Gimp users make scripts, and you can easily download all sorts of scripts from various web sites. Maybe it's not that easy to get started with scripting in Gimp, but the power it offers is so much stronger that it's well worth the trouble. Read "Web" on page 878 for further information reading scripting in Gimp.

Pre-press

In this area, Photoshop is much better than Gimp. Gimp pre-press capabilities are very limited because it can only handle RGB, grayscale and indexed images. Working with pre-press and Gimp will require some planning, and it's way too much to write about here. We have devoted a whole chapter to pre-press and Gimp so please read "Pre-press And Color In Gimp" on page 197 and you will know what to do if you are in the pre-press business and still want to use Gimp.

If you already have a UNIX version of Photoshop, we recommend that you use Gimp until you reach the stage where you would normally convert the image to CMYK. Instead, save the image and switch over to Photoshop to make the CMYK conversion and other preparations for print.

Some Final Notes

We have not covered every single difference between Gimp and Photoshop, but we have discussed the major ones. You should also keep in mind that Gimp has a lot of functions that aren't available among the Photoshop stock programs. Reading this overview will not make you a master of Gimp. This chapter should be seen as a means to help you quickly move over the basics so that you can concentrate on the fun stuff, which is exploring the more advanced Gimp functions.

A migration is never easy, and it will take some time before you are adjusted to your new favorite. We can only say that we have never regretted that we switched from Photoshop to Gimp.

PART III

Basic Functions

- *Files And Preferences*
- *Selections*
- *Paint*
- *Edit*
- *Transform*
- *Text*
- *Brushes And Other Dialogs*

CHAPTER 6

Files And Preferences

In this chapter, we will discuss how to save, open and create files, and how to set preferences. We will also cover how to list the file formats supported by Gimp and how to print from Gimp.

THE FILE MENU

In Gimp, you can get to the **File menu** in two different ways: by clicking on the File command at the top of the toolbox, or by clicking the right mouse button in an image window and moving your mouse cursor down to the File command. The menus are slightly different in the two places; in the *toolbox* File menu, you will find the following menu items:

- New
- Open
- About...
- Preferences...
- Tip of the day
- Dialogs
- Quit

And in the *right-click* File menu, you will find:

- New
- Open
- Save
- Save as
- Preferences...
- Close
- Quit
- Mail image
- Onroot
- Print

In the *Xtns* menu (in the toolbox), you will find:

- DB Browser
- Guash
- Screen Shot
- Waterselect
- Script-Fu
- Web Browser

With the exception of the **Dialogs** and **Script-Fu** menu entries, we'll discuss every entry in these three menus. You will find information on the dialogs for Brushes, Gradients, Palettes and Patterns in "Brushes, Gradients, Palettes And Patterns" starting on page 171. Script-Fu will be discussed in "Script-Fu:

Description And Function" starting on page 687 and in "Mike Terry's Black Belt School Of Script-Fu" starting on page 697.

CREATING IMAGES

Let's start by creating our first image. Click on the File menu in the toolbox, and select **New**. This will bring up the dialog box shown to the right.

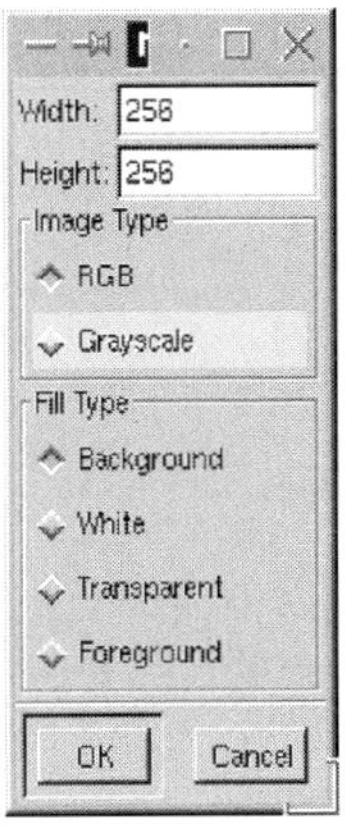

Figure 6.1 *The New file dialog*

The dialog box allows you to decide the size of your image in pixels, whether your image should be grayscale or RGB and what color it should be filled with, or whether it should be Transparent (alpha-enabled).

As you can see, three solid backgrounds are available: Background, Foreground and White. **White** will produce a white background, and **Background** will produce a colored background based on the background color in the toolbox (more about choosing a color from the toolbox background/foreground swatches can be found in "The Color Selection Dialog" on page 143.*)* **Foreground** will create a background using the foreground color in the toolbox. **Transparent** results in a checkerboard-like background that signifies transparency, or the presence of an alpha channel (a convenient feature for creating transparent GIFs).

For now, let's stick to the default values; just click on OK. Now you have a workspace to work in. Close the image by choosing `right-click|File|Close`. Note that `right-click|File|Quit` will both close your image and quit Gimp.

You may wonder why you can't create an *indexed* image (an image with a small, fixed set of specific colors) right away. After all, it would be great for that nice GIF you're trying to make for your web site. The reason for this is that you haven't chosen a set of colors, and Gimp can't predict which colors you'll use in your image.

It's almost always a very bad idea to start out with an indexed image. You should create GIFs by converting your completed image from RGB to indexed (see "RGB, Grayscale And Indexed" on page 266*)*. The rule of thumb is: Always work with RGB (or with whatever color model you need) and don't convert it until you're finished.

GUASH

One of Gimp's most useful features is **Guash**. If you have worked on a UNIX system before, you have probably used **xv** and its Visual Schnauzer. **Visual Schnauzer** displays thumbnails of images, and allows you to browse through the thumbnails and load images using a graphical interface. Or if you're a former Macintosh and Photoshop user, and you're used to the small thumbnails in an image directory, then you're going to love Guash. Guash lets you browse your home directory and see all of your images as small thumbnails.

To start Guash, select it from the Toolbox menu `Xtns|Guash`. When you first start Guash, it will scan your home directory, looking for image files that Gimp can read. If it finds a **PostScript** file, a dialog box will appear in which you can press **Load** to load the image, or select **Cancel** to skip that file. This is a nice feature, because loading PostScript files can be slow. In addition, because PostScript files are sometimes very large, they can take up a great deal of space in the `gimpswap` file, the temporary file that Gimp creates when it opens a file.

Tip: Load PostScript files only if you need to, and only load the first page in any case.

Guash's directory scanning can take quite some time (five minutes or even more), depending on the number of images in the directory being scanned. Once the scan has completed, simply double-click on a thumbnail to load it (the first click will select it; the second opens it), and the image will open in a regular Gimp window.

Guash only displays a set number of directories or images at a time. To change Guash's default behavior, you need to edit the `gimprc` file in your `.gimp` directory. Look for (or add) the following entries:

- `guash-ncol "5"` changes the number of columns (valid range is 4 to 10)
- `guash-nrow "3"` changes the number of rows (valid range is 2 to 10)
- `guash-keybindings "emacs"` enables Emacs-style key bindings

If you click on a Guash thumbnail, it will become selected and will be highlighted with a red frame. If you click once more on the highlighted image, it will be loaded into Gimp. To select or deselect more images, hold down the Shift key and click on their thumbnails.

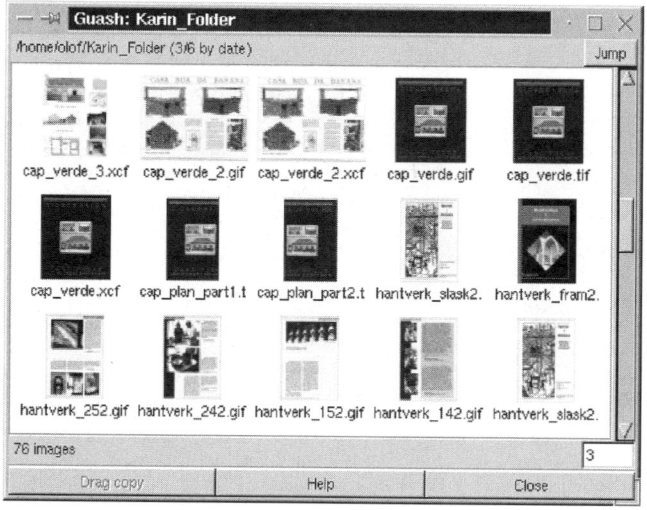

Figure 6.2 *The Guash window*

If no images are selected, pressing the right mouse button will bring up a **root menu**. If any images are selected, a right-click will produce a **select menu**, which allows you to perform various operations on the selected images.

All of the items on the menus are easy to use and learn. To get the root menu when images are selected, hold down Shift and press the right mouse button.

In Guash, you can do all the usual file management sorts of things (moving, copying and deleting images, and creating directories). You can even apply UNIX commands and, more importantly, Script-Fu "commands" to your images from either the root or select menu.

The **Jump** button (at the top-right corner) allows you to quickly change directories. The Jump menu also includes shortcuts to directories you've already visited. You can also bring up a file dialog, which makes it simple to move quickly to another directory. We recommend using the Jump menu, because moving around within Guash can be quite slow, because Guash scans each directory you visit for images.

Opening Files

Next, we'll open an image using File|Open. This will pop up the **Load Image** dialog box, which allows you to browse file names so you can select the image you want. In the **Determine file type** pull-down menu, you can choose what kind of file you want to open, or let Gimp do it automatically (by leaving it at Automatic).

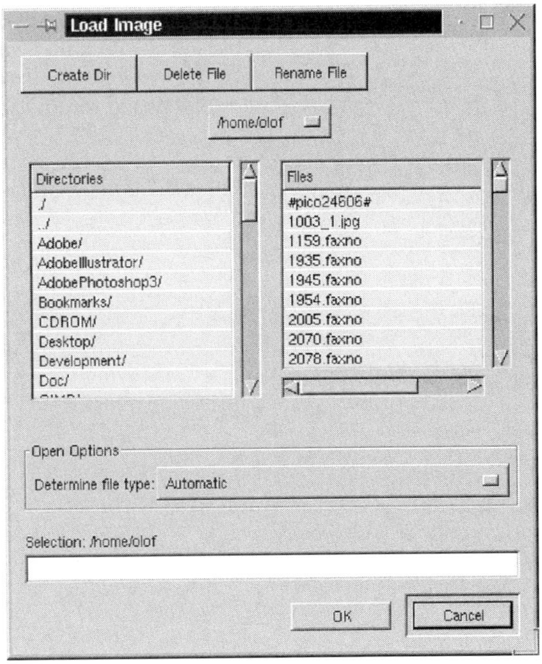

Figure 6.3 *The Load Image dialog*

In general, it's a good idea to let Gimp figure out the file type. If Gimp is having a hard time with a particular file, then you can step in and lend a hand by manually specifying the file type.

Familiarize yourself with the interface by opening some images in common formats like GIF, JPEG and TIFF). Later in this chapter, we'll discuss what kind of formats Gimp can read and write.

Tip: Gimp can automatically **expand** your file name, so you only have to enter enough of the name to uniquely identify the file. Then, press the Tab key to fill in the rest of the file name, just as you can do in certain UNIX shells.

The Load Image dialog box also allows you to delete (**Delete File**) and rename (**Rename File**) files. To do this, simply click on the file to select it and press the corresponding button. This will bring up a **confirmation** dialog box. To create a directory, press the **Create Dir** button and a dialog box will prompt you for the name of the directory.

If you've just created a new directory (or have made any changes to the files in the displayed directory), remember to double-click on the current directory symbol (./) to update the file listing; otherwise, you won't see the changes. The ability to create directories in the **Load Image** or **Save Image** dialogs is actually quite handy, as you'll often find you'll want to save images for a new project in a new directory.

Opening PostScript And PDF Files

If you select a PostScript or PDF file in the Load Image dialog box, and then click on OK, Gimp will pop up a **Load PostScript** dialog box, as shown. Our advice is to not change any values here if you're going to print it at home or in the office — the default values are fine when displaying the paper formats that are normally used for PostScript files.

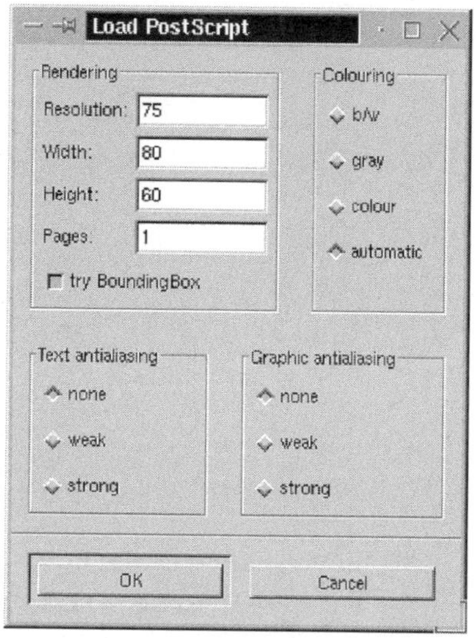

Figure 6.4 *The Load PostScript dialog*

If you lower the **Resolution**, you'll also have to reduce the **Width** and **Height** of the image canvas (and vice versa, if you increase the resolution). Note that if you don't change the width and height when you increase the resolution, only part of your PostScript file will be displayed. On the other hand, if the width or height exceeds the size of your PostScript file, the display will automatically be adjusted.

If you uncheck the **try BoundingBox** checkbox, the pages will be stacked over each other; otherwise, they will be displayed side by side. The **Pages** entry allows you to specify what page or page interval to display; for example, `1-99` specifies pages 1 to 99, and `75` specifies page 75 (if your PostScript file has fewer pages than the numbers you specify, the numbers will be adjusted automatically).

Selecting **b/w** will produce a black-and-white image from a color PostScript file. **Gray** or **color** will produce a grayscale or a colored image, respectively. **Automatic** will produce whatever type of image the PostScript file was created as. Of course, you can't obtain a colored image from a black-and-white PostScript file, even if you select color. Gimp is good, but it's not that good!

You can also specify the level of **antialiasing** for text and graphics. If you only want a quick look at your file, then select **none** or **weak**. On the other hand, if you're done working on the file and you're going to press, then select **strong**.

Saving Images

Gimp lets you save the images you've created. Isn't that wonderful? A ***free*** program with save abilities! Compare this to using Photoshop for free in demo mode, where *"save and print are disabled, this is a demo copy."*

You can access the **Save Image dialog** by pressing the right mouse button in the window that contains the image you want to save: `right-click|File|Save As`. The Save Image dialog is exactly the same as the **Load Image** dialog, except that the Determine file type menu is a bit different. In this context, the default is By extension.

By extension means that the format of the resulting image depends on the image file's extension. For example, if you name your image `hello.gif`, it will automatically be saved in GIF format. You can of course choose to save `hello.gif` in TIFF format, by selecting TIFF in the **Determine file type** menu, but this is not a good idea, because it tends to confuse people. If you want to save a file without an extension, then you *must* choose the file type from the menu.

Note: Remember to **flatten** the layers in your image *before you save it*, unless you are saving in **XCF** format (Gimp's native file format) or creating a **GIF** animation.

Gimp supports many different file formats; the exact number depends on which plug-ins you have installed. Yes, as with most things in Gimp, file format support is implemented with **plug-ins**. Examples of plug-ins are the **mail** and **print** plug-ins, and all of the **filters**. We will discuss plug-ins in general later on in this book. Right now, we will concentrate on the file format plug-ins included in the base Gimp distribution.

SUPPORTED FILE FORMATS

Table 6.1 shows some of the file formats that Gimp supports for reading and/or writing. Notice that your Gimp may not support all of these formats, because special software libraries must be supplied for some file formats.

Table 6.1 *File Formats*

Format	Write	Read	Format	Write	Read
BMP	X	X	PCX	X	X
bzip	X	X	PIX	X	X
CEL	X	X	PNG	X	X
FaxG3		X	PNM	X	X
FITS	X	X	PSD		X
FLI/FLC	X		PostScript	X	X
GBR	X	X	SGI	X	X
GIcon	X	X	SNP		X
GIF	X	X	SunRas	X	X
gzip	X	X	TGA	X	X
Header	X		TIFF	X	X
HRZ	X	X	URL	X	X
JPEG	X	X	XCF	X	X
MPEG		X	XWD	X	X
PAT	X	X	XPM	X	X

Let's take a quick look at each of the different file formats.

- **XCF**: The native Gimp format. It supports layers and other Gimp-specific information. If you save your image in a different file format, all Gimp-specific information will be lost, and you won't be able to open and edit your layers anymore. Note that GIF files can be considered to support layers (since each layer becomes a frame in a GIF animation). In general, however, you should keep your work in XCF format until you're completely finished working on it. ***Keep in mind that only the active layer is saved when you save an image in formats other than XCF and GIF***. So, for example, if you want to save a layered image in TIFF format, make sure you flatten it before you save it.
- **BMP**: An uncompressed bitmap format used by Microsoft Windows for displaying graphics. Color depth is typically 1, 4 or 8 bits, although the format does support more.
- **bzip**: Allows you to open and save bzipped images. The name of the file must be `<name>.<well-known extension like tiff>.bz`. This format is ideal for saving large, multi-layered XCF images. bzip compression is slightly more efficient than gzip.
- **CEL**: The file format used by KISS programs.
- **FaxG3**: The format used by faxes. It's very useful if you have a fax connected to your UNIX workstation.

- **FITS** (Flexible Image Transport System): Mainly used in astronomy; for example, it's used by NASA.
- **FLI/FLC**: The file format used by many animation programs. Gimp reads both FLI and FLC file formats. The main difference between the two is that FLI only supports 64 colors at a resolution of 320x320 pixels, whereas FLC supports 256 colors at a resolution of 64Kx64K pixels.
- **GBR**: Gimp's native brush format. You will learn how to make brushes in "Creating A New Brush" on page 173.
- **GIcon**: Gimp's native icon format, used for the icons in the toolbox. This format only supports grayscale images.
- **GIF** (Graphics Interchange Format): Trademarked by CompuServe, with LZW compression patented by Unisys. GIF images are in 8 bit indexed color and support transparency (but not semi-transparency). They can also be loaded in interlaced form by some programs. The GIF format also supports animations and comments. ***Use GIF for transparent Web graphics and GIF animations***.
- **gzip**: For opening and saving gzipped images. The name of the file must be `<name>.<well-known extension like tiff>.gz`. This format is ideal for saving large, multi-layered XCF images.
- **Header**: C programming language header files. This format is for programmers who want to include their image in a C program.
- **HRZ**: This format is always 256x240 pixels and it was used in amateur slow-scan TV broadcasts. The format does not support compression; it's just raw RGB data.
- **JPEG** (Joint Photographic Experts Group): This format supports compression and works at all color depths. The image compression is adjustable, but beware: Too high a compression could severely reduce image quality, since ***JPEG compression is lossy***. Use JPEG to create TrueColor Web graphics, or if you don't want your image to take up a lot of space. JPEG is a good format for photographs.
- **MPEG** (Motion Picture Experts Group): A well-known animation format. You can load an MPEG movie into Gimp and play it with the Animation Player plug-in. You can also open an MPEG movie and save it as a GIF animation (be sure to remove all unnecessary frames beforehand). However, you can't (yet) save an animation created in Gimp as MPEG.
- **PAT**: Gimp's native pattern format.
- **PCX**: The Zsoft file format, mainly used by the Windows Paintbrush program and other PC paint programs.
- **PIX**: A format used by the Alias/Wavefront program on SGI workstations. It supports only 24 bit color and 8 bit grayscale images.

- **PNG** (Portable Network Graphics): The format that is supposed to replace the GIF format and thus provide a solution to GIF's trademark and patent issues. Indexed color, grayscale, and truecolor images are supported, plus an optional alpha channel. PNG also uses compression, but unlike JPEG it doesn't lose image information.
- **PNM** (Portable aNyMap): PNM supports indexed color, grayscale, and truecolor images. PNM images can be converted to many other formats with the programs that come with the netpbm or pbmplus distributions. Use this format when you know that you will want to change the image later with a PBM program.
- **PSD**: The format used by Adobe Photoshop. Great if you are a former Photoshop user and have lots of images in PSD format. (Note that Gimp will now preserve PSD layers.)
- **PostScript and EPS**: Created by Adobe, PostScript is a page description language mainly used by printers and other output devices. It's also an excellent way to distribute documents. This plug-in can also read PDF (Acrobat) files. Most printing firms can handle PostScript files, so if you're going to have your image professionally printed, choose PostScript.
- **SGI**: The original file format used by SGI graphic applications.
- **SNP**: the format used by MicroEyes for its animations. You can load this format and then save the resulting image as a GIF to obtain a GIF animation.
- **SunRas** (Sun rasterfile): This format is used mostly by different Sun applications. It supports grayscale, indexed color and truecolor.
- **TGA**: The Targa file format supports compression to 8, 16, 24 or 32 bits per pixel.
- **TIFF** (Tagged Image File Format): Designed to be a standard, TIFF files come in many different flavors. Six different encoding routines are supported, each with one of three different image modes: black and white, grayscale and color. Uncompressed TIFF images may be 1, 4, 8 or 24 bits per pixel. TIFF images compressed using the LZW algorithm may be 4, 8 or 24 bits per pixel. This is a high quality file format, perfect for images you want to import to other programs like FrameMaker or CorelDRAW.
- **URL** (Uniform Resource Locator): With this plug-in, which is dependent on GNU wget, you can download a picture off the Internet directly into Gimp. The format of the "filename" (i.e., URL) that you must enter into the open dialog is `ftp://<address>/<file>` or `http://<address>/<file>`. For more information on specifying files by URL, see "Obtaining Gimp" on page 48.
- **XCF**: The native Gimp format. Use this format to store all your Gimp images (if you have enough disk space). Consider using bzip or gzip compression on your XCF files.
- **XWD** (X Window Dump): The format used by the screendump utility shipped with X.

- **XPM** (X PixMap): The file format used by color icons in X. Gimp's XPM plug-in supports 8, 16 and 24 bit images.

Save Dialogs

When you save a newly created image, selecting the **Save** or **Save As** command will open the **Save Image** dialog box. Under **Save Options**, you can specify a file format for the saved image, which will in turn set the kind of compression and many other options for your saved image. We will now take a look at the different choices you have for image formats, and discuss what impact each format's parameters will have on the saved image.

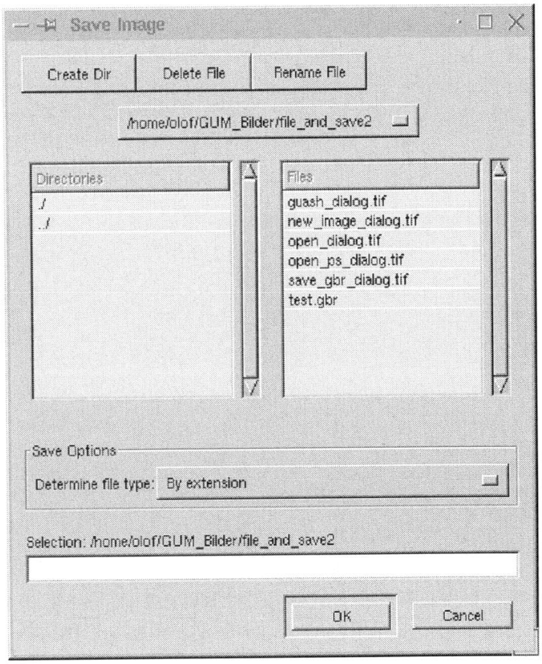

Figure 6.5 *The main Save Image*

GBR

The GBR **Save As Brush** dialog allows you to save your own images as a brush. **Spacing** refers to the default spacing your brush will have as shown in the Brush dialog (more information on brushes is provided in "Brushes" on page 172).

Description refers to the name for your brush in brush-related dialogs, so it's a good idea to enter something descriptive, like "My test brush."

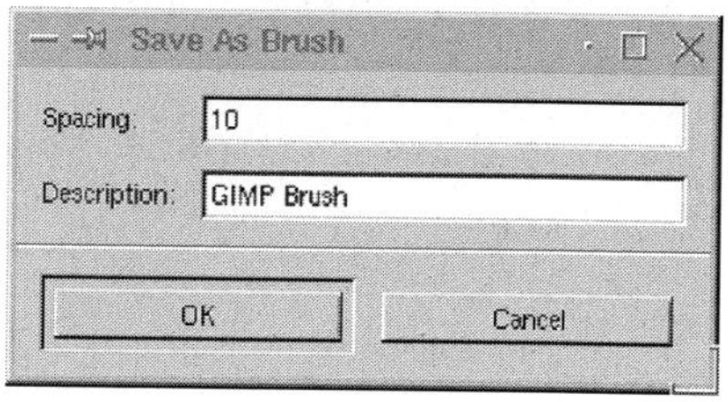

Figure 6.6 *The GBR Save As Brush dialog*

GIcon

All you need to enter in the **Save as GIcon** dialog is the name of your icon. Note that this is not the file name; it's the internal name of the icon as Gimp sees it, so keep it short and descriptive.

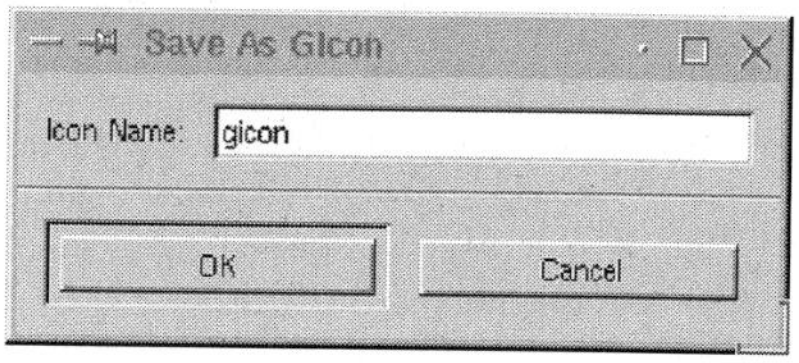

Figure 6.7 *The Save As GIcon dialog*

GIF

The **Save As GIF** dialog has many options. If you've flattened your image, you can save it as an **interlaced** GIF image, which enables it to be loaded incrementally by some applications (such as Netscape). You've probably seen this on the Web, when the image appears blurry at first but gradually becomes sharper.

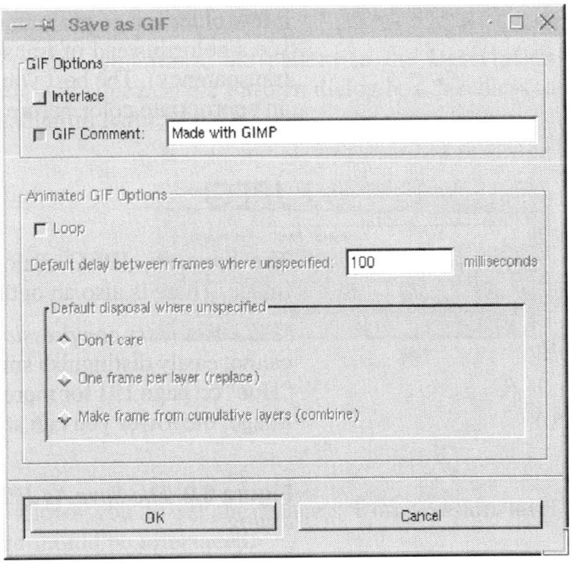

Figure 6.8 *The Save As GIF dialog*

You can also set the **GIF Comment** stored in the GIF file to anything you want, like, "Made by Karin with Gimp." Note that if you want to change the default GIF comment ("Made with GIMP"), you'll need to edit the GIF plug-in source code.

Note that you'll need to convert your image to indexed color (`right-click|Image|Indexed`) before you can save it as a GIF.

If your image contains layers, you can create a **GIF animation**. If you want the animation to play only once, uncheck the **Loop** box; otherwise, it will loop forever. The **Default delay between frames where unspecified** field is the delay between frames in your animation. The checkboxes in the **Default disposal where unspecified** section control the following actions:

- **Don't care** and **Make frame from cumulative layers** have the same effect: The animation starts by displaying the first layer in the GIF image. Subsequent layers are then displayed "on top of" each other. This mode is useful when creating, for example, a logo that you'd like to appear one letter at a time.
- **One frame per layer (replace)** will use the first layer as the first frame, the second layer as the second frame and so on, just like in a movie. This mode is useful when creating an image of a moving object, such as a spinning globe.

If your GIF image is transparent, the transparency will be retained when you save it. Transparency works in both flat and layered images. ***Note that GIF does not support semi-transparency***; pixels are either 100 percent opaque or 100 percent transparent.

Textual Informations lets you include information about the image, such as Description, Author, etc. This is a good thing if you want to prevent anyone from stealing your image, but you should be aware that the information can be removed.

Figure 6.12 *The Textual Informations tab*

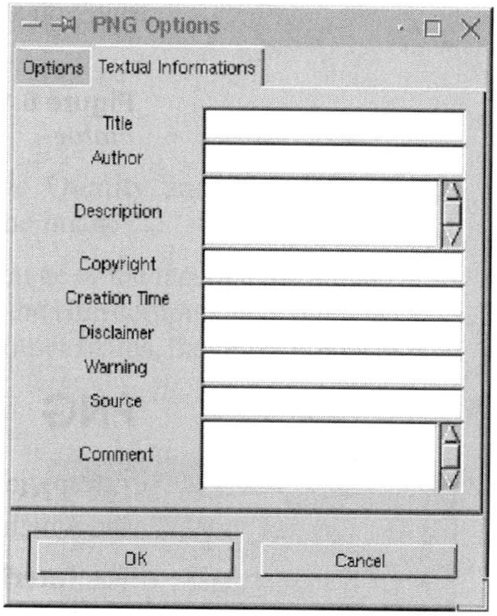

PNM

The **Save As PNM** dialog is fairly self-explanatory. **Raw** means that the file is saved in binary format, whereas **Ascii** will cause the file to be saved as a sequence of printable characters. You'll probably always want to save PNM files in **Raw** format, as it's smaller (eight times smaller, in fact) and saves faster than **Ascii** format.

PNM is a UNIX image format. It is often used to translate images to and from other formats. PNM is also used as an image format within programs, so if you are a programmer you have to choose whether to use Raw or Ascii in your program.

Figure 6.13 *The Save As PNM dialog*

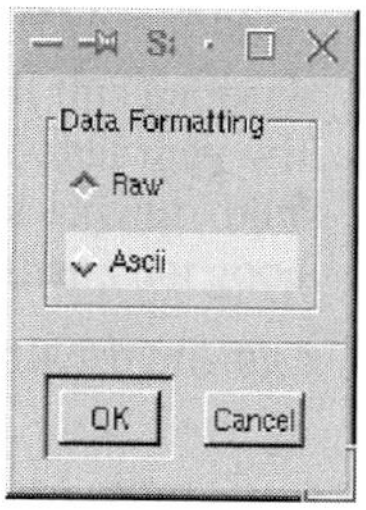

POSTSCRIPT AND EPS

Saving your image as **PostScript** is significantly different from saving it as TIFF, GIF, JPEG, etc.

When you save an image as PostScript, you must specify the **Image Size**. Think of it as if you were specifying the size of the paper on which the image will be printed. Choose a reasonable image size. In other words, a 300x400 pixel image won't look very good if you stretch it out to the default size of 11.30x7.87 inches. You will almost always have to alter the paper size. To do so, change the **Width** and **Height** fields.

Figure 6.14 *The Save PostScript dialog*

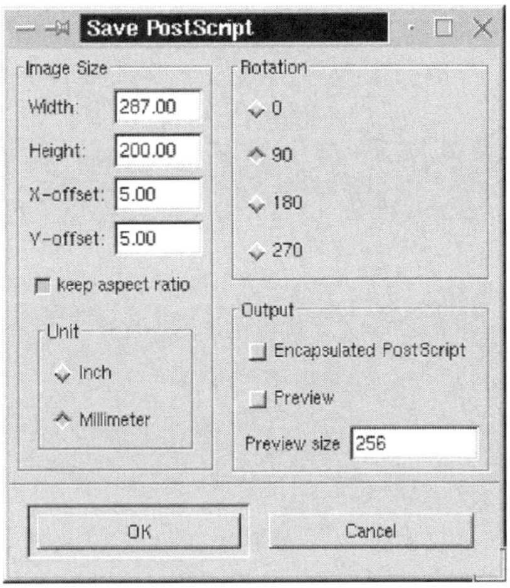

The **X-offset** and **Y-offset** fields can be thought of as the *margin* of your imaginary paper. Checking the **keep aspect ratio** checkbox means that the image size will be automatically adjusted to be the same relative shape as your image, so that the image won't be stretched out.

For example, let's say you are going to save a 300x400 pixel image, and that you decide that the resolution is going to be 100 pixels per inch (suitable for printing to a 300 dpi laser printer). The image area would be 3x4 inches. If we add a margin of 0.2 inches on top and bottom, and 0.2 inches on each side, then the total image size will be 3.4x4.4 inches. So, let's set **Width** to 3, **Height** to 4, **X-offset** and **Y-offset** to 0.20, **Unit** to **Inch** and **Rotation** to 0. This will result in your image being saved in *portrait* mode.

If you want to rotate your image by 90 degrees, you'll have to switch values in Width and Height, and the image will be saved in *landscape* mode. If you rotate your image by 180 degrees, you'll get an upside-down *portrait* mode, and if you rotate by 270 degrees you'll get an upside-down *landscape* mode. You can read more about resolution and printing in "Pre-press And Color In Gimp" starting on page 197.

Clicking the **Encapsulated PostScript** checkbox will create an Encapsulated PostScript (.eps) file instead of a plain PostScript (.ps) file. EPS is useful for **importing** an image into a page layout or an illustration program. Encapsulated

Postscript is also a commonly requested file format when you print at a professional printing company.

If you're going to import your EPS file into another program, it is wise to check the **Preview** box. If you don't, the program may not show what your image looks like on screen (it will either be displayed as a gray square or at very low resolution) and the image will only appear when you print it out.

SunRas

This is the SunRas save dialog When you save a SunRas file, you'll get a dialog box asking if you want **RLE** compression or **Standard** format (no compression). RLE compression is lossless so it's generally a good idea to select this option, but note that RLE format supports only 4 or 8 bits per pixel. This will have no effect on the image, except that you can't save Indexed images in SunRas.

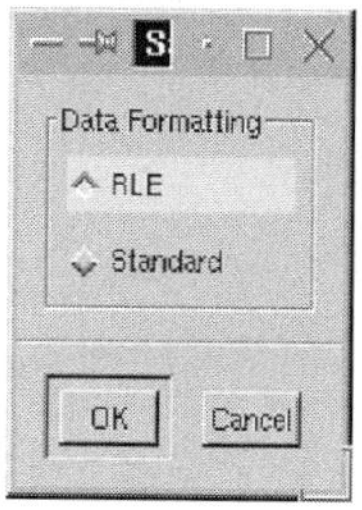

Figure 6.15 *The SunRas Save*

TGA

When you save a Targa image, the **Save As TGA** dialog box asks if you want RLE compression or no compression (RLE compression is not checked). Like SunRas compression, RLE is generally a good idea, since it will save disk space.

Figure 6.16 *The Save As TGA dialog*

TIFF

The **Save As TIFF** dialog asks what kind of compression you want. Since TIFF compression is **lossless**, you might as well use it. Use **LZW** with 4, 8 and 24 bit images and **Pack Bits** with 1 bit (bitmap) images like FaxG3 images, because Pack Bits is only designed to work on 1 bit images (B&W).

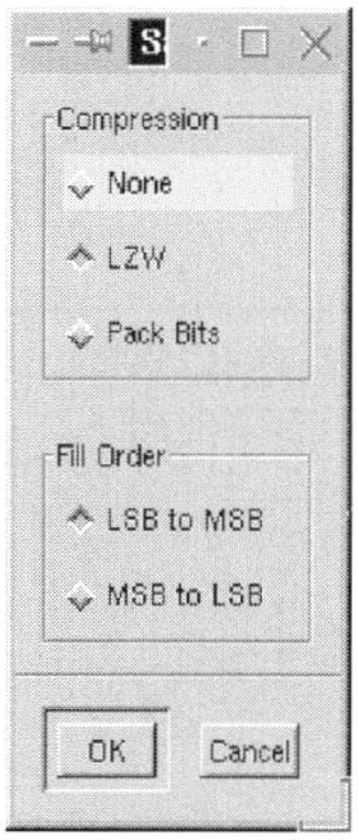

Figure 6.17 *The Save As TIFF dialog*

The **Fill Order** determines how the bits in your image are filled. The first option is Least Significant Bit (**LSB**) to Most Significant Bit (**MSB**), the default order on little-endian machines (for example, machines with Intel X86 processors). It is also known as **PC filling**.

The other option selects a reverse fill order: **MSB** to **LSB**. This is the default order on big-endian machines (ones with Motorola and SPARC processors, for instance). This is also known as **Mac filling**.

If you want to import the image into FrameMaker or a similar program, set **Compression** to **None** and set **Fill Order** depending on the type of machine that the program runs on. Most programs are fairly flexible when it comes to importing files, but this way you are safe.

XPM

The **Save As XPM** dialog appears when you save an image that has alpha (transparency). **Alpha Threshold** determines which alpha values should be considered transparent and which should be considered opaque.

For example, a threshold of 0.5 means that all alpha values under 128 will be transparent and all over 128 will be opaque (128 is half of the maximum channel value 255). According to the source code, 16 bit and 24 bit XPM images are supported on 16 bit displays; code for 8 bit images exists, but has not been tested.

Figure 6.18 *The Save As XPM dialog*

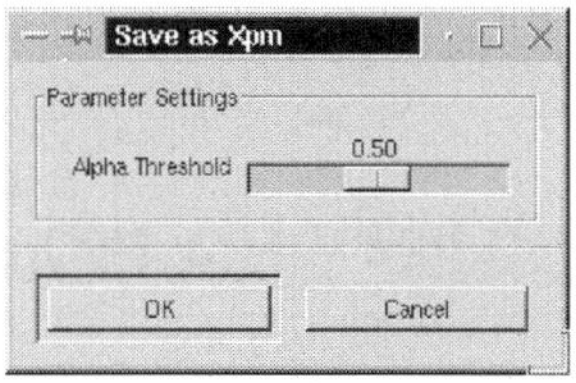

Other Image Formats

The other image formats that Gimp supports, such as BMP, CEL, FITS, FLI, HRZ, HTL, Header, PCX, PIX, SGI, XCF, XWD, bzip2, gzip, etc., have no options at the time of this writing. Therefore, we can't supply any special information on how to save in those formats.

Mailing Images

Gimp can mail images. This is a handy feature, particularly if you work in more than one location. Then, you can mail your image home or to work. You can also use it to send digital Christmas cards to your friends and family. Note, however, that mail administrators may not be very happy if you mail large images, so use this feature with care.

`Right-click|File|Mail Image` to pop up the **Send to Mail** dialog box. The **To** field is the email address of your friend. **Subject** is the subject of your email. **Comment** is a comment for the image, like "Here's a nice picture of my new pet gnu." **Filename** is the file name of the image that you want to send; it should have the format `filename.well-known_extension`.

You also have to choose the mail message's **Encapsulation or coding type**; you can choose either **Uuencode** or 64 bit **MIME**. It's usually better to use MIME because it's supported by most mail programs.

Figure 6.19 *The Send to Mail dialog*

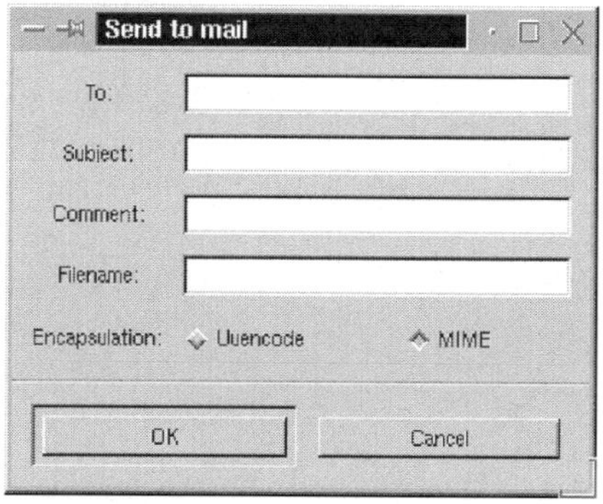

Displaying Images In The Root Window

`Right-click|File|Onroot` lets you display an image as a repeated background pattern in the root window.

The root window is the "background" of your X Window System desktop. On start-up, most X desktops set the background to a specific color or image. The background is normally set using a GUI application, or by changing a line in a file. The next time you start the desktop, the new background will be displayed (many desktops allow you to do this without having to restart your desktop).

This setup will suit most ordinary users who only want to choose from a set of preconfigured backgrounds. But since Gimp is an image manipulation program and you are an image manipulator, you will probably want to create your own background, and here's where the **Onroot** feature comes in handy. With Onroot, you can easily put the image you're working with in the root window to see how it will look. If you're not happy with the result, you can keep manipulating it, displaying it in the root window again and again until you are satisfied. Then, you can use your window manager to display the finished image.

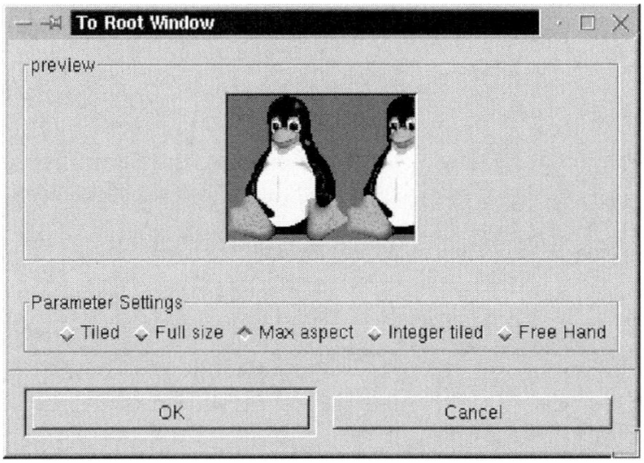

Figure 6.20 *The To Root dialog*

Onroot also has a dialog box where you can specify how the image will be displayed on the root window. There are five different options/settings. There is also a preview screen, so you can easily see what it will look like. A quick overview of the options is as follows:

- **Tiled**: This option will place your image (in its original size) in the upper-left corner, and place copies from left to right until the entire row is filled. Then, it will put a copy of the image under the first and fill the second row. This will go on until the whole screen is filled. Since the image hasn't been scaled, it will probably be cropped at the right side and in the bottom of the screen.
- **Full size**: This option will stretch your image so it will cover the entire screen. Unless the image is very large, it will (probably) lose its original ratio and become blurry, since it will be stretched to fit the screen.
- **Max aspect**: This option will stretch your image with its ratio intact. This will most likely result in a cropped duplicate of your image unless its aspect ratio exactly matches that of your screen.
- **Integer tiled**: This option is nearly the same as **Tiled**. The difference is that there will be no cropped images as they will be stretched to fill the window.
- **Free Hand**: With this option you can place your image at any position on the root window. Initially, the image is placed in the center of the preview screen. You can then drag it to the location of your choice.

Not every desktop environment can handle each of these options, so when you're creating the right background image, take into account the background options your desktop has to offer.

PRINTING IMAGES

Before you start to print from Gimp, you should know that only the **active layer** of a layered image will be printed, so you must first *flatten* (`right-click|Layers|Flatten Image`) your image before printing. We're not going to discuss UNIX printing subsystems, spooling methods and the like, as it's beyond the scope of this book.

What kind of printer does Gimp support internally? To find out, open an image and select `right-click|File|Print` to pop up the **Print** dialog box. If you click on the **Setup** button and then on the **Driver** pull-down menu, you'll find that Gimp supports the following printers:

- PostScript printers (including PostScript level 2)
- HP DeskJet 500, 500C, 520, 540C, 600C, 660C, 68xC, 69xC, 850C, 855C, 855Cse, 855Cxi, 870Cse, 870Cxi, 1200C and 1600C printers
- HP LaserJet II, III, IIIp, IIIsi, 4, 4L, 4P, 4V, 4Si, 5, 5FS, 5L, 5P, 5SE, 5Si, 6L and 6P printers
- EPSON Stylus Color, Color Pro, Color Pro XL, Color 400, Color 500, Color 600, Color 800, Color 1500, Color 1520 and Color 3000 printers

OTHER PRINT SETTINGS

Gimp supports most common printers internally, so you probably won't need to use **GhostScript**.

GhostScript is a program that is often used to convert PostScript to another printing language, such as PCL, which is used by HP printers. Since PostScript is the most common printing output for UNIX programs, GhostScript is often set up as a filter that interacts with the printer system to convert the output on the fly from PostScript to PCL, which is fed to the HP printer.

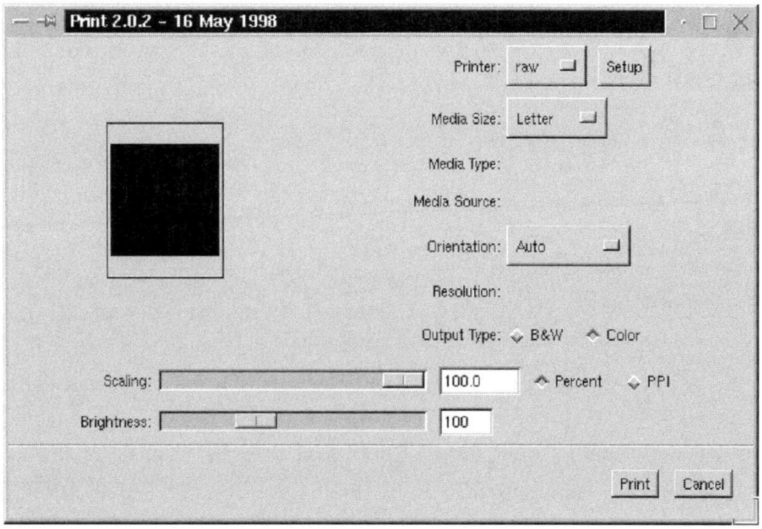

Figure 6.21 *The Printer dialog*

However, if you have GhostScript installed and use it as a printer filter for your printers, then you'll probably want to print using the **PostScript Printer** option. We recommended that those of you with Ghostscript installed create a raw printer device and let Gimp print directly to it, at least temporarily, so you can follow the examples in this manual more closely.

SETUP

Before you can print, you must enter the **Setup** dialog. Setup tells Gimp what type of printer you are using. As you might imagine, this is crucial information when it comes to printing.

Figure 6.22 *The printer Setup dialog*

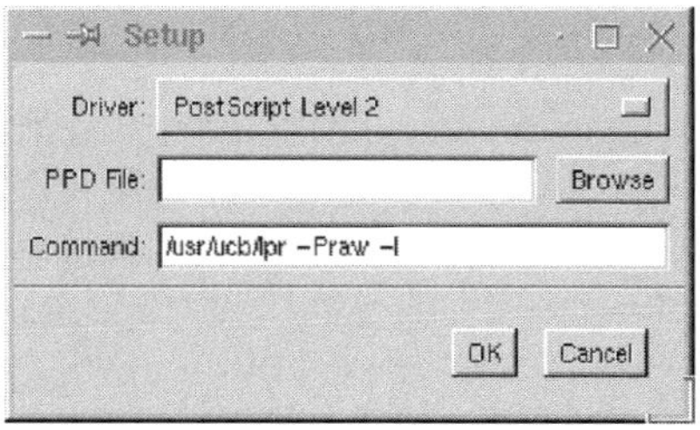

First, specify the **Printer** (actually the printer's queue) you'd like to print to in the drop-down menu, then click on the Setup button to access the Setup dialog box.

In the Setup **Driver** pull-down menu, you specify what type of printer you're using. If you have a PS or PS level 2 printer, you can provide your printer with a **PPD File**.

Tip: A PPD file is a file that describes your printer's capabilities. By providing a PPD file specific to your printer, you'll be able to use your printer's special features (like resolution, media source and media type).

Just browse and choose the PPD file that comes with the printer driver for Windows, or you can download it from Adobe's FTP site.

Gimp doesn't come with PPD files, so you have to get them yourself. Usually, you get it from the Windows driver for your PostScript printer, but sometimes it can be hard to extract the PPD file from the Windows driver. If that is the case, you can get the PPD file from `ftp.adobe.com/pub/adobe/printerdrivers/win/all/ppdfiles`. The files at Adobe's FTP site have the following format; `brand_name_of_printer.exe`, so you either need Windows or an emulator to unpack the driver (execute the file).

If you don't have a PostScript printer, just choose one of the printers supported by Gimp from the drop-down menu.

In the **Command** input field you'll see the print command that will be used when you print. Normally this is determined when you compile the print plug-in. But if the command is wrong, you can correct it here. Once everything is correctly set, press OK. If you don't have a command field, don't worry; Gimp has been set up so well that there is no need for it.

THE PRINT DIALOG

The main dialog box may now have changed its appearance depending on what features your printer supports. We will describe all of the options, but don't be surprised if your printer only supports a few of them.

- **Media Size**: The *size* of paper you use in your printer. Gimp supports **Letter**, **Legal**, **Tabloid**, **A4**, **A3** and other paper sizes.
- **Media Type**: Refers to the *type* of paper you use, such as **Transparent**, **Glossy**, etc.
- **Media Source**: The way to specify the tray containing the paper on which you'd like to print. As you might imagine, this is heavily dependent on your printer's capabilities.
- **Orientation menu**: Lets you select whether you want to print in **Landscape** or **Portrait** mode. You can also let Gimp decide by selecting **Auto**.
- **Resolution**: Provided because different printers support different resolutions. In this field, you can specify what resolution you want to use for your print job. This option can come in handy; for example, you probably don't want to use high resolution when printing a draft. We'll discuss resolution in more detail a bit later when we talk about scaling.
- **Output type**: If you have a color printer, use **Color mode**; otherwise, use **B&W** (you can also use **B&W** on a color printer, of course).

- **Brightness** is set by default to 100, which is fine for printing to lasers and black-and-white inkjets. Usually, though, you will have to increase this value when printing to a color inkjet. The author of Gimp's printer interface recommends a setting of 125 to 150, but for us, that's too bright. We use 110 for our Deskjet 870Cxi. The bottom line is that you will have to experiment a bit to find out what setting gives the best results on your printer.
- **Scaling**: When you open the Print dialog box, Scaling is set to the default value 100, and the image will be stretched to cover the entire page (with a margin of 6 mm on each side, and 13 mm on top and bottom). *If you use this scaling factor on a small image, it will get so enlarged that it will look jagged and ugly, because the effective resolution (in pixels per inch) will be extremely low.*

The nice thing about Gimp's printer interface is that you can set the scale in **PPI**. As we have already mentioned, PPI stands for **pixels per inch** and represents the *resolution* of the printed image. *We recommend that you always use the PPI option; otherwise, you will have little control over print quality.*

So, what PPI value should you use? Well, it depends on your printer. A suggestion is to use 72 ppi for a 300 dpi laser printer and 110 ppi for a 600 dpi laser printer. Note: If you can set the resolution in the printer dialog, remember to also change the PPI value.

But our suggestion is not absolute. For example, if you have a PostScript printer that uses AM screening, the PPI should be around 1.6 to 2 times the **LPI** (**lines per inch**) of the printer.

As you may have noticed, the more we discuss this topic, the more you'll need to understand. We strongly recommend that you read "Pre-press And Color In Gimp" on page 197, where we discuss the complex subject of printing in more detail.

However, we can give you a few simple guidelines. A 300 dpi *laser* printer will need at least 60 ppi, and a 600 dpi *laser* printer will need 100 ppi (minimum). A general rule is that inkjet printers get away with a lower ppi than laser printers, so try 50 ppi for a 300 dpi *inkjet* printer and 90 ppi for a 600 dpi *inkjet* printer.

If you find this printing jargon confusing, stick to our guidelines or read "Pre-press And Color In Gimp" starting on page 197. If you have an inkjet printer it might also be a good idea to read "Scanning, The Web And Printing" on page 259.

If you'd like to use the **Percent** option, remember that small images (set at 100%, which means 100% of the paper size) will print at a very low resolution. In order to get a nice printout, the image will have to be relatively large and you will have to scale it down to increase the resolution. Read more about this in "Pre-press And Color In Gimp" on page 197. A 300x400 pixel image will look fine with a scaling of around 30% (assuming that you use A4 paper and a 300 dpi printer). The procedure is the same as when we saved in PostScript format.

Tip: If you are making a draft of a large image, like a poster, you will probably start by working with a small image in order to avoid heavily loading your computer. If you just want a quick printout of the draft, use the Percent function and enlarge the image. Since it is a draft, you only want a quick look anyway, so the quality is not that important.

There's also a **print to file** choice in the **Printer** pull-down menu. When you select File, the data that would normally go to your printer will instead be saved to a file. When you press the **Print** button, a file dialog will appear where you can specify the output file name (and path). Printing to a file is quite handy as an alternative to saving the file as **PostScript**. In our opinion, it's often easier to print to file (in PS mode) than to save as PS, mainly because you don't have to mess with the **Save As** settings. However, even if you print to file, it's still important that you set the resolution correctly.

Printing to a file is also an option when you want to print your image at the local printer. You only have to get a copy of its printer's PPD file and install it on your system. When the Print dialog appears, enter the setup in "print to file" mode. Choose the PPD file provided by your print house and click on OK. Now you can set the options that its imaging hardware supports. Once you've "printed" your image to a file, simply deliver the PS file to the local print house for printing. Read more about this in "Pre-press And Color In Gimp" on page 197.

GIMP PREFERENCES

In the **Preferences** dialog box (`right-click|File|Preferences`), you'll find a lot of Gimp-related settings. There are four tabs: **Display**, **Interface**, **Environment** and **Directories**.

To save any changes permanently, click on the **Save** button; if you press **Cancel**, all your changes will be discarded. If you press **OK**, your changes will affect Gimp at once, though not all values will be affected (dir values like swap will have no effect). If you press OK and not Save, your changes will only affect the currently running Gimp and will not be saved for future Gimp sessions.

Note: To enable your Saved modifications you must first quit Gimp and then start it up again. We recommend that you use Save and then restart Gimp instead of taking a chance with OK.

DISPLAY

On the **Display** tab, you can set the default size for new images (in pixels), and the default image type (**RGB** or **grayscale**). You can also set the **Preview size**. If your computer has a small screen and is low on system resources (like RAM and processor speed) you'll generally want to keep the Preview size set to small.

Check Size lets you choose the size of the checks in the checkerboard on an image composition screen that is used to represent transparency, and **Transparency Type** lets you specify the grayscale tone of the checks. The default values should be fine for just about any work.

INTERPOLATION

When you scale an image to make it bigger, Gimp has to calculate what kind of pixels it needs to insert between the original pixels (in order to make the image bigger). This is called *interpolation*. **Linear interpolation** is faster and also leaner on system resources, but it does not produce as high a level of detail in the output image as **cubic interpolation** does. To get a nice-looking image with a lot of detail when you scale it, check the Cubic interpolation checkbox. If your system is not up to running with cubic interpolation enabled, make sure the Cubic interpolation checkbox is not checked. Gimp uses linear interpolation by default.

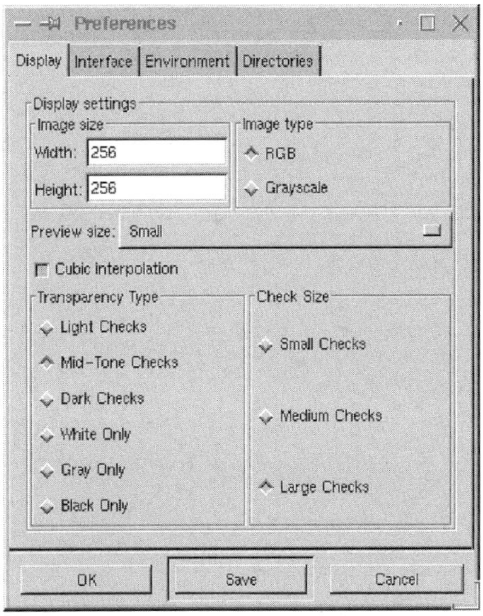

Figure 6.23 *The Display tab*

INTERFACE

On the **Interface** tab, you can set **Levels of undo**. Setting it to a high number (over 10) requires a lot of disk space, so use with care if disk space is low on your system.

Resize window on zoom means that the canvas size will always adapt to the amount of zoom you use, so you'll always be able to see the entire image regardless of zoom level. Our advice is to keep this option unchecked because you can easily enable and disable it in the **Zoom Options** dialog box. Read more about this in "Zoom" on page 150.

Show tool tips is a nice feature; Gimp will automatically pop up small tips about the tool when you move the mouse over the tool. We recommend that you enable tool tips until you have learned every tool *(i.e., never)*.

By default Gimp changes the cursor symbol. For example, if you use the Move tool, your cursor will be the move symbol. However, this consumes system resources, so if you are extremely low on resources, check the **Disable cursor updating** checkbox. Bear in mind that this can be unwise because you won't be able to see what mode you are in.

You can also set the speed of the "marching ants" (the blinking dots that appear whenever you make a selection). The value in the **marching ants speed** input field is the amount of time between updates (in milliseconds), so a lower value makes the ants march faster.

Figure 6.24 *The Interface tab*

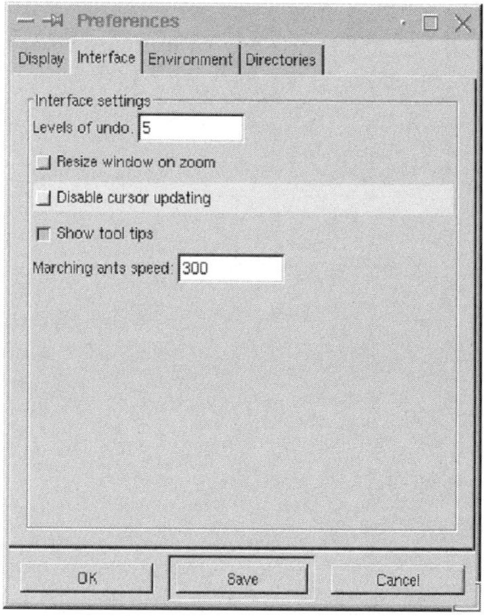

ENVIRONMENT

On the **Environment** tab, you'll see the **Conservative memory usage** checkbox. Gimp will usually trade memory consumption for improvements in speed. Checking Conservative memory usage will make Gimp more concerned about memory, but it will also slow things down, so only use it when memory is scarce.

Tile cache size is the amount of memory that Gimp consumes in order to ensure that it doesn't damage the tile memory when Gimp moves memory to and from disk. Gimp uses its own swap file on disk to handle memory; this is the *tile memory*. Since Gimp has its own swap file, you can edit really large images. The only restraining factor is disk space.

We all know that keeping program memory on disk makes the program slow, so we don't want the memory that Gimp uses to edit an image to be on our disk. This is where the *tile cache* comes in. You can specify the amount of tile memory that you want to put in our computer's main memory. The rest will stay in Gimp's tile memory swap file. Setting this value high will make Gimp faster, because it doesn't need to keep all that information in the swap file. We recommend setting it to 32 MB on a computer with 128 MB RAM, 16 MB on a 64 MB system and 10 MB on a smaller system (note that Gimp will continue to work even if you set the Tile cache size to 0). *Note that a big tile cache will only affect Gimp's speed on large images*. Using a 64 MB tile cache when you work on a 2 MB image will not make Gimp faster.

If you're working on an 8 bit display, you'll definitely want to use the **Install colormap** option. Because most of the 256 available colors on your 8 bit display will have already been claimed by other applications (such as the window manager, Netscape, etc.) Gimp, and the images it displays, will only be allowed to use the leftover colors. As you probably realize, under such conditions Gimp will be quite useless.

Colormap cycling affects the "marching ants" selection border. If you check this option, the "ants" will be replaced with a smooth line. This line is dark as you drag the selection, and turns bright when you release the mouse button.

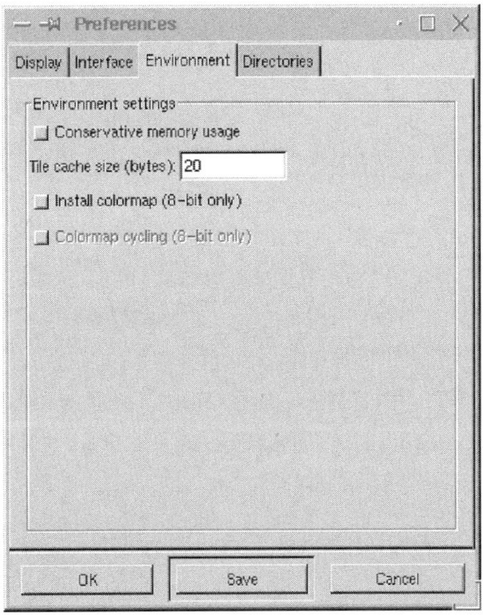

Figure 6.25 *The Environment tab*

DIRECTORIES

The most important directories that you can manipulate in the **Directories** folder are Temp and Swap. The **Temp** directory is where Gimp stores all of its temporary data, like working palettes and images. The **Swap** directory is where Gimp keeps its swap file for the tile-based memory system.

Figure 6.26 *The Directory tab*

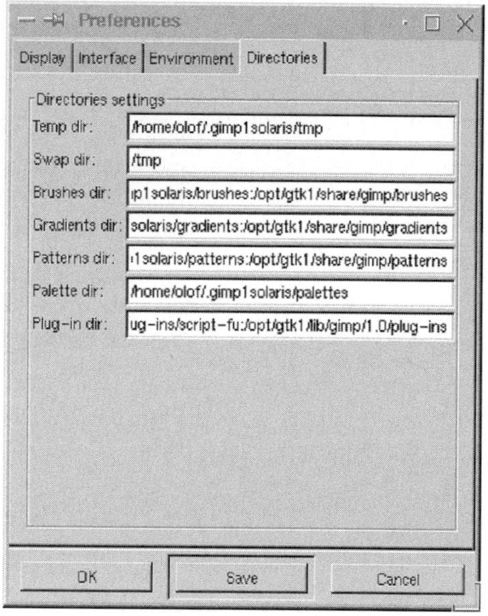

Suggestions

How should you configure these directories for optimal performance? If you are on a system that mounts home directories from a **server** over **NFS** and/or you have only a fixed **quota** of disk space that you can use, you will probably want to place your Swap directories on a local temporary directory such as `/tmp`. Otherwise, you won't have any disk space left to save your images, because the swap file can (almost always) get *very* big. Another reason to do this is that if you have to send image data to and from a swap file over the Net, Gimp will be terribly slow because it has to wait for network traffic to finish before it can proceed.

Temp is a bit different. Most of the files here will disappear when you exit Gimp, but some will remain (such as working palettes) so you will probably want a Temp directory that you don't share with other people, and that isn't cleared if you reboot your workstation. A good idea is to make a personal directory under `/usr/tmp` or `/var/tmp`. For example, in a terminal window create a temp directory with the command:

```
mkdir /usr/tmp/<your_user_name>
```

Set this directory to be your **Temp** directory.

The other directories for brushes, gradients, palettes, patterns and plug-ins may be left as they are, or modified to suit your special needs. If you change them, remember to move your Gimp add-ons to the right place. If you don't, you may not have any plug-ins available the next time you start Gimp.

Miscellaneous Features And Extensions

Tip Of The Day

In the toolbox, click on `File|Tip of the day`. The **Tip of the day** is a handy feature for new Gimp users. You can browse the tips by clicking **Prev. Tip** and **Next Tip**. To turn off Tip of the day, uncheck the **Show tip next time** checkbox on the Tip of the day dialog box. The file containing all the tips is in the Gimp system-wide data directory and is called `gimp_tips.txt`, so if you are a system administrator, you can edit this file and add new tips for the Gimp users on your system.

DB Browser

In the DB browser you can search for Gimp **PDB calls** and **routines**. This feature is mainly for people that deal with scripts and plug-ins. Even if you are not writing scripts or plug-ins, this can be a good source of information on Gimp's internals. You can search the database for both PDB **procedure names** and **information** about the procedure. If you call the **DB Browser** from the Script-Fu Console, you can also apply the PDB command to the console.

PDB Help

This is another interface to the Gimp PDB. With this extension you can run a specific PDB call on your image. To do this, simply click on **Run**, which will bring up a dialog asking for information. As with the DB Browser, this extension is mainly for developers.

GimpTcl Consolio

Gimp's main scripting language is **Scheme**, which is one of the many scripting languages available for **UNIX**. Consolio is written in **Tcl**, and you can use it when you create Tcl scripting for Gimp.

Scripting

If you are familiar with Tcl or Perl, you probably don't want to bother to learn Scheme. If you are a user without technical background, you may well ask yourself, "Why should I bother learning some obscure UNIX scripting language?" Well, let's first state that there is no absolute requirement to learn a scripting language to use Gimp. You can happily use Gimp without giving a thought to learning any scripting language. But if you find yourself performing a certain operation over and over again, wouldn't it be nice to automate it?

Take the **Drop Shadow** Script-Fu, for example. You can make a drop shadow by hand in Gimp, but isn't it nice that you have a script to do it for you? Situations like this make it worthwhile for ordinary users to learn a scripting language. At the time this was written, Gimp supports **Scheme**, **Tcl** and **Perl** as scripting languages. Each of these languages is well documented in a variety of different books, so feel free to choose whichever language you like. If you are totally new to computer languages and scripting, then we suggest that you learn Scheme, as it is Gimp's native scripting language. But Perl is also a good candidate because it's officially a part of the upcoming Gimp 1.2.

Screen Shot

In the toolbox, click on `Xtns|Screen Shot`. The Screen Shot utility can take **screen dumps** directly into Gimp. You have three alternatives: grab a single window *with* window decorations (the frame that a window manager creates around your window), the same window *without* window decorations or the *whole screen*.

To take a dump of the active window, check the appropriate options and press **OK**. Your mouse pointer will now change into a cross symbol. Use it to select the window that you want to grab by moving it within the window and clicking.

When you want to take a dump of the entire screen, check the appropriate options and press **OK**. After a few moments, a new Gimp window with your screen dump will appear. All screen shots in this book have been taken with this tool.

Figure 6.27 *The Screen Shot dialog*

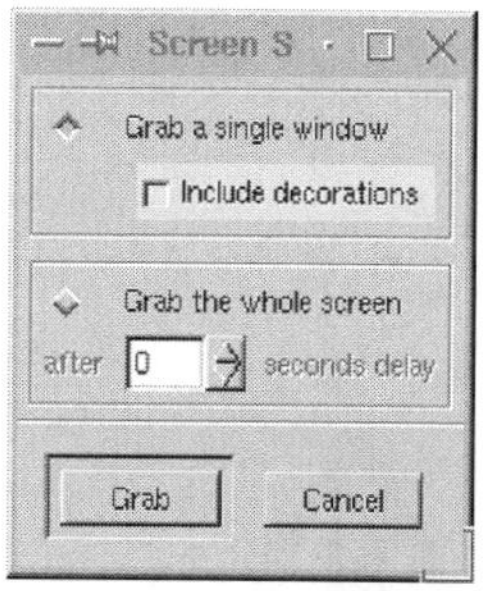

Waterselect

Waterselect is an alternative to the **Palettes** or the **Color Select** dialog. This tool resembles the little water cup you use for blending colors when you're making a watercolor painting.

The interface is simple. At the top you'll find the last ten colors that you mixed. Press one of these colors, and it will be activated. If you want to mix a color, simply move the mouse over the color scale while pressing the left *and* right mouse buttons.

Figure 6.28 *The Waterselect dialog*

The left mouse button, which mixes to **darker** colors, overrides the right mouse button. If the color gets too dark, temporarily release the left mouse button so that you only press the right mouse button while moving the mouse. The color will get lighter, just as if you had added more water. Release both mouse buttons when you're satisfied, and the chosen color will appear in the active color swatch in the toolbox. Press OK or Cancel to close the Waterselect window.

WEB BROWSER

The **Web Browser** (`Xtns|Web Browser`) allows you to open a web site from within Gimp. You'll find a few shortcuts to important locations like Gimp.org, the Plug-in Registry, Gimp news and so on. You can also open the online version of the *Gimp User's Manual* this way.

To open a site that is not available in the shortcut menu, select **Open URL**. This option pops up a dialog box asking you about the site. You can also choose whether you want to open the site in an existing Netscape session, or whether you want to open a new Netscape window. Naturally, for this to work, Netscape must be installed and in your path.

If you want to change or add a shortcut, you have to edit the script that controls the behavior of this extension. The script is called web-browser.scm and is usually located in `/usr/local/share/gimp/scripts/`, but this is naturally site-dependent. Just copy it to your personal gimp script directory (`cp/usr/local/share/gimp/scripts/web-browser.scm/your/home/.gimp/scripts)` and edit it in a text editor.

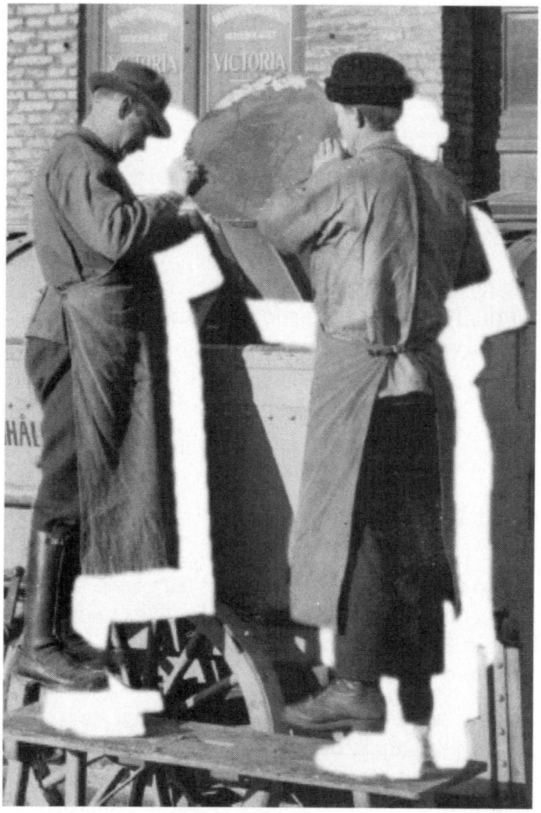
VICTORIA
VICTORIA

CHAPTER 7

Selection Tools

In this chapter, you'll learn about making selections, and how to use the different selection tools. We'll also explain why strange things happen when you try to move your selection for the first time.

Basic Controls

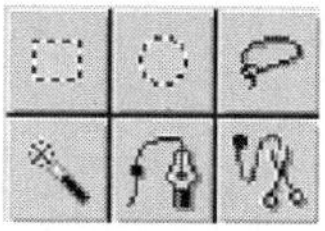

The first six tools in the toolbox are **selection tools**. In order to manipulate a specific part of your image, you first need to **select** that area. The trick is to find the right selection tool (or the right combination of tools) to make your selection correspond as exactly as possible to the part of the image you want to work with. Even the untrained eye can pick out a sloppy selection, so it's important that your work looks convincing. The selection tools in the toolbox are used for quick, simple selections. For really advanced selection work, read "Select Menu" on page 307 and "Channels And Duotones" starting on page 351.

Toggle

When you have made a selection, the **boundary** of the selection becomes a blinking dotted line, often referred to as *"marching ants."* Your selection is now the only active part of your image; the rest of the image is masked and will not be affected. If you find the blinking line distracting, Gimp allows you to switch it on and off with `right-click|Select|Toggle` menu. Note that the yellow-dotted **layer** boundaries are also affected by the Toggle command.

Selection Control

If you're not happy with your selection, just make a new one; the first will instantly disappear and be replaced by your new selection. If you regret making selections at all, just click once in your image (with the rectangular, ellipse or lasso tool active) and the selection will be gone. However, you might want to make more than one selection, or combine several selections into one — for that you'll have to use the Shift and Ctrl keys.

Pressing the Shift key as you create a selection allows you to **add** a selection. If the selections touch, they will be combined into one single selection (a **union**).

Figure 7.1 *Selection union*

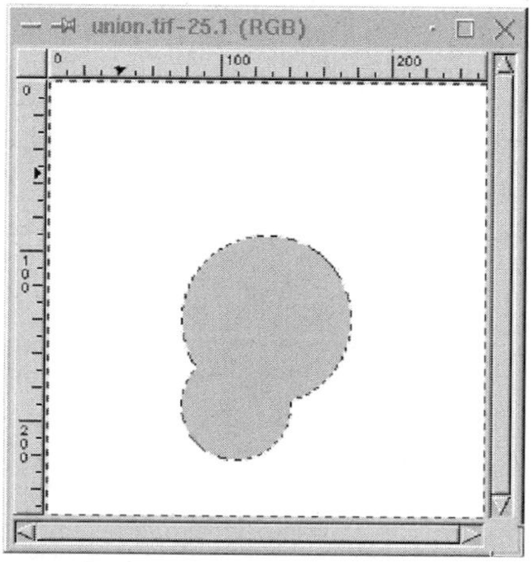

Pressing the Ctrl key will do the opposite; dragging a second selection that overlaps the first will **subtract** that area from the first selection (leaving you with the difference). Just pressing Ctrl while drawing selections won't do anything — the selections have to touch each other.

Figure 7.2 *Selection subtraction*

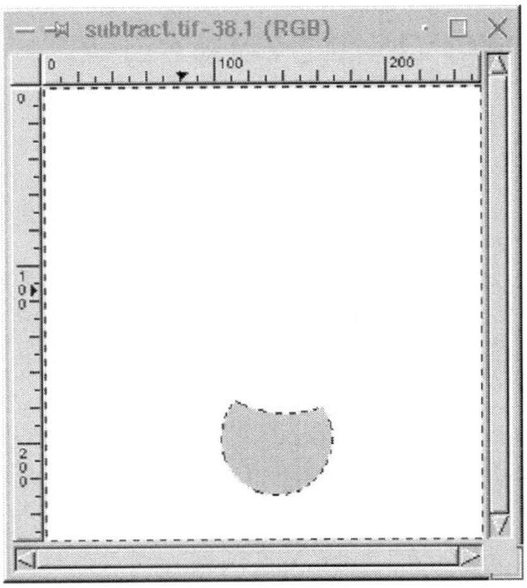

If you press both the Ctrl and Shift keys simultaneously, you'll get the **intersection** of the two, i.e., only the portion that is part of both selections.

Figure 7.3 *Selection*

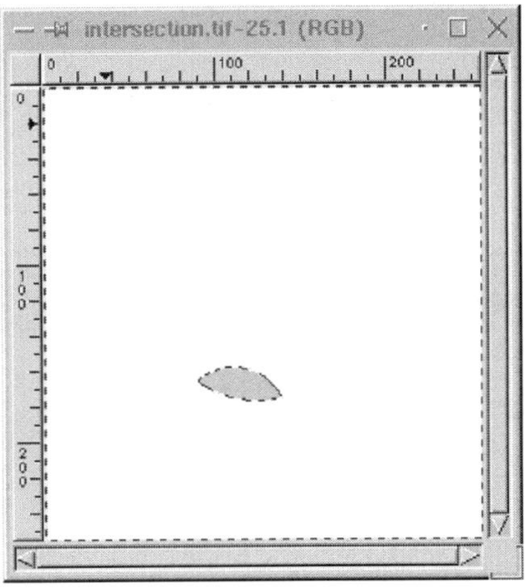

While making **additions** or **subtractions**, remember "to err is human." It's a good idea to keep your middle finger prepared to press the **right mouse button**. If you do this and then *release* the **left mouse button**, the selection you are drawing will disappear.

The ability to **Undo** a selection before it's finished is useful, particularly when performing these kinds of selections. When you decide you don't like the selection you're drawing, you can undo that selection without also erasing the other "good" selections. You can, of course, do this afterwards with Ctrl+Z, but it's a bit quicker to do it with the mouse.

MOVING SELECTIONS

Moving selections in Gimp is not entirely intuitive, so you may initially become somewhat confused. When you've made a selection in Gimp, the cursor will automatically turn into a **move symbol** (crossing arrows), and you'll find that you can move the selected part of the image, although the **Selection tool**, not the **Move tool**, is still active. What you may not have realized is that this action makes your selection *float* — that is, the image information in the selection has been separated from the background and "floats around" until you either anchor it to the background or to a layer of its own. To learn more about floating selections, read "Floating Selections" on page 331.

Figure 7.4 *Floating selection*

To leave the floating selection where it is, click on the image and it will merge with the rest of the image in the position you left it in. To place the floating selection in a layer of its own, open the `right-click|Layers|Layers & Channels` dialog and double-click on the blue **Floating Selection** bar, or click the **New Layer** button. See "Layers And Floating Selections" starting on page 315 for more information on Layers.

Note: To move a selection without making it float, you have to select the Move tool and press the Alt key as you drag the (empty) selection to another position. If you try to use the Move tool on a non-floating selection without pressing the Alt key, you will just move the entire layer or background.

Selections Within Floating Selections

If you have already moved the floating selection once, you can't do it a second time without switching to the Move tool. If the Selection tool is still active, you'll just form a new selection inside the float. However, this isn't really a selection as you know it — the dotted outline is gray instead of black, it doesn't blink and most importantly, the rest of the floating selection seems to have disappeared!

Figure 7.5 *Selections within floating selections*

The appearance of such a selection can be quite annoying if you created it by mistake (which is not uncommon). Don't panic — just press Ctrl+Z (Undo) and you'll be back to where you started.

Note that this doesn't happen when you move floats that are **text selections** or **pasted objects**, because then no Select tool is active.

The Old Way Of Manipulating Floating Selections

This effect is a remnant from the time before **Layers**, when floating selections and channel operations were the only tools for working with composite image information. Making selections within the float was used as a quick, but rather ineffective, **mask** effect. Now that Gimp supports **Layers**, which is much more sophisticated, there is really no need for this kind of operation anymore.

However, because this behavior has confused many users, we'll explain how it works:

What happens is that the contents in the floating selection become invisible, so that you can see the background through it. It's only inside the boundaries of the gray-lined subselection(s) that you'll be able to see the original contents of the float. This part of the float is now the only area that can be affected by paint, filters or other operations. The rest of the float is *masked*, and will not be changed. You can make a new subselection at any time, in which case this selection will replace the old one, and the new selection area will show another part of the floating selection.

This gray **subselection** won't turn into a normal selection until you *save* or *delete* the floating selection. To sum up, you have three options for floats:

- As we mentioned earlier, you can *save* a float in a new layer by double-clicking on the thumbnail bar, or by pressing the **New Layer** button in the `right-click|Layers|Layers & Channels` dialog.
- You can *delete* it with the **Delete Layer** button, in which case the entire content of the float will be *erased.*
- The third option is to click on the **Anchor Layer** button, which will merge the floating selection with the background (the same effect as clicking in the image). Anchoring will cause everything in the floating selection to be erased except the information inside the subselection.

In all of these scenarios, the subselection will become a normal selection.

GUIDES

To place your selections exactly where you want them, use the **horizontal** and **vertical guides**. Guides are vertical or horizontal dotted lines that you can drag into the image canvas from the rulers. Because selections and layers will snap to guides, they are a great help when you want to align different image objects. The guides will not show up in your output image. They are only visible on the computer monitor and in Gimp's native file format (XCF). To switch the guides on and off, click the **Toggle Guides** radio button in the `right-click|View` menu.

With a selection tool, drag the guide down from the top ruler or across from the left ruler. Use the **Move** tool to change the position of the guides (notice how the **move symbol** changes into a **pointing hand** when it touches a **guide**). **Snap to guides** is set by default in the **View** menu. If this option is checked, moving any kind of selection close to the guides causes it to "stick" or snap to it.

You can also use the guides to specify exactly where you want your square or ellipse selection to start. If you use the Ctrl key and start dragging close enough to the point where the guides cross, that will be the center of the new selection. Without Ctrl, the selection will start from the cross and continue in the direction you drag.

You can easily adapt the size, shape and position of a rectangular or elliptical selection to the guides by drawing it within the frame of two vertical and two horizontal guides (just using the guides as visual references).

Rectangular And Elliptical Selection Tools

It's pretty obvious what these selections will look like. If you click the mouse and drag, you'll get normal **rectangular** or **elliptical** selections starting from the corner where you first pressed the mouse button. If you want to create **circles** or **squares** or make your selection **spread from the center**, you must use the Ctrl and Shift keys:

- The Shift key constricts the selections to perfect **squares** and **circles**. The selection starts from the **corner** and continues in the drag direction.
- The Ctrl key draws normal **rectangle** and **ellipse** selections, but with this key, selections will emanate **radially** from the point where you start dragging. This point is now the **center** of your selection.
- Using both Shift and Ctrl results in circles or squares (as with Shift), but they grow from the center and out (as with Ctrl).

Note: To make this work, **first** press the mouse button, **then** hold the key and drag.

Now, if you want to use Shift and Ctrl for adding, subtracting or intersecting selections, and at the same time use Shift and Ctrl for the operations mentioned above, it gets a bit complicated — but not impossible.

First, you must decide what the selection will be used for:

- If you want to make **many selections**, or **add** to an existing selection, use Shift.
- If you want to **subtract** a selection from another selection, use Ctrl.
- If you want to make an **intersection** of two selections use Shift and Ctrl.

When you have decided, hold that key and then press the mouse button. Then, release the key but not the mouse button. Then, press Shift, Ctrl or Shift+Ctrl and drag. This time the key determines what **shape** or **starting point** you want for your selection (as delineated above). Table 7.1 on page 116 charts the different key stroke options.

This procedure makes it easy to add a rectangle to a selection, or make subtractions with squares or circles. It is, however, rather tricky and if you want to do serious work using these commands, you need to plan ahead, and always use the guides and rulers to place new selections correctly.

You can, of course, always use **Channels** to perform such operations. By making white circles in a channel and putting black ones on top of them, you'll subtract a circle without having to remember what key to use, except Shift for circle. Read more about making selections in "Channels And Duotones" starting on page 351.

Table 7.1 *Selection control*

	Key2=Shift Circle	Key2=Ctrl Center	Key2=Both Circle+Cent er	No Key 2
Key1=Shift Adding	Add circle from corner	Add ellipse from center	Add circle from center	Add ellipse from corner
Key1=Ctrl Subtracting	Subtract circle from corner	Subtract ellipse from center	Subtract circle from center	Subtract ellipse from corner
Key1=Both Intersect	Intersect circle from corner	Intersect ellipse from center	Intersect circle from center	Intersect ellipse from corner
No Key 1	Create circle from corner	Create ellipse from center	Create circle from center	Create ellipse from corner

SUMMARY

To create selections:

1. Press mouse
2. Press key and drag

To add, subtract or intersect with other selections:

1. Press key
2. Press mouse and drag

To create a selection of a certain shape or from a certain direction, *and* use that selection to add/subtract/intersect:

1. Press key 1 to determine effect
2. Press mouse
3. Release key 1, but not mouse
4. Press new key 2 to determine shape or direction, and drag

SELECTION OPTIONS

If you double-click on a button in the toolbox, you'll see a little window showing you that tool's options. For example, if you double-click on the **Select elliptical regions** button in the toolbox, you'll see the **Tool Options** dialog shown in Figure 7.6 . Once you have accessed the Tool Options dialog, you don't have to repeat this procedure to view the tool options for another tool. The dialog will stay on screen, but it will change when you select another tool, displaying the options available for that tool.

Figure 7.6 *Selection option dialog*

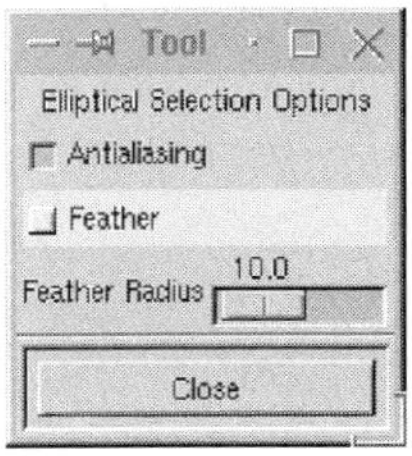

ANTIALIASING

For most select tools, you have the option of **Antialiasing**. Antialiasing is an effect used on curves and boundaries of high contrast areas, which makes the curve or boundary look softer and smoother. The most common use is the anti-aliasing of letters in bitmapped images, because it takes away the **jaggies** (the visible jagged and pixelly edges of the letter's curves in low resolution). It softly blends the edge pixels with the background, which will make curves look a lot better, but also a bit blurred. So you gain in smoothness, but lose in sharpness.

Figure 7.7 *The difference between using and not using antialiasing*

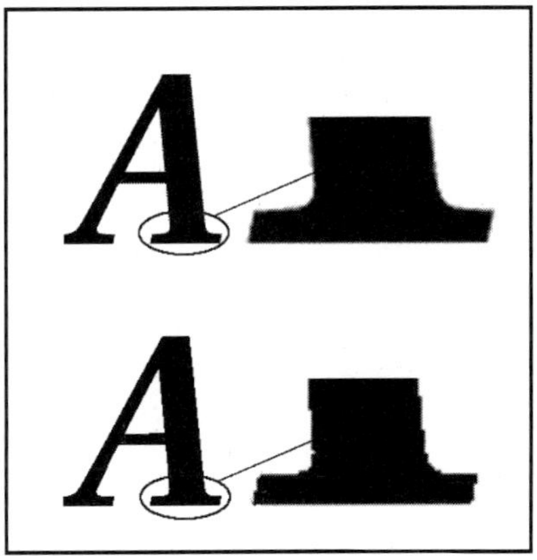

FEATHER

For the **Rectangular select** tool, the only option is **Feather**. Feather means that you can choose to make the peripheral parts of your selection transparent. It will be opaque in the middle, and get more and more transparent as you get closer to the edges. This is very useful if you want to make something look soft and blurry, like soft shadows or glowing edges, or if you'd like to use collage techniques with the **Paste** or **Paste Into** commands.

Figure 7.8 *An example of feathering*

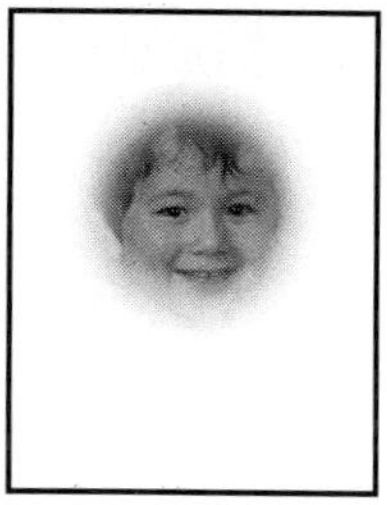

An image you paste into a feathered selection will get soft and transparent at the edges and blend in nicely with your background. It is also usually a good idea to use a small amount of feather (a Feather Radius of around 5-10 pixels will do in most cases) if you want to select something that is to be **copied**, **moved** or **cut** and **pasted**, because the feathered edges will compensate for an imperfect selection edge and make it blend into the background.

The Free-Hand Selection Tool

The **Free-hand selection** tool, or lasso, lets you create a selection by drawing a free-hand form with it. You close a free selection by ending in the point you started from. If you draw an open shape, this selection tool will close it for you.

Tip: Usually, you can't select a complex area with just one selection tool. Use more than one and add the selections together.

The lasso is an excellent tool for fixing up selections. If you see that you've missed some pixels, it is easy to correct this with Shift+ or Ctrl+ lasso. As we explained earlier in "Selection Control" on page 110, Shift+ a selection tool will add to the selection, and Ctrl+ a selection tool will subtract from a selection.

As I'm sure you have noticed, the mouse isn't a very sophisticated drawing instrument. The good news is that the Gimp now fully supports **digitized tablets** (like the Wacom ArtPad), and pressure-sensitive pencils. X programs have supported such devices as a substitute for a mouse for a long time. This means that you could use a Wacom device as a pointer or pencil, but the pressure-sensitive feature was not available. Gimp now has patches to make this work. Believe me — working with lassos, pencils and brushes is dramatically different with an accurate tool.

Options

The options for the Free-hand selection tool are the same as for the **Ellipse selection** tool: **Antialiasing** and **Feather**. Read about them in "Selection Options" on page 116.

FUZZY SELECT

The **Fuzzy Select** tool looks like the Photoshop magic wand and works much the same way. **Fuzzy Select** selects adjacent pixels of similar color. It starts selecting when you click at a spot in the image. The wand will select the color on that spot, and continue outwards until it thinks the color gets too different.

FUZZY SELECT OPTIONS

The options dialog doesn't provide a control button for controlling the wand's sensitivity. To control the wand's sensitivity, after you position the cursor and press the mouse button, drag the cursor (without releasing the mouse button) from the upper-left corner, either to the right or straight down (it doesn't matter) to increase from a small, stingy selection to a very generous one.

Figure 7.9 *The Fuzzy Selection option dialog*

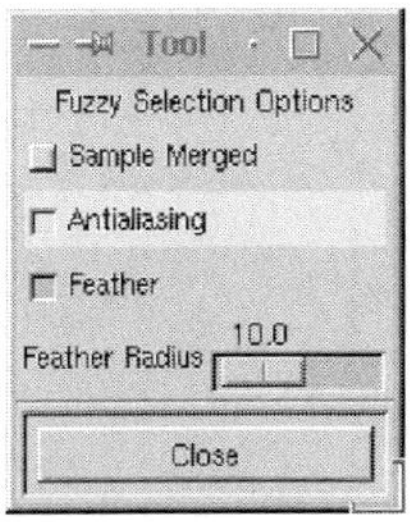

Be careful where you start. If you select the wrong spot, you might get the inverted selection of what you wanted. In other words, selecting the wrong spot may make the wand select everything except your choice. (If you have a black, antialiased object on a white background, you can end up with a white to gray selection instead of a black to gray one if you are not careful.)

The wand is the perfect tool to select sharp-edged objects in an image. The wand is easy and fun to use, so the beginner often starts out using the wand a lot. A more experienced user will find that tools like the **Bezier** tool, **Color Select** or **Alpha Channels** are often more efficient for selection, and use the wand less. Still, it's very useful for selecting an area within a contour, or for touching up imperfect selections. The wand is also very efficient for removing the remains of the background color from a cut and pasted selection.

The **Fuzzy Selection Options** dialog includes a checkbox called **Sample Merged**. This option becomes relevant only when you have several layers in your image, and the active layer is either semi-transparent or is set to another **Layer Mode** than *Normal*. If this is the case, the colors present in the layer will be different from the colors in the composite image. If the Sample Merged option is unchecked, the wand will only react to the color in the **active layer** when it creates a selection. If it is checked it will react to the composite color of all visible layers.

THE BEZIER SELECTION TOOL

In our opinion, the **Bezier** selection tool is one of the most useful tools. You'll find **Bezier curves** in all major drawing or imaging software packages.

USE BEZIERS AS A SIMPLE DRAWING TOOL

The Bezier selection is the equivalent of "Pentool Paths" in Photoshop. Most drawing in programs like Corel, Illustrator, Freehand or even 3-D programs is done with Bezier curves. Because Gimp is based on **bitmaps** and not on **vector graphics** (like Corel or Illustrator), you can't draw with Bezier curves, but you can make advanced selections.

Figure 7.10 *The motorcycle image that we will use in our Bezier selection example*

As far as drawing with Bezier tools goes, I don't count using **Stroke** (`right-click|Edit|Stroke`) on a Bezier curve, or making a **Border** from a bezier selection with `right-click|Select|Border`, and then filling the border, as drawing. If you just want to add a simple drawing, this can be quite sufficient, but if you want to create a more advanced drawing, use the **Gfig** plug-in in the `right-click|Filters|Render` menu, or do it in a commercial drawing program, convert it to suitable format and import it to Gimp.

CONTROL POINTS

You use the Bezier select tool by clicking out **splines** or **anchor points** in a rough approximation of the shape you want. You click, move the cursor and click again to make straight lines and click and drag to make curves. Don't bother to try to make curves at this stage though, unless you're an experienced user. Just click out a rough, angular shape and make sure you close it by placing the last point over the first and clicking.

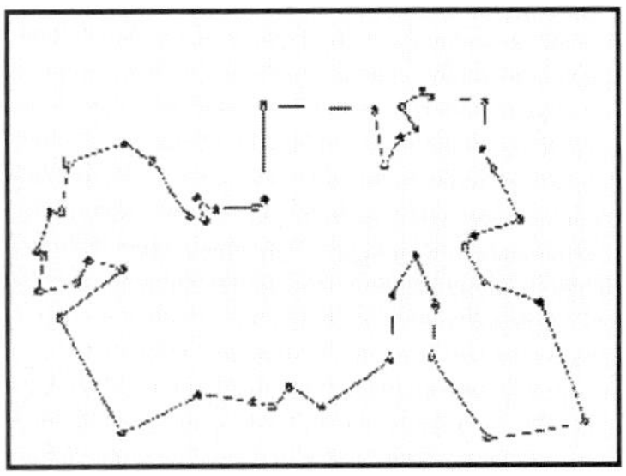

Figure 7.11 *A first rough Bezier selection*

Tip: Be careful about where you place anchor points, because you can't remove or add anchor points with this tool. This reduces the control you have over your curves. You can't change anything, so watch out where you put your splines!

Also, don't use too many splines. You only need one for each curve segment, so adding too many to the Bezier curve will just make it harder to create the final selection shape.

MODIFYING CONTROL POINTS

Now, you can start to make curves out of the straight lines. When you click on an anchor point, two little **handles** appear. If you pull the handles, they will change size and direction and shape a curve from the lines.

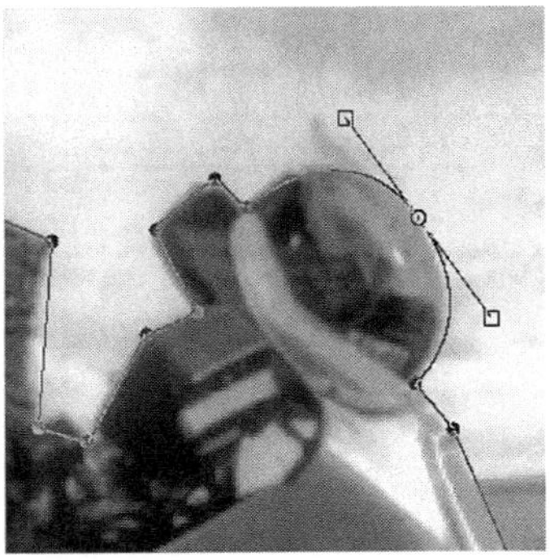

Figure 7.12 *A control point with handles*

Long handles result in a flattened curve, and short ones in a steeper curve. Turn the handles in the angle and direction you want them by clicking and dragging with the mouse.

Moving Splines

The first thing you'll want to do is *move* the splines to their correct position. By pressing Ctrl, you can drag and drop an anchor point any way you like.

The other important thing to do is determine what splines are to be **soft**, and which are to be **sharp** or angled. By default, the handles have equal length and create curves with round corners.

When you need a **sharp corner**, press Shift. Then, each handle can be controlled separately, and you have total control over the shape of your curves.

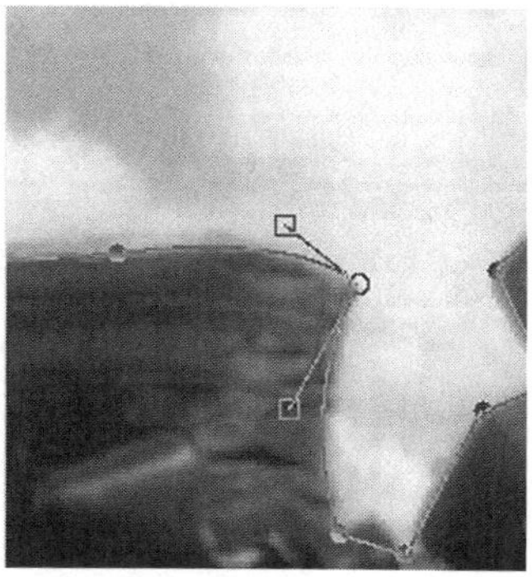

Figure 7.13 *The control point with its handles — notice the sharp corner*

The Final Touch

When you're happy with your curve, click inside the curve and it will turn into a selection.

Figure 7.14 *The Bezier selection saved in an alpha channel*

Remember to always preserve a complex selection like this in an **alpha channel**. You'll probably need it again.

An **alpha channel** is a storage place for selections. Selection information is interpreted as transparent (unselected areas), semi-transparent (fuzzy selection edges) or opaque (selected areas). The `right-click|Select|Save to Channel` command will save this selection information as a grayscale image in the **Layers & Channels** tab. The selection stored in the Alpha channel can be invoked at any time with the **Channel to Selection** command. For more information on Alpha channels, see "Channels And Duotones" starting on page 351.

Options

The options for the Bezier tool are **Antialiasing** and **Feather**. Read more about them in "Selection Options" on page 116.

Intelligent Scissors

If you're using Gimp v. 1.0.x, this feature is not fully developed, and will not work very well.

The **Intelligent Scissors** tool is a very interesting piece of equipment. It will *guess* the edges that you're trying to select.

It's quite hard to fully control the **Free-hand** tool, unless you're extremely dexterous. This is where Intelligent Scissors comes in. This tool lets you draw the *outline* of an object, just like the Free-hand tool (you can be a bit sloppier), but when you have defined your selection, it will automatically seek out the edges of the object that you are trying to select. If it's not a perfect selection, you have the option to convert the Intelligent Scissors selection to a **Bezier** curve, and make the necessary adjustments.

Sounds wonderful, doesn't it? Sorry to say, the current version of Intelligent Scissors (Gimp v. 1.0) is not in full working order, but let us show you how it's *supposed* to work when it's functional again.

Open a Gimp image, make an IS selection around a clearly defined object in the image (like you would with the Free-hand tool). Hopefully, you'll now have a nearly perfect selection. If you want to adjust the IS selection, double-click on the IS tool. This will bring up the **Intelligent Scissors Options dialog**. Press **Convert to Bezier Curve** and make the final adjustments.

Activation And Shortcuts

You may have noticed that there is no *marching ants border* in an IS selection. IS is just like **Bezier** select — you have to click inside the shape to create a selection. After you have activated your selection, all the usual selection shortcuts (creating unions, subtractions, intersections, etc.) work as they do with an ordinary selection.

Options

There are several options in the Intelligent Scissors option dialog: Edge-Detect Thresh. (for Threshold) and Elasticity are the most important ones.

- **Edge-Detect Thresh.** controls how *sensitive* Intelligent Scissors is to the edges in your image. The higher the value, the more sensitive IS will be.
- **Elasticity** controls how *willing* IS is to *bend away* from the curve you have drawn and snap to the edge.

These two options more or less control the entire functionality of Intelligent Scissors.

For selecting solid objects with well-defined edges, you can set both **Elasticity** and **Edge-Detect Thresh.** to a high value, because there is only one edge, and you want to make a quick and sloppy selection. The clear contours will enable IS to easily snap away from what you have "selected" to the edge of the square.

On the other hand, if you're trying to select a certain edge in an image that is full of edges, you have to be more careful in your drawing, and also lower the **Elasticity** value so the section won't snap to another edge than the one you wanted.

There are also a few other options. **Curve resolution** controls the roughness of the selection. If you have a lot of curves in your selection, a low curve resolution will make the curves *rough* or uneven. A higher curve resolution will make the curves much *smoother*. **Antialiasing** and **Feather** work like they do for all the other selection tools.

Using Undo With Intelligent Scissors

An Intelligent Scissors drawing doesn't turn into a selection until you click in it, and there are some advantages to this. You can **Undo** what you did *before* the IS operation without destroying your IS selection. After you have used IS to create a selection, but before enabling it, press Ctrl+Z to undo the previous action (but not your IS selection). When you're finished, click inside the IS selection (or convert to Bezier curves for further adjustment) to turn it into an active selection.

This will, for example, enable you to run some of the `right-click|Filters|Edge-Detect` filters (see "Edge-Detect Filters" starting on page 485) to enhance edges before you start using IS.

CHAPTER 8

Paint Tools

To be able to use the more advanced functions in Gimp, you must first learn to control Gimp's basic paint tools. You will soon find that you can achieve much more using the basic paint tools than by applying any of the instant paint filters.

THE COLOR PICKER

The **color picker** is used for choosing colors. If you don't want to use any of the **palettes** available (read more about palettes in "The Color Picker" on page 128), you can just pick a color in your image or in any other images that are currently open in Gimp, so you have many color choices. Just click on a color in an image, and this color will appear as the **foreground** or **background** color at the bottom of the toolbox.

THE COLOR INFORMATION WINDOW

A small information window shows the **RGB** and **Alpha** values (see "Alpha Channels" on page 353) of your chosen color. **Alpha N/A** means that your image contains no alpha channel (see "Alpha Channels" on page 353), or that transparency is not enabled. Invoke the **Add Alpha Channel** command in the `right-click|Image|Alpha` menu or the `right-click|Layers` menu to add transparency information to your image. Now, when you erase, cut or clear, you'll get transparent areas instead of the background color in the toolbox. For more information on alpha channels, see "Channels And Duotones" starting on page 351.

The **Hex Triplet** is the color coded in hexadecimal. The hexadecimal format can be used to set colors in web pages, because hex is used for coding color in HTML. For a **Grayscale** image the information box displays an **Intensity** value ranging from 0 to 255, where 0 is black and 255 is white. An indexed image also has an **Index** number for the specific color. Note that the alpha value of an indexed image is either 0 or 255; there's nothing in between.

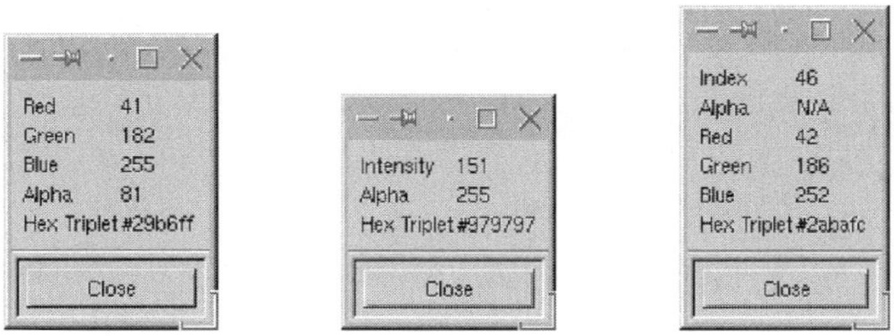

Figure 8.1 *Indexed, grayscale and RGB color info dialogs*

OPTIONS

If you double-click on the Color Picker icon in the toolbox, you'll access the **Color Picker Options** dialog. The only option is a **Sample Merged** checkbox. If the active layer isn't opaque, or if it's set to another Layer Mode than *Normal*, the colors in the composite image will be different than the colors that are present in the layer. Check the Sample Merged checkbox if you want to pick a color that represents the color you see on the monitor, not just the color in the active layer. *Only colors in visible layers are used.*

Figure 8.2 *The Color Picker Options dialog*

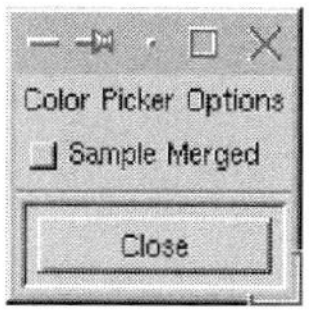

PALETTES

When you want to pick a color to work with, you can always use the **color picker**, but most of the time you'll be working with a **Color Palette**. You can choose one of the many ready-made palettes, but you can also create your own palette.

Another option is to create a palette from an indexed image using `right-click|Image|Save Palette`. You can use a temporary **Indexed Color Palette** (if you're using an indexed image) with the command `right-click|Dialogs|Indexed Palette`.

Figure 8.3 *The Color Palette*

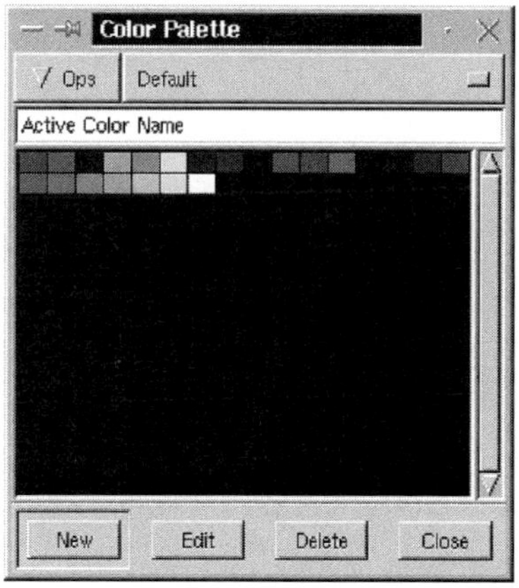

CREATING A PERSONAL PALETTE

To create a personal palette, open the **Color Palette** (from the toolbox, `File|Dialogs|Palette` or press Ctrl+P). You'll find a **Default** palette in the palette window, which contains some standard CMYK/RGB colors and a range of grayscales. You can add colors to this or another custom palette, or you can create and name a new palette by selecting **New** from the **Ops** menu.

To add colors from an image, drag the color picker over the image until you find a color you want to add to the palette (look in the *foreground color square* — you'll see the colors change as you drag). When you've got the right color, release your mouse button. Then, click on the **New** button at the bottom of the Color Palette dialog. The color square will appear on the palette. To add a color with a specific RGB or HSV value, double-click in the foreground color square to access the **Color Selection dialog**. More information about the Color Selection dialog box is in "The Color Selection Dialog" on page 143.

You can name and save your new palette, and you can edit or delete colors. To use colors in a palette, you don't need to select them to the foreground color square with the picker — just click on a new color with whatever paint tool you're using at the time. More information about palettes can be found in "Palettes" on page 176.

THE BUCKET FILL

This tool fills a selection with the current **foreground color**. If you Shift+click and use the Bucket tool, it will use the **background color** instead.

The Bucket tool will fill a layer that already contains color and alpha information. The amount of fill depends on what **Fill Threshold** you have specified.

Figure 8.4 *The Bucket Fill Options dialog*

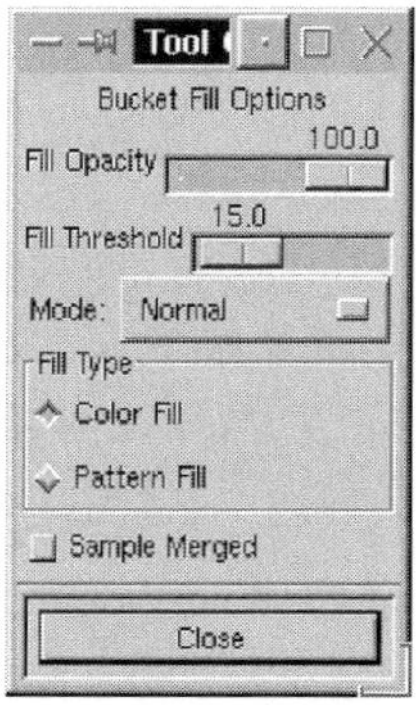

The fill threshold determines how far the fill will spread (similar to the way in which the magic wand works). The fill starts at the point where you click and spreads outward until the color or alpha value becomes "too different."

BUCKET FILLING IN TRANSPARENT LAYERS

When you fill objects in a transparent layer (such as letters in a text layer) with a different color than before, you may find that a border of the old color still surrounds the objects. This is due to a *low fill-threshold* in the **Bucket Fill options dialog**. With a low threshold, the bucket tool won't fill semi-transparent pixels, and they will stand out against the fill because they have kept their original color.

However, if you want to fill areas that are totally transparent, you have to choose `right-click|Select|Select All`, and make sure that the layer's Keep Trans button (in the Layers & Channels dialog) is unchecked. If the Keep Trans button is checked, only the opaque parts of the layer will be filled, and if you don't use the Select All command, only the opaque "island" that you clicked on will be filled. To read more about the layers and channel dialog read “The Layers & Channels Dialog” on page 317.

Options

The **Fill Opacity** slider allows you to set the transparency of the fill. The dialog also includes a **Mode** option (read more about modes in “Modes” starting on page 335).

Under **Fill Type**, the **Pattern Fill** radio button enables you to fill your selection with a pattern instead of a color. Use the commands `right-click|Dialogs|Patterns` or `File|Dialogs|Patterns` to open the Pattern dialog, where you can choose a fill pattern.

Sample Merged means that the bucket fill reacts to the color borders in the *entire composite image*, and not just the ones in the active layer (however, it will only fill in the active layer).

Filling Feathered Selections

In a feathered selection, the bucket will make a soft concentric fill, which can be made more intense by clicking several times. If you use different colors each time, they’ll blend softly into each other in an opalescent effect.

The Blend Tool Or Gradient Fill

This tool fills the selected area with a gradient blend of the foreground and background colors by default, but there are many other options in the Gimp Blend tool. To make a blend, drag the cursor in the direction you want the gradient to go, and release the mouse button when you feel you have the right position and size of your blend. The softness of the blend depends on how far you drag the cursor. The shorter the drag distance, the sharper it will be.

Options

Double-click on the Blend tool to see the **Blend Options** dialog.

The Blend tool has an **Opacity** option. Using a semi-transparent opacity value, and then dragging several times in different directions, gives an interesting shimmering, bubbly surface to a background.

Tip: Also check out the **Difference** option in the **Mode** menu, where doing the same thing (even with full opacity) will result in fantastic swirling patterns, changing and adding every time you drag the cursor. To understand Modes, read "Modes" starting on page 335.

The Offset slider controls the fuzzyness of the blend. A high offset value gives a harder, sharper blending edge, and the foreground color becomes more dominant. Offset moves the blend's point of departure in the image (the point where the foreground color starts to blend with the background color). Offset works with all gradient types, *except for Linear and Shapeburst*. Increase the offset value if you want to control the appearance of fluorescent, shiny or metallic objects created with the Blend tool.

The Blend Options dialog offers the standard **RGB** option, as well as the **FG to BG (HSV)** option (HSV stands for **H**ue, **S**aturation and **V**alue).

Figure 8.5 *The Blend Options dialog*

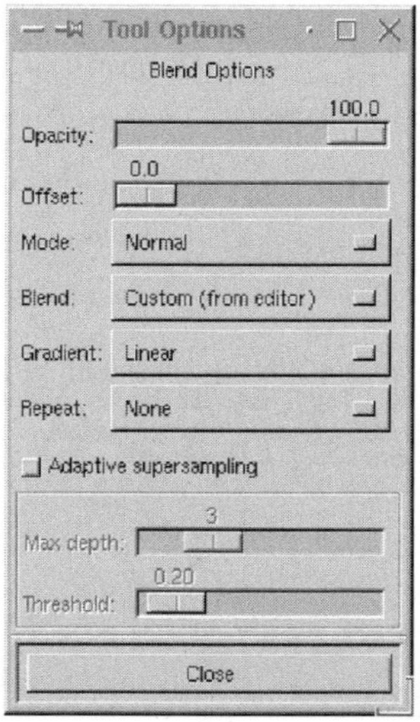

HSV Gradients

HSV is a color model based on a 360-degree **spectrum circle**. This means that a gradient using an HSV blend will not simply make a transition from red FG (foreground) to blue BG (background) via shades of violet.

HSV starts with red and follows the color circle clockwise through yellow, green and cyan until it reaches blue. The gradient will go clockwise if FG is in the right part of the semicircle, and counterclockwise if FG is in the left half.

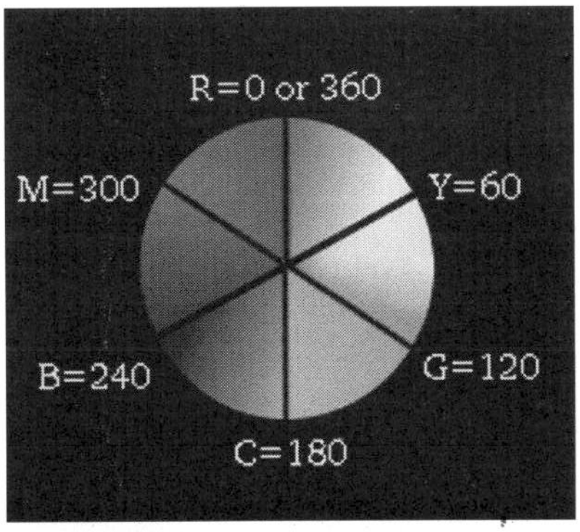

Figure 8.6 *HSV circle*

Figure 8.7 *HSV gradient blending from red FG to a red/magenta BG*

FG to Transparent only uses one color for the gradient blend. It gradually changes the alpha value (see "Alpha Channels" on page 353) from 255 to 0, causing the color to become increasingly transparent. This option is very useful for working with softly blended collages or fog effects.

You can also choose to use one of the custom gradients (as described next) or make your own gradient with the powerful **Gradient Editor** (`right-click|Dialogs|Gradient Editor`).

Gradient Types

You can choose from nine different gradient types, as follows:

- The default gradient type is **Linear**, which produces a smooth linear transition from one color to another.

Figure 8.8 *Linear gradient*

- **Bilinear** *mirrors* a linear gradient blend. In other words, Bilinear places the FG color in the middle, and then makes the transition to BG color both ways. The result often resembles metal pipes, especially if you only drag for a short distance.

Figure 8.9 *Bilinear gradient*

- **Radial**, as the name implies, makes a radial transition from FG (in the middle) to BG (peripheral). The radial gradient type is necessary for certain gradients in the Gradient Editor, such as "*Eyeball*."

Figure 8.10 *Radial gradient*

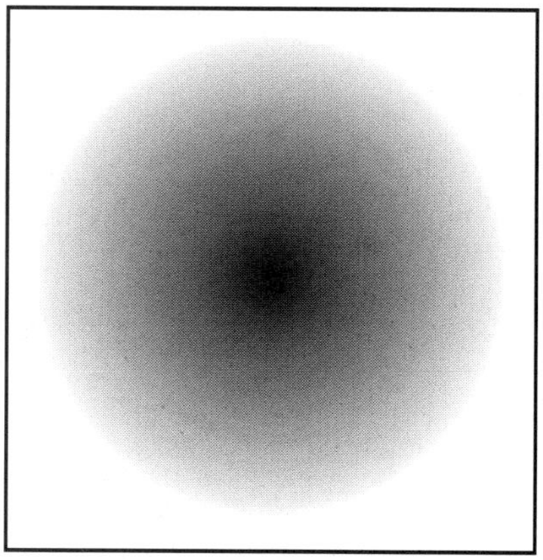

- The **Square** gradient produces a square blend, imitating the visual perspective of looking down a corridor.

Figure 8.11 *Square gradient*

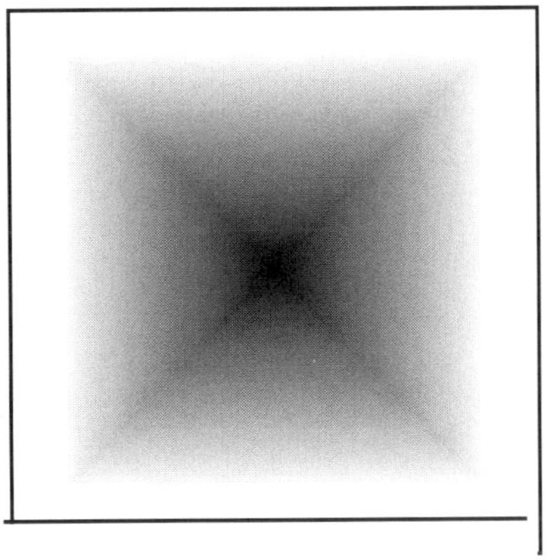

- The effect of the **Conical (symmetric)** and **Conical (asymmetric)** gradients is like looking at a 3-D cone from above. The dragging distance is irrelevant for conical gradients. The two things that affect a conical gradient are *the point of departure*, which determines where the top of the cone is placed, and the *drag direction*, which determines from where the FG color (which represents light or shadow) is coming.

Conical (symmetric) creates a cone with an even shape.

Figure 8.12 *Conical symmetric gradient*

The **Conical (asymmetric)** gradient imitates a "drop shaped" cone, i.e., a cone with one sharp edge.

Figure 8.13 *Conical asymmetric gradient*

- **Shapeburst** gradients give a three-dimensional look to a defined shape or selection. Shapeburst gradients are not affected by drag direction, distance or position. **Spherical** gives a flatter, rounder looking surface than **angular** or **dimpled** (which produces a sharp topographic surface). You can see examples of the different shapeburst gradients here below.

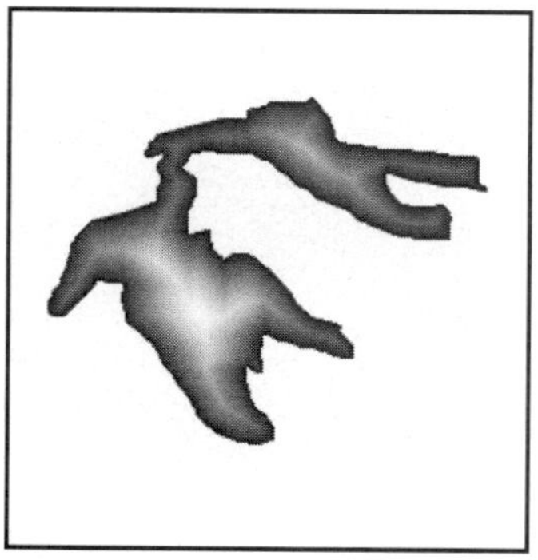

Figure 8.14 *Spherical*

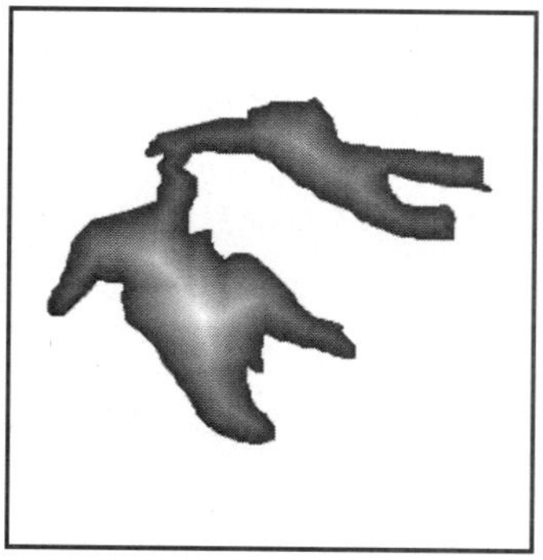

Figure 8.15 *Angular*

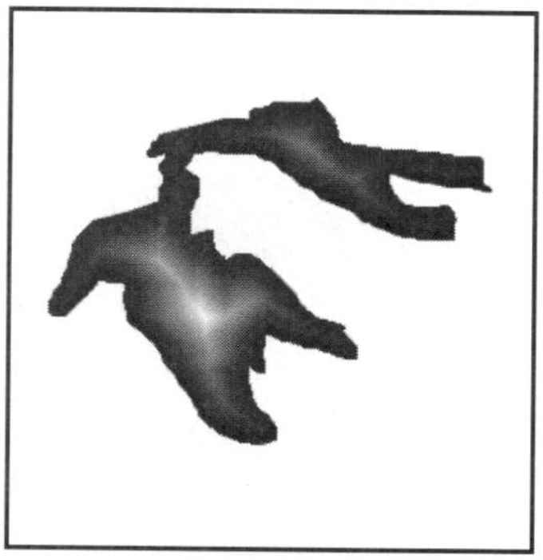

Figure 8.16 *Dimpled*

The **Repeat** options (**Sawtooth wave** and **Triangular wave**) allow you to repeat a gradient fill. The shorter the drag distance, the more often the fill repeats. The examples below show the sawtooth and triangular repeating options with a linear gradient.

Note: Repeat can't be used with Conical or Shapeburst gradients.

Figure 8.17 *Sawtooth*

Figure 8.18 *Triangular*

Adaptive supersampling is an option which slightly improves the smoothness of the blend by adding a few intermediate colors. The effect is often quite subtle, unless this option is used for very small selections (especially when using Shapeburst), with a gradient from the editor. You can read more about the **Gradient Editor** in "The Gradient Editor" on page 177.

THE PENCIL AND PAINTBRUSH

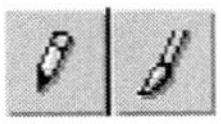

The **pencil** and **paintbrush** are similar tools. The main difference between the two tools is that although both tools use the same **Brush Selection** (`File|Dialogs|Brushes` or `right-click|File|Dialogs|Brushes`), the pencil tool will not produce fuzzy edges, even with a very fuzzy brush.

If you want to draw straight lines, use Shift and click the mouse at the point where you want the line to go (don't drag the mouse).

Tip: the Shift+click option also works for the **eraser**, the **airbrush**, the **clone tool** and the **convolver**.

PAINTBRUSH OPTIONS

The paintbrush has a Fade Out option and an Incremental option. **Incremental** only affects semi-transparent paint, so in order to see it, you must change the opacity value in the **Brush selection** dialog. Incremental allows you to increase opacity in the area where two brush strokes cross, somewhat like painting with watercolor.

Fade Out means that a continuous sweep of the brush, without releasing the mouse button, will cause the paint to become increasingly transparent until it is completely invisible, as if you made a real brush stroke and ran out of paint. The amount of Fade Out determines where the fading starts as well as the length of the "comet tail."

The lowest Fade Out value you can get by dragging the slider manually is 34.5, but you can get more exact values by using the left and right arrow keys on your keyboard. The brush stroke will start to fade after reaching the specified length (in pixels); it will fade to near transparency after reaching double that amount of pixels; and it will completely fade out when the stroke is about three times as long as the initial pixel value. More information on brushes is included in "Brushes" on page 172.

Figure 8.19 *Paintbrush Options dialog*

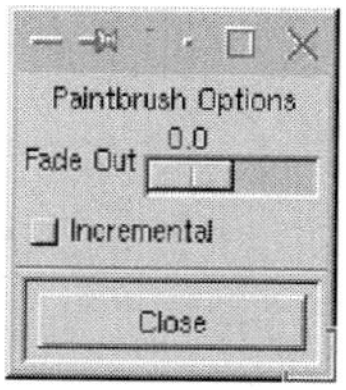

BRUSH SELECTION

Brush Selection (`File|Dialogs|Brushes` or `right-click|Dialogs|Brushes`) isn't only available for the Pencil and Paintbrush tools, but also for the eraser, airbrush, clone tool and convolver.

You'll find a variety of brushes available. Besides **Mode** and **Opacity** options, a **Spacing** option allows you to separate the brush stroke into a line of individual brush-shaped objects. You can also make your own brushes and add them to the **Brush Selection** dialog. More information on the Brush Selection dialog is available in "The Brush Selection Dialog" on page 172.

Figure 8.20 *The Brush Selection dialog*

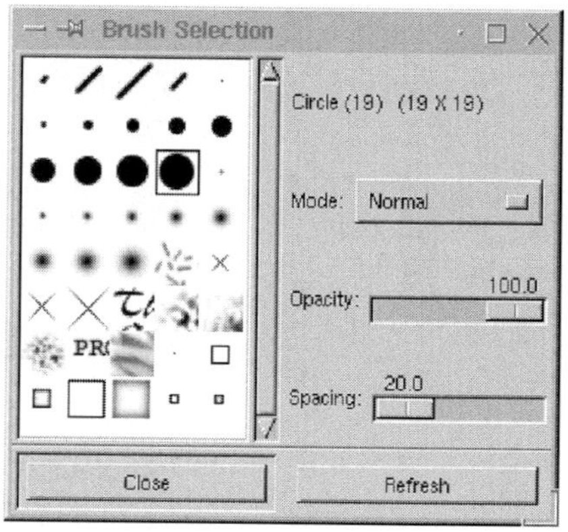

THE ERASER TOOL

Just as you can paint with pattern-shaped brushes, you can also **erase** with the same patterns. This is a great way to create convincing **texture** effects, especially if you use it in many layers. The **Incremental** option is only effective when the brush opacity is less than 100. Incremental allows you to increase transparency in the area where two brush strokes cross, somewhat like adding more water to a watercolor painting. The **Hard edge** option removes fuzzy edges on all brush types (like the Pencil tool).

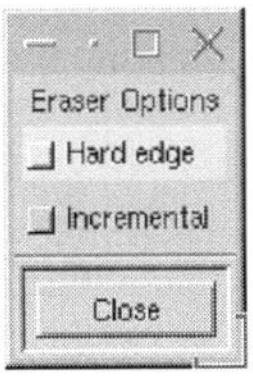

Figure 8.21 *The Eraser Options dialog*

Tip: To isolate a complex selection, use the Eraser tool to erase the background around the object's outline, then use the **wand** or **lasso** to easily select either the object or the surroundings and delete or cut them away.

HINTS

You can change the size and shape of **Floating selections** with the eraser tool. This happens because the eraser tool affects alpha values (see "Alpha Channels" on page 353), and those values determine the area of a floating selection. You can, for example, reduce the selection by trimming its edges or cutting holes in it with the eraser tool. If you'd rather increase the floating selection area than reduce it, you can do this by choosing `right-click|Select|Invert` before floating. That way, you'll trim the surrounding areas instead, thus increasing the size of the original float. To re-select the old float (which you have now added parts to) you just invert it back again, using the same command.

THE AIRBRUSH TOOL

The **airbrush** tool creates soft, semi-transparent spray strokes. There are two options in the Options dialog: **Rate** and **Pressure**. The **Rate** value determines how spray distribution follows movement. A low value produces a smooth, even brush stroke (pausing does not affect it). With a high value, this tool behaves more like a real airbrush: If you pause in mid-stroke, the airbrush will keep on spraying and leave a darker stain at that position.

Figure 8.22 *The Airbrush Options dialog*

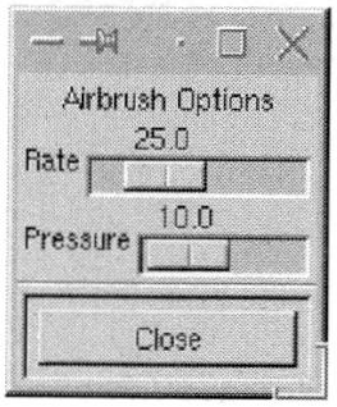

Pressure regulates how much paint there is in the "spray." Note that low pressure isn't the same as low opacity on the brush. Low pressure is more uneven (or "airbrushy" looking) compared to the smoother appearance that results from high pressure and low brush opacity.

THE CLONE TOOL

The **Clone tool** gives you the ability to paint with *patterns* or with *parts of an image* instead of just a solid color. To paint with a pattern from the **Pattern Selection** dialog (see "Palettes" on page 176), simply click on the pattern you want and start painting.

CLONE OPTIONS

Use the **Aligned** option if you want a continuous pattern. If the Aligned option is not checked, you will paint a new part of the pattern every time you let go of the mouse button and start again.

Figure 8.23 *The Clone Tool Options dialog*

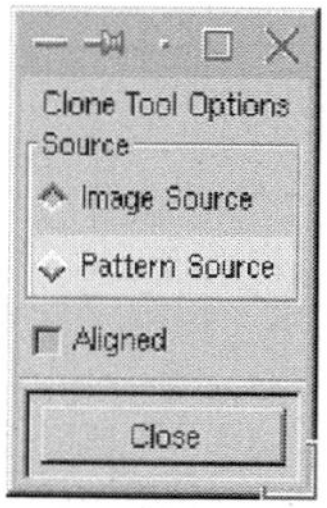

If you use the **Image Source** option, note that in Gimp you use Ctrl instead of Alt (Photoshop) to choose the point of departure from the image source. Press the Ctrl key and click on the part of the image that you want to clone, return to the image you wish to retouch and start cloning. You can choose to clone from another part of your image, from one layer to another or from a completely different image.

Retouching Hints

Needless to say, the **Clone** tool is the ultimate **retouching** instrument. For example, if you would like to retouch a birthmark from a face, it would be hard, almost impossible, to imitate the complex color varieties of skin texture with regular paint or blends. The cloning of skin in another part of the face is the only way to make it look good. We're not saying that cloning is easy, though; to make it look convincing you may well have to clone from different directions, with different brushes, and maybe even in different layers with appropriate opacities and modes.

THE CONVOLVER

The **Convolver** tool allows you to blur or sharpen your image. **Pressure** regulates the strength of the convolve effect.

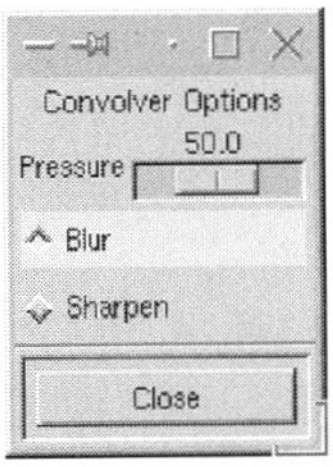

Figure 8.24 *The Convolver Options dialog*

CONVOLVER BLUR

The convolver's **Blur option** is somewhat similar to *Smudge* in Photoshop, though not quite as smeary. It softens sharp edges and blurs whole areas as you use it. The blurring effect always produces a darker color than the original. Blurring transparent areas with the convolver will transform those areas to an opaque color. The convolver tool will use the nearest color and smear it to full opacity.

Figure 8.25 *The original image and the blurred one*

CONVOLVER SHARPEN

The **Sharpen** option doesn't really sharpen in the traditional sense of the word; its effects are too "dotty" or "pixelly."

If you want to sharpen something that is out of focus, you should use `right-click|Filters|Enhance|Sharpen` or `right-click|Filters|Enhance|Unsharp Mask`. However, the convolver's Sharpen will produce some very interesting graphic results (especially in a grayscale image) resembling engravings, prints or ink drawings.

Figure 8.26 *The sharpened image*

THE FOREGROUND/BACKGROUND ICONS

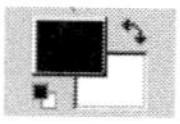

The **foreground/background** color selector is at the bottom of the toolbox. The *foreground* color is the color with which you paint or bucket fill. The *background* color is the color you'll get if you **erase**, **cut** or **edit/fill** a piece of your image. Note that if you perform these operations on an image that contains an alpha channel (see "Alpha Channels" on page 353), you'll get transparency instead of the background color.

Pressing the **double arrow** symbol swaps the foreground and background colors. You can also swap the colors by pressing X, or you can choose to restore the default values (Black/White) with D (the mouse cursor must be in your image as you use these shortcuts).

The Color Selection Dialog

Double-clicking on the **foreground** or the **background** icon brings up the **Color Selection dialog**, where you can easily change to another color.

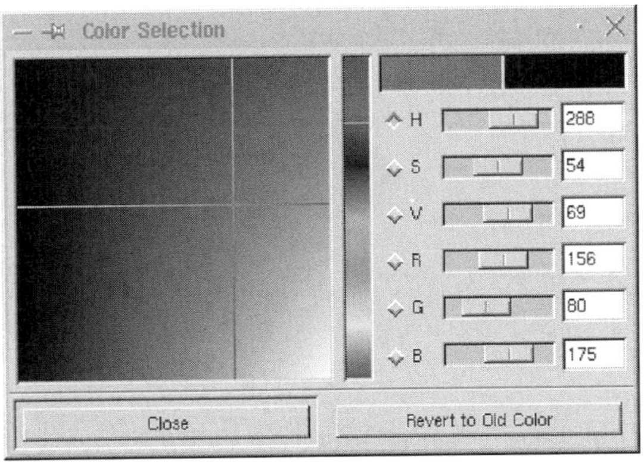

Figure 8.27 *The Color Selection dialog*

You can change the color manually, by clicking on a hue in the spectrum color field to the right, and then dragging the cross in the large color box on the left to the exact color you want.

If you want a specific RGB or HSV color, you can type the exact value in the **HSV** or **RGB** parameter fields, or you can drag the sliders to specify a color.

The **H** (Hue) channel is displayed in the color fields by default when you open the Color Selection dialog. However, you can choose to search in another channel for the color you want. If you'd like a pastel or neon color, you can click on the **S** (Saturation) radio button to search by saturation instead of by hue. If you want washed out or gloomy colors, click on the **V** (Value) radio button. You can also search using the **R** (Red), **G** (Green) or **B** (Blue) channels to find the shade you want.

When you search in another channel than the Hue channel, the spectrum color field will change into a smooth gradient, where you specify an approximate channel value. Clicking in this gradient is the same thing as dragging the channel slider. The large color box will then display all colors with this specific channel value, so dragging the cross will change the value of all the other channels, but it will not affect the value of the selected channel.

CHAPTER 9

Edit And View

This chapter covers the basic functions found in the Edit and View menus. Some of these functions are well-known to users of similar software, but some features are quite unique to Gimp.

Cut, Copy And Paste

These three commands (all located on the `right-click|Edit` menu) are so common that they shouldn't need much explanation. As with ordinary word processing, cutting and copying a part of an image will place that selection in a local **buffer**. When you choose **Paste**, Gimp takes that selection from the buffer and turns it into a **floating selection**, which you can either **anchor** to a layer, or put into a layer of its own.

Note that the default shortcut keys for these commands are the same as in most Windows programs: Ctrl+x for **Cut**, Ctrl+c for **Copy** and Ctrl+v for **Paste**.

You may have noticed the fantastic possibilities of **dynamic key bindings** in Gimp. If you don't like the default settings, you can choose any shortcut key you like for a certain command by simply typing the new shortcut in the menu! Read more about it in "Default Shortcuts And Dynamic Key Bindings" starting on page 9.

Paste Into

`Right-click|Edit|Paste Into` is a very useful command when you want to insert an image into a defined shape in another image. To use it, you first need to copy or cut the image you want to paste. Then, you make a selection shape in the target image (if you use a little feather, you'll get wonderfully soft edges to your selection). Choose Paste Into and the image you copied will appear inside the selection. Click on the **Move** tool and you can place the selection exactly where you want it, before you anchor it by clicking elsewhere on the image.

Cut, Copy And Paste Named

You're probably accustomed to being able to cut/copy and paste only one image at a time. In other words, as soon as you copy or cut something new, the old copy will be replaced by the new one.

Cut Named, **Copy Named** and **Paste Named** allow you to use a **buffer** that can hold a great number of cut images. If you're repetitively cutting/copying and pasting a lot of images, this is an extremely convenient feature.

Select an image or part of an image that you want to cut or copy. Select the command `right-click|Edit|Copy Named` or `right-click|Edit|Cut Named`. A small dialog box pops up and prompts you to enter a name for your selection. After you enter a name and click on the OK button, your selection will be placed in a buffer.

When you want to paste one of the selections you have named and put in the **named buffer**, choose `right-click|Edit|Paste Named`. This command brings up a dialog which displays a list of all the selections you have saved. To paste a selection, just choose its name and press **Paste**, and your selection will appear as a floating selection in the active image.

Figure 9.1 *The Paste Named Buffer dialog*

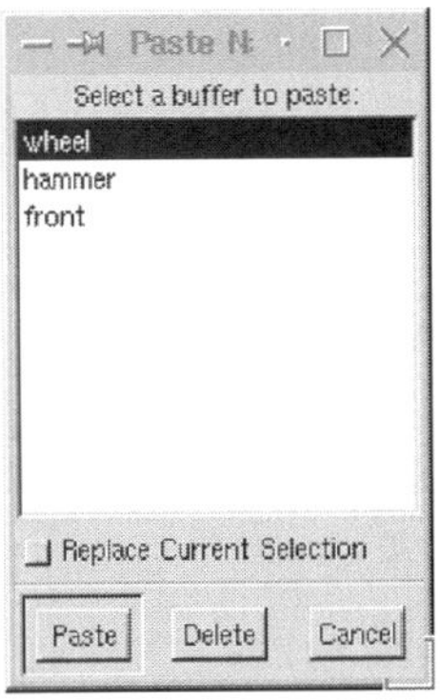

Note: The named buffer only exists as long as your Gimp session. If you want to save a selection more permanently, you need to save it in a separate layer in your image.

The option **Replace Current Selection** allows you to replace a non-floating selection in the image with a selection from your list. Replace Current Selection unchecked gives the same result as **Paste Into**, if you already have a selection in the image. If you try to use this option with a floating selection, the float will be anchored to the image. The selection from your list will turn into a new float in the same place as the old one.

You can also delete a selection from the list if you no longer need it.

Figure 9.2 *These images were created using Cut, Copy and Paste Named.*

Paste As New Image

This is a very useful function. When you apply `right-click|Edit|Paste as New Image` to a selection, the image information within the selection will be copied and pasted into a new image with the same size and proportions as the selection. The selection itself will also be copied.

If your image has several layers, all layers present within the selection will be copied into the new image (small layers outside the section will not be copied). All layer information such as **visible layers**, **grouped layers**, **layer masks** and **alpha channels** will also be copied to the new image. To learn more about layers read "Layers And Floating Selections" starting on page 315.

Copy Visible

`Right-click|Edit|Copy Visible` will copy all visible layers to a flat copy which you can paste into a new image. It's like executing both **Copy** and **Merge visible layers** at the same time. This function is quite handy when you don't want to alter the original layers, but only work with a quick copy. The copy can then be pasted into a new image.

Multiselect

The `right-click|View|Multiselect` function is used to break up an image into several smaller images. This is ideal for preparing your work for being published on the Internet, since web graphics are often cut up in a grid system to make them fit in an HTML table. Before invoking the Multiselect command, you must prepare the image by dragging **guides** (See "Rulers And Guides" on page 151) to the exact position where you want the image to be partitioned off.

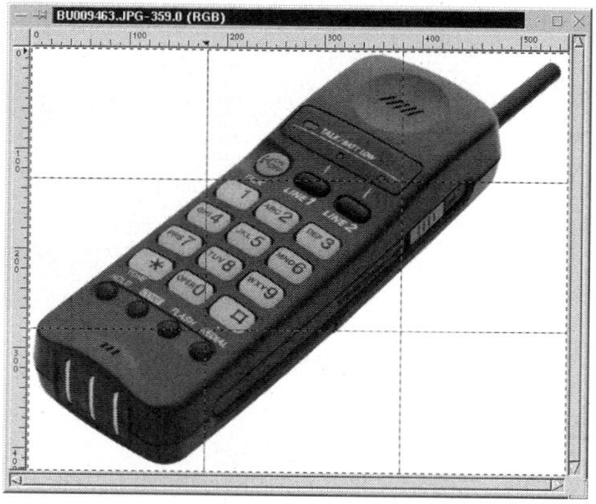

Figure 9.3 *The image is ready to be cut up by Multiselect; note the guides*

When you apply the Multiselect command, the sections indicated by the guides will be selected and copied into new images. As with the **Paste as New Image** function, all layers and layer attributes are also copied. A layered image cannot be save as a JPEG file, so if you are designing for the Web, we recommend that you **flatten** the image (merge all layers) before applying Multiselect. This saves you the trouble of flattening all of the small Multiselect images separately.

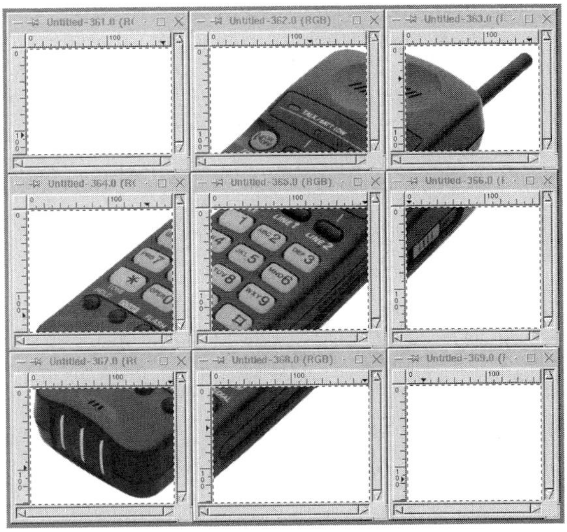

Figure 9.4 *The image after applying Multiselect*

Clear, Fill And Stroke

Clear

`Right-click|Edit|Clear` is a powerful command that *cuts without saving what you cut away*. Used in a layer, it will delete everything and leave an empty, transparent layer. Used on a selection, it will delete or cut everything inside of it, leaving only the "marching ants." Used on a non-alpha background, it will delete all background information, and leave only the **background** color that you see in the toolbox's background color swatch. If your image has an alpha channel (see "Alpha Channels" on page 353), the background layer will become transparent.

Fill

`Right-click|Edit|Fill` is the equivalent of the **Bucket Fill** with a maximum fill threshold. It's not as sophisticated as the Bucket Fill, but it's quick, easy and efficient. Note that this command always uses the background color in the toolbox color swatch, whereas the Bucket Fill uses the foreground color.

STROKE

`Right-click|Edit|Stroke` creates a **colored edge** around the selection. This edge, or contour, is based on what brush you're using and what brush options you have set in the **Brush Selection dialog**. Stroke can be used for creating simple drawings from selection shapes, or for manipulating selection edges by using Stroke with different artistic brushes and different settings for **Spacing**, **Mode** and **Opacity**.

Figure 9.5 *This example was created with Stroke using the swan brush*

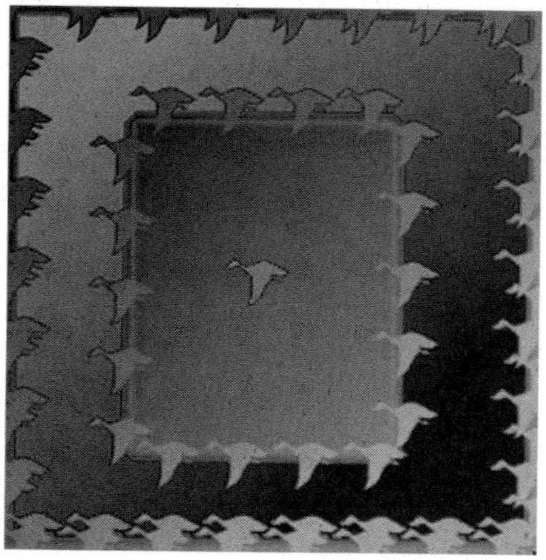

ZOOM

If the **Magnify** tool is active, you can click in an image to zoom in, and Shift+click to zoom out. To zoom a specific part of the image, drag diagonally across that part (draw a rectangle), and release the mouse button. You can also **pan** a zoomed image by clicking and dragging on the image with the **middle** mouse button.

Even if the Magnify tool is not active, you can zoom with the `right-click|View|Zoom in` and `right-click|View|Zoom out` commands. The default keyboard hotkeys are - (the minus sign or hyphen) for **Zoom out** and = (the equal sign) for **Zoom in**. Since Gimp supports **dynamic key bindings**, you can change = to + (the plus sign), if you like that better. Pressing `1` on your keyboard will return the view to 1:1 scale.

The `right-click|View|Zoom` command allows you to choose from nine different zoom scales: 16:1, 8:1, 4:1, 2:1, 1:1, 1:2, 1:4, 1:8 and 1:16. 16:1 is the lower limit and 1:16 is the upper limit for zooming in Gimp.

Pressing - zooms in smaller steps than zooming using the scales. In other words, to display your image in a scale of 1:3, press - three times.

MAGNIFY OPTIONS

Allow Window Resizing means that the canvas size will always adapt to the amount of zoom you use, so you'll always be able to see the entire image regardless of zoom level. If you don't want to use this option, you can press Ctrl+e for **Shrink Wrap**, which will also adjust the canvas to the image size.

Figure 9.6 *The Zoom Options dialog*

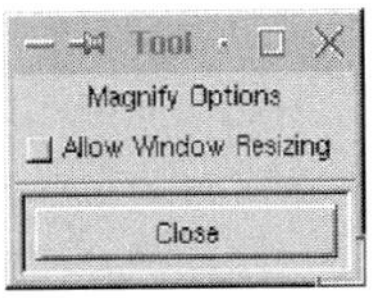

RULERS AND GUIDES

RULERS

At the top and left sides of the image frame, you'll see the Gimp **rulers**. As you drag the cursor over an image, a horizontal and a vertical arrow will appear inside the rulers, showing the current cursor position.

In Gimp, all images are measured in **pixels** by default, so the ruler unit is pixels. You can change the ruler unit to millimeters or inches by editing your `.gimp|gimprc` file (see "Gimp Start Flags And rcfiles" starting on page 785).

However, there is not much point in doing so, because in Gimp v.1.0 you can't set image resolution and canvas size the way you can in Photoshop. Size (and therefore resolution) for a printed image is determined by the **Print** dialog or **Save as (Postscript)** dialog (see "Printing Images" on page 96 and "PostScript And EPS" on page 91). The reason for this is that Gimp is hard coded to handle all images in 72 ppi (dpi) which is the default for things like web images, but is quite insufficient for printing.

GUIDES

Horizontal and vertical **guides** can be dragged straight from the left or top rulers. You can easily adapt the size, shape and position of a selection to the guides by drawing it within the frame of two vertical and two horizontal guides.

You can also use the guides to set the exact point of origin from which you want a selection to start. If you press the `Ctrl` key and start dragging close enough to the point where the guides cross, that spot will be the center of the new selection. Without `Ctrl`, the selection will start from the cross and continue in the direction you drag.

To change the position of a guide, use the **Move tool**. *Notice how the move cursor symbol changes into a pointing hand when it touches a guide, and that the guides will change color from blue to red when they are touched.*

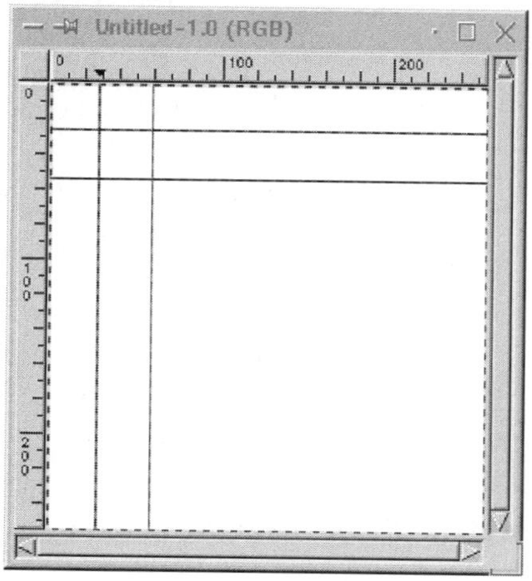

Figure 9.7 *A screen shot of two guides dragged into the drawing area from the horizontal and vertical rulers*

Toggle And Snap

Right-click|View|Snap To Guides is enabled by default. If this option is checked, moving any kind of selection close enough to the guides automatically causes the selection to "stick" or snap to the guides.

If you don't want to use guides and/or rulers, they can be toggled on and off with the right-click|View|Toggle Guides or right-click|View|Toggle Rulers commands.

Undo And Redo

These options should be self-explanatory. Because you'll use them often, you should learn their keyboard shortcuts by heart. The shortcut for right-click|Edit|Undo is Ctrl+z and the shortcut for right-click|Edit|Redo is Ctrl+r.

New View, Shrink Wrap And Window Info

New View

The right-click|View|New View command opens a new window that displays the same image you're currently working on. This enables you to watch your creation from several windows, each with different focus and zoom if you so desire. However, it is still the same picture, and the changes you make will appear in all of the New View windows. If you want to try out different versions of your image, press Ctrl+d to **Duplicate**. Unlike New View, duplicate windows are separate, changeable copies of your original image. Changes made in one window won't appear in the other windows.

Shrink Wrap

`Right-click|View|Shrink Wrap` will cause the canvas size to expand or shrink based on your zoom, so you'll be able to see the entire image regardless of zoom level. If you want this to happen automatically every time you change the zoom level, click on **Allow Window Resizing** in the **Magnify tool** options dialog (double-click on the Magnify tool to display the Magnify tool options dialog).

Window Info

The **Window Info** dialog (`right-click|View|Window Info`) displays up-to-date information on the active window, such as **Dimensions**, **Scale Ratio** and **Display Type**.

Figure 9.8 *The Window Info dialog*

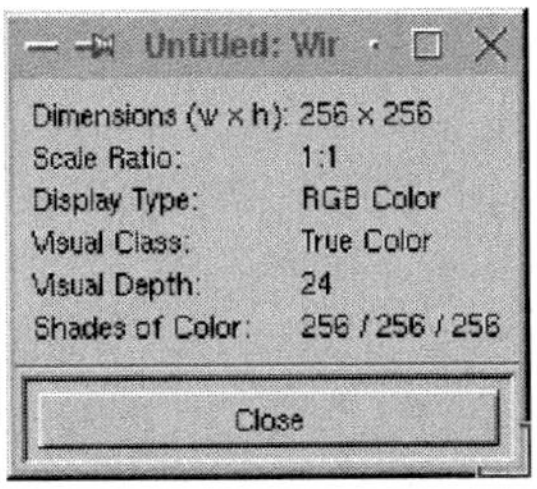

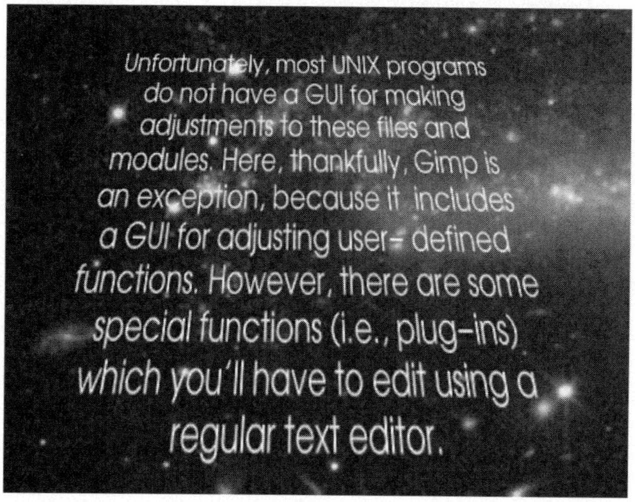
Unfortunately, most UNIX programs do not have a GUI for making adjustments to these files and modules. Here, thankfully, Gimp is an exception, because it includes a GUI for adjusting user-defined functions. However, there are some special functions (i.e., plug-ins) which you'll have to edit using a regular text editor.

CHAPTER 10

Transform Tools

In this chapter, we'll take a look at the different transform tools, including the Move tool and the Crop tool.

The Move Tool

The **Move tool** can move the entire image or layer, guides, floating selections or empty selection shapes. Please read "Layers And Floating Selections" on page 315 for information about layers.

Moving Without Using The Move Tool

In "Selection Tools" starting on page 109 we discussed the fact that Gimp displays a **move symbol** when you move your cursor over a selection, although a selection tool (and not the Move tool) is active.

If you move your selection using this move symbol, the selection will become a **floating** selection. You can only move it once, because the move symbol will disappear as soon as you let go of the mouse button. To move your selection a second time, you must switch to the Move tool.

You can also ignore the selection tool's move symbol and go straight to the `right-click|Select|Float` command. This procedure will make your selection float without moving it from its current position. Should you decide to move it, you can use the Move tool in the normal way.

Moving Floating Selections

When you use the Move tool on a floating selection, you'll notice that the **double-arrow** symbol becomes a **single arrow** when the pointer is outside of the selection. If you click your mouse when the single arrow is visible, the floating selection will **anchor to** (merge with) the layer that was last active.

Moving The Entire Image Or A Single Layer

If you don't have a selection, the Move tool will move the **entire image** outside the drawable area. If your image has more than one layer, the Move tool will move the **active layer**.

Moving Transparent Layers

The Move tool can't move an empty, transparent layer. If you try to do that, the Move tool will move the top layer in the layer stack instead! This happens because the Move tool needs something solid to grab onto. Of course, you could paint a dot of color in the empty layer, turn off all the other layers (see "Layers And Floating Selections" starting on page 315) and then move the layer (by grabbing the layer by the dot), but this isn't a very convenient technique.

The solution to this problem is to press the Shift key as you drag. When you see the yellow **layer boundary** turn blue, you'll know for sure that you're moving the right layer.

Moving Grouped Layers

Also notice that if you have **grouped** one or more layers (with the little anchor symbol), they'll all move, regardless of which layer is currently active. For example, if you have grouped a text layer with a drop shadow layer, you'll have to ungroup them or merge them before moving another layer, otherwise you'll move all three layers. See "Layers And Floating Selections" starting on page 315 for more information on working with layers.

Moving Empty Selections

If you just want to adjust the position of a selection area, press the Alt key as you move the selection. With this technique, only the empty form of the selection moves, and not the contents.

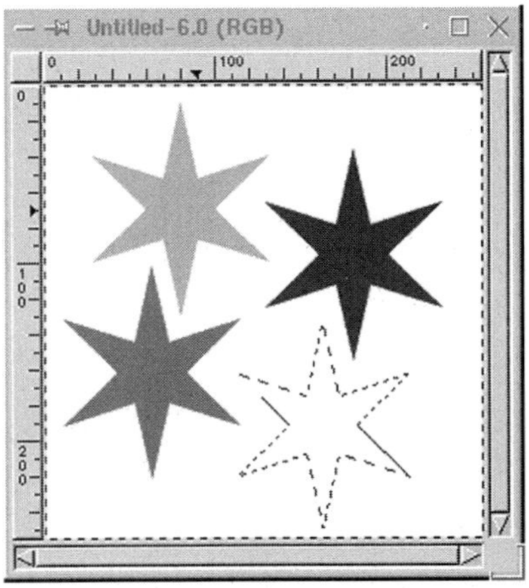

Figure 10.1 *Duplicating a star shape by moving a selection*

Note that this option only works for the normal (empty) selections you make with a selection tool. You can never move a floating selection using the Alt key.

This option allows you to use the selection as a template: You can move the selection around and fill it every time you move it. Note that the Move tool or a selection tool must be active for this technique to work.

Hints

The Move tool has an extra feature that allows you to *nudge* (move in small, precise increments) a floating selection or a layer with the keyboard's **arrow keys** when the Move tool is active. Pressing the Shift key as you press the arrow keys will increase the length of these steps. To nudge an empty selection, press the Alt key and the arrow keys.

Note that when you make multiple selects, Gimp treats them as a **unit**. That means that you can't move one selection closer to another with the Move tool, because all of the selected areas will move together as one.

THE CROP TOOL

The **Crop tool** corresponds to the "scissors" in Photoshop. You can crop an image if you just want a part of the picture. To crop, click and drag the marquee diagonally. Release the mouse button when you are satisfied and the **Crop Information** dialog box will appear. See the next section for more information on the dialog box.

The cropmarks can be placed very accurately. You can move the crop square by dragging on the lower-left or upper-right corners, or resize it by dragging on the upper-left or lower-right corners.

You can also move (nudge) the crop area using the arrow keys on your keyboard. Alternatively, you can set **guides** (make sure that the Snap To Guides checkbox is checked in the `right-click|View` menu) to position the crop area.

Figure 10.2 *Screen shot showing the Crop tool in action*

Press the **Crop button** in the toolbox, or click inside the markings, and the portion of the image inside the cropmarks will be your new image.

THE CROP INFORMATION DIALOG

This dialog displays the crop area's **X** and **Y Origins** and **Width** and **Height** in pixels. If you have created a selection in your image, you can click on the Selection button in the dialog box. This will automatically place the crop area as close as possible to your selection.

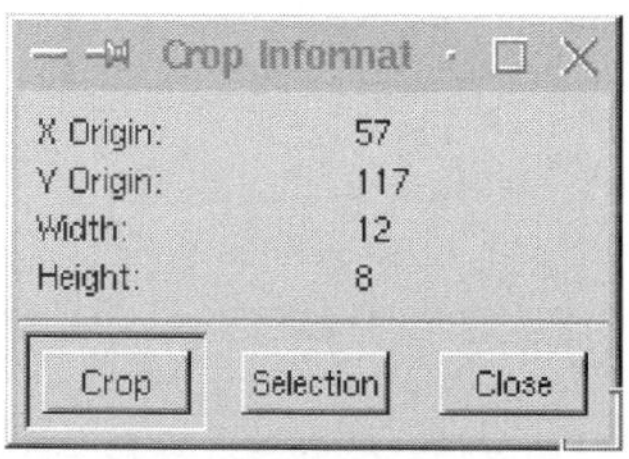

Figure 10.3 *The Crop Information dialog*

THE TRANSFORM TOOL

The **Transform tool** is much like the "Effects" menu in Photoshop. Double-click on the Transform tool to see the Transform Tool Options dialog box, where you can choose whether you want to **rotate**, **scale**, **shear** or **distort** a selection.

ROTATE

When you're transforming using **Rotation**, you drag the mouse to rotate the selection. Note that parts of the image will end up outside the drawable area, so you may have to resize the image afterward.

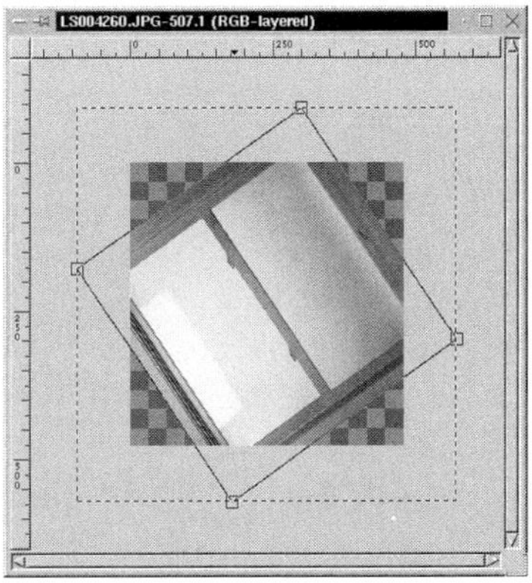

Figure 10.4 *Screen shot showing that you may need to resize the image after rotating it*

As you use the mouse to rotate the image, the **rotation angle** will be displayed in a small dialog box. You can't insert numbers into the dialog; it just displays how much you've rotated the image (this is not a very precise tool). However, you can press the `Ctrl` key and drag on the image with your mouse, which makes the selection rotate in 15 degree increments.

If you want to rotate a layer or image 90 or 270 degrees (for example, if you scanned an image in portrait mode and you want landscape) the `right-click|Image|Transforms|Rotate` option is a better choice.

If you need to specify the exact rotation angle, use the `right-click|Layers|Transforms|Rotate Any Angle` option. Note that you can't get exact values by just dragging the slide bar in the Rotate Any Angle dialog. Click the mouse button to the left or right of the slider to change the angle in one degree increments for every click.

Figure 10.5 *The rotation angle dialog*

SCALE

Choose **Scaling** from the Transform Tool Options dialog and then click on the image to see the Scaling Information dialog. The Scaling Information dialog provides you with information on both the **Original Height** and **Original Width** of the selection, as well as the **Current Width** and **Current Height**.

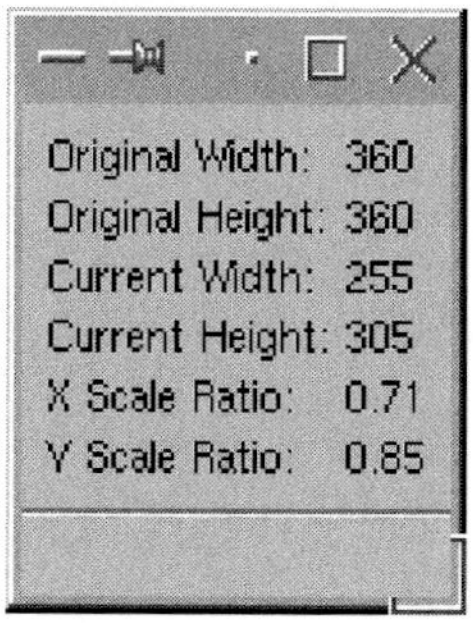

Figure 10.6 *The Scaling information dialog*

Drag on the image with your mouse to scale the image. The **X Scale Ratio** and **Y Scale Ratio** tell you how much you've altered the size and proportions of the original image.

The Ctrl key locks the scale's **X axis**, so you can only affect the height of the image. Shift locks the **Y axis**, so you can only affect the width of the image. Ctrl+Shift forces the image to scale **proportionally**.

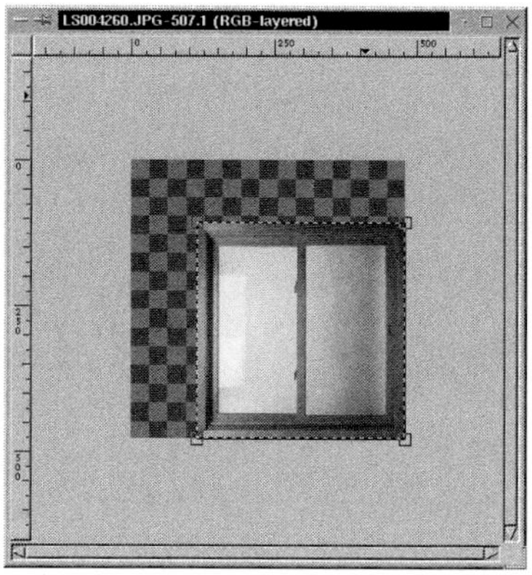

Figure 10.7 *Screen shot of a downscaled image*

SHEARING

Shearing will *deform* an image in either the horizontal or the vertical plane. In other words, it will turn a rectangle into a parallelogram.

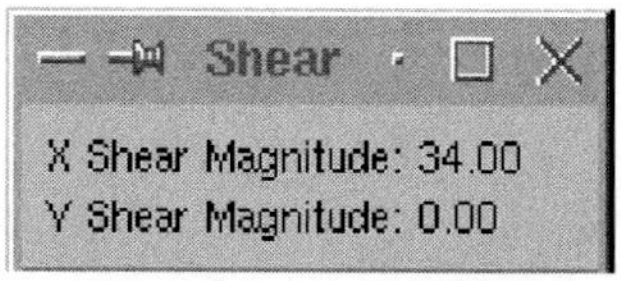

Figure 10.8 *The Shear info dialog*

Click on the **Shearing** option in the Transform Tool Options dialog, then click on your image to see the **Shear Information dialog**. Shear your image by clicking and dragging on the corners. Dragging up and down shears in the Y direction, and dragging on the sides shears in the X direction. You can shear along either of the X or Y axes, but only on one at a time. In other words, if the X Shear Magnitude is other than zero, then the Y Shear Magnitude must be zero.

Figure 10.9 *A screen shot of Shear in action*

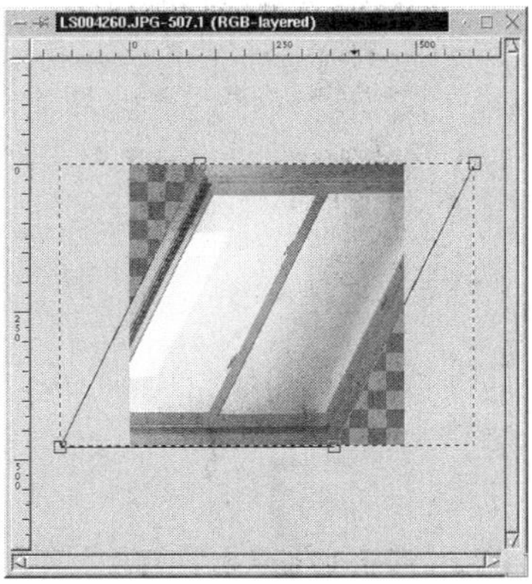

Tip: If you want to shear a selection both ways, you have to change to another tool icon, and then return to Transform.

PERSPECTIVE

The last option on the Transform Tool Options dialog is **Perspective**. The term perspective isn't quite accurate, because no actual perspective transformation takes place (making the image small in the far end and large in the other).

It is better described as a *distortive* effect, since you can move all four displacement points (the corners) independently. You can certainly make a rectangular selection look like a perspective, but you have to do that manually.

Figure 10.10 *A screen shot showing Perspective in action*

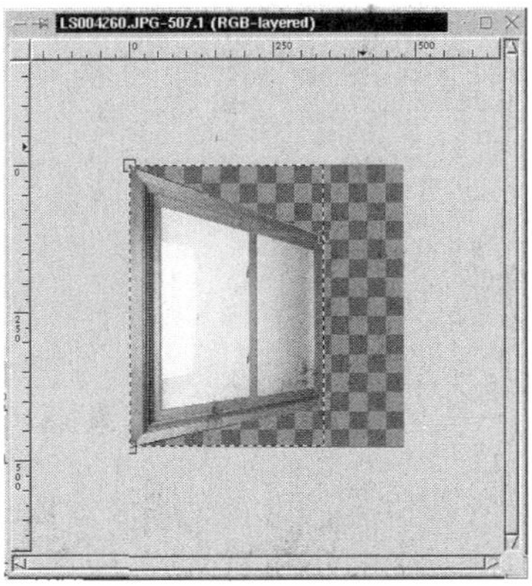

Observe that you can turn the "perspective" inside out if you like. If you let the lines of the perspective square cross or top each other, you'll mirror and wrench the selection so much it will eventually become unrecognizable.

Transform Smoothing

On the Transform Tool Options dialog, the Smoothing checkbox provides an **antialiasing** option, which will make distorted edges look better. If you don't use Smoothing, your selection might turn out very rough and pixly on the edges. On the other hand, the Smoothing option can make edges very blurry, so you should take that into consideration as well.

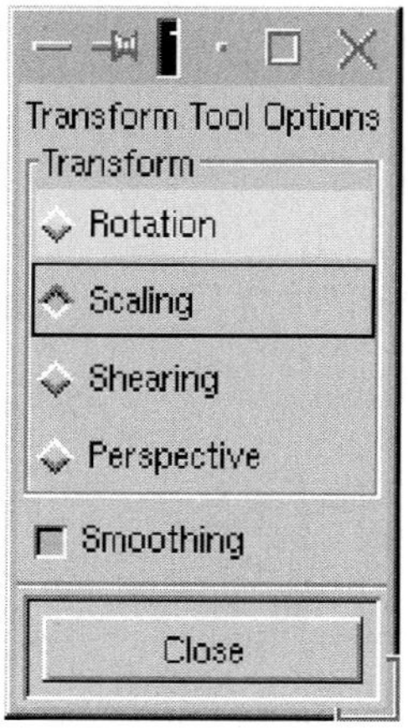

Figure 10.11 *The Transform Tool Options dialog*

THE FLIP TOOL

On the toolbox, the Flip tool does exactly that — it **flips** the image, or more accurately — the Flip tool **mirrors** the selection **horizontally** or **vertically**. If you are working with an image where you want the illusion of reflection (whether in water, glass or metal), this is the tool to use.

THE MAGNIFY TOOL

Please turn to "Zoom" on page 150.

CHAPTER 11

Text And Fonts

Gimp's support for text is based on how the X Window System manages fonts.

THE TEXT TOOL

To insert text in a Gimp image, click on the **Text tool** in the toolbox and then click at a spot inside the image. The Text Tool dialog box will open and display a list of the installed fonts. Type in the text you want in the text box in the bottom of the dialog. Click on the font you want, set the parameters if you want to change the default values and click OK.

Now your text string will appear as a **floating selection** in your image. The text will have the same color as the **foreground** color in the toolbox. If for some reason you aren't happy with the text — if it's too small, too large or if the font just doesn't look right — you can delete the floating text selection by pressing the cross (**Delete Layer**) button in the **Layers & Channel** dialog.

MOVING AND ANCHORING TEXT

To move the text selection to another position, place the cursor on top of the text so that the **move symbol** appears, then click and drag the text. You can move and drop the text as many times as you like, and you don't have to switch to the Move tool.

When you're satisfied with the position of the text, you have two options. You can either anchor the text to the last active layer, or place it in a layer of its own. To merge the text with the image, press the **Anchor Layer** button in the **Layers & Channels** dialog. To create a text layer, press the **New Layer** button or double-click on the **Floating selection** icon bar.

Once you've anchored the text to the image, you can't edit it anymore. However, if you choose to place it in a transparent text layer, it's easy to move the entire text layer with the Move tool.

CHANGING THE TEXT COLOR

It is also simple to change the color of the letters in a text layer. First, make sure that the **Keep Transp.** radio button is checked in the text layer. Choose `right-click|Select|All`, click in the foreground color field in the toolbox to access the **Color Selection** dialog and choose another color. Then select the **Bucket fill** tool and click in the layer.

Tip: If you want to be able to edit the text, you should use a great plug-in called **Dynamic Text** instead of the Text tool. Read about this plug-in in "Dynamic Text" on page 588.

Options

At the top of the Text tool dialog, the current **Text Size** is shown in either **pixels** or **points** (you can choose which you prefer from the pull-down menu). A pixel is the smallest component in a bitmap image, and all measures in pixels depend on the **screen resolution**. A point, however, is a fixed value — one inch is the same as 72 points.

Points are used to measure fonts. For example, 12 points is the standard size of body text in most word processing programs.

Standard screen resolution is often 72 pixels per inch, in which case text in pixels will be the same size as text measured in points. However, on a high-resolution screen, such as one with a resolution of 90 pixels per inch, setting the text to points will render a larger text than setting the text to pixels. For example, there are 90 pixels for every 72 points, so a text size of 50 points will be 63 pixels wide, because there are 1.25 pixels for every point.

Antialiasing is an effect used to smooth edges in bitmapped images. It is often used on artistic text, because it softens the **jaggies** (the jagged pixel edges of the letter's curves in low resolution). It will blur the edge pixels to transparency. This will make curves look smoother, but the edges will become unsharp and less distinctive.

The **Font list** displays all fonts installed on the local X server. Click the name of a font to change the text in the text box. Note that some of the more unusual fonts (such as Chinese or Japanese fonts) may bring X to a near-crashing halt simply because so many characters are involved. As a rule, be careful using fonts with Asian names, or avoid them entirely. To learn how to install new fonts, read "How To Get Fonts To Gimp" starting on page 759.

Font Parameters

There are eight font parameters (**Foundry**, **Weight**, **Slant**, **Set width**, **Spacing**, **Registry**, **Encoding** and **Border**) in the Text Tool dialog box.

Figure 11.1 *The Text tool dialog*

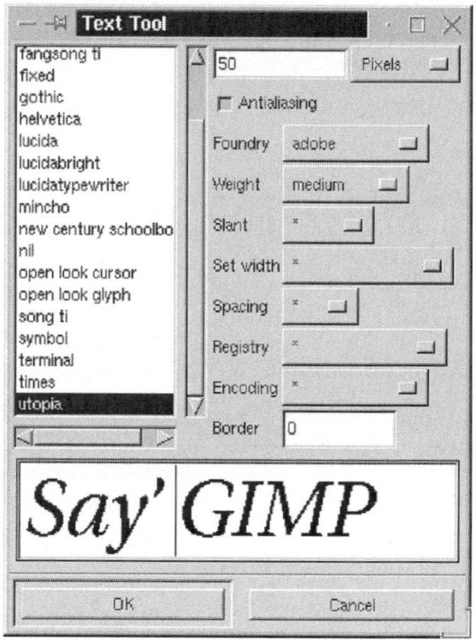

Foundry

Foundry refers to the **origin** of your font (usually the manufacturer). This parameter has to distinguish different fonts with the same name that are from different companies. This is important, because many different versions of well-known fonts exist and you need to specify which one you mean if you have several versions installed.

Weight

Weight shows what typographic "blackness" options you have for the font you have chosen (*black*, *bold*, *demibold*, *medium* and *regular*). Options that aren't available for the chosen font are grayed out.

Slant

Slant is the "posture" option. The letter **r** (**Roman**) signifies *upright* posture. The letters **i** (**italic**) or **o** (**oblique**) are two different *slanted* postures. **i** produces a good representation of the letters and **o** gives a simpler, more jagged italic type. The available posture depends on the font.

Set Width

This is an option if your font includes the built-in possibility of modifying the horizontal width. Sometimes, the same font will come in wider and narrower versions, typically called *black*, *semi-condensed* and *narrow*.

Spacing

Spacing displays what types of built-in spacing your font allows: **c** for **character cell**, **m** for **monospaced** and **p** for **proportional**. The **c** and **m** fonts are mainly for programmers and are used in terminal display windows. In these fonts, every character takes up the same amount of space. The proportional fonts are what you might consider to be "normal" typographical fonts, because they are not constrained to a fixed width. Each character can take up a different amount of space.

Registry And Encoding

These are options for advanced users, and you'll probably never have to bother about these parameters. For additional information read "How To Get Fonts To Gimp" starting on page 759.

Border

The Border option will increase the size of the text layer that is created when you press the **New Layer** button or double-click the **Floating Selection** icon bar in the Layers & Channels dialog. Border is useful when you plan to put your text in a text layer, and feel that you'd like some extra space around the letters.

As you may know, when you place a floating selection in a layer of its own, Gimp will optimize the layer size to be as small as possible. When you have placed the text in a layer (click on the text layer's icon bar to make it active), you'll see a yellow-dotted rectangular box around your text. This is the **layer border**.

The default value, which is a border of zero pixels, fits text very snugly, whereas larger borders increase the size of the layer. Change the Border parameter if you need some space for **kerning** your letters by hand (adjusting the spacing between the letters), or if you just want to move each letter around separately. If you find that the layer size wasn't large enough after all, you can always change it by using **Resize Layer** in the **Layers menu**. More information on floating selections and how to move letters is included in "Moving Objects In A Floating Selection Layer" on page 332.

CHAPTER 12

Brushes, Gradients, Palettes And Patterns

How to use these basic tools, and how to create your own brushes, palettes, patterns and gradients.

BRUSHES

The **Brush Selection** dialog is accessible from the toolbox (`File|Dialogs|Brushes`) or from `right-click|Dialogs|Brushes`.

The Brush Selection dialog displays all the available brushes. You may notice some unusual brushes, like artistic text, little flourishes or doodles, etc. Such brushes are not very difficult to make yourself. In this section, we'll discuss how to create a brush. First, however, we'll take a look at the Brush Selection dialog.

THE BRUSH SELECTION DIALOG

When you select a brush, its name and size in pixels will be displayed at the top of the dialog. The **Mode** pull-down menu lets you select what kind of mode your brush will use (more information about modes is included in "Modes" starting on page 335).

Tip: If you can't see the whole brush, click and hold on the brush square and the entire brush will appear (and disappear when you release the mouse).

The **Opacity** slider sets the amount of transparency. With the max value of 100, your brush paints with a solid color. An Opacity of zero gives you total transparency (or invisible paint).

Spacing is the distance between your brush marks. If you set the spacing to zero, the brushmarks will create a solid, brush-shaped line.

Figure 12.1 *The Brush Selection dialog*

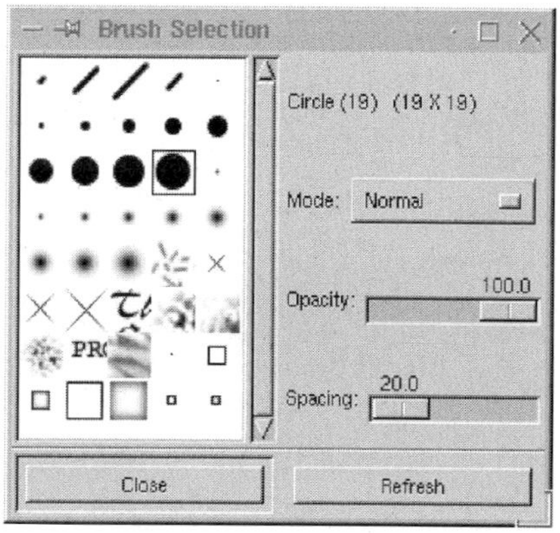

Test one of the **Circle brushes** and set the spacing to 150. Your brush stroke will now consist of a dotted line. The larger spacing makes it clear that the brush shape is circular, but if you had used the default spacing, you wouldn't be able to see it.

Now, try a decorative brush like the **Guitar** pattern. Change the spacing value to 10 or less (mouse-click the Spacing slidebar and use the arrow keys to set exact values) and see what happens. Normally, you'll want to use low spacing values, but when you paint with special brushes a bit of spacing can be useful.

Creating A New Brush

1. Create a new image using **Image Type:** *Grayscale* and **Fill Type:** *White.*
2. Use the **Pencil tool** to draw an X inside the image frame.
3. Invert the image with `right-click|Image|Colors|Invert`.
4. Rescale it to 20x20 using `right-click|Image|Resize`.
5. Use `File|Save` as to save the image as xxx.gbr. In the **Save as Brush** dialog, set the **Spacing** to *15* and set the **Description** to *New Brush.*
6. Move xxx.gbr to your `.gimp/brushes` directory.
7. Open the **Brush Selection** dialog (`right-click|Dialogs|Brushes`) and press the **Refresh** button. The new brush will now appear in your Brush Selection dialog as *New Brush (20x20).*

Tip: To make good-looking brushes, make them large and then resize them to the size you want.

Note that creating the brush in a solid black color (before inverting) makes your brush look hard. If you use a gray color, the brush will look softer. The same effect occurs when you create a brush with lots of blur; the new brush will have soft edges. Experiment with different kinds of brushes. Create them with or without blur, soft edges, etc. until you achieve the effects that you want.

Patterns

You can fill selections or backgrounds with a **pattern** instead of with a solid color. Gimp includes many preset custom patterns. You can also find patterns at many Gimp users' home pages. If you're interested in finding more patterns, look through **http://www.gimp.org/patterns.html** and/or search the web using your favorite search engine for terms like *gimp* and *patterns.*

Click on `right-click|Dialogs|Patterns` to access the **Pattern Selection** dialog. If you can't see the whole pattern, click and hold on the pattern square and the entire pattern will appear. Once you've clicked on a pattern, it is selected. You can see the name of the selected pattern in the upper-left corner of the dialog.

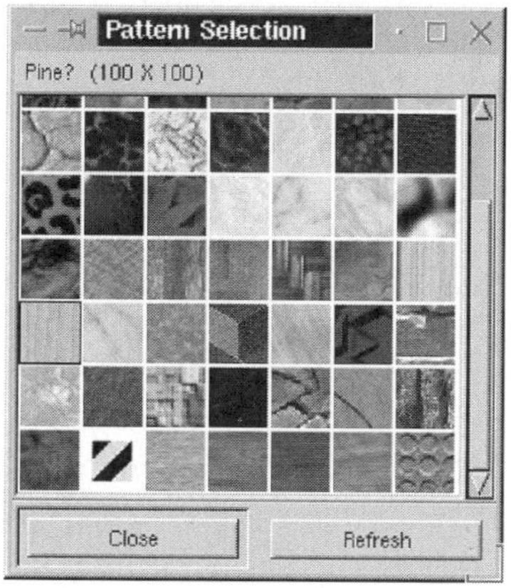

Figure 12.2 *The Pattern Selection dialog*

To use a selected pattern, double-click on the Fill tool icon to display the **Bucket Fill Options** dialog. Under **Fill Type**, select *Pattern Fill*. Now you can click on a selection to fill it with your selected pattern. You can also paint with patterns, using the **Clone tool**, but you can't use patterns with any other tools.

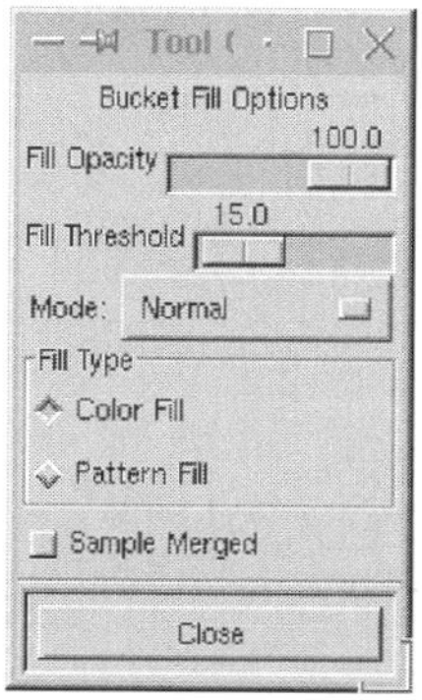

Figure 12.3 *The Bucket Fill Options dialog*

MAKING A NEW PATTERN

To make your own pattern:

1. Open a new RGB image and set an appropriate size for your pattern tile.

   You may want to make two versions of your pattern, one larger (say 256x256) for pattern filling in high resolution/large images, and a smaller version (such as 64x64) for filling smaller images (like GIFs for the web).

2. Create a pattern tile by painting something interesting, or by pasting part of a scanned photograph into your image.

3. Your tile will reproduce itself in a rather stiff perpendicular grid, so if you want a wallpaper effect with a simple repeated shape, it's a good idea to use the `right-click|Image|Channel Ops|Offset` command to modify your pattern.

   This is how you do it:

- First, check out what your present pattern will look like by opening `right-click|Filters|Map|Small Tiles`. This filter is more than useful when you create patterns, because it gives you a sneak preview of what your pattern will look like, as well as the opportunity to modify it (read more about this filter in "Small Tiles" on page 558).

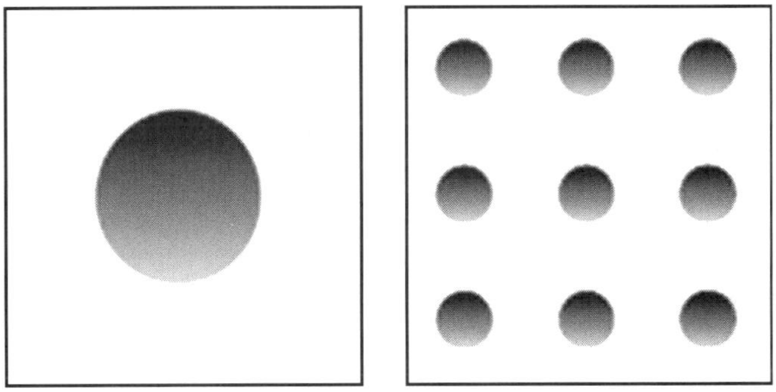

Figure 12.4 *A single dot will not render a good pattern*

- Open the **Layers & Channels** dialog box and **duplicate** the pattern layer.
- Open the **Offset** dialog box and offset the top layer by x/2 and the bottom layer by y/2. (This is not the same as offsetting the original image with the Offset by (x/2),(y/2) button!)

  Set the top layer in **Multiply Mode** (if the background color is other than white, the pattern element must be created in a transparent layer on top of the colored background layer), then **flatten** the image and take a look at your pattern once again with the **Small Tiles** preview.

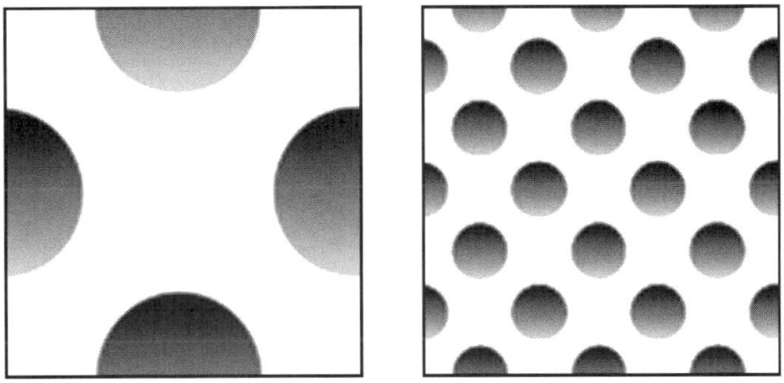

Figure 12.5 *If you use Offset you will get a better pattern, as you can see in the final outcome (right)*

4. If you have created a more complex pattern or have used a photograph (for example, a wood structure), you will also need to use the **Offset** option to remove visible seams between tiles. This is described in more detail in "Offset" on page 294. The `right-click|Filters|Map|Make Seamless` filter is also a useful tool, but the result is often a bit

blurred (see "Make Seamless" on page 550 for more information about this filter).

You can also take an existing pattern and change it. System patterns are in `usr/local/share/gimp/patterns` (of course, this location varies, depending on site setup).

5. When you're satisfied with the tile, resize the image to fit the tile size of the pattern you want to create. Use `File|Save As` to save the image as a PAT file in the `.gimp/patterns` directory.
6. Click on `right-click|Dialogs|Patterns` to view the **Pattern Selection** dialog. Press the **Refresh** button and your newly created pattern will be available for use.

Palettes

Use `right-click|Dialogs|Palette` or `File|Dialogs|Palette` to display the **Color Palette** dialog.

Palette Options

Select **New Palette** from the **Ops** pull-down menu to create a new palette, and name the new palette. The same pull-down menu allows you to *refresh* and *delete* palettes. When you create a new palette, you always start with an empty (black) palette.

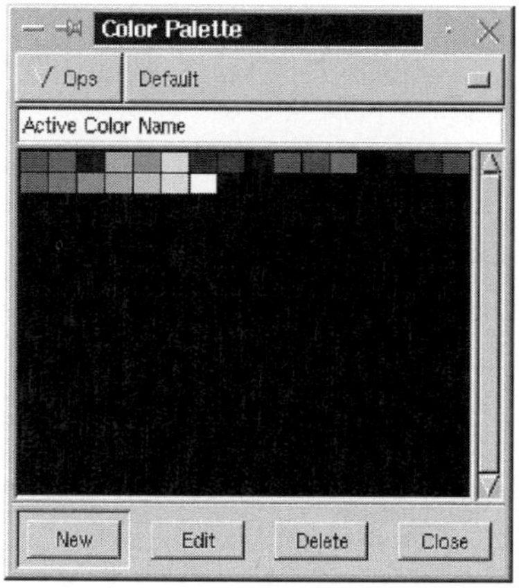

Figure 12.6 *The Color Palette dialog*

To add a color to the new palette, use the **Color Picker** tool to select a color from an image, or specify a color in the **Color Selection** dialog (open this dialog by double-clicking in the foreground color swatch in the toolbox). The chosen color is always visible as the **foreground** color in the toolbox. Press **New** to add this color to your palette.

Edit a color in your palette by selecting it and pressing the **Edit** button, which will open the Color Selection dialog (see "The Color Selection Dialog" on page 143). You can delete a color by selecting it and pressing **Delete**.

As soon as you edit a **system palette** (any palette other than your personal palettes), it will move to your *personal palette directory*. You can't delete a system palette; Gimp will simply acknowledge that you don't want to use it in this session. However, if you delete a **personal palette**, it is gone forever.

Note that if you have added a large number of palettes to the palette directory, it will take some time before they are all displayed in the pull-down menu.

Creating A Palette From An Indexed Image

You can create a palette from an indexed image. This is quite handy if you only want to use the specific colors contained in the image. Here's how you do it:

1. Convert the image to Indexed mode with `right-click|Image|Indexed`.
2. In the **Index** dialog, select how many colors your palette should comprise and click `OK`.
3. Save the palette with `right-click|Image|Save palette`.
4. Name the palette and press OK.

Your palette now exists, but Gimp will need to re-read all the palettes. Use `right-click|Dialogs|Palette` to display the **Color Palette** dialog. Click on **Refresh Palettes** in the **Ops** pull-down menu, and your new palette will become a choice in the list of available palettes on the Color Palette dialog.

Hints

Tip: Use palettes when you want to create images with a fixed number of colors, for example, when you are creating icons.

If your screen depth is only 8 bit (256 colors), you'll need to be concerned about whether the created icons use up all 256 colors. If your icon manager reduces the number of colors it may look awful. You'll need to create a palette with a limited number of basic colors for your icons and then create the icons using those colors.

The palette file format is similar to the format of the rgb.txt file used by the X Window System. Each color has a line for the RGB number values of the color and then the name of the color. This means that you can edit palette files in an ordinary text editor.

The Gradient Editor

When we mention gradients, the **Blend tool** may come to mind. The Blend tool lets you "flood" a selection or image, starting with one color and smoothly changing into another.

Gimp allows you to do even more complex blends with a tool called the **Gradient Editor**. The Gradient Editor comes with a number of *preset* **custom** gradients, but you can also create your own gradients or edit one of the custom gradients with this tool. The Gradient Editor is a flexible tool that can create very advanced gradients.

To apply a gradient from the Gradient Editor you double-click on the Blend tool icon in the toolbox and select **Custom (from editor)** from the **Blend** pull-down menu in the Blend Tool Option dialog.

The custom gradients from the Gradient Editor can be very useful. You can use them in advanced fountain fills or patterns, and you can also create objects with them, like an eyeball, a hole or a pipe. For tips on how to make the best use of the gradients in the Gradient Editor, read about the Blend tool, which is described in "The Blend Tool Or Gradient Fill" on page 131.

Figure 12.7 *This example shows how a gradient was used to create pipes.*

The Gradient Editor Dialog

Click on `File|Dialogs|Gradient Editor` or `right-click|Dialogs|Gradient Editor` to open the Gradient Editor. The user interface is shown in Figure 12.8. You'll find a list of all available gradients under **Gradients**, and the currently selected gradient can be seen in a preview window.

The buttons to the right let you create, copy, delete, save and refresh gradients. If you click the right mouse button in the gradient preview window and hold it down, a menu of editing tools will appear for that gradient. You can also *zoom* the gradient with the **zoom buttons** present in the main dialog.

The **Save as POV-Ray** button allows you to save a gradient in POV format. POV-Ray is a popular ray tracing software program.

If you have downloaded a gradient and placed it in `.gimp/gradients`, you will have to press the **Refresh gradients** button to see and use it.

Edited system gradients will be saved to your personal gradient directory (.gimp/ gradients) . So if you want to use the original system gradient, and not the edited copy, just delete or move the edited copy from your personal directory.

If you delete a system gradient, it just means that you don't want to use it in this session. However, as is the case with personal palettes, if you delete a personal gradient it will be gone forever.

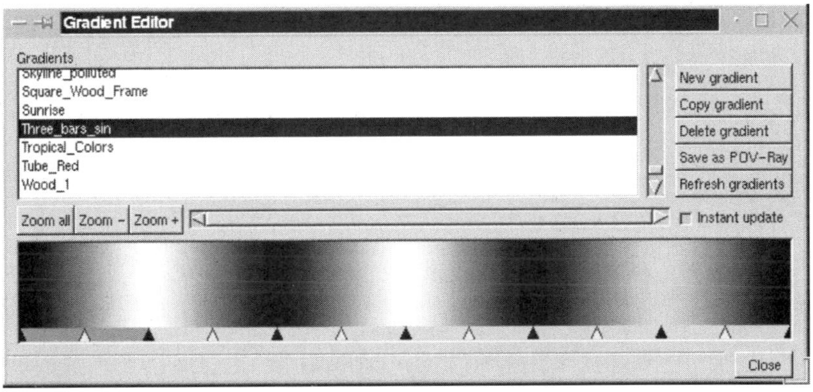

Figure 12.8 *The Gradient Editor dialog*

So, What Can You Do With The Gradient Editor?

Start by copying a gradient and playing around with it. Select a gradient and click on the **Copy gradient** button. This will bring up the Copy Gradient dialog, which will ask you to name the new gradient. Name the copied gradient and click OK. If you edit a system gradient, it will now be copied to your personal gradient directory, as when you edit system brushes or palettes.

Note: There is no undo option in the Gradient Editor.

THE GRADIENT PREVIEW WINDOW

The *triangles* at the bottom of the gradient preview window are **color section** markings. Two kinds of marks exist: black **endpoints** and white **midpoints**. The area between two black points is called a **segment**. In the gradient shown in Figure 12.8 a segment has been selected by clicking on it. A selected segment turns a darker shade of gray.

Adjusting Endpoints And Midpoints

- You can **move** an entire selection by clicking in the darker gray field and dragging, but you can only move it as far as the next midpoint to the left or right.

- If you move a *white midpoint* (by clicking and dragging on it), you will see the **color transition** shift as the balance between the two end colors is being changed.
- Dragging a *black endpoint* (not the ones to the extreme left or right, because you can't move them) will **stretch** the area between that endpoint and the midpoint, making it **wider** or **narrower**. The stretch limit is the next midpoint to the left or right.
- If you click on an *endpoint*, then press Shift and drag, you will **compress** or **expand** the entire selection in the drag direction. This deformation will also include the neighboring midpoint, which will move along until you reach the next endpoint.
- You can **extend** or add to a selection by pressing the Shift key and clicking on another segment.

Any of the described manipulations can be used on extended selections (more than one segment).

The Popup Menu

As mentioned before, if you press the right mouse button in the gradient preview window, a menu will appear for editing the colors in the selected segment.

Editing An Endpoint's Color

You can edit the color of the endpoints by selecting either **Left endpoint's color** or **Right endpoint's color** from the popup menu. This will bring up a **color select** dialog where you can select a new color.

Figure 12.9 *The popup menu*

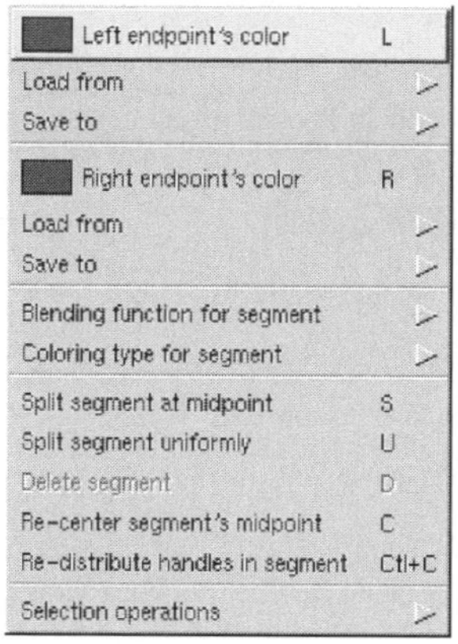

The **Load from** and **Save to** menu options allow you to *load* a color from an RGBA channel to an **endpoint**, or to *save* an existing endpoint color to one of the preset RGBA channel swatches, so that you can load that color later.

The **Load from** command allows you to load some nice basic colors and transparent backgrounds. The **Save to** option is useful if you want to use a particular endpoint color in another part of the gradient.

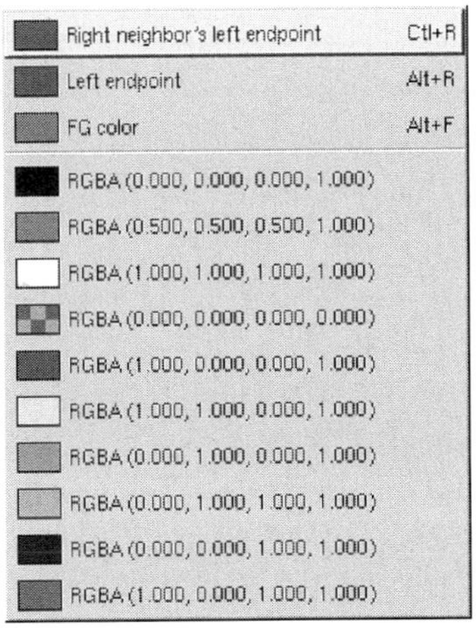

Figure 12.10 *The endpoint's Load from menu*

Blending Functions

In the **Blending function for segment** submenu, you will find some functions that control how the appearance of the gradient in your selection:

- **Linear:** This is the default function, and it causes the color to change at a constant rate from one endpoint to another.
- **Curved:** Causes the end sections' colors to change at a different "rate" than the colors in the middle section. Think of it as a semi-circle where the color changes more at the ends and less in the middle.
- **Sinusoidal:** This is the opposite of *Curved*, so the rate of change is slow at the ends and fast in the middle.
- **Spherical increasing:** Causes the color change rate to be faster on the left and slower on the right.
- **Spherical decreasing:** The opposite of spherical increasing; the color change rate is slower on the left side and faster on the right side.

Coloring

The **coloring type for segment** submenu lets you choose a color model for your selection or segment. You can choose **Plain RGB** and two kinds of **HSV**. See "Color Models" starting on page 187 for more information on the different color models.

Segments

The **Segment** commands will work on the selected segment. If you have selected more than one segment, they will not be treated as a unit. Each segment will be treated separately:

- **Split segment at midpoint:** Puts an endpoint at the midpoint and then divides the two new segments with new midpoints.
- **Split segment uniformly:** Lets you specify how many splits you want to make in the selected area.
- **Delete segment:** Deletes the entire selection, not just the segment you press the right mouse button in.
- **Re-center segment's midpoint:** Re-centers the midpoints in all of the selected segments.
- **Re-distribute handles in segment:** Evenly distributes all the points in the segment. This is useful if you have selected several segments and want a smooth gradient in the selection.

Selection Operations

The **Selection operations** submenu allows you to *flip* or *replicate* the segment and also allows you to *blend* the endpoints' colors and/or opacity:

- **Flip segment:** Lets you flip or reverse a segment or selection. Flip can be used to change the order of two segments. First, select two segments and flip both together. Deselect one segment and flip the other one. Select the first segment and flip that one, too. Now you have changed the order of your segments. This can be done to more than two segments, and gives you the freedom to change the structure of the gradients.
- **Replicate:** Provides a small dialog in which you can copy the selected segment(s) as many times as you like. The copies will be squeezed into the original segment's space.
- **Blend endpoints' colors:** Only works if you have selected more than one segment. It will blend the color in the endpoints of the selection, and will subsequently "merge" your segments so they blend gradually from the selection's left handle to the right handle, thus changing the color of the endpoints inside the selection.
- **Blend endpoints' opacity:** Works the same way as blending colors. This command will create a soft transition from the opacity (transparency) in the left endpoint to the opacity in the right endpoint of a multi-segment selection.

PART IV

Pre-press Knowledge

- *Color Models*
- *Pre-press*
- *Scanning*

CHAPTER 13

Color Models

If you want to work seriously with digital imaging and/or pre-press, you need to understand color — how it works in real life and how it works in your computer.

Color models are used to classify and standardize color. In this chapter we'll discuss a few of the more popular models: RGB, CMYK, indexed, HSV and NCS.

RGB

RGB stands for the three colors used in the RGB system: *red*, *green* and *blue*. Perhaps an "**L**" for "*light*" should be included as well, because this color model is very much based on light.

Figure 13.1 *The RGB color model*

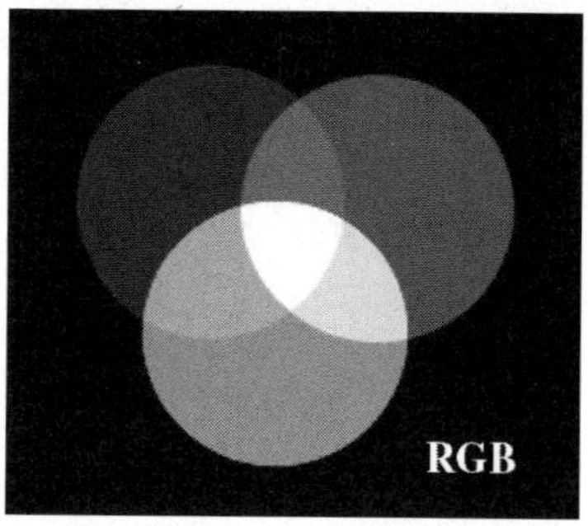

Imagine three spotlights (a red one, a green one and a blue one), directed at the same spot on a white screen. Because each spotlight adds more light, the intersection of two spots will be brighter than just one. The brightest spot is where all three spots intersect; that intersection is white.

As you may know, the RGB model is used by televisions and computer monitors. The colored spots on a TV screen are red, green or blue, and the interaction of the colors determines what the eye perceives. If the color spots shine with equal strength, the visual impression is of white or gray.

RGB is called an **additive** color model, because light is *added* to light, which results in brighter colors. In the RGB model, every color is represented as a set of three values: a value for red, a value for green and a value for blue. Each color value can range from 0 to 255. If all three color values are 0, the resulting color is black; if all three colors are 255, the color is white.

If you think of this model as spotlights, then it's easy to understand that weak lights (low values) mean darker colors, while strong lights (high values) result in brighter colors.

RGB can represent more than 16 million colors (which is often called **True-Color**). The calculation is simple:

256 red values x 256 green values x 256 blue values = 16,777,216 colors

However, RGB can produce only 256 shades of gray, because gray only occurs when all three color values are equal. If your computer only has 8 bit color, this doesn't matter, because you'll never be able to see more than 256 colors anyway.

The reason why there are 256 RGB color values — and not, for example, 1024 — is that Gimp was programmed for 8 bit color channels. In most cases, 16 million colors is quite satisfactory, but there are certain highly specialized image manipulation programs that can handle 16 bit color channels. There is also a new version of Gimp under development called GIMP HOLLYWOOD that will include 16 bit color channels. In this book, we will focus on 8 bit (256 value) color channels since that is what you'll work with in Gimp.

CMYK

CMYK is another important color model. CMYK stands for **cyan**, **magenta**, **yellow** and **black** (**K** for **key** color). These colors are sometimes called **process** colors, because they are used in four-color process printing. If you have a color printer, you may have noticed that the toner in the machine consists of these primary colors.

Figure 13.2 *The CMYK color model*

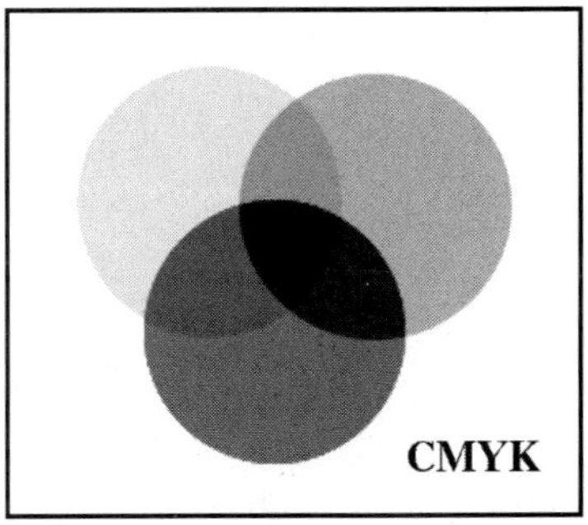

All other colors can be created by mixing these primary colors. Cyan, magenta and yellow are theoretically all you need, but to make a print look sharp and crisp, a black plate is also used in the printing press.

CMYK is called a **subtractive** color model, because the process ink pigments "subtract" light when mixed, or absorb certain colors and reflect others (which are seen by your eyes).

INDEXED

Indexed or mapped color works with a fixed color value for each pixel. Each color used in a given image is put in a **color table** or **color map**, which is part of an indexed image file. This color table is then used to map the appropriate color to each pixel to be displayed.

Figure 13.3 *An RGB image*

Indexed image files contain less data and therefore require less memory to store. If you are designing graphics for the web, you should keep in mind that many computers can't display 24 bit color. Many people out there use monitors that are limited to 256 colors. Therefore, your beautiful, "millions of colors" image may be indexed to a measly 256 colors when it is reproduced on their monitor. It may not look very good, and it will take the same amount of time to download.

GIF format images, which are often used on the web, are indexed to contain no more than 256 colors.

Figure 13.4 *An Indexed image*

Two kinds of image file formats are commonly used on the web: JPEG and GIF. Both formats have advantages and disadvantages, but we won't get into a big discussion about GIF vs. JPEG here.

The important point to remember is that GIF images are indexed and JPEG images aren't. Among the many reasons to use GIFs, the most important is that indexed images are small files.

Also note that if you assign a **web-indexed palette** to a GIF image, you can be sure that "what you see is what you get." In other words, everyone who downloads the image will see almost exactly the same colors, without any strange substitutions. Those images will always look almost exactly the same in a particular browser, whether displayed with 8 bit, 16 bit or 24 bit output.

Don't index your image before you're finished with it. And always save and keep an RGB copy of your original before converting the image to indexed color — you'll need the original for any future image editing. Most of the image information is lost forever as soon as you convert it to indexed format, and you regain any of the information by converting back to RGB. Also note that you can't work on an indexed image with most filters.

HSV

HSV stands for **Hue**, **Saturation** and **Value**. The HSV color model is used in most options in the Image dialog for Colors (`right-click|Image|Colors`) and Channel Ops (`right-click|Image|Channel Ops`). It is also used in certain filters and color modes.

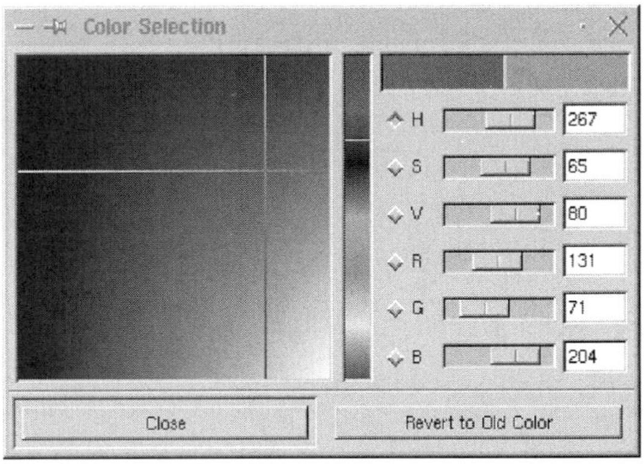

Figure 13.5 *The Color Selection dialog*

This color model is best understood if you open the **Color Selection** dialog (click on the **foreground/background** icon at the bottom of the toolbox) and look at the three top sliders marked **H**, **S** and **V**. Drag these three sliders as you read this passage, and notice how the color is affected. The **R**, **G** and **B** sliders display the equivalent values for the RGB color model. Let's take a look at each of these three parts of the HSV color model, starting with H for Hue.

Hue

Hue describes where a color lies along the **spectrum**, or what "rainbow color" it is: for example, red, orange, indigo or green. As in a rainbow, the starting and ending color is red. Hue values are organized into a color circle, with red at 0 degrees, yellow at 60 degrees clockwise, continuing with green, cyan, blue, magenta and red again at 360 degrees.

Figure 13.6 *The HUE color circle*

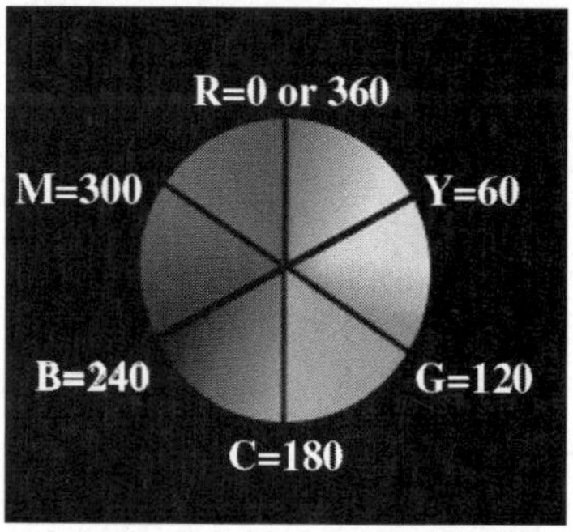

SATURATION

Saturation is how **pure** or "loud" the color is. The saturation value goes from 0 (grayscale) to 100 (maximum purity). A low value will provide a neutral, dull color, and a high value means a strong, pure color.

VALUE

Value is another way of saying **brightness**. A value of 0 means completely black, while 100 is the brightest value that a color can have. Maximum value doesn't mean white, however (unless saturation is zero). Maximum value is simply the brightest value a color can have at a particular saturation.

NCS

NCS (the *Natural Color System*) is the system used by architects and interior decorators. This is also often the system that's used when you buy paint for your house (unless you live in the U.S., where you might see the *Munsell* system instead). The NCS color model is based on the six **elementary** colors: yellow, red, blue, green, black and white.

Figure 13.7 *The NCS circle*

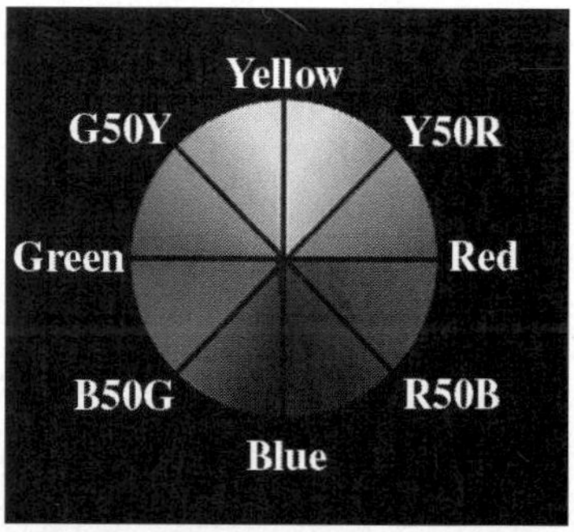

All colors can be described by how closely they resemble the elementary colors. The elementary colors and the color scale between them form a **three-dimensional** spindle-shaped body (like two cones put together). From the color body, a **color circle** and **color triangles** can be derived. In the color circle (a horizontal "slice" of the color body), the colors are arranged according to their position in the spectrum, evenly distributed between the four basic colors; yellow, red, blue and green.

For every color in the circle, a vertical section, shaped like a triangle, shows the different shades of a color: **whiteness**, **blackness** and **colorfulness** (saturation).

Colors are then identified according to the following scheme: **Y70Rs70c20**.

Y stands for yellow and **70R** means 70% red. This indicates a position in the spectrum circle somewhere between the elementary colors yellow and red. It also tells us that this orange color is composed of 30% yellow and 70% red, i.e., a bit like a blood orange. Likewise, **R70B** would indicate a bluish violet color, and **G70Y** a lemon yellow. Note that the first letter in the color code always refers to the first primary color (clockwise) in the color segment, and that the color percentage always refers to the second primary color.

With the notation **s70**, we have turned from the color circle to the color triangle. It means that our orange color has 70% blackness, which gives us a dark brown color (whereas a blackness value of 10 would produce shades of peach). Finally, we have **c20**, which means that our color has 20% colorfulness, which is not very intense. So **Y70Rs70c20** indicates a color best described as a dark, washed-out maroon.

You can get a fair idea of what this color looks like by opening the **Color Selection** dialog and adjusting the **HSV** slidebars. In HSV space, red is at 0 and pure yellow is at 60 degrees. Consequently 70% red and 30% yellow would be placed at 18 degrees in the Hue field. Set the Saturation field to 20, and Value to 30 (100-70=30). Note that the match isn't perfect because the color systems aren't compatible. This is only an approximation, and you can't use this method instead of an NCS color chart. (The largest difference is cause by Hue.)

Even if you don't use NCS on your computer, you should still understand it, because it is the most widely used color system for professional designers and architects in many European countries. If you get an assignment in Europe where a client wants you to suggest different colors for a pattern, an object or a building (using a program like Gimp or Photoshop) you should be prepared to discuss those colors in terms of NCS values, and not RGB or HSV.

Spot Color

Spot colors or **custom colors** are colors defined in a commercial custom color system and are normally used for printing in color when four-color process printing won't do. For example, you may want to use a non-rasterized smooth silver gray for text on a poster; in that case, you'd have to specify a predefined spot color. Pantone and Truematch are the most common custom color systems used by professional printers. Read more about spot colors in "Using Channels For Spot Color Separation" on page 355.

Grayscale And Line Art

From the name, it should be pretty obvious what a **grayscale** image is: an image consisting solely of shades of gray (with a maximum of 256 different shades). Therefore, grayscale images are small files, compared to **RGB** files, and they can convey more detail than **indexed** color images.

It would seem that an indexed image with a 256-entry color table would be equivalent, and if we mean 256 shades of gray, that's quite true. However, for an indexed image in color, a palette of 256 colors is quite crude for most photographic images.

Figure 13.8 *The grayscale image to the left was converted to a line art image on the right*

Line art is the simplest and smallest bitmap file that can exist. A line art image consists only of white or black pixels. Such images are extremely simple, but can be quite expressive. You can scan in line art or use `right-click|Image|Colors|Threshold` or `right-click|Image|Colors|Posterize` to convert a grayscale image into a line art image, as we did in Figure 13.8 .

Complementary Or Inverted Colors

Complementary colors are two colors that produce a neutral gray when mixed together. Complementary colors in real life are not the same as on your monitor. Most people are taught as children that mixing yellow and blue results in green. This is perfectly true if you're talking about inks, oil paint and pigments, but it doesn't apply to the RGB color model.

To illustrate this point, try painting yellow in a layer on a blue background and watch it in 50% opacity — no green appears, just a neutral gray. Do the same thing with watercolor or oil paint and you'll definitely get a greenish color!

To understand this, look at the **RGB color circle**. In the circle model, the complementary colors are opposite each other. In the RGB color system the opposite of red is cyan, the opposite of yellow is blue, and so forth. In other words, the **inverted** or complementary value equals 255 minus the original value in the RGB model.

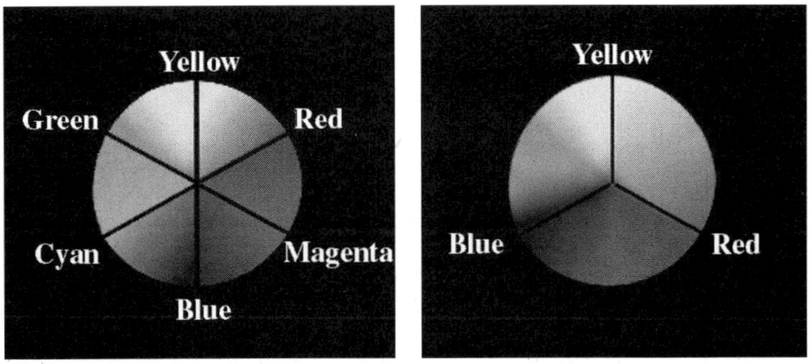

Figure 13.9 *RGB model on left and natural color model on right*

However, this doesn't work with pigments in real paint. In the **natural color circle**, which you'd need to use for real paint pigments, you can see that the complementary color of yellow isn't blue but violet, and the complementary color of blue is orange.

Watercolor artists often add a complementary color to neutralize an overstrong background without dulling it. A real life example: Why do you think some old ladies have "blue" hair? They (or their hairstylists) are trying to neutralize the unwanted red/yellow shades in their gray hair by using a dye containing the complementary color, blue or violet.

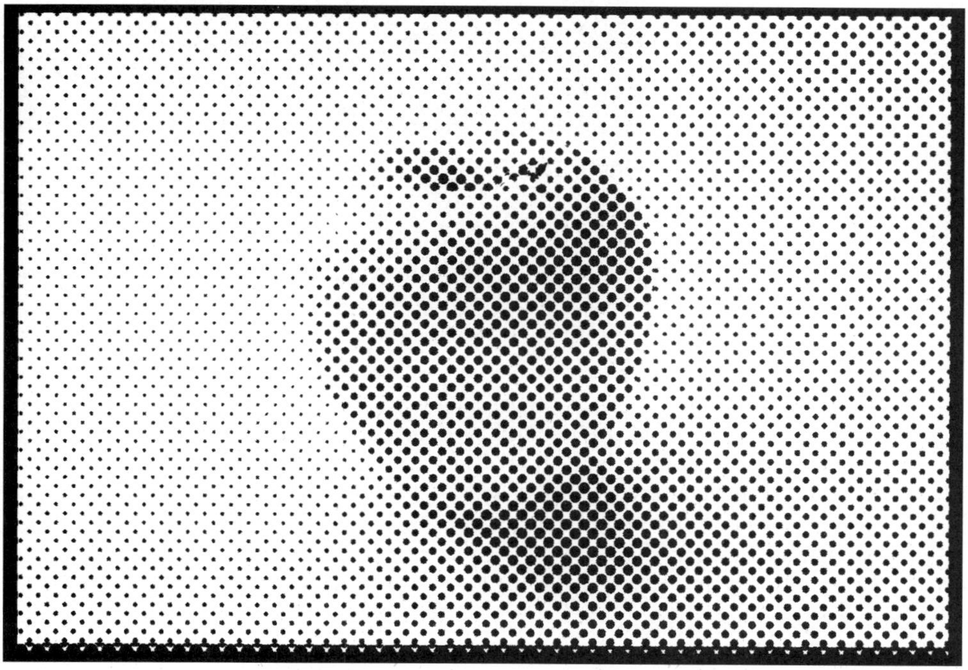

CHAPTER 14

Pre-press And Color In Gimp

This chapter will help you prepare your Gimp images for the printing press. You will also learn some simple color calibration techniques for your monitor.

What Is Pre-press?

When people think about **pre-press**, they are usually thinking about taking their image or book to the local printer so it can go to press. For a long time, the digital pre-press business has been dominated by a company with an apple in their logo. Programs for pre-press have also traditionally been provided by companies such as Adobe, Corel and Macromedia, and tight bonds often exist between **graphics software** and **printing hardware**. This system means that it is very easy for the average Macintosh user to create digital designs and send them to pre-press.

Since the market has been dominated by Apple for so long, most of the scanners, printers and monitors come with drivers and calibration tools adjusted and written for Macintosh. The only thing the graphic designer has to do is get a printing profile from the print house, put it in the program, and everything is set as it should be. People can argue about whether this is the right way to go, or whether the user should have more control over settings or parameters, but using preset Mac profiles is certainly very handy.

When you meet with pre-press people for the first time, you'll hear a lot of buzzwords (*lpi, dpi, ppi, Pantone colors, etc.*). You'll also have to solve the problem of how to format your Gimp images for Mac users and Mac print shops, and figure out how to transfer large image files.

In this chapter, we will try to answer these questions and sort out some of the buzzwords. And relax, you really don't need a Mac or a Windows box to prepare for pre-press. All you need is Gimp and UNIX.

Printing From Gimp

Gimp is not as intuitive as Photoshop is about pre-press issues. Gimp is more focused on web design. In Gimp, you always see the image size as the web surfer would see it.

Why? By default, images with no resolution information provided in the file will be opened at 72 ppi (pixels per inch). This is the case for Netscape, and for most other programs. Gimp doesn't provide any dialogs for incorporating **printing values** before you start creating your design. Don't worry; it isn't very difficult if you just plan ahead a little. You simply have to use your good sense and a few calculations.

If you want to **adjust** or **calibrate** your scanner, monitor, etc., you'll need to do it by hand. If you don't calibrate, it's very likely that you will be disappointed when you see the printed outcome of your work. Even if you don't have a top-of-the-line calibration kit, the printout will probably be closer to what you see on the screen than before the calibration. We'll cover calibration in detail later in this chapter, but let's begin with a discussion of file types.

File Formats for Printing

Many image file formats exist, but most professional printers use only two: **EPS** (Encapsulated PostScript) and **TIFF** (tagged image file format). Some print shops can also manage JPEG and compressed EPS.

If you don't want to save your image into one of these formats, you can import the image file into a **layout program**. Most print shops that accept PC files can support programs like Adobe FrameMaker, Adobe Illustrator and Corel Draw. If you import your image to a such a program and save it in the program's native file format, the print shop will be able to print from that file instead.

PostScript Files

If your local print shop can manage **EPS files**, you should probably use that format. EPS is device and platform independent, and you can be sure that the outcome will look just like the image you created (assuming that you calibrated your monitor and that you're printing to a **PostScript** printer).

If you use EPS, make sure that your print shop can handle **color adjustment** in an EPS file, and that they are able to **preview** it. If they can't, you'll need to be sure that all settings and colors in your file are perfect from the start, because the printer won't be able to fix it for you afterwards.

If you have a large print job, you also need to know whether they can **rearrange** the pages in the PostScript file. If they can't, you may have to pay for two printing plates instead of just one. This has to do with the type of binding you want to use. In a DTP program there are automatic functions that will rearrange the pages so that they will fit your choice of binding. For example, in a "saddle" binding, the first and last pages will be printed on the same large piece of paper (this paper is then folded like a roof or saddle). Only the pages in the middle of the document will actually be placed on the printing plate in the order that you see them in the original text file.

Gimp includes a powerful PostScript file saver in which you can specify paper size and resolution as well as the type of PostScript.

To create an EPS file, check the **Encapsulated PostScript** checkbox on the **Save PostScript** dialog box (`right-click|File|Save As` and then choose **PostScript** from the **Determine file type** pull-down menu). Most print shops can take plain PostScript files, so this may also be a option for you, but you still have to specify all parameters as you do when you save a PS file.

You can also use the `right-click|File|Print` command and **print to file.** You can adjust the PostScript file so that the options that the print house printer or image setter understand are included in the PostScript file. You do that by asking what **ppd** (printer parameters description) file you should use for that printer, or even better, ask to get the ppd file from the print house. When you have the ppd file, enter the setup dialog from the printer dialog window. Here you'll set the printer to Postscript Level 1 or 2 depending on what kind of printer the print house is going to use. The next step is to specify which ppd file to use in the ppd field; simply press the **Browse** button and "open" your ppd file. The PostScript file generated will now support the options available for the print house printer.

The file output will be PostScript and not EPS. You also have to talk to your print house to see if they can take plain PostScript files instead of EPS files.

TIFF Files

If your printer doesn't support EPS or PostScript, you'll have to save your image in an ordinary image format like TIFF or JPEG. Be aware that some image formats (for example, TIFF) differ in PC and Mac environments. The advantage of using TIFF is that you can make a high-quality proof even on a non-PostScript printer. Also, TIFF is a good choice if your image's background is white, because EPS sometimes has a tendency to produce a weak tint in large white areas.

If you ship your images as ordinary image files, you must remember to tell your printer in what **size** you want the images to be printed. This is important, because printers normally expect plain image files to be created in Photoshop. In Photoshop, the image size and resolution is included in the image file. However, Gimp only supports (so far) one resolution (72 ppi or monitor resolution).

Resolution And Image Size

As we have stated before, Gimp images only have one resolution: 72 ppi (pixels per inch), which is the unspecified default screen resolution. Obviously, this is ideal for web publishing, because web surfers are viewing images on their monitors. However, 72 ppi resolution is far too low for any kind of serious printing.

For example, suppose that your printer tells you that to make your 50x60-inch poster look good, you need a minimum resolution of 100 ppi. To provide the 100 ppi resolution, you'll need to create a larger image in Gimp and then scale it down when you save it as a PostScript or EPS file (or the printer will do it when they import the image into one of their programs).

In the `File|New` dialog, you always specify the image size in pixels, so it's not very difficult to calculate the size you need for a certain resolution. Using the figures in this example, we'll just multiply the image width and height (50x60 inches) by 100 (the resolution) and insert those values as **Width** and **Height** in the **New Image** dialog box.

50 x 100 equals 5000 pixels and 60 x 100 equals 6000 pixels. The standard equation is simple:

Note: Gimp image size = desired ppi desired height or width in inches

As a rule of thumb, always adjust the image size *before* you start making the image. Ask your printer for the required resolution, and calculate the image size you need to produce a nice printed output.

If you need a high resolution for your print job, your images will be huge on the screen. The good news is that Gimp is smart enough to adjust the canvas size so it will never be bigger than your display.

So, how can you fix it if you didn't do the necessary calculations before creating the image, or if the printer tells you that your image resolution is too low? Don't panic, there is a way out of this dilemma. You can **scale** the image a certain amount, because Gimp can *interpolate* the image.

Interpolation means that when you enlarge an image by scaling it, Gimp compares neighboring pixels, makes an assessment of their color and calculates an intermediate color for the new pixels. This works well if you only have to resize the image a small amount, but don't try it for scaling the image to double its size or more. The image will end up looking blurred and fuzzy at the edges. For better (but slower) interpolation, check the **Cubic interpolation** checkbox on the **Display** tab in the **Preferences** dialog (`File|Preferences`).

Preparing For The Press

DPI, LPI, PPI And Scanning Resolution

If you've never done a high-end print job before, the first thing you should do is make some phone calls to local print shops and ask a few questions. For example, if you want to print a 22x34-inch poster, you'll need to make sure that the print shop can print that size and in the resolution you want.

People often think that a higher resolution is automatically a better choice, but that's not always true. For a poster, you need to consider the *viewing distance.* For a large image, like a commercial poster, the beholder will observe it from a certain distance and will never see the coarse halftone dots unless he or she gets very close to it. For that reason, you don't have to print a poster in a very high resolution. On the other hand, if you're making a cover for a monthly fashion magazine, then you'll need a very high resolution, indeed.

Lpi And Dpi

You have probably often heard the expression **dpi** (*dots per inch*) in reference to home or office printer resolution (for example, a 600 dpi laser printer or a 300 dpi inkjet printer). However, the term "dpi" is not as commonly used in professional printing.

Lpi is the most widely used term in professional printing for printer resolution, and one you'll encounter as soon as you enter the print shop. Lpi stands for *lines per inch*, and is used for **screening**, the fine **halftone** pattern you see when you look closely at a picture in a newspaper. The higher the lpi, the more (and smaller) halftone dots are squeezed in per inch.

Each halftone dot is made up of very small "dpi dots." **Dpi** can simply be described as the maximum number of these microscopic dots that the printer can manage to print per inch. Inexperienced users tend to think that 600 dpi in a printer is equivalent to 600 ppi in an image file, but they are not equivalent. It takes a lot of dpi to represent a ppi.

For more information about the relationship between dpi and lpi, see "Printer Table" and "Image Table" on page 217. These tables can serve as a guide for the lpi needed to produce different types of printed material and/or which output device can produce an lpi suitable for your needs.

Ppi And Scan Resolution

After you've chosen an appropriate lpi (lines per inch) for your print job, you can calculate the **ppi** (*pixels per inch*) resolution you'll need in your digital image. In the following example, we will make a 15"x15" poster out of a 4"x4" photograph.

First a general rule of thumb: ***image ppi = 1.6xlpi*** (assuming that the image file and the printed output have a 1:1 ratio). This equation is not exact, because it depends on what kind of quality you want (see "Lpi Table" on page 216).

We chose an lpi of 150, which is good enough for a poster. If we wanted to make a life-size print of the 4"x4" photo (1:1 ratio), we would scan the image in at 240 dpi (1.6x150). *Note that scan dpi is the same as ppi.*

To make a large print from a small scanned image, we'll need a much higher resolution. We want to produce a 15"x15" printed poster from a 4"x4" photo, so we will need to scan the photo in at a higher resolution than the 240 ppi.

The calculation to use is: **scan resolution = desired ppi x (wanted size/ actual size)**.

If we insert the figures from our example into this algorithm, we'll get: 240x (15/4), which equals 900. This means that you need to scan the photo in at 900 dpi to be able to print the 15"x15" poster at 150 lpi.

Note that when we're talking about scan resolution, we mean the *optical scan resolution*. When you read a sales brochure about scanners, and it says that a certain scanner can scan at a resolution of 9,000 dpi, this figure usually refers to the software *interpolated resolution*. The real scan resolution may be as low as 300 dpi. Always make sure that you scan in optical resolution. If you want to interpolate a scanned photo, Gimp will do a much better job than the scanner software (SANE, which is the scanner program we recommend to use with Gimp, only scans in optical resolution).

Scan dpi is *not* the same as printer dpi, so don't think that you have to scan at 600 dpi to print to a 600 dpi laser printer! Scan resolution is measured in "scan dpi," which is equivalent to ppi (pixels per inch).

After having made these calculations, we can start calling the local print shops, asking if they can print a poster that is 15"x15" large, using an lpi around 150.

If you need to know more about lpi, dpi, ppi and screening, in-depth information is provided later in "Resolution" on page 212. If you have a inkjet printer you can also read about that kind of printing in "Scanning, The Web And Printing" on page 259.

At The Print Shop

Why The Colors That Looked So Good On Your Monitor Don't Match The Color Of The Output

Never give your image file to the printer and simply ask them to print it. If you do, you can more or less rely on the colors being screwed up. **Color calibration** of your computer environment is one of the stumbling blocks when it comes to image production. If your monitor is not calibrated correctly, you can't predict what colors will actually be printed.

The most simple solution to this problem is to make a small **proof** at home on a color inkjet printer. If the proof's color is correct as far as you're concerned, bring this example to the printer and ask them to adjust the color so that the printed outcome will match your proof. We will describe how to calibrate scanners, monitors and the like later in this chapter, but remember that it's always a good idea to bring a proof or dummy to the printer as a reference. If you bring a proof, you can demand a reprint if the colors of the printed product are incorrect.

Spot Color

If you can only afford one or two color plates, or if a part of your design doesn't look good in halftone pattern, there is another way of handling the problem of getting the right color. You can use **spot colors** from a commercial color system like **Pantone** or **Truematch**. Instead of using the four-color process inks cyan, magenta, yellow and black on the printing plates, you can choose any color you like from a custom color chart, and apply that ink to a plate. Such inks are called spot colors.

Gimp doesn't natively support spot colors, so if you want to use custom colors with Gimp you'll have to buy a custom color map. Decide which spot color you want to use, and give a **grayscale file** and a **spot color specification** to your printer. If you want to use more than one spot color and you don't have a spot color separation program, you must give the printer an appropriate grayscale file for each color plate. Read more about spot colors in "Color Models" starting on page 187 and "Channels And Duotones" starting on page 351.

How To Transfer Images To The Print Shop

Removable Drives

A common method of transporting images to a printer is by using removable drives, such as SyQuest and Ezdrive by SyQuest and Jaz and Zip drives from Iomega.

The Iomega Zip drive, which can store 100 MB of data, is the most common removable drive in the PC world. To decide what drive you should buy, phone your local printers and ask what kinds of drives they support. Based on that information, decide what kinds of drive you should buy.

Based on our own experience, we suggest a SCSI Zip drive because the Zip drive is fast and the old SyQuest drives are expensive and on their way out. New drives from SyQuest have not been as successful as Iomega drives, and most printers these days support Zip drives.

CD-ROM

CD-Recordable (CD-R) prices have also fallen, so CD-Rs can be considered as a delivery medium for images. If you want to use CD-Rs, the best strategy is to record in ISO9660 format without any extensions, which allows only 8.3 (MS-DOS format) file names. When you're working on a project, it is more convenient to have it on your hard drive. When you're done, transfer it to the CD. This practice will make it easier to keep a large number of images without having one or more very large hard disks.

CD-R quality is not as high as an ordinary CD. In the archive world, the CD-R medium is not trusted. Most archives re-record CD-Rs at regular intervals (because of concern about the medium and also because the machines that read the medium are not likely to be around forever).

According to the National Swedish Archives, CD-Rs should be re-recorded every five years (in contrast, they estimate that ink lasts 1,000 years!). An ordinary CD has a guaranteed lifetime of 20 years, so remember to re-record your stock photo library at regular intervals.

Internet And BBS

Many print shops have some sort of Internet connection or a Bulletin Board Service (**BBS**). If they have an Internet connection, they can probably support file upload using the **FTP** protocol. If they do, all you need is an FTP program and their address so you can upload files to their server.

If they have a BBS, then you need a **modem** and a **terminal program** that supports their BBS. You'll need to ask them what kind of program you need to use. Several modem/terminal programs are available for UNIX/Linux including **Kermit** and **Seyon**.

Tip: Although this doesn't apply to U.S. phone lines, it can be expensive to use this kind of file transfer in Europe, where local calls aren't free.

We don't suggest uploading files over 20 MB if you only have an ordinary modem. Some printers also charge you for each MB you upload, adding even more expense.

Email

We don't recommend that you email the file to the printer, because you're probably starting with a fairly large image file, and the coding of the file as an email attachment makes it even larger. Therefore, the "upload" time will last even longer. Also, it is not uncommon for files to become damaged when they are sent as email.

File System Format

What kind of **file system format** should you use? Nearly all print shops support **FAT** (File Allocation Table, an MS-DOS file system format) even if they use a Mac. If they don't support FAT, you'll have to use the Internet or BBS to transfer files.

Why FAT? Most UNIX system supports FAT, and Linux can even run on top of a FAT file system. Support for the native Mac file system (HSPF) is rare in the UNIX world. And don't think that your local print house will support any native UNIX or Linux file system, so we suggest that you stick to FAT.

If your print house doesn't support FAT, we think you should seriously consider finding another printer who does. If they support FAT, you can create a FAT file system on your removable drive (Zip and Jaz PC disks come preformatted for the FAT file system).

If you are running a **Linux** system, nice freeware (OSS) tools exist that make it easy to manage Zip and Jaz drives using a GUI interface. Helpful how-to documents also exist for using both Iomega and SyQuest drives with Linux. For more information, see `http://metalab.unc.edu/LDP/HOWTO/HOWTO-INDEX-3.html`.

Scanning Using A UNIX Or Linux System

Free Scanner Programs

Because we are working with Gimp, Sane (Scanner Access Now Easy) is the best scanner interface to use. Sane will run as a stand-alone program, but it can also act as an **extension** to Gimp. If you're running Sane as an extension to Gimp, you can open Sane from Gimp and scan straight into Gimp. Using Sane in this manner is like having a **Twain** interface under Photoshop or a similar program in a Mac or Windows environment.

Sane supports a wide range of scanners on nearly all major UNIX/Linux platforms and includes an attractive interface in which you can adjust nearly everything (for example, gamma, color curves, resolution, and more). To learn more about Sane read "Scanning And Scanners" starting on page 219, which is a whole chapter devoted to scanning with Sane.

Naturally, there are other freeware scanner programs, but most of them do not include a capable GUI interface like Sane does. If you have a **Mustek scanner,** you can try a program called **Tkscan** (`http://muon.kaist.ac.kr/~hbkim/linux/tkscanfax/`).

If you have a scanner that isn't supported by Sane, look through the SunSite Linux Information Repository (`ftp://metalab.unc.edu/pub/Linux/apps/graphics/capture`) for another program that supports your scanner. It's better to have a plain CLI (command line interface) to scan with than no program at all.

Commercial Scanner Programs

Of course, there are many commercial scanner programs available. **XVScan** (`http://www.tummy.com/xvscan/`) is a very nice program that supports **HP scanners**, and it isn't expensive. XVScan is integrated with the xv graphics program and it supports all of the functionality of a modern scanner program. We've used both Sane and XVScan for this manual and we've been equally satisfied with both.

In the professional class of scanner software, you can choose from scanner programs from **Caldera Graphics** (`http://www.caldera.fr`) and **Mentalix** (`http://www.mentalix.com`). Both companies offer everything from scanner interfaces to complete graphic studios with programs that are Gimp-like but focus on pre-press.

If you're considering serious pre-press in a UNIX/Linux environment, you may want to buy one of these programs. Mentalix sells "light" versions (with less functionality, but at a lower price) of its programs for Linux.

In the future, we'd like to obtain copies of these programs so we can give you a full review of their capabilities here, but for now the only available information is on their web sites. Other scanner programs exist for UNIX, but we don't know of any others for Linux.

Calibration

Gamma Calibration

Every monitor has a **gamma** value. We will not go into the background of gamma, but we can tell you that a gamma curve describes the distribution of darkness/brightness values. When you scan an image using SANE, its gamma value is set to 1 (if you haven't altered the default value), and that may not be suitable for your monitor.

Tip: Before you calibrate anything, turn on your monitor and let it warm up for at least 30 minutes. Also, make sure that you have a normal light in your room (not too dark or too light).

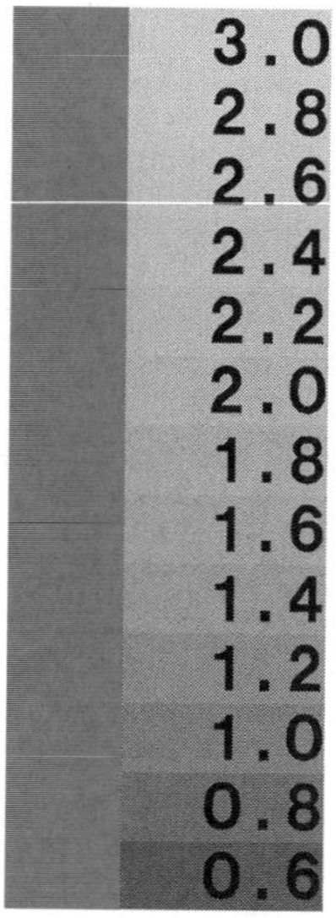

Figure 14.1 *Gamma calibration image*

Calibrating Your Monitor's Gamma Value

1. To find out your monitor's gamma value, download the file:

    ftp://manual.gimp.org/pub/manual/GUM_PrePress_Calibration_Images.tar.bz2 x

2. **Decompress** and **untar** the file with the following commands:

```
bunzip2 GUM_PrePress_Calibration_Images.tar.bz2
tar xvf GUM_PrePress_Calibration_Images.tar
```

3. Change to the `PrePress` directory created by untarring the file:

```
cd PrePress
```

   An `ls` command will display the following files: `gamma.tif`, `color-cal.tif`, `black_lev.tif` and `white_lev.tif`.

4. Open the gamma.tif file in **Gimp**, and decide which of the numbered squares on the right matches the brightness of the long vertical strip to the left.
5. Open the gamma.tif image in a program that lets you alter the gamma by value, such as ImageMagick's **Display**. If you're using Display, the following command will open the file:

```
display gamma.tif
```

6. Click your left mouse button to produce a pop-up menu. Select `Enhance | Gamma`. Enter the gamma value that matched the vertical strip in Gimp, and press the **Gamma** button. Save the file with a new name. Open the new file in Gimp.

If your gamma is okay, the 1.0 square should now have the same brightness as the vertical strip on the left.

If you know your monitor's gamma value, you can apply that value when you scan images, so they will display correctly when it comes to gamma. It won't affect color mismatch, but it's much better than no correction at all. Otherwise, you will often end up adjusting levels in the scanned image, and it's better to correct this as you scan in order to save time.

Black Level And White Level Adjustment

Besides the gamma value, the **black level** is one of the most important things to adjust.

Adjusting The Black Level

1. Open the `PrePress/black_lev.gif` file in Gimp. Adjust your screen until the image covers most of it *(do not adjust the image size--adjust the screen resolution).*
2. Access the **brightness** control on your monitor. Adjust (turn up) the brightness until the *gray stripes* marked 1, 2 and 3 are visible. Gently turn

down the brightness until strip 1 fades away. Carefully turn up the brightness until strip 1 is just visible again.

Figure 14.2 *Black level*

Adjusting The White Level

1. Load the `white_lev.gif file` into Gimp. Adjust the contrast until the *gray bars* in the middle square have **equal density**, that is, until the gray field looks like a uniform gray field without bars. This is tricky, so don't adjust too much. Stop immediately when the gray bars start to disappear.
2. Now re-check the black level, because black and white levels are interdependent. For the same reason, re-check the white level again.

Note: If you have a old monitor or if it's low quality, you will never be able to achieve perfect results for both the black and the white level. You'll have to choose something that is compromise between the two

COLOR CALIBRATION

There is no easy way to do color calibration, so you will have to buy a **color calibration kit**. When you buy your kit, make sure that it is either platform-independent or designed for your version of UNIX.

PLAIN COLOR CALIBRATION SYSTEMS

Simple color calibration kits are usually made up of *a printed color image*, a *color image slide* and a *color image file*. You load the color image from the file, compare it with the printed image and adjust your monitor until the colors match (for more specific information, read the instructions that came with the kit).

To calibrate your **scanner**, scan the slide or the printed image and compare it with the image file. To calibrate your **printer**, compare the output from your printer with the printed image from the kit, and adjust it accordingly.

Color calibration is a very time-consuming task, but until you've calibrated your hardware, you can't trust your system's color fidelity. Even if you have made all of these corrections, the color calibration is still not a sure thing, because humans are subjective about color representation.

CMS

If absolute color correction is a high priority for you, you need to get a **CMS** (Color Management System).

CMS systems are available for UNIX. Caldera Graphics (`http://www.caldera.fr`) sells CMS-like systems. Mentalix (`http://www.mentalix.com`) also provides CMS. These products work for most UNIX systems, including Linux. Other providers exist for UNIX systems, but we don't know of anyone else who provides CMS for Linux systems.

Color correction kits are expensive. CMS systems are *very* expensive. However, if you own or work for a commercial company dealing with advanced image manipulation and pre-press, the best solution for color correction is a real CMS system.

Figure 14.3 *Color calibration image (see color section)*

Poor Man's Color Calibration

If you can't afford or get hold of a real calibration kit, here's a cheap and easy (but not very exact) method. Simple color calibration is better than none. However, don't think that your system is properly calibrated by this technique. It helps, but it can never compare to a professional color calibration.

Famous **brand names** always use a specific color in their product name or logotype. Volvo uses a very special "Volvo blue" color, Marlboro cigarettes has its "Marlboro red," Sun uses their own particular color in the Sun logotype, etc. These colors can often be downloaded in images from the companies' web sites, and the printed color can be picked up by a phone call or a visit to their sales office.

When you have the color on file as well as in print, you can calibrate just like you would with a plain color calibration kit.

Please don't expect miracles from using this method. This provides only a rough approximation of real color calibration.

Why Don't The Colors Look Right Even After Calibration?

When you work at your computer monitor you work in **RGB** mode, and when you print your file at a print shop or at home you work in **CMYK** mode. Every RGB color can't be exactly equivalent to a CMYK color (for more information on this, read the "In-Depth Information" on page 210).

Because Gimp is more focused on creating images for the web, it doesn't have a **CMYK preview** through which you can find out whether your color image can be printed without some loss in the RGB information.

Tip: Be careful when using highly saturated colors in your image, because they probably aren't CMYK safe. Always make a proof before giving the file to the print shop. If you want to use colors that you suspect aren't CMYK-legal, choose a high-quality printer to print a proof, because a home-office printer doesn't have the capacity to make a good translation from RGB to CMYK.

In-Depth Information

Color Management

Before reading any further, read "Color Models" starting on page 187.

RGB And CMYK

Here's a common question: Why don't the colors on my monitor match the output from my printer?

As we've discussed before, the answer is that monitors are based on the **RGB** color system and printers are based on the **CMYK** color system. Because monitors and printers use different **color models**, it is impossible to print the monitor data directly to the printer. When you print your RGB image it will automatically be converted to CMYK.

Gamut

Gamut is the total number of colors a device can produce. The human eye can perceive a higher gamut than a 24 bit color monitor (RGB) can produce, but the gamut of a monitor is still higher than the gamut of a color printer (CMYK).

Figure 14.4 *Color gamut; see the Color Section for a better view of this figure*

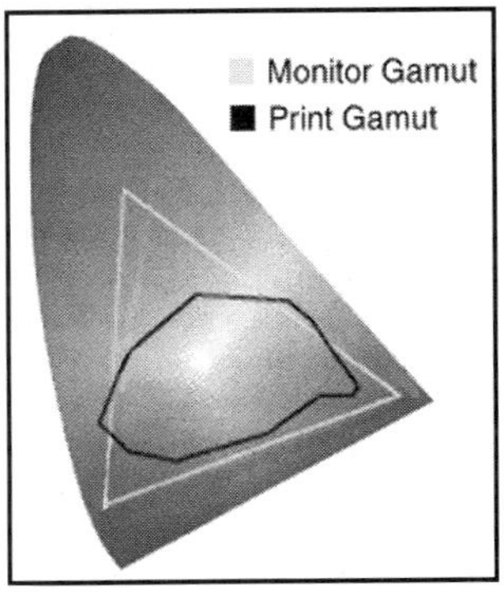

You now understand that all colors in an RGB image can't be represented in a CMYK image. An RGB color that can't be represented in CMYK will therefore be **converted** to the *nearest* CMYK color.

The success of the conversion depends on the software you're using (that is, the printer driver, which is **GhostScript** in most Linux systems). Gimp also provides a *built-in printer driver.* If you decide to use the Gimp printer driver, the conversion quality will depend on the quality of Gimp's native printer driver.

CMS

A CMS system provides the appropriate **gamut mapping** between the different devices on the system. **Profiles** of different devices are made by color scientists using special equipment, based on factory defaults. As a device ages, the profile is no longer correct, and a *recalibration* is necessary. Even if the device is brand new, variations in manufacturing quality often make a recalibration necessary.

Profiles

All of the **preset profiles** are used by the CMS system as the image travels from the scanner to the monitor and finally to the printer. The CMS system often uses an independent **color space** when the images are transmitted from one device to another. This results in consistent colors, even if the devices have different color systems. Sometimes it's impossible to keep the colors consistent (for example, you can't reproduce a highly saturated monitor image with CMYK ink, wax or toner).

The printer gamut area is simply too small to cover highly saturated colors (see Figure 14.4). This type of RGB color is not *CMYK safe*. When a non-CMYK safe color has to be reproduced, the system does a gamut mapping, that selects the nearest reproducible color.

High-quality CMS systems often provide you with the option to select a certain type of rendering for the gamut mapping, because there is a vast difference between reproducing images and reproducing business graphics.

Resolution

Resolution is the quality of images that are made up of pixels. A digital image appears to be of good quality when you can't see the individual pixels that form the image. If the resolution drops (for example, when the image is magnified), individual pixels will be visible to the eye, and the image will become "jaggy" or of low quality. In other words, image quality is based on the total **number of pixels** and the **size** of the image. These two factors determine the resolution.

Printed material such as a newspaper looks good when you view it from a reading distance. If you look at a newspaper with a magnifying glass, however, you will see the halftone dots that make up the images. Therefore, the perceived resolution of printed material is affected by the **distance** from which it is viewed as well as how smooth it is.

The resolution of the print and the resolution of the digital image must conform to each other. If the image resolution is higher than the output machine can handle, the **ripper** (the device that creates the halftone pattern) discards much of the information that it doesn't need.

The quality of the selection (determining what parts of the image information should be discarded) depends on the quality of the ripper. It is always better to create the image with the proper resolution, because then the ripper won't have to choose what information it should discard. On the other hand, if the image resolution is too low, the image pixels will be visible in the print. Even if you can't see the halftone dots, the print will look jaggy and cheap.

LPI, DPI And Screen Frequencies

Screening is a common printing buzzword. Imagesetters make a print based on **halftone screens**. These halftone screens are measured in **lpi**, or lines per inch, and the resolution or quality of an imagesetter or laser printer is often measured in **dpi**, or dots per inch.

The halftone screen can be represented by a **grid**. A halftone **cell**, capable of holding one halftone **dot**, is in each grid square. A superimposed grid called the *resolution grid* is over the halftone grid. The resolution grid includes a high number of grid squares for each cell. The amount of squares in the resolution grid determines the imagesetter's resolution in dpi.

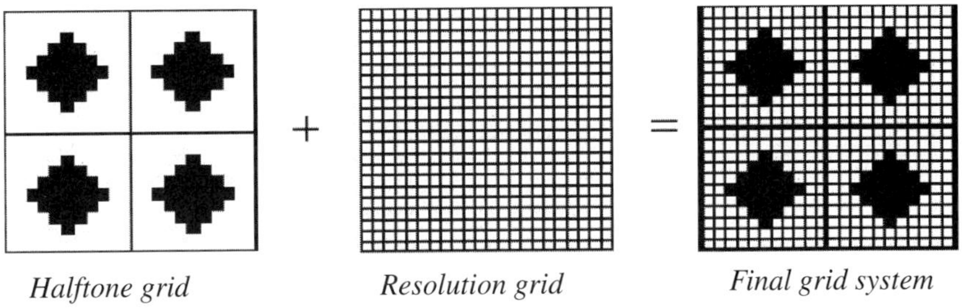

Figure 14.5 *Resolution grid system*

Halftone Dots

If you look closely at a newspaper, you will see that it's made up of different **half-tone** dots (see Figure 14.6). A halftone dot can vary in size from very tiny to the full size of the halftone cell. The tiny ones represent a light gray and the big ones represent a dark gray.

Each halftone dot consists of a number of smaller dots, and each square in the half-tone screen is built up of a subgrid (the halftone cell matrix), with a fixed number of available squares to put the small "dpi" dots in (see Figure 14.7).

The image "roughness" depends on how large the halftone cells are, and the number of grayscales (how many shades of gray can be represented) depends on how many small dots you can fit into the cell matrix.

Figure 14.6 *Different sized halftone dots*

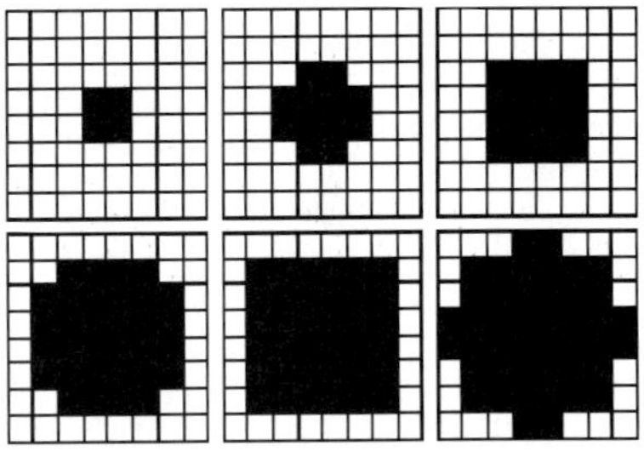

A halftone **matrix** is measured in 1x1, 2x2, 3x 3, 4x4, 5x5 grid squares, etc. A 3x3 matrix is capable of holding ten shades of gray. A 5x5 can hold 26 shades, an

8x8 matrix can hold 65, and so on (there is an extra shade, because all of the squares could be empty).

Figure 14.7 *Different sized matrixes*

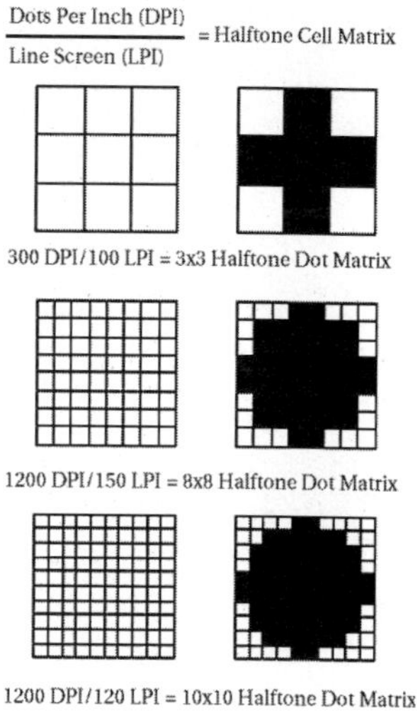

The number of grid squares in a halftone matrix can be calculated like this:

dpi/lpi = N x N halftone matrix

Therefore, a 300 dpi printer combined with an lpi of 100 only produces a matrix that is 3x3 and contains 9 grayscales (not very impressive). An image produced from 10 shades of gray looks quite bad.

A better setup combines the 300 dpi printer with an lpi of 60, which gives you 16 shades of gray (equivalent to the print in a cheap newspaper).

Now, if we took a 600 dpi printer and set it to 100 lpi, we would get a 6x6 matrix capable of producing 35 levels of gray.

So you see, dpi isn't everything. To achieve the really high quality of 256 shades of gray with an lpi of 133 (magazine standard), you'll need a 2,400 dpi printer.

Why Doesn't My Inkjet's Print Look Like Halftone Screens?

When we discussed screening in the paragraph above, we were talking about **halftone** screening, which is also called amplitude modulation (AM) screening. Although it isn't completely accurate, you could say that inkjet printers use **stochastic** screening, which is also called frequency modulation (FM) screening. AM screening uses different sized dots in a fixed grid. FM screening dots are exactly the same size, but the distance between the dots varies.

Stochastic screening is called **FM screening** because it is based on the dot *frequency*. Halftone screening is called **AM screening** because it is based on dot size or *amplitude*. FM dots are usually 1-2 percent of the size of halftone dots.

FM screening's advantage is that you can achieve a higher level of detail, even with a low resolution printer (for example, a 600 dpi printer). Other advantages of FM screening include the fact that it doesn't produce **rosette** and **moire** patterns, like AM screening can.

You also don't need the same level of resolution in the images that you provide for printing. Usually half the resolution that you would have used for AM printing suffices to produce excellent results with FM printing.

If FM screening is so great, why doesn't everybody use it? Until recently, the biggest problem has been to get printing press machines to produce small enough dots. This has become a minor problem, and it is now quite common to print using FM screening. Please read about inkjet printing in "Scanning, The Web And Printing" on page 259.

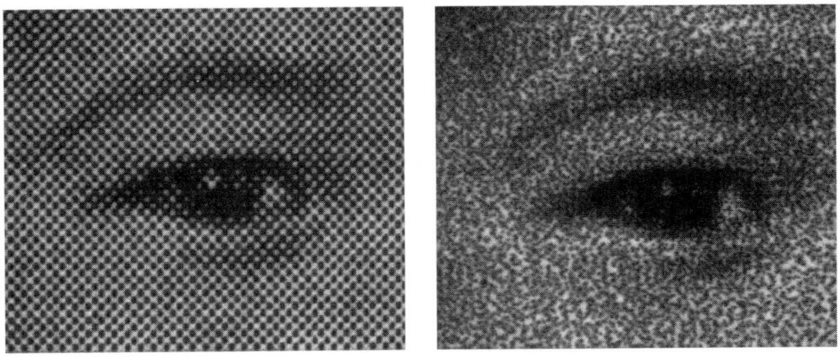

AM screening *FM screening*

Figure 14.8 *The difference between AM and FM screening*

TABLES

LPI TABLE

Table 14.1 *Lpi values*

Document Type	Paper Type	Necessary lpi
High-end advertisements and high-end brochures, fine art books and fine art reproduction. High-end magazines	Sheet-fed/coated	150 to 300 lpi (median 200 lpi)
Catalogs, monthly magazines, commercial-grade advertisements, ordinary books	Heat set web/coated	100 to 150 lpi (median 133 lpi)
Newsletters, forms and flyers	Sheet-fed/uncoated	100 to 133 lpi (median of 100 lpi)
Small magazines, catalogs, direct mail	Heat set web/uncoated	90 to 133 lpi (median of 100 lpi)
Newspaper supplements of high quality	Newspaper/coated	65 to 100 lpi (median of 90 lpi)
Newspaper supplements of ordinary quality	Newspaper/uncoated	65 to 100 lpi (median of 65 lpi)
Newspaper, low-quality spare parts catalogs	Newspaper/newsprint	65 to 100 lpi (median of 65 lpi)

PRINTER TABLE

Table 14.2 *Dpi/lpi printer values*

Printer Resolution	Recommended lpi	Best Choice/Number of Gray Shades
2,400 dpi	133 to 150 lpi	150/257
1,200 dpi	90 to 110 lpi	100/145
600 dpi	60 to 80 lpi	75/65
300 dpi	40 to 55 lpi	53/33

Image Table

Table 14.3 *Lpi/ppi image values*

lpi	Recommended Image ppi	Median
150	240 to 300	240
133	210 to 266	210
100	160 to 200	160
75	120 to 150	120
53	85 to 100	85

Shades Of Gray

$$Z = \left(\frac{Y}{X}\right)^2 + 1$$

X = screen frequency

Y = printer resolution

Z = number of gray shades

Screening Matrix Geometry

$$X = \frac{Y}{Z}$$

X = X x X halftone dot matrix

Y = printer resolution

Z = line screen

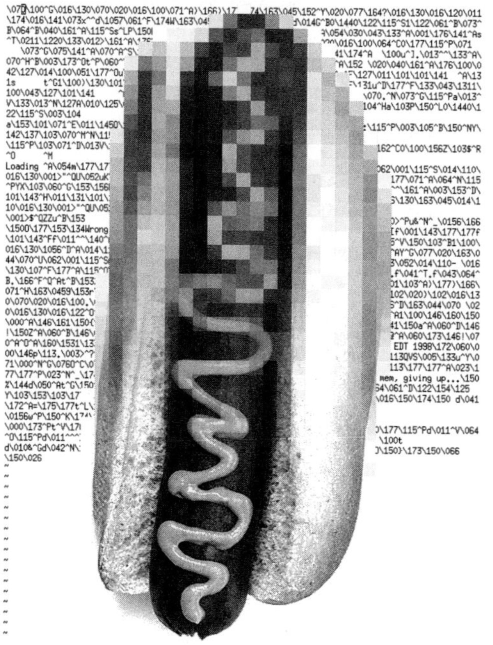

CHAPTER 15

Scanning And Scanners

This chapter will give you some tips on how to use scanners with Gimp. We will focus on Sane, which is a UNIX/Linux scanner program that can act as a plug-in to Gimp. We will also take a brief look at things you need to know if you're planning to buy a scanner.

Scanning In Gimp

There are a number of scanner programs available for UNIX/Linux, see "Scanning Using A UNIX Or Linux System" on page 205. This chapter is only going to discuss **Sane** (Scanner Access Now Easy), which in our opinion is the only "sane" way to scan with Gimp.

For a list of Sane-supported scanners and operating systems, take a look at the Sane scanner list on page 870. In this chapter, we will discuss how to install Sane for **Linux** and **Solaris**.

We will also cover usage and configuration of the *Umax Astra 1200S* flatbed scanner and the *HP Photosmart* slide scanner (SCSI model). Note that this doesn't mean that we advise the reader to buy a specific brand or type of scanner. It will suffice to say that we are satisfied with the functionality that the reviewed scanners provide, and that they are adequate for our use here at Frozenriver. The *HP Photosmart* support in Sane is still rather undeveloped, and will therefore not be discussed here, although it will serve as an example for configuring Sane.

What Scanner To Buy

First of all, you can forget all cheap *parallel port* scanners, because they are not very well supported under Sane or Unix/Linux.

Secondly, as far as Sane is concerned, you can also omit USB *(Universal Serial Bus)* scanners; they are even less supported than parallel port scanners. The USB interface may well be a good one, but Linux just got its USB stack as of Kernel 2.2.7. At the time of writing (July 99) Sane doesn't support USB scanners, and the Linux USB stack is, as we mentioned before, still very "young." However, the situation may change later on; both Sane and Linux may well have excellent support for USB scanners in the future.

Other UNIX versions, such as Solaris, IRIX and AIX, don't support USB, because there are no USB ports available for their hardware (well, the BSD versions of UNIX have some USB support). Let's just overlook USB for the time being, because there is no current support in Sane for USB scanners (besides, SCSI scanners are much better).

So to make it short, the only scanners that we can recommend for use with Gimp are scanners that use the SCSI interface to deliver data.

How Do You Want To Use Your Scanner?

First, ask yourself why you want a scanner. Is it intended for collecting graphics for web design, is it for easy desktop publishing, is it to digitalize drawings or documents, is it to put all your slides and negatives into the computer or is it just for you and your family's sheer enjoyment?

Well, the purposes are many and the answers are just as many. Because this book concerns Gimp and how to use Sane in Gimp, we will only discuss a small fraction of the possible fields of application, and when we do, we will try to group them in categories where the demands on the scanner are identical.

Not many years ago, scanning was something you did for a living. Scanners were expensive equipment, and only professional service bureaus could afford them. Scanning was also a complicated procedure, which meant that you had to be an expert to be able to operate a scanner.

Today, the scanner (for most us) is a tool, much like a word processor or a screwdriver. We use the scanner when we need it, i.e., when we want a digital copy of an image, drawing or document.

The different fields of application (which are relevant for use within Gimp) can be divided into the following categories:

- Web images
- School use, low-level desktop publishing, SOHO (Small Office, Home Office) scanning and printing
- Semi-professional desktop publishing
- Drawings and image composing
- Professional desktop publishing
- Scanning of slides and negatives

The modest scanner requirements are at the beginning of the list, followed by the high demands required by advanced applications. Before we go into what scanner qualities are relevant for each group, we need to discuss and analyze what different scanner specifications really mean.

What All Those Specs Really Mean

When you buy a scanner today, most salespeople think of it as just another piece of hardware or computer accessory. Because scanners have become really cheap compared to a few years ago, the computer store will not make as much money from selling a scanner as it used to. This means that the salesmen aren't specialized in the scanners they sell, so you'll have to do all the research yourself.

There are several ways to do the research (start by checking if the scanner is supported by Sane). Try the scanner manufacturer's web site, read computer magazines (a small suggestion is to only read magazines that focus on DTP or image manipulation), browse the web for reviews, and finally, my personal favorite: Search Usenet for comments about the scanner you're interested in.

During your investigation you will most likely face several new terms in the scanner specification or review/tests. The most common ones are:

- **Bit depth (bpp):** Stands for the maximum numbers of bits each RGB channel can have. For example, a 24 bit (8 bit grayscale) scanner can have 2^{24} different colors and 2^8 shades of gray. A scanner with a high bbp can capture more information in dark and light areas of the image than a scanner with a lower bpp. However, note that it's very common to cheat with this value, and there are very few scanners today that are 30 bit or higher in reality.

- **Optical resolution:** Typically specified as 600x600 ppi (or dpi). This expression is often used for the optical sampling rate of the scanner in X-direction (across the page) and the maximum hardware sampling rate in Y-direction (down the page). The important factor is the X-direction to the *optical sampling rate* (more commonly referred to as **resolution**). As with *bit depth*, it's very easy to cheat with those values, and today, very few flatbed scanners are truly capable of producing 1,200 ppi or higher.
- **Hardware resolution:** Typically specified as 2,800x2,800 dpi (for a flatbed scanner). This value is normally the maximum hardware *interpolation* that the scanner can deliver. As you may realize, this figure is of little interest because it doesn't tell us how good the scanner is at resolving details.
- **Maximum resolution:** Typically specified as 9,600 dpi. In nearly all cases, this term refers to the maximum *interpolation* that the bundled scanner *software* is capable of producing. This is a figure of no interest at all. You can make a better job in Gimp and it's only limited by diskspace storage. Furthermore, every interpolation exceeding 3 times the image size is very questionable and something that we don't recommend.

Bit Depth

Let us consider this example; we have a 24 bit scanner (8 bit grayscale) and a 30 bit scanner (10 bit grayscale). In the 24 bit scanner the signal-noise ratio is 1:X. Noise is false or incorrect scanning information, and signal noise ratio is the ratio between the signal and how much noise the signal carries. If the advertised 30 bit scanner is indeed a 30 bit scanner, then the signal-noise ratio must be decreased to a fourth of the noise factor X in the 24 bit scanner.

The scanner manufacturer can achieve that end in several ways: The light source intensity can be increased, a more sensitive CCD (the device that captures the image) can be used or a longer exposure time could be implemented (i.e., make the scanner move slower in order to capture more "light").

The first two alternatives are expensive and the third is no good because it will slow down the scanning and the CCD will get too much light. The best thing is probably to integrate a more sensitive CCD and a better lamp, but as we mentioned, it costs.

The signal in a scanner is analog and it's converted to a digital signal by an AD (analog-to-digital) converter. In an 8 bit (24 bit color) scanner this is done with an 8 bit AD converter and in a 10 bit (30 bit color) scanner this is done with a 10 bit AD converter.

Since bpp is a sales argument these days, the simplest way for the manufacturer to improve a system is to just buy a new 10 bit AD converter and not bother to adjust the rest of the system (this is naturally the worst-case scenario), and all you'll get for your money is 2 bit of extra noise instead of 2 bit of extra details.

This is not necessarily true for all 30 bit scanners, but it's a reminder that you can't take bpp figures for granted.

Optical Resolution

You can apply the same conclusions for optical resolution as for bit depth when you want to increase the optical resolution from, for example, 300x300 to 600x600, because the light gathered by a pixel in a 600 ppi scanner is 1/4 of the light in a 300 ppi scanner.

Again, the light source and the CCD device are the bottlenecks that must be replaced in order to achieve a higher resolution. The manufacturer must include a new CCD to increase the optical sampling rate, but he may choose to get a CCD of lower quality.

Why Are Some Scanners Cheaper Than Others?

Given these facts we can easily understand why two different 600x600 optical resolution scanners can have very different price tags. The more expensive ones (besides the added cost of a well-known brand) are most likely to have much better CCD, lamp, optical lenses and mechanics, and they will also most likely be provided with better electronic contrivances inside.

The truth is that most cheap scanners with excellent specifications will not match your expectations. A good 300 ppi scanner may well do a much better job of computing details than a 600 ppi scanner with a lower price tag.

Different Types Of Scanners

So far we have only discussed scanners in general, as if all scanners were flatbed scanners. There are naturally other types of scanners:

- **Handheld scanners:** This is the sort of scanner that you drag by hand over a page in order to capture the image. Handheld scanners were quite popular several years ago, when flatbed scanners were expensive. This type of scanner will not even be able to stand up to very modest demands, such as scanning images for the web. However, if you are into mobile computers, then this type of device can be of interest, because you can take it with you and make fast, sketch-quality scans of documents or a page in a book.
- **Sheetfed scanners:** These are scanners of fax-type; you feed your image or paper into a slot. This is the most common type of scanner for fax machines (yes, a fax is in fact a scanner). This type of scanner can be used to scan simple text documents, but it is obviously not suitable for acquiring images for Gimp.
- **Flatbed scanners:** These are the most versatile of the scanner types described here. They resemble a copy machine, since they also have a platen (the optical document glass) where you place your original. It is

probably this type of scanner you will need for scanning images and drawings for Gimp. The only disadvantage is the size; a flatbed scanner is big and cumbersome compared to the other scanner types.

- **Slide and Film scanners:** These are specialized for scanning 35mm negatives or positive film strips. The usage is limited to this type of original, but it's a very useful device if you're a photographer. The quality of the scan is also much better than the quality that you can get from scanning a paper copy in a flatbed scanner. We will discuss this type of scanner a bit later in the chapter, because some rules don't apply to this type of scanner. This is the scanner to get if you both like to take photos and work with Gimp.
- **Drum scanners:** These are expensive scanners for professional work, and the price is beyond most people's reach. A drum scanner will produce top-quality, high-resolution images. If you need that type of quality, you can always buy it from a service bureau. If you are working with desktop publishing, you can work with low-resolution scans until the last stage when you order the high-quality drum scans from a service bureau.

The conclusion is that the best choice of scanner, for an image manipulation program like Gimp, is a flatbed scanner. Optionally, you can get a slide scanner if you like to be able to scan slides or negatives.

What Scanner Quality Do You Need?

The recommendations in this section aren't absolute, we are just trying to make your scanner choice a little bit easier by providing some general information. Note that Gimp doesn't support higher bit depth than 8 bit grayscale and 24 bit color even if Sane supports higher bit depths. Assuming that the ppi and bpp specifications are correct (which they often aren't), we can give you the following advice:

300 ppi Scanner

- Scanning of photographs 1:1 scale and 2 to 4 times real enlargement
- Scanning of logos, low-end drawings and artwork
- Scanning for usage in web pages
- Scanning for faxing, OCR, document storage and to use as a copy machine for your printer

600 ppi Scanner

- Scanning of photographs for real enlargement beyond 4 times
- Scanning of drawings for high-quality reproduction or enlargement
- Scanning of large transparencies such as 2x2 and 4x5; note that you'll need a transparency-enabled scanner

1,200 ppi (Or More) Scanner

- Scanning of 35mm slides or negatives

24 bpp Scanner

- Scanning of photographs
- Scanning of drawings and artwork
- Scanning for web publishing

30 bpp Scanner

- Scanning of bad photographs; e.g., under- or overexposed photos
- Scanning of slides and negatives

36 bpp Scanner

- If you are a professional, you might use a 36 bpp scanner for scanning large slides

PRICES

The prices of scanners are falling constantly, so keep in mind that these guidelines may not be accurate if you read this passage after 1999, when this edition was published.

- **Flatbed scanner for non-professional work:** You can find a good letter scanner for less than $500. If the retail price falls below $175, the scanner's quality is questionable.
- **Professional flatbed scanners:** You will get a really good letter scanner for around $700 and up.

Prices may be dropping, but what won't change as fast is the fact that really cheap scanners are often not much more than cheap junk. Cheap scanners are also often parallel port scanners, which aren't supported very well under Linux/UNIX.

SCSI CARDS

Keep in mind that the SCSI card that comes with the scanner is often useless in a Linux/UNIX environment, because there are no drivers for it. You can get a nice cheap SCSI card that is supported by Linux for around $50 to $100. On UNIX workstations, SCSI is more or less standard; all Sun workstations (except Ultra 5 and 10) come with a SCSI interface.

Remember to assign a high SCSI-id to your scanner (since it doesn't need a low SCSI-id, which has a faster response time). Some scanner SCSI interfaces are also of *SCSI one* standard, and should be placed at the end of the SCSI chain.

SUMMARY

- For the average user, a 600 ppi, 24 or 30 bpp scanner will suffice for almost any job.
- It's often better to buy a more-expensive, but lower-specified scanner than a cheap one with higher figures, because those figures are likely to be bogus.
- Don't buy an ultra cheap scanner, you will soon come to regret it.
- Buy a flatbed scanner if you aren't into photography, in which case a dedicated slide scanner is a good option.
- Even if you are a professional graphic artist, you may not need a very expensive professional scanner. If you are working with web publishing, you definitely won't need it. If you plan to use the scanned images as a component or base for further image manipulating, then you might be satisfied with the result of a good scanner and not need to invest in an advanced professional scanner.
- If you don't use Windows or a Mac, you don't need to pay attention to bundled software, and the quality of that software. However, if you do use Windows or a Mac, then the scanner software is of high importance.

INSTALLING SANE

Compiling and installing Sane isn't difficult. The part that can be a bit more troublesome is the configuration, especially the configuration that enables network scanning.

One of the smartest things about Sane is the network interface, which allows several graphic workstations to share a common scanner, which is attached to one of them. This is very practical; having a dedicated workstation just for scanning can be very distressing in a busy office.

SCSI MODULES

The fist task you must take on is to install a generic SCSI module driver under Solaris or to load a generic SCSI module under Linux (alternatively recompiling your kernel to support generic SCSI access).

Without a generic SCSI interface (which is provided by the generic SCSI module), Sane will not be able to send SCSI commands to the scanner, and you will not be able to scan.

Solaris 2.x

There are at least two generic SCSI drivers for Solaris. One that is free, made by Joerg Schilling, and one that you have to pay for, made by Kevin Sheehan. The commercial SCSI driver is more secure, but with some configuration, we can work around that problem in the free version. In this chapter, we will describe how to install the free SCSI driver.

First of all, download the SCSI driver; see "Sane" on page 881 for a download location. Note that if you have a Solaris 7 system, you have to follow *Joerg Schilling's* instructions. We will provide you with information for Solaris 2.4 to 2.6.

If you have a Sparc system; download `SCHILYscg.sparc.tar.Z`, and if you use SolarisX86 on a PC, download `SCHILYscg.i386.tar.Z`.

Here is a guideline to help you install the driver.

```
[olof@whopp olof]$ uncompress SCHILYscg.sparc.tar.Z
[olof@whopp olof]$ tar -xf SCHILYscg.sparc.tar
[olof@whopp olof]$ su
Note: You must provide the root password here.
[root@whopp olof]# pkgadd -d .

The following packages are available:
  1  SCHILYscg     SCSI General Driver
                   (sparc) 3.1

Select package(s) you wish to process (or 'all' to process all
packages). (default: all) [?,??,q]:
Note: Answer "1" and press Enter.
Processing package instance <SCHILYscg> from </home/olof>

SCSI General Driver
(sparc) 3.1
  Copyright 1995 Joerg Schilling, all rights reserved.

The author is not deemed to have made any representations as to
the suitability of this software for any purpose nor is held
responsible for any defects of this software.
THERE IS ABSOLUTELY NO WARRANTY FOR THIS SOFTWARE.

Where should the driver objects be installed [/kernel/drv] [?,q]
Note: Just hit Enter.
```

```
It will be necessary to do a reconfiguration reboot after driver
installation. Execute 'reboot -- -r' to reboot after installation.

## Processing package information.
## Processing system information.
## Verifying disk space requirements.
## Checking for conflicts with packages already installed.
## Checking for setuid/setgid programs.

This package contains scripts which will be executed with
super-user permission during the process of installing this
package.

Do you want to continue the installation of <SCHILYscg> [y,n,?]
Note: Answer "y" and hit Enter.
Installing SCSI General Driver as <SCHILYscg>

## Installing part 1 of 1.
[ verifying class <devlink> ]
/kernel/drv/scg
/kernel/drv/scg.conf
/usr/include/sys/scsi/targets/scgio.h
[ verifying class <drv> ]
## Executing postinstall script.

Installation of <SCHILYscg> was successful.

The following packages are available:
  1  SCHILYscg     SCSI General Driver
                   (sparc) 3.1

Select package(s) you wish to process (or 'all' to process
all packages). (default: all) [?,??,q]:
Note: Answer "q" and hit Enter. The driver is now installed.
```

If you work with an X86 system, just substitute `SCHILYscg.i386` for `SCHILYscg.sparc`.

All you have to do now is reboot to reconfigure your driver settings, and to rebuild `/dev`. This operation will be executed automatically in Solaris if you enter the following commands:

```
[olof@whopp olof]$ su
Note: You must provide the root password here.
[root@whopp olof]# touch /reconfigure
[root@whopp olof]# init 6
Note: The system will now reboot when the machine is up and work-
ing and you've logged in.
[root@whopp olof]# su
[root@whopp olof]# rm -f /reconfigure
```

The driver is now ready to use; we will configure the driver interface later: See "Setting Device Permissions" on page 238. But for now, this is all we have to do.

Linux

There are two options in Linux: either you load a generic SCSI module (recommended) or you recompile your kernel with generic SCSI support. Recompiling your kernel is beyond the scope of this book. We will describe how to load the **generic SCSI** module.

You must also have a Linux-supported SCSI card, and please remember that most SCSI cards that come with the scanner aren't supported by Linux. We will not describe how to enable your SCSI card; you have to check in your Linux distribution manual or in the **Linux SCSI How-to**. See "Sane" on page 881. Here is how to load the SCSI module:

```
[olof@whopp olof]$ su
Note: You must provide the root password here.
[root@whopp olof]# insmod /lib/modules/2.0.36-0.7/scsi/sg.o
[root@whopp olof]#
```

The example above is from Red Hat Linux 5.2, so it may be different if you have another distribution. The key value is `2.0.36-0.7`, which must be replaced with your kernel version (if your distribution uses **rpm** it will probably also have an rpm version number like the `-0.7` above). Use `uname` to find out your kernel version:

```
[olof@whopp olof]$ uname -r
2.0.36
[olof@whopp olof]$
Note: In this case the kernel version in use is 2.0.36.
```

When you have loaded the module without any problems, it may be wise to put it in a *start up* file, like `rc.local`, to ensure that you load your module every time you restart your Linux computer.

Here is an example from a RedHat Linux 5.2 `/etc/rc.d/rc.local` file. The `insmod` of the **sg** module is executed in the last line of the file:

```
    echo "$R" >> /etc/issue
    echo "Kernel $(uname -r) on $a $(uname -m)" >> /etc/issue

    cp -f /etc/issue /etc/issue.net
    echo >> /etc/issue
fi

insmod sg
```

Note that this is not the preferred way to load a generic SCSI module. Modern Linux kernels can use a *load-on-demand* schedule in which the module is loaded only when it's needed, i.e., when you want to scan. Consult your Linux distribution manual for instructions on how to enable this feature. Otherwise, just use **kedit** or **gedit** to edit the file *(you must be the root user to edit the rc.local file).*

Configuring For Compiling

It's quite easy to configure and build Sane — just remember that you will need the development **header** files when you compile, not just the needed libraries. Take a look at "Compiling Plug-ins" starting on page 769 for general tips if you have problems compiling or configuring Sane.

- First of all, you must **download** Sane, see "Sane" on page 881 for where to get your copy of Sane.
- **Configuring** Sane to make it ready for compilation is easy. All you have to do is to run `./configure` in the Sane distribution directory. Because we will use Sane with **Gimp** and **Gtk** (the toolkit library that Gimp needs to show items such as menus), we will have to provide Sane with a configure program where Gtk is installed.

- To find out if Gtk and Gimp are installed under `/usr` or `/usr/local` enter: `which gimp`, and this command will echo either `/usr/bin/gimp` or `/usr/local/bin/gimp`. You don't need to tell Sane's configure program anything. It will find Gimp and Gtk anyway.
- However, if you have installed Gtk and Gimp somewhere else, such as `/opt/gimp`, then you will have to provide the configure program with that information. If you run into problems when you configure, you can examine the `config.log` file present in the same directory as `configure`. You can also invoke `configure` with `--help` like this:

  ```
  ./configure --help
  ```

  and configure will display all of its options.

Here is an example of how to **extract** and **configure** Sane:

```
[olof@whopp olof]$ gunzip sane-1.0.1.tar.gz
[olof@whopp olof]$ tar xvf sane-1.0.1.tar
[olof@whopp olof]$ cd sane-1.0.1
[olof@whopp sane-1.0.1]$ ./configure \
--with-gtk-prefix=/opt/gimp  --disable-gtktest
```

If Gimp Is Not Installed In A Standard Directory

If you have Gimp in a standard location, i.e., `/usr` or `/usr/local`, Sane's configure program will find Gimp automatically. When you have compiled Sane, it will be able to function as a Gimp plug-in.

If you have Gimp installed somewhere else, such as `/opt/gimp`, Sane's configure program will not find Gimp, and the possibility to compile and later run Sane as a plug-in to Gimp will be disabled.

However, if both Gimp and Gtk are installed under the same location, this is very easy to fix. Just edit the **Makefile** in the **frontend** directory in Sane with gedit (or kedit). You'll find `frontend/Makefile` in the top directory in the Sane distribution directory.

You have to add `-DHAVE_LIBGIMP_GIMP_H` in the `CPPFLAGS` line and `-lgimp` in the `GIMP_LIBS` line.

Here is an example of how it looked after adding these command lines:

```
INCLUDES = -I. -I$(srcdir) -I$(top_builddir)/include -
I$(top_srcdir)/include \
        -I/usr/local/include -I/opt/gimp/lib/glib/include -I/opt/
gimp/include -
I/usr/X11R6/include
DEFS = -DHAVE_CONFIG_H
CPPFLAGS =  -D_GNU_SOURCE -DHAVE_LIBGIMP_GIMP_H  \
-DHAVE_LIBGIMP_GIMP_H
Note: Here is the line we changed. Notice that you must not remove
any entries in the line, just add the "-DHAVE_LIBGIMP_GIMP_H" .
You must also add -lgimp to the GIMP_LIBS line:
GIMP_LIBS = -lgimp
```

Preparing For Security

Well, we don't want to jump ahead, but there are some adjustments you can do now that will enable you to raise the security level later on.

You may have *dependent* libraries in *non-standard* locations, for example, Gimp and Gtk could be installed under `/opt/gimp`, and `libjpeg` could be installed under `/usr/local`.

After having raised the *security* by enabling **sgid** (**s**et **g**roup **id** on execution) on the scanner program, the scanning program (e.g., **xscanimage**) will not find all of the libraries that it needs, because they are located outside the standard library directories. Why? Well, when you read "Setting Device Permissions" on page 238 you will understand what we are doing here.

- On **Solaris**, *outside standard libraries* means outside `/usr/lib` or `/lib`.
- Under **Linux**, you have to check the `/etc/ld.so.conf file` to find out which standard directories will be searched for library files when the scanning program starts.

The solution is to add the command `-R/where-you-have-libraries` when you **link** your program.

In the following example we will include:

```
-R/usr/local/lib
```

in the `LIBS` line in the **Makefile** (in the *frontend* directory). Because we had Gtk and Gimp installed under `/opt/gimp`, we must also add `-R/opt/gimp/lib` to the `GTK_LIBS` line.

```
LIBS = -R/usr/local/lib -ldl -lsocket -lnsl -ljpeg -lintl -lm
GTK_LIBS = -L/opt/gimp/lib -L/opt/X11R6.3/lib/ \
-R/opt/X11R6.3/lib/ -R/opt/gimp/lib  -lgtk -lgdk -lglib \
-lXi -lXext -lX11 -lsocket -lnsl -lm
GIMP_LIBS = -lgimp
```

It's very easy to find out if any libraries are missing. Just enter `ldd`, for example, `ldd xscanimage`, after the program has been built and "sgid'ed", and `ldd` will tell you which libraries the program can't find.

All you have to do now is include the directory where the library is with a `-R` in the Makefile (in the frontend directory).

Run `make clean` and then `make` in the frontend directory. This will rebuild the program and find the dependent libraries.

Compiling

You must have **make**, **gcc** or **cc** (the compiler), **ld**, etc., in your *path*. Under Solaris those tools are in the `/usr/ccs/bin` directory, and that directory must be in your path.

gcc must also be in your path, and you have to find out under which directory it is installed (this depends on which precompiled version of gcc you downloaded). When you know the gcc directory (in this example, gcc was installed under `/usr/local`), enter:

`export PATH=/usr/ccs/bin:/usr/local/bin:$PATH`

In Linux, this is no problem as long as you have installed the necessary programs; they will be in your path automatically.

If you have problems later on, when running Sane, you can add the following flags when you run configure:

`--disable-shared`, `--disable-dynamic` and `--enable-preload`

Normally, you don't need to do that under Linux or Solaris.

You are now ready to build and install Sane. The configuration above will install Sane under `/usr/local`. To change it, use:

`--prefix=/where/to/install/sane`

Lets build and install Sane:

```
[olof@whopp sane-1.0.1]$ make
[olof@whopp sane-1.0.1]$ su root -c "make install"
Note: You must provide the root password here.
```

Sane will now hopefully be installed under `/usr/local`. If you have experienced any problems, you can read "Compiling Plug-ins" starting on page 769 to get more information on how to compile in general.

RUNTIME CONFIGURE

Before you can use Sane to scan on your local workstation (we will discuss network scanning under "Network Access" on page 241), you will need to *configure* Sane. Sane's configure files are located under `/usr/local/etc/sane.d/` if you installed it under `/usr/local`.

To help you find out which device your scanner is attached to, and what type of scanner you have, the Sane team has created a program called **find-scanner**. This program is located in the *tools* directory in the Sane distribution directory (in the tools directory in the main directory where you compiled Sane). `Find-scanner` will locate your scanner and find out what model it is.

Here is how it can look under Solaris

```
[olof@whopp sane-1.0.1]$ su
Note: You must provide the root password here.
[root@whopp sane-1.0.1]# tools/find-scanner
# You may want to run this program as super-user to find all
# devices. Once you found the scanner devices, be sure to adjust
# access permissions as necessary.

find-scanner: found processor "HP C5100A R032" at device \
/dev/scg0c
find-scanner: found scanner "UMAX Astra 1200S V1.3" at device \
/dev/scg0e
```

And here is how it can look under Linux:

```
[olof@whopp sane-1.0.1]$ su
Note: You must provide the root password here.
[root@whopp sane-1.0.1]# tools/find-scanner
# You may want to run this program as super-user to find all
# devices. Once you found the scanner devices, be sure to adjust
# access permissions as necessary.

find-scanner: found processor "HP C5100A R032" at device \
/dev/sg0
find-scanner: found scanner "UMAX Astra 1200S V1.3" at device \
/dev/sg1
```

This tells us that we have an **HP** scanner under `/dev/scg0c` (or `/dev/sg0` for Linux) and a **UMAX** scanner under `/dev/scg0e` (or `sg1` for Linux). All we have to do now is configure Sane to query `/dev/scg0c` for the HP scanner and `/dev/scg0e` for the UMAX scanner. Before you proceed, it is advisable to test if Sane works as it should: `cd` down to `/usr/local/etc/sane.d/` and as root user (`su root`) edit `dll.conf` and comment out every line except the `pnm` line.

Here is an example of a bit of the file:

```
#microtek2
#mustek
#pint
pnm
#qcam
#ricoh
#s9036
```

Now, run `/usr/local/bin/xscanimage` as user root:

```
[olof@whopp olof]$ xhost localhost
localhost being added to access control list
[olof@whopp olof]$ su
Note: You must provide the root password here.
[root@whopp olof]# /usr/local/bin/xscanimage --display \
localhost:0.0
```

If Sane works (the dynamic loading of modules), a dialog will appear where you can set which pnm device to use. Click OK and continue. You will now access xscanimage's main scanner window.

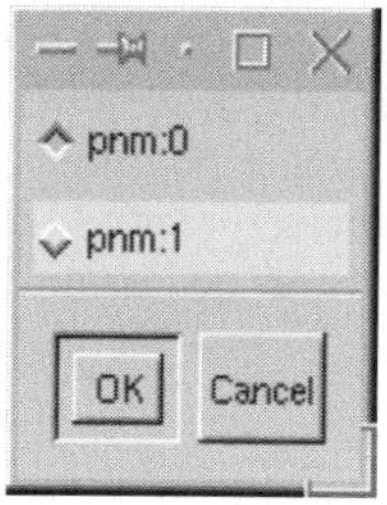

Figure 15.1 *The device dialog*

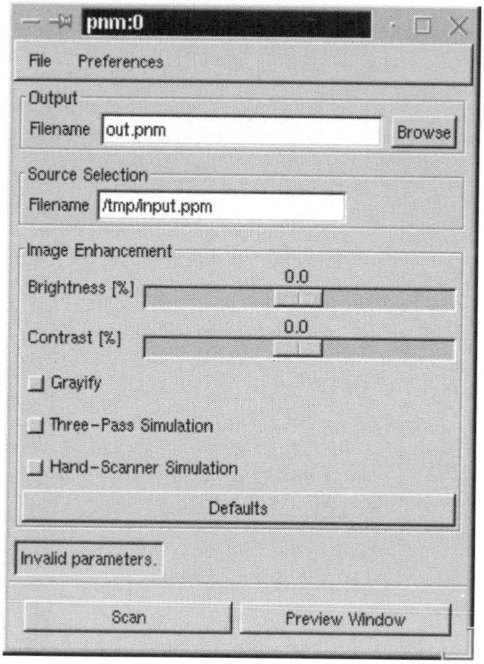

Figure 15.2 *Xscanimage's main scanner window for the pnm test interface*

If these dialogs appear, Sane is probably working just fine. Now, edit the `dll.conf` file and remove the # from hp and umax and comment out `pnm`. If you have another brand of scanner you should of course not use the hp or umax entries; instead, remove # from your scanner brand. Also check the compatibility list, see the Sane scanner list on page 870, because sometimes, for example, a Nikon scanner is really a UMAX scanner with a Nikon brand. The compatibility list will tell you exactly which entry to uncomment.

Now, it's time to use the device information extracted from `find-scanner`. If you installed Sane under `/usr/local/` you will find a `config` file for all backends (scanners) supported by Sane in the `/usr/local/etc/sane.d` directory (otherwise, `/where/you/installed/Sane/etc/sane.d/`).

In our case, we have to edit `hp.conf` and `umax.conf`. The changes in the config file regard what device that the scanner is attached to, such as `/dev/sg1` (Linux) or `/dev/scg0c` (Solaris). Note that if you uncommented epson instead of hp and umax in the `dll.conf` file, then you have to edit the `epson.conf` file instead.

Here is an example from our umax.conf file:

```
scsi UMAX * Scanner
scsi LinoHell Office
scsi LinoHell Office2
scsi LinoHell SAPHIR2
scsi Nikon AX-210
/dev/scg0e
```

The last line tells the scanner that your scanner is attached to /dev/scg0e. Normally when you install Sane from scratch, this line will say /dev/scanner. All you have to do is exchange /dev/scanner with your interface.

Still as root, run /usr/local/bin/xscanimage. Because we have two scanners, we will get a device dialog just like the one we got for the pnm test devices. Just click OK; this tests that everything is working. If everything is fully functional, you will access the main scanner interface for your scanner.

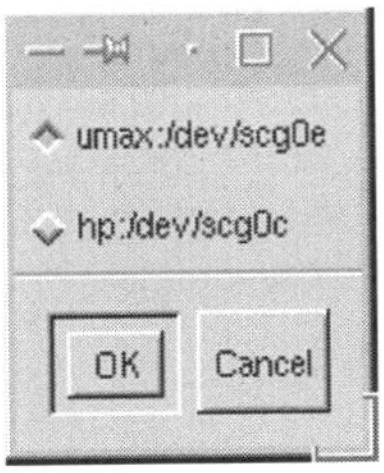

Figure 15.3 *The device dialog for the UMAX scanner and the HP slide scanner*

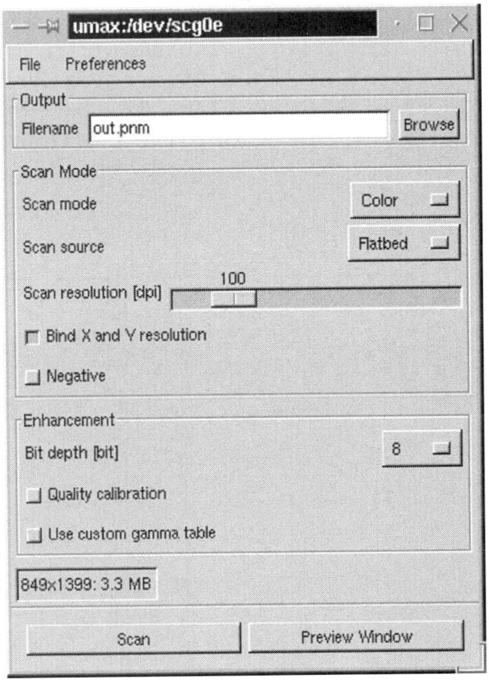

Figure 15.4 *The main scanner window for the UMAX interface*

Setting Device Permissions

The problem that we have to face now is that no ordinary user can scan, because `/dev/sg1` or `/dev/scg0` is owned by root, and only root has the authority to read and write. Under Linux, this is no big problem, but under the Solaris interface, it's a bit more troublesome. All you have to do under Linux is change the access rights from `/dev/sg1` to `777`, and everyone will be able to scan.

Here is how to do it in a shell:

```
[olof@whopp olof]$ su root -c "chmod 777 /dev/sg1"
```

Note: You have to type the root password here.

The problem is that if you do the same on the Solaris interface, *everyone* will have the right to write and read to *every* device on that SCSI interface. This means that if you have SCSI disks on the same interface, someone (or you by mistake) can send an *"erase everything"* command to one of your disks. As you probably understand, this is not a good solution for solving this problem.

The answer is to create a special user and group that have read and write access to the device, e.g., `/dev/scg0`. Then, you let the system automatically set the group ID to that special scanner group every time you invoke a scanner command. We must enable sgid (set group id on execution) on every scanner program.

This is also the safe way to do it under Linux. Also, you will need the user and group to enable network scanning later on.

Adding a user is beyond the scope of this book, because there are a lot of ways to manage users. Please consult your operating system's manual. A good hint is to read the `useradd` manual page. Remember to lock the account so that no one can log in as the new user. Let's say that you have created a new user Sane, and a group Sane.

Under Linux, enter:

```
[olof@whopp olof]$ su
Note: You must provide the root password here.
[root@whopp olof]# chown sane:sane /dev/sg1
[root@whopp olof]# chmod 660 /dev/sg1
[root@whopp olof]# chown root:sane /usr/local/bin/xscanimage
[root@whopp olof]# chmod 2755 /usr/local/bin/xscanimage
[root@whopp olof]# chown root:sane /usr/local/bin/scanimage
[root@whopp olof]# chmod 2755 /usr/local/bin/scanimage
[root@whopp olof]# chown root:sane /usr/local/bin/xcam
[root@whopp olof]# chmod 2755 /usr/local/bin/xcam
```

Doing the same thing under Solaris will include finding out the real device name of `scg0`. Solaris keeps all real devices under `/devices`. The `/dev` directory only holds symbolic links to the real device.

This example will show you how to find out the real device name. Notice that we do it on `scg0`. The "e" in `scg0e` is only the SCSI id; "e" in this case means that our scanner has SCSI id 4.

```
[olof@whopp olof]$ ls -l /dev/scg0
lrwxrwxrwx   1 root     other        81 Apr 19 14:53 /dev/scg0 ->
../devices/iommu@f,e0000000/sbus@f,e0001000/espdma@f, \
400000/esp@f,800000/scg@0,0:
Now we chown and chmod the real interface.
Note: "\" means that there is no line break.
[olof@whopp olof]$ su
Note: You must provide the root password here.
[root@whopp olof]# chown sane:sane /devices/iommu@f, \
e0000000/sbus@f,e0001000/espdma@f,400000/esp@f,800000/scg@0,0:
[root@whopp olof]# chmod 660 /devices/iommu@f, \
e0000000/sbus@f,e0001000/espdma@f,400000/esp@f,800000/scg@0,0:
```

The rest is like the Linux example. You can now try to run the xscanimage program as an ordinary user. If you added the right directories with the `-R` flag when you compiled Sane, everything will work fine. But you may get this kind of error:

```
ld.so.1: /opt/gtk1/bin/xscanimage fatal: libjpeg.so.62: can't \
open file: errno=2  Killed
```

This means that when you compiled xscanimage, you forgot to add all directories (with the `-R` flag) that have libraries that xscanimage needs. (See "Preparing For Security" on page 232). To find out whether any more libraries are missing, invoke `ldd`, like this:

```
[olof@tinyjump olof]$ ldd /opt/gtk1/bin/xscanimage
        libsane.so.1 =>  /opt/gtk1//lib/libsane.so.1
        libgimp.so.1 =>  /opt/gtk1//lib/libgimp.so.1
        libgtk.so.1 =>   /opt/gtk1//lib/libgtk.so.1
        libgdk.so.1 =>   /opt/gtk1//lib/libgdk.so.1
        libglib.so.1 =>  /opt/gtk1//lib/libglib.so.1
        libXi.so.6.0 =>  /opt/X11R6.3/lib//libXi.so.6.0
        libXext.so.6.3 =>        /opt/X11R6.3/lib//libXext.so.6.3
        libX11.so.6.1 =>         /opt/X11R6.3/lib//libX11.so.6.1
        libsocket.so.1 =>        /usr/lib/libsocket.so.1
        libnsl.so.1 =>   /usr/lib/libnsl.so.1
        libm.so.1 =>     /usr/lib/libm.so.1
        libdl.so.1 =>    /usr/lib/libdl.so.1
        libjpeg.so.62 =>         (not found)
        libintl.so.1 =>  /usr/lib/libintl.so.1
        libc.so.1 =>     /usr/lib/libc.so.1
```

As you see, only the jpeg library wasn't found, but naturally, many more libraries could have been missing. You'll never know, until you run `ldd` on the program.

Now, you must find out where the missing library is installed on your system. When you have that information, you can rebuild the scanner program: `cd` to the Sane distribution directory (i.e., the directory where you build Sane). Edit the `frontend/Makefile` and include the missing directory (the one where the jpeg library is) with a `-R` flag, as you did in "Preparing For Security" on page 232.

When you have edited the `frontend/Makefile`, enter:

```
[olof@whopp sane-1.0.1]$ cd frontend && make clean && make
[olof@whopp frontend]$ su -c "make install"
Note: You must provide the root password here.
```

After that, you have to run chmod and chown in the scanner programs (the permission and owner of the files are not the same, because you have recompiled and installed them):

```
[olof@whopp olof]$ su
Note: You must provide the root password here.
[root@whopp olof]# chown sane:sane /dev/sg1
[root@whopp olof]# chmod 660 /dev/sg1
[root@whopp olof]# chown root:sane /usr/local/bin/xscanimage
[root@whopp olof]# chmod 2755 /usr/local/bin/xscanimage
[root@whopp olof]# chown root:sane /usr/local/bin/scanimage
[root@whopp olof]# chmod 2755 /usr/local/bin/scanimage
[root@whopp olof]# chown root:sane /usr/local/bin/xcam
[root@whopp olof]# chmod 2755 /usr/local/bin/xcam
```

Sane should work now. If it fails anyway, you'll have to check everything again and make sure that you didn't make any mistakes.

Network Access

One of the most amazing capacities of Sane is that you can scan over the network. In fact, every Sane-controlled scanner can be a network scanner. To make this work, you have to configure both the clients (the workstations that will use the network scanner) and the Sane server (i.e., the scanner server).

This involves:

- Setting up network access rules for Sane
- Configuring server start-up through the inetd super server
- Configuring your scanner clients to request scanning from the right hosts

Inetd — The Super Server

The easiest way to create a Sane network server is to use **inetd**. Inetd is the server that provides you with Telnet (or rlogin). Every time you make a Telnet (or rlogin) to a host, the inetd server on that host starts the Telnet (or rlogin) server on the same host to answer your Telnet (or rlogin) demand.

To enable the **saned** scanner server to start (on client request), you have to edit the `/etc/inetd.conf` file by adding *saned* as a server that *inetd* should start when a client wants to scan over the network.

You also have to edit the `/etc/services` file on both clients and Sane servers to include the new scanner service.

There are inetd servers *with* **tcp wrappers** (standard on most Linux distributions) and *without* tcp wrappers. (Tcp wrappers are used as a way of controlling the access rights of all your inetd controlled servers). The configuration entry in the `inetd.conf` file is slightly different in these two versions.

This is how it will look in `/etc/inetd.conf` if you don't have tcp wrappers:

```
sane stream tcp nowait sane.sane /usr/local/sbin/saned saned
```

and this is how it looks when you have tcp wrappers:

```
sane stream tcp nowait sane.sane /usr/sbin/tcpd/usr/local/sbin/saned
```

Just add the appropriate line at the end of your `/etc/inetd.conf` file, using your favorite editor such as kedit or gedit. Remember that you must be *root* when you perform this operation. Did you also notice the *sane user* and *sane group* in the `inetd.conf` lines above? It is not very smart to run *saned* as root. If you do you will open security holes that hackers can use to compromise the workstation security.

Note that Solaris only accepts *user,* not *group* in the `/etc/inetd.conf` file. Just remove "`.sane`" from the `inetd.conf` lines above.

The /etc/services File

The next step is to add a line in `/etc/services` to tell which port to use when you want Sane to start up (the closest non-technical comparison would be a *door*; in order to talk to the right person, you must know on which door you should knock). This needs to be done on both clients and servers. Here is the line to add to the end of your `/etc/services` file :

```
sane 6566/tcp # SANE network scanner daemon
```

All you have to do now is restart the **inetd** server. This is done by sending a `SIGHUP` signal to the server. First, you have to find out the running inetd server's **pid** (every program running on a UNIX-like computer has a unique number pid for identification). This is how you do it:

Under Linux

```
[olof@whopp olof]$ ps aux | grep inetd
olof     10033  0.0  0.2   836   348  p9 S    21:47 0:00 grep inetd
root       290  0.0  0.0   776    76  ?  S    Apr 24 0:00 inetd
```

Under Solaris

```
[olof@tinyjump olof]$ ps -ef | grep inetd
```

Notice that it is the `root` line that you should read; the `olof` line is simply me using `grep` to reach for **inetd** in the program listing. Now, we will send the `SIGHUP` signal, and here is how to do it. Notice that your pid number may be different than the one in these examples:

Under Linux

```
[olof@whopp olof]$ su root -c "kill -SIGHUP 290"
Note: You have to provide the root password here
```

Under Solaris

```
[olof@whopp olof]$ su root -c "kill -SIGHUP 112"
Note: You have to provide the root password here
```

Access Control

There are now three ways of allowing hosts to access the *saned* server.

- `saned.conf`
- `/etc/hosts.equiv`
- `/etc/hosts.allow` and `/etc/hosts.deny` if you have tcp wrappers installed

You can use any of these methods, but `/etc/hosts.equiv` is the one that is most insecure. The `saned.conf` file present under `/usr/local/etc/sand.d/saned.conf` must be edited both for plain `saned.conf` access control and for tcp wrapper access control. For plain `saned.conf` access control, at the end of the file, simply add all the hosts that should be able to scan.

Here is an example of how it may look (host names are naturally site dependent):

```
# matching is NO LONGER case-sensitive.
#
#scan-client.somedomain.firm
#localhost
#
# NOTE: /etc/inetd.conf and /etc/services must also
# be properly configured to start the saned daemon as
# documented in saned(1), services(4) and inetd.conf(4)
#
# for example, /etc/services might contain a line:
# sane  6566/tcp        # network scanner daemon
#
# and /etc/inetd.conf might contain a line:
# sane stream tcp nowait root /usr/local/sbin/saned saned
whopp.frozenriver.nu
tinyjump.frozenriver.nu
ultra.frozenriver.nu
niceriver.frozenriver.nu
```

Here, we have enabled `localhost` (always wise to do that) plus some other host within the `frozenriver.nu` domain. If you don't use long hostnames, you only have to specify the short name; for example, `whopp.frozenriver.nu` will be written as "`whopp`" if you use short hostnames. The # shows that the line is a comment, and will therefore be ignored by the saned server.

If you have tcp wrappers installed, we recommend that you use them. The configuration of tcp wrappers is beyond the scope of this book, but you can read about it in the man pages; enter `man tcpd` and `man -S 5 hosts_access`. The `host_access` man page will describe in detail how to set up host access control with tcp wrappers. If you have tcp wrappers that haven't configured yet, now is the time to do it. The only thing you have to do after you have configured tcp wrappers is add a + sign at the end of `saned.conf`.

Here is an example of what the file will look like:

```
## NOTE: /etc/inetd.conf and /etc/services must also
# be properly configured to start the saned daemon as
# documented in saned(1), services(4) and inetd.conf(4)
#
# for example, /etc/services might contain a line:
# sane  6566/tcp        # network scanner daemon
#
# and /etc/inetd.conf might contain a line:
# sane stream tcp nowait root /usr/local/sbin/saned saned


+
```

The `/etc/hosts.equiv` file is a very unsafe way of controlling host access in Sane (or for that matter, all host access control to your workstation or server). It's a fast lane to lowering the security of your workstation.

Its purpose is to make it easy to log in to different UNIX workstations within a UNIX domain. The function makes sense if you are in a well-secured UNIX-only network.

Suppose that a user name is present on a remote UNIX computer (host, client) UNIX-like computer and on your workstation (server). If the remote login host is specified in the `/etc/hosts.equiv` file, this user will be able to make a remote login to your workstation without providing a password. Obviously, there is a security concern with the file. We recommend that you don't use a `/etc/hosts.equiv` file if your computer is connected to the Internet.

We assume that you will now have selected a safe way to enable secure scanner access to your workstation.

Network Client Configuration

Start by installing Sane on the network client, as we did in "Configuring For Compiling" on page 230. You also have to edit the `/etc/services` file, as we did in "The /etc/services File" on page 242, but you don't have to restart the inetd server.

Now, you have to edit the `/usr/local/etc/sane.d/dll.conf` file as root with your favorite editor, such as gedit or kedit. You have to remove the hashmark "#" that is present in the net line. It's also recommended to comment out all other lines with a hashmark. Here is how our `dll.conf` file looks at one of our clients (workstations):

```
# enable the next line if you want to allow access through the net
net
#abaton
#agfafocus
#apple
#artec
#canon
#coolscan
#dc25
#dc210
#dmc
#epson
```

The next file you have to edit is the `/usr/local/sane.d/net.conf` file. It is in this file that you specify which servers to call when you want to scan. Sane can't guess which hosts are provided with the Sane network scanning service. You can specify scanners on the server, but we suggest that you just put the hostname there, which will enable you to access all scanners on the Sane scanner server.

This is an example of a client `net.conf` file:

```
# This is the net config file.  Each line names a host to attach
# to. If you list "localhost" then your backends can be accessed
# either directly or through the net backend.  Going through the
# net backend may be necessary to access devices that need special
# privileges.
# localhost
tinyjump
```

If you use a long hostname, you have to exchange `tinyjump.frozenriver.nu` for `tinyjump` (naturally the name should match your Sane server's hostname).

You are now ready to test the network scanning with the `scanimage` program. Putting an `-L` flag in this command will list all available scanners, and you should be able to see your network scanner.

This is how it looks on our site:

```
[olof@whopp olof]$ /usr/local/bin/scanimage -L
device `net:tinyjump:umax:/dev/scg0e' is a UMAX Astra 1200S \
flatbed scanner
device `net:tinyjump:hp:/dev/scg0c' is a Hewlett-Packard C5100A \
flatbed scanner
```

If you get a similar list that shows the scanner(s) available on the Sane scanner server, you will know that network scanning is working.

Installing Xsane

Well, we could start using Sane right away. The default GUI to Sane which is called **xscanimage**, is nice, but there is a program that is even better — namely **Xsane**. Xsane has several advantages over xscanimage. It's easier to use and you can, for example, save gamma correction settings. Another nice thing with Xsane is that it allows you to use your scanner as a copy machine. Xscanimage is not as sophisticated; it's a bit more powerful, but also harder to use. Therefore, we will go ahead and show you how to configure and compile Xsane. Start by downloading Xsane; see "Sane" on page 881 for where to get your copy.

Configuring And Compiling

Xsane follows the same path as Sane when it comes to configuring and compiling. If you run into difficulties, please take a look at "Compiling Plug-ins" starting on page 769.

Configuring Xsane to make it ready for compilation is easy. All you have to do is run `./configure` in the Xsane distribution directory. Because we will use Xsane with Gimp and Gtk (the toolkit library that Gimp needs to show items such as menus), we will have to provide Sane with a configure program where we have Gtk installed. If Gtk and Gimp are installed under `/usr` or `/usr/local` running the command `which gimp` will render in either `/usr/bin/gimp` or `/usr/local/bin/gimp`.

You don't need to tell Xsane's configure program anything; it will find Gimp and Gtk anyway. But if you have installed Gtk and Gimp under another directory, such as `/opt/gimp`, then you will need to provide the configure program with that information.

This example shows how to extract and configure Xsane:

```
[olof@whopp olof]$ gunzip xsane-0.21.tar.gz
[olof@whopp olof]$ tar xsane-0.21.tar
[olof@whopp olof]$ cd xsane-0.21
[olof@whopp xsane-0.21]$ ./configure \
```

If you have installed Gimp in a non-standard directory (i.e., not `/usr/local` or `/usr`), it's the same story with Xsane as with Sane — configure will disable Gimp plug-in support. Since we will also run Xsane as a sgid-enabled program, we will have to include `-R/where/you/have/dependent/libraries` in the `frontend/Makefile` file, as we did in Sane.

Xsane is dependent on a few Sane libraries found under `/usr/local/lib/sane/` (if you installed Sane under `/usr/local`). This means that you have to include that directory with an `-R` flag in the Makefile.

Here is how the `frontend/Makefile` will look after it's changed:

```
CPPFLAGS = -D_GNU_SOURCE -DPATH_SANE_DATA_DIR=$(sanedatadir) \
-DV_MAJOR=0 -DV_MINOR=21\337 -DSANE_V_MAJOR=1 \
-DHAVE_LIBGIMP_GIMP_H
Note: We added -DHAVE_LIBGIMP_GIMP_H above.
CFLAGS = -O2 -fpcc-struct-return -mcpu=v8 -Wall
LDFLAGS =
LIBS = -lsane -ldl -ltiff -lpng -lz -ljpeg -lintl -lm \
-R/opt/gtk1/lib -R/opt/gtk1/lib/sane -R/usr/local/lib
Note: You can see that we have added several -R flags.
GTK_LIBS = -L/opt/gtk1//lib -L/opt/X11R6.3/lib/ \
-R/opt/X11R6.3/lib/ -lgtk -lgdk -lglib -lXi -lXext -lX11 -lsocket
-lnsl -lm
GIMP_LIBS = -lgimp
Note: The last change was to include the gimp library.
```

You can now build Xsane in the xsane distribution's top directory, and this is how it looks:

```
[olof@whopp xsane-0.21]$ make
[olof@whopp xsane-0.21]$ su root -c "make install"
Note: You must provide the root password here.
```

If you experience any problems, please read "Configuring For Compiling" on page 230, because the way of configuring and compiling described there is very similar.

Installing On A Server And A Network Client

The last thing you need to do before using Xsane is to *sgid* the xsane program file. Here is how you do it (it is just like what we did for Sane's program files):

```
[olof@whopp olof]$ su
Note: You must provide the root password here.
[root@whopp olof]# chown root:sane /usr/local/bin/xsane
[root@whopp olof]# chmod 2755 /usr/local/bin/xsane
```

You can now try to run Xsane as an ordinary user. If you want to use Xsane on scanner network clients, you will have to install Xsane there as well. It's no different from installing it on the Sane server, which we just did.

Using Sane In Gimp

You can, of course, use Sane (or more precisely, **xscanimage** and **Xsane**) as a stand-alone program, but using Sane with Gimp is so much better. Together with Gimp, xscanimage and Xsane will be much more powerful, because all of Gimp's image manipulation functions will be available. (The only exception is if you want to scan with a higher bit depth than 24 bit color or 8 bit grayscale.

The **xcam** program, which also comes with Sane, is for use with equipment like Connectix QuickCam, according to the Sane web site. We will not go into the usage of xcam in this book.

Scanimage is a CLI program, and we have used it to list available devices. Its field of application is, however, much wider. It can, for example, be used in shell scripts to achieve all sorts of things. Since it can't be used with Gimp, we will not discuss it further. There is, however, a very good man page in the Sane distribution. If you have the Sane man pages in your `MANPATH`, just enter the command `man scanimage` to access this information.

Installing The Plug-in

To use Xsane and xscanimage as Gimp plug-ins, you must install them as such. The easiest way (and the right way to do it) is to make a symbolic link from `xscanimage/xsane` to your Gimp plug-in directory. Here is how you do it (of course, the location of both Gimp plug-ins and Sane is site-specific):

```
[olof@whopp olof]$ su
Note: You have to provide the root password here.
[root@whopp olof]# ln -s /usr/local/bin/xscanimage \
/opt/gimp/lib/1.0/plug-ins/xscanimage
[root@whopp bin]# ln -s /usr/local/bin/xsane \
/opt/gimp/lib/1.0/plug-ins/xsane
```

Running Gimp With Sane

You will now be able to access Sane from Gimp. You only have to start (or restart) Gimp, and **Xsane** and **xscanimage** will act as plug-ins, letting us scan directly into Gimp where we can continue to edit the image.

Xsane can be accessed from `Xtns|xsane` and xscanimage is in `Xtns|Acquire Image`. Under each menu item you will find a list of the available devices (scanners). To use a scanner, you only have to select that device in the menu.

Notice that if you change the scanner configuration, you must remove the `pluginrc` file, and let Gimp rebuild it when it starts up the next time. Just enter `rm ~/.gimp/pluginrc`, restart Gimp and your new scanner (configuration) will be visible as a menu item under both Acquire Image and Xsane.

We have chosen to use Xsane and not xscanimage in the following examples, because Xsane introduces some very useful basic scanner manipulations. The principal advantage of xscanimage is that you can set the gamma correction curves manually, just like in the curve dialog under Gimp. This feature enables you to adjust the gamma curve in all directions, instead of specifying a fixed gamma value with a slider or in an input field.

Scanning With A Flatbed Scanner

We will describe how to scan with a UMAX Astra 1200S flatbed scanner. However, the chief functions in the scanner interface will be similar to what you'll find in many other flatbed scanners. Sane has adopted the standard approach to providing generic scanner functions, such as gamma correction, levels, ppi, bit depth, preview, etc. The ppi (resolution) and bpp (bit-depth) specifications are, of course, scanner-dependent, but all flatbed scanners operate in a similar fashion.

Essentially, things that differ among scanners are the special functions, such as the Photosmart scanner's ability to eject the filmstrip.

The Scanner Interface (UMAX)

Start up the Gimp UMAX Xsane interface; in our case, `Xtns|Xsane|net:tinyjump:umax'dev'scg0e`

You will now be presented with the main Xsane scanner interface. We will make a quick description of what all the controls and menus are about, starting from the top in the main dialog.

- The **Checkerboard** symbol menu determines the scan mode: Color, Grayscale or Lineart (Black&White). The number of possible choices in this menu depend on the capacity of your scanner.
- The **Scanner** symbol menu lets you specify the *scan source;* for example, if your scanner has a sheet feeder (don't touch this control menu if your scanner doesn't have any such options).
- The **Halftone dots** symbol slider controls the optical resolution in ppi (dpi).
- The Γ (**gamma**) slider sets gamma correction.
- The **Sun** control slider controls the scanning brightness.
- The **Half-moon** control slider controls the scanning contrast.

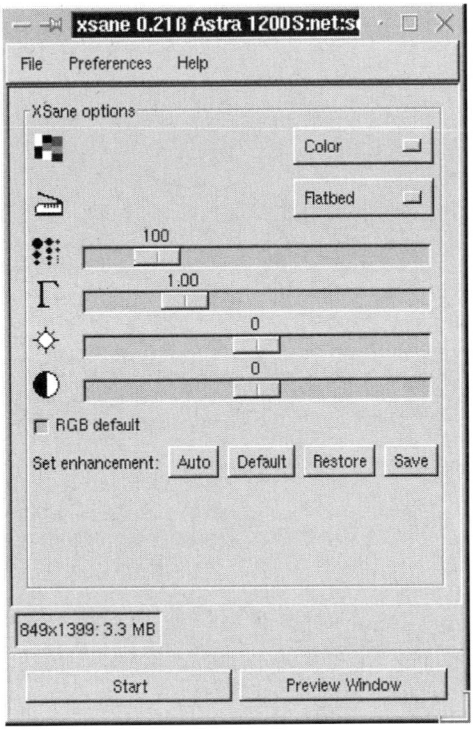

Figure 15.5 *The main Xsane scanner interface*

Below the sliders, you will find some buttons for scan enhancement: **Auto**, **Default**, **Restore** and **Save**. If you uncheck the **RGB default** checkbutton, you can set the *gamma*, *brightness* and *contrast* for each RGB channel separately. The interface will then look like Figure 15.6 .

Figure 15.6 *The Xsane scanner interface when RGB default is unchecked*

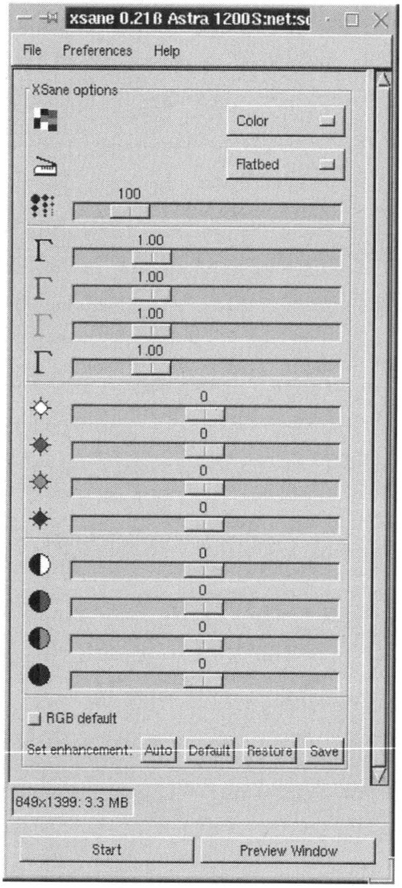

In the top menu bar, you'll find three menus called **File**, **Preferences** and **Help**. Under File, you'll find info about the Xsane creator and general info about the device you are using. In the Preferences menu, you'll find entries for Setup, Advanced and Standard options. You can also view a scanning histogram and save device settings. We will talk more about these settings a bit later, but let us concentrate on basic "Sane'ing" for a while.

The Preview Window

We're sure you know what a preview is meant for. To open the preview window, press the **preview** button. (If you checked Save preview in the Preferences, then you will see the last preview when you open the preview window.) When you first open the preview window there will be nothing but a white board. Place a photo on the document glass and press **Acquire Preview**.

Sane will now make a rapid low-resolution scan of the photo. While the preview scan occurs, all options in Xsane will be grayed out, and the only thing you can do is press **Cancel Preview**. We don't recommend canceling the preview or any other scan for that matter (it's a bit buggy). Just let Sane finish the scan job; you can always dump the image later on.

One of the advantages of **Xsane** over **xscanimage** is that you can preview how your adjustments in the main window will affect the final scan. To limit the scanning area, click and drag the mouse in the preview window to create a selection. You will now see a dotted selection outline, and Sane will only scan the contents within that rectangle.

When you are satisfied with your selection (a rough selection will do, because it's much easier to crop the image in Gimp), press the **Scan** button in the main dialog. Sane will now scan the image and display it in Gimp.

Figure 15.7 *The Xsane preview window*

Options

The Preference menu offers both Standard options and Advanced options as well as a Histogram option. Most options are quite scanner-specific, but we will mention some of them.

- **Use Custom Gamma Table:** If your scanner supports hardware gamma correction you can enable it with this button. Furthermore, if your scanner supports more than 8 bit color, then the custom gamma table will make the gamma correction with that number of bits. The conclusion is that if your scanner supports more than 8 bpp and/or has hardware gamma correction, then it's a good idea to use it.

It's also worth mentioning that xscanimage has more features dealing with gamma curves. The gamma curves in xscanimage are built up in the same way as Gimp's Curves command (`right-click|Image|Colors|Curves`).

- **Bit depth 8 or 10 bpp:** If you are using Xsane or xscanimage within Gimp, you can only use 8 bpp because Gimp only supports 8 bpp. If you scan with 10 bpp you will only get errors.
- **Histogram:** This works like Levels in Gimp (`right-click|Image|Colors|Levels`). It's a very useful option when you want to correct errors in both color and lightness. If you have unchecked the RGB defaults button, you can also set the histogram for each RGB channel.

Scanner Modes

Most flatbed scanners support *lineart*, *grayscale* and *color* scanner modes.

Lineart

The result of scanning in lineart mode is often unpredictable, so to retain a high level of detail, we suggest that you scan in grayscale mode, and then manipulate the grayscale image by *indexing* to black and white.

Alternatively, use `right-click|Image|Colors|Threshold` or `right-click|Image|Colors|Levels` to gain better control of where the black and white pixels end up in the lineart image.

Grayscale

Grayscale scan mode is, of course, useful if you want to scan grayscale (B&W) photos. Scan a grayscale image in color, and you have to worry about the scanner's color balance. If you want to colorize the image later, it's better to convert from grayscale to RGB mode in Gimp.

Scanning a color image in grayscale mode is not unusual. If your color image is destined to be printed in black-and-white, you might think that it is pointless to scan in color mode, but that's not always true. It depends on how good your scanner is.

For example, a yellow color is perceived by the human eye as being lighter than a blue color with the same intensity (value). Gimp makes quite a good conversion from color to grayscale and compensates for the human factor by converting the yellow color to a brighter shade of gray than the blue color. If your scanner can manage to produce an equally good or better grayscale image than Gimp, then scan in grayscale mode. Otherwise, scan in color and make the grayscale conversion in Gimp.

Color

Color mode is color mode, and there's not that much to say about it. Naturally, you should be concerned about color correctness and dropout color, but if you have a bad scanner, we can only recommend that you try to correct it with the different color correction functions in Gimp.

Auto Correction

Xsane has a very useful feature called **Auto Adjust** (the Auto button in the main dialog). Auto Adjust will correct a poorly exposed photo automatically in the scanning process. The correction calculations are based on the highlights and shadows of the selected part in the preview. It is therefore very important that you don't select any part of the white scanner lid. This auto function is even more useful when you want a particular part of an image to be correctly "exposed." For example, you may want a person's face to be correctly exposed in a portrait. The trick is to select the face in the preview image, press Auto and then select the entire area that you want to scan in the preview window. Of course, an Auto Adjust function will never be able to correct an image with the same accuracy as a well-trained professional. We use it as a starting point for further correction, but in general, Auto Adjust does a really great job and leaves us nothing or very little to correct manually.

Figure 15.8 *Before Auto Adjust*

Figure 15.9 *After Auto Adjust*

Gamma Correction

In our opinion, there is no scanning correction that is more important than **gamma** correction. Most people believe that gamma correction is a correction of some fault in the scanner, but that's not it. Gamma correction compensates for the imperfections of output devices, such as computer monitors or printers. Gamma correction is a *tonal* correction (light/darkness), and it refers to a special gamma curve that is used to perform that correction.

To find out which gamma correction is needed for your display, read "Gamma Calibration" on page 206. When you know that gamma value, drag the gamma slider to that value. Your scan will now be gamma correct — the lightness in the photo will be the same on the original as on the scanned image displayed on your monitor. Notice that gamma correction will not make a bad picture good, it will only correct it so it looks equally bad on your monitor. There are other correction functions to help improve your photos (gamma can naturally be used as a correction function here, too, in the sense that you will alter the gamma to *not* match your monitor).

Figure 15.10 *With and without gamma correction — as you see, the difference is huge*

Tonal Correction

We have already discussed tonal correction to some extent in the previous paragraph. We mentioned that setting the gamma value to the correct value according to your monitor isn't always that good. If the original image was overexposed to begin with, the scanned image will be equally overexposed, unless you *lower* the gamma value to compensate for the faulty exposure (and vice versa for an underexposed photograph).

When you scan older color photographs, you will often have to deal with different kinds of color tone problems. A well-known problem with aging photographs is that they often attain a tonal shift towards blue or red. To rectify unwanted tonal shift, you can uncheck the RGB default button in the main Xsane window, and suppress the color channel that is overly dominant in the image. Move the gamma control slider of the channel that is overrepresented until you're satisfied with the result.

If the photo's tonal range shifts toward cold, blue shades, and you want to make your image look a bit warmer, then you should increase gamma value in the red channel (and also a little bit in the green channel). This technique is commonly used to increase the warmth in the skin color of a model's face.

Likewise, if you have a photo that you want to adjust toward a cooler color range, then you should either increase the gamma value in the blue channel, or lower the gamma in the red channel (or a combination of the two).

SCALING

When you talk about scaling and scanning, it's not just a question of scaling to make the image bigger; you must also consider the final output device (the printer or monitor).

Let's scan an ordinary 4x6 photo:

- If you decide to print that photo in a 1:1 scale with a resolution of 300 ppi (not dpi!) you will scan with a 300 ppi resolution.
- If you'd like to make the print twice as large as the original (2:1) using the same resolution (300 ppi), then you need to scan with a 600 ppi resolution.
- If your final target is a web page with a 72 ppi resolution, then to get the same size as the original photo, you have to scan with a 72 ppi resolution.
- Likewise, if you want a 2:1 resolution, you have to scan at 144 ppi.

As you probably have understood by now, the scaling factor depends on the final output.

Scaling Limits

Using a 300 ppi scanner, you are not advised to scale an image more than 4:1. If you have a 600 ppi scanner, you can scale beyond that (but it is not sufficient to scale 35mm slides).

Generally, the quality of the source (the photo) sets the limit for how much you can scale an image. If the scanned photograph was of poor quality, you will see the structure, or grain, even with a relatively modest scaling. Obviously, there's no point in including photographic artifacts such as grain and structure.

Any scaling beyond 4:1 using a 300 ppi scanner will only render in a high noise ratio in your image, so don't think that you can scale a small photo (or slide) with a 300 ppi scanner.

A final big tip is that you should always scale with the scanner. Never scan at 100 ppi and then scale the image in Gimp. When you scale in Gimp, Gimp will interpolate (guess) what would be an appropriate color between pixels. So always scale with the scanner!

Scanning Drawings And Printed Images

Scanning drawings and printed material involves artifacts such as **moiré** patterns and **aliasing** effects. So, why does it look so bad when you scan an image from the newspaper?

Moiré Effects

A book, magazine or newspaper is printed with a certain **lpi** (lines per inch), also know as **line frequency**. According to digital sampling theory, you must sample at least twice the frequency of the source in order to capture accurate information of the signal (in this case, the signal is the printed halftone dots). This is called the Nyquist rate or Nyquist frequency. So, to capture a book printed in 150 lpi you must scan it in at 300 ppi. Because most 300 ppi scanners aren't really capable of making true 300 ppi scans, it's clear that such a scanner can't be used to scan a book printed in 150 lpi, because it is not capable of resolving the frequency that is needed to scan a 150 lpi source.

Figure 15.11 *Before and after moiré correction*

Fixing Up Moiré Patterns

Even if you scan with the right resolution (300 ppi for a drawing or book that has a line frequency of 150 lpi) the moiré pattern problem will pop up again when you resize the image to make it fit your layout. The solution is to:

1. Add some Noise: `(right-click|Filters|Noise|Noisify)`
2. Then add a little Gaussian Blur: `(right-click|Filters|Blur|Gaussian Blur (IIR))`
3. Then sharpen it up with Unsharp Mask (a lot): `(right-click|Filters|Enhance|Unsharp Mask)`
4. Now you can resize and print your image

The result isn't perfect, but this is as good as it gets without running one of the anti-moiré programs available on the market.

Aliasing

Having gained a basic knowledge of sampling frequency, you now understand that the same effect will occur when you scan a line drawing. A drawing consists of lines, so imagine that we take all of those lines and calculate how many lines will fill one inch. That is the "lpi" of the drawing. We must scan at a resolution twice as big as that lpi to get an accurate result.

If you scan at a lower resolution, you will not resolve every detail of the source. This may render lines in the drawing that weren't there to start with. This unwanted effect is called **aliasing**, and is due to the fact that you can't resolve all of the lines with such a low sampling frequency. The thin lines you see in an aliased image do not represent the thinnest lines in the original; it's an aliasing effect built up from several of the thinnest lines.

To learn more about lpi and printing, read "Pre-press And Color In Gimp" starting on page 197.

Scanning, The Web And Printing

In the pre-press chapter (see page 197), we discussed printing from a more professional point of view. But there are probably a lot of readers out there who only use Gimp in a SOHO (Small Office, Home Office) environment. This means that you will probably print to an inkjet printer with a "resolution" somewhere between 300 dpi and 1,400 dpi, or perhaps you have a 300 dpi or 600 dpi laser printer.

Inkjet Printers

Inkjet printers are quite different compared to laser printers, because they use **FM screening**. FM screening (see "Why Doesn't My Inkjet's Print Look Like Halftone Screens?" starting on page 214) can yield excellent results with a much lower image resolution than the halftone dpi equivalent printer (note that you can't really talk about dpi when you discuss FM screening printers; see "Resolution" on page 212).

A very rough rule of thumb is to use 125 ppi for every 300 dpi in the output device (printer):

- 300 dpi inkjet printer; scan at 100 ppi
- 600 dpi inkjet printer; scan at 200 ppi
- 720 dpi inkjet printer; scan at 240 ppi
- 1,440 dpi inkjet printer; scan at 480 ppi

This table is not absolute; it's a guideline that will help you get a good result after running some tests. Also try lowering the scanning resolution when you scan in very high resolution. For example, test to scan in 150 ppi for your 600 dpi inkjet printer (instead of 200 ppi) and see if the result is acceptable. Naturally, if you don't use the full capacity of the printer (for example, if you print with a resolution of 300 dpi on your 600 dpi printer) you should scan in 100 ppi, not 200 ppi.

When you print your image from Gimp, always make sure to use the **ppi option** in the **Printer** dialog, and print with the scan resolution (e.g., 100 ppi for a 300 dpi inkjet printer).

Laser Printers

The list above covers inkjet printers, but it will most likely also apply to your SOHO laser printer. However, it may be wise to try a few different resolutions. To get a really good result, you need to figure out what **lpi** your printer uses (or set an appropriate lpi if you have that option). The lpi will determine what ppi you'll need for scanning and printing. Please read "Resolution And Image Size" starting on page 200 to understand lpi and halftone printing.

Web Pages

Scanning for web publishing is generally very simple — just scan in 72 ppi. This resolution will suffice for color photos that don't require a high level of detail.

If you scan items where detail is important, such as drawings, you have to scan at a much higher resolution (see "Scanning Drawings And Printed Images" on page 258). This will produce huge web images, but if you scan in a lower resolution you won't be able to capture the details.

There is no simple solution to this problem. However, you can try this trick: Apply the Unsharp Mask filter (see "Unsharp Mask" on page 498) to enhance all edges and details in the high-resolution image. After that, you can resize the image to a more web-friendly size.

Scanning Other Objects

If you have a flatbed scanner, you are of course not limited to scanning photographs. You can scan almost all flat objects, and with a few cunning tricks, you can also scan certain 3D objects.

It's very easy to scan textures, but you may have to increase the exposure time (if that option is available). Alternatively, you can add more light or increase the gamma, since a texture doesn't reflect as much light as a paper or a photograph.

We suppose that many of you have tried to photocopy 3-D objects, such as your hand. The result is often quite disappointing. The reason for this is that the focus of the scanner/copy machine is optimized to the distance of the document glass. Another reason is that the amount of light doesn't suffice to reflect 3-D objects back to the CCD.

If you want quality images of 3-D objects, then you should get a digital camera or even better, a real 35mm camera. Good digital cameras are very expensive (at the time of writing), you will not get ahold of a good digital camera for less than $1,200, and then we are talking about cameras that are good enough for SOHO usage. If you want a professional camera, we're talking about $10,000 or more.

We mentioned that you could make some limited 3-D object scanning. Well, you can, but the result will not be very professional (if you don't want some special effect). Still, to get a decent result, you have to put some sort of box over the object, don't think that you can squeeze it in between the platen and the lid. Get a cardboard box, preferably white inside. Place the object on the platen and the box over the object. Now, you can try scanning using a slightly higher gamma than you normally would.

Here is the outcome of a scan using the "white box" technique:

Figure 15.12 *Julius' favorite pussycat "Missen" was placed on the scanner platen inside a white shoebox. The result is quite pleasing, don't you think?*

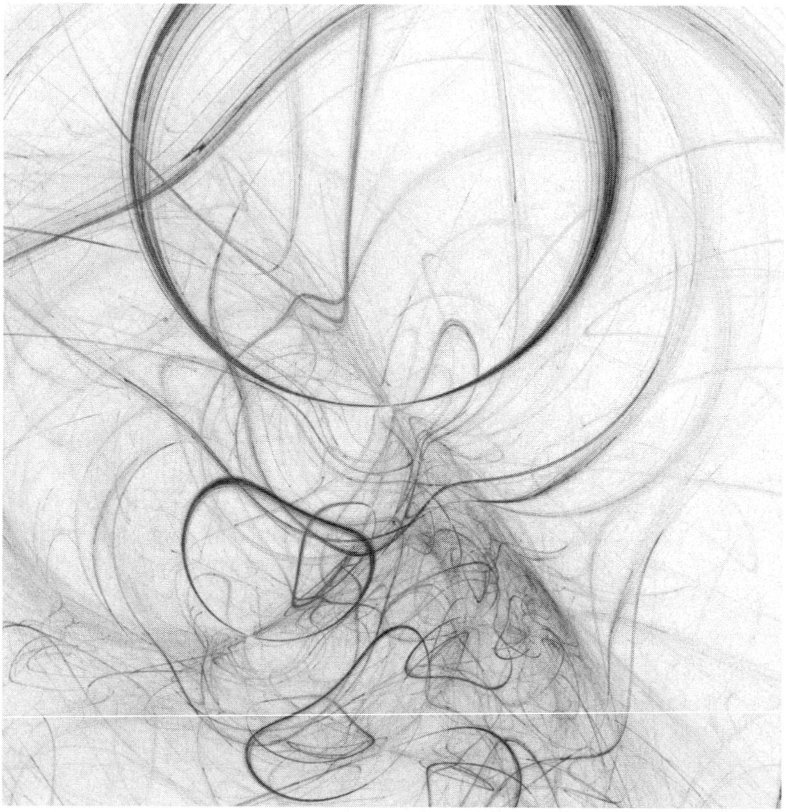

PART V

More Gimp Functions

- *Image Menu*
- *Selection Menu*
- *Modes*
- *Layers*
- *Channels*

CHAPTER 16

Image Menu

The Image menu offers some of the most useful image manipulating functions in Gimp. In this chapter, we're going to discuss what you can do within the image menu. The Colors, Channel Ops and Alpha submenus will be covered in separate chapters.

RGB, Grayscale And Indexed

`Right-click|Image|RGB`, `right-click|Image|Grayscale` and `right-click|Image|Indexed` are the three conversion options you have for your image. Normally, you'll work on an image in RGB color.

If you know that you want a grayscale or indexed image, you can easily convert your image later. Some commands, filters and Script-Fus require grayscales, whereas others require RGB images.

Tip: All color information is irreversibly lost as soon as you convert to Grayscale, and a lot of color information is lost when converting to indexed.

Most commands, filters and Script-Fus give poor results or no result at all when used on **indexed** images. If you are using an indexed image, convert it to RGB immediately, and don't convert it back to indexed until you're finished with it! For more information on RGB, grayscale and indexed images, review "Color Models" starting on page 187.

Indexed Palette Options

Select the `right-click|Image|Indexed` command to convert an RGB or grayscale image to indexed. This will open the **Indexed Color Conversion** dialog box.

When you think of indexed images, you probably think about GIF images with a maximum of 256 colors. In general, however, you are free to specify any number of colors for an indexed image. To set the number of colors, press the **Generate optimal palette** radio button and type the number of colors you want into the **# of colors** box.

If you are doing web design, you should use the **WWW-optimized** palette to map the colors. You can also choose a **custom palette** from the drop-down list, or create a *line art* image by using a black/white palette for color mapping. The **Enable Floyd-Steinberg dithering** option helps to make indexed images look "good" even if they only include a few colors.

Without dithering *With dithering*

Figure 16.1 *The difference between indexing without and with dithering*

Resize and Scale

Resize

The `right-click|Image|Resize` command is used to change the size and aspect ratio of the "canvas" where your image is placed. The scale and aspect ratio of the actual image and the layers within it are not affected. There are basically two reasons for changing the canvas size:

A. You're happy with the layers you have, but you need a new canvas size to make space for *new and larger* layers. When you resize the canvas, all new layers that you create will have this size and aspect ratio, unless you specify another width and height in the **New Layer** dialog box. The old layers, however, will remain as before.

B. You find that your layers are too *small* to contain things you want to add to them, or perhaps you wish to change the shape (aspect ratio) of your image without distorting the information within it. To resize an old layer, use the **Resize Layer** option in the Layers menu you get from right-clicking in the **Layers tab** (`right-click|Layers|Layers and Channels|<layers>|Resize Layer`).

Figure 16.2 *The Resize dialog*

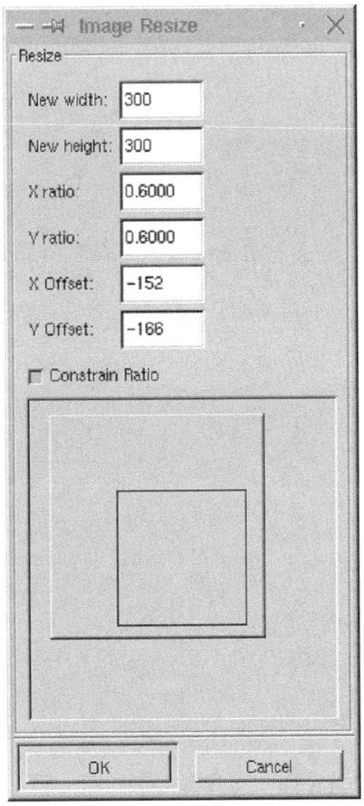

The Resize Dialog Options

The dialog box displays a preview of what the proposed changes in size, aspect ratio or offset will look like. Set where on the canvas you want to place the image by dragging at the gray “image rectangle” in the dialog window, or by specifying a value in the **X Offset** and **Y Offset** fields.

If you check the **Constrain Ratio** checkbox, the proportions of the old canvas will be kept. If you uncheck Constrain Ratio and then change the proportions, Resize will either *crop* or *add* a transparent area to the image to fit the new size.

SCALE

`right-click|Image|Scale` changes the **size** and **aspect ratio** of your image. Scale makes *everything* in your image larger or smaller, including layers.

If you check the **Constrain Ratio** checkbox, the proportions of the old image will be kept. If you uncheck Constrain Ratio and then change the proportions, Scale will *stretch* or *compress* the image to fit the new size, thus **distorting** the image.

Interpolating With Scale

When you enlarge your image with Scale, Gimp **interpolates** the new image. This means that when you add new pixels to an image, as you must when you make it larger, a process called *interpolation* will calculate the color and value of the new pixels based on the properties of the neighbor pixels. That is, an additional pixel between black-and-white original pixels will get a gray color.

The consequence is that the enlarged image will look better than the original image zoomed to the same size, but it will also lose sharpness and clarity. Read “Interpolation” on page 100 to get more information about interpolation in Gimp.

Figure 16.3 *The Scale dialog*

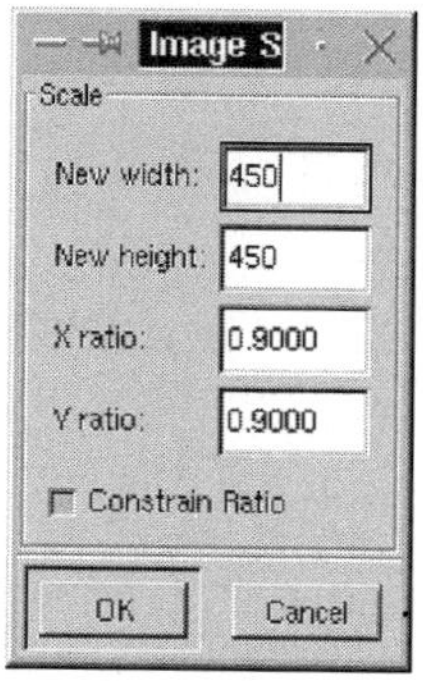

HISTOGRAM

`Right-click|Image|Histogram` gives you valuable *statistical* information on the channel values for an entire image or for a certain pixel range in a channel.

The Histogram always refers to the **active layer**. Every **spike** in the histogram represents pixels with a defined value. The higher the spike, the more pixels of that value in the image. The 256 spikes, one for every value, are ordered in a sequence from left to right, starting with low values to the left and continuing with increasing values to the right. You can chose a certain value or value interval by clicking on a spike or clicking and dragging at a part of the histogram.

Figure 16.4 *The Histogram window*

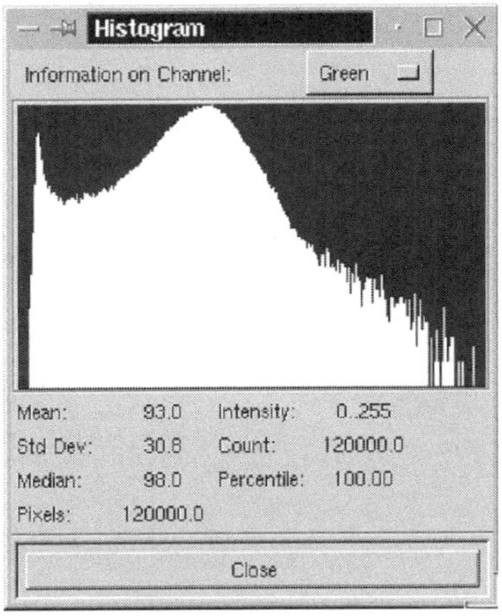

Histogram Parameters

- **Mean** is the mean value of that interval. This figure will give you an approximate value of the range you're interested in.
- **Intensity** tells you the value (from 0 to 255) of the chosen pixel spike, or the value of the *first* and *last* spike in a chosen interval. You can, for example, select an interval where there seems to be a large number of pixels and find out where on the brightness/darkness scale those pixels are.
- **Std Dev (Standard Deviation)** is how homogeneous the pixel spike height is in a certain range. It tells you whether the pixels in a certain interval are equally distributed over that range (this usually means that there are many different shades and soft transitions in the image), or whether you can only perceive a few shades within a certain value or color range.
- **Count** refers to the number of pixels a spike or interval represents.
- **Median** is the median of the interval, i.e., the value of the fiftieth spike if you have chosen an interval of 100 spikes.
- **Percentile** is the percentage of the total number of pixels in a selected range. This tells you how large that part of your image is.
- **Pixels** tells you the total number of pixels in the active layer.

Save Palette

Right-click|Image|Save palette will create a palette of colors from an indexed image. When you are manipulating indexed images, this option lets you *save* the colors in your images, so that you can organize colors and easily pick the color you want.

When you convert an image to indexed (right-click|Image|Indexed) you set the number of colors you want in the **Indexed Color Conversion** dialog box. This also sets how many colors will be in a palette created from that indexed image.

Creating A Palette From An Indexed Image

Select right-click|Image|Indexed to convert your image to indexed. Choose how many colors you want for your palette and type that number into the **# of colors:** box. Click on the **OK** button and your image will be converted to indexed format.

Right-click|Image|Save palette will display the **Export GIMP Palette** dialog. Type in a name for the palette, and press the OK button (the dialog is already in your personal palette directory so there's no need to change the directory).

Back on your image, press Ctrl+z to **Undo** the indexed conversion and return your image to RGB.

Open the **Color Palette** dialog (with either right-click|Dialogs|Palette or File|Dialogs|Palette). Choose **Refresh Palettes** from the **Ops** pull-down menu to refresh the palettes. Now, the palette you just created should appear in the pull-down palette menu, and be available for you to use.

Transforms

Autocrop

Right-click|Image|Transforms|Autocrop crops images **automatically**. If you paint or paste something onto a large solid or transparent background, you may find that you have too much space around the image object.

Autocrop will *crop* your image so that everything but the important parts are cut away. Note that if you work in a **layer**, Autocrop will crop the entire image with no concern for the other layers.

Image

Right-click|Image|Transforms|Image|Rotate 270 or |Rotate 90 lets you **rotate** the entire *image* either 270 degrees or 90 degrees. This is useful for changing scanned images to either **landscape** or **portrait** mode.

Layer

`Right-click|Image|Transforms|Layer|Rotate 270` or `Rotate 90` allow you to **rotate** a *layer* 270 degrees or 90 degrees. Remember that when you rotate a large layer, portions of it will disappear outside of the image boundary.

Mirror

`Right-click|Image|Transforms|Mirror` reflects your image as a mirror would. The difference between *Mirror* and the *Flip tool* is that with Mirror, you can flip all layers at the same time by checking the **Mirror the whole image** checkbox.

Rotate

`Right-click|Image|Transforms|Rotate` provides a simple way to rotate your image or selection 0, 90, 180 or 270 degrees. **Rotate** is very convenient for reorienting scanned images.

Zealous Crop

`Right-click|Image|Transforms|Zealous Crop` works much like the **Autocrop** filter, but there are some significant differences. While Autocrop cuts away any peripheral parts of the image that have no variation in color or alpha, Zealous Crop *moves objects closer together* (but not on top of each other) before cutting.

When Zealous Crop finds objects of a different color on a solid or transparent background in the same layer, it moves the objects as close to each other as possible without them overlapping, so that they remain in the same relative positions to each other. Zealous Crop lets you keep all of the objects in your image, but reduces the size as much as is possible without scaling the image.

Zealous Crop works on all layers, but only compresses the objects in the **active layer**. Zealous Crop always crops the *upper-left* part of inactive layers, while Autocrop crops *all* layers in the position determined by the active layer.

CHAPTER 17

Image Menu: Colors

The Image menu offers some of the most useful image manipulating functions in Gimp. In this chapter, we're going to discuss what you can do with Colors in the Image menu.

COLORS

The first part of the `Image|Colors` menu deals with how image pixels are mapped to different RGB values; the second part deals with color correction; and the third part contains useful filters for auto-correction of scanned photos. Remember that you're likely to get much better results adjusting scanned images in a professional image manipulation program like Gimp, than in the scanner program.

EQUALIZE

`Right-click|Image|Colors|Equalize` is often used to correct overexposed or underexposed photos. Equalize finds the darkest and lightest pixels in the image and sets the darkest value to black and the lightest to white. Intermediate colors are then translated to the corresponding **histogram** values on the new scale. This action adjusts the image pixel colors to a wider scale or spectrum. The resulting image is usually harder and much clearer, with more saturation and contrast, but often with less fine detail.

Figure 17.1
Comparing dark and light images before and after Equalize has been invoked

Dark input *Output after Equalize*

Light input *Output after Equalize*

Tip: Equalize can be used to find "hidden" colors in old, fading photos, because colors are also equalized.

For example, if there is a weak shade of green somewhere in a seemingly solid blue area, Equalize will find it and strengthen it, while the blue color will lose intensity. Sometimes, this results in colors looking a bit unnatural after equalization. You might have to correct the image using color correction tools like **Color Balance**.

For adjusting old photos, it is sometimes better to use other commands such as `right-click|Image|Colors|Auto-Stretch HSV`, `Auto-Stretch Contrast` and `Normalize`. Try all of them and see which one is most suitable for your picture.

INVERT

`Right-click|Image|Colors|Invert` creates a color negative of your image (or a positive of your negative). Invert is very useful if you have a **slide scanner**, because then you never have to worry about expensive developing. You need only develop the negative film, and then you can do your own developing with your computer.

Figure 17.2 *Invert is shown on the right side*

The calculations are quite simple: The inverted RGB value of a pixel is 255 minus the former channel value. Read more about inverted or complementary colors in "Complementary Or Inverted Colors" on page 194.

POSTERIZE

`Right-click|Image|Colors|Posterize` is a way of creating an "indexed" image, in which the colors are derived not from the image, but from the number of possible combinations the three RGB channels can produce. The available colors depend on what you set as **Posterize Levels** in the **Posterize dialog**.

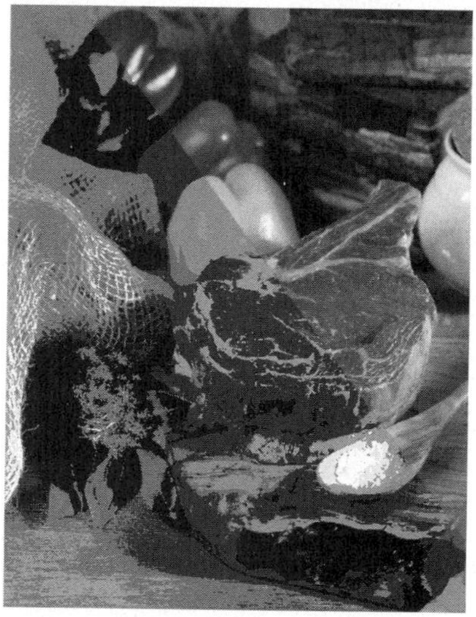

Figure 17.3 *Posterize is shown at the bottom-left side*

For a grayscale image, it's easy. Posterize Levels 0, 1 and 2 produce the minimum of possible colors: black and white only. For each level, you get one more grayscale. Posterize Levels 4 equals four shades of gray, Posterize Levels 16 equals 16 shades of gray, etc.

For an RGB image, Posterize Levels 4 equals four different shades in each color channel. So Posterize Levels 4 equals 4x4x4, or 64 colors. Those 64 colors were chosen by dividing the color value of each channel into even multiples of 4, so only the values 0, 85, 170 and 255 are used.

As those colors may not be similar to the original colors in the image, only a few of them will be used in the image. A posterized image will be a lot less representative, but (perhaps) will be more "artistic" than an indexed image, where the chosen colors are taken from the image.

THRESHOLD

The `right-click|Image|Colors|Threshold` dialog displays a brightness histogram of the image. Each spike in the histogram represents a value ranging from 0 to 255. The longer the spike, the more pixels that have that particular value. In the preview window, you can see where those pixels are situated in the image.

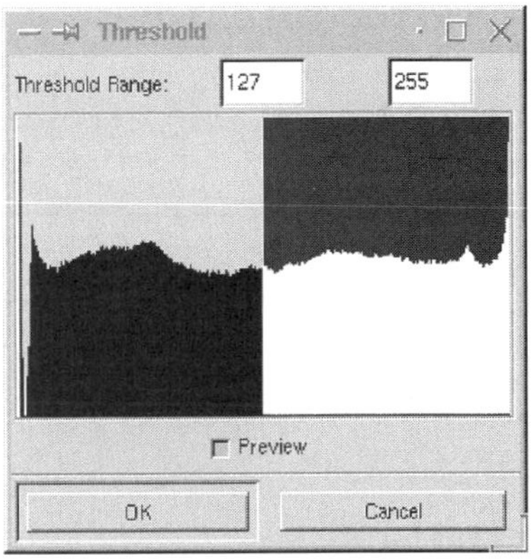

Figure 17.4 *The Threshold dialog*

Clicking on a single spike displays only the pixels with that particular value. If you drag from one spike to another, Gimp will display all pixels with a threshold range from the first value to the second.

You can use the **Threshold** command to make a **line art** (black and white) image. Threshold is also an excellent tool for **selecting by value**. If you copy your image to an **alpha channel**, and use Threshold on the alpha channel (see "Channels And Duotones" starting on page 351 for more information on alpha channels) you can, for example, select all pixels dark enough to represent a certain shape and use that to make a selection.

Figure 17.5 *Line art created with Threshold*

COLOR BALANCE

`Right-click|Image|Colors|Color Balance` allows you to adjust the **color levels** in your image. Color Balance changes colors in the image, but not as drastically as **Hue-Saturation**. Use Color Balance when you want to make subtle changes in color.

Figure 17.6 *The Color Balance dialog*

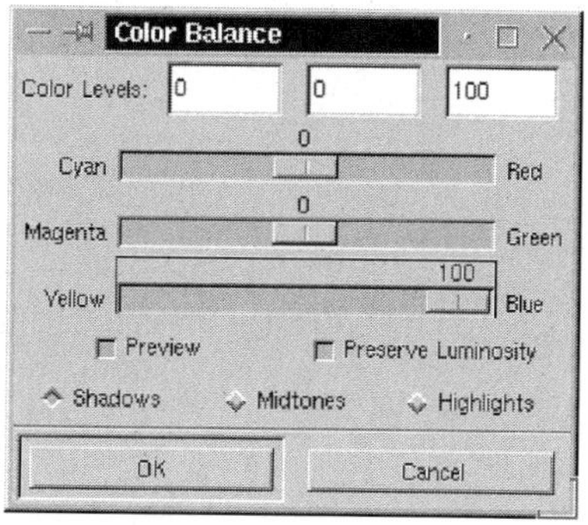

In the Color Balance dialog, you'll find three slide bars ranging from the three **RGB** colors to their complementary colors (**CMY**). As you know if you read "Image Menu: Colors" starting on page 273, the sum of two complementary colors is neutral gray. You can consider your current pixels "neutral" (or zero) and any change you apply will move the pixel color either toward **Red** or **Cyan**, **Green** or **Magenta**, **Blue** or **Yellow**.

Moving all three sliders towards the CMY *(subtractive)* colors will darken your image, while moving them toward the RGB *(additive)* colors will lighten the image.

The dialog includes three radio buttons: **Shadows**, **Midtones** and **Highlights**, which respectively correspond to the *darkest* pixels, the *medium* pixels or the *brightest* pixels. Click on the button corresponding to the pixels you want to affect.

If you click on the **Preserve Luminosity** checkbox, the brightness value of your image doesn't change. By default this option is unchecked, because the image's colors can become very unnatural-looking if you insist on keeping the original values while changing the color balance.

Figure 17.7 *Output from Color Balance is shown at the bottom-left side*

BRIGHTNESS-CONTRAST

`Right-click|Image|Colors|Brightness-Contrast` is easy to understand. The zero values represent the current values of your image.

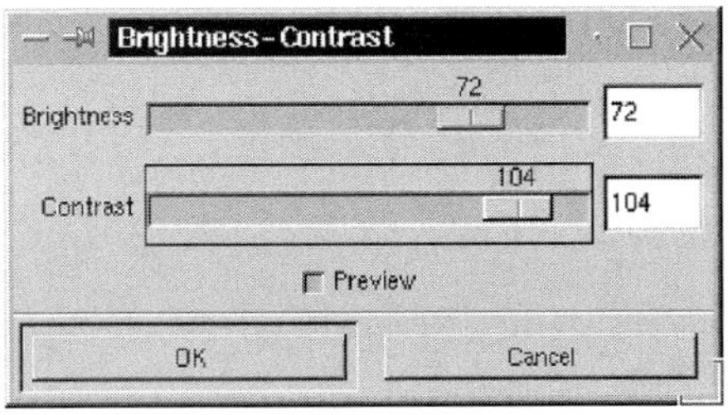

Figure 17.8 *The Brightness-Contrast dialog*

From that "neutral" point, you can raise or lower the amount of **Contrast** and **Brightness**.

Figure 17.9 *Image corrected on the right with Brightness-Contrast*

HUE-SATURATION

The `right-click|Image|Colors|Hue-Saturation` dialog lets you adjust **Hue**, **Saturation** and **Lightness** (or Value). You should understand that this option is entirely based on the **HSV** color model, as explained in "HSV" on page 191.

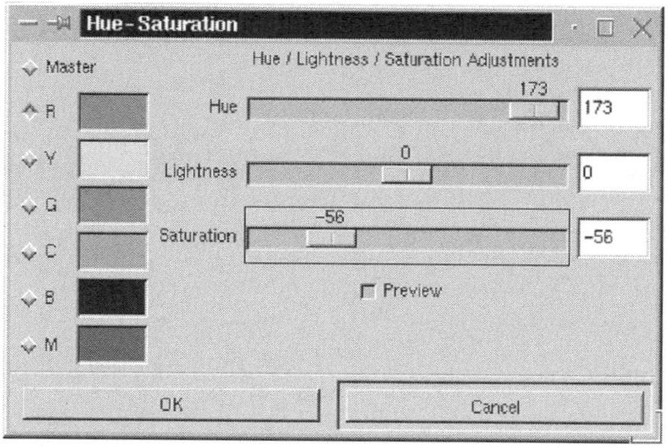

Figure 17.10 *The Hue-Saturation dialog.*

You can adjust the sliders by dragging on them with your mouse, by typing values into the boxes or using the left and right arrow keys on your keyboard.

When you change **Hue** with the **Master** checkbox checked, *all* pixels in the image or selection will change color according to how many degrees you have turned the HSV color circle. If you just want to change part of the spectrum, you can choose any one of the color radio buttons (**Red**, **Yellow**, **Green**, **Cyan**, **Blue**, or **Magenta**).

Remember, HSV is the color model being used here (not RGB). Because it is HSV, checking the **Yellow** button and changing its value won't necessarily change the yellow parts in your image.

Figure 17.11 *The hue circle*

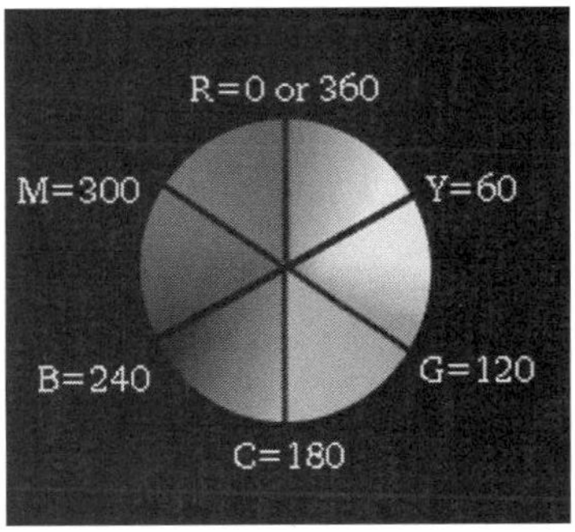

In HSV, the **yellow swatch** starts at 100% pure yellow on the HSV color circle (no orange shade whatsoever is allowed) and continues toward **green**. Everything in the yellow to green slice is affected by changes to hue, saturation or value. Yellow pixels get the color you see in the swatch, and greenish pixels get the next swatch color (clockwise), and so on, as they get greener.

So, if you want to affect yellow pixels that are slightly to the red side, choose the **red swatch** instead. The red swatch changes all color between pure red and yellow. Because of this, Hue-Saturation is unsuitable for certain images. For most images, it's very useful indeed, but if you have trouble with it, try **Colormap Rotation** in the `right-click|Filters|Colors` menu instead (there are very few things you can't achieve with that filter).

Figure 17.12 *The truck has had its color changed by Hue-Saturation (right side)*

CURVES

The `right-click|Image|Colors|Curves` tool is an advanced instrument for changing the **color**, **contrast** and **brightness** of an image, or a certain color/brightness range in an image.

Figure 17.13 *The right side of the image has been adjusted with Curves*

Simply put, the image's **RGB values** (and possible **alpha values**) are represented by **curves**, and you can change a curve any way you like by dragging at different parts of it.

When you first open the **Curves** dialog, you'll see a straight, linear curve. This curve is called **Value** and represents the values of all three RGB channels of the current image. Value here does not mean value as in HSV. Curves is based entirely on RGB values.

Remember the **Threshold** command? When you looked at your image with Threshold, you could choose an area from spike A to spike B, and that area represented pixels of intensity A ranging to intensity B.

Curves works the same way. The leftmost segment of the curve represents the darkest pixels in the image, and the rightmost segment represents the lightest pixels.

The vertical grayscale gradient to the left of the curve displays what **brightness value** the curve follows.

Figure 17.14 *The Curves dialog*

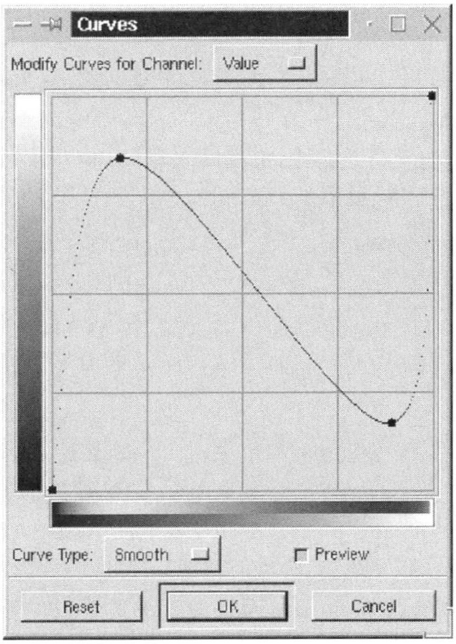

CHANGING BRIGHTNESS AND CONTRAST

To understand Curves better, open an image and try it out. Try dragging the **middle** of the curve up and down. While you are doing this, take a look at the gradient below the curve.

The gradient and the preview image show that dragging *down* makes your image **darker**, and dragging *up* makes it **lighter**. The middle of the curve represents pixels with **midvalues**. By creating a soft curve in this fashion, you have changed the general brightness values a lot, but you have only changed *highlights* and *shadows* a little, so you have **less contrast** now.

Reset the Value curve, and drag the **right** part of the curve (representing highlights) *up*, and the **left** part (representing shadows) *down*, until your curve is shaped like an S. With this procedure you have made bright parts lighter and dark parts darker; you've **increased the contrast** without changing the brightness in the image.

On the lower horizontal gradient, you'll see that the balance of dark and light has been changed and you can also see where on the scale it happened and how much. If you are in a color channel (select **Red**, **Green** or **Blue** from the **Modify Curves for Channel** pull-down menu), this procedure will make pixels more or less green, red, or blue.

In a color channel, *dark* means pixels with *little* of that color, and *light* means pixels with *a lot* of that color in them. If you are changing alpha, it works the same way. Dark means a low alpha value, or very transparent. Light means a high alpha value, or very opaque.

Adjusting Curves

You may have noticed that there is a **dot** at each end of the curve. Drag at one of the dots. You'll find that the line created to the left or right of the dot is perfectly straight. In practice, this means that dragging the **left dot** constrains a range of dark pixels to the same value, whereas dragging the **right dot** constrains a range of light pixels to the same value. How *large* this range or interval will be depends on the **horizontal** length of the line. The darkness or lightness of the pixels depends on where you put the dot on the **vertical** scale.

Click on different points on the curve. Each click produces another dot, and you can move each dot independently of the others. You can move them up, down or along the curve. These dots are like **Bezier anchor points**, but without handles. This means that by moving a dot, you'll produce a little curve between the two nearest dots. This way you can easily pick a suitable **pixel range**, and only change the values within that range.

To **remove** dots, drag them toward one of the end dots. You can remove all of the dots except one, but if you only have one dot, your curve will be flat. A flat curve causes all values to be the same. If all of the values are the same, your image will turn gray and disappear (or, for example, if you're in the red channel, all pixels will get the same red value).

The option **Curve Type: Free** lets you create or modify your curve with a pencil, which offers unlimited possibilities of fine-tuning colors or values. The **Smooth** option will produce a smoother version of the same curve. Experiment with Curves to learn more.

Unwanted Side Effects

Because the value is based on **RGB**, you can sometimes produce an unwanted change in color when you only wanted to change the pixel brightness. This effect happens when you try to make extreme changes, like lightening a very dark object without disturbing the other colors in the image. If you try to do this, you'll **invert** the color, and you'll just end up with something red if the object was green. Instead of using Curves to produce this effect, you should isolate the object in a selection and use `right-click|Filters|Colors|Value Invert`. This filter works in **HSV**, and inverts Value without changing Hue or Saturation.

Levels

`Right-click|Image|Colors|Levels` is another way of manipulating **RGB** properties. Levels is an excellent tool for creating **highlights** or **shadow** areas, which enhance 3-D effects in your image.

Levels is also useful for adding emphasis to dark or bright areas in the image. Whereas *Curves* allows you to manipulate pixels within **defined ranges**, *Levels* affect the **entire range** of pixels. You normally use *Levels* for changing the general balance between bright and dark parts in the image or selection, and *Curves* when you only want to affect certain color or value ranges.

Using Levels In All Channels

When you open the **Levels** dialog, you'll see a **histogram** of your image's Value (all RGB channels) or of the Red, Green, Blue or Alpha channel if you switch channels in the Modify Levels for Channel drop-down menu.

Figure 17.15 *The Levels*

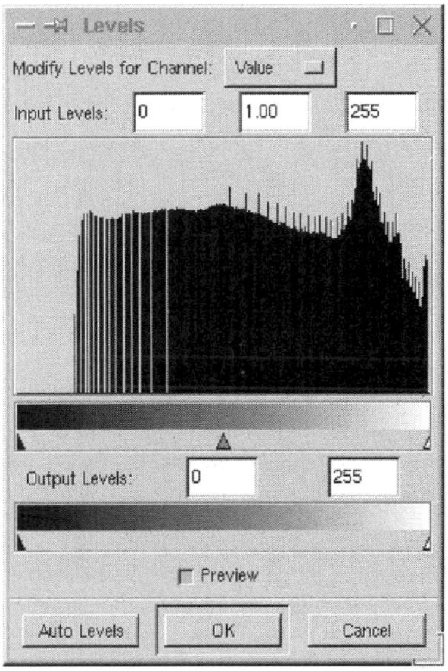

Input Levels

The histogram shows the *input* levels of the image. For example, the histogram shown in Figure 17.15 shows an image that has no black or really dark areas. The black arrow below the histogram represents the **minimum** value (0) in the RGB channels, the white arrow represents the **maximum** value (255) and the gray arrow represents the **mid** value (127 on the RGB scale). The area between the black-and-white arrows always defines a pixel value range from 0 to 255.

If you're working with a **grayscale** image and you drag the white or black arrows, every pixel to the *left* of the black arrow turns black, and everything to the *right* of the white arrow turns white. Each spike between the black-and-white arrows represent pixels of different shades of gray, and the pixels with mid value (127) are in the spike above the gray arrow. You can change the balance of light and dark pixels by moving the gray arrow.

Move the white-and-black arrows toward the center. The result will be *more* **contrast** and *less* **detail**, because the gray transitional range between black and white is narrowing. Move the gray arrow. Moving it to the left adjusts the brightness balance so that more and more of the gray pixels end up in the range between medium gray and white (they get brighter), and vice versa.

If you're working with an **RGB** color image, the pixels to the left of the black arrow will turn into either black or one of the **additive primary colors** (red, green or blue). Pixels to the right of the white arrow will turn into either white or one of the **subtractive** primary colors (cyan, magenta or yellow).

For an image with low contrast, if you drag the black arrow to the start of the histogram (the first spike), the white arrow to the end of it (the last spike) and put the gray arrow in the middle, you have pretty much done the same thing that `right-click|Image|Colors|Equalize` does, i.e., broadened the **spectrum** of the image.

Output Levels

The **Output Levels** gradient controls the overall brightness value. As you drag the black or white arrows on the Output Levels gradient, the new values define the brightest/darkest value in the image. As a result, the entire image becomes darker or lighter. The output is always more dull than before, because there will be less contrast when the value for the darkest and/or brightest pixel is being moved towards the gray mid values.

Figure 17.16 *Contrast has been lowered on the right side, using Levels*

Adjusting Levels In A Single Channel

When you switch from **Value** to a **Color channel** in the **Modify Levels for Channel** drop-down menu, remember that we're no longer talking about dark and light. We're now discussing the **quantities** of color in the image.

RGB Output And Input Levels

In the **Output Levels** gradient, dark means *low* values of the color in question, and light indicates that pixels have *a lot* of that color in them.

The Output Levels gradient controls the value range that pixels can use for a certain color. In other words, if you modify the levels for the Green channel by setting the Output Levels to between 100 and 120, all pixels with a little green in them (even if it's a very low value) will shift to a new green value of at least 100. No pixel's green value can be greater than 120. Dragging the white arrow to the left causes the image to have less green (i.e., more red). The opposite is true when you drag the black arrow to the right.

The result of moving the **Input Levels** arrows in a color channel isn't as obvious as with **Value**. The result depends on how much of the color is in the image, and in what range most of the color is found.

Levels And Alpha Channels

The alpha channel works the same way as RGB: Dark means *low* alpha (or transparent) and white is *high* alpha (fully opaque).

Modify **Levels** for the alpha channel on feathered or otherwise semi-transparent selections or layers, i.e., on areas with great variation in alpha values. Examples of this are selections created from an **alpha mask channel** or layers where you have applied a **Layer mask**.

Example: Making Carved Text With Levels

To help you understand what you can do with Levels, work through this example:

1. Create a new image with a white background. With the command `File|New`, choose **Fill Type White** (you can just leave the Fill Type at **Background** if the background color in the toolbox is set to white).
2. Create a white layer in this image. Use the command `right-click|Layers|Layers & Channels` to open the Layers & Channels dialog. Click on the **New Layer** button. In the New Layer Options dialog, click on **Layer Fill Type White** and click OK.
3. Click on the **Background** in the Layer & Channels dialog, so you're working in the background layer. Choose the **Text tool** and write a few (black, not gray or colored) letters on the white background. In this example we used white text on a black oval. You may have to click "off" the **eye icon** on the new layer so that you can see the background. With the letters still selected, apply some `right-click|Filters|Blur|Gaussian Blur`. The more blur you apply, the more bevel and softness you'll get in the bumpmap image you'll create next.

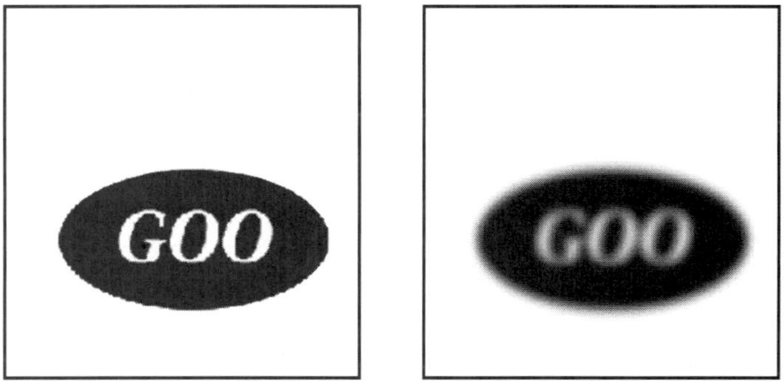

Figure 17.17 *White letters before and after Gaussian blur*

4. Activate the white layer (click on it in the **Layers & Channels** dialog, and click "on" the **eye icon** so you can see the white layer). Select `right-click|Filters|Map|`**`Bump Map`**.
5. Choose the background layer of your image from the **Bump map** pull-down menu and click OK.
6. You should now have a nice **3-D image** of the letters in your layer. Use Gaussian blur if you think the shadows are too hard, and **Duplicate** the 3-D layer. One of these bumpmapped layers will be the highlight layer and the other will be the shadow layer.

Figure 17.19 *The newly bumpmapped image*

Figure 17.20 *The highlight layer*

7. Activate the top layer and open `right-click|Image|Colors|`**`Levels`**. Move the **black** and **gray** arrows below the **Input Levels** gradient to the right, until you see the bright highlights of the letters on top of a black background. Click OK.
8. Activate the middle layer, and open the Levels dialog again. Move the **white** and **gray** Input Levels arrows to the left, until you see the shadows on top of a white background. Click OK.

Figure 17.21 *Shadow layer*

Figure 17.22 *The finished image*

9. Click on the *highlight* layer. Select **Screen** from the **Mode** pull-down menu to change the mode of the highlight layer to Screen.

10. Change the mode of the *shadow* layer to **Multiply**.
11. Fill the background with a suitable color or pattern using the **Bucket Fill** tool.

Desaturate

`Right-click|Image|Colors|Desaturate` removes color from a layer or selection without disturbing the rest of the composite image. This command is useful when you want to put emphasis on a certain object in an image by draining the color from everything else. This option also gives you the possibility to work with grayscale in certain layers, and with color in others. **Desaturate** does not turn your image into a grayscale. Your image is still RGB, even if there is no visible color.

Auto-Stretch Contrast

`Right-click|Image|Colors|Auto-Stretch Contrast` works just like **Auto-Stretch HSV**, but within RGB color space. This command is a wonderful image enhancer. It is great for removing undesired color tints in poorly developed or aging photos.

Figure 17.23 *The right side was corrected with Auto-Stretch Contrast*

Auto-Stretch HSV

`Right-click|Image|Colors|Auto-Stretch HSV` makes an automatic contrast stretch of your image. It finds the lowest and highest values of each **HSV** channel and stretches them to the full contrast range. This is similar to **Auto-Stretch Contrast**, but Auto-Stretch Contrast works with RGB values.

Figure 17.24 *The right side was corrected with Auto-Stretch HSV*

Auto-Stretch HSV is a great filter for enhancing or correcting old pictures. Test it on some old, faded images. If that doesn't work, try `right-click|Image|Colors|Equalize`.

NORMALIZE

`Right-click|Image|Colors|Normalize` is similar to **Auto-Stretch Contrast**, but it won't allow the RGB channels to stretch **independently**. Instead, they are treated as a **union**. Technically, the difference is that with Normalize, all of the channels will not stretch over the whole range from 0 to 255, so just the highest values go to the edges. This filter is an excellent image enhancer for scanned images.

Figure 17.25 *The right side was corrected with Normalize*

Colorcube Analysis

`Right-click|Image|Colors|Colorcube Analysis` is a great tool for **indexing**, since it informs you of the compressed and uncompressed sizes, dimensions and the number of unique colors in an image.

If you're working on a GIF image (which is already indexed), this tool will help you keep track of the image size as you bring down the number of colors.

If you're preparing an RGB or grayscale image for indexing, you can use this tool after running the `right-click|Filters|Colors|Quantize` filter on chosen selections to keep informed on the total number of colors in the image (or before running it to determine the number of colors in the selection).

CHAPTER 18

Image Menu: Channel Ops And Alpha

The Image menu offers some of the most useful image manipulating functions in Gimp. In this chapter, we're going to discuss what you can do with Channel Ops and Alpha in the Image menu.

THE CHANNEL OPS MENU

The `right-click|Image|Channel Ops` commands were once the only way of handling composite image information. Now that Gimp supports effective layer handling, the few commands in this menu are all that remain of the channel options. Nevertheless, the items in this menu contain some very powerful and useful features.

DUPLICATE

`Right-click|Image|Channel Ops|Duplicate` *copies* all layers and channels in a composite image, so that a complete replica of your image is created. Be sure to use it every time you want to experiment with different solutions and variations on an image.

OFFSET

`Right-click|Image|Channel Ops|Offset`, which tiles and rearranges the edge pixels in your image, only affects the active layer/channel. It can be used to place layers or floating selections to a specific position in the image.

Offset is useful if you want to move layers a very exact amount, or if you'd like to move them without extending the **layer border**. The other important application of this command is to create **seamless tiles** for patterns.

Figure 18.1 *The Offset dialog*

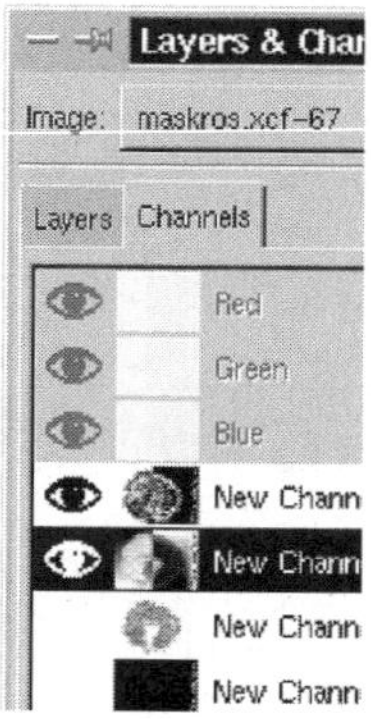

If the **Wrap-Around** button is checked, after you offset the layer or selection, the parts of the image that moved outside the layer border will turn up on the other side of the image. If you don't want this, you can choose to fill the empty area with the **background** color or with **transparency**.

Using Offset To Adjust Pattern Tiles

Offset allows you to make *seamless tiles*. If you want to make a wallpaper pattern of your image, it's a good idea to check how well the edges fit, before you tile it.

If you click on the **Offset by (x/2),(y/2)** button with the **Wrap-Around** checkbox checked, you'll split your image into *four equal tiles*.

To create a seamless tile, you need to erase the sharp borders between the tiles. There are many ways of doing this, depending on how complicated the image is. You can use the **Clone** tool and the **Transform** tool; you can **Paint**, **Copy** and **Paste** suitable selections with different opacities; or you can use special filters.

When you're satisfied with the results, click on the **Offset by (x/2),(y/2)** button again, and your image will return to normal, but now with seamless edges that will produce a perfect result when tiling the image.

The `right-click|Filters|Map|Make Seamless` filter also produces seamless tiles. Tiling looks very good with this filter. The problem with **Make Seamless** is that you can never get really sharp patterns with it. Everything looks a bit blurred and double-exposed.

You can also try the `right-click|Filters|Blur|Tileable Blur` filter, which creates softer, if not entirely seamless, edges.

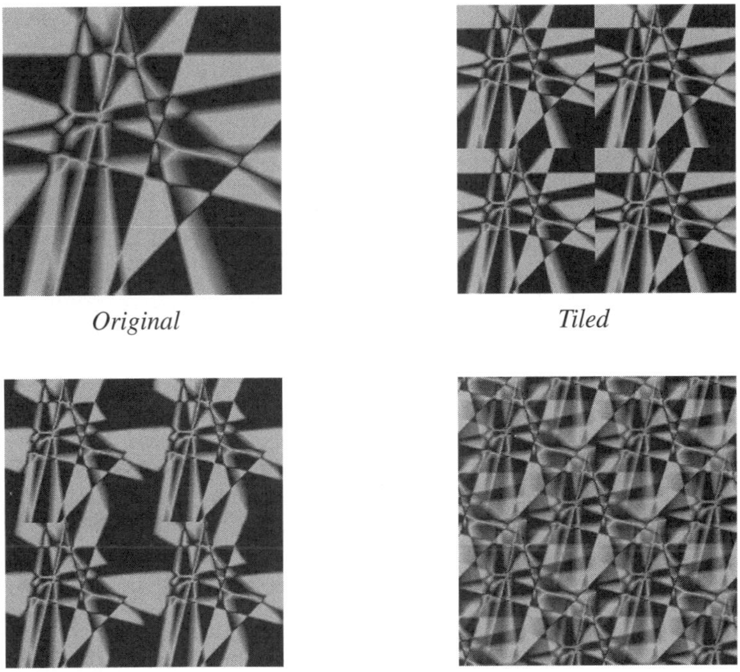

Original *Tiled*

Offset and Tiled *Make Seamless and Tiled*

Figure 18.2 *Here, you can appreciate the difference between using Tiled, Offset and Tiled and Make Seamless and Tiled*

Correcting Tiles

Follow this example to get an idea of how the Offset tool can be used to create seamless pattern tiles.

Figure 18.3 *This is a nice picture of a brick pavement. I'd like to use this image to make a pattern.*

Figure 18.4 *I apply the Small Tiles filter to get a preview of what a pattern would look like using this image. Sorry to say, it doesn't look very convincing when I tile it.*

Figure 18.5 *When I use Offset by (x/2),(y/2) on my image, it's clear that the tiles don't match very well*

Figure 18.6 *Now I've manipulated the offset image by copying and pasting bricks into positions that will erase the sharp borders. I used the Clone tool to smooth edges, the Paint tool to make the colors blend and the Rotate Transform tool to make the pasted selections fit the pattern. This time it looks much better!*

Figure 18.7 *When I'm satisfied with the Offset adjusted image, I can rest assured that the pattern rendered from this image will look alright*

Compose And Decompose

`Right-click|Image|Channel Ops|Compose` merges at least three grayscale images into one color image. **Decompose** is a way of **extracting channels** from an image. You can break up your image into its constituent channels, by extracting RGB, HSV, CMY(K) or alpha information.

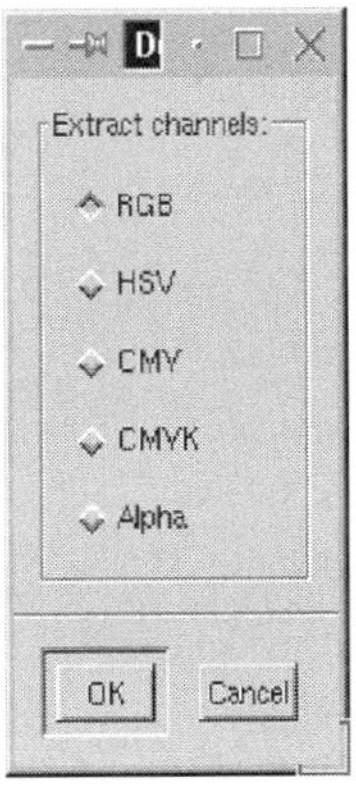

Figure 18.8 *The Decompose dialog*

RGB Decomposing

Decomposing to RGB is the same as activating a color channel in the **Layers & Channels** dialog, but now you'll get the color channels in the form of three different grayscale images. You can do a lot of things with decomposed images. The first thing that comes to mind is to edit them in different ways, and then use **Compose** to put them together again.

This option lets you manipulate color channels in ways that the **Channels** tab folder does not allow. If you *decompose* your image, there is, for example, no problem in performing operations like cutting/copying/pasting, or moving selections in a single RGB channel.

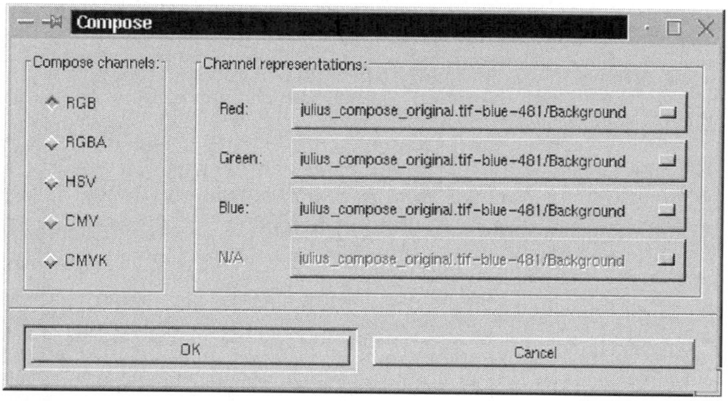

Figure 18.9 *The Compose dialog*

You can use an extracted *decomposed* grayscale as a **selection** or **mask** by saving it in a **channel** (`right-click|Select|Save to Channel`). Sometimes, there is very little of a certain color in the background compared to an object in the image. This gives you the perfect opportunity to create very exact selections of intricate objects. You can also play around with Compose/Decompose to create interesting patterns.

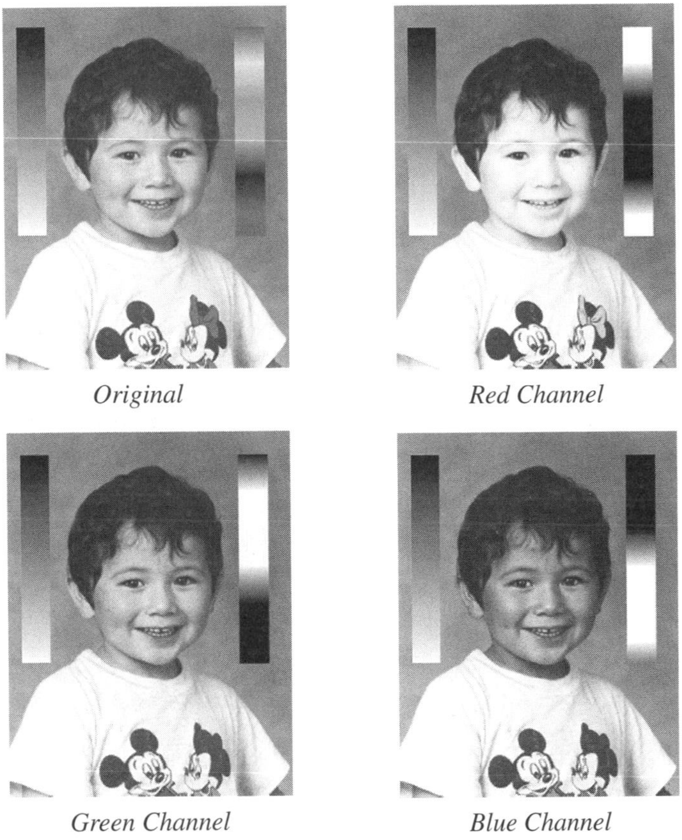

Figure 18.10
Example of an RGB image decomposed to three grayscale images; each grayscale represents a color channel, such as the red, green and blue channels

HSV Decomposing

The **HSV** decompose option creates three different grayscales: one for **Hue**, one for **Saturation** and one for **Value**.

It may seem strange that a grayscale image can describe color, as in **Hue**, but consider the HSV color circle. Imagine a circular gradient where white and black meet in the starting and ending points on the circle. Pure black and white represent red, which is on top of the HSV color circle. Dark gray equals orange or yellow, and medium gray tones represent green or cyan. Accordingly, light grays represent blue and magenta.

The **Saturation** and **Value** grayscales are easier to understand. White represents pure, strong color (Saturation) and maximum brightness (Value). Black means completely desaturated gray (Saturation) and black (Value).

Therefore, if you want something to be white in an HSV-based image, Saturation in that area must be set to black, and Value to white.

The big difference between **RGB Compose** and **HSV Compose** is that grayscale information means very different things for Hue, Saturation and Value, whereas gray in RGB channels just represents the concentration of a certain color.

This also explains why it is possible to manage with just one grayscale, when you are *composing* to HSV. If you were to use the same grayscale for composing RGB, the result would be exactly the same as the original grayscale. If you did the same for CMYK, you'd just end up with an overbright negative of the image.

To show the great difference between the HSV-extracted grayscales, we have decomposed an image to HSV and composed it again using Value in the place of Hue, and vice versa. See Figure 18.11, below.

Figure 18.11 *The same RGB image, but decomposed in HSV space*

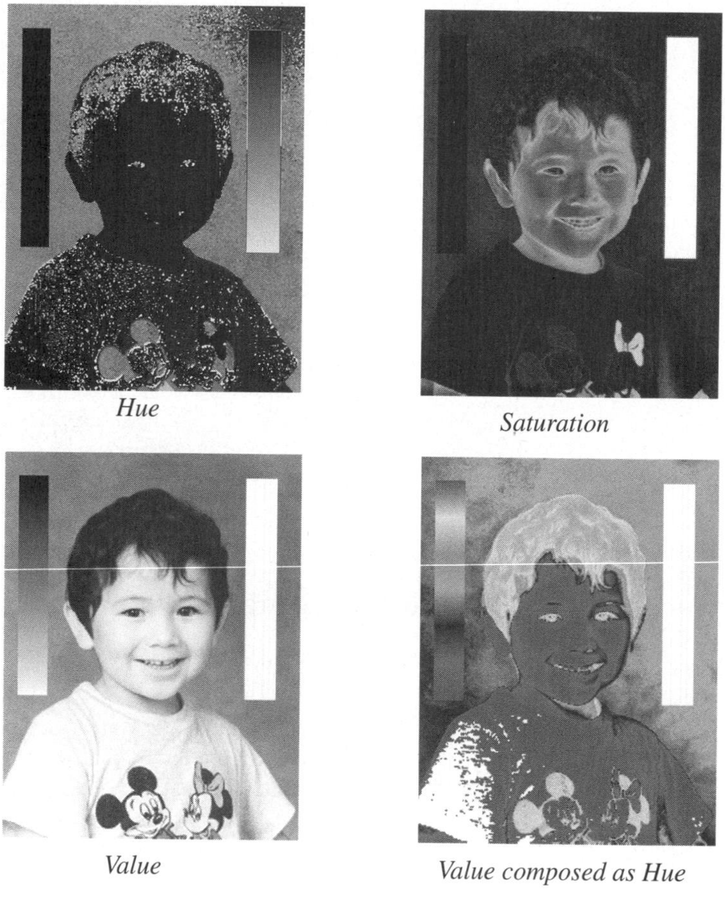

Hue *Saturation*

Value *Value composed as Hue*

CMYK And CMY Decomposing

The **CMY** or **CMYK Decompose** options are interesting if you are planning to print your work. The difference between CMY and CMYK decomposing is that CMY doesn't decompose to black, and therefore creates darker (more saturated) grayscale separations.

Using CMYK Decompose is actually the same as making your own color separation for four-color printing plates (see Figure 18.12). In principle, you can use CMYK Decompose, print the outcome on a laser printer, and give it to a professional print shop, but the professional printer will most likely do a much better separating job than you can. However, you can certainly achieve very interesting results with CMY/CMYK decomposed images, even if you don't use them for printing purposes.

Alpha Decomposing

Alpha Decompose is a fast and easy way of converting a semi-transparent layer to an equivalent grayscale. You can accomplish the same effect by using a **Layer Mask**, but Compose/Decompose lets you decompose a layer to alpha as well as to RGB, and then compose a new RGBA image from the edited grayscales. This allows you to edit all channel information, not just transparency.

It's a very convenient way to edit layers with transparency information, and a worthwhile alternative to editing using commands from the **Layers & Channels** menu.

Figure 18.12 *The same RGB image decomposed to CMYK; the four images at the bottom show what the outcome of each process plate would look like if it was printed on paper*

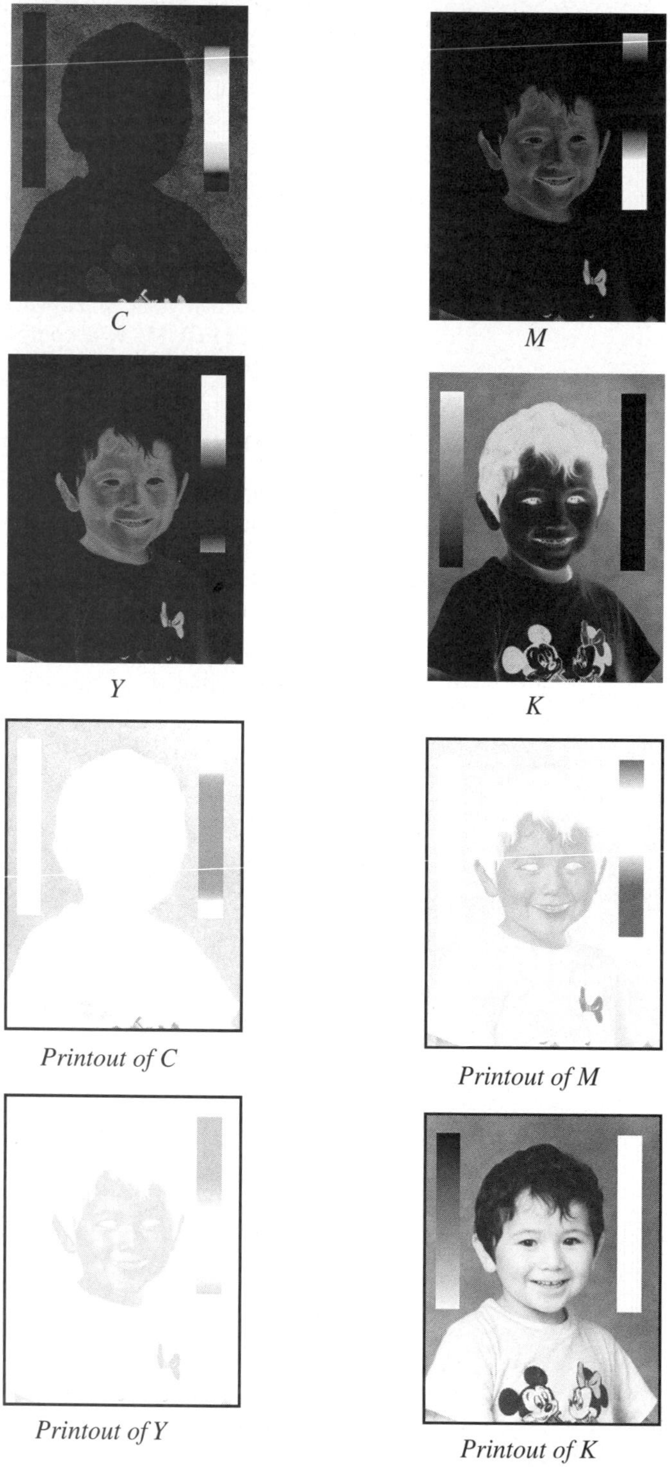

Alpha

Add Alpha Channel

If you wish to add alpha information (be able to work with transparency) to the background layer, you can use this option. **Add Alpha Channel** is also available in the `right-click|Layers` menu and in the menu you get when right-clicking in the **Layers & Channels** dialog. See "Channels And Duotones" starting on page 351 for more information on alpha channels.

Holes

This command requires a **layered image**. As you may have noticed, indexed images like GIF *don't* support **semi-transparency**. Holes creates a rather convincing illusion of semi-transparent pixels (at least if you compare it to a dithered Netscape image in 8 bit mode).

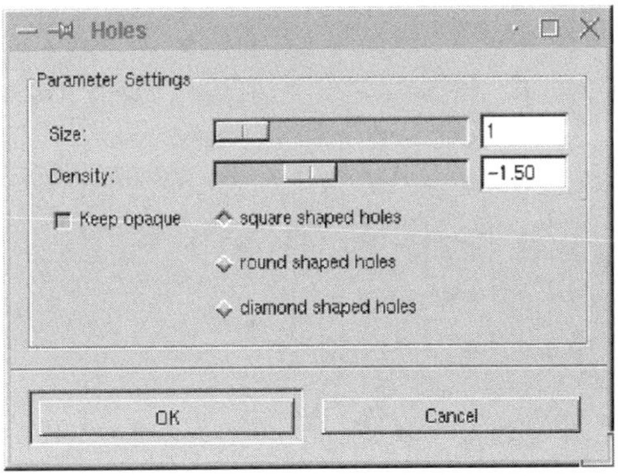

Figure 18.13 *The Holes dialog*

You can, of course, use **Dissolve** to achieve a similar effect, but this is slicker. In order to make this look good, you must use a small **Hole Size** (like 1) and a *medium to low* **Density** (like -1.50).

Make sure the **Keep Opaque** checkbox is checked. If you don't use Keep Opaque, you'll risk getting spillout or "dot pollution" on the transparent areas of the image. This is undesirable behavior if you're trying to create a semi-transparent look in a GIF, but if you're not, this option can result in quite nifty effects.

Depending on what effect you want, you can change the **shape** and **size** of the holes. You can choose from *square*, *round* and *diamond*, though round- and diamond-shaped holes require a minimum size of 2.

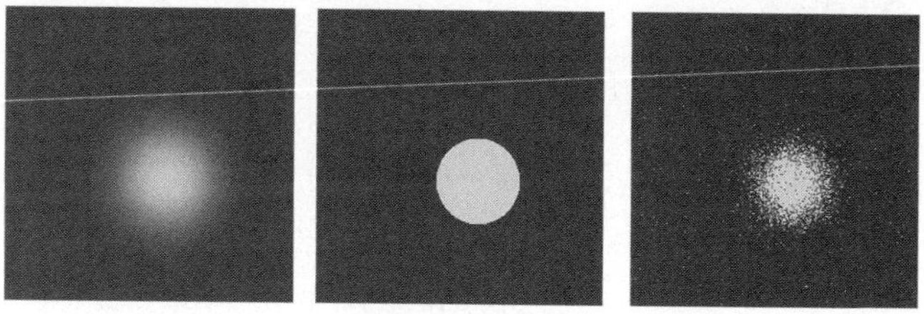

Original *Without Holes* *With Holes*

Figure 18.14 *A semi-transparent image converted to GIF with and without Holes*

THRESHOLD ALPHA

The `right-click|Image|Alpha|Threshold Alpha` filter only works for images which contain an alpha channel. Select **Add Alpha Channel** from the same menu to enable transparency.

Threshold Alpha lets you remove pixels by their **alpha value** or transparency. The resulting image is always totally transparent or solid and never semi-transparent, so it's a great tool for controlling the appearance of an image that you want to save as a transparent GIF. The slider value determines which values you want to remove. If you set a high value, only pixels with even higher alpha values (less transparent pixels) will remain after the filter is applied.

CHAPTER 19

Select Menu

Here, we will explore how Gimp allows you to make advanced selections using the commands in the Select menu.

CREATING SELECTIONS

TOGGLE

`Right-click|Select|Toggle` allows you to turn the "marching ants" border around layers and selections *on* or *off*. This border is sometimes distracting, and prevents you from seeing what you are doing, so this is a nice option.

INVERT

Use `right-click|Select|Invert` to select everything *except* your current selection — usually the background or surroundings of selected objects. Select what you *don't* want to include, then click on Invert to unselect the current selection and select the remainder of the image. Note that feathered selections will still be feathered when inverted, but the feathering will now do the "fuzzying" inwards, toward the object border.

ALL AND NONE

`Right-click|Select|All` selects everything in your image or layer. If you have several objects in a transparent layer and want to fill all of them at the same time (most commonly a text layer, where you want to select all of the letters), use **Select All** with the **Keep Trans.** checkbox on the **Layers & Channels** dialog checked.

You may also want to use this command to select an entire layer (with Keep Trans. unchecked) if you want to fill all of it with paint and discard the objects in it.

`Right-click|Select|None` unselects everything. You could just click on the layer with the rectangular or ellipse selection tools to get the same result, but if you drag the tool while doing this, you will transform the selection to a float. This option is quicker and safer.

FLOAT

Use `right-click|Select|Float` when you want your selection to **float**, but not to **move**. As previously discussed, you can transform a selection to a float by moving it when the Select tool is still active.

Moving it like this will change the position of the selection, at least a little bit. The effect will be even more obvious if you took the float from the background, so a "hole" now exists in the background image where the float used to be. Read more about floating selections in "Channels And Duotones" starting on page 351.

Adjusting Selections

Sharpen

`Right-click|Select|Sharpen` removes the **fuzziness** on the edges of a feathered selection, leaving a sharp-edged core. **Sharpen** will not restore any edge detail to a feathered selection, however.

Use Sharpen when you change your mind about feathering a selection. Perhaps more commonly, use Sharpen when you have added a fuzzy fill and want to enhance it by making a sharp fill or paste inside of the fuzzy one (a sharp selection is always smaller than a fuzzy selection).

Border

`Right-click|Select|Border` creates a new selection surrounding the outline of the old one. The new selection is a hollow border area or frame that covers an area both outside and inside the original selection edge.

Border is useful for applying special effects to text, or when you want to make drawings or frames from selections.

The Difference Between Border And Stroke

The effects of `right-click|Edit|Stroke` may seem similar to applying **Border** and filling the new selection. However, the Stroke outline is based on the shape, size, fuzziness and other parameters of the currently selected brush in the brush dialog.

A Border selection has fuzzy edges by default, the more so the wider the border is. This means that you may sometimes have to use Sharpen on the border before filling it, to remove unwanted blur effects.

Feather

`Right-click|Select|Feather` produces a selection with fuzzy edges. In other words, a feathered selection becomes more and more transparent until it reaches the edges of the selection. Feather allows you to blend a color or image softly with the background.

On the **Feather dialog** you select how much you want to feather the selection by. A low value produces a selection with a bit more softness to the edge than usual. The maximum value produces a very fuzzy selection; it will be so soft that you can fill it with patterns, then with colors, and then paste images into it, and all these things will blend together. If the **Keep Trans.** checkbox on the **Layers & Channels** dialog is checked, filling or painting within the selection will only affect areas that have an alpha value greater than zero (i.e., that are not fully transparent).

Feathering reduces the *detail* of the selection's shape. **Edge detail** disappears in a fuzzy fog, and a hand-shaped selection with fingers will look like a softball mitt at best. You can use this to your advantage if your selection isn't as smooth as you'd like. Use **Feather** to smooth, use **Grow** to make the selection a little bigger (compensating for the loss in size from feathering), and lastly use **Sharpen**.

Grow And Shrink

Grow and **Shrink** allow you to modify the size of the selection by a specified amount. If the selection edge has fine details, they will disappear if you shrink or grow too much.

If you want your selection to be bigger or smaller, but otherwise look the same, you should instead save the selection to a layer and apply the **Scale Layer** command from the menu you get by right-clicking in the `right-click|Layers|Layers & Channels` dialog.

Special Selection Commands

Save To Channel

If you are working with a complicated image, you should use `right-click|Select|Save To Channel` almost every time you make a selection. By saving the selection as a channel, you're storing the selection's shape and transparency in an **alpha channel**. After saving it as a channel, you can later activate the channel and use the selection again if you need it. You can also do very advanced selection editing using alpha channels. For more information, read "Channels And Duotones" starting on page 351.

By Color

Select By Color is a very advanced tool. You can use it to modify an existing selection, or you can create entirely new selections with it. This tool is based on color, but it works fine for grayscale or indexed images.

Click on By Color to display the **By Color Selection** dialog. Click on an area in your image. All pixels with that color or a similar color will be selected.

Figure 19.1 *An image with a color selected, and the By Color Selection dialog*

The **Fuzziness Threshold** slider lets you control how generous the "similarity" classification will be. A low Fuzziness Threshold value selects only pixels of that exact (or nearly exact) color. A high Fuzziness Threshold value accepts many similar shades/colors.

While you are selecting by color, you see a grayscale representation of your current selection in the By Color Selection dialog. This preview works just like an **alpha channel**. White parts represent solid selections (opaque), gray parts are for more or less feathered selections (semi-transparent) and black areas represent unselected areas (wholly transparent).

Selection Modes

The four **Selection Modes** are *Replace, Add, Subtract* and *Intersect.*

- **Replace** is the standard mode, and also the most important one. Use Replace Mode to choose the **basic color range** for your selection. If you are not happy with the basic selection, you can click on another place in your image to select a different spot, or change the Fuzziness Threshold value and then click on another spot.
- **Add** and **Subtract** are used to modify the basic selection. Click on the Add radio button and then click on an unselected part of the image and the new color or color range will be added to the selection.

- **Subtract** will **deselect** areas of unwanted color from your selection. Click on the Subtract radio button and then click on areas in your image to remove them from the selection.
- **Intersect** is a little trickier to understand. Intersect chooses areas of intermediate color between the original selection color and an adjacent color that you click on. If you click on a color that isn't directly adjacent to the original selection in the image, you'll end up with no selection at all. Using Intersect usually results in selecting thin, antialiased edges between different shapes.

Options

When you're using select By Color, you can see its **Tool Options** dialog by clicking on `File|Dialogs|Tool Options`.

Figure 19.2 *The By Color Selection options dialog*

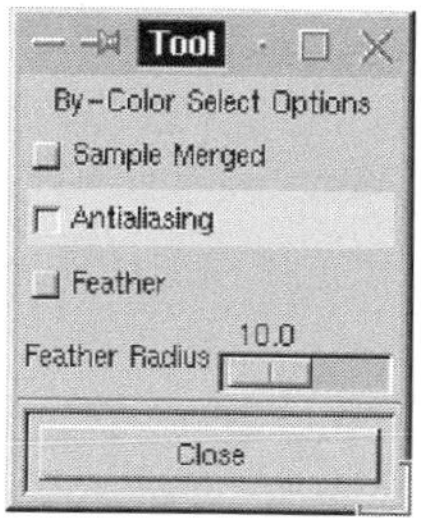

If you click on the **Sample Merged** option, you base the color selection on the entire composite image instead of just the colors in the active layer. This is useful if the active layer is slightly transparent or has another layer mode than *Normal*. Then, the colors of the composite image will be different than the colors present in the active layer.

The **Antialiasing** checkbox is checked by default. If you uncheck it, the selection will become sharp with absolutely no feathering.

The **Feather** option is quite interesting. Watch the selection preview window closely when you select with this option. You'll create soft cloudlike selections with *Replace*, and lightning or metal highlight effects with *Intersect*. Feel free to experiment with the Feather option checked. The results are always interesting.

If you like the grayscale selection preview and want to work with it as an image, you can save it using the **Save To Channel** command, and then copy and paste that channel to a layer.

Floating Selection
Floating Selection
Background copy
Background copy
Original Background

CHAPTER 20

Layers And Floating Selections

Layers and the use of layers are the foundation of effective image manipulation.

Introduction

If you're new to image manipulation, the concept of layers may not seem obvious, but using layers is really as simple and straightforward as wearing layers of clothes on your body. Once you have started to use layers, you won't understand how you could ever do without them.

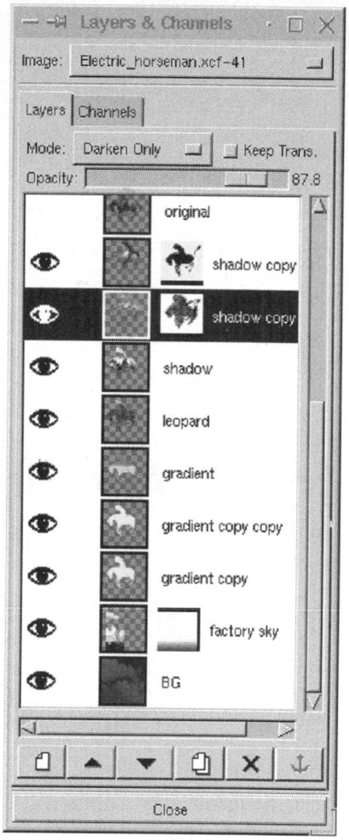

Figure 20.1 *The Layers dialog*

Composite Image Information

An image created or manipulated in Gimp usually consists of several image objects. You may, for instance, have copied and pasted parts of other images into your image, or perhaps you have added a text string. Instead of placing all of these things onto a single background, you can paste or paint them in different layers.

These layers are just like a stack of transparent plastic sheets placed on top of one another, creating a **composite** image. This means that you can easily manipulate the contents of a certain layer without affecting the rest of the image. You also have artistic freedom with the possibility to adjust the transparency in a layer, or to composite it with other layers using **Layer Modes**.

Optimal Layer Size

Contrary to other graphics programs where all layers have the same size as the image, Gimp has the ability to **optimize** the layer size. When you turn a selection (for example, a text string) into a layer, the new layer is never larger than the selection itself. This saves both disk space and valuable processing time. The edges of the small layers appear as a yellow dotted line, and can easily be distinguished. It is also a great advantage to be able to move an entire layer and its contents with the **Move** tool, instead of first having to select the image object and then move it within the layer.

THE LAYERS & CHANNELS DIALOG

Open the Layers & Channels dialog (`right-click|Dialogs|Layers & Channels` or `right-click|Layers|Layers & Channels`). There are two tabs: **Layers** and **Channels**. Channels will be discussed in "Channels And Duotones" starting on page 351.

The Layers Tab

The Layers tab includes **Image** and **Mode** pull-down menus, an **Opacity** slider and a **Keep Trans.** (Keep Transparent) checkbox.

The **Image** pull-down menu is at the top of the dialog, and will display the name of your image. If you are working with several images, the Image pull-down menu is very useful, because all open images are listed in it and you can choose the one you want to work with by clicking on its name.

Six buttons are at the bottom of the dialog: **New Layer**, **Raise Layer**, **Lower Layer**, **Duplicate Layer**, **Delete Layer** and **Anchor** floating selection. All of these buttons will be discussed later in this chapter.

Each layer has a **bar** corresponding to it in the dialog window. The bar contains a **thumbnail icon** of the layer. An **eye icon** is to the left of the thumbnail, and if your image only contains one layer, your image/layer will be called **Background**.

BASIC LAYER OPERATIONS

NEW LAYER

If you right-click on a layer's bar, another menu will appear that includes a few more options than the `right-click|Layers` menu. Choose the first option on the list — **New Layer —** or click the left toolbar button.

When you choose New Layer, the **New Layer Options** dialog will appear. Name your layer in the Layer name box. For example, you could call the layer "shadow" if you are going to create a shadow of an image object in this layer. Always name your layers if you work with a lot of them, especially when you use similar layers with different functions.

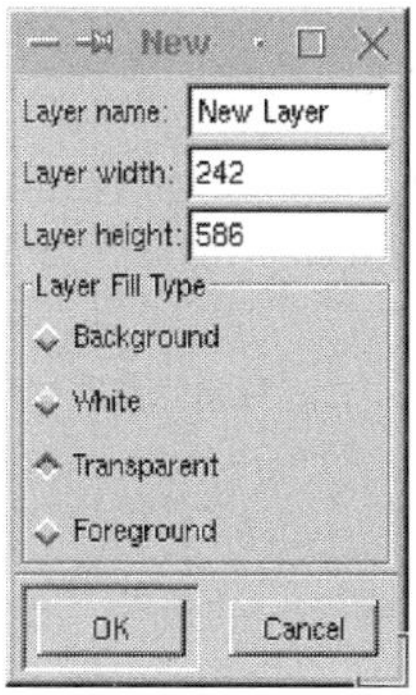

Figure 20.2 *The New Layer Options dialog*

If you don't want the new layer to be the same size as the background, you can specify the size of the layer by filling values into the **Layer width** and **Layer height** boxes.

You also need to decide on a **Layer Fill Type**. Your options are **Background** (the current background color in the toolbox), **White**, **Transparent** and **Foreground** (the current foreground color in the toolbox). White is the default fill. Click on the radio button for the fill you want and click on the OK button. Now, you have created a new layer on top of your background.

THE ACTIVE LAYER

When you have two ore more layers, it's really important to know which one is the **active layer**. As soon as you have several layers in an image, Gimp's actions are in the active layer, so you can only work in one layer at a time. The active layer's bar in the dialog is marked with blue. If you click on another layer's bar, it will become the active layer.

If a layer is smaller than the background layer, you can also make it active by clicking in it (in the image) with the **Move** tool. If you want to move a **transparent** layer, or just make sure that you move the right layer, press the Shift key as you drag. With the Shift key pressed, only the active layer will move. When the selected layer's boundary changes color from yellow to blue, you know that it's safe to move it. For more information about the Move tool, see "The Move Tool" on page 156.

THE BACKGROUND LAYER

Remember that your original image was automatically named Background? The **background layer** doesn't act exactly like other layers. The background layer is a fixed and solid area for other layers to work against. The background works the same way that it did when you didn't have any other layers. When you cut parts of it, or use the eraser, the background color shows, and not a transparent surface.

You also can't use **Layer masks** (see "Add Layer Mask" on page 322) on the background layer, and you can't **raise** the background layer. Normally, you won't need to do any of these things with a background layer, but if you want to (for transparent GIFs, for example), double-click on the background layer's bar, and **rename** it. From then on, it will act like any other layer. To achieve the same result, you could also use `right-click|Layers|Add Alpha Channel`, or duplicate the background, keep the copy and delete the original.

Symbols And Explanations

The Eye Icon

The eye icon allows you to **toggle** the visibility of layers on and off, so you can work with a particular layer without having to see all other layers. Click on the **eye icon** and the image/layer will disappear if you have more than one layer in your image. Click again and it returns. If you press the Shift key and click on an eye icon, all of the layers except that one will be hidden from view. If you press Shift and click on that eye icon again, the other layers will return.

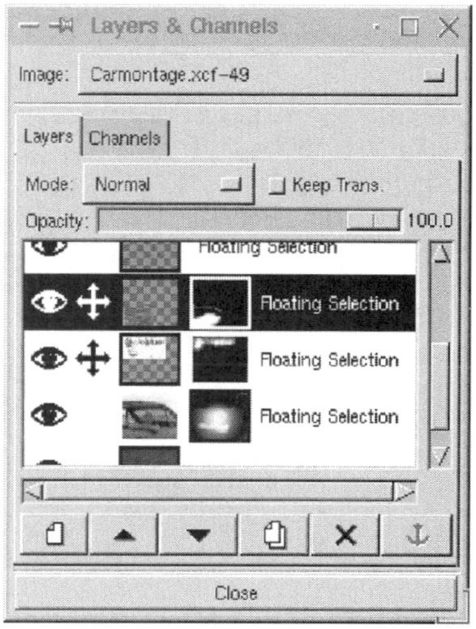

Figure 20.3 *Symbols in the Layers dialog*

Linking Layers

If you click between the eye icon and the thumbnail icon, you'll see a crossed **arrows** symbol (like the Move cursor). The cross symbol *links* layers. **Linking** layers means that all layers with the cross symbol are locked or **grouped** in relation to each other, so you can't move one layer without moving the others at the same time.

Remember to unlink layers before moving another layer; otherwise, you'll move all of the layers even if the linked layers aren't active.

Keep Transparent

To understand the **Keep Trans.** button, you'll need to have something drawn in a transparent layer. Make the layer active, and paint something with the **Paintbrush** tool (with Keep Trans. unchecked, which is the default). Then check Keep Trans., change the color of your paint, and start painting again. You will only be allowed to paint the **opaque** areas, i.e., the areas that you already painted.

Keep Trans. protects the boundaries of opaque shapes in a transparent layer. It also makes it very easy to change opaque shapes' colors, because you never have to worry about painting outside of their edges. If you want to use a filter on a layer, you normally won't want to have this option checked, because if Keep Trans. is checked, the filter will only affect the interior of opaque objects in the transparent layer.

Naming

You can **rename** a layer by double-clicking on the layer's old name. The **Edit Layer Attributes** dialog will allow you to type in a new name.

Figure 20.4 *The Edit Layer Attributes dialog*

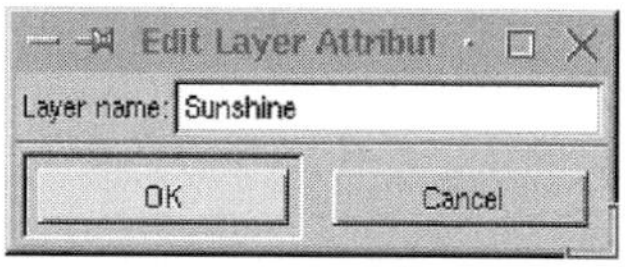

The Layer Toolbar Buttons

New Layer

Creates a new layer, as described in the paragraph "New Layer" on page 317.

Raise Layer And Lower Layer

These commands (and the corresponding buttons on the **Layers & Channels** dialog) move the active layer to a higher or lower position in the layer hierarchy. You can only raise or lower a layer one step at a time. The background layer can't be raised, unless you **rename** it or apply **Add Alpha Channel** (see "Add Alpha Channel" on page 325).

Duplicate Layer

Makes a **copy** of the active layer, and places it immediately above the original.

Delete Layer

Deletes the active layer.

Anchor Layer

Anchor Layer is used to **merge** floating selections with a layer (the layer that was active before you placed the float). If you don't know what a floating selection is, read "Floating Selections" on page 331.

Usually, all you need to do is click in a floating selection to make it stick to a layer. Sometimes, the **Move** tool needs to be active for this to work (for example, when you are trying to anchor a floating text string). However, the **Anchor Layer** command always works and is quick, especially if you use the shortcut key (Ctrl+h, unless you've changed your hotkeys).

THE LAYER DIALOG MENU

If you right-click on a **layer's bar**, the **Layer Dialog** menu will appear. The first five commands (and Anchor Layer) on the Layer Dialog Menu have already been discussed in "The Layer Toolbar Buttons" on page 320, and the more complex options, such as Layer Mask and alpha commands, will be discussed in the next section.

Scale Layer

Shrinks or enlarges the layer *and its contents*, to measurements that you specify.

Resize Layer

Changes the **size** of the layer, *but not its contents.* If the contents of the layer are larger than the new layer size, the image or selection will be cropped to fit the new layer size. You can use **X Offset** and/or **Y Offset** to place the original layer in a particular spot inside a larger resized layer.

Figure 20.5 *The Resize Layer dialog*

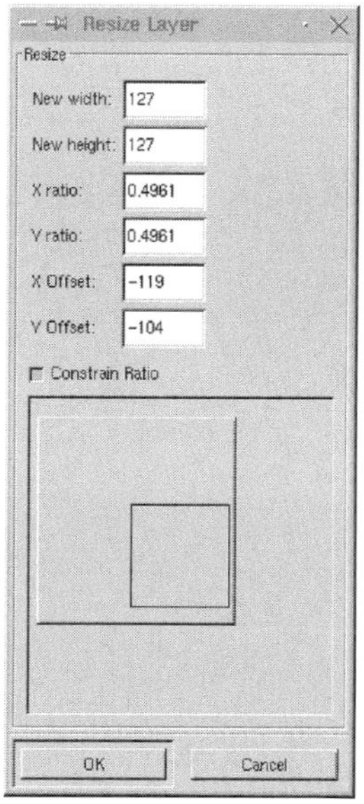

Merge Visible Layers

This function *combines* all layers that have the eye icon turned on. Invisible layers are not affected. The options **Expanded as necessary** and **Clipped to image** have the same result: The merged layer is just big enough to fit all layers, but no larger. **Clipped to bottom layer** results in a merged layer with exactly the same dimensions as the bottom layer.

Figure 20.6 *The Layer merge option dialog*

ToBot, ToTop

The active layer is moved to the *top* or *bottom* position.

Flatten Image

Flatten Image merges *all* layers without exception. Remember that you must use Flatten Image before saving your image, if you want to save it in any image format other than XCF and GIF formats. Also remember to *erase* your **alpha channels** (see "Alpha Channels" on page 353) if you have made any in the Channels folder. Many image formats and printers don't understand alpha channels.

Mask, Alpha And Selection Operations

Open the `right-click|Layers` menu to find these commands.

Add Layer Mask

Add Layer Mask is an advanced option, used for changing the **alpha** (transparency) values in a layer. If you don't know what alpha values are, read "Alpha Channels" on page 353.

When you add a layer mask to a layer, you always work with a **grayscale** image (you can use colors, but they will appear as shades of gray in the mask). In the layer mask, black means transparent and white means opaque. After you create a layer mask, the objects in that layer will be more or less transparent, based on the values of white and black in the layer mask.

After you click on Add Layer Mask, the Add Mask Options dialog will appear. You'll need to choose which initial **fill** you want: White, Black or the Layer's Alpha Channel. If you choose **Black**, you start with a *transparent* mask, **White** gives an *opaque* mask and **Layer's Alpha Channel** means that the mask will use the layer's alpha values.

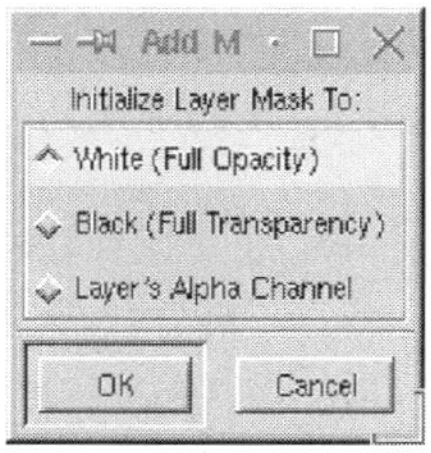

Figure 20.7 *The Add Mask Options dialog*

After you've chosen the initial fill, a small layer mask thumbnail appears next to the layer thumbnail. To switch between layer mask and layer, click on the appropriate thumbnail.

Mask Display Options

You need more than the **mask thumbnail** to edit the mask. Press the Alt key and click on the mask thumbnail, and you'll see the grayscale mask in place of your image. *Note that the mask thumbnail is now outlined in* ***green***. When you want to check the result of the mask, press Alt and click on the thumbnail again and you'll see what your image looks like with the mask effect.

To see your image *without* the mask, press the Ctrl key and click on the mask thumbnail. *The thumbnail will be outlined in* ***red***. Press Ctrl and click on the thumbnail again to view the mask again.

You can alternate between the two display options (the mask alone and the image alone) by pressing on the Alt key and clicking, but to enter and exit this alternating mode, you'll need to Ctrl and click first.

Layer Masks Made From Gradients

A very useful mask can be made from a **gradient fill** (see Figure 20.8). A gradient results in the top layer gradually blending with the background. You can paint areas of transparency where you want them, or use a filter or pattern to create an interesting mask. You can use selections or paste an image into the mask.

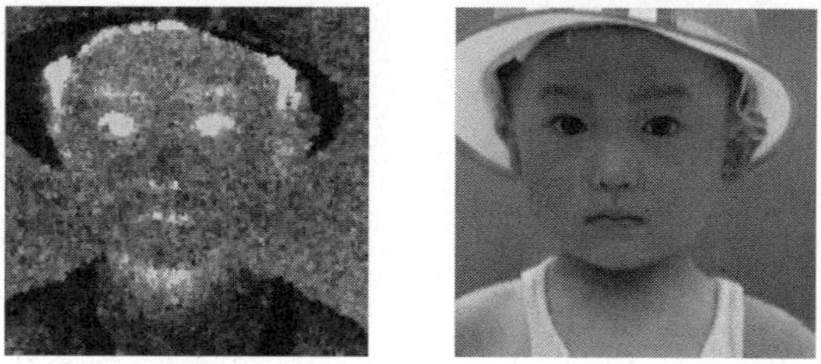

In the examples shown here, we have used two different layer masks to create two different effects. The first layer mask was created by copying the boy's face into the mask, inverting it and adding some noise to it.

The second layer mask was made from filling square selections with different gradients. The layer was set in Value Mode.

Figure 20.8 *Different ways of using the layer mask function*

Apply Layer Mask

Click on **Apply Layer Mask** when you're ready to apply your mask or if you don't like it and you want to discard it. If you discard it, the mask will be removed. If you cancel, you will only cancel the operation itself.

Figure 20.9 *The Layer Mask dialog*

Alpha To Selection

Use the **Alpha To Selection** command to transform opaque or semi-transparent shapes in a transparent layer into a selection.

This command is so useful that you'll use it nearly every time you work with a layered image. When you work with different layers, you mostly work within the *shape* of an object.

For example, if you're working with an image of a saucer, you'll want a copy of the saucer shape underneath the actual saucer to create a saucer-shaped *shadow*. You'll also want another saucer copy to accentuate *highlights* in the porcelain, another to show dark areas, another with a special pattern on it, etc. For every copy of the saucer, you just want the empty shape or the selection of the saucer, not a copy of the entire image with a saucer in it. The shape of the selection applies to all layers. Just activate the layer you want to work in, and start working.

Mask To Selection

Mask To Selection is the equivalent of **Alpha To Selection**, but for masks. This command isn't used as often as Alpha To Selection, but if you've made a good mask it's nice to be able to use it again in another layer.

Add Alpha Channel

Use Add Alpha Channel if you want to enable **transparency** in the background layer. There are other ways to accomplish this, but Add Alpha Channel is fast and easy.

LAYER ALIGN, ADJUST AND MOVE OPERATIONS

ALIGN VISIBLE LAYERS

`Right-click|Layers|Align Visible Layers` is used to *position* layers in a very exact way, especially if you're working with a lot of small layers. For example, Align Visible Layers is ideal for correcting frames in *GIF animations*. Align Visible Layers only works on **visible** layers (which have the **eye icon** turned on).

Horizontal Style

Horizontal style controls how layers are positioned **horizontally** in relation to each other. The consequence of this is that horizontal style *aligns vertically*, although it cannot change a layer's vertical position. The choices for horizontal style are:

- **None:** No change in horizontal position.
- **Collect:** The top layer controls where the lower layers end up. The lower layers' **horizontal bases** snap to the horizontal coordinate of the top layer's horizontal base.

Figure 20.10 *Horizontal style*

- **Fill (left to right):** Places the layers from left to right, starting with the top layer. The distance from the horizontal base of a layer to the next layer is always the same. If the top layer's horizontal base is already to the left of the others, it will not change horizontal position.
- **Fill (right to left):** The same as **Fill (left to right)** except that the layers are set from right to left.
- **Snap to grid:** The chosen edge will snap to the nearest **horizontal grid line**. A chosen corner *(left edge and top edge makes a corner)* will snap to the nearest **node** in the grid system you made.

Horizontal Base

Horizontal base controls what *horizontal* edge the layers snap to or fill from: the Left edge, the Center or the Right edge.

Vertical Style

Vertical style controls how layers are positioned **vertically** in relation to each other, so that they *align horizontally*.

- **None:** No change in vertical position.
- **Collect:** All of the lower layers snap their **vertical base** to the vertical coordinate of the top layer's vertical base.

Figure 20.11 *Vertical style*

- **Fill (top to bottom):** Places the layers from *top* to *bottom*, so the distance from the vertical base of one layer to the next is always the same. If the top layer's vertical base is over the top of the others, it will not change vertical position.
- **Fill (bottom to top):** Works the same way as **Fill (top to bottom)**, except that it works from bottom to top.
- **Snap to grid:** Snaps the vertical base to the nearest **vertical grid line**. A chosen corner will snap to the nearest node.

Vertical Base

Vertical base controls what *vertical* edge the layers snap to or fill from: the Top edge, the Center or the Bottom edge.

Collect

Use Collect to **stack** objects in horizontal or vertical rows. To place your layers exactly on top of each other, choose **Collect** from the Horizontal style and Vertical style pull-down menus, select **Center** from both the Horizontal base and Vertical base pull-down menus, and click on the OK button.

Fill

Fill is useful for **animations** where you want to move an object in equal steps frame by frame. If the layers are placed on top of each other, or very close together, you'll need to move them apart before you use Fill.

Figure 20.12 *Fill*

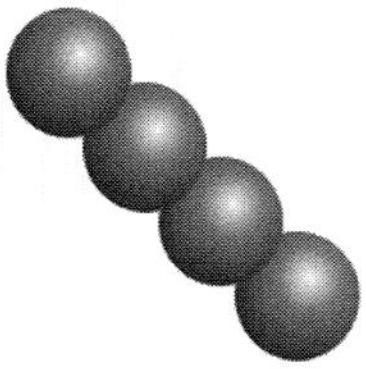

Moving small layers is very easy. If you click on a small layer with the **Move** tool, that layer automatically becomes active, so you can drag and drop layers easily without having to choose them in the **Layers & Channels** dialog.

You can't precisely control the distance between layers, but if you spread the layers as far apart as possible before alignment, you'll get the maximum separation between them after the alignment. As you align using Fill several times, the distance between layers reduces. Each time you use Fill, the layers move closer together until the layers' chosen edges touch.

Tip: Link the layers (with the cross symbol in the layer bar) after using Fill. You can then move all of the layers as a group.

Snap To Grid

Snap to Grid is indispensable for planning an **animation**, with one problem: The grid created with **Grid size** is *invisible.*

So first, you need to make the grid *visible*. To do this, create a new full-sized layer. Create a grid with `right-click|Filters|Render|Grid` and set the **X Size** and the **Y Size** to the same sizes used as Grid size for the invisible alignment grid.

Figure 20.13 *Snap to Grid*

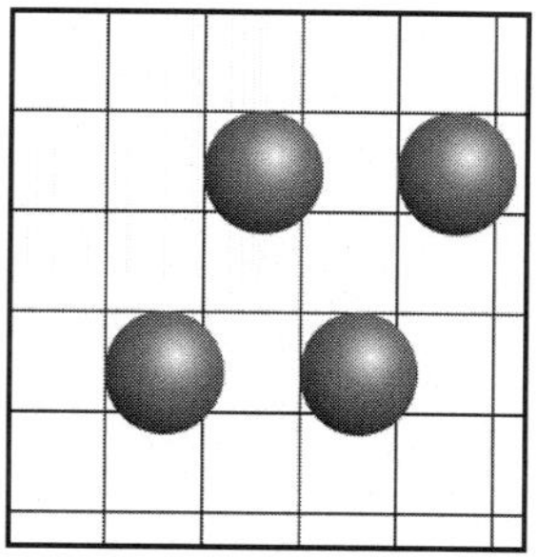

Remember that different layers may snap to different nodes in the grid, because each layer will snap to the node/line that is nearest to its chosen edge/corner. The best way to work with Snap to Grid is to place the layers close to where you want them, and *then* align them perfectly with Snap to Grid.

If the grid doesn't work for you, you can always correct positions afterwards using **Guides**; see “Guides” on page 151.

Other Align Visible Layers Parameters

The Ignore the bottom layer even if visible checkbox is checked by default. This is wise in most cases. When you have created layers with a fixed background, you normally don't want the background to start moving.

The Use the (invisible) bottom layer as the base checkbox is not checked by default. If you check it, then the background or bottom layer is treated like any other layer and is aligned as you align the other layers. Use this option if you want to make a GIF animation with transparent background.

The Grid size slider and/or box allow you to set the size of the invisible grid. The grid squares can measure up to 200 pixels.

Adjust Layers

When you add a small layer to an image, you may want to adjust that layer in relation to another layer or the image border. **Adjust layers** will help you do this in several ways. You must first choose the layer(s) or image border to which you want the adjustment to be relative. Then, you need to specify the layers you want to adjust. The adjustments are controlled by four checkboxes. As you see in Table 20.1, there are sixteen different combinations of the four checkboxes.

Table 20.1 *Adjust layers*

Left	Right	Top	Bottom	Result
X				Adjust to the left. No vertical change.
	X			Adjust to the right. No vertical change.
X	X			Center layer horizontally. No vertical change.
		X		Adjust to the top. No horizontal change.
X		X		Adjust to the top-left corner.
	X	X		Adjust to the top-right corner.
X	X	X		Center layer horizontally and adjust to the top.
			X	Adjust to bottom. No horizontal change.
X			X	Adjust to the bottom-left corner.
	X		X	Adjust to the bottom-right corner.
X	X		X	Center layer horizontally and adjust to bottom.
		X	X	Center layer vertically. No horizontal change.
X		X	X	Center layer vertically and adjust to the left.
	X	X	X	Center layer vertically and adjust to the right.
X	X	X	X	Center layer in all directions.

You can also select a layer in the pull-down menu. You should keep the **Layers & Channels** dialog up, so you can set the layers that should be **linked**, **visible** or **active**. All these functions make it easy to adjust several layers against the image border or another layer. You can, for example, use a combination in which you adjust *all linked layers* against *all visible layers*.

Move Layer

Move Layer can be used to move one or several layers in a more precise way than can be done by hand with the **Move** tool.

Select a layer to move from the pull-down menu. The sliders set the distance and direction of the movement. If you want to move more than one layer you have to check **Affect visible layers**, **Affect linked layers** or both. If you don't check any of these buttons, only the layer selected in the pull-down menu will be affected. You must also choose how to move the layers: Relative or Absolute.

Relative will move the layers with the selected layer's *current position* as reference. **Absolute** will move the layers with the image *border* as reference.

IMPORT LAYERS

Import Layers can **import** one or more layers from another image. The **source** image can be bigger or smaller than the **target** image. There is a menu where you select an image to import layers from, and several options for selecting what layers you want to import. You can make importing easier by bringing up the **Layers & Channels** dialog.

As you can see in the interface, you can import the layers in the way they appear in the source image, or in reverse order. You can also choose what layers you want to import: **linked** (ones with the little cross), **visible**, **selected** or **all layers**. To import a layer, press OK or Apply. Pressing Apply will keep the dialog open after importing, so you can continue importing layers from other images.

TRANSFORMS

The Layers Transforms option is very similar to the graphic "drag and see what it looks like" Transforms tool, except that it doesn't show you a preview. You can specify each value in a coordinate system for very exact transforming, but you must know in advance what is going to happen when you specify those values.

PERSPECTIVE

The Perspective option allows you to change the position of each corner in the original layer by dragging the sliders or typing a coordinate value in the value field. As is the case with the `Transforms|Perspective` command, *skew* would perhaps be a more appropriate name than *perspective*. Still, this tool is quite useful for making exact perspective or skew transformations.

ROTATE 3-D

Contrary to the Perspective commands, Rotate 3-D is a *true* **perspective** filter. It is based on simple plane geometry, so it's not difficult to understand. Imagine your image as a plane rotating on a ball joint, so that it can be turned in any direction. The x-parameter flips it around the horizontal axis and the y-parameter does the same around the vertical axis. The z-parameter makes the image rotate like a wheel.

The **Depth** option allows you to add more depth to the perspective, as if you were smaller or the object was larger. An object that is enormous compared to the beholder (like a football field) will appear to vanish in the horizon, whereas a small piece of paper in the beholder's hand will not show much perspective effect at all, even though you see them from the same angle.

Rotate Any Angle

Rotate any angle is the perfect complement to the **Rotate** tool in the toolbox. This tool allows you to specify the exact rotation angle (instead of relying on manual rotation or on 15 degrees of rotation at a time). Note, to make one degree increments, don't drag at the slider; click on the left or right side of the slidebar push button.

Scale

Scale makes your layer larger or smaller in both the X and Y directions. This function also **moves** your layer as it scales it, so watch out for its *new position!*

Shear

Shear is a great complement to the **Shear** tool, because it allows you to specify a precise shear angle, in the same way as the **Rotate any Angle** command does.

Floating Selections

What Is A Floating Selection?

When you first place a text string, move a selection or choose `right-click|Select|Float`, your free, empty selection is transformed to a **floating selection** with a pixel content.

This means that the selection contains information that isn't attached to any layer. It *floats* independently. Changes to a floating selection won't affect the rest of the image (note on the **Layers** tab on the **Layers & Channels** dialog how all of the layers are grayed out).

What Can You Do With A Floating Selection?

You are restricted by the "marching ants" selection border, but you can affect your float in the following ways:

You can change the **color** by using the `right-click|Image` options or by using `right-click|Filters` on your selection. You can use the **Eraser** tool to reduce the selection, you can **edit** it with cut/copy/paste and you can **move** the selection.

You can't use any of the **Select** commands on a floating selection. You can, however, make a selection *inside* the floating selection, and use Select commands on that selection. Read more about moving and selecting within a floating selection in "Selections Within Floating Selections" on page 113.

Anchoring A Floating Selection

In the **Layers & Channels** dialog, you can choose **Anchor layer** (the button or from the right-click pull-down menu) and the float will *merge* with the layer that was active before you placed the float.

The simplest way to anchor a floating selection is to click your mouse anywhere in the image (*outside* the floating selection if the **Move** tool is active).

You can save a float as a *new layer* by right-clicking on the Floating Selection bar in the Layers & Channels dialog and clicking on **New Layer**, or simply by clicking the New Layer button. The new layer's size will be the same as the float.

In Photoshop, all layers are the same size as the image, but Gimp saves disk space by adapting the layer size to the size of the floating selection. The dotted yellow layer border, which you'll see around your floated layer, constitutes the boundaries of the drawable surface in a layer. You can't paint or make a selection outside of this border in that layer, and if you use the **Move** tool on that layer, you'll move the entire layer around.

Moving Objects In A Floating Selection Layer

To move an image object in a layer made from a floating selection (like a character in a text string), you must first select it (the **Lasso** or the **Wand** tools are good choices). When you try to move the selection, it will turn into a new floating selection.

When you have moved the selection and released the mouse button, you need to immediately activate the **Move** tool, or you'll just get irritating subselections (as discussed in "Moving Selections" on page 112). To avoid this, don't move the selection with the first automatic move cursor that appears as soon as you've made a selection and you move your mouse cursor over the selection. Instead, use `right-click|Select|Float` to select the float, then activate the Move tool and move your float.

When you're happy with the position of the float, anchor it to the layer with the Anchor button or with `right-click|Layers|Anchor Layer`. Remember that the text layer will be very small and snug unless you specified a **Border** in the Text tool dialog. In order to anchor single text characters to the text layer, you may have to increase the layer size with the **Resize Layer** command (from the popup menu that appears when you right-click on a layer in the **Layers & Channels** dialog).

Working With Floating Selections

If you want to apply any of the selection options in the Select menu to create special effects to a floating selection; a text string, for example, you should remember the following guidelines.

Put The Float In A Layer Of Its Own

There are two ways of doing this. Click on the **New Layer** icon in the bottom of the Layers & Channels dialog or select New Layer from the right-click menu and you'll place the floating selection in a new transparent layer called **Floated Layer**. If you double-click on the Floating Selection bar in the Layers & Channels dialog, you'll place the floating selection in a new transparent layer called **Floating Selection** or **Text layer** if you're placing a text string. As in any other layer, you can't use Select menu options until you select something.

Select Menu Options In A Floated Layer

To apply effects like `right-click|Select|Border` or `right-click|Select|Feather`, you must first *select* the image object (e.g., text) inside the transparent layer with the `right-click|Layers|Alpha to Selection` command. This results in an ordinary non-floating selection, because this command selects everything with an alpha value greater than zero (everything opaque or semi-transparent in the layer). If a pixel's alpha value equals zero, that pixel is transparent.

If you have used Select menu options that will create a *larger* selection size than the original object selection, you'll have to *uncheck* the **Keep Trans.** button in order to apply paint to all parts of the new selection. This is because Keep Trans. *preserves* all transparent pixels.

The Keep Trans. option allows you to paint an image object *without selecting* it. If you use the **Bucket fill** tool instead of a brush, you should remember to Select All to paint all letters at the same time.

The Size Of Floating Selection Layers

Since the **Floating Selection** layer is reduced in size, filter effects and large selections may be cut off by the layer border. Also, if you make too many changes in the original layer, the pure form of the shape (especially for letters) will soon disappear.

This is why it's usually a good idea to use a different layer for each effect. Change to a *lower* layer to create special effects (the selection goes through all layers, and you can choose any layer you want to work in). In a full-sized transparent layer, you need not worry about such restrictions.

CHAPTER 21

Modes

Modes are powerful instruments for applying layers and paint. Gimp provides many different ways of combining layers and they're all very useful. If you learn how to use modes, you have learned a lot about computer graphics.

What Are Modes?

Blending Modes or *Transfer Modes* control how the pixels in a foreground layer blend into the background layer(s). Modes are mainly used with layers, but they can also be used more directly as Paint Modes with the **Bucket tool**, the **Blend tool** or any tool that uses **Brush Selection**. Gimp provides 15 different modes:

- Normal
- Dissolve
- Multiply
- Screen
- Overlay
- Difference
- Addition
- Subtract
- Darken Only
- Lighten Only
- Hue
- Saturation
- Color
- Value
- Behind *(not available for layers)*

The modes that are available for any of the painting tools are available from the Mode pull-down menu on the **Brush Selection** dialog `right-click|Dialogs|Brushes` or `File|Dialogs|Brushes`.

The modes used for layers are available from the Mode pull-down menu on the **Layers & Channels** dialog (`right-click|Layers|Layers & Channels`).

Normal

Normal Mode is the default mode, and doesn't do anything special, as you might expect. A Normal Mode layer covers all other layers, unless there are **transparent** or **semi-transparent** areas in it.

Figure 21.1 *Normal Mode*

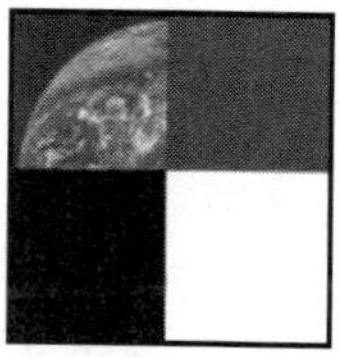

Dissolve

Dissolve Mode is very similar to Normal Mode, but this mode is used for **semi-transparency**. It displays pixels as either completely transparent or completely solid, according to the level of opacity you set. In order to see the effect of this mode, you must first make the layer or paint transparent with the **Opacity** slider.

Figure 21.2 *Dissolve Mode*

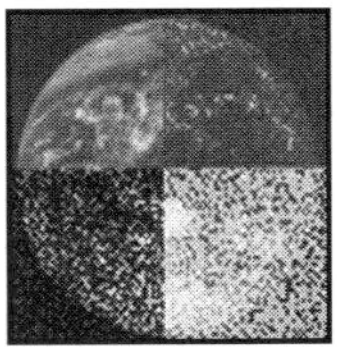

If you're painting in Normal Mode at 50% opacity, you'll get a smooth semi-transparent surface. Dissolve Mode will instead produce noise effects similar to grainy film or granite rock. Instead of using semi-transparent pixels, Dissolve Mode produces either entirely *opaque* or entirely *transparent* pixels, 50% of each (if 50% is the **Opacity** value).

As you probably know, GIFs only include transparent or non-transparent pixels. If you want a transparent GIF to look semi-transparent, you can use Dissolve Mode (or **Holes** in the `right-click|Image|Alpha` menu to achieve the effect. This is good for rough, grainy effects, but a soft or smooth semi-transparent surface (glowing text for example) will probably look much better with a solid background that is indexed to match the background on your page.

This mode is used with semi-transparency, where it displays pixels as wholly transparent or fully solid, according to the level of transparency.

Multiply

Multiply amplifies **shadows** or dark areas of the image. You can compare it to putting two slides on top of each other on a light table. White areas are transparent, dark areas on top of dark areas become darker. Colors act as if they were layers of colored glass on top of each other, or as color works in the CMYK color model (for example, yellow + magenta = red).

Figure 21.3 *Multiply Mode*

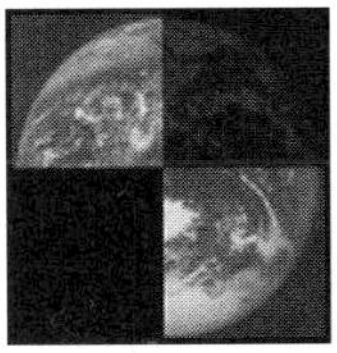

This mode works with shadow, much like putting two slides on top of each other.

Screen

Screen is the mode you should use to create **highlights** in an image, and is in many ways the opposite of **Multiply**. You can compare it to projecting two slides onto a film screen.

This mode depends on *light*, so black is transparent (just like a black spot on one slide will allow the image on the other slide to show) and *the result is always lighter*. Accordingly, the darker a layer is, the less it will affect the composite image, and vice versa.

In Screen Mode, white covers everything, gray shades get more transparent the darker they get, and color is only visible if the other layer's color permits it (we are talking about RGB color, so yellow + magenta = white, just like on your computer monitor or television set). Read more in "What Is The Difference Between Screen, Addition And Lighten Only?" on page 346.

Figure 21.4 *Screen Mode*

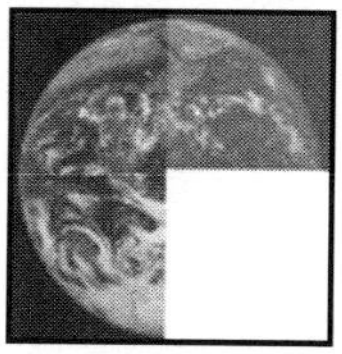

This mode works with light, much like projecting two slides onto the same screen.

Overlay

Overlay Mode is something of a combination of **Screen** and **Multiply**. Medium gray is transparent in this mode. The background is the most important layer; the overlay layer is only used for modifying the background.

Light and dark areas in the foreground affect the background by intensifying **highlights**, **color** or **shadows**, so white, black or RGB|CMY parts of the background are not affected. In other words, you can't intensify the shadow of black, you can't highlight white areas and you can't intensify a color with maximum color value. Basically, the foreground affects the background (which dominates) by intensifying color, highlights or shadows.

Figure 21.5 *Overlay Mode*

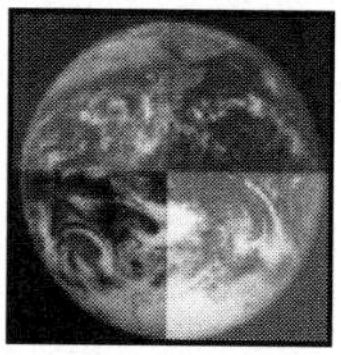

In this mode, all **foreground** colors appear paler and more washed out. Overlay color and saturation depend mostly on the **background**. You can say that the foreground intensifies or modifies the background color; a green foreground on a green background makes the image a little bit greener, whereas a red foreground would make the green color slightly less green (but green nevertheless).

Overlay Mode is good for adding shadows and highlights to an image, or for changing the color temperature. It adds information to the existing brightness Value in your image, so you can "paint with light." Hue and Saturation are also changed, but add no more effect than a cold shadow or reddish sunlight would.

The foreground affects the dominating background by intensifying color, highlights or shadows.

DIFFERENCE

The Difference Mode displays the difference between the RGB values in two layers. Foreground and background pixels have a dramatic effect on each other. When you paint in Difference Mode, the corresponding pixels in both the foreground and the background are evaluated and the **difference** between them is calculated.

If grayscale pixels are in one of the layers, the outcome is easy to predict. If the foreground pixel is brighter than the one in the background layer, the background pixel is **inverted**. If the foreground pixel is darker, the background pixel keeps its color. However, a grayish cast is added to the image, and the further the grayscale pixel is towards white or black, the weaker this shade of gray gets.

Figure 21.6 *Difference Mode*

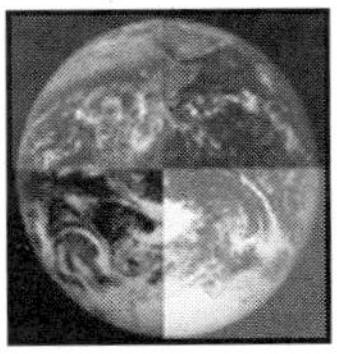

If the pixels are colored or grayscale in both layers, the result is harder to predict, but it works the same way:

| FG - BG | = outcome

In other words, the result is the absolute value of the difference between the foreground pixel and the background pixel. Black pixels in either the foreground or the background are transparent (have no effect). White pixels have the most effect (a white pixel always *inverts* the correspondent pixel).

Difference Mode is usually very colorful, and can produce psychedelic results, but it is also a powerful tool for displaying the *differences between two layers.*

For example, if you wanted to compare the size, shape and relative position of grayscale masks in different layers, you could use **Difference** Mode. Where the results are black, the layers are **identical**. Any small difference will appear very clearly in this mode.

This mode displays the difference between the RGB values in the two layers.

Addition

Addition Mode is similar to Screen Mode. Addition Mode adds the RGB values of foreground and background pixels. The result is *always lighter* and often has white areas and unsharp edges.

Figure 21.7 *Addition Mode*

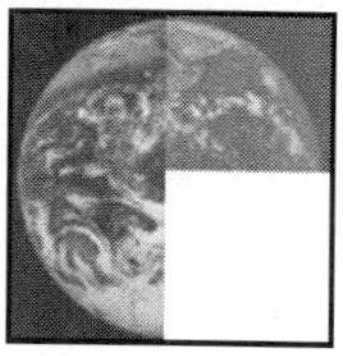

This mode adds the foreground RGB value to the background RGB value.

Subtract

Subtract Mode is the *opposite* of Addition Mode and sometimes produces results similar to Difference Mode. Subtract Mode subtracts the foreground color (RGB value) from the background color (RGB value). If your background is white (255,255,255), and you subtract red (255,0,0), the result is cyan (0,255,255).

Figure 21.8 *Subtract Mode*

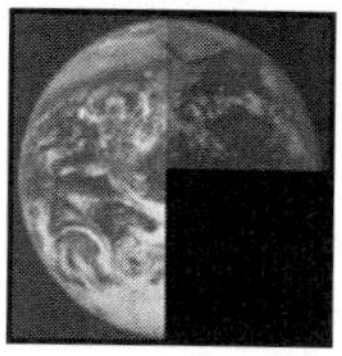

In Subtract Mode, a white shape in the upper layer against a white background will produce a black shape. So far, the result is the same as for Difference. As soon as a foreground value exceeds the background value, however, **Difference** and **Subtract** produce different results, because a zero value in Subtract Mode can be a *negative* value in Difference Mode.

This mode subtracts the foreground RGB value from the background RGB value.

Darken Only

Darken Only Mode compares the foreground and background pixels and displays the one with the **lowest** RGB value. Darken Only is somewhat similar to Multiply Mode. Color can only get darker, but Darken Only will usually produce lighter colors than Multiply.

If Darken Only worked on two pixels — one bright red (243,83,47) and one turquoise blue (47,239,201) — the result would be (47,83,47), a dark moss green. If you had used **Multiply** Mode, the result would have been a similar, but somewhat darker green (44,77,37).

Figure 21.9 *Darken Only Mode*

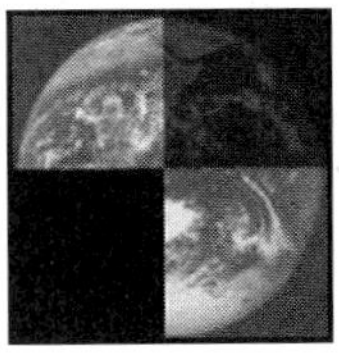

This mode compares the foreground and background pixels and chooses the lowest RGB value.

LIGHTEN ONLY

Lighten Only compares foreground and background pixels and displays the **highest** RGB values. It is the *opposite* of **Darken Only**.

Using the same example, the result of Lighten Only used on the bright red and turquoise pixels, would be (243,239,201), an eggshell bright beige. The result of Lighten Only is similar to Screen Mode but is always lighter.

If you had used **Screen** Mode instead, you would get a similar, but somewhat brighter color (246,245,211). If you'd used **Addition** Mode, you'd get a similar but *much* brighter color (255,255,248) as a result.

Figure 21.10 *Lighten Only Mode*

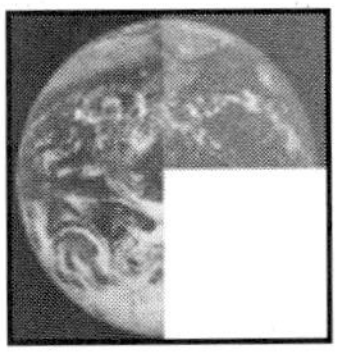

This mode compares the foreground and background pixels and chooses the highest RGB value.

HUE

Hue Mode results in a composite image that uses the background pixels' values for Value and Saturation information, while using the foreground pixels' values for determining Hue information.

Hue Mode allows you to change the shade of an object without changing brightness or saturation; it only affects **color**. The foreground color is the color you'll get, but you'll keep the general feeling in the image; for example, a loud green on soft dark blue will be translated into a loud yellow on soft dark yellow. White, black or grayscale information in the background is not affected and can't be tinted. Note that you cannot shift a color to grayscale in this mode. Grayscale information in the foreground comes out as a scratchy red.

Figure 21.11 *Hue Mode*

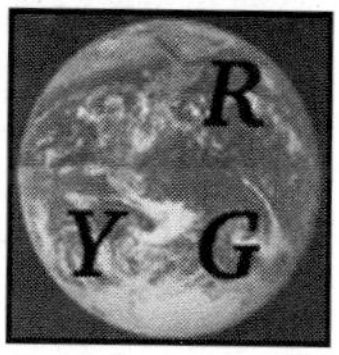

A word of warning, or perhaps a tip, if you want to use this mode to tint a background with **complementary** colors next to each other (see "Complementary Or Inverted Colors" on page 194). Around the edges where complimentary colors meet and blend, there will always be shades of gray. Because Hue cannot tint gray, using Hue Mode on top of such a background will produce thin, gray contours around the objects (like a microscope would).

The composite image uses the background for Value and Saturation information, while the foreground is only used for determining Hue.

SATURATION

In Saturation Mode, the composite image uses the background values for Hue and Value information and the foreground values for determining Saturation. You may use any color in the foreground. The background color won't change, but the background Saturation will, because it assumes the same saturation as the **foreground** color.

Figure 21.12 *Saturation Mode*

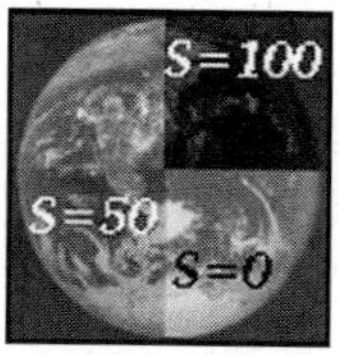

The Hue can't be changed, unless you have a pure grayscale background, which will become shades of red if the foreground contains color. Because you can change Saturation, this mode is often used with gray, white or black paint because this desaturates the background.

The composite image uses the background for Hue and Value information, while the foreground is only used for determining Saturation.

COLOR

Color Mode uses the foreground values for hue and saturation information and uses the background values to determine value information. Black or white background pixels are not affected, but all other colors (grayscale or not) will get the hue and saturation of the foreground color. Color Mode does not affect the Value (brightness) of the background; dark and light information are left intact.

Figure 21.13 *Color Mode*

Color Mode is useful for tinting grayscale photos if you want strong, clear colors. For a softer tinting, or the look of an old photo, consider using Overlay Mode instead.

The composite image uses the foreground for Hue/Saturation information, while the background is only used for determining Value.

VALUE

In Value Mode, the composite image uses the background values for Hue and Saturation information and uses the foreground information for determining Value. Value is the same as *Luminosity* in Adobe Photoshop. Value Mode won't change the Hue or Saturation of the image, but will affect **brightness** and **shadows**; i.e., the structure or 3-D-quality of the image.

Figure 21.14 *Value Mode*

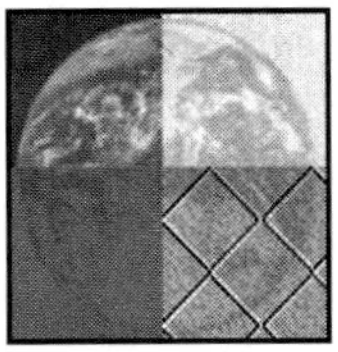

Unlike Overlay Mode, Value Mode can't distinguish a dark red from a bright red. All shadows or highlights disappear from the background and Value Mode doesn't deal with a grayscale background at all (because background value is ignored).

Value Mode is useful for correcting overbright or overdark colors, or it can be used to transfer patterns or structures into an image, without changing the color of the image.

The composite image uses the background for Hue/Saturation information, while the foreground is only used for determining Value.

Behind

Behind Mode is only used for **painting** *(and not for layers)*. Don't try to use this mode on anything solid, because it only affects **transparent** or **semi-transparent** areas. When you paint in Behind Mode, it's like painting on the *other side* of the layer. If you pretend the layer is a wall with windows in it, the Behind paint is applied to the outside of the house and is only visible through the windows. If the windows are dirty (i.e., are semi-transparent), the dirt will show against the Behind color.

This is a Paint Mode where only transparent areas are affected by the paint. (It does the opposite of Keep transparent in the Layers dialog.)

Comparing Different Modes

The test squares shown in Figure 21.15 demonstrate the effect of different modes. The black-and-white test squares range from black (intensity 0) to white (intensity 255) and are placed on top of a medium gray background (intensity 127), which explains why the sixth square (also intensity 127) is invisible in **Normal Mode**. The colored test squares range from black through dark red to bright red. The colored background is a soft green.

As you can see, **Screen** maintains the value variation of the grayscale squares, but all shades are brighter than in the original. **Lighten Only** hasn't changed the brightness of the visible squares, but all dark squares have become invisible. **Addition** brightens up so much that most of the squares have turned entirely white, and black is invisible for all three modes.

Multiply, **Darken Only** and **Subtract** (grayscale) are the dark equivalents or opposites of **Screen**, **Lighten Only** and **Addition**.

Overlay is only subtly different from the original. Note that medium gray is invisible in **Overlay** Mode. **Difference** shows the difference between foreground and background values. The dark colors represent a small difference between foreground and background.

The **Color** and **Hue** test squares have assumed a uniform red color, so these modes obviously use the Hue of the foreground, but not the Value. As you see, **Color** uses the Saturation of the foreground and **Hue** uses the Saturation of the background.

The **Saturation** test squares have turned uniformly green, so this mode uses both the hue and value of the background. Only the saturation is controlled to be the foreground. The **Value** test squares have turned softly green like the background, but the values come from the foreground

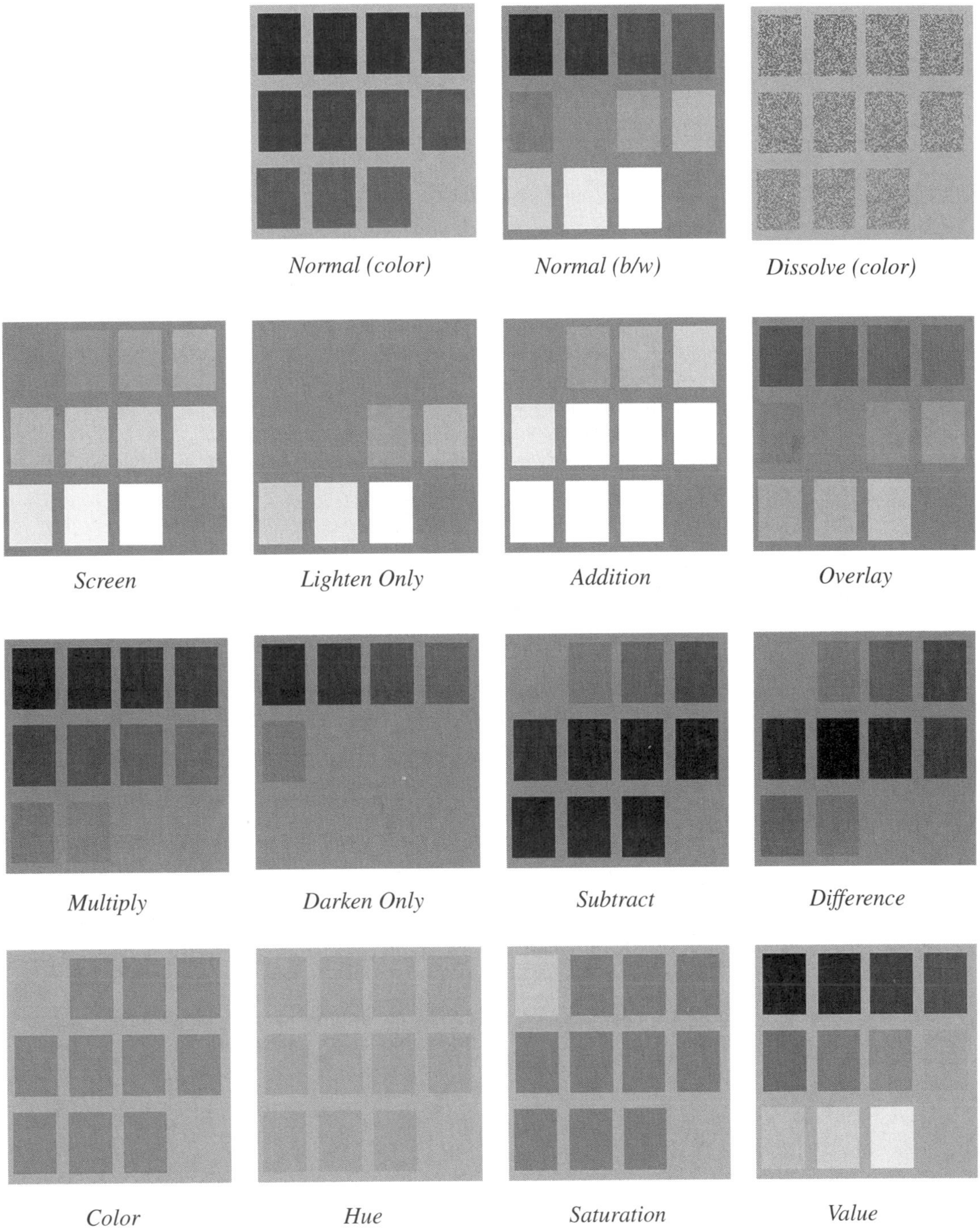

Figure 21.15 *Comparing modes*

What Is The Difference Between Screen, Addition And Lighten Only?

Screen, Addition and Lighten Only Modes may appear very similar. Sometimes, their effects are almost as if they are the same mode, but certain important differences exist between them.

Lighten Only compares the foreground and background RGB values, and chooses the *higher value* in each channel.

Addition *adds up* all values, so it ends up with a brighter image.

Screen *maps* the foreground against a background scale from 0-255 in each channel, with the foreground pixel mapping its value to 0 (black) on the scale.

Imagine that two scales of equal length are on top of each other. The background scale goes from 0 to 255, while the foreground scale goes from x (the foreground value) to 255. The composite value is somewhere on the foreground scale, and is determined by the background scale. If the background is a grayscale with an intensity of 100 (a medium dark gray), and the foreground's intensity is 178 (a medium light gray), the composite value can be calculated as follows:

The formula for Screen: composite value = FG + ((255 - FG) x BG) / 255.

An example:

- The background scale consists of 255 equal parts.
- The foreground scale consists of 77 equal parts, because 255 - 178 = 77.
- For 100 on the background scale, the foreground scale can be calculated as: 100/255 = FG scale/77.
- FG scale = (77 x 100)/255, so in this case the FG scale = 30.
- The composite value = 178 + the FG scale value, so 178 + 30 = 208.

The most obvious difference between the three modes is that Screen color is *darker* than Addition color, but *lighter* than Lighten Only.

The main practical difference between *Lighten Only* and *Screen* is that Screen is brighter, and it allows more shades than Lighten Only does. This effect occurs because Lighten Only is seldom affected by dark colors. It will just choose the lighter color in all RGB values, if there is one.

The advantage of *Screen* Mode over *Addition* Mode is that Screen colors don't "white out" as often as Addition colors (Addition colors white out because 255 is often the result from adding the values).

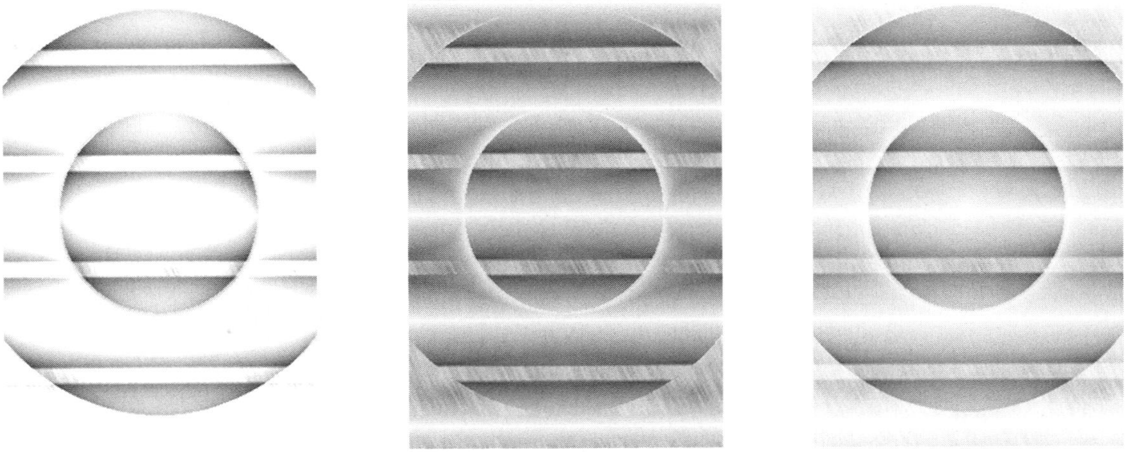

Addition *Lighten Only* *Screen*

Figure 21.16 *What's the difference between Addition, Screen and Lighten Only?*

What Is The Difference Between Multiply And Darken Only?

These two modes often result in similar outcomes, but **Multiply** is always a little *darker*. As you know, **Darken Only** chooses the darkest RGB values in each channel to produce its result. The differences and similarities between *Multiply* and *Darken Only* can be compared with the differences and similarities between *Screen* and *Lighten Only* (note that Subtraction can be thought of as corresponding to Addition, if you inverted the top layer).

Multiply is mathematically the opposite of **Screen**. In Screen, the foreground value is mapped to zero and up, but in Multiply it is mapped to 255 and down. Therefore, the foreground value is the lightest possible value and its darkness is determined by the background value. ***The algorithm is simple: the composite value = FG x (BG/255)***.

For grayscale images, the difference is much more evident. If you take a look at the pictures portraying these modes, you'll find that Darken Only looks semi-transparent, whereas Multiply looks as transparent as a slide. Multiply Mode is darker and shows a lot more of the background. In color images, you'll get more color variation (for lighter colors) with *Multiply* than you would with *Darken Only*.

Darken Only

Multiply

Figure 21.17 *What's the difference between Darken Only and Multiply?*

What Is The Difference Between Color And Hue?

Hue and **Color** sometimes produce similar results, because in both cases the **foreground** controls the composite *Hue*, and the **background** determines the *Value*. The difference is based on which layer controls *Saturation*. In **Hue** Mode, the background controls the saturation and in **Color** Mode, the foreground controls the saturation.

Generally, Hue and Value are the most important parameters in an image. If Saturation is roughly the same in both layers, it will be hard to tell the difference between *Hue* and *Color* Modes.

You will be able to tell the difference if one of the layers is grayscale, or if there is a lot of variation in the Saturation of a layer. Another way to think of it: *Color* Mode is often used to **add color** to a grayscale, so it's important that the top layer controls Hue and Saturation, but it must not interfere with the dark or bright values of the background.

Hue Mode, on the other hand, is often used for *changing* the **existing color** of a certain object. In that case, you don't want to change the *Saturation* in the background, because then the object would look very unnatural.

Figure 21.18 *In Color Mode, you can see the leaf pattern of the foreground clearly, although no brightness value from the FG has been used in the composite image*

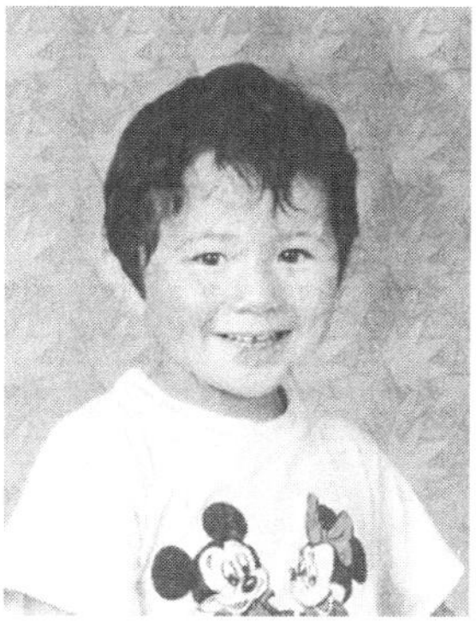

Color

Figure 21.19 *In Hue Mode, the only visible effect of the foreground is the green color of the leaves (see the color section); because saturation is taken from the background, the only part of the image that is really green is the face (which had the highest saturation)*

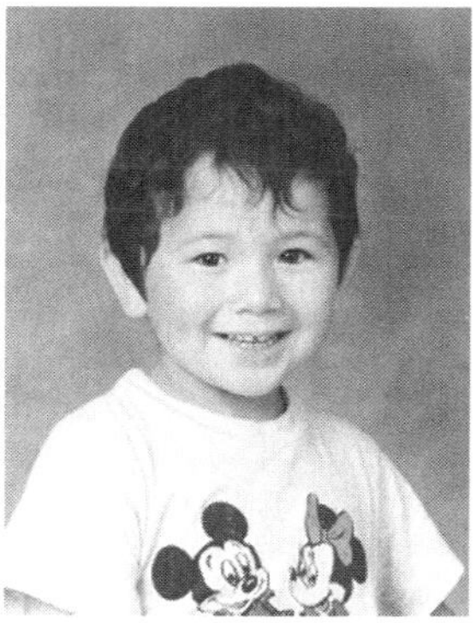

Hue

CHAPTER 22

Channels And Duotones

Channels are a resource that beginners often leave unused in programs with channel capability. Learn how to use them, and you won't be able to live without them!

RGB CHANNELS

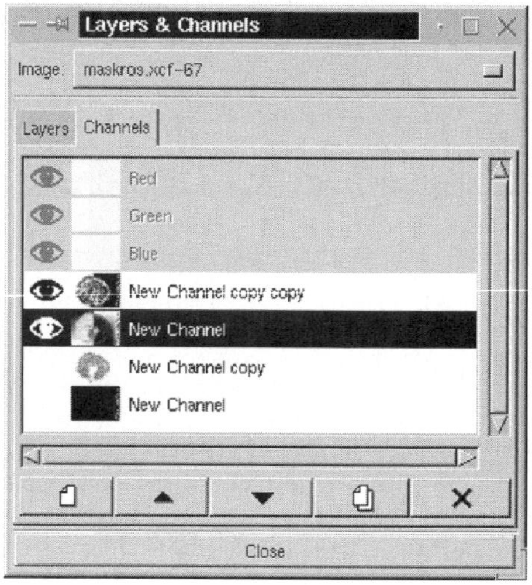

Figure 22.1 *On the Layers & Channels dialog (right-click|Layers|Layers & Channels), click on the Channels tab.*

COLOR CHANNELS

The **Channels** tab displays the three RGB channels, showing the current red, green or blue color values of each pixel in your image. The RGB channel **thumbnails** are grayscale representations of each color channel, where *white* represents 100% color, and *black* represents no color.

The RGB channels each have an **eye icon**, so you can look at your image in a single color channel. Click *off* the eye icon in the Blue and Green channels, so that only the **Red** channel is visible. Bright red in the red channel is the equivalent of a maximum red value for that pixel; black means that the pixel has no red in it at all. If all three channels have maximum values for an area, that area is *white*.

The RGB channels are always active when a layer is active, and they display the color values of *all* visible layers, not just the active one. Unlike **layers**, the RGB channels can all be active at the same time. You can also choose to work in one or two specific color channels, by clicking on the appropriate channels to activate the ones you want and deactivate the ones you don't want.

Normally, working directly in RGB channels isn't that useful. However, if you are very skilled and you like to experiment with patterns and advanced coloring, they can be of interest. For example, you can erase or add things to the red channel, or try a filter on the blue channel, etc. Remember that although the channel shows all visible layers, the operation only affects the *active* layer.

Also note that you can't use the standard edit functions (like Cut, Copy and Paste) in a single RGB channel. You can move selections in a color channel without moving the content of all three RGB channels. If you want to do either of these things, use `right-click|Image|Channel Ops|Decompose` and `right-click|Image|Channel Ops|Compose`.

Alpha Channels

Alpha Values And Transparency

An alpha value describes the amount of *transparency* in a pixel. Every pixel has a value for the Red, Green and Blue channels in the RGB system, and if there is an **Alpha channel** (RGBA) every pixel also has an *alpha* value.

Note: Unlike the RGB channels, you can't see the true alpha channel or grayscale representation of your image's current alpha values. It is not displayed in the Channels tab, and should not be confused with the static alpha mask channels.

If you'd like to see a grayscale representation of your image's current alpha values, you can do so by *decomposing* your image with the `right-click|Image|Channel Ops|Decompose` command and decompose to RGBA. You can also use the `right-click|Layers|Alpha To Selection` command followed by the `right-click|Select|Save To Channel` command to save the current alpha values in a new channel.

Just like the RGB values, alpha values range from 0 to 255. The maximum value (255) represents 100% *opacity* in that pixel, and 0 represents total *transparency*. You can check this out with the **Color Picker** (eyedropper tool) in the toolbox. The transparency or alpha values will be displayed in the little Color Picker dialog box that appears when you click on different parts of the image. If the Picker dialog shows **N/A**, it's because your image contains no alpha channel and therefore cannot display transparency, just as an image without a red channel would not be able to display red color.

Enabling Transparency

When you *erase* or *cut* such an image, the "holes" you make will only display the background color (the background color swatch in the toolbox). Now, if you add a new layer to this image, you will find that it is different from the background layer. All layers that you add to an image contain alpha information, so when you use the eraser on the new layer, you will see the underlying layers through the transparent hole you just made.

To enable transparency in the background layer, you must first select the **Add Alpha Channel** option in the **Layers** menu. If you choose **Transparent** as **Fill Type** when you create a new image, none of this will be necessary because this command will produce an **RGB-alpha** image with a transparent background.

Alpha Mask Channels

The real reason to use the channels is the ability to *store* and *edit* selections in alpha mask channels. Whenever you make a selection that is more complex than a square, you should save it in a new channel so that you can use it later.

When you open the **Channels** dialog and create a **New Channel**, you create a *mask,* which can be translated to a selection and applied to a layer. These channels, which we can refer to as *alpha mask channels*, have nothing to do with the actual alpha values present in your image.

RGB channels display the color values in each pixel in the image, and consequently change automatically when the image is altered. Alpha mask channels are nothing like that. They are static **storage channels** that won't change with your image. Just like in the RGB channels, black represents an alpha value of zero, or full transparency, and white represents areas where the alpha value is 255, which is the same as full opacity.

Note: A layer and an alpha mask channel can't be active at the same time. That's why the three RGB channels are grayed out as soon as you click in an alpha mask channel. To return to your image, you must switch to the Layers tab and click in one of the layers.

If you turn off all layers (and other channels) and only look at one channel, you'll see it the way it looks in the thumbnail — a clean black-and-white representation of the Alpha channel. The way channels appear on screen, should you choose to display them together with other channels or layers, can be compared to putting slides on top of each other. White mask areas (which represent opacity) look transparent, and black areas (which represent transparency) appear as opaque as the **Fill Opacity** value that you have specified.

Note that the way the channel values appear on screen is quite the *opposite* of the alpha values they represent. This means that loading an alpha channel selection on a white layer and filling it with black will result in an image that is a negative of the channel image. You can also choose another color than black as mask color, in which case this color will appear on screen instead; see "Adding Color To A Channel" on page 355.

When you activate an alpha mask channel with the **Channel To Selection** command (right-click in the Channels dialog to access the Channels menu), you have created a *selection* where black mask areas remain unselected, white areas represent fully selected parts and the shades of gray in between represent different levels of "selection." When you apply this **selection mask** to a layer, the operations performed will only affect the areas where the channel image was bright. The dark areas of the mask will protect the original image.

Storing Selections As Channels

The `right-click|Select|Save To Channel` option allows you to save a selection as a channel. Create a selection, click on `right-click|Select|Save To Channel`, and open the Layers & Channels dialog (`right-click|Layers|Layers & Channels`). A new channel will now appear: **Selection Mask copy**.

Selection Mask copy is a grayscale version of the selection you just made. Don't forget to rename the channel, because selections stored in channels may be hard to recognize. To name the channel, double-click on its old name and the **Edit Channel Attributes** dialog will appear. Name the new channel whatever your selection represents (or will represent when you have edited it).

You can set a **Fill Opacity** value in the Edit Channel Attributes dialog, but it won't affect the alpha values in your channel. The reason you set the fill opacity to a transparent value in this dialog is that this will enable you to see your image through the dark parts of the channel. If the mask wasn't somewhat transparent, it would be impossible to edit the channel properly. The channels are displayed with a 50 percent opacity when you make them visible (with the eye icon), but this is just a default value.

When you want to use the selection you just stored, click the right mouse button on the channel's name, and a popup menu will appear. Choose the last option on the list: **Channel To Selection**. Channel To Selection will create a selection based on your channel. Switch to the Layers tab, click on one of the layers to make it active, and your selection will be available for use. Remember to toggle off the visibility (eye icon) of the channel, so that it will not disturb you when you work with the new selection.

Editing Alpha Channels

The buttons in the bottom of the Channels dialog box, or in the popup menu you see when you right-click on a channel, should be easy to understand. You can create a new channel, raise or lower a channel in the channel hierarchy, duplicate or delete a channel and change channels into selections (only in the popup menu).

You can't *merge* channels, unless you first copy them and paste them into layers. Merge those layers with the `right-click|Layers|Merge Visible Layers` command, then you copy or cut the layer and paste it into a channel again.

As you see, the contents of alpha channels and layers can be edited just as in ordinary images. You can paste an image or a layer into an alpha channel, and vice versa. You can paint, adjust image values, make selections or use filters on alpha channels. These capabilities make channels the most powerful tool available for creating advanced selections.

Just remember that alpha channels belong to Gimp's native file format **XCF**. As long as your image contains alpha mask channels it is considered to be *Layered.* You can't **flatten** an image with alpha channels, and because layered images can't be converted, you'll have to *delete* all alpha channels before converting your image to a working file format like TIFF or GIF.

Using Channels For Spot Color Separation

Adding Color To A Channel

You can change the mask color of an alpha channel by clicking the color swatch in the **New Channel Options** dialog, if you create a *new* channel, or the **Edit Channel Attributes** dialog (accessed by double-clicking the Channel bar), if you wish to edit an *existing* channel.

Warning: This will only change how the channel is displayed on your monitor. Your alpha channel is still a grayscale representation of a selection, not a color channel.

When you replace the black *mask color* with another color, this color and brighter (but never darker) shades of it are now the only things the channel can add to the monitor display. This is similar to the way a **printing plate** adds ink to a paper. If you toggle off the visibility for all layers, you'll see what such a plate would look like.

Take a look at Figures 22.2 and 22.3 to appreciate the difference between a **colored layer** and a **colored channel**. For example, a yellow channel and a yellow layer look just about the same. However, if you were to copy the yellow mask channel and paste it into a grayscale image, it would look like Figure 22.3 — crisp, clear and entirely *black* in areas that were 100% yellow in the colored channel. Figure 22.2 shows what the yellow layer would look like if you did the same thing. The yellow brightness values have been translated to light shades of *gray* without contrast.

This means that you can use *channels* but not *layers* as originals for making **printing plates**. Only channels will reproduce this image faithfully with the specified yellow ink.

Figure 22.2 *A yellow layer comes out as pale gray when it is converted to grayscale. If this image file is used for making a printing plate, the printed result will be much paler than the original yellow layer.*

Figure 22.3 *This is the grayscale representation of a channel with the same yellow color as in the layer. This image will produce a plate capable of printing the same shade of yellow that was specified in the channel.*

Spot Colors

Printing plates were mentioned because colored alpha channels can be used to create **spot color** separations.

Spot or custom colors like PANTONE or TRUMATCH are used when you don't want, or can't afford, four-color CMYK printing. Custom colors come in all possible shades, including special inks and varnishes (like gold, silver or fluorescent inks). Designs for spot colors can be very attractive, and have the great advantage of letting you print a solid color without a **halftone** pattern. When you're printing a smaller series, it is cheaper to use fewer plates than four, and it will often look much better than a plain black-and-white print.

Duotones

What is a duotone? Simply put, a *duotone* is an image where you use the same grayscale image to produce two (almost) identical printing plates.

The difference is that the screen angle is set differently, so that the little ink dots will not end up in the exact same spot. Remember that when you're using several plates to compose one image, you have to use less ink (especially black ink) to prevent the printed result from getting too dark.

The result is often a very eye-pleasing, softly tinted image, with more depth to it than a plain black-and-white image. Typically, duotones are created with one black plate and one colored plate, often blue or sepia brown (the classic inks used in traditional ink drawing and lavure painting).

You don't need Channels to create a **duotone** or a **multitone**, but you'll need them to *edit* and *preview* your work, and you'll definitely need them if you want something more than a uniform color distribution.

Figure 22.4 *Duotone created with two colored channels*

Checklist

Before you create a spot color multitone, you should consider a few things:

What spot colors should be used?

You can choose from a great variety of custom colors, so this problem can be solved in two different ways. You can go to your local print shop, take a look at its **color charts** and ask it to make a **color calibrated proof** of your chosen colors to take home, or you can buy an expensive PANTONE color chart and specify (to your printer) the custom colors that look most like the RGB colors you chose for your alpha channels.

Remember that the color in the alpha channels is for preview only — as we have already explained, all channels are really grayscale.

In what order should the plates be printed and the channels be placed?

Always ask your printer's advice about this. Ask them in what *order* they prefer to print the different inks, and the approximate *density* of the last ink to be applied. You should probably also discuss what *screen angle* and *dot gain* your printer thinks would be appropriate for this print job and whether you should use *AM* or *FM screening*. As always, make a color proof that you're satisfied with and tell the printer to adjust the final settings to look like your proof.

For more information on printing procedures and pre-press, see "Pre-press And Color In Gimp" starting on page 197.

How To Create A Duotone

Preparing Your Image

Open the image you want to turn into a duotone. If the image contains color information, you should first **desaturate** it (`right-click|Image|Colors|Desaturate`) and *increase* the **contrast** somewhat.

The image should be black where you want full ink coverage (`right-click|Image|Colors|Brightness-Contrast`).

Figure 22.5 *The original image*

Copy the image and then **Clear** it so that only a *white* background remains (`right-click|Edit|Copy` and `Edit|Clear`). This way you'll know that the target image is exactly the same size as the image you have just copied, but you can just as well create a new white image and paste your picture in a channel there.

Make sure that the **eye icon** is turned on in the *white* background layer on the Layers & Channels dialog (`right-click|Layers|Layers & Channels`). The *white* layer represents the paper color, and is necessary to display the colors.

Creating A Colored Channel

Open the **Channels** tab and create a new channel. In the **New Channel Options** dialog, set this channel to 100% **Fill Opacity**. Click the *black* **color swatch** to access the **Color Selection** dialog, and choose a nice color (this will be the first plate to be printed). **Name** the channel "navy blue" or the like, depending on what color you chose. Click on the **OK** button.

Paste (`right-click|Edit|Paste`) the image into this channel. Then create a *new* channel and repeat these steps for this channel (which is the second plate to be printed), only this time set the **Fill Opacity** to 85% (or to the value that your printer thinks is closest to the density of this ink). Name this channel, e.g., "tawny yellow".

Now you can manipulate the contents of the channels. Figures 22.6 and 22.7 show how we adjusted our channel images for a nice artistic output.

Figure 22.6 *Screenshot of the blue spot color channel*

Figure 22.7 *Screenshot of the yellow spot color channel*

Adjusting Color With Mask Channels

Sometimes you only want *one* of the custom inks in a duotone to show in a certain part of the image.

In this case we want the text *Dandelion* to be printed with a pure blue, that is, without a trace of the yellow ink. To achieve this, we wrote the word *Dandelion* in a **transparent** layer and selected this text string using the `right-click|Layers|Alpha To Selection` command.

Figure 22.8 *The Text mask channel*

Then we *stored* the text in a new channel with `right-click|Select|Save To Channel`. We named the new channel "Text Mask", and loaded the text selection from the Text mask channel by right-clicking on the Text mask channel icon and selecting Channel To Selection.

Then, we clicked on the Blue channel icon and filled the selection with **black** color (because black will display as 100% of the mask color, which in this case is blue). Then, we turned to the Yellow channel with the selection still active, and filled it with white color (because white displays as transparent).

This way we made sure that the text was placed in the exact same position in both channels, and that the blue plate would print a full coverage of blue ink exactly where we wanted it, and that the yellow plate wouldn't put any ink at all in the same spot.

Converting Channels To Grayscale Images

When you're satisfied with the duotone image, it's time to convert the channels into something that will be useful to your printer. They will need two **grayscale** images to print your duotone, one for each plate.

Duplicate the image file (Ctrl+D), then copy and paste the contents of the two channels to the white background layer of each file. When this is done, you delete all other channels and layers and convert the images from **RGB** to **grayscale** (`right-click|Image|Grayscale`). Save grayscale number 1 as *blue.tif* and grayscale number 2 as *yellow.tif.*

Instructions To The Service Bureau

Give the files and a proof of what the final print should look like (make a *screen grab* of your image with the `Xtns|Screen Shot` command and print it on an ordinary inkjet printer) to your printer or service bureau, specify the custom colors for "blue" and "yellow" and tell them in what *order* the plates should be printed. Ask your printer to set an appropriate screen angle and dot gain. Remember that they are the experts, so you are well advised to follow their instructions.

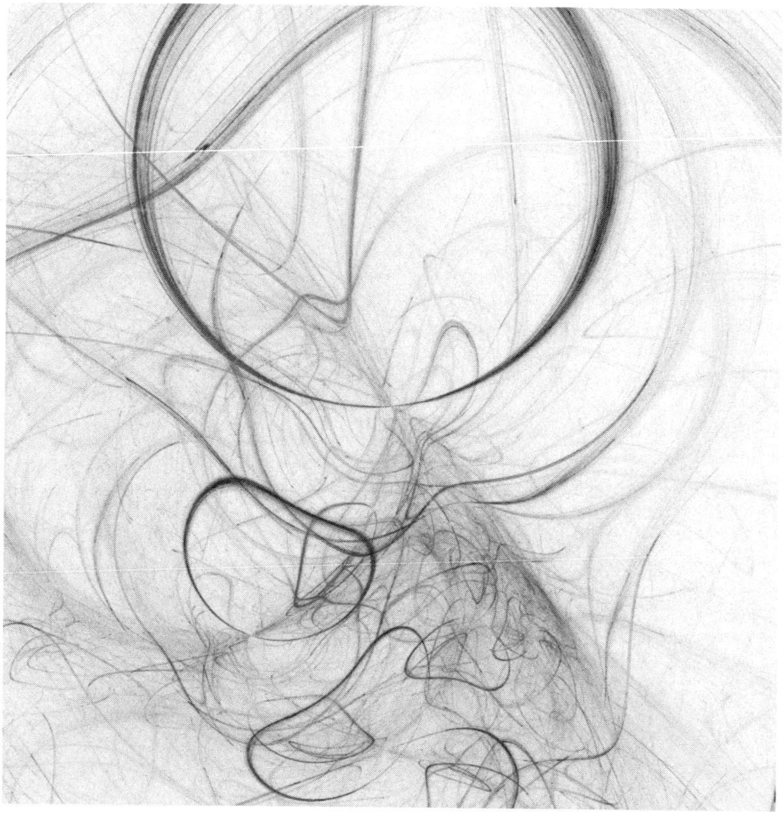

PART VI

Filters

- ANIMATION
- ARTISTIC
- BLUR
- COLOR
- COMBINE
- CRYPTOGRAPHIC
- DISTORT
- EDGE-DETECT
- ENHANCE
- GENERIC
- GLASS EFFECTS
- LIGHT EFFECTS
- MAP
- MISCELLANEOUS
- NOISE
- RENDER

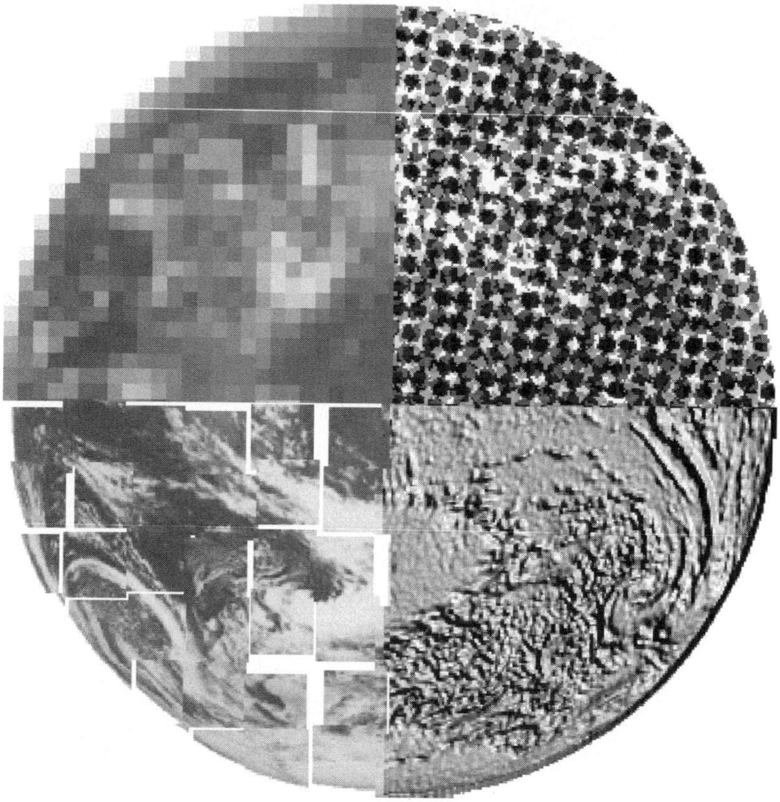

CHAPTER 23

An Introduction To Filters

A short description of how filters generally work in Gimp.

Plug-ins

When a Photoshop user thinks of *plug-ins*, things like Eye Candy and Kai's Power Tools come to his or her mind. Gimp plug-ins are similar: They permit the user to add *extra features* to Gimp. By features, we mean **filters**, **printer drivers**, **mail interfaces**, **save/write modules**, etc. Gimp is very modular; nearly every function besides the basics is done by plug-ins.

Many Gimp users/developers have written Gimp plug-ins and made them available to the Gimp community. We encourage you to do the same. If you create your own plug-in, submit it to the Gimp community under the GPL license. Your plug-in will make Gimp even better.

In these chapters, we will discuss the **Filters** menu. We are going to call these filters **plug-ins**, because that's what most people think of when they hear the word "plug-in". The **Script-Fu** menu is similar to the Filters menu because Script-Fus can be applied as ordinary filters to your images. You'll find that you can make your own filters quite easily, without expert knowledge of C programming or GTK+ libraries.

Because plug-ins and scripts develop rapidly in the Gimp community, this chapter can't be as up-to-date as we would like. We encourage developers to send us mail about their new or changed plug-in so that we'll have an easier job updating this chapter. In "Compiling Plug-ins" starting on page 769, you'll find some tips on how to compile plug-ins. You may also want to visit the filter developers' home pages to get up-to-date information about the filter.

Please note that the screen shots of the plug-in dialogs won't necessarily display the same values that we used to generate the resulting image. This is because we sometimes need to exaggerate a bit so that you can really see the effects of the filter.

Main Categories

The **Filters** menu includes the following submenus, which group plug-ins by function:

- **Animation:** Includes an animation player that lets you play Gimp animations and an animation filter that can optimize your animation, so that it uses much less disk space.
- **Artistic:** Includes filters to create instant artistic effects. You can easily create cubist paintings, mosaic patterns, etc. This kind of filter is mainly used for adding special effects to an image, but you can also create nice patterns with it.
- **Blur:** Includes many different types of blur filters. Blurring is useful when you want to soften part of a picture. Real shadows are seldom hard and solid, so to create realistic shadows you'll want to soften them up with an appropriate blur filter. A portrait may look too honest and show all the imperfections and wrinkles of the model, so blurring the portrait will help.

- **Colors:** Includes tools that can manipulate color and HSV values, just as if you were standing in a darkroom.
- **Combine:** Provides many different ways of combining several images to create a new image.
- **Crypt:** These filters allow you to sign, encrypt/decrypt your image or send hidden files Notice that this item is not a part of the core Gimp distribution.
- **Distorts:** Creates the kinds of effects you'd find in a hall of mirrors. Some of these filters are great for adding special effects to an image, like making ripples in a water surface. If you want to create textures, you'll find many useful filters here.
- **Edge-detect:** These filters help you find the edges or color boundaries in an image, which can be quite useful when you work with layered images and you want to strengthen or smooth the contours of an object. You can also use edge-detect filters for making easy selections with the magic wand, or easy fills with the Bucket fill tool.
- **Generic:** Includes mathematical filters that use a matrix for image manipulation. You can perform all kinds of manipulation with these filters, but you may need some math up your sleeve.
- **Glass Effects:** Includes filters that create different kinds of lens or curved mirror effects.
- **Light Effects:** These filters add a little glamour (extra shine, lustre, glitter or star reflections) to your designs.
- **Map:** Includes filters that allow you to bump map, displace or alter your image in relation to an image map.
- **Miscellaneous:** Includes filters that don't fit anywhere else. Currently, these include stereogram filters and video screen simulation.
- **Noise:** These filters will add noise effects to your image, like monitor noise, film graininess or just pointillistic artistry.
- **Render:** These filters will render all kinds of shapes or objects, and are extremely useful for creating textures or patterns.

Notice the handy shortcuts: Shift+Alt+f will bring up the last plug-in you used and Alt+f will apply the last filter again.

CHAPTER 24

Animation Filters

Descriptions of the different animation filters and functions available as well as a description of GIF animation.

Animation Filters In The Filters Menu

Animation Playback

Animation Playback will display your **layers** or **GIF animation** as if it were a piece of film. If the layers don't contain specific animation information, each layer will be run in **Combine mode**. You can also step through each frame.

This plug-in can also show you a *preview* of what an image will look like in a web page. You can grab the image in the playback frame, drag it out of the frame and drop the image on another window (including a browser window). Just click on the image and drag it to where you want it to go.

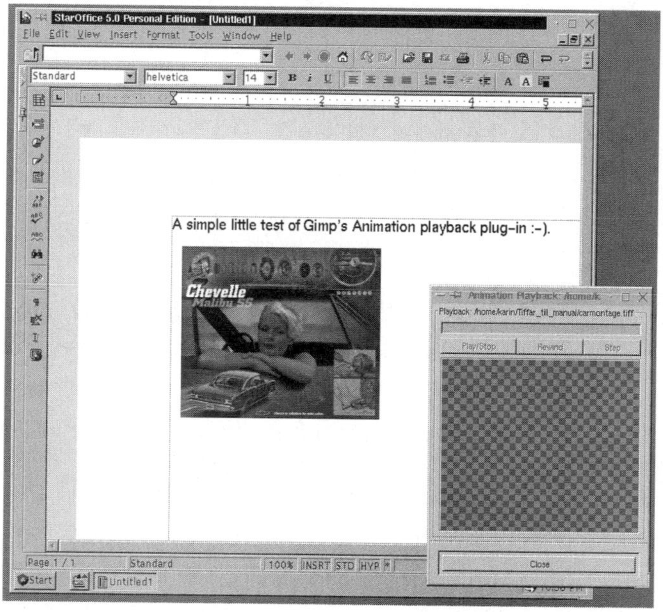

Figure 24.1 *Animation Playback's preview function; this illustration shows an image being dragged into the StarOffice canvas*

Note that the image doesn't need to be layered (i.e., a playable image) in order to use this function. You can use it on any ordinary JPEG, GIF or TIFF image.

Animation Optimize

A GIF animation is built of many layers. Some of the layers will probably repeat much of the information in the previous layer (the previous frame in your animation). Wouldn't it be great if you could skip all that unnecessary information? This would be difficult and time-consuming to do by hand, but there is a filter that can do it for you.

Open your animation file and apply `right-click|Filters|Animation|Animation Optimize`. Now look at your layers. The layers will be much smaller, because only *additional* or *diverging* information is displayed. This filter will make GIF animations much smaller and faster to download. You can also use this filter on large, multi-layered XCF files to reduce their size.

Animation Unoptimize

After you have optimized an image (using Animation Optimize or by hand), it is usually quite hard to scale and your manipulations will often produce an ugly result. The Animation Unoptimize filter solves this problem, so use this filter before you make any alterations to an optimized image.

Filter All Layers

Filter All Layers is used to create animations with the **GAP** plug-in (see "Advanced Animation With Gimp Or How To Use AnimFrames" starting on page 639), but you can apply it to any kind of multi-layered image. When you select this filter, a browser will appear. The browser is much like the **DB Browser**, except that only plug-ins are listed.

Select the filter that you want to apply, and specify how you want to apply it, by selecting *constant* or *variable*. When you have made your choice, a filter dialog will pop up asking for values. If you chose **constant**, the dialog will appear only once, and the values you specify will apply to all layers. If you chose **variable**, the dialog will appear for every layer so you can apply different values to each layer.

How To Create A GIF Animation

Gimp is a great tool for creating GIF animations. Gimp treats each layer as a **frame**. The Background layer is Frame 1 and each new layer is a new frame. When you add a new layer to the background layer, name it Frame 2, Frame 3 and so on.

Specifying The Delay Of Each Frame

Edit the layer name by double-clicking on a layer in the **Layers & Channels** dialog. Rename it **Frame X (xxxxms)**, where *X* is the frame number and *xxxx* is the delay in milliseconds. Naming a frame **Frame 5 (100ms)** will give that frame a delay of 100 ms.

Figure 24.2 *The Layer dialog, showing the frame(layer), name, time and how to combine it.*

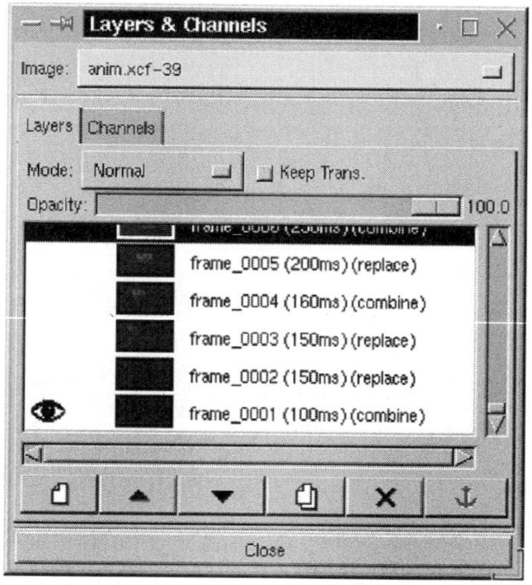

Combining Frames

To make a layer combine with the previous layer (combine means that Frame 2 will be added to Frame 1 (the background), Frame 3 will be added to Frame 2 and Frame 1, and so on), name the layer **Frame X (xxxxms) (combine)**.

Replacing Frames

To make the animation work like a real movie (i.e., each new frame replaces the former), add (**replace**) instead of (**combine**). You can (combine) and (replace) in any order.

Note that when you save your GIF, you'll see a dialog box that asks you about **Default disposal where unspecified**. Don't check **Don't care** because that will make the layers combine without showing up in the Gimp layer dialog as (combine). Just choose **combine**, and the settings in the layer dialog will still be preserved.

An example of five layers/frames:

- **Background (100ms) (replace)**
- **Frame 2 (100ms) (combine)**
- **Frame 3 (100ms) (replace)**
- **Frame 4 (100ms) (combine)**
- **Frame 5 (100ms) (replace)**

The previous five frames will be played back in this order with a 100 ms delay between each frame:

- Background
- Frame 2 + Background
- Frame 3
- Frame 4 + Frame 3
- Frame 5
- Background

and so on until you stop it.

Note: **Combine** combines the frame with the previous frame, but if you have set the background layer to combine, it will not combine with the top layer. The background layer will always replace the top layer when the loop starts over again.

AVTVNNO

CHAPTER 25

Artistic Filters

Artistic filters create instant artistic effects like oil paintings or mosaic floors. In general, they are ready-to-run filters that demand little input from the user.

Apply Canvas

Apply Canvas adds a canvas texture to your image or selection, which will make it look more like a painting. You can specify four different canvas directions, as well as how "rough" the fabric should be.

The **Depth** slider controls the canvas roughness. A high value will produce a very rough and prominent canvas texture, whereas a low value results in a softer, smoother canvas.

Figure 25.1 *The Canvas filter has been applied to the left side of the image*

Apply Carpet

Apply Carpet adds **texture** to an image, like the Canvas filter. This filter applies a *rug-like* appearance to an image or selection. The **Depth** parameter controls the weave pattern or canvas bottom of the rug. **Noise** adds random noise for a long or coarse pile rug illusion. **Shift** displaces pixels vertically (for each repeat session), which controls the pile length. **Repeat** allows you to repeat the effect up to five times.

Figure 25.2 *The Carpet filter was applied to the bottom-left side of the image*

Cubism

Cubism transforms your image into cubist art. If you check **Use background color**, the background color will appear between your tiles; otherwise, this area will be black. **Tile Size** determines how "cubist" you want your image to be; higher values result in a more abstract image. The **Tile Saturation** value specifies how *colorful* the image will be.

Tip: To achieve interesting effects, try applying Cubism to several layers with different modes over the original image.

Figure 25.3 *Cubist cat at the bottom-left side*

GAG

Genetic Algorithms for Gimp, or GAG, is a pattern-generating Render filter like `right-click|Filters|Render|Qbist.`

When you open GAG, the display shows nine randomly chosen patterns from the GAG *pattern library*. Pressing the **New Generation** button will generate new patterns.

Each pattern swatch is equipped with a small **Weight Scale slider**. This slider determines the *weight* or influence of this pattern for the next generation, so when you have found one or more patterns or themes that you like and would like to see more variations of, set the sliders in accordance to your preferences and press the New Generation button.

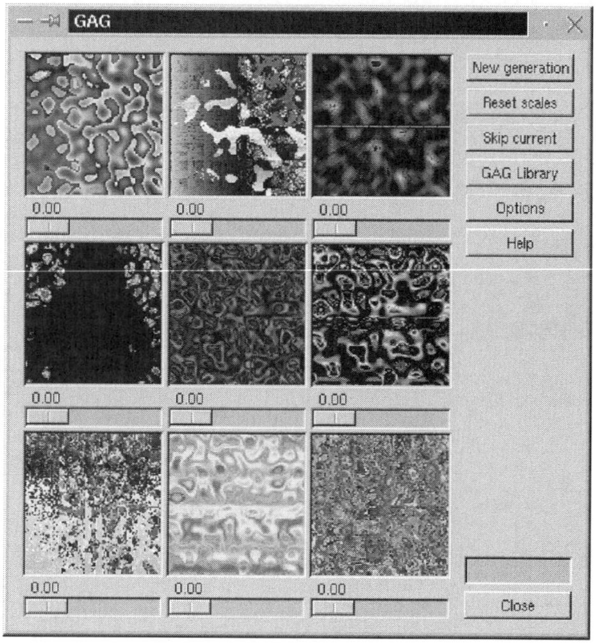

Figure 25.4 *The GAG main dialog*

The GAG Right Mouse Button Menu

To slightly mutate a single pattern, press the *right mouse button* inside the pattern box and select **Mutate**. The amount of mutation can be set in the **Options** dialog in the **Mutation** tab with the **Probability of Mutation** slider.

To get an entirely different pattern, right-click and select **Random**, and GAG will generate a new, randomly chosen pattern.

If you are an experienced Scheme programmer, you can try to modify a pattern by hand by selecting the **Edit by hand** option in the right-click menu. To get a better view of the pattern, select the **Magnify** option. This opens an X Window that displays the pattern magnified by 2.5.

To render the pattern into an existing image, select the **Render picture** option and choose an image or layer from the **Render to drawable** pull-down menu. If the chosen image contains a selection, the pattern will render to that selection only.

The Tabs

The **GAG library** contains a number of nice preset patterns. To see previews, double-click the pattern's name and right-click to access the pull-down menu.

The **Options** dialog box allows you to specify a wide range of settings.

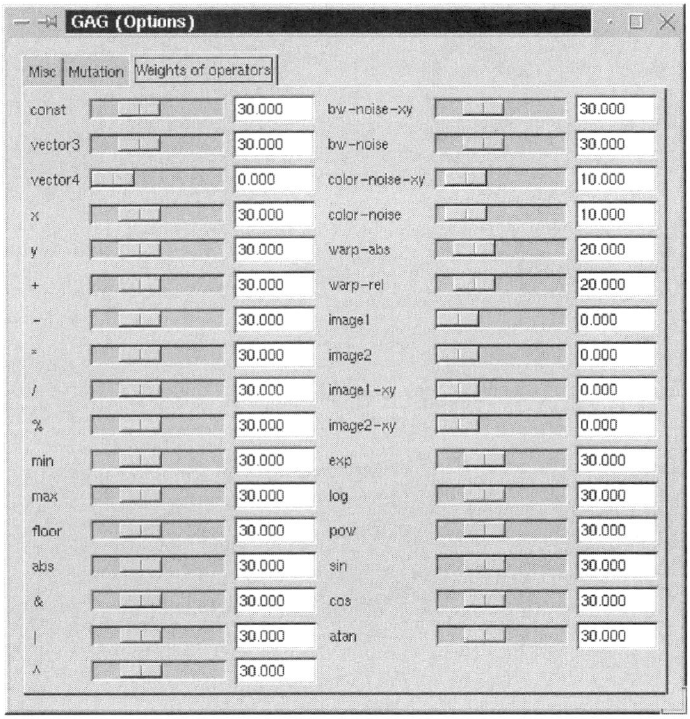

Figure 25.5 *The GAG Options dialog*

As mentioned before, the *Probability of Mutation* slider controls the mutation rate, or how different the "children" will be from their "parents."

The most useful option is probably **Image as Function** on the **Misc** tab. With this option, you can make one or two given images affect the outcome of the generated patterns. However, to make this work properly, you must remember three things:

- You must first open the **Weight of Operators** folder and set the sliders of **image 1 (2)** and **image 1 (2)-xy** to high values.
- Always choose simple or strictly geometrical pictures (preferably in black and white) as source images. A photographic image is much too complicated to influence a GAG pattern in a recognizable way.

- As soon as you recognize the influence of the source image(s) in one of the patterns, "breed" on this pattern by moving its Weight slider and pressing New Generation. It may take a few generations before a visible influence of the source image is discernible.

Figure 25.6 *The original on the left was used to generate the two images on the right*

GIMPRESSIONIST

Gimpressionist is a sophisticated *instant artist* filter. It is designed to imitate *Impressionist* painting, so it's a good choice when you want to add a "hand painted" look to an image.

Figure 25.7 *Gimpressionist invoked on the right part of the image; as you see, the girl that the boy is talking to is now quite impressionistic*

Paper

The first tab in the Gimpressionist dialog concerns the "paper" that you wish to use for background *structure*. If you use maximum value for **Stroke Density** (on the **Placement** tab) and you want the paper quality to be clearly visible in the painting, you'll have to increase the **Relief** value. The **Scale** factor is used to control the graininess or density of the paper structure. You can also apply an **Overlay** option which means the paper will not be embossed into a relief. The **Invert** option simply inverts the grayscale values in the paper.

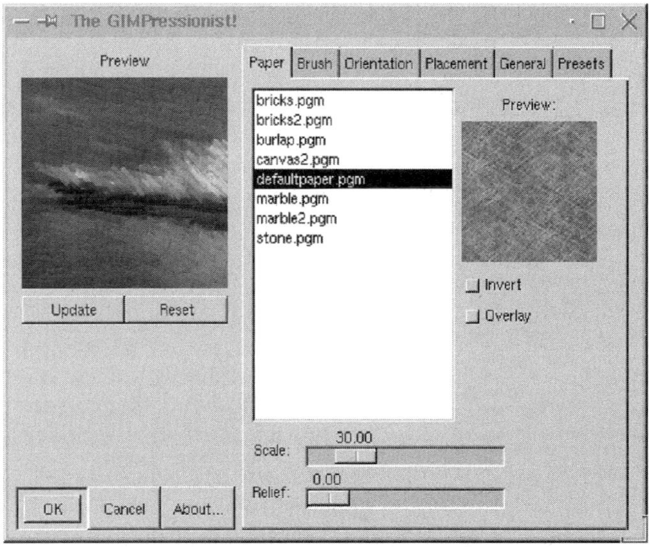

Figure 25.8 *The Gimpressionist main window where you control the paper type*

BRUSH

The **Brush** tab lets you set the **Size**, **Aspect ratio**, **Relief** and **Gamma** of a paintbrush. If you don't want to use a brush from the list, you can select another Gimp image, and use that as a brush.

To understand **Relief**, think of thick oil paint that is *scratched* or *smeared* onto the painting with a palette knife. Keep in mind that a high relief value may cause the image to appear so abstract that it will be hard to make out what it represents (the same goes for large brush sizes).

The **Gamma slider** below the brush window controls the intensity of the brush strokes (or how much paint you put on the brush).

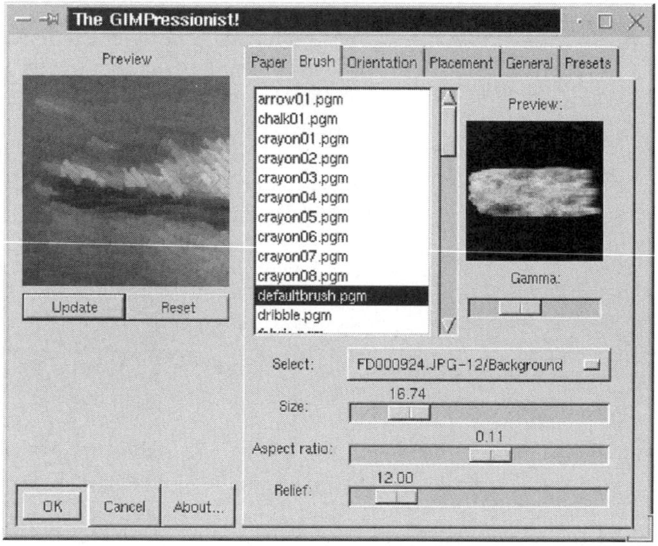

Figure 25.9 *The Gimpressionist Brush tab*

Size controls the size of the brush measured in horizontal pixels. The **Aspect ratio** slider controls the proportions of your brush. You can deform the default shape of the brush to make it thin and long or short and thick.

Select lets you select an open Gimp image as a brush type. (Be careful with this option and only use small images.) We recommend that you use the ordinary brush types that comes with Gimpressionist and only use Select when you're designing new brushes for Gimpressionist.

ORIENTATION

Orientation sets the *direction* of the brush strokes. The three top parameters determine how strict your brushwork should be. In a gravure, for example, there are only a few brush directions (or just one), usually 0 and 90 degrees, and sometimes also 45 and 135 degrees. In a free pencil drawing, however, all sorts of directions are used and those directions are often chosen to accentuate a certain shape or movement in the image.

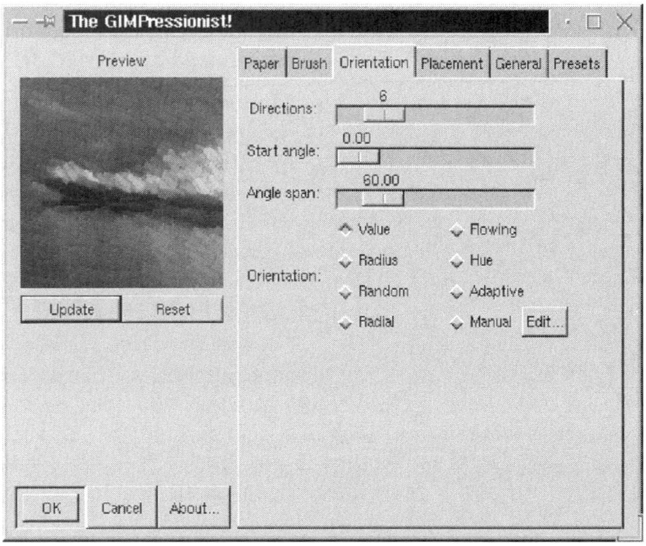

Figure 25.10 *The Gimpressionist Orientation tab*

On the **Orientation** tab, you can set the number of brush directions, the angle that those directions should be constrained to, and from what angle the specified angle span should start.

Note that in this filter 0 (zero) signifies horizontal lines, and 90 means vertical lines.

Orientation specifies the *style* of the brush strokes. To use a very simple example, you could say that Van Gogh (even though he was an Expressionist) would often use the kind of sweeping brush movements that the **Flowing** orientation option offers, and that **Random** orientation is more characteristic of late Monet paintings:

- **Value:** Sets direction by the *brightness* value. Bright brush strokes are painted at different angles from dark ones, resulting in a somewhat stiff, but consistent, paint direction for uniformly colored areas.
- **Radius:** Produces a *sinus-shaped* sweeping brushwork, where strokes of all colors more or less follow the same wave form.
- **Random:** Sets a different direction for each brush stroke, producing a mottled, dynamic surface.
- **Radial:** Lets all strokes emanate from a central direction, giving this brush orientation a very strong illusion of movement.
- **Flowing:** Provides the same sweeping kind of brushwork as **Radius**, but this is a less restricted kind of movement, where the paint is allowed to flow in different directions in different parts of the image.
- **Hue:** Sets direction by *color*. You shouldn't use this orientation for grayscale images unless you only want one brush stroke direction.

- **Adaptive:** Is the most realistic-looking orientation mode. This orientation makes object-oriented brush strokes, where each shape is accentuated by a certain stroke direction.
- **Manual:** Lets you make a really advanced painting. You can specify your own brush stroke orientation by setting different angles and orientations for different parts of the artwork. Before you can apply Manual orientation, you must *edit* the stroke directions. Press the **Edit** button, which will bring up the **Orientation Map Editor**.

THE ORIENTATION MAP EDITOR

As the name implies, you can specify how each brush stroke will be applied. In the **Vectors** window you can see the position and angle of your vectors (brush strokes). The currently active vector is highlighted in red, all other vectors are grayed out. In the **Preview** window you'll see how the different vectors will affect the image field.

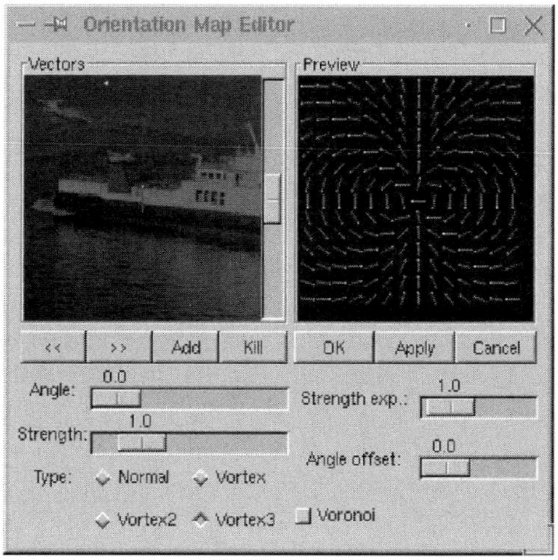

Figure 25.11 *The Orientation Map Editor*

You can use several vectors, or just one as it fits your purpose. To *add* a vector, press the **Add** button. To *delete* an unwanted vector, press the **Kill** button. To *navigate* from one vector to another, press the ">>" and "<<" buttons.

To set the base angle of a vector, drag the **Angle** slider. To set an exact angle value, left-click on either side of the slide button to change the value one degree for every click.

The **Strength** slider controls the strength of the selected vector (brush stroke).

The vector type can be set with the Type check buttons. The easiest way to find out how they work is to press them and look in the **Preview** window.

The **Strength exp.** slider controls the exponent of all vectors, i.e., you can change the overall strength of all brush strokes.

The **Angle offset** slider will rotate the angle of all vectors.

If you want to try out your settings, press **Apply** and then **Update** in the main window. You will now be able to preview the effect of your brush stroke settings in the Gimp image. When you are satisfied with your settings, press **OK**. With this command, you will exit the editor and apply your changes. **Cancel** simply exits the editor without saving your settings.

If you want to keep your settings for another Gimpressionist session, you can save them in the **Preset** dialog.

PLACEMENT

On the **Placement** tab, you can change the **Stroke density** and set the distribution of brush strokes to **Even** or **Random**. Use a low stroke density if you want to create a *crayon* or *charcoal* type of artwork, where the paper (or other background) is fully visible in unstroked areas. A high stroke density painting will cover all of the paper (only the structure or relief will show through). **Centerize** will make your strokes focus around the center of the image.

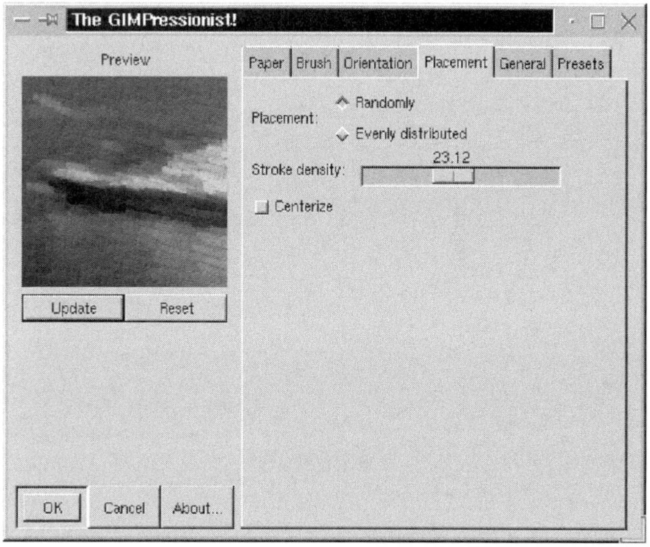

Figure 25.12 *The Gimpressionist Placement tab*

Set **Placement** to **Evenly Distributed** only if you want to create a very strict drawing (like an engraving). Otherwise, use **Randomly**, which produces a more naturalistic, hand-painted look.

GENERAL

On the **General** tab, you can change the weight of the dark edge of the brush strokes, thus increasing the relief effect of thick oil paint. Note that if the **Paint edges** button is left unchecked, the paint strokes will not cover the edges of the painting; instead, it will leave a fringe of the background visible in that area.

The **Background** option allows you to choose what kind of background should show through at a low stroke density: the **original** image, the **paper**, a **solid** background color of your choice or a **transparent** background. You can also make your image tileable by checking the **Tileable** button. This is a very handy option if you're creating a background for a web page.

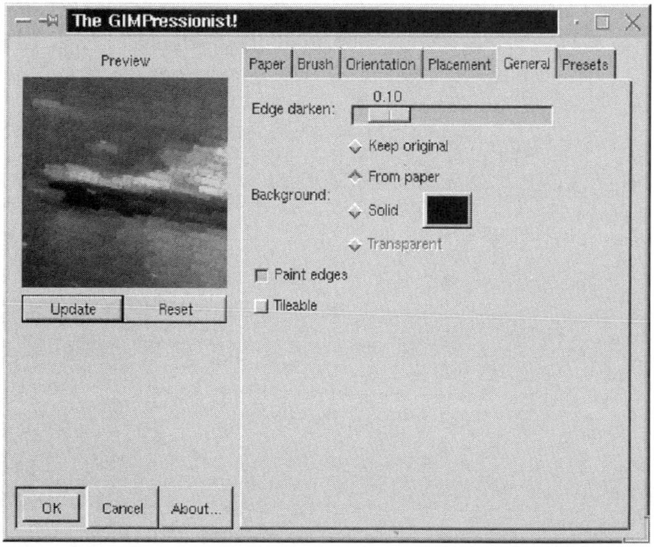

Figure 25.13 *The General tab*

PRESETS

The **Presets** tab contains a number of nice presets like *Cubism*, *Flowerbed* or *Weave*. You can also name and save your own settings in the **Presets library**. If you import Preset files into Gimp's preset directory, don't forget to press **Refresh**; otherwise, you will not see the new files. The preset directory will probably be called `~/.gimp/gimpressionist/Presets` or `/usr/local/share/gimp/gimpressionist/Presets` (site specific). Under the `gimpressionist` directory you will also find the `Brushes` and `Paper` directories where you can store additional brushes and papers that Gimpressionist can use.

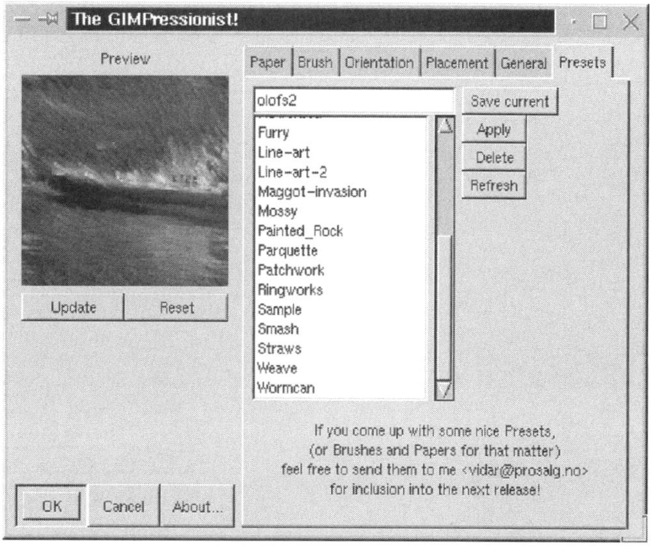

Figure 25.14 *The Presets tab*

Mosaic

The **Mosaic** plug-in allows you to imitate everything from a stained glass window to a ceramic mosaic floor.

Parameter Settings

This plug-in has many parameters that let you control the final result: the **Tile Size** and **Tile Height**, the **Tile Spacing**, and the **Tile Neatness,** which controls the appearance of the stones.

Light Direction controls how *light* will appear to shine on the mosaic edges. **Color Variation** adjusts how much the color is allowed to fluctuate. With a low value, the original color from the image will be preserved. If you set a low **Neatness** value and a high **Color Variation** value, you will get a very abstract mosaic.

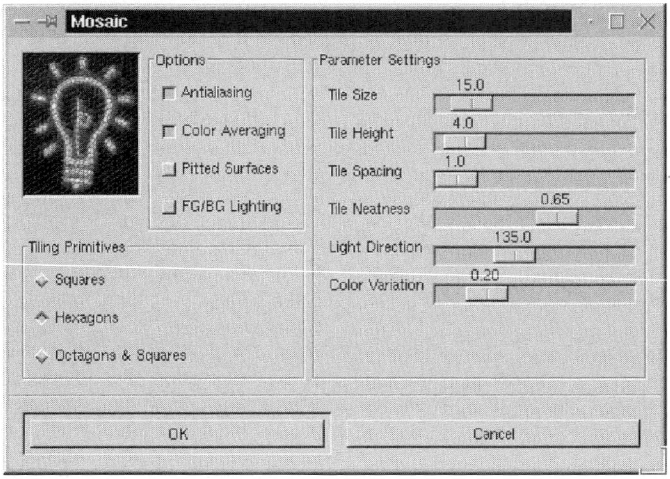

Figure 25.15 *The Mosaic dialog*

Tiling Primitives

Tiling Primitives determine the kind of mosaic tiles you want to use as a base for your mosaic. If you choose a **Hexagons** shape from the Tiling Primitives and lower the neatness value, the hexagonal structure will fade, and the stones will look more like natural stones.

Options

Antialiasing produces smooth edges. **Color Averaging** creates a true mosaic. If this option is unchecked, the original picture will only get a mosaic texture. **Pitted Surfaces** will produce a surface that looks old and used. **FG/BG Lighting** controls edge color. If unchecked, Mosaic will use the foreground and background colors from the toolbox.

Figure 25.16 *Mosaic filter invoked at the bottom-left corner*

You can create very interesting surfaces with Mosaic. For example, you can take a stone pattern and combine it with Mosaic to get something that looks like an old stone floor, or use another combination, perhaps a cracked glass/windshield.

NEWSPRINT

Newsprint creates *halftone screen patterns* similar to a newspaper print. You may have used a similar Adobe Photoshop filter called *Color Halftone*. Like many Gimp plug-ins, this filter is much more advanced than the Photoshop equivalent.

Figure 25.17 *Newsprint applied on the left side*

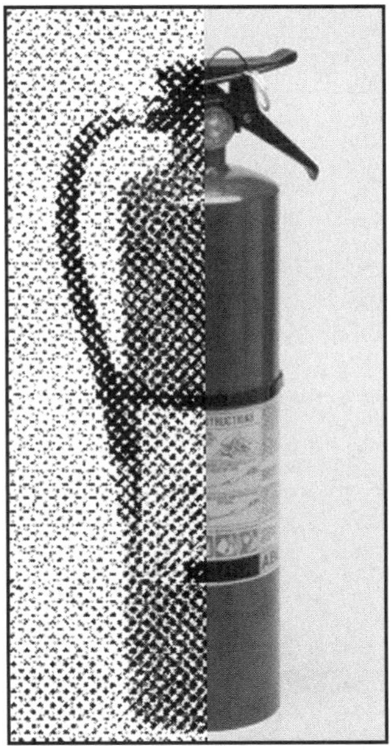

The **Newsprint** dialog includes a variety of parameters that control the outcome of the filter.

Note: The Input SPI (samples per inch, meaning pixels per inch or image resolution) and Output LPI (lines per inch) sliders are provided so this filter can be used in the future as a ripper for imagesetters. Until that is possible, don't bother about SPI or LPI and just use the Cell size slider.

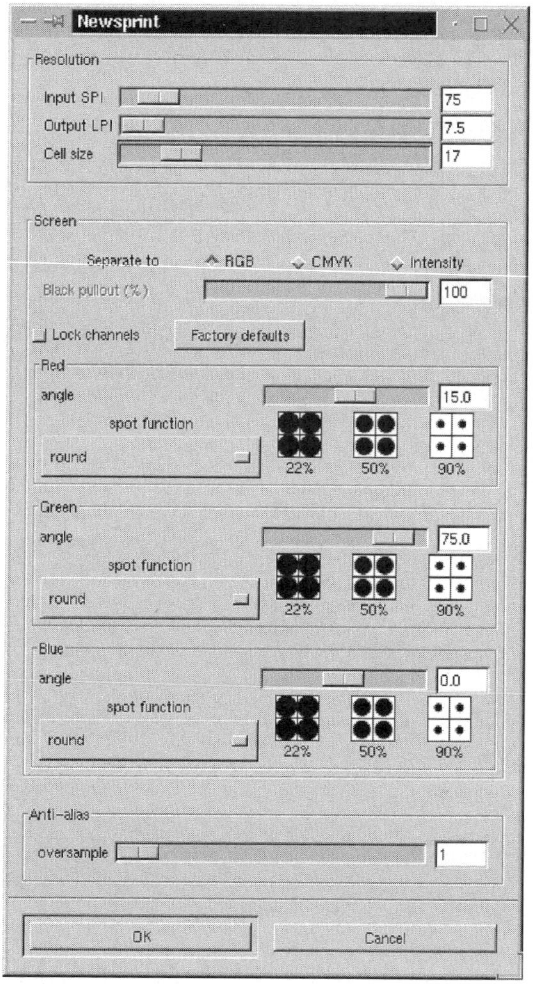

Figure 25.18 *The Newsprint dialog*

SCREEN

In the screen control area, you can select whether to separate to **RBG**, **CMYK** or by **Intensity**.

Intensity will map black halftone dots to the brightness value in the RGB image and place those dots on top of the original image. This is a rather neat trick to apply halftone likeness to a color image without having to simulate the colors with coarse CMY rosettes.

The **RGB** screening takes place in the red, green and blue channels, where black halftone dots appear at the specified screen angles. Black in a channel signifies the absence of color, so the color is actually in the area *surrounding* the black dots. Because the RGB color system is *additive*, the sum of the three RGB colors equals white, so the final effect of this screening is one of cyan, magenta and yellow dots on a white background. Of course, real printing is *subtractive* and no process inks are red, green or blue, so this only works on the screen.

The **CMYK** screening simulates halftoning in CMYK channels (because Gimp does not yet support CMYK channels). The effect is the opposite of RGB screening, because CMYK is a *subtractive* color system. Here, the sum of C, M and Y equals black, and the "black spots" in the channels become holes where the white background shows through. The black K (key color) channel is an intensity channel where the amount of black can be regulated against the black CMY overlap with the **Black Pullout** slider.

The screen control area will display one channel control for each independent color channel. Each channel has its own spot function and screen angle specified. For *grayscale* images, a smaller dialog with a single **Gray** channel will appear.

Angle

The default screen angle for the different color channels is set at the traditional process color print angles, which will produce a rosette of dots. If you want your image to look as if it was taken from a newspaper, you should not change these values. However, if you just want to experiment with interesting patterns, feel free to change the screen angles as you see fit.

Spot Functions

There are several different spot functions to choose from:

- The **Round** function produces circular dots.
- The **Line** function can be used for special effects at 90 or 0 degrees for grayscale images (compare it to the `right-click|Filters|Distorts|Engrave` filter) or at crossing "fishnet drawing" angles for RGB images.
- The **Diamond** spot is symmetrical and therefore its own inverse. At 50%, it forms a checkerboard pattern with all four corners touching for the first time.
- The **Euclidean** spot function is probably the most common spot function, because it is both symmetrical and tends to produce round dots most of the time.
- The **PostScript** diamond function grows from a small round spot to a diamond, and then back to an inverted round spot.

OILIFY

As you might guess, **Oilify** makes your image look like an oil painting. **Mask Size** controls the outcome. A high value gives the image less detail (as if you had used a larger brush).

Figure 25.19 *Oilify invoked at the bottom right in the image*

Tip: This tool is nice to use with several layers. You can also use this filter to help you select intricate objects by running it on a duplicate layer; a simplified shape is much easier to select.

VAN GOGH (LIC)

Van Gogh can be used to blur an image or to add texture. This plug-in has more in common with the texture or displace filters than the artistic ones, even though you can achieve artistic results with it.

- To create a **blur**, check **Convolve with source image** before applying the filter.
- To create a **texture**, check **Convolve with white noise**.

GENERAL PARAMETERS

Whether you want to make a pattern or a blur effect, you must first create a **map image**. **Effect channel** determines which HSV channel should be used (brightness is generally best). **Effect operator** controls the direction of the pattern or blur. **Derivative** sets the direction opposite of **Gradient**. If your map image has a certain direction, the effect operators work much the same way as the **Flip** tool in the toolbox.

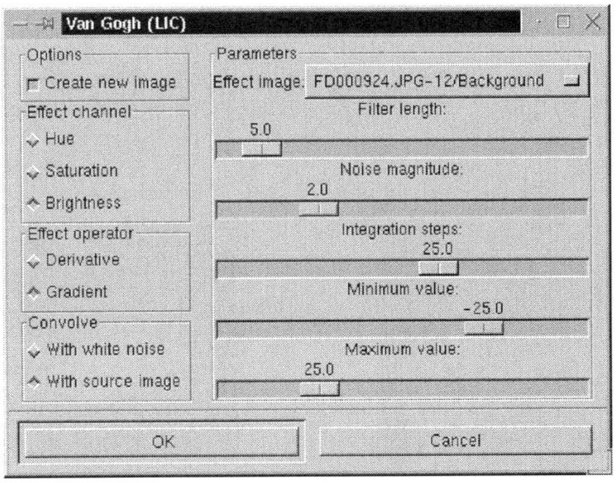

Figure 25.20 *The Van Gogh (LIC) dialog*

BLUR

The advantage of this filter is that the map image determines the direction of the blur effect, which means that you can adapt a gradient to create variation, movement and a sense of direction in blurring. A **radial** gradient creates a circular blur movement, a **horizontal** linear gradient (like dragging left to right) puts an emphasis on vertical lines in the image because it blurs horizontal lines, and vice versa.

A solid color object in the map image doesn't create a blur effect (except for the antialiased edges); you must use some sort of **gradient** in the areas you wish to blur. You should probably use the default settings, with the exception of **Filter length**, which controls the strength or depth of the blur, and in some measure also **Integration steps**. Use a black/white gradient map and nothing else (you can use all sorts of image maps, but in most cases it won't accomplish more than a general blur over the entire image).

Figure 25.21 *These examples illustrate the effect on a target grid-line image using different maps with blur or texture setting*

The Derivative Shapeburst illustration shows the result of using Derivative instead of Gradient Effect Operator. The Filter Length, Blur image shows what the Radial Blur image would look like using a higher Filter Length value.

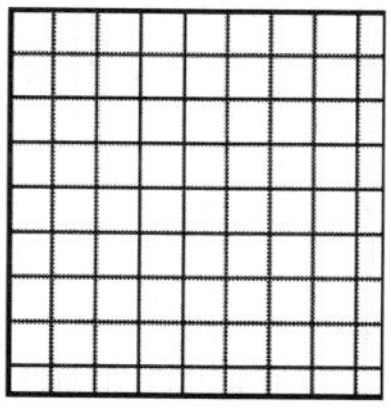

Target image

Horizontal Map

Square Map

Vertical Map

Radial Map

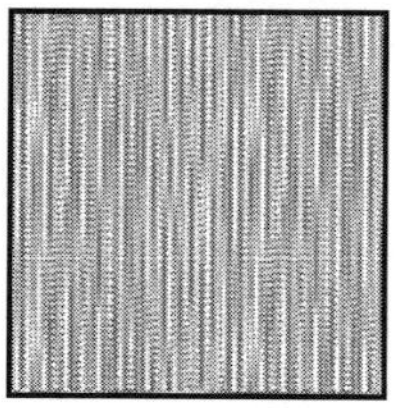

Horizontal Pattern

Shapeburst Pattern

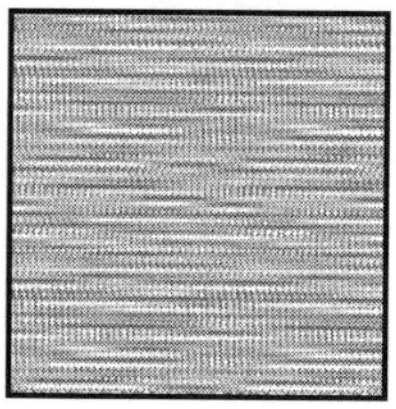

Vertical Pattern

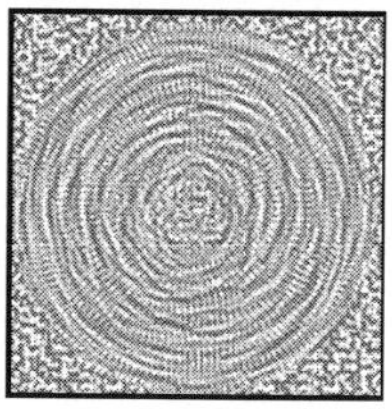

Radial Pattern

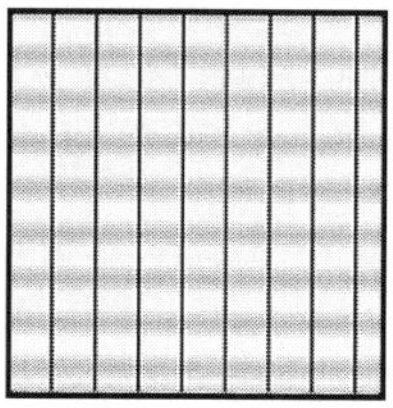

Horizontal Blur

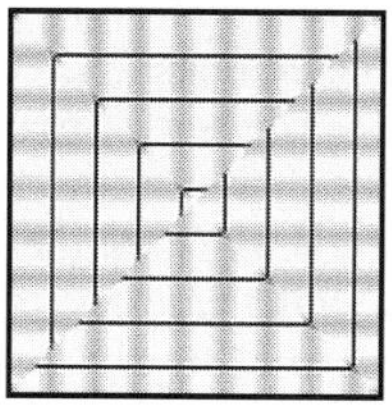

Shapeburst Blur

Vertical Blur

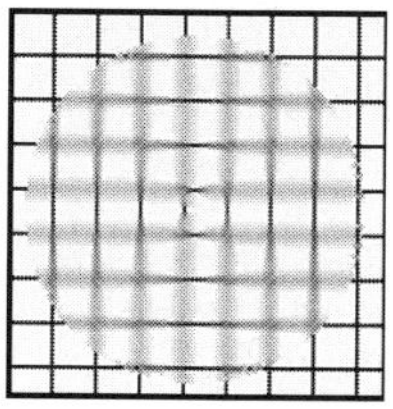

Radial Blur

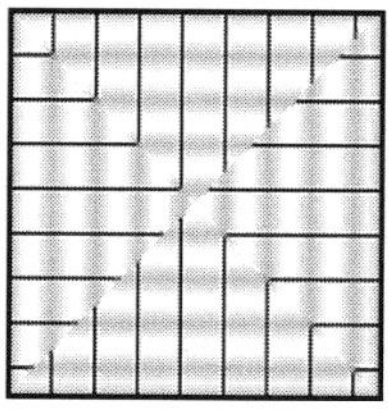

Derivative Shapeburst Blur

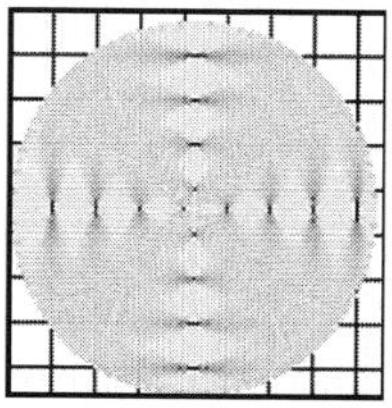

Filter Length, Blur

TEXTURE

Van Gogh is especially good for making patterns that look like woven or knitted textiles or fabrics. Use a target image with a solid color or a color pattern you think would fit your texture. Use a grayscale gradient or blurred mask as a map image, set **Integration Steps** a bit higher than default and experiment with the other settings to get the sort of texture you want.

When you use this filter as a texture maker, the settings are more important than when you use it for blurring:

- **Max/Min Value:** Controls contrast. If the Max/Min range is large, contrast is low. The contrast increases when you shrink the interval. *This setting does not affect blur.*
- **Integration Steps:** Controls how much the map gradient is allowed to influence the shape of the pattern (a large integration = a large influence). Don't set this parameter too low for blur; the default is probably fine.
- **Noise Magnitude:** Controls the amount and size of **random noise** (which breaks up the regularity of the pattern). Low values produce finely grained surfaces (sand), and high values produce coarser materials (large bumps and holes). *These values do not affect blur.*
- **Filter Length:** Controls depth just like the `right-click|Filters|Distorts|Emboss` filter. Low filter length gives you a smooth surface; high filter length provides a rough surface. This value controls the strength of the blur (compare the two images at the bottom of Figure 25.21 — *Radial Blur* and *Filter Length, Blur* — to appreciate the difference between low and high filter length)

Creating A Burlap Cloth Texture

Run the Van Gogh filter *twice* on a **white** image to produce two separate images. Both times, check **White Noise** (for pattern), select a quite small interval for **Max/Min** and put the other sliders somewhere in the middle (higher to create a coarser fabric). Use a *diagonal linear gradient* as the map.

Figure 25.22 *Cloth texture*

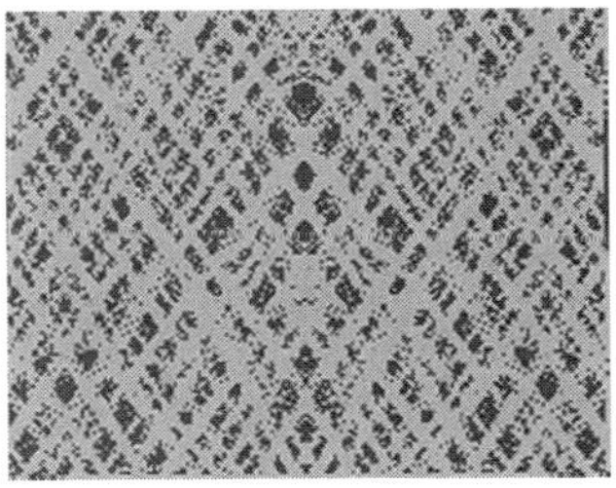

Set **Gradient** the first time and **Derivative** the second time (which will invert the direction of the pattern). Paste the *second* resulting image to a new layer in the first resulting image, and set **Lighten Only** mode (or another suitable mode).

WARP

Warp can produce effects that are a lot like the patterns you might have made as a child with a spoon in a bowl of thick cream and juicy berries. To make Warp work properly, you'll need a **Displacement map** (see the explanation of "Displace" on page 542 to get a good understanding of displacement maps).

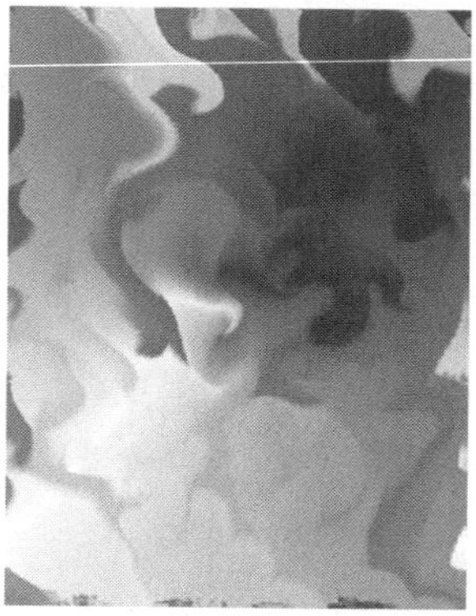

Figure 25.23 *Warp*

For example, to create juicy curls, you should use the **Solid Noise** filter (`right-click|Filters|Render|Solid Noise`) for a displacement map.

The more detail and small turbulences you have in the map image, the more smaller and frizzier curls you'll get. Make sure that the map image is the same size as the image you want to work the filter on. If you only want to warp a small part of the image, you can **erase** or **cut** part of the map image, and only leave an area that is about the same size and shape as the area you want to **warp** in the target image. When you want to specify a more exact position, size and shape of the warpable area, use a magnitude map instead.

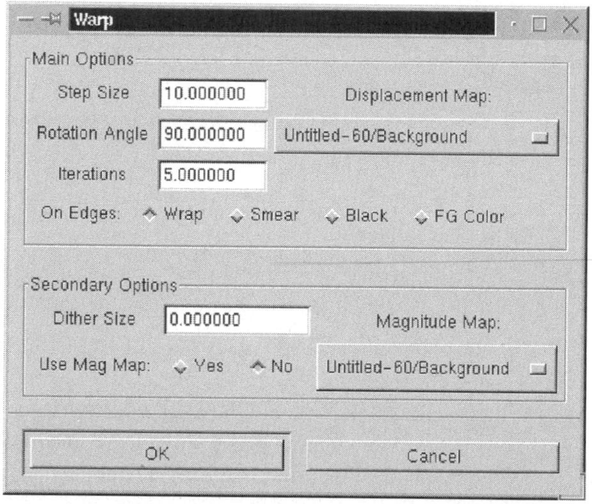

Figure 25.24 *The Warp dialog*

Main Options

- **Step Size:** Controls the amount or *strength* of the filter. The value you set here affects the image for every iteration, or warp step, you make.
- **Iterations:** Sets the number of times the filter should repeat the effect.
- **On Edges:** Refers to the way the plug-in deals with background color at the distorted edges (see "Displace" on page 542).

Secondary Options

- **Dither Size:** Causes pixels to displace randomly, thus decomposing the image. A moderate Dither Size just makes the warp curls look more grainy. Larger values scale from fuzzy particle clouds to total disintegration of the image.
- **Rotation Angle:** Determines what the "curls" will look like. A 90-degree rotation, the default setting, makes them look like small whirlpools. A 0-degree rotation looks more like the kind of solid distortion you'd see through a bathroom window. Other angles are combinations of these two, more or less so depending on how close they are.
- **Substeps:** Increases calculation time for each flow step. Raising the number of substeps gives a slight improvement in detail, but it also slows down the process.
- **Magnitude Map:** A more subtle way of controlling what parts of the image should be warped and by how much. The Magnitude map should be a grayscale image, where areas you do not wish to affect are black. Warp magnitude is determined by a brightness scale. White represents 100% (or normal warp), black stands for no warp at all and the different shades of gray weaken the warp effect.

Warped Image *Magnitude Map* *Displacement Map*

Figure 25.25 *This example shows the warped image, and the map images needed to achieve the warp effect*

OTHER OPTIONS

Besides the Warp displacement map, you can add a **Gradient** displacement map. This map will not displace in the curly warps you have seen before. Here, displacement depends on the direction of the gradual transition that makes the distortion straight and angular. The **Gradient Scale** sets the amount of influence the gradient map should have.

You can also displace along a fixed direction by using a **Vector** map. This option lets you displace a chosen map one step per iteration in a certain direction. **Vector Magnitude** determines by how many pixels the image should move for each iteration, and the direction is specified in the **Angle** swatch. A Vector map is something in between a Displace and a Magnitude map. It protects black areas and the rest of the image moves along the vector direction. The smoothness of the stretch is determined by the number of pixels specified. A low value gives a smooth disfigurement of the image.

Figure 25.26 *Thes e examples illustrate the result of using the same map with different options*

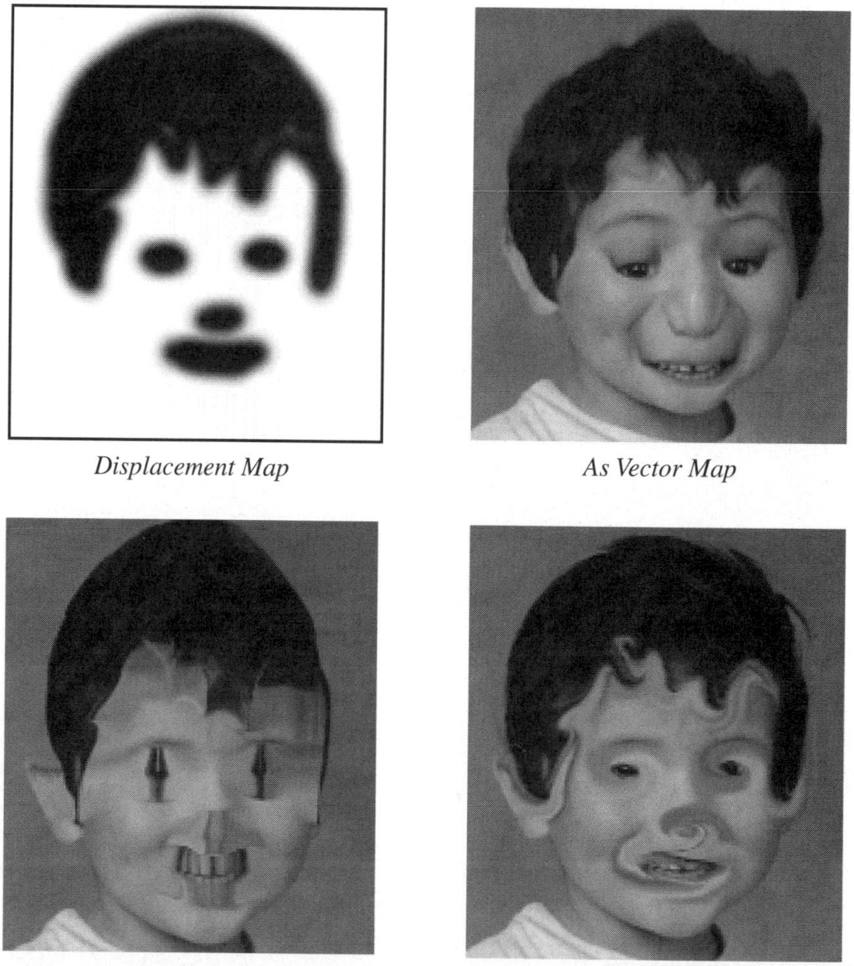

Displacement Map — *As Vector Map* — *As Gradient Map* — *As Normal Warp Map*

CHAPTER 26

Blur Filters

Gimp provides many ways to create blur effects. This chapter tells you how you can learn what filter to use and how to get the kind of blur you want.

Blur filters are often used on certain parts of an image to shift the focus to the sharper parts, to soften hard edges or to create an illusion of depth or distance.

ANTIALIAS

Antialias is an effective little filter for smoothing jagged edges. Antialias will find the edges and smooth the boundary between areas of different color or contrast, but it won't blur the entire image as other blur filters will. This filter is used by the `right-click|Filters|Blur|Antialias...` script that is described later in this chapter, so if you'd like to change any parameters, we suggest you use the **Antialias...** script instead.

BLUR

Blur makes your image look soft and out of focus. Several settings can be adjusted in the Blur dialog.

Figure 26.1 *Blur was applied to the right side of this image*

Blur causes *random displacement* of pixels. The **Randomization%** can be adjusted from 0% to 100%. A high value will render in a high level of blur. You can also specify if you want the filter to be repeated only once, or up to 100 times. Don't use too high repeat values, because this will make your image very unfocused.

You can set the **Randomization Seed** to the current time, or you can set it yourself in the input field as an **Other Value**. With Other Value you will get the "same" initial random value for each repeat; with current time you will get a different value for each repeat step.

Gaussian Blur

Gaussian Blur (IIR)

Gaussian Blur (IIR) is a variable blurring method, based on the **radius** of the blur. Higher radiuses produce a higher amount of blur (values less than 1.0 are invalid).

Figure 26.2 *Gaussian blur was applied to the right side of this image; blur is a good tool if you want to have a softer image*

You can also choose to blur vertically, horizontally or both by checking the appropriate checkboxes. These parameters make it possible to create a *motion blur* with this filter.

The Gaussian Blur (IIR) blur type is best for **scanned images** and other natural (photographic) images.

Gaussian Blur (RLE)

Gaussian Blur (RLE) works the same as Gaussian Blur (IIR) and provides the same parameters in its dialog. Gaussian Blur (RLE) is the blurring technique you should use for **computer-made images**.

Motion Blur

Motion Blur simulates a snapshot of a moving object.

Figure 26.3 *The Motion Blur dialog*

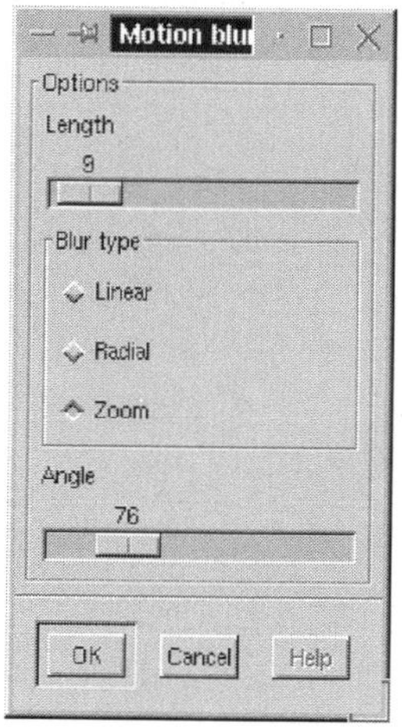

Linear Motion Blur

If you check the **Linear** radio button in the **Blur type** field, the image will look as if the object was moving *beside* you. The **Angle slider** sets the *direction* of the motion and the **Length** slider controls the *speed* of the motion (the more Length the higher the speed).

Figure 26.4 *Linear Motion Blur was applied to the upper parts of the sprinter to accentuate the impression of motion and speed*

Radial Motion Blur

If you check the **Radial** Blur type radio button, the image or selection will appear to be *rocking* or *spinning* in front of you.

In this case, **Angle** determines the amount of radial motion. A high value for Angle will make the image spin. **Length** determines how *fast* the object appears to be rocking/spinning.

Figure 0.1 *The upper gear has been blurred with Radial motion blur, which makes the gear appear to be in movement, while the chain and lower gear remain still. This is naturally impossible in real life, but Gimp makes the illusion seem real enough.*

Zoom Motion Blur

If you check the **Zoom** Blur type radio button, the objects in the middle of the image will look as if they are moving *towards* or *away* from you. Here, **Length** is the apparent speed at which the object is travelling. **Angle** seems to have no impact on this blur mode.

Figure 0.1 *We have blurred the surroundings of the running man (inverted selection of the man) with the Zoom blur, making him seem to be flying toward us at the speed of light*

PIXELIZE

Pixelize makes your image look as if it was made of really large pixels. You have to set the new pixel size. In other words, a **Pixel Width** of 3 makes an area made up of a 3x3 pixel block look like a single large pixel.

Figure 26.5 *Pixelized secret agent*

SELECTIVE GAUSSIAN BLUR

Selective Gaussian Blur is very useful for removing *noise* from scanned images. It works by adding blur to the parts of the image where focus is low.

The **Max Delta** parameter controls the size of the image area that will be blurred. A high value (>70) will blur larger areas, while low values (<40) will only blur small portions of the image. This means that using a high value for Max Delta will cause more details to be blurred.

The **Radius** parameter controls the amount of blur that is applied to selected parts. High values (>7) produce a high level of blur, and low values (<4) produce a weaker blur effect.

When you use this filter to remove noise, we recommend that you start with the default values (5, 50). If the default values prove too strong, then lower the Max Delta parameter until you are satisfied. If this still doesn't remove your noise, then raise the blur Radius. If a higher blur level should reduce details in the image, then lower the Max Delta value.

Another application for this filter is for accentuating the focused part of the image. Since Selective Gaussian Blur removes noise, it will also smooth less focused parts of the image, thus adding **depth** to the image, and highlighting the focused parts. This function is ideal when you work with amateur portrait photographs.

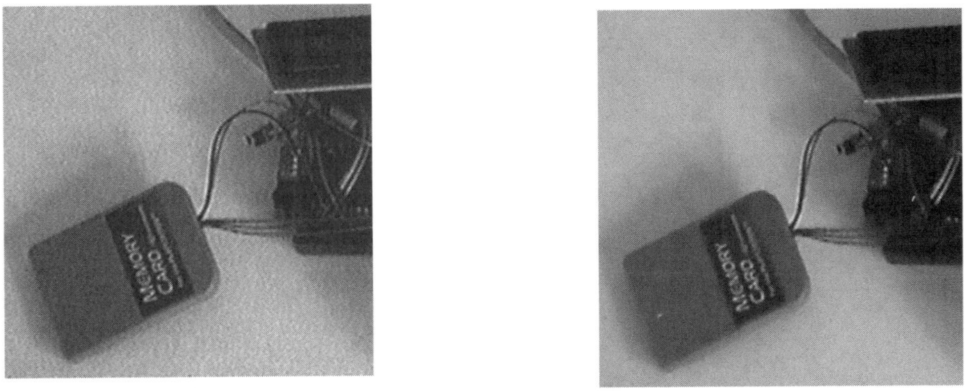

Before *After*

Figure 26.6 *Selective Gaussian Blur before and after; notice the background (table), which has a high degree of noise before but not after; this is a very useful tool for smoothing out noise and still getting a high level of detail*

TILEABLE BLUR

Tileable Blur is an excellent tool for softening the tile seams in images you want to use in tiled backgrounds. Tileable Blur compares the pixels that will end up next to each other when the image is tiled, and compensates for this by blending/blurring those edges as if they had been adjacent.

The **Blur Vertical/Horizontal** and **Radius** functions are the same as described in the **Gaussian Blur** filter. The **RLE** and **IIR** options are for computer-generated and photographic images, respectively, just as with **Gaussian Blur RLE/IIR**.

To avoid blurring the entire image, use `right-click|Select|Feather` to select the important parts of the image (the parts that you don't want to blur) and `right-click|Select|Invert` the selection before you apply the filter.

Note that Tileable Blur is a **script**, so it can't be reversed with Undo.

VARIABLE BLUR

Variable Blur is much like ordinary blur, but it allows you to regulate the amount of blur by adjusting the **Mask Size**. A large Mask Size will result in a high amount of blur, and vice versa.

Figure 26.7 *Variable Blur was applied to the left part of the image*

ANTIALIAS...

This **Antialias... script** allows you to fine-tune the *contrast* in the softened (antialiased) border. The antialiasing border is always 2 pixels wide, but you can set a preference for what the contrast should be between those pixels. The default value (0.33333) produces a normal antialias border, with an even distribution of 1/3 of the new color in the first pixel and 2/3 in the second pixel.

A lower value results in low contrast between the two pixels because they'll both get a similar *intermediate* color, while high values will increase the contrast between the pixels. This script uses the **Antialias filter** described in the beginning of this chapter.

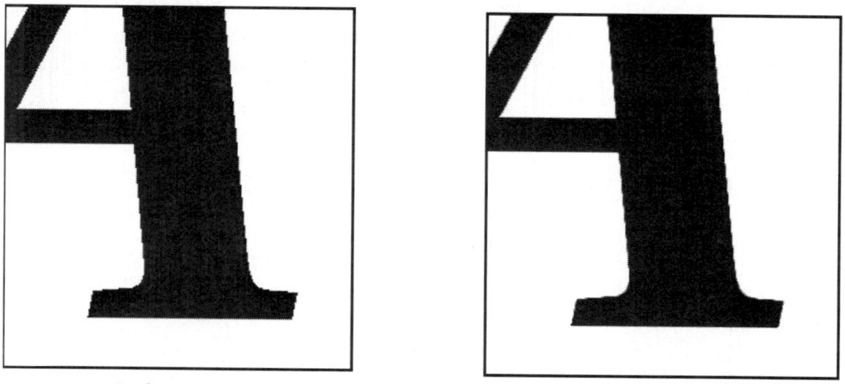

Before *After*

Figure 26.8 *Applying antialias to a blocky edge will produce a smoother output*

CHAPTER 27

Color Filters

Welcome to the color darkroom! With these filters you can achieve effects that you would create in a darkroom: changing colors, masking colors and more.

ADJUST FGRD. - BKGRD.

Adjust Fgrd. - Bkgrd is a simple **color map** function. The pixels in the image will be mapped against the toolbox foreground and background color swatches. The darkest pixels in the image will be mapped to the foreground color, and the lightest to the background color in the toolbox. Also, pixels with the same color as the foreground will be mapped to *black*, and pixels with the same color as the background will be mapped to *white*.

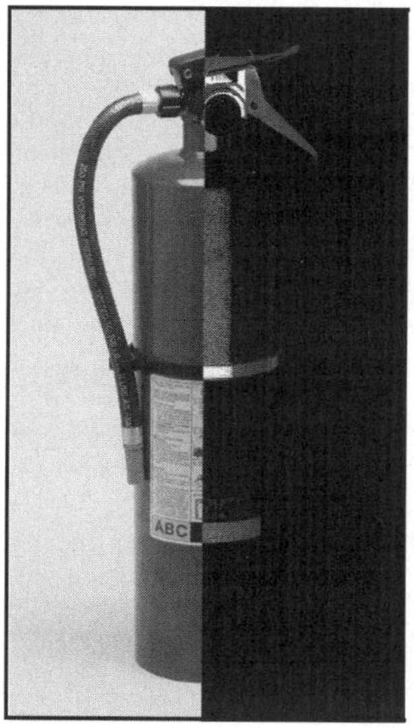

Figure 27.1 *The right part of the image was mapped with Adjust Fgrd-Bkgrd*

ALIEN MAP

Alien Map applies trigonometrical functions to **RGB channels**.

FUNCTIONS

The Cosine Function

Let's take the *Red* channel and see what we can do with it. First, set *Green* and *Blue* to **None** (i.e., Linear), set **Phase** displacement to 0.00 and **Frequency** to 1.00 for all channels. Last, uncheck all **Inversion** buttons.

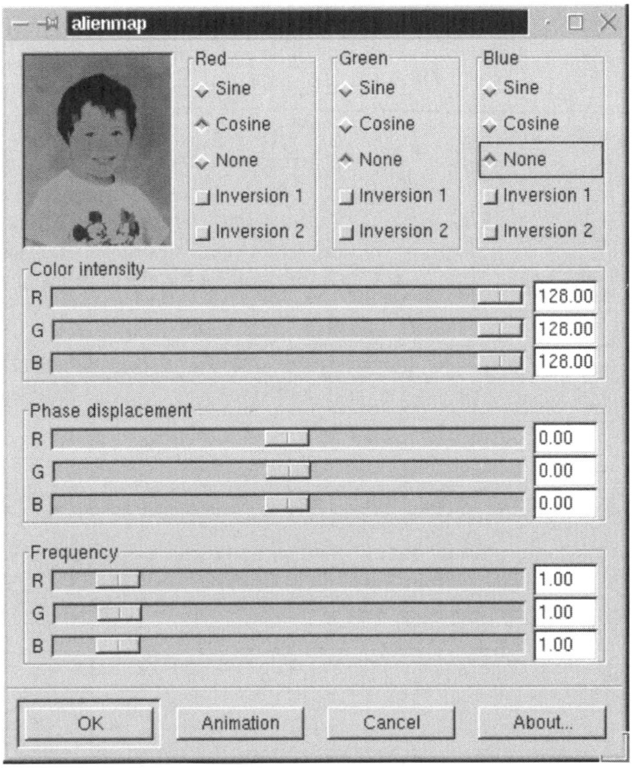

Figure 27.2 *The Alien Map dialog*

If you now check **Cosine** in the Red channel, the image will get a lot redder.

Figure 27.3 *The Cosine function applied to the red channel will boost red middle values and subdue high values for red*

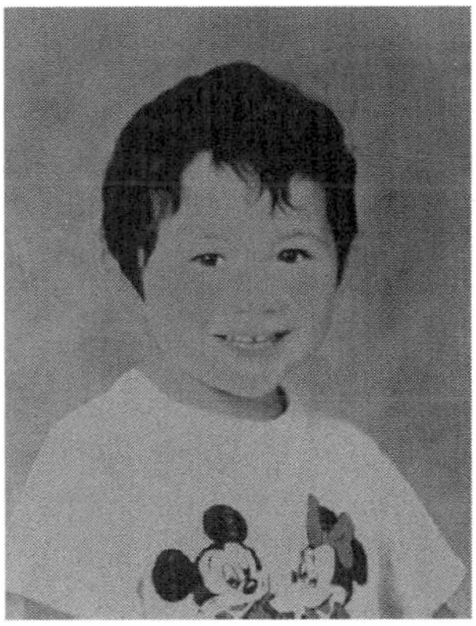

Why? Well, the original picture contains a lot of medium red skintones. As you can see in Figure 27.3. Cosine will *boost* those "middle" red values. *Remember that medium gray areas also contain middle values of red.* You may also notice that the parts with **high** value for red have been subdued. Maximal values for red are often found in *white/bright* areas, which assume a **cyan** tint when the red is removed.

What happens if we set all three channels to Cosine? The same principle applies here. Middle tones get *boosted*, which means that those areas turn brighter. Bright areas turn dark, because those areas are *subdued*. Dark areas stay dark, and if a certain color is very saturated, that color will either turn dark or change into one of the primary colors: blue, red or green.

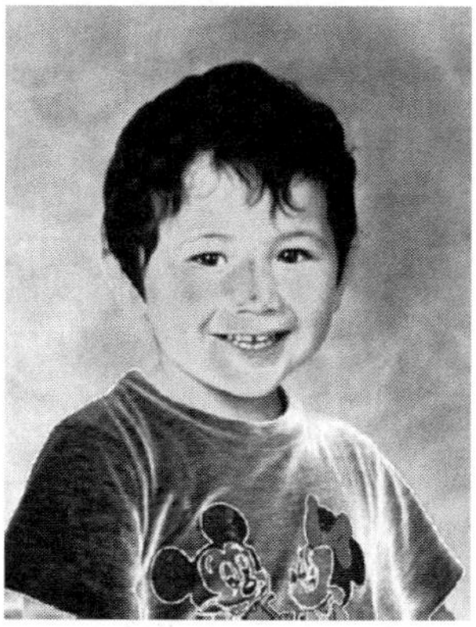

Figure 27.4 *The Cosine function applied to all three channels.*

The Sine Function

If you check **Sine** you'll notice that the image will get considerably *less* red. This is because **Sine** does not change middle RGB values much. Note that really dark parts such as the hair and eyes have become more red, while most of the medium/low red values (the background) have been subdued. Medium/high red values are boosted (the face), as are the bright parts of the T-shirt, while the truly white areas shift toward cyan. Sine in all channels results in higher contrast in medium values and lower contrast in bright/dark areas.

Figure 27.5 *Sine in the red channel*

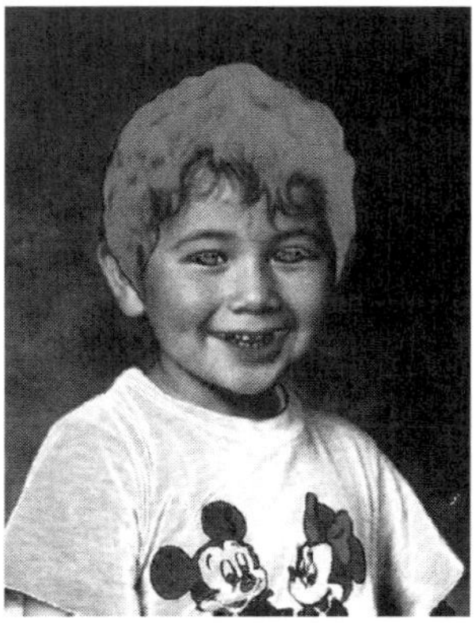

Figure 27.6 *Sine in all three channels*

Figure 27.7 shows a cosine and a sine wave over the Red channel interval from 0 to 255. With a *cosine* function, red color with a value of 128 (medium red) will be mapped to 255 (maximum red). With a *sine* function, medium red tones can get very different red values depending on what side of 128 they are on.

Figure 27.7 *The Cosine and Sine curves show how values in the original image will be mapped*

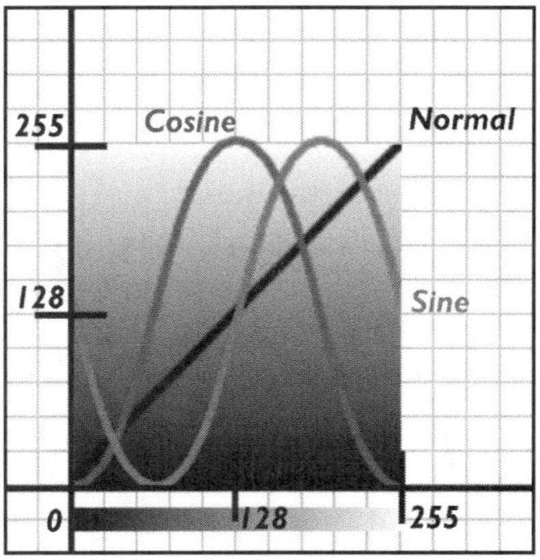

Parameters

Inversion 1 will invert the color values before the Alien Map function has been applied. **Inversion 2** will invert the colors after Alien Map has applied the sine or cosine function.

Color intensity is easy to understand; with the RGB sliders you can adjust the intensity of each channel. But **Phase displacement** and **Frequency** are perhaps a bit harder to understand.

Frequency

Lets start with *frequency,* using the settings of the Sine example in Figure 27.5. Changing the frequency of a sine function can produce dramatic effects.

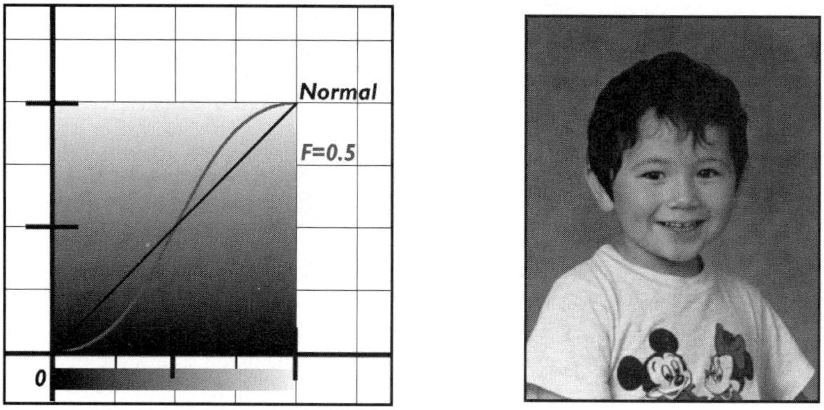

Figure 27.8 *Half frequency*

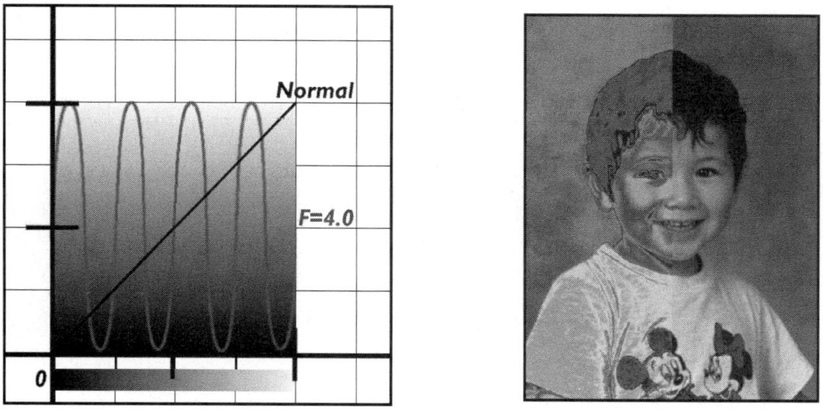

Figure 27.9 *Quad frequency*

If you set the frequency to 0.5, as in Figure 27.8, you can only fit a *half* sine wave over the 0 to 255 interval. This will make the red values follow the normal curve pretty well, so this will only increase the **contrast** in the image. If, on the other hand, you set the frequency to 4 or more, you will fit four sine waves over the interval, which will map the maximum value to four different red values in the image.

Phase Displacement

If you change the **Phase displacement** slider, you will drag the sine wave **sideways** in the 0 to 255 interval. This naturally will affect the mapping so that a higher value will be mapped to 255 if you slide it in a positive direction. If you slide it in a negative direction, a lower value will be mapped to 255. Notice that the effect is circular because the outcome is the same for both maximum and minimum values.

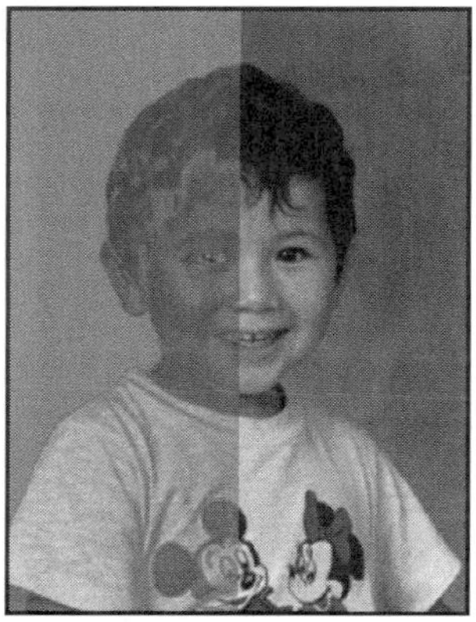

Figure 27.10 *In this example, the Phase was displaced to 3.00 in the positive direction*

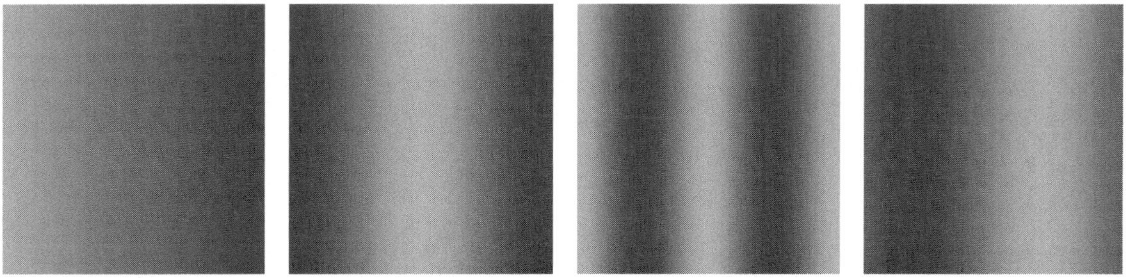

Original *Cosine* *Frequency = 2* *Phase disp = 1.25*

Figure 27.11 *These images show the effect of the cosine function, using different parameter settings*

ALIEN MAP2

Alien Map2 is also based on *trigonometrical* functions, but it is more versatile than the **Alien Map** filter. The difference is that you can switch between **RGB** and **HSV** (HSL) space. Otherwise, the parameters in this filter are the same as in Alien Map, so we recommend that you first read "Alien Map" on page 412, to understand Alien Map2.

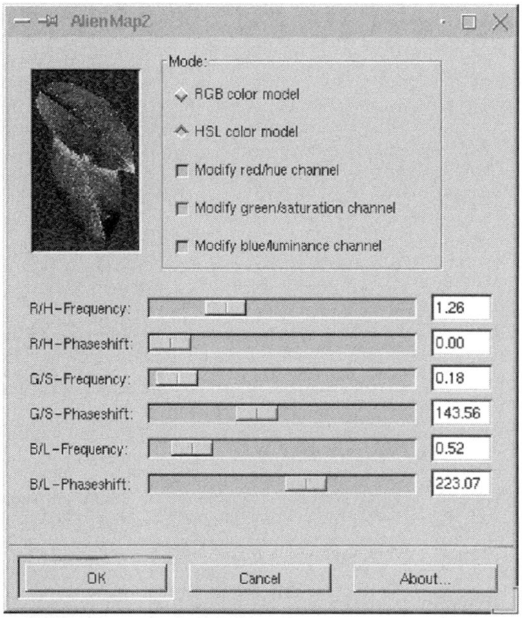

Figure 27.12 *The AlienMap2 dialog*

Figure 27.13 *The top leaf was mapped to autumn colors with AlienMap2*

FREQUENCY AND PHASE

In RGB space, each color channel can be adjusted by tuning the **Frequency** and **Phase displacement angle**. Frequencies around 0.3 to 0.7 provide a curve that is similar to the linear function (original image), only darker or with more contrast (see Figure 27.8). As you raise the frequency level, you'll get an increasing variation in pixel transformation, meaning that the image will get more and more "alien" (see Figure 27.9).

The phase change will alter the value transformations. You'll find that 0 and 360 degrees are the same as a **sine function** and 90 is the same as a **cosine function**, while 180 inverts sine and 270 inverts cosine.

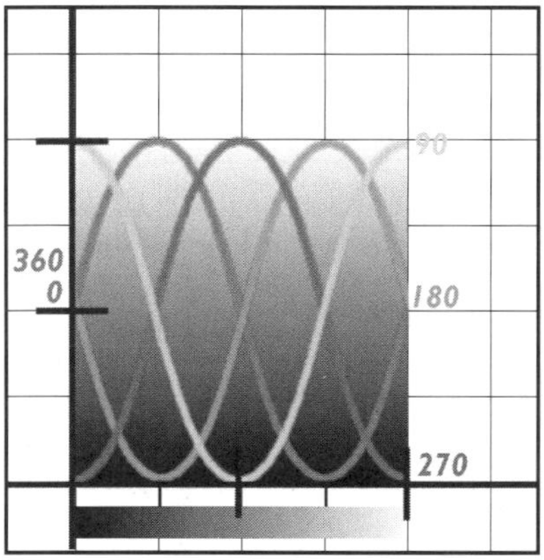

Figure 27.14 *This illustration shows how a sine curve can be transformed with different phase displacement angles*

HSV Manipulation

In HSV space, the most notable difference is the **Hue** channel. The sine curve follows the color distribution of the HSV color circle, and a change in frequency will produce psychedelic results. The **Saturation** and **Value** (Luminance) channels can be manipulated in the same manner.

Border Average

The **Border Average** tool is used to calculate the **background** color of web pages. The idea is to find a web page color that differs as little as possible from the *edge* pixels in your image.

Use Border Average to calculate the most common (mean) color in a border around the current selection, or an image if there is no present selection. The border is an imaginary image border that is X pixels wide. Set the border width in the **Border Size Thickness** field. The **Bucket Size** parameter controls the number of colors that are used to calculate the average color. A high Bucket Size value gives you better precision in these calculations.

Color Mapping

The **Color Mapping** filter is a plain **color map** filter. You can map two colors in your image to two new colors. The interface is simple to understand. Just press the **From** and **To** buttons to set the colors that you want to swap.

Figure 27.15 *The right side of this image was mapped with Color Mapping*

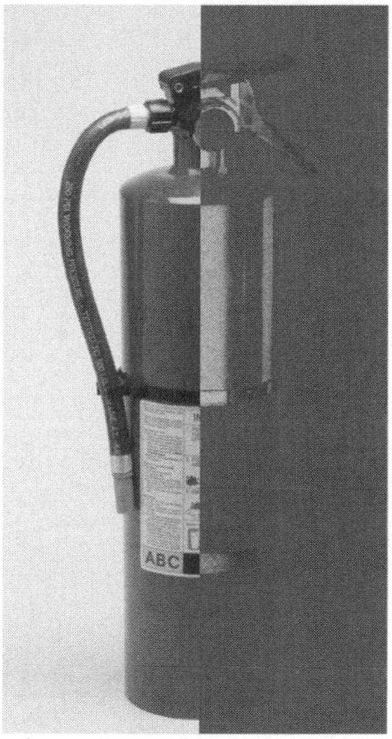

Color Exchange

Color Exchange is a lot like the **Colormap Rotation** filter (see "Colormap Rotation" on page 422) but it is simpler and faster.

Figure 27.16 *The bottom-left part of this image was altered with Color Exchange*

Define the color to exchange (the **From color**) by setting the slider for each **RGB channel** and a **threshold** fuzziness as you did in `right-click|Select|By Color` to define the color range that will be affected. The **To color** slidebars specify the RGB values of the new color.

Tip: Always keep the Color Select dialog up as you're adjusting the RGB sliders, so that you can choose a color there and insert the given RGB values in the Color Exchange dialog.

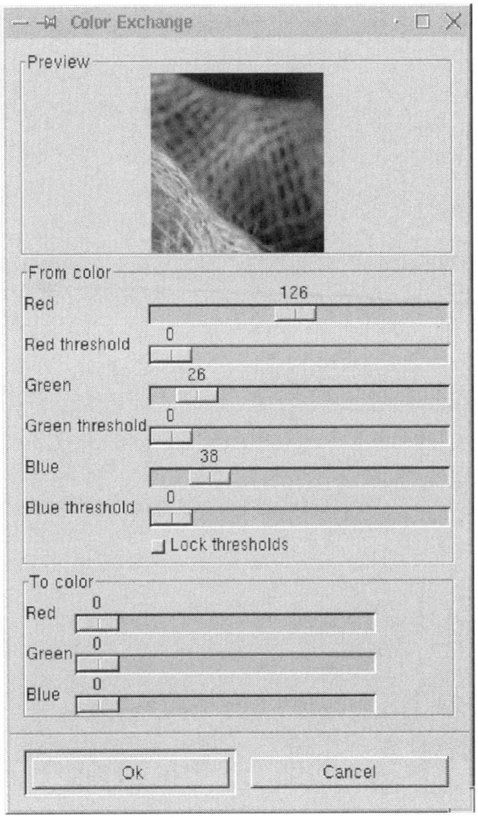

Figure 27.17 *The Color Exchange dialog*

COLORIFY

Colorify makes your image look like it is being viewed through colored glass. Predefined colors are provided, but you can also set a color of your choice by clicking on the **Custom Color** swatch.

Figure 27.18 *The left part of the image has been treated with Colorify*

COLORMAP ROTATION

Colormap Rotation lets you exchange one color interval for another.

THE MAIN TAB

In the **From** and **To** color circles, define the color range that you want to rotate from and the color range you want to rotate to. By default the range is going *counterclockwise*, so if you define a range that you want to rotate, the rotation will map your pointers in the **From** and **To** color circles. If one of the fields is switched to *clockwise*, the first pointer in a field will map the second pointer in the other field.

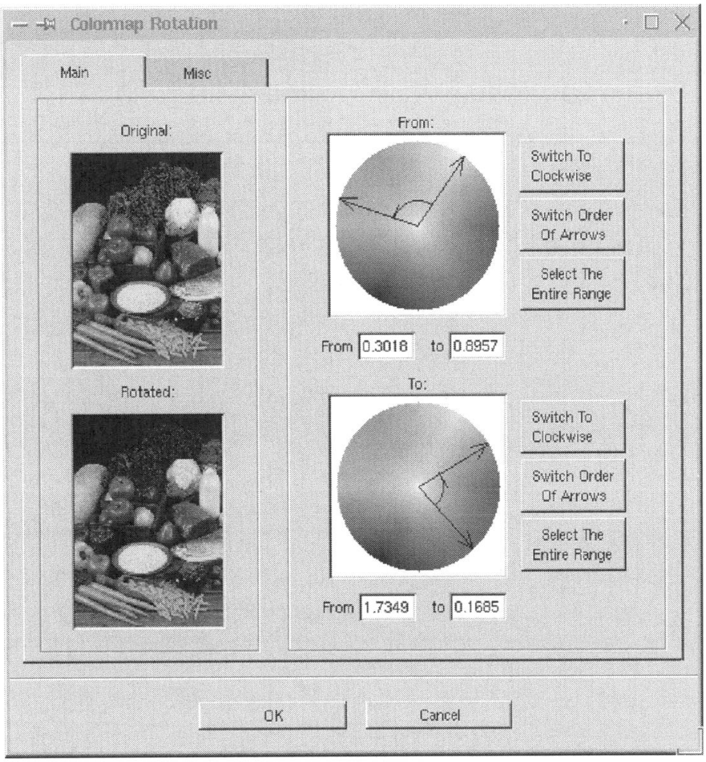

Figure 27.19 *The Colormap Rotation dialog*

Example

In the **From** circle, select a range from cyan to magenta and select *counterclockwise*. In the **To** field, select the same range (but *clockwise*). Then, all cyan colors will be rotated to magenta, and vice versa.

If you press the **Switch Order of Arrows** button, the range will be *inverted.* When, as in the example above, your selection range goes from cyan to magenta over blue, Switch Order of Arrows will change the selection range to go from magenta to cyan over red and green.The **Select The Entire Range** button will select the whole range. Colormap Rotation makes it easy to rotate an entire color range to another shade or color range.

Original

Rotated

Figure 27.20 *The lettuce has turned red instead of green — the same goes for all green parts of the image*

The Misc Tab

What Is Gray?

In the **Misc** tab, you can specify how to treat gray "colors." By default, gray is considered colorless and is not affected by the rotation. But gray can also be defined as other shades, such as a very washed-out shade of green, and should therefore by definition be affected by the rotation.

How saturated a color has to be for it to be affected depends on the settings of the **Treat As This** or **Change To This** parameters.

Gray Settings

So let's find out how to define what gray is, and how to deal with it.

The field **What is Gray?** is where you specify what saturation range you think should be considered "gray." You define this in a **Saturation scale** from 0 to 1 (pure gray is 0).

Zero saturation is often too narrow, so you will probably have to set gray to less than or equal to 0.1 or 0.2. As you set this value, the circle in the **Gray** color circle will expand and cover more saturation values.

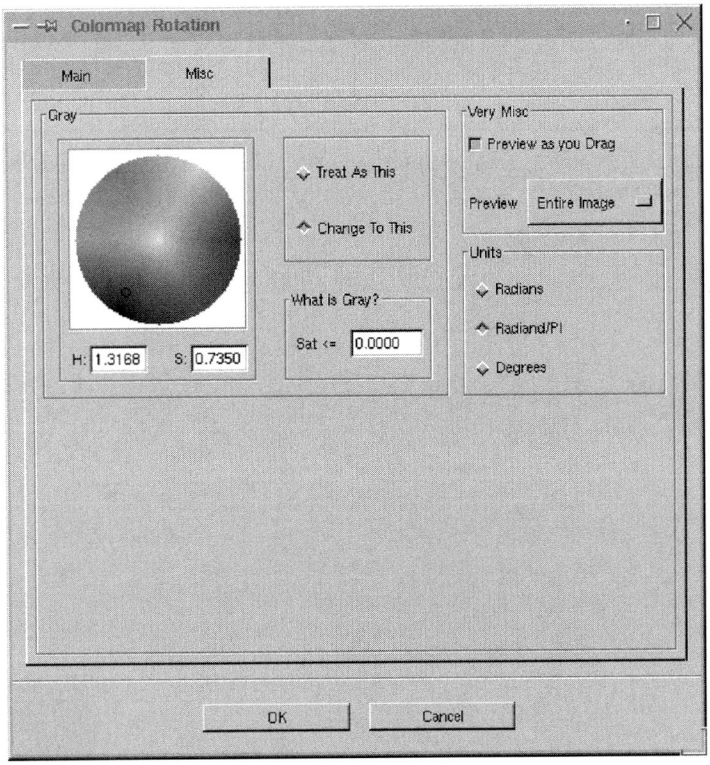

Figure 27.21 *The Misc tab*

The radio buttons **Treat As This** and **Change To This** determine what you want to do with the gray areas you defined in the What is Gray field.

If you've checked Treat As This, you're telling the plug-in what color you want gray *to be like*. You do this by *paning* the little circle cursor in the Gray color circle. For example, you can drag the define circle to the red part of the color circle, and all gray shades will be treated as red when you perform a color rotation.

If you check Change To This, all gray shades will be changed to the color you have selected within the gray define circle.

Other Parameters

You can also select what kind of **Units** you want to use — **Radians**, **Radiand/PI** or **Degrees** — when you view and drag the pointers in the rotation dialog.The **Preview** can be set to **Entire Image**, **Selection** or **Context**.

Context is a smart preview option if you have a selection. Instead of just displaying the selection, the Context option will let you see the selection in its context, as if you had *zoomed out* a little bit from the selection. Check the **Preview as you Drag** checkbox if you want the preview to change as you drag in the rotation dialog.

Filter Pack

Filter Pack is a real darkroom tool in which you can do most of the things that you would do in a real lab. Although you can perform all of these functions using other tools in Gimp and maybe even with better precision, this tool has a natural interface. It's perfect for fixing up old and faded pictures, or for correcting other kinds of color problems.

Select Pixels By And Affected Range

First, in the **Affected Range** field, decide what **brightness** values you want to work with: *Shadows*, *Midtones* or *Highlights*. By selecting Shadows, only the darkest pixels in the image will be affected by the Filter Pack operations.

The **Select Pixels By** *Hue*, *Saturation or Value*, buttons determine what HSV channel the selected range should affect. The default setting is **Value** (brightness), but there are occasions where you may wish to operate on the Hue or Saturation channels. To illustrate this point, we have decomposed an image to HSV in Figure 27.22. Figure 27.23 shows how an image can be manipulated using Select Pixels By Hue.

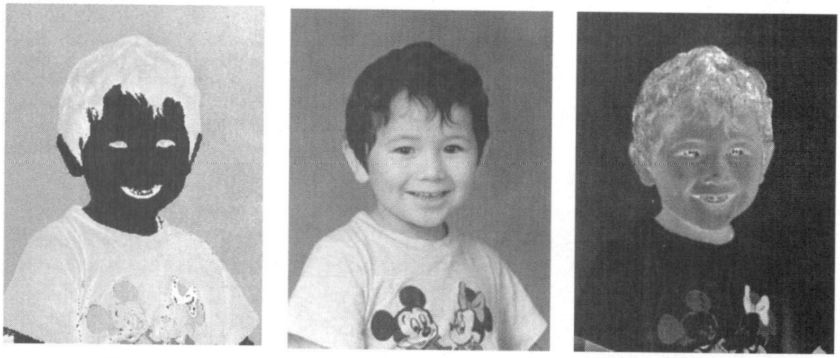

Hue *Value* *Saturation*

Figure 27.22 *Thes e pictures show the original image decomposed to HSV; as you see, selecting pixels by value, hue or saturation will select totally different parts of the image*

Figure 27.23 *The fair and the dark boys were created from the same image by selecting Shadows in the Affected Range field, and then selecting pixels by Hue; this way, only the face was affected by color and value changes*

The blond hair was made by selecting pixels by Value, and making those areas lighter in the Value Window

Show And Roughness

Show sets what you want to preview. If you're using a selection, you can click on the **Selection Only** radio button to preview only the selection.

Selection In Context is a smart preview option if you have a selection. Instead of just viewing the selection, the **Context** option will let you see the selection in its context, as if you had zoomed out a little bit from the selection.

The **Roughness** slider controls how much the image will be altered. The higher the value, the less precision you'll have.

Figure 27.24 *The main Filter Pack dialog*

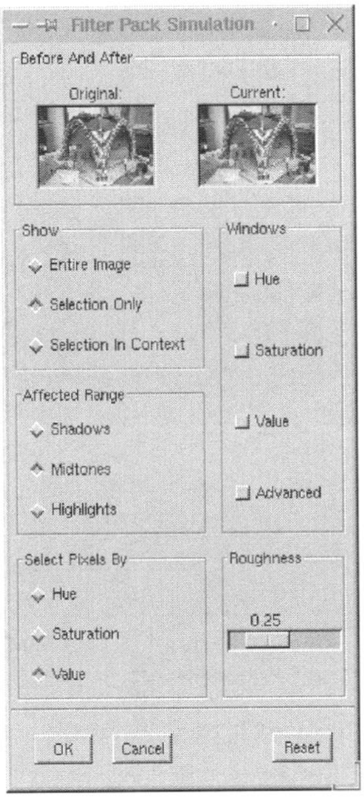

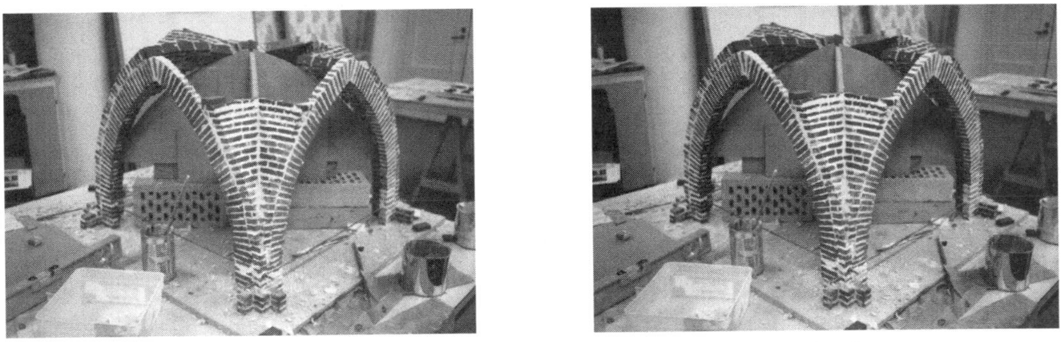

Original *Fixed*

Figure 27.25 *Filter Pack is a perfect tool for adjusting images with incorrect color tone*

WINDOWS

The **Windows** settings determine what kind of values you are interested in changing (**Hue**, **Saturation**, **Value** or **Advanced**) and therefore want to view.

- **Hue** lets you change the *color* of the image. If you want your image to look a bit more blue, just press the blue preview in the Hue window.
- **Value** lets you change the amount of *light* in the image.
- **Saturation** lets you alter the color *dullness/loudness*.

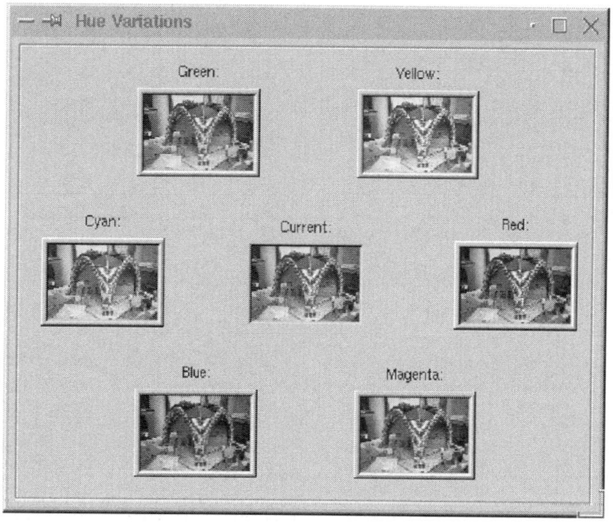

Hue

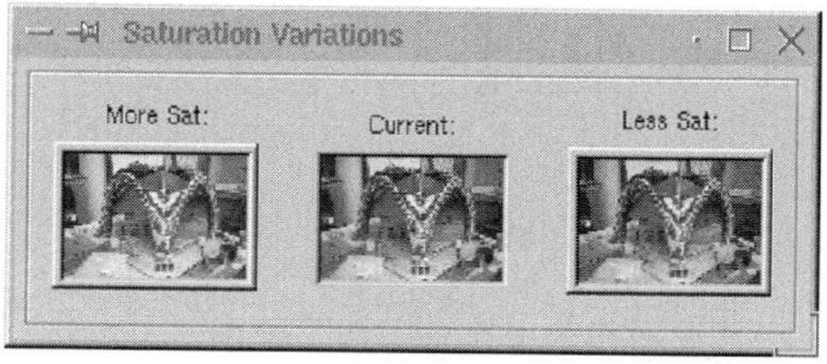

Saturation

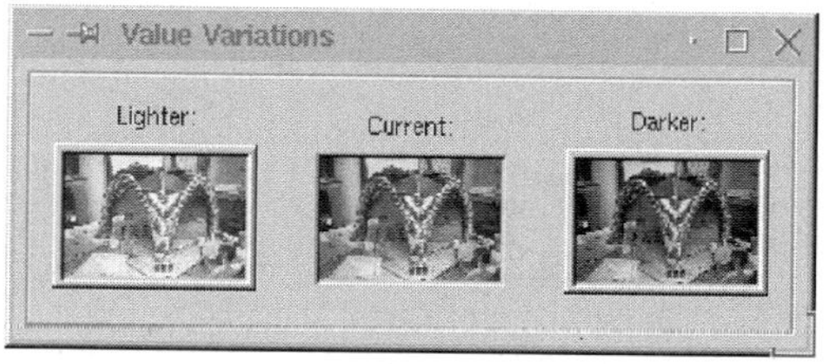

Value

Figure 27.26 *Filter Pack's HSV Variations windows*

Advanced Options

In **Advanced Options,** you can set the **Preview** size (useful if you have a large screen).

You can also check the **Pixel Selection Menu**, which lets you select the HSV value that you want to change. The pointers in the curve let you alter the range of shadows, midtones and highlights in a brightness scale from 0 to 255.

The slider alters the **smoothness** of the transition from one shade to another. If you set it to zero, only the selected range *(shadows, midtones or highlights)* will be affected by your interaction. If you set it to 1, every range will be affected. A value in the middle is the most appropriate choice to create a smooth transition.

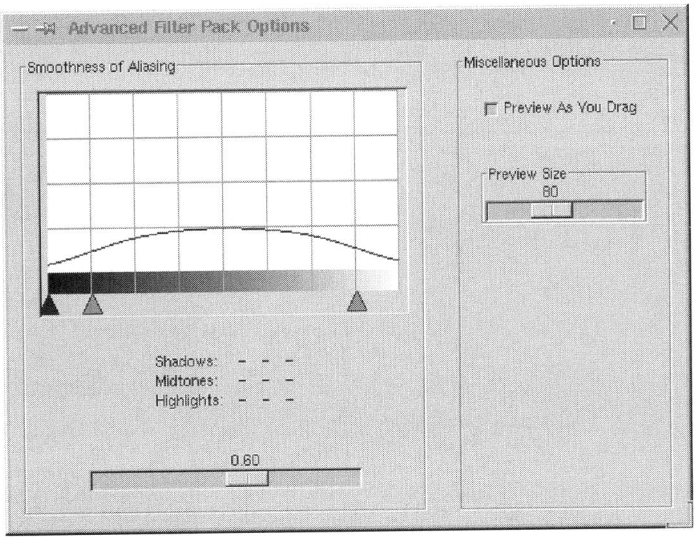

Figure 27.27 *The Advanced Filter Pack Options dialog*

FS-Dither

FS-Dither is used for preparing images that are going to be **indexed** (such as GIF images). This filter was created as an alternative to Gimp's built-in Dithering function, which is less advanced. With this filter, you can select which color channel to dither, which gives you a better control of the dithering process.

Options And Advice

The **Number of Shades** option refers to the number of colors in each channel. If your image is a grayscale, you should set the same amount of colors in the **Index** dialog as you did in **No. of Shades**.

If your image is an RGB image, you should multiply the No. of Shades number by three, and add two shades for white and black. Set this number in the Index dialog.

Remember to index against **Optimal palette** in the Index dialog, because that's what FS-Dither uses for a palette when it dithers. If you index against something else, the FS-Dither will not work as well as it is supposed to. Naturally, you should uncheck the **Dither** option in the Index dialog when you have applied FS-Dither.

To get a better view of how much better **FS-Dither** is than Gimp's dither, take a look at the reference images below. Both gradients have been dithered with three shades.

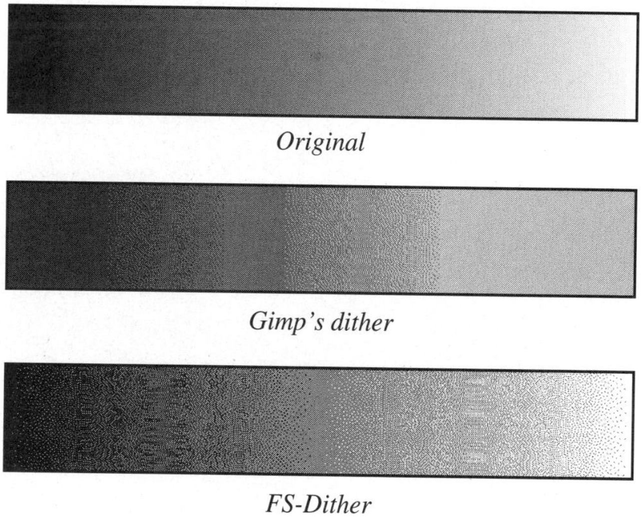

Figure 27.28 *The difference between Gimp's built-in dither and FS-Dithering*

Gradient Map

Gradient Map allows you to map the image against the **active gradient** in the **Gradient Editor**. The lightest pixel in the image will get the color on the right in the Gradient Editor, and the darkest pixel will get the color on the left (except for transparent areas).

Before applying this filter, you'll want to open up the Gradient Editor `right-click|Dialogs|`**`Gradient Editor`** or `File|Dialogs|`**`Gradient Editor`** and select a gradient.

Think of the effects of Gradient Map as mapping the **luminosity** (Value) of your image against the **gradient** in the Gradient Editor. Say that in your image, the luminosity stretches from 50 (dark) to 235 (light). Pixels with a luminosity value of 50 will get the left end color, pixels with a luminosity of 51 will get the next color to the right (from the left end) in the Gradient Editor and so on until you reach 235, which will get the right end color.

The examples in Figure 27.30 to Figure 27.32 may help you understand how this filter works.

Figure 27.29 *Examples of two different gradients mapped against the same image*

Figure 27.30 *Original*

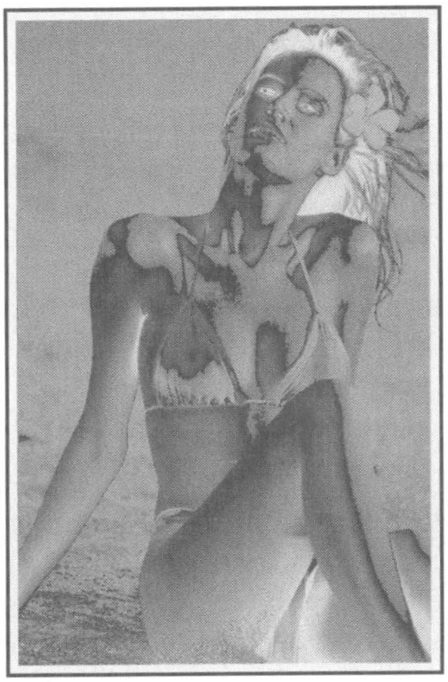

Figure 27.31 *Mapped with Cold Steel*

Figure 27.32 *Mapped with Burning Transparency*

HOT

Hot will identify pixels that can be hard or troublesome to show on an **NTSC** or **PAL** monitor. You can do this on the original image, or as a new layer on top of your image if you check the **Create New Layer** checkbox. You can reduce the pixels' *luminance* or *saturation* or simply make them black.

Figure 27.33 *Hot's dialog*

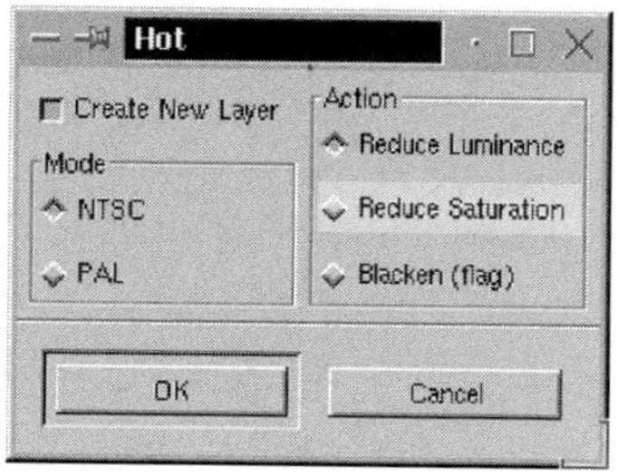

It's generally a good idea to use this filter when you publish images on the web, but the obvious drawback is that different surfers use different monitors.

MAX RGB

Max RGB goes through the pixels in the image, detects which **RGB** channel has the highest or lowest value and maps each pixel to either pure red (255,0,0), pure green (0,255,0) or pure blue (0,0,255). Figure 27.34 displays the effects of Max RGB.

If you check the **Hold the maximal channels** radio button, you select by *maximal* value. If **cyan, magenta** or **yellow** values exist in your image, those colors will remain even after the filter has been applied, because those colors already have maximal values for two RGB colors (the filter doesn't know which color to choose).

If you check **Hold the minimal channels** you select by *minimum* value. With this button checked, process colors will not show, because the filter will choose the lowest value, which is 0 for one of the RGB channels. Black and white will remain in both cases, because they have no RGB value that is lower or higher than another.

QUANTIZE

The effect of **Quantize** is similar to making an **Indexed** image from an **RGB** image, but now you can stay in RGB space.

Use Quantize when you want to selectively reduce the number of colors in an image (for example, when you prepare to make a small GIF that's fast to download). Because you're still in RGB space, you can select an area where you feel color is less important and Quantize those colors. Then, you can keep more of the "important colors" when you index the image.

You can choose between two different color spaces: **CIE** or **RGB**. You can check **Principal Quantization** if you want the filter to Quantize to slightly different colors. Which method to use depends on the colors in the original image; try both!

Figure 27.34 *Result of applying Max RGB with max and min on the original image.*

Original

Min

Max

RGB Displace

This filter will create an illusion of double-vision, dizziness, or movement in the image. Instead of just applying a Motion blur, you **displace** the color channels.

RGB Displace works by displacing the R, G or B channels in different directions. You can displace each channel independently in both the X and Y axes. To displace a channel horizontally or vertically, drag the channel's X or Y slider, or type in the value. There's a preview window, so you'll see the displacement take place as you drag the sliders.

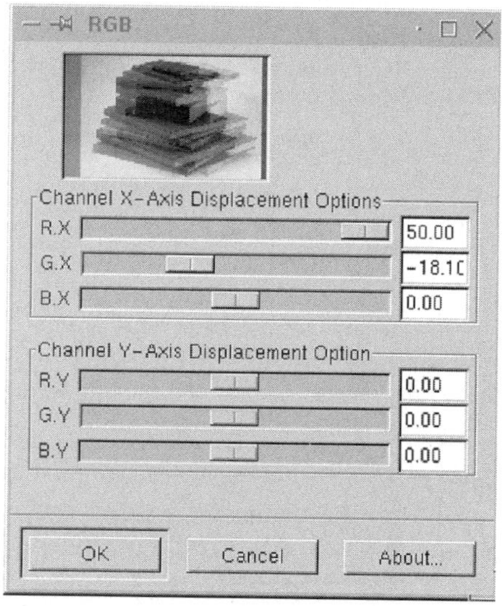

Figure 27.35 *The RGB Displace dialog*

Figure 27.36 *An example of RGB Displace*

SAMPLE COLORIZE

Sample Colorize is *the* tool to use if you want to **colorize** old black-and-white images. All you have to do is to select a portion of a black-and-white image, map a color source image against the selection and there you are! You have colorized the old image.

In the example shown in Figure 27.37, the target image is an old black-and-white portrait photograph. We used a modern portrait as a color source for the skin tones.

As you can see in Figure 27.38, it's not bad for a few minutes work. Adding some extra pre-adjustments to the retro image (such as adjusting the color balance to a brown shade instead of gray) would have made it even better.

Image to colorize *Source image*

Figure 27.37 *We used the modern woman's face as a color source when we colorized the old retro image*

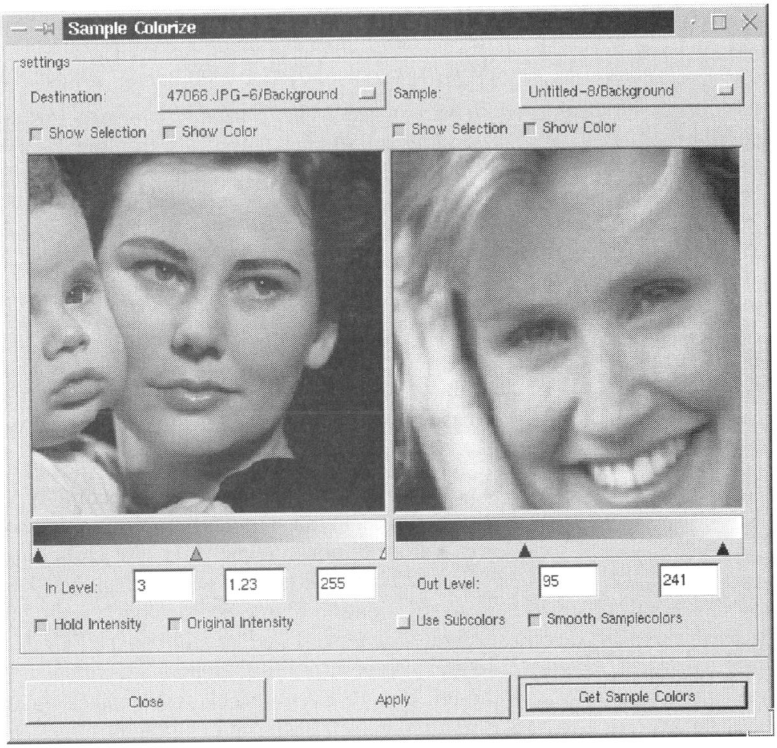

Figure 27.38 *The Sample colorize dialog — the image to colorize at the left side, and the color source to the right*

So How Does This Filter Work?

An important note is that your black-and-white (grayscale) image must be converted to RGB before you will be able to colorize it.

In short, to use this filter, you select the part that you want to colorize, in this case the face of the mother in the old photo. Then, you select the color source, in this case the woman's face in the modern color photo. Then, bring up the filter and start adjusting the image.

Destination And Sample Images

Destination is the target image that will be colorized. It is also the image from which you invoke the filter. **Sample** is the source image or source gradient.

Start by specifying the Destination and Sample images (in our case, the source is a color image, but you can also use a gradient as source). The **Show Selection** and **Show Color** options can be toggled on and off. You can easily switch between viewing the entire image or just the selection. You can also switch between grayscale and color view as you work.

Selecting Sample Colors

To get the colors from the color sample, press the **Get Sample Colors** button. If you don't have any sample colors (you have not pressed the Get Sample Colors button yet) the **Apply** button will be grayed out and you can't apply the filter.

When you press Get Sample Colors, the gradient bar below the Sample preview window will display a gradient with the colors present in thc source. If the source selection/image only holds a few colors, you will also only get a few colors in the Sample gradient. If you check the **Smooth Samplecolors** checkbox, the filter will calculate the missing colors between the colors present in the sample; that is, Smooth Samplecolors will produce a *smoother* sample gradient.

Because we map against a black-and-white (grayscale) image, we can only map colors against value. A grayscale image only holds information on **Value** (brightness/darkness). Since several colors in the sample can have the same brightness value, you must decide whether you want to mix all such colors or if you just want to use one of them to map against a specific value.

For example, there are 16 pixels in the destination image that have the value 127. In the source sample, there are a number of colored pixels that have the value 127. Furthermore, in the sample there are ten red, five green and only one blue pixel of that value. If you uncheck the **Use Subcolors** checkbox, then the dominating color (red in our example) will be mapped against all the sixteen 127-value pixels in the destination image. If you check Use Subcolors, all colors will be used in a weighted scheme. In our example ten 127-value pixels will be mapped to red, five to green and one to blue. There is no way to tell whether you should use subcolors or not. You'll have to check and uncheck the button as you're looking at the preview to determine what will be the best choice for your image.

Out Level controls what source colors should be used. Color outside the chosen range is not used for mapping.

In Level controls what level (intensity) the destination image will get after the mapping.

If the **Hold Intensity** checkbox is unchecked, there will be no real colorization. Instead, the sample color will be mapped as a semi-transparent layer over the destination image (just toggle the button and watch what happens).

You can use the original intensity or you can use the adjusted In Level intensity. If you check the **Original Intensity** checkbox, the adjusted In Level intensity will not affect the mapping.

Using Gradients For Color Mapping

We have shown how we can use a source image to colorize a grayscale destination image. However, if we wanted to colorize the baby's clothing in Figure 27.37, we could use a **gradient** to do this instead of a source image.

Let's make the baby's shirt baby blue with the help of a gradient. First, bring up the Gradient Editor to choose a suitable gradient. Select the baby's clothing with the **Bezier** tool and bring up the **Sample Colorize** dialog.

As you can see in the screenshot in Figure 27.40, the sample image preview window is *grayed out* when we select a gradient as our sample. Also notice that we have unchecked the **Original Intensity** button in order to be able to map a more saturated color to the clothing (otherwise, it would have been very pale). A little cloning on the edges of the shirt, and the colorization is ready.

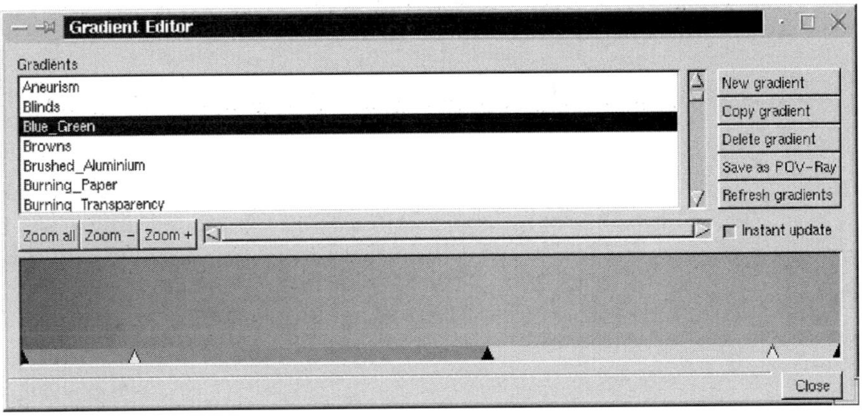

Figure 27.39 *The Gradient Editor dialog. You have to select the active gradient before invoking Sample Colorize.*

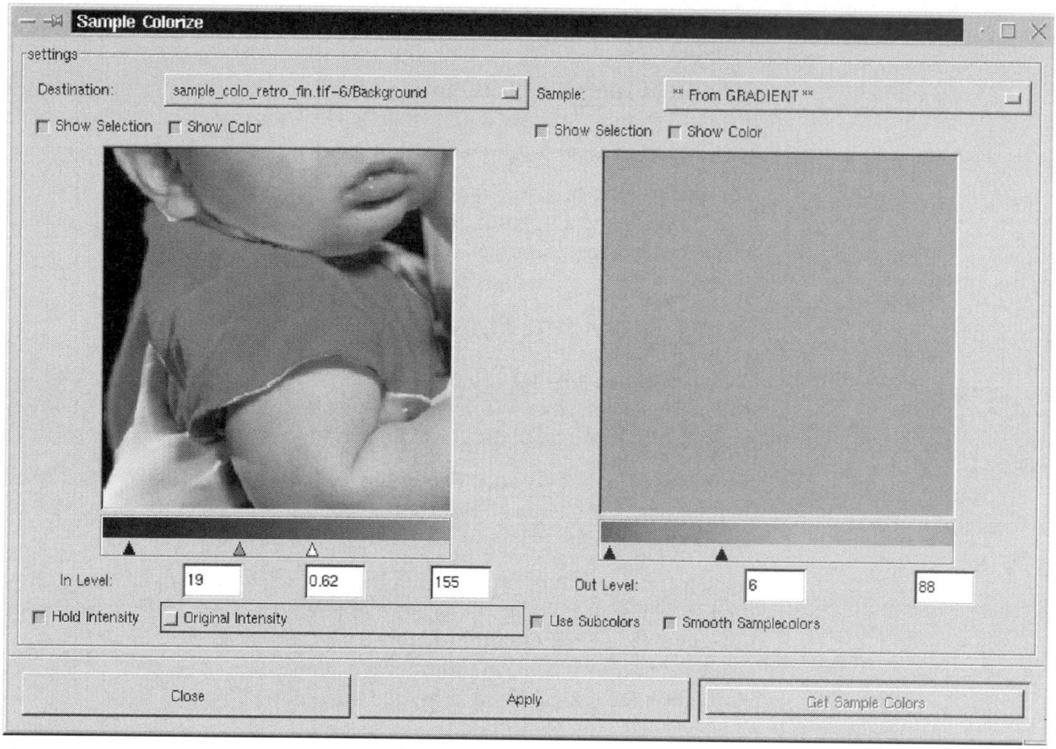

Figure 27.40 *The Sample Colorize dialog, as it appears when you use a gradient as a color source*

Figure 27.41 *The final result*

SCATTER HSV

Scatter HSV is a powerful and sophisticated tool for creating **noise** in an image. Sliders are provided for how much you want to scatter each of the HSV components.

Figure 27.42 *The two leaves to the left have been scattered with Scatter HSV*

Hue changes the color of the pixels in a random pattern. The color spread starts with the colors nearest to the original color in the HSV color circle, and continues to spread until all colors are available. The **Saturation** slider increases saturation, and the **Value** slider scatters Hue-changed pixels. *(If Hue is 0, Saturation/ Value will only affect a few random pixels.)*

The **Holdness** slider controls how far the scattering is allowed to go, or how different the new value is going to be compared to the original value. A low Holdness value allows maximal scattering; a high Holdness value results in a subdued noise effect.

SEMI-FLATTEN

Semi-Flatten is an extremely versatile filter for *web graphics.*

To make use of the filter you must have alpha (transparency) enabled in your image; otherwise, the filter will be grayed out in the menu.

Many of the images on the web are **indexed** GIF images, because GIF supports transparency. A transparent image looks good when you do things like place a logo over the background color in a web page.

Most of the time this works fine, but just try to create a **semi-transparent** glow around your logo. When you convert the image to indexed, you'll find that the image looks horrible.

What happened? Isn't GIF supposed to handle transparency?

Yes, indexed GIF images do handle transparency, but only *total* transparency (alpha value = 0). Every other alpha value will automatically be converted to either fully opaque or completely transparent. So, indexed images don't make a smooth transition from solid color to transparency.

Semi-Transparency In Web Images

This filter will save your day; all you have to do is apply the filter and then convert the image to indexed.

The Semi-Flatten filter works like this: Every pixel with an **alpha value** between 1 and 254 is flattened/merged to the current **background** color in the toolbox. Set the background color to the color your image will be placed on. If your semi-transparent logo will be placed on a white web page, then you need to set the background color to white, then apply the filter.

To appreciate the difference this filter makes, take a look at Figure 27.43.

Figure 27.43 *Examples of how useful Semi-Flatten can be when you work with transparent GIF images.*

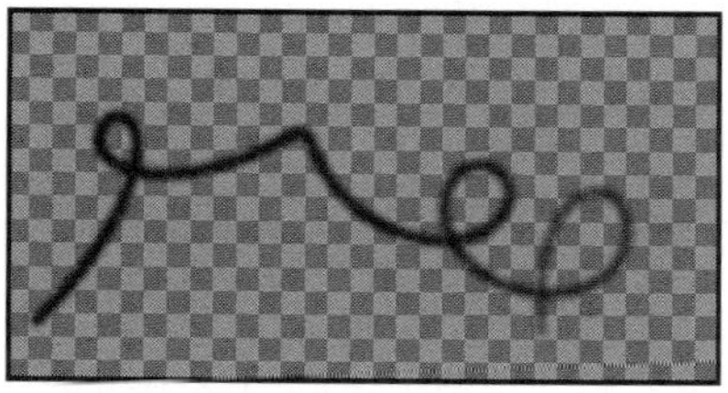

Original

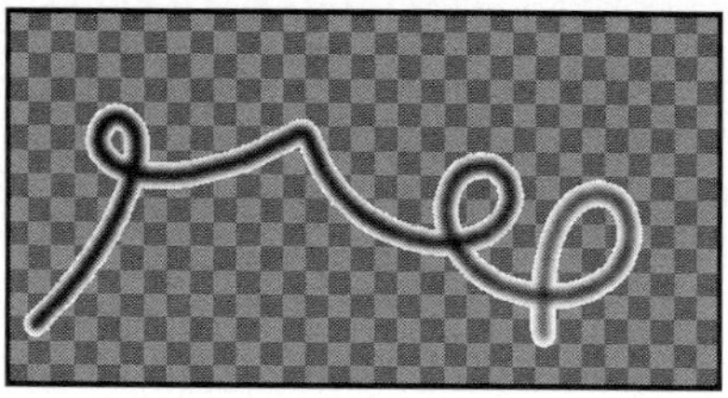

Indexed with Semi-Flatten

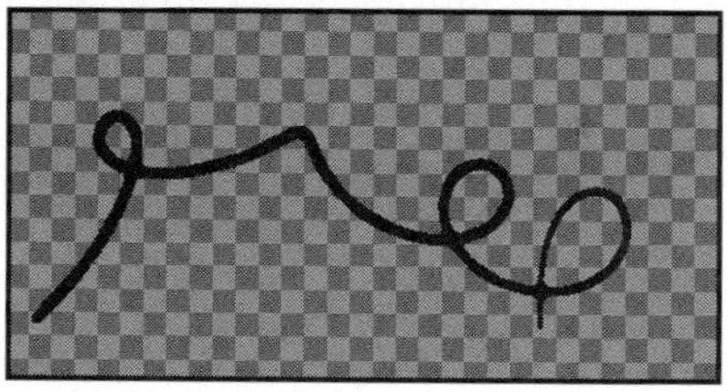

Indexed without Semi-Flatten

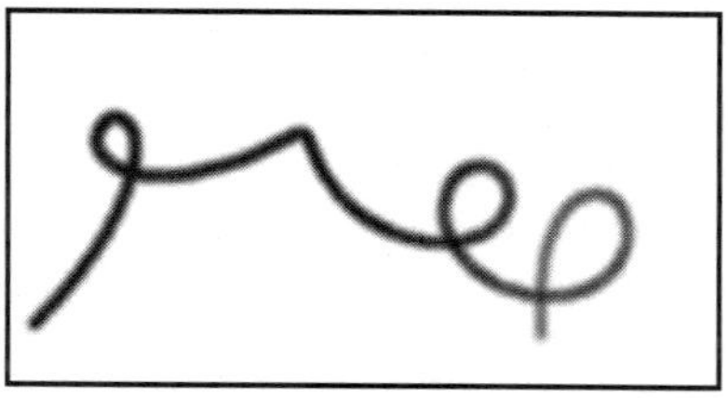

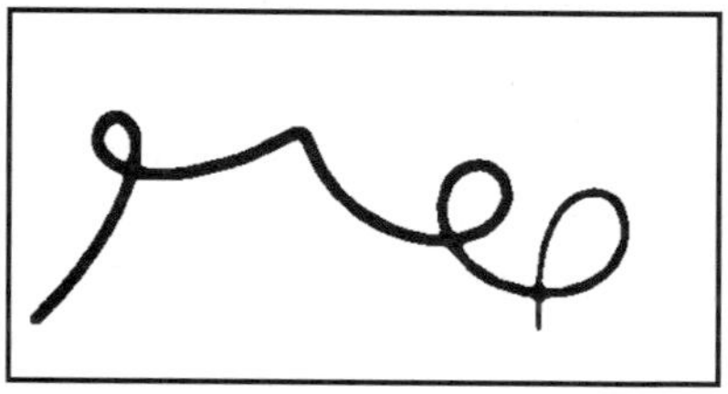

Smooth Palette

Smooth Palette creates a *striped palette* from the colors in your image. The palette is helpful for when you want to see what kinds of colors you have used in an image, but the main purpose of this filter is to create **colormaps** for use with `right-click|Filters|Render|Flame` (see "Flame" on page 592).

Value Invert

Value Invert inverts the image in **HSV space**. It will not alter *Hue* and *Saturation*. It just inverts the brightness value without changing the basic colors in your image.

The effect can be very useful if you are using **Curves** to change a certain value dramatically, and you get stuck with the wrong (inverted) color.

Figure 27.44 *Value Invert was applied to the right side of the image*

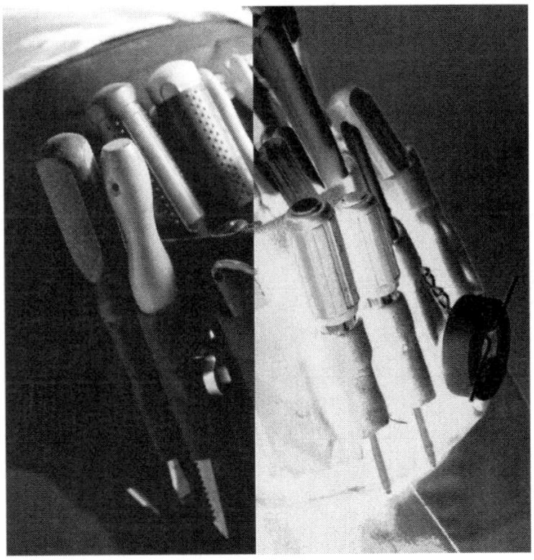

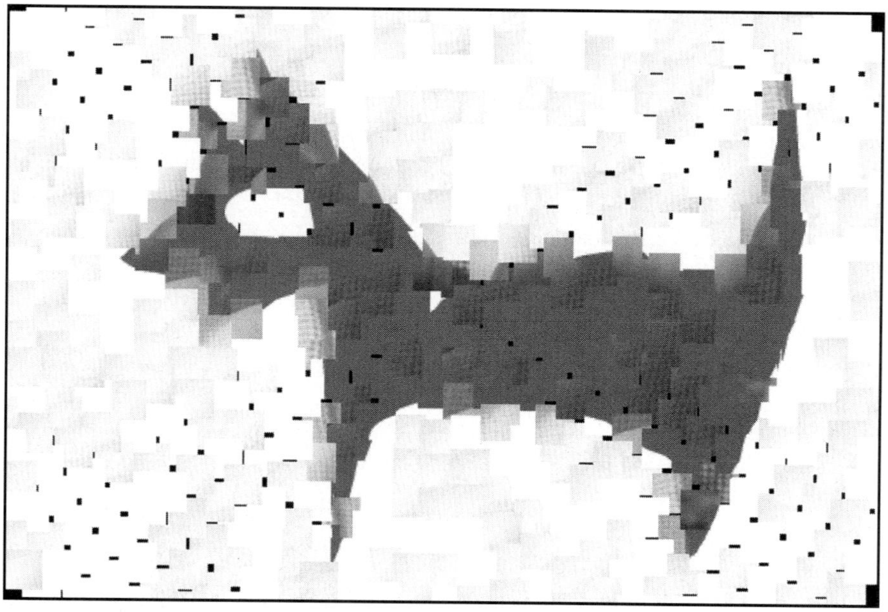

CHAPTER 28

Combine Filters

The smash-them-together factory. If you want to combine several images into one, fade images into each other or even create a piece of celluloid film, these are the filters to use.

Depth Merge

Depth Merge is a very nice tool for **combining** two images. The combination is accomplished with the help of two **map images**. The maps should be *grayscale* images (so you can better control the outcome).

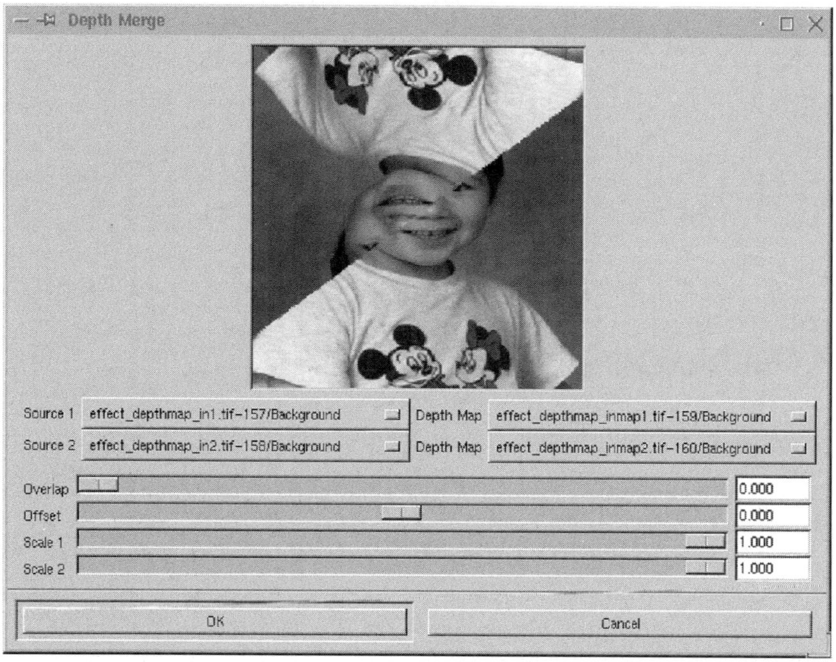

Figure 28.1 *The Depth Merge dialog*

Example

This example will hopefully make matters more clear:

1. Start with two images of equal size. Then create two new empty images that are the same size as the original images.
2. In one of the empty images, use the **Blend** tool to blend from black in the top-left corner to white in the opposite corner. For the other empty image, do the opposite: Blend from black at the bottom right to white at the top left.
3. Now, bring up the **Depth Merge** dialog. Set **Overlap** to 0, set **Offset** to 0 and set **Scale 1** and **Scale 2** to 1.000. Use one of the first opened images as **Source 1** and the other one as **Source 2**.

4. Set the first blended image as **Depth Map** for **Source 1**, and the other blended image as the **Depth Map** for **Source 2**. The preview window will display the two images *combined* and a sharp border will appear diagonally from the top right to the bottom-left.

How Does Depth Merge Work?

What causes this effect? Well, the plug-in looks at both map images, and compares every pixel. The map with the darkest pixel will win, and the source to that map will show its image pixel. When we created our grayscale images, a clean line diagonally from top right to bottom left separates where the darkest pixels changed from one map to the other.

Now that you understand the basics, you can create all kinds of maps.

Parameters

Let's see what the **sliders** can do for us. As you saw in our example, there was a sharp border between the images. This was because **Overlap** was set to zero. If we slide it up a bit, you will see that the border becomes more fuzzy and transparent. Use Overlap if you want to create *soft transitions*.

Offset changes the darkness value of your maps. If you slide it to a negative value, the map to Source 1 will become *darker* and therefore control more of the resulting image. If you slide it to a positive value, the other map will get darker and will control more of the resulting image.

The **Scale 1** and **Scale 2** sliders make the Depth Map for Source 1 and the Depth Map for Source 2 darker or lighter. They have the same effect as Offset, but they are more sensitive. When you scale to a lower value, it will affect the map image's value, making it darker and thereby more dominant in the merge; that is, you will see more of the image that the map is serving.

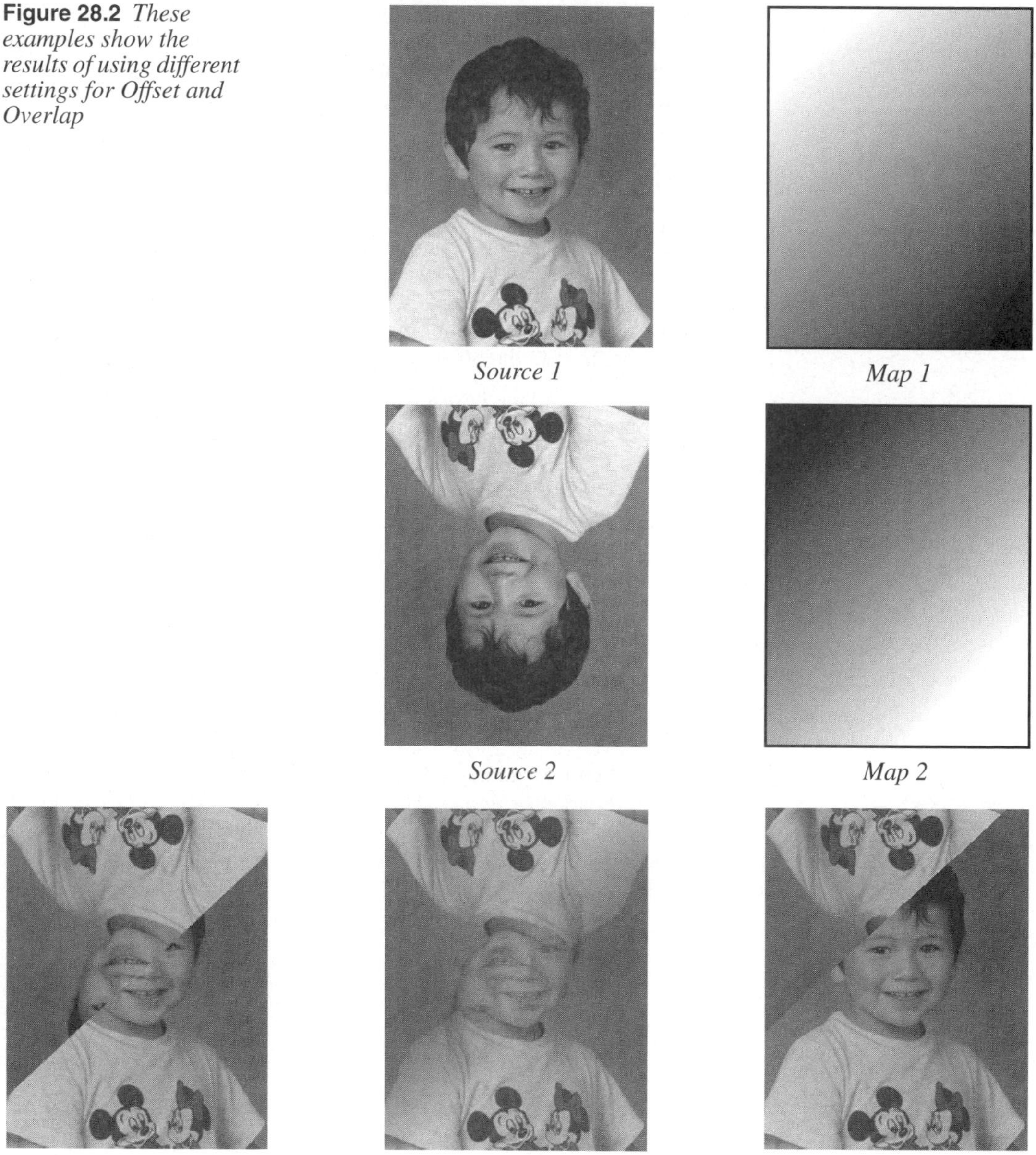

Figure 28.2 *These examples show the results of using different settings for Offset and Overlap*

Source 1 *Map 1*

Source 2 *Map 2*

No Offset or Overlap *Overlap* *Offset*

FILM

Film creates a film celluloid of one or more images; a nice special effect.

Figure 28.3 *The Film filter*

HOW TO USE THE FILM FILTER

Film's user interface is quite simple. Under **Available images**, you have a list all available images. Select an image and click **add** to use it in your film.

On film shows the pictures on your film. To change the order of the pictures, you have to add and remove pictures.

Height is the height of the outcoming film.

Color is the film color (black). The plug-in will automatically adjust your images so that they will fit.

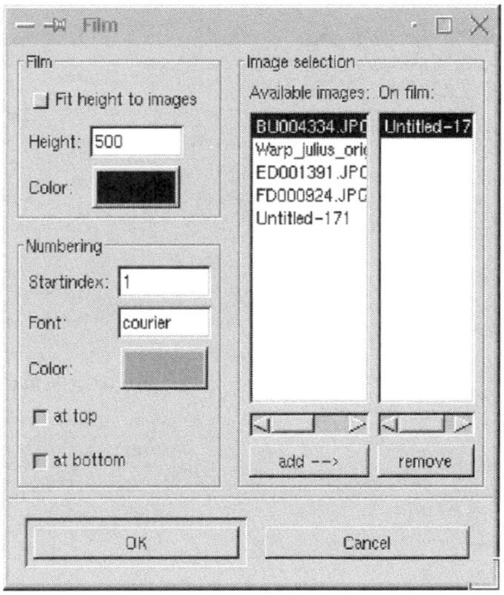

Figure 28.4 *The Film dialog*

Numbering lets you specify a start number on the roll. Set numbering to Numbering/Startindex.

Font lets you choose the font that is showing the frame numbers in the film (you have to have the font installed).

Color is the color of the frame numbers in your film (orange by default). Both the color of the film itself (usually black) and the color of the numbers can be changed by clicking on the color swatches.

Check the **at top** and **at bottom** checkboxes if you want numbers there; otherwise, leave them unchecked.

FUSE

Fuse creates a new image from **tiles** of one or several input images. You can use this filter in two ways.

TEMPLATE

First, you can use the **target image** as a **template**. The result will be an image that looks like a mosaic or cubist version of the original image, where the mosaic stones or cubes consist of pieces of the input image (a little like modernist collage art where you create a composite image by cutting and pasting pieces of a newspaper).

Figure 28.5 *Fused used as a template*

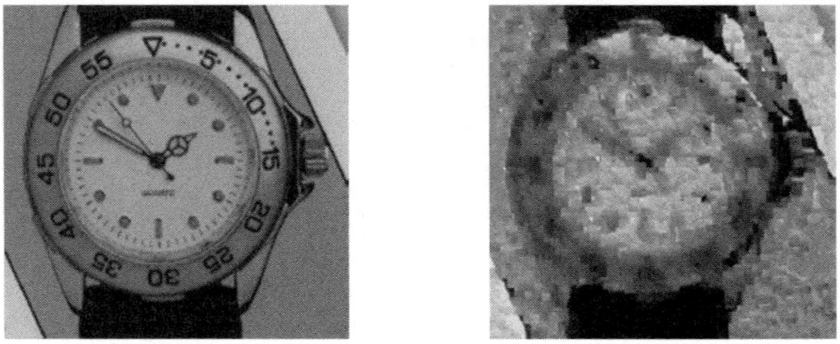

Original *Fused as template*

FUSING

You can also create a new shape by **fusing** one or more images. This filter uses *associative image reconstruction*, meaning that it will search out pieces that match where they overlap, thus creating a pattern with more or less "solid objects" in it. The new pattern is a random mix of matching tiles from the source images, with a direction tendency toward the center of the image.

Figure 28.6 *These pictures show the difference between fusing the original with itself and fusing the original with another image*

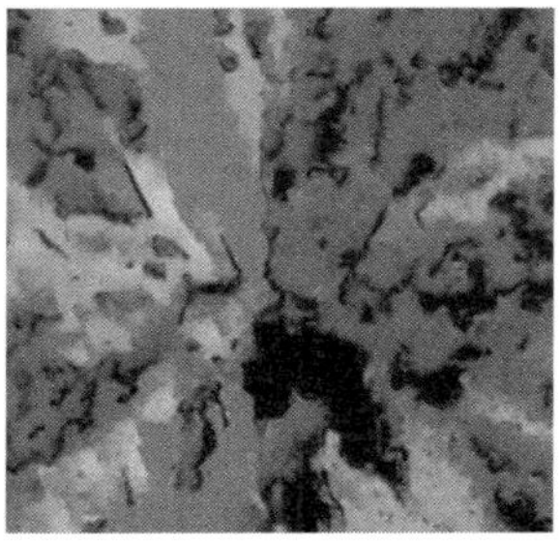

Fused original only

Fused original + other image

The Fuse dialog displays a window at the top of the dialog with a list of available images *(note that indexed images are not accepted)*. You can select one or all of the images in this list by clicking on them. Click on them again to deselect them.

Note: The image you opened Fuse from is not used in the fusing process unless you select it in this menu or check the use target as template checkbox.

PARAMETERS

The parameters list starts with **Tile Size**, which controls the size in pixels of the square tiles. Small tiles produce smoother images, but will make the operation very slow.

Figure 28.7 *The Fuse dialog*

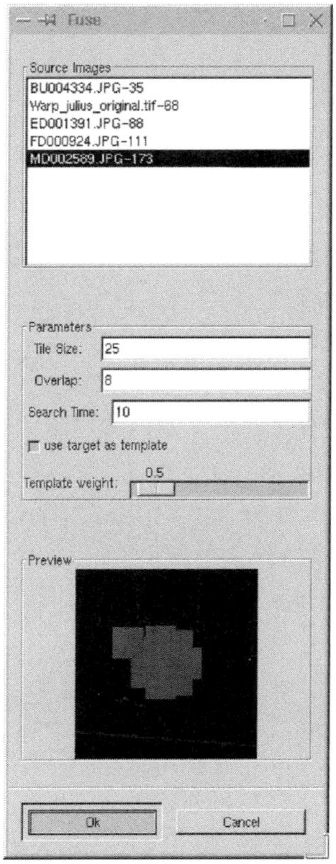

Overlap determines by how many pixels the selected tiles should overlap in the fused image. If Overlap is too low, you'll get small black gaps in the composite image, and if it's too high, the process will slow down a great deal. The recommended amount of Overlap is somewhere between a quarter and a third of the Tile Size.

Search Time refers to how long the filter should search for the tile that best fits the Overlap. Search Time also slows down the process, but results in a smoother output.

When you check **use target as template**, Fuse has to determine whether it is more important to find a tile that matches the template, or a tile that matches the Overlap.

If you set the **Template weight** slider to a high value, you'll get a good representation of the target image, but the image will look much more *"cubist"* than a fused image without the template (but with the same parameter value). If you set the Template weight lower, you'll get a smoother image, but it will not bear as much resemblance to the template image.

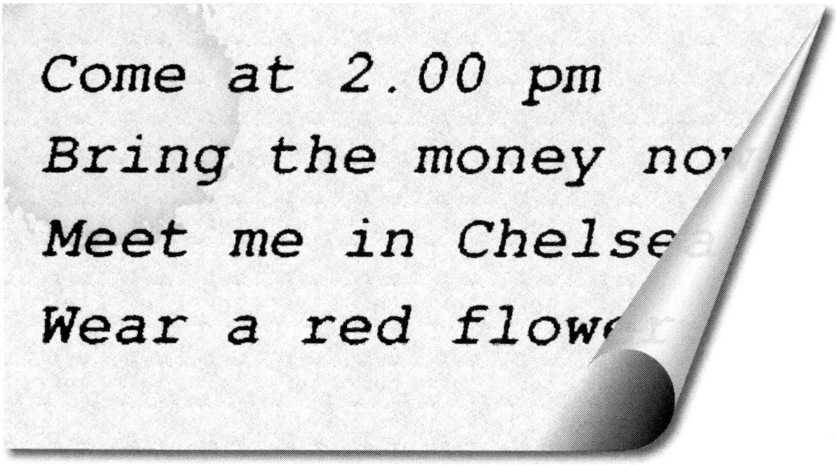
Come at 2.00 pm
Bring the money no
Meet me in Chelse
Wear a red flow

COLOR SECTION

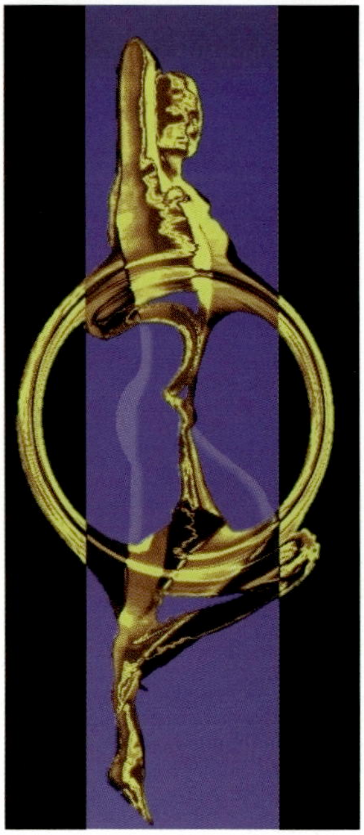

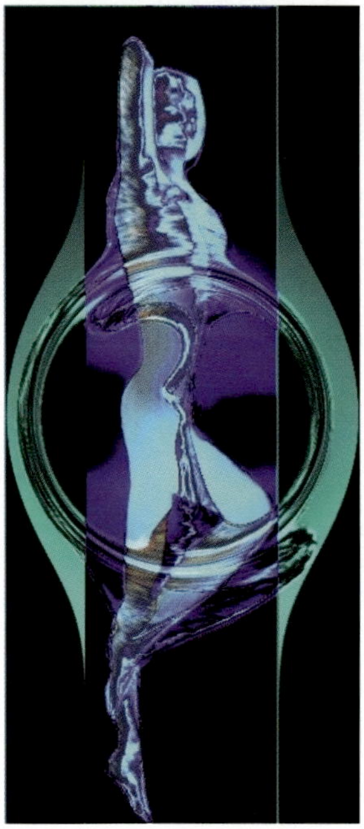

THE GALLERY

Creating objects: You can easily create different versions of the same basic design by using different color modes, or by applying a gradient map.

Creating the illusion of glass, water and reflection using 2-D image manipulation requires some skill and planning. The main difficulty lies in making the composition convincing in the areas where water meets an object, and in keeping the balance between reflection, glitter and shadow.

Transforming a photo into a drawing is a simple way of creating stunning graphics. A sketch is also much more personal than an ordinary photograph. To achieve this end, there are many different techniques ranging from cartoon style to crayon drawings. Just remember that you are the artist, and not the computer.

As you can see, the different red, yellow and white layers really make the horse glow. ***The key, as usual, is to create several layers and combine them***.

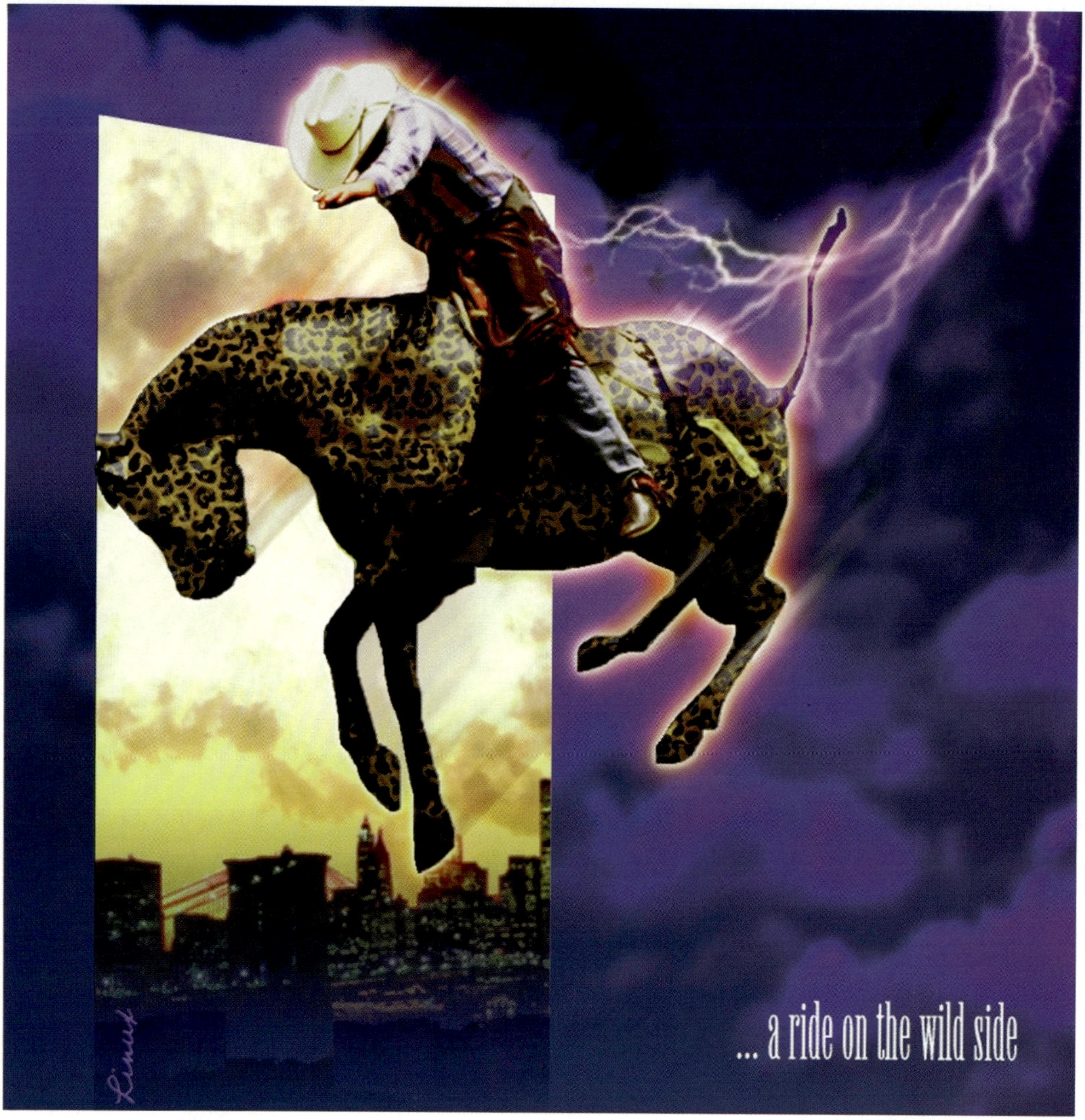

FX is another favorite. Light effects are powerful eye catchers and sometimes you may want to maximize your image as in our "wild ride" image. To make things a bit more surreal, we have turned a horse into a leopard. Layers is the key to creating images like this one. All effects are created by combining a multitude of layers in different ways.

The Chevelle photo montage is a classic poster art work. The technique of making montages is commonly used by graphic designers in advertisements. The method of blending two or more images using layers and layer masks is the tool that makes this possible. The standard procedure when you create this kind of design is to work with a combination of an illustration program and an image manipulation program. If you use both program types you can easily change type face and other objects that are better represented as vector drawings. We wanted to show that you can do all of that within Gimp.

PAINT TOOLS

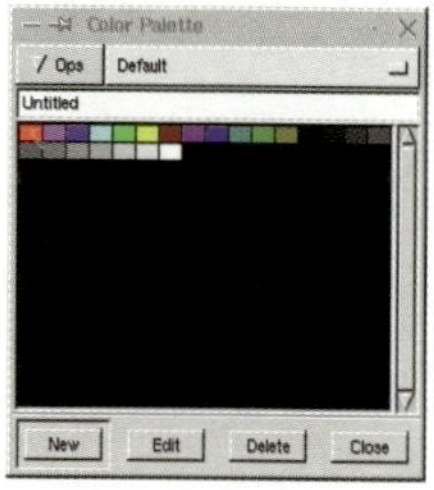

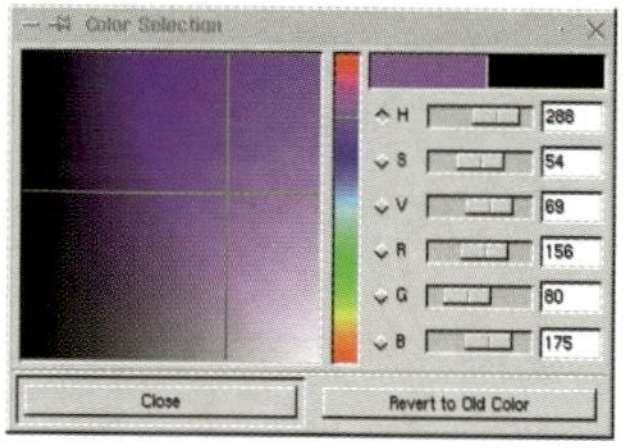

When it comes to color tools, the ***color palette*** is among the more useful. Think of it like the palette that you use for making ordinary paintings. Choosing colors from the color dialog is much too ineffective, and you can't be that sure that you get the same color each time.

GRADIENTS

The ***Gradient Editor*** is the key to making smooth color transitions, and it is used as a base for many kinds of important operations in Gimp. You can use gradients to blend two images through layer masks, or as a distort map image. The Gradient Editor allows you to create your own gradients where you'll have absolute control over all parameters, so this is a very useful tool for advanced image manipulation.

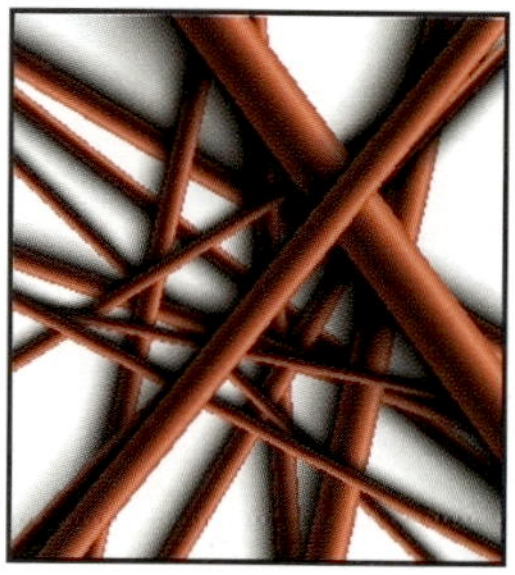

COLOR

If you want to learn to use an image manipulation program like Gimp to its full capacity, you must learn how colors work in the digital world and to understand the different color models. These pictures will help you understand the ***Color Models*** and ***Pre-press*** chapters.

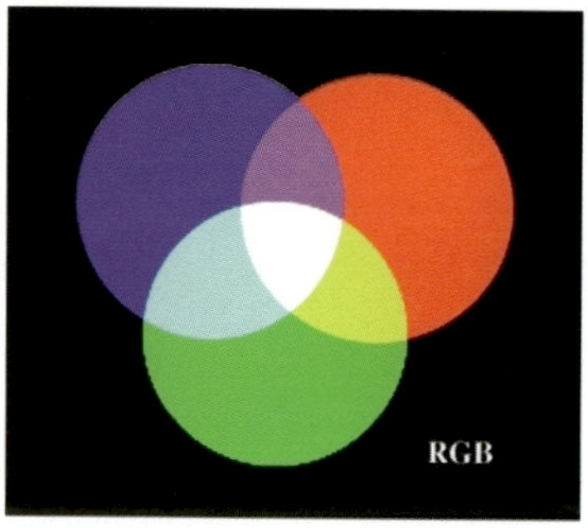

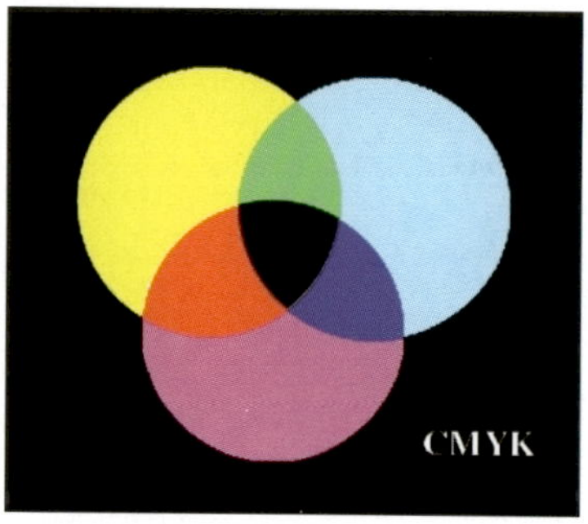

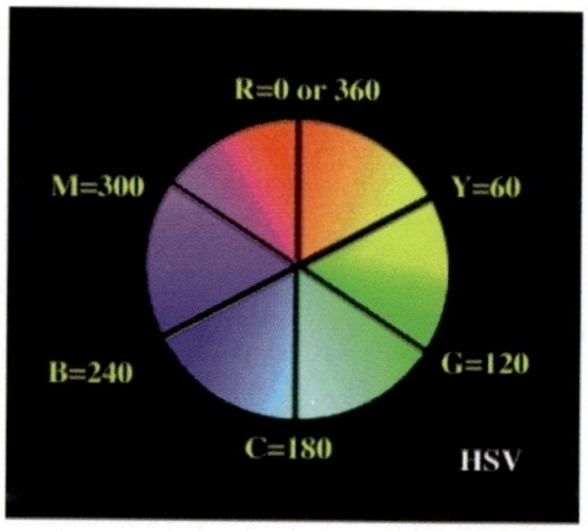

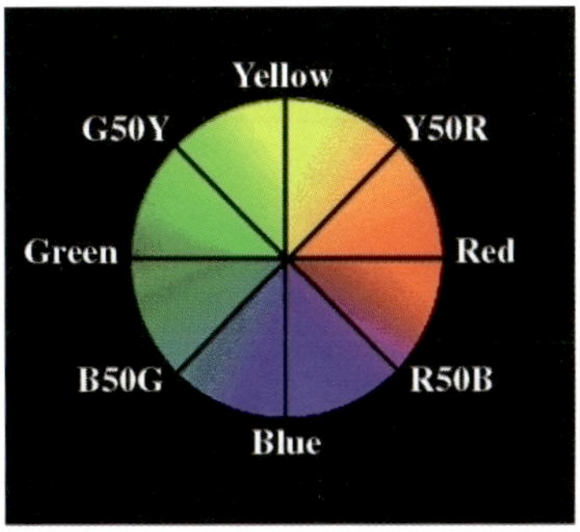

NCS color model

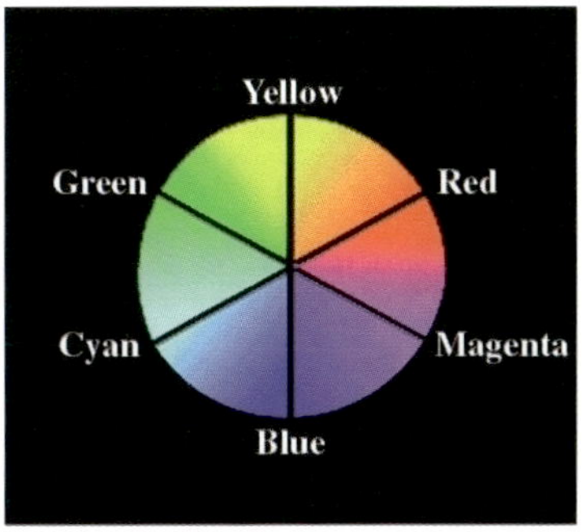

Complementary colors, RGB model

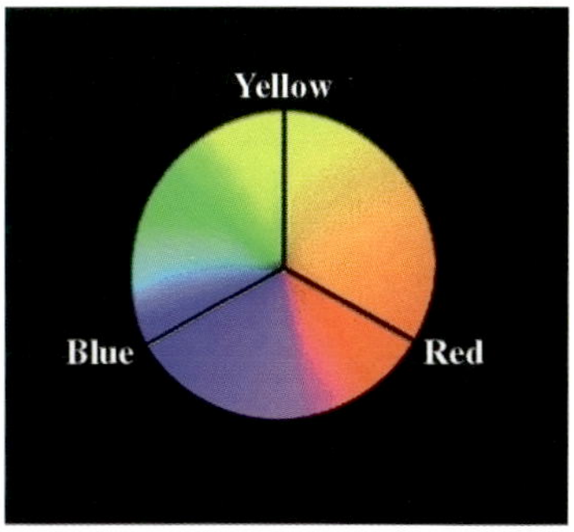

Complementary colors, Natural model

It is essential to understand that different color models/devices have different gamut areas. An RGB monitor can display many more colors than a printer (CMYK) can. Finally, you can perceive more colors with your eyes than a monitor can display. The image below visualizes these facts.

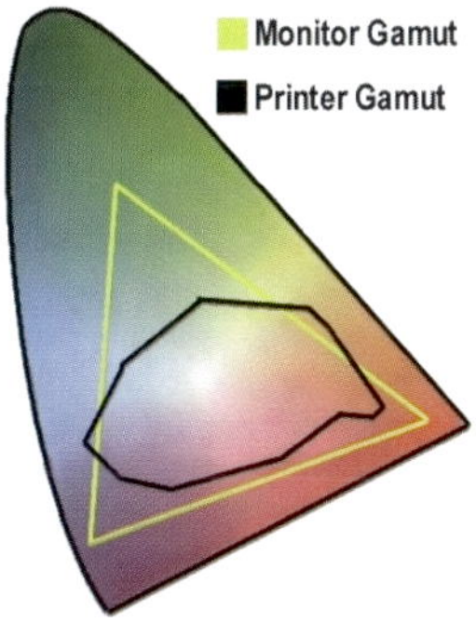

IMAGE MENU

The Image menu commands execute most operations in either RGB or HSV color space.

The Equalize command can be used enhance contrast and to find "hidden" colors in old, fading photos.

Dark input

Output after equalize

Light input

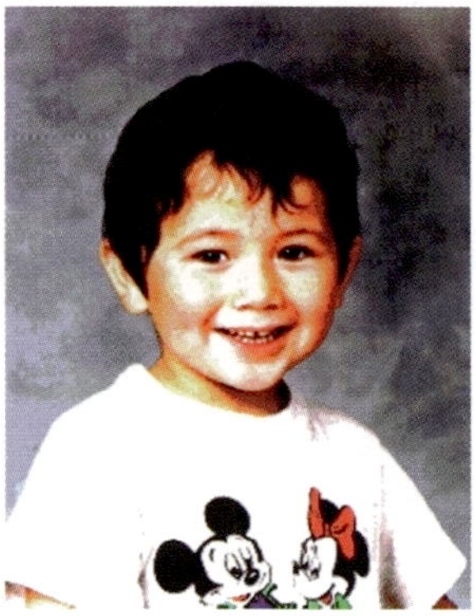

Output after equalize

Invert will make a color image look like a photo negative. This means that if you have a slide scanner, scan the negative film and "develop" it to positive images using the Invert command. With the Posterize command you can reduce the number of colors/shades in an image, making it less naturalistic.

Invert

Posterize

Color balance is a useful color correction tool if your image has distorted colors, or if you want to change the colors, like we have done with the blue duck.

Hue-Saturation is perhaps an even better tool for correcting color problems. It's also a great tool for changing colors. As you can see, our yellow truck has turned blue without any change in the other colors in the image. Curves is another color control tool. Here, we have turned day into night, or is it the other way around?

Hue-Saturation

Curves

Levels is an excellent tool for enhancing 3-D effects by adding highlights or shadow. You can also use it the other way around and make the image flat, using less contrast when it comes to color, highlights and shadows. Desaturate takes away the color information, but you are still in RGB space. Desaturate is excellent when you want to accentuate a certain part of the image. If the surroundings are desaturated, the colored part will catch the viewer's focus.

Levels

Desaturate

Normalize, ***Contrast Auto-stretch*** and ***Auto-stretch HSV*** are three ways of enhancing faded or dull color photos.

Normalize

Contrast Auto-stretch

Auto-Stretch HSV

Compose and ***Decompose*** in the Image/Channel Ops menu let you compose and decompose images to and from different color models. The RGB original to the left has been used for all decompose operations. All decomposed images are grayscale images, because they are representation of the color models' different channels.

RGB original

Value composed as Hue

C

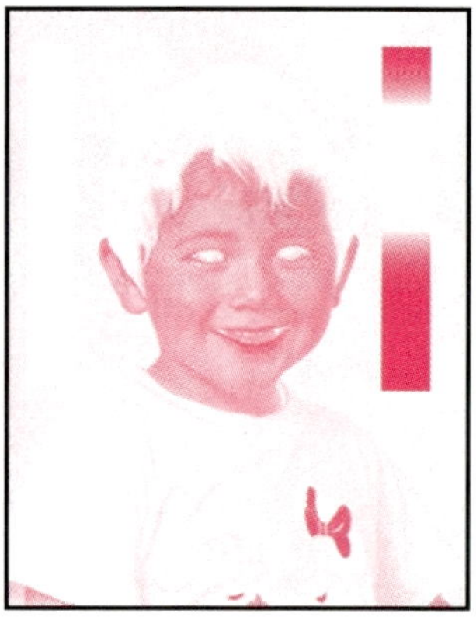

M

Y

The printed result of each CMY plate.

MODES

The color images shown here are a necessary complement to their black-and-white counterparts, which are shown in the ***Modes*** chapter.

Normal Mode

Dissolve Mode

Multiply Mode

Color

Screen Mode

Overlay Mode

Difference Mode

Value

Addition Mode

Subtraction Mode

Darken Only

Lighten Only

Hue

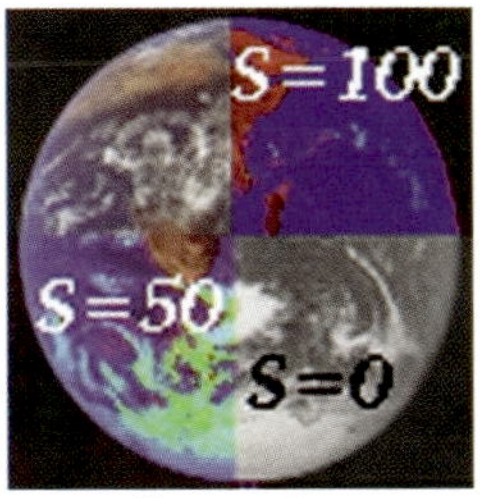

Saturation

Comparing Modes

Normal Mode (color)

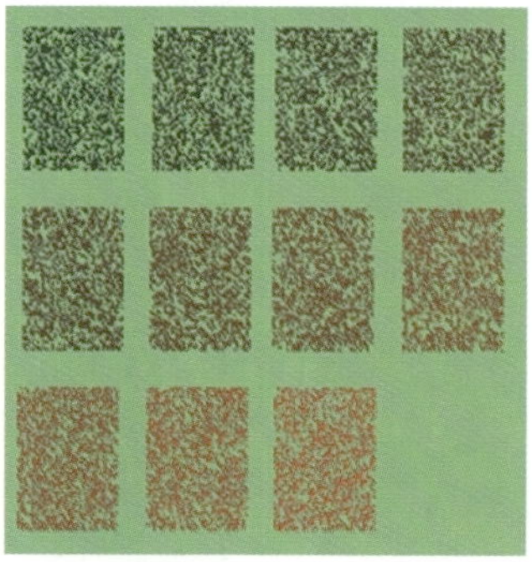
Dissolve Mode (color)

Color

Hue

Saturation

Value

A layer containing a green leaf pattern was combined with the portrait layer. These images show the difference between ***Color*** and ***Hue*** mode.

Color

Hue

CHANNELS

These figures show the result of adding color to a channel. The yellow channel would look like the black-and-white image to the right if you copied and pasted it to a new image. If the yellow image had been a regular layer, it would look like the gray image (after desaturation).

This duotone image was created using a blue and a yellow channel.

Plug-ins

Plug-ins, commonly referred to as *filters* are an important part of Gimp. Many filters use color transformation, or affect the colors in the image in other ways.

Artistic Filters

All of the artistic filters affect color. However, only the ***Newsprint*** filter changes the way that color is used. The Newsprint filter separates colors either to RGB or to CMYK mode in order to build the half-tone pattern of an AM-screening printer.

Color Filters

Naturally, color filters must be shown in color. This section should be your companion when you read the color filters chapter.

Adjust Fgrd. - Bkgrd *is a simple color-rotating filter*

Alien Map is a psychedelic color-rotating filter that rotates and phase displaces colors using cosine and sine functions. Alien Map only works in RGB color space.

Alien Map

Original

Frequency = 2

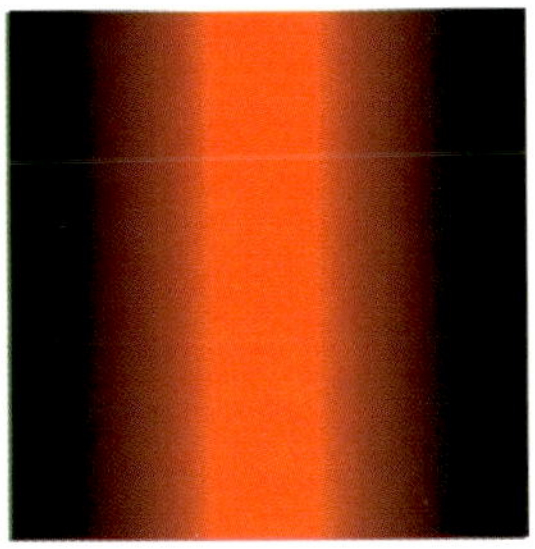

Cosine

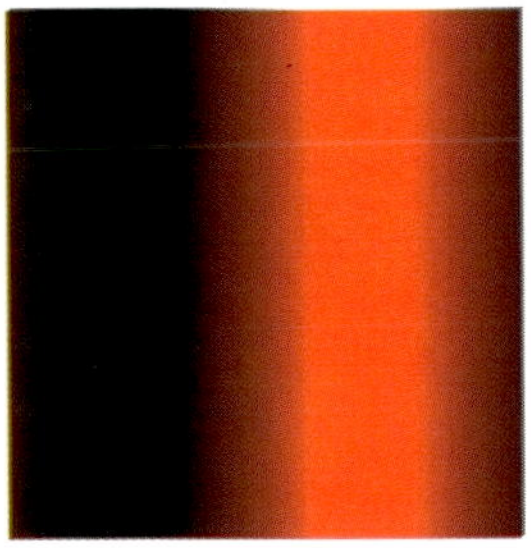

Phase disp = 1.25

Alien Map2 has nearly the same functions as Alien Map, but this filter also works in HSV color space. Here we have aged a green spring leaf prematurely.

Color Mapping is a more "advanced" implementation of Adjust Fgrd. - Bkgrd.

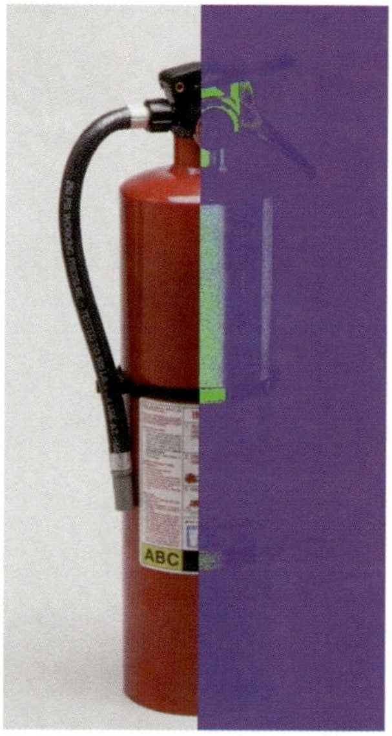

Color Exchange lets you exchange one color to another. You can set the width of the desired color spectrum, i.e. how many shades should be exchanged for the specified color.

The ***Colorify*** effect is like putting a transparent color slide on top of your image.

Color Map Rotation is a powerful color exchange filter.

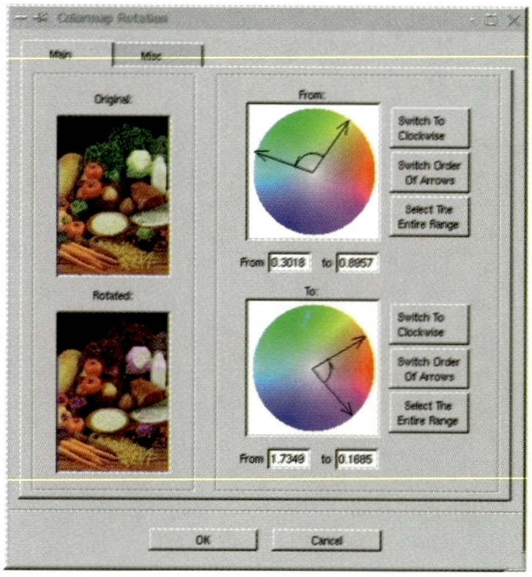

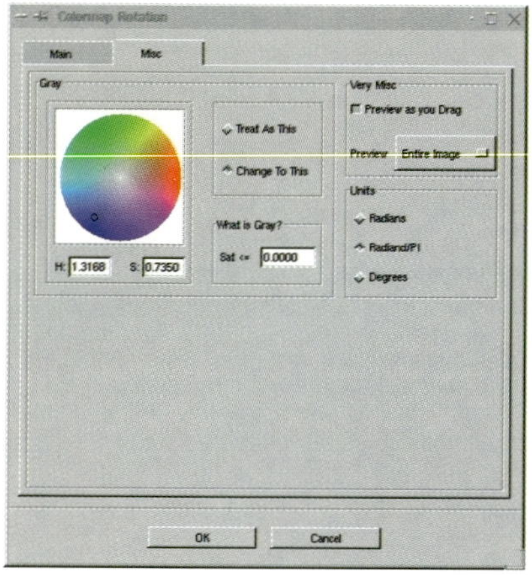

Original

Rotated

Filter Pack is the darkroom filter. It's perfectly suited for adjusting miscolored photographs.

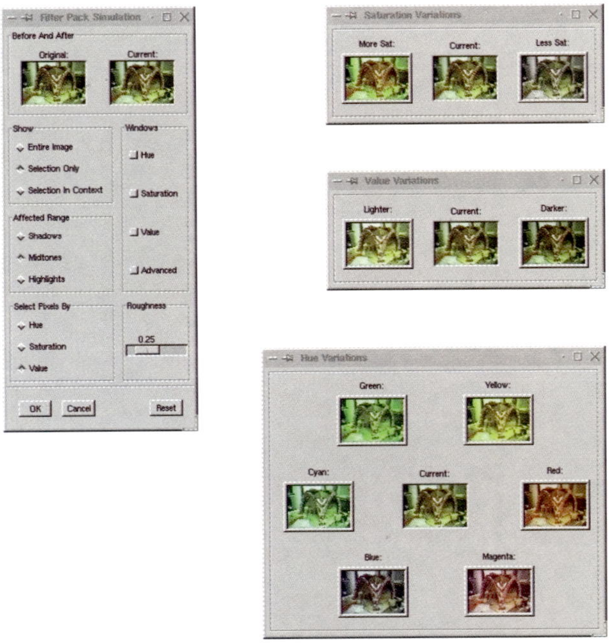

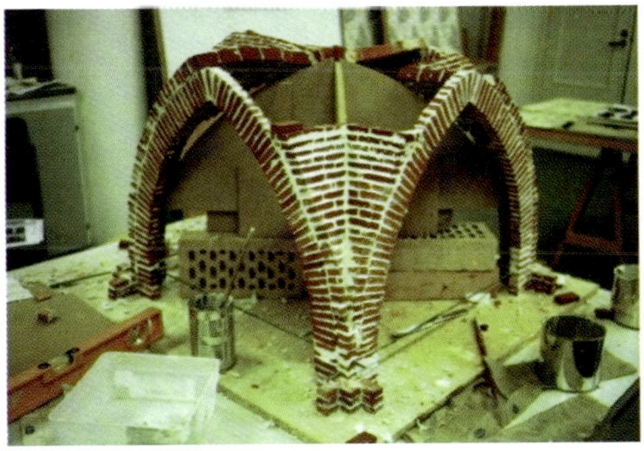

Original

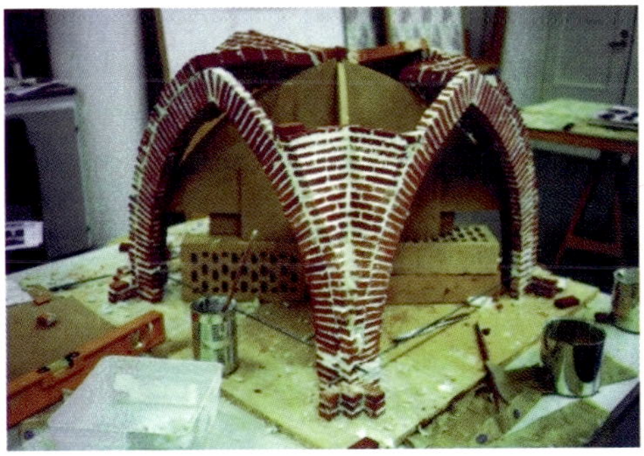

Adjusted

The ***Gradient Map*** filter will map an image against a gradient in the Gradient Editor.

Burning_Transparency

Cold_Steel

Max RGB will only display the color that has the highest or lowest value.

Original

Min

Max

If you want to colorize an old black-and-white photo, then ***Sample Colorize*** is the tool to use. You use a sample (a color photo) as source for colorizing an old black-and-white photo.

But you can also use a gradient, as we have done by coloring the baby's shirt.

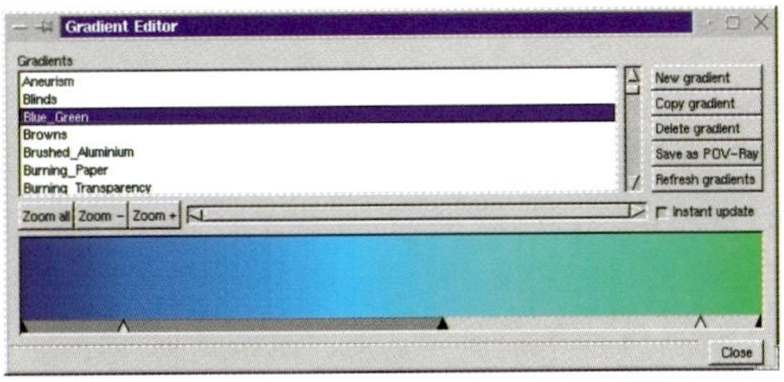

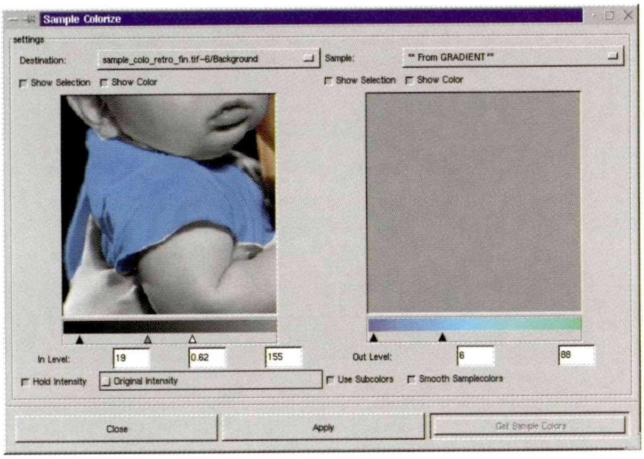

Scatter HSV adds color noise to the image.

Instead of inverting the colors like in the `right-click|Image|Colors|Invert` command, the ***Value Invert*** filter will invert the brightness value of each pixel.

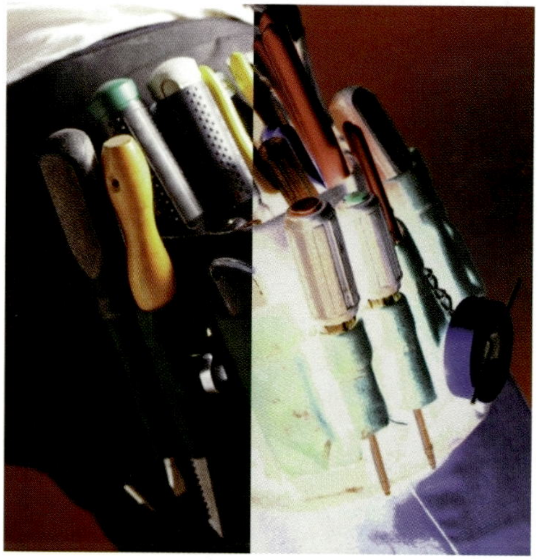

EDGE DETECT

All of the edge detect filters produce colorful edges.

Edge

Laplace

Sobel

And with the ***Log*** filter you can make instant cartoon pictures.

Light Effects

Most of the light effects such as ***Flare FX, GFlare*** and ***Super Nova*** produce color lens/light effects.

FlareFX

GFlare

Super Nova

Render

Most of the render filters affect color in one way or another. Here are some examples of the outcome of the fantastic ***IFS Compose*** filter.

CHAPTER 29

Cryptographic Filters

So, you want to be a secret agent? You may want to use these filters to encrypt and hide your information.

Digital Signature

Digital Signature lets you make or read an invisible *signature* in the image. In order to read a signature just press the **Read** button.

If you want to create a signature, you have to fill in the information in the dialog and press the **Write** button. Then, you'll need to save the image in a non-destructive format like TIFF. If you save it as a JPEG the signature will be destroyed.

The option **Restricted image distribution** will create a signature that states that your image is not free for distribution. The **Adult contents** option will create a signature stating that the image has adult contents.

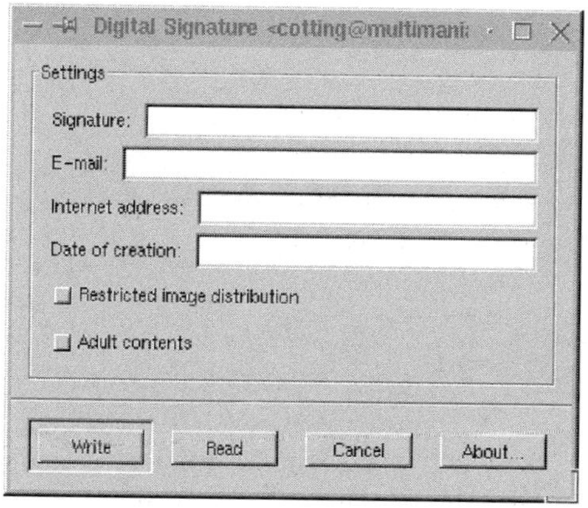

Figure 29.1 *The Digital Signature dialog*

Encrypt & Decrypt

Encrypt makes it possible to *encrypt* your images, so no one besides yourself can see them. To encrypt the image, bring up the filter and type in a **Password**. To **decrypt** an image, bring up the filter again, type in your password and the image will be decrypted.

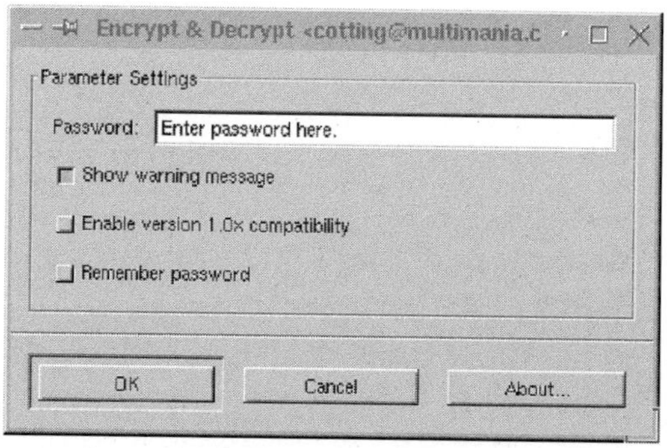

Figure 29.2 *The Encrypt & Decrypt dialog*

The author of this filter, Daniel Cotting, warns that he can provide no guarantees that this filter will work (but for us at Frozenriver, this filter has worked just fine). Remember not to save the image in a destructive file format, such as JPEG.

You can enable backward compatibility with the 1.0 versions of this plug-in by clicking on the appropriate checkbox, but we suggest that you stick with 2 and not enable this feature unless you have images that are encrypted with the 1.0 version.

You can also enable the plug-in to remember your password, but don't forget that passwords are best kept in your own mind where no one can see them.

GIMP MASK

Gimp Mask works by masking the entire image or selected parts of it. *Unmasking* is performed by running the filter once again on the selected area, using the correct *code word* for **CP** masks or by reversing the direction for **MEKO** masks. In most cases, you also have to fine-tune the **Offset** coordinates on the **Adjustment** tab to get the two masks to fit.

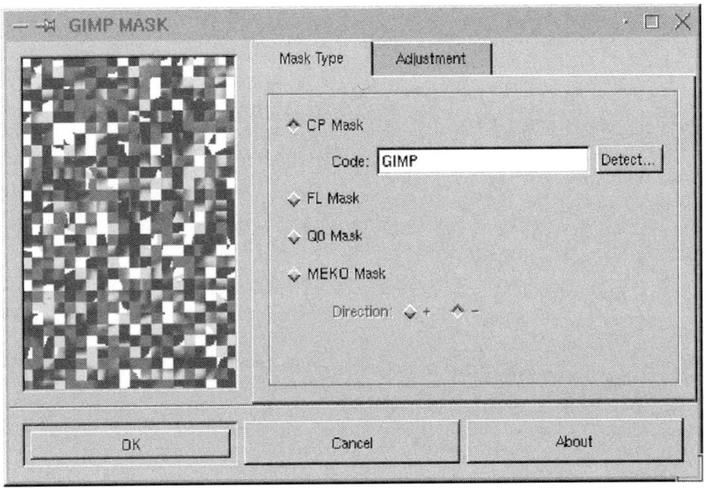

Figure 29.3 *The Gimp Mask dialog*

Use the **Rectangle** selection tool when specifying the mask area. Other selection shapes may not create the mask area properly. When you **reselect** the masked area (in order to unmask it), an overlap of up to seven pixels is acceptable. This means that it's OK to make a slightly bigger selection to cover all of the mask. If you should fail to get a perfect fit when you reverse the masking process, click on **Cancel** and try again, this time with a smaller selection.

Note that the CP code is not compatible with JPEG files, so if you're using the JPEG file format, you should choose another mask type.

STEGANO

The **Stegano** filter lets you **hide** or **read** a *hidden file* inside your image. To *read* the hidden file, press **Read**. To *hide* a file, press **Write** and then **Browse** (to find the file). There is no restriction concerning the file type that you want to hide.

Remember that if you want to hide a big file, you'll need to use a big image. And just like with the other encrypt filters, you can't save your image in a destructive file format like JPEG. This filter is perfect for secret agents like 007. ;-)

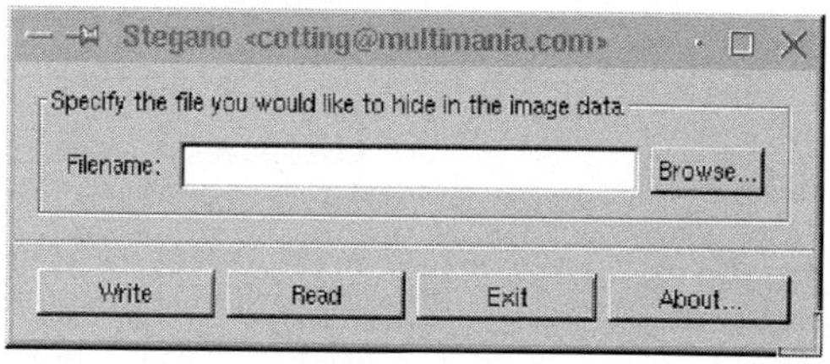

Figure 29.4 *The Stegano dialog*

CHAPTER 30

Distort Filters

Do you feel that your image lacks a certain something? Here are the ultimate distort tools provided by Gimp.

BEND

Bend can *bend* the contents of a layer or the entire image *(but it can't bend a selection)*. However, because the size of the layers increases when you run this filter, full-sized layers will end up being larger than the image area and some clipping will be required.

Figure 30.1 *The Bend dialog*

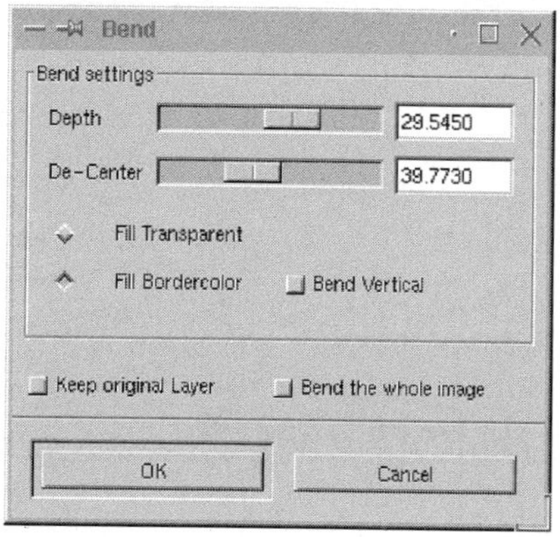

BEND ORIENTATION PARAMETERS

The **Depth** parameter controls the *amount* and *direction* of the horizontal displacement (or vertical if you check the **Bend Vertical** checkbox).

A depth of 100 or (-100) means that the layer width (or height for Bend Vertical) will stretch to double its original size, but it will stay centered around its original position. *Negative values* bend from top to left instead of from top to right, and from left to top instead of from left to bottom (Bend Vertical).

De-Center controls the center of gravity of the displacement. The maximum value (100) will reverse the directions mentioned above. Instead of bending from the top and down, the layer content will bend from the bottom up, and Bend Vertical will bend from right to left. With the mid-value (50), the layer content will bend in a perfect U-shape, and the curve will be drawn toward the new center of gravity for higher or lower values.

OTHER PARAMETERS

The **Fill Bordercolor** option will fill the background (vertically or horizontally) with the color of the edge pixels of the original layer. You can also fill with transparency by checking the **Fill Transparent** checkbox instead.

The **Keep Original Layer** checkbox will keep the original image, and create a new layer for the bent image. This can be handy if you want to create several bends from the same image.

Bend the whole image will show the entire (bent) image. Normally, some of the bent parts will be clipped when you bend the entire image instead of just bending a small layer. If you check this option, the canvas size will automatically be enlarged so that you'll be able to see all parts of the image.

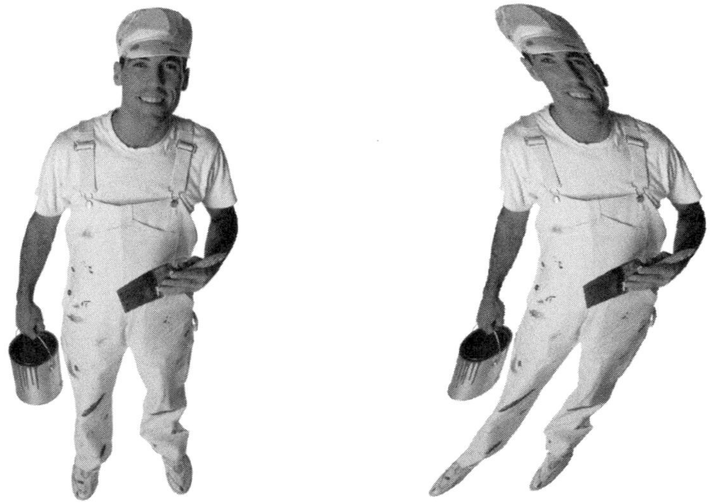

Original *Bent*

Figure 30.2 *The original image, and the result after applying Bend*

BLINDS

Applying **Blinds** is like slicing your image or selection in shreds and then pasting the slices to the different sections of window blinds.

Figure 30.3 *The right part of the image has been altered with Blinds*

PARAMETERS

If you want a transparent background, you'll need to work in layers or add an *alpha channel* (`right-click|Layers|Add Alpha Channel`) to the background. Otherwise, the background will be the background color in the toolbox, and the **Transparent Background** checkbox will be grayed out, so you can't check it.

You can create either **Vertical** or **Horizontal** blinds; just check the appropriate button.

The **Displacement** parameter refers to the open *angle* of the blind. A zero degree angle closes the blinds. A 90 degree Displacement angle opens the blinds as much as possible.

The **Num Segments** parameter controls how many sections the image will be cut into by the blinds.

CURTAIN

The **Curtain** filter makes it appear as if you are looking at your image through the fabric of a thinly woven curtain. Only, this curtain has a pattern printed on it, and that pattern is your image.

When you apply this filter **vertically**, the image is copied. This copy is rotated 180 degrees, thinly slashed and then combined with the original image.

If you choose **Apply horizontal curtain**, the same effects will be applied, but from a horizontal perspective. You can choose to apply the filter both horizontally and vertically at the same time.

Figure 30.4 *Curtain*

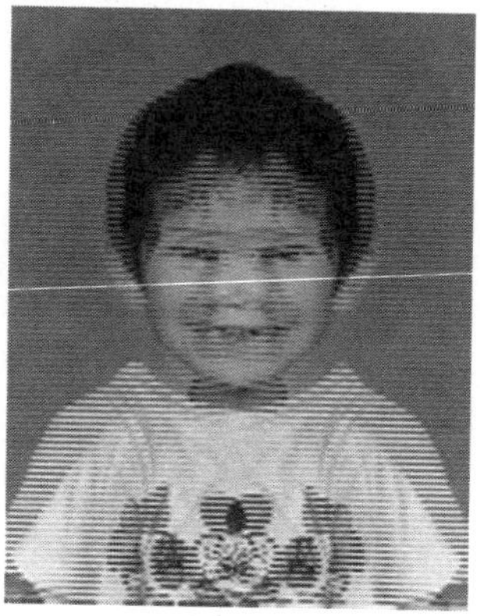

EMBOSS

Emboss *stamps* or *carves out* a three-dimensional look to your image. *Note that Emboss only works for RGB images.*

PARAMETERS

The direction of the **stamp** (inward or outward) is determined by the original brightness values of the image. Bright parts will appear to be *raised*; dark parts will appear to be *carved.*

The **Azimuth** and **Elevation** sliders control the direction of the light. Azimuth can be described as the direction from which the sun rises in the morning. Think of Azimuth as a shining satellite, moving around your image; the light in the image will change as it moves.

If Azimuth was the sun in the morning, think of Elevation as the *time of day*. Think of the sun when it reaches its zenith and doesn't create any shadows. Elevation works the same way.

Depth determines the embossed carve depth. If your depth is large, the lowest parts will look like black holes (this filter is good at detecting edges). When the sun falls or rises, the shadows will get longer or shorter, and the direction of the shadows will also change.

EMBOSS AND BUMP MAP

As you may have noticed, Emboss will make your image gray. If you compare Emboss with the similar filter called **Bump Map** (`right-click|Filters|Map|Bump Map`), you'll find that Bump Map keeps the color information, but the *carving* will not appear as deep as with Emboss.

Figures 30.5 and 30.6 illustrate this fact. The images have been embossed and bumpmapped with the same values, so you can see the difference. Emboss makes a surface look like metal or rock. Bumpmap just adds more depth to your image, like an impression on paper or leather.

Figure 30.5 *The right side of the image was altered with Bumpmap*

Figure 30.6 *The right side of the image was altered with Emboss*

Engrave

Engrave makes your image look like an *etching*.

The **Height** slider determines the depth of the engraving. For more realistic etchings, use low Height values (close to 3). In order for Engrave to work you must have an image with alpha enabled (transparency); a plain RGB or grayscale image will not work. Try `right-click|Layers|Add Alpha Channel` to enable transparency.

The **Limit line width** checkbox will limit the number of allowed line widths, thus reducing the visual impression of having many *shades of gray* in the image. You will get more contrast if you don't check this button, and the etching will look more realistic. On the other hand, you can get quite interesting results with this option checked.

Figure 30.7 *Engrave was applied to the right part of the image*

IWARP

IWarp is Gimp's answer to Kai's Power Goo. IWarp is quite an amazing distort filter.

Figure 30.8 *Well, do we need to say more? The cat is certainly not a cat anymore!*

You can set the amount of distortion (the Deform Amount) and how large the deformation zone should be (the Deform Radius).

To create a distortion, click on the radio button for the desired effect, and drag the mouse in the preview image where you can watch the distortion take place. If you are not satisfied with a distortion, click the **Reset** button and the image will return to its original state. Similar to Power Goo, you can also animate the distortions you've just made and play them like a film.

The Settings Tab

- **Deform Radius:** Sets the size of the distortion area around your mouse pointer. The Deform Radius is the *radius* in pixels from the center of the mouse pointer.
- **Deform Amount:** Sets the amount of deformation on a scale from 0.00 to 1.00.
- **Move distortion:** Allows you to *stretch* parts of the picture. For example, you can stretch a tiny nose into something a witch could be proud of.
- The **Grow** and **Shrink** distortions should be self-explanatory.
- **Swirl:** *Twists* a part of the image, either clockwise or counterclockwise.
- **Remove:** Removes an entire distortion effect, or just part of the effect. Remove is the perfect tool for adjusting a distortion. Remove allows you to avoid pressing **Reset** (and starting again) if you failed to create the effect you wanted. *Note that if you are making an animation, the correction will appear in one of your frames.*
- **Reset:** Simply resets the image to its original state.
- **Bilinear:** If checked, the warping effects will become more smooth.
- **Adaptive Supersample:** An option that slightly improves the smoothness of distortion by adding a few intermediate colors. The effect is often quite subtle, unless this option is used for very small areas.

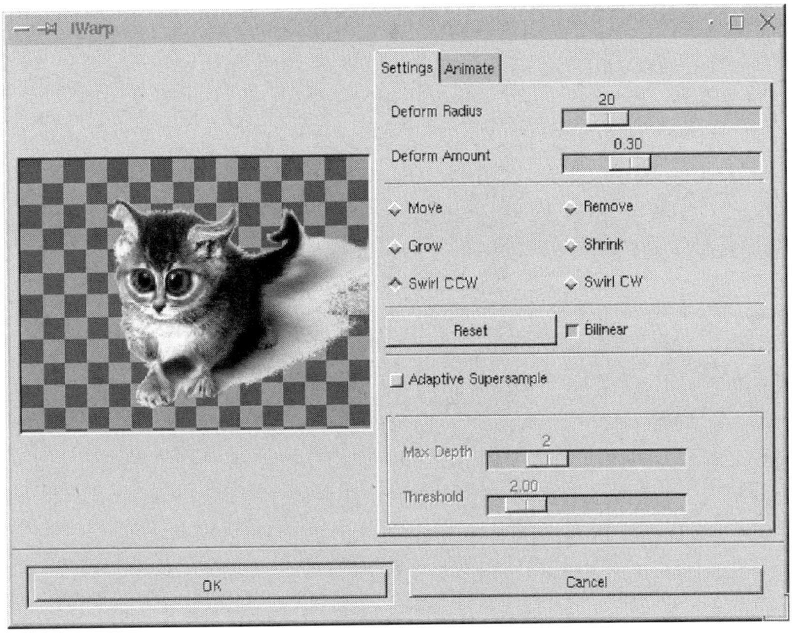

Figure 30.9 *The main IWarp dialog*

THE ANIMATE TAB

The parameters on the Animate tab control the distortion animation that you can create with IWarp.

If you check the **Animate** button, you will create a layered image, ready for making GIF animations. You can set the number of frames and in what order you want to play the frames of the film.

If you don't check **Reverse** or **Ping Pong**, you'll play the animation in **normal mode**: The first frame is the original image, and the following frames are gradually distorted until the last frame, which displays the fully distorted image you made in the preview window.

Reverse will play the animation backwards from the fully distorted image to the original image.

The Ping Pong effect creates the following frame sequence: original image...distorted image...original image, etc.

Reverse and Ping Pong together create the following sequence: distorted image...original image...distorted image, etc. With Reverse and Ping Pong together, you must remove the background layer after you have applied the filter to make it work properly.

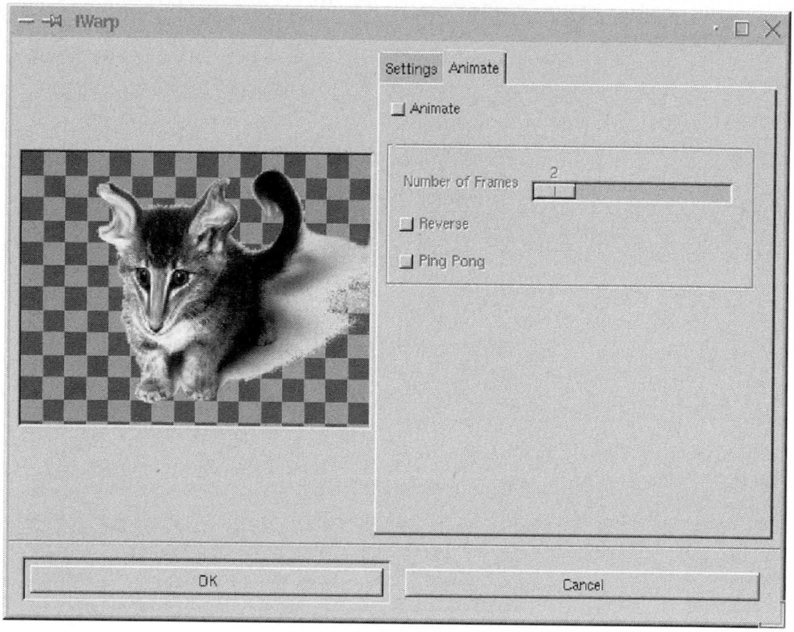

Figure 30.10 *The IWarp Animation*

Click on the **OK** button and IWarp will warp the frames for the animation. You can use `right-click|Filters|Animation|Animation Playback` to view the animation.

Don't worry about how to save the animation. Because the animation is built up on layers, it will be saved if you save the image in a file format that understands layers (such as XCF and GIF).

PAGECURL

Pagecurl allows you to lift and curl a corner of your image.

To be able to use Pagecurl, you must have at least two **layers** (including the background layer) or an alpha-enabled **background** in your image (select `right-click|Layers|Add Alpha Channel`). By invoking the *Add Alpha* command, or by adding a new layer, you have made it possible to use transparency in the image, and that is needed by the Pagecurl plug-in.

The **top** layer will *curl* and the **bottom** layer will *show* under the curl. If your image is only a background layer with alpha, the background will curl up to show the transparency.

The color of the back of the curled page is controlled by the current colors in the toolbox. The background color will be the highlight, or the middle part of the curl gradient, and the foreground color will be the shadow, or the first and last parts of the curl gradient. You can also check the **Use current Gradient instead of**

Figure 30.11 *The Pagecurl dialog*

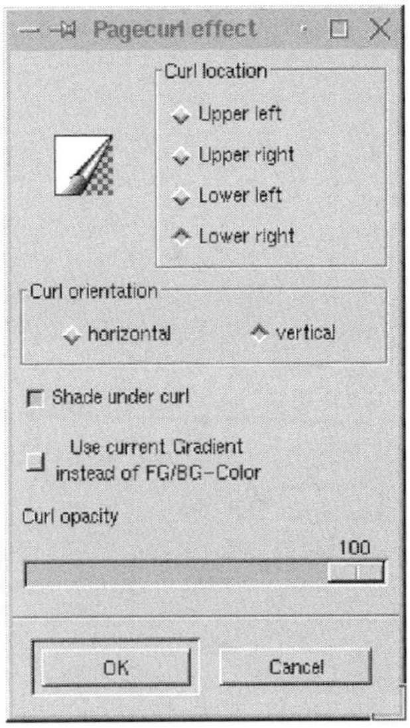

FG/BG-Color checkbox. With this option, the current gradient (determined by the settings in the Gradient Editor) will be used instead of the foreground and background colors.

The Pagecurl dialog also allows you to put a shade under the curl by checking the **Shade under curl** checkbox and to set the opacity of the curled page using the **Curl opacity** slider.

If you just want to curl a small part of the image, make a selection and then Pagecurl the selection. This allows you to make a small curl, as if the glue didn't stick properly to that corner of the image.

Figure 30.12 *An example of Pagecurl*

POLAR COORDS

Polar Coords can be used to create distorted **circular** or **rectangular** representations of your image.

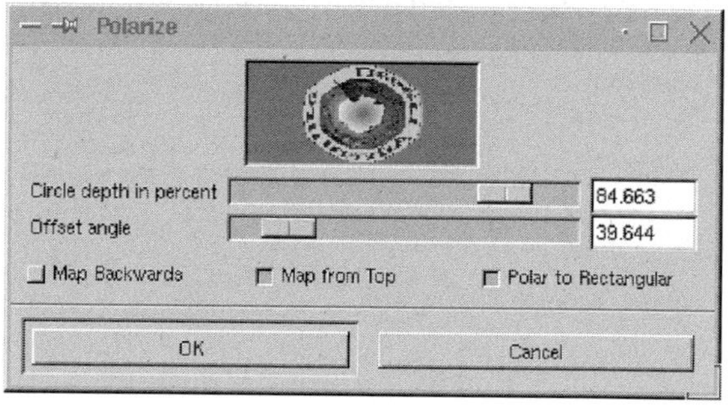

Figure 30.13 *The Polarize dialog*

EXAMPLES

To create a powerful but rather unsophisticated text curve, you can apply this plug-in to a text string. You can also make a target circle out of some lines, or you can make rectangles out of straight lines.

The Sliders

The **Circle depth in percent** slider controls how round the curve will be.

If you apply the filter to your image like the one in Figure 30.14 and set this option to a high value, you will make it circular (Figure 30.15); a lower value makes it rectangular (Figure 30.16).

The **Offset angle** slider controls where the circle/half-circle will start in degrees (see Figure 30.17).

Figure 30.14 *Original image*

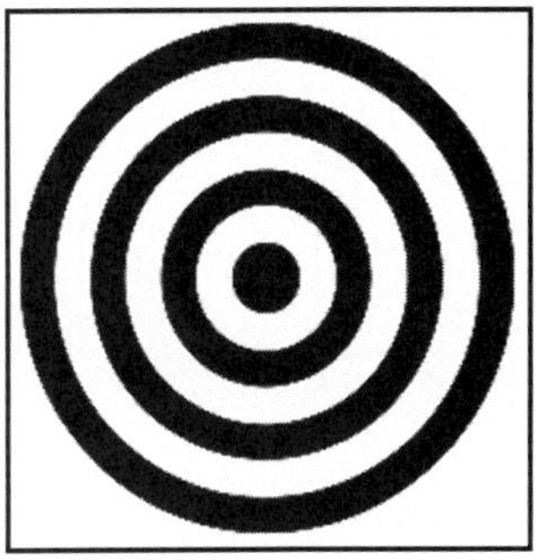

Figure 30.15 *High values for circle depth*

Figure 30.16 *Low values for circle depth*

Figure 30.17 *The offset angle*

The Buttons

The **Map from top** button controls where the lower part of the original image (Figure 30.18) will turn up. If the Map from top button is checked, the bottom part will end up in the center (Figure 30.19). If it is unchecked, the bottom part will be distributed around the edges of the image, as in Figure 30.20.

The **Map Backwards** option is a mirror function. The effect is the same as flipping the image with the Flip tool in the toolbox.

The **Polar to Rectangular** button sets whether the image should be mapped to a circular or rectangular shape. Press this button and the original image (Figure 30.18) will map to rectangular Figure 30.21.

Figure 30.18 *Original image*

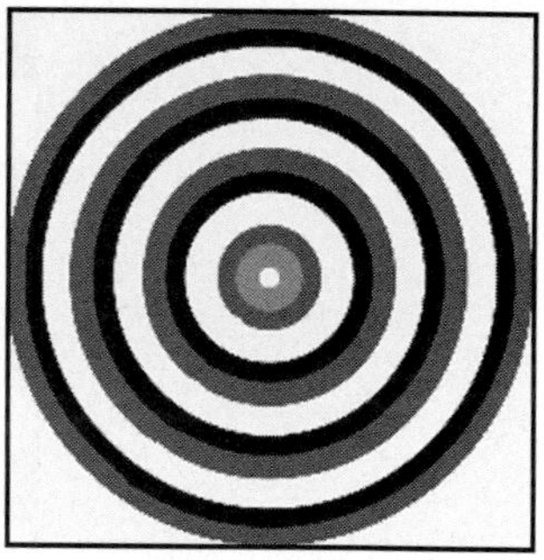

Figure 30.19 *Map from top checked*

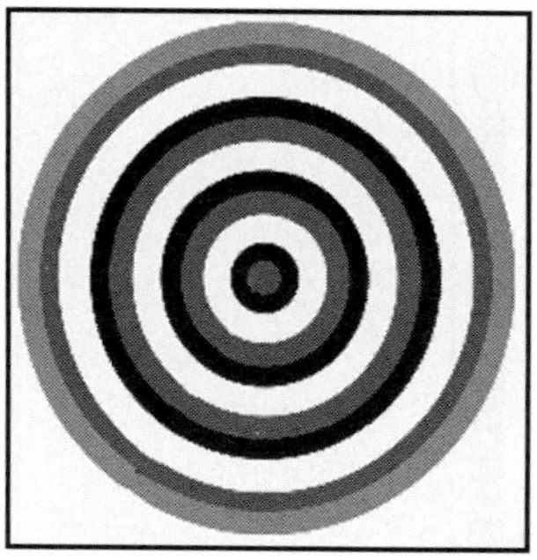

Figure 30.20 *Map from top unchecked*

Figure 30.21 *Polar to Rectangular checked*

Figure 30.22 *The effect of Polar Coords is very evident in these images, but you should keep in mind that it's not just a start and go filter; you often have to choose an appropriate image or prepare the image before you apply the Polar Coords filter*

Original

After applying Rectangular coordinates

Ripple

Ripple displaces the image or selection in waves or ripples so that it looks like a disturbed water surface.

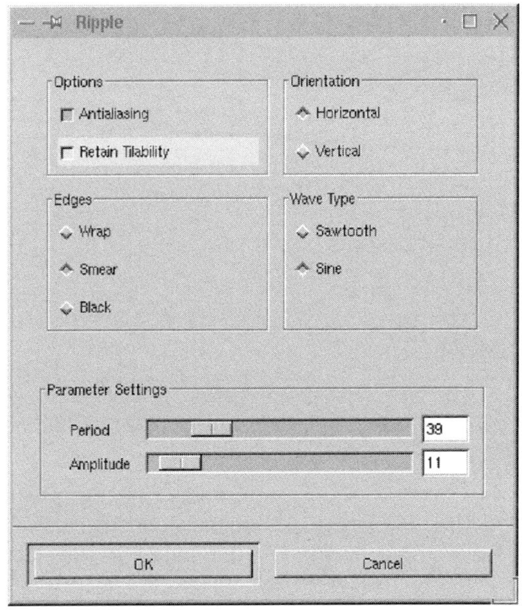

Figure 30.23 *The Ripple dialog*

Parameter Settings

You can displace the image in **Sine** or **Sawtooth** wave form. You can ripple in either a **Horizontal** or **Vertical Orientation**. Use the sliders to specify the **Period** (length) and **Amplitude** (height) of the wave.

The **Edges** parameters **Wrap**, **Smear** and **Black** have the same functions as they do in the `right-click|Map|Displace` plug-in (see "What Are Black, Smear And Wrap Good For?" on page 548 for an explanation of their functions).

If you uncheck the **Antialiasing** checkbox, the wave pattern will get rough edges. This is normally not what you want, so we recommend that you keep this button checked.

If you check the **Retain Tileability** checkbok, a tileable image (pattern) can still function as a seamless pattern after you have rippled it. If this checkbox isn't checked, the edges will not fit when you try to tile the image as a pattern.

Figure 30.24 *The cat's head is being rippled away*

SHIFT

Shift creates a random displacement of each **pixel row**, horizontally or vertically.

The **Shift Amount** slider sets how much a row should be displaced. You can't control whether it will displace left or right/up or down; you can only control the amount of displacement.

Figure 30.25 *Shift was applied to the top of this image*

TWIST

Twist is a versatile plug-in that provides a variety of geometric image distortion functions.

How Does It Work?

Twist distorts the image by translating the original pixels according to a 2-D vector field, which is determined by the selected distortion function. Certain parameters (up to eight, depending on the function type selected) can be adjusted, resulting in different effects.

Twist's output is a geometrically distorted image. The effect of a selected parameter setting can be viewed in a **preview window**. Each selectable function provides eight predefined effects that can help the inexperienced user get a feeling for the settings. Currently, eight different distortion functions are available.

Note that you cannot distort **indexed** images. Convert your indexed image to RGB or grayscale before you use Twist on it.

Twist's dialog is divided into four sections: **Preview image**, **Parameter settings**, **Functions/Effects** and **Cutoff function**.

Figure 30.26 *The right side of this image was altered with Twist*

Functions/Effects

Under **Functions/Effects**, you can choose from several distortion functions in the **Functions** pull-down menu. After you choose a distortion function, you must choose parameter settings that, in combination with the chosen distortion function, achieve the effect you want.

There are two ways to define a parameter set. The first and easier way is to select one of eight effects from the **Effects** pull-down menu under Functions/Effects. The parameters defining the effect will be displayed in the **Parameter settings**. The effect on the image can be seen in the Preview image at the top-left corner of the dialog.

PARAMETER SETTINGS

The second way to choose a parameter set is to manually set the **Parameter settings sliders**. Note that some of the sliders may not be available for certain functions; those parameters will not affect the image distortion effect. The labels of the sliders depend on the distortion function.

To get a feel for the parameters of each distortion function, you should experiment with the sliders. If you feel that the preview image is too small, go ahead and execute Twist by pressing the OK button at the bottom of the dialog. Twist will remember all the parameters you selected when it is started again, so you can fine-tune an effect.

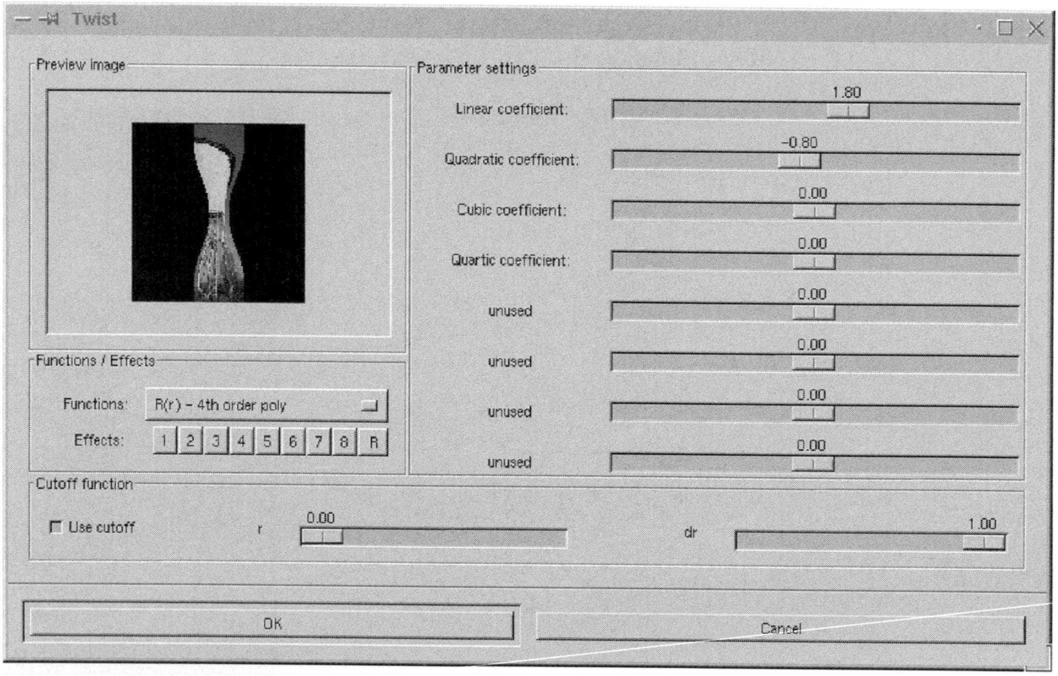

Figure 30.27 *Twist's dialog*

Cutoff

The **Cutoff function** provides a mechanism for dampening the image distortion function, depending on the distance **r** from the image's center. So if the **Use cutoff** checkbox is checked when Twist is activated, the image distortion is a product of the selected distortion function and of the Cutoff function.

Some of the predefined effects use the Cutoff function, so be sure to notice if it is used when you're trying to figure out which parameters will yield an effect that you like.

Value Propagate

Value Propagate *spreads* (or propagates) certain value ranges in a specified direction.

Propagate Modes

More White And More Black

The first two parameters, **More White** and **More Black**, have a large impact on *scanned photographs* (see Figure 30.28). You might describe the effect as a *swelling* of bright (or dark) areas where the contrast is high. When you run the filter several times, those areas will clog together in large square clusters, but middle values will remain relatively unaffected.

The result is often quite artistic. The More White effect resembles oil painting, and More Black looks like watercolor. This filter is also very good for drawings. A black-and-white line drawing made on the computer will look more like a real ink pen drawing if you use More White on it. More Black will just thicken the lines.

Other Propagate Modes

The other Propagate modes work best with *drawings* and computer-made images with distinct edges. Scanned photos are either hardly affected, or the result is strange and unpredictable.

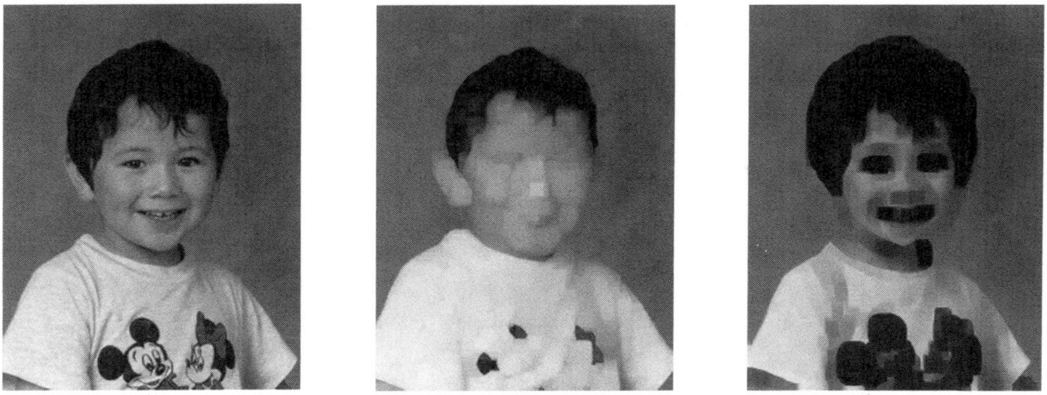

Original *More White* *More Black*

Figure 30.28 *Value Propagate can create very interesting effects. The boy definitely looks more chubby when you apply Value Propagate with More White. More Black, on the other hand, makes him lose a few pounds.*

- **Middle value to peaks:** Creates and propagates the transitional color (blend of object's edge color and background color) and blurs the image. It will blur more each time you use it, because the transitional color will be created from the new edge color.
- **Foreground to peaks:** Draws a fine contour (with the current foreground color) around defined objects or shapes in the image. If the object border is fuzzy, the foreground outline starts where the object color fades out.
- **Only foreground:** Propagates areas that match the exact shade of the foreground color in the toolbox. Soft and fuzzy edges don't propagate well with this option.

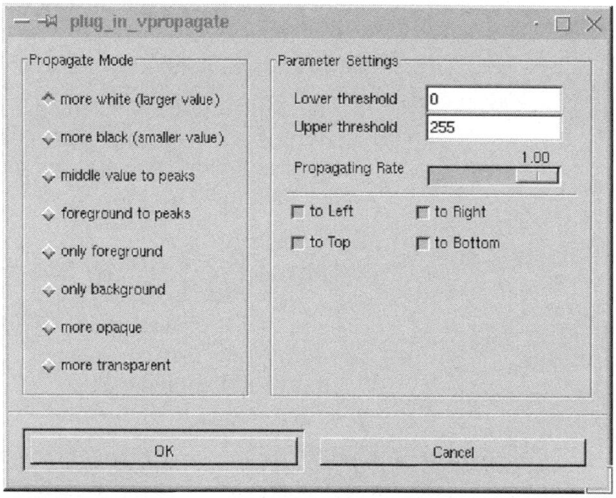

Figure 30.29 *The Value Propagate dialog*

- **Only Background:** Does the same thing with the background color. Sometimes, these options cause pixels of the chosen color to spread in an asymmetric way so that large lumps or clusters grow. This can occur when you spread soft brush lines, or when you run the filter several times.
- **More opaque** and **More transparent:** Only apply to images with an **alpha channel** (a layer or an alpha-enabled background). Those options work exactly the same way as More White and More Black, but white is replaced by opaque and black by transparent.
- **Lower threshold** and **Upper threshold:** Can be set to certain values if you only want to propagate areas in a certain range, like only very dark areas or only middle values. You can also set the **Propagating Rate** (the amount) and the direction (**to Left**, **to Top**, **to Right**, **to Bottom**) of the spreading.

- **Propagate Alpha** and **Value Channel:** Can be unchecked and thereby prevent that the alpha and/or value channels are affected by the propagation.

WAVES

Waves simulates the effect that you get when you throw a stone in a pond (if the **Reflective** checkbox is unchecked).

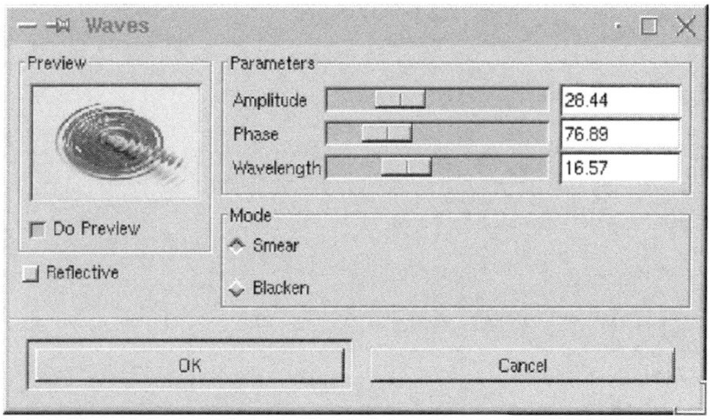

Figure 30.30 *The Waves dialog*

PARAMETER SETTINGS

- The **Amplitude** slider controls the *height* of the waves.
- The **Phase** slider sets the position in the wave.
- The **Wavelength** slider controls the length of the waves.
- The **Smear** and **Blacken Modes** work the same as they do in `right-click|Filters|Map|Displace` (see "What Are Black, Smear And Wrap Good For?" on page 548 for an explanation of Smear and Blacken).
- If you check the **Reflective** checkbox, you will not get the simple "thrown stone" effect. Instead, your wave will create an interference pattern.

Figure 30.31 *The difference between non-reflective waves and reflective waves*

Original

Nonreflective waves

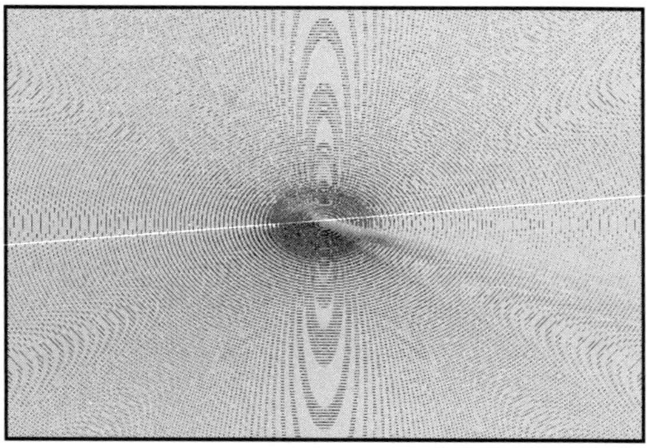

Reflective waves

WHIRL AND PINCH

Whirl and Pinch distorts your image in a concentric way.

Whirl distorts the image much like the little whirlpool that appears when you empty your bath.

Pinch can be compared to applying your image to a soft rubber surface and pressing it in different ways. If the **Pinch amount** slider is set to a *negative* value, it will look as if someone tried to push a round object up toward you from behind the rubber skin. If Pinch amount is set to a *positive* value, it looks like someone is dragging or sucking on the surface from behind, and away from you.

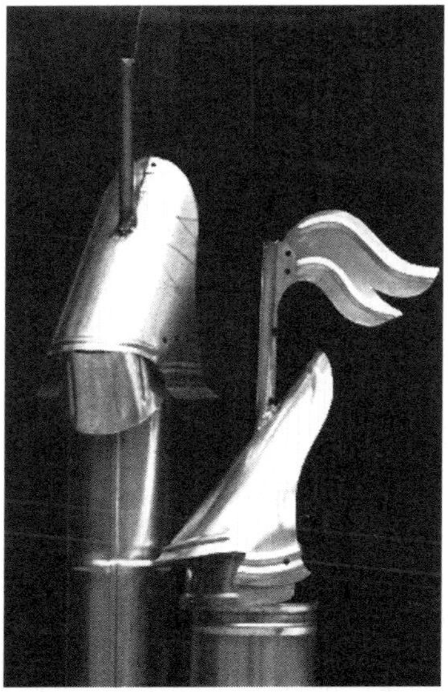

Original

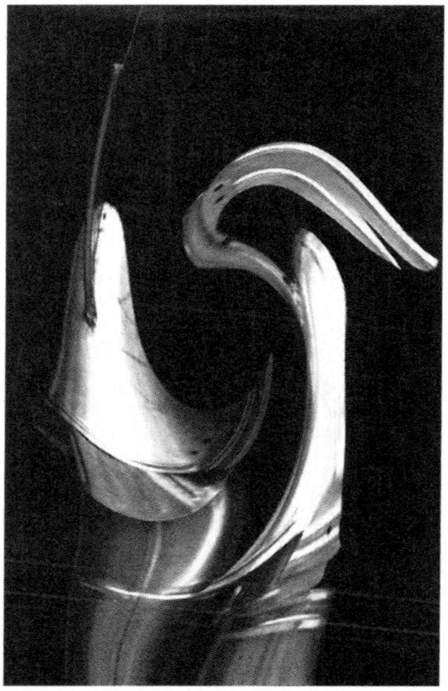

Whirled

Figure 30.32 *The effect of Whirl can be quite surreal*

Parameters

The **Whirl angle** slider controls how many degrees you want to *rotate* your image.

The **Radius** slider sets how much of your image will be affected. If you set Radius to 2, the entire image will be affected. If you set Radius to 1, half the image will be affected. If Radius is set to 0, nothing will be affected (think of it as the radius in a circle with 0 in the center and 1 halfway out).

Tip: To create a really realistic whirlpool, combine Whirl and Pinch.

Figure 30.33 *The Whirl and Pinch dialog*

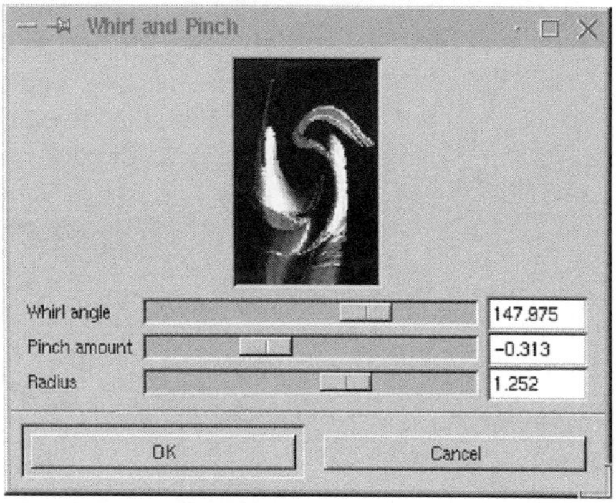

WIND

The **Wind** filter can be used to create **motion blur**, but it can also be used as a general distort filter. What's characteristic about this filter is that it will render thin black or white lines.

Wind will detect the edges in the image, and stretch out thin white or black lines from that edge. This is why you can create the illusion of motion, because the edges are what will be blurred in a photograph of a moving object.

Let's take a look at the train in Figure 30.34. There is no motion in the original image, but in the second image we added some wind to get the train started. First, we created a new layer, we copied the train into this layer and invoked the Wind filter. The final step was to blur the windows with the convolver tool.

No wind, no motion — *Wind results in motion*

Figure 30.34 *Wind was used to create a feeling of motion*

Parameter Settings

The interface is quite simple. You can set the **Strength** of the wind and a **Threshold** value. Threshold will restrict the effect to fewer areas of the image.

Strength controls the amount of wind, so a high value will render a storm. You can also increase the effect by setting the **Style** to *Blast,* which will produce thicker lines than *Wind.*

You can only set the wind in two directions, either *Left* or *Right*. However, you can control which edge the wind will come from using the commands **Leading**, **Trailing** or **Both**. Because Trailing will produce a black wind, it creates a less convincing motion blur than Leading, which will produce white wind.

Figure 30.35 *Wind was applied to the same image using Leading, Trailing and Both*

Leading *Trailing* *Both*

CHAPTER 31

Edge-Detect Filters

Living on the edge? Gimp provides you with a few edge-detect filters to help you find your edge.

Introduction

Edge-Detect filters search out the borders between areas of different color, so they can trace the contours of objects in the image.

For the **Edge**, **Laplace** and **Sobel** filters, the background is black or transparent, and the contours are either white or have the same color as in the original image. The results are actually a lot like sgrafitto or other artistic scratching techniques, where you cover an image with thick oil paint or crayon and then scratch the contours with a knife or needle so that the original colors appear in the scratch marks.

The **LoG** filter, however, is strictly black and white with a black contour on a white background.

Edge-Detect filters are often used to make *selection* easier, but they can also be used for artistic purposes or to achieve effects like simulating a hand-drawn sketch.

Edge

Edge will produce a dark image with (mostly) white contours.

You can set the **Amount** of edge-detect. A high value results in a black, high-contrast image with thin, sharp edges. A low value will produce thick, coarse edges with relatively low contrast and lots of color in the dark areas.

The **Wrap**, **Smear** and **Black** options aren't operational, so you might as well leave those as they are.

Figure 31.1 *The left part of the image was altered with Edge*

LAPLACE

Laplace creates a black image with extremely thin (1 pixel wide) colored edge lines.

Note: When applied on a layer, Laplace and Sobel result in a transparent image with thin black edge lines.

Laplace is very useful when you want to put emphasis on the contours of an image, or make a photograph look like an ink drawing. To achieve this effect, duplicate the image and use Laplace or Sobel on the top layer. For the best result, apply some blur to the image before running this filter (such as **Gaussian Blur** with a radius of 0.5 to 5.0).

Figure 31.2 *The left side of the image was altered with Laplace*

LOG

LoG is a very useful *edge-detect* and *tracing* filter. You shouldn't compare it to tracing programs like Corel Trace or Adobe Streamline for vector drawing programs, but if you want to use a similar feature in a bitmap application like Gimp, LoG is an excellent tool.

How To Use LoG

The LoG filter transforms scanned or computer-made images into black-and-white **line art** drawings, where each line is a closed curve. This makes it possible to create simple yet effective drawings by filling the closed curves with color, using the **Bucket Fill** tool.

You can also use it as a *template* or aid for hand-painted images. However, retouching to erase unwanted contours and close certain curves, in order to define the desired fill area, will be necessary in most cases.

Original *LoG'ed* *LoG'ed and colorized*

Figure 31.3 *Example showing how you can use LoG to create a cartoon-like image*

PARAMETERS

You'll need to set several parameters before applying this filter successfully.

Edge-Detect Lines

Allowable PA *(percentage of allowable aliasing energy),* or the tolerated amount of aliasing, is used to specify how edges are treated.

A high PA gives you a higher level of edge-detecting, which will result in a more precise line art output of your image. A high PA is recommended on complicated images where detail is important. Use a low PA on simpler images, or when you want a clean output.

Figure 31.4 *The LoG filter dialog*

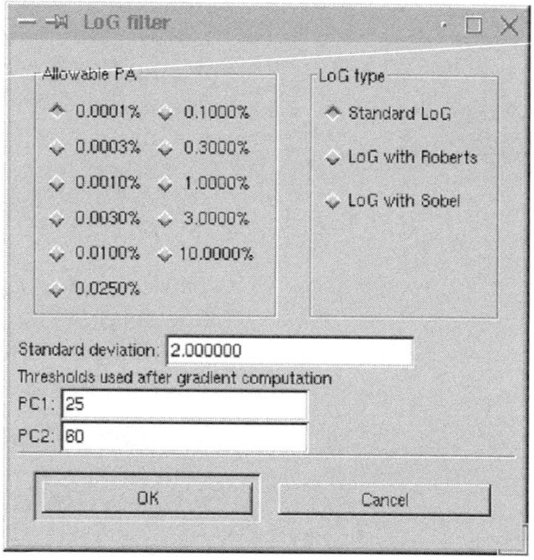

LoG Rendering Types

There are three types of LoG rendering: **Standard LoG**, or **LoG with Roberts** and **LoG with Sobel**.

Standard LoG is perhaps a bit crude, but graphically clean and very powerful in its simplicity. Standard LoG creates a thick, closed border around objects; the higher the **PA**, the thinner the contour border.

Roberts and **Sobel** trace fine contours without borders and with more realism in the penwork. They make use of **gradients** to filter out spurious contours in the image. Their results are *cleaner* to look at, but important parts of the image are often lost.

Adjusting The Level Of Detail

To rectify this loss of image information, you should specify an appropriate **Threshold range** in the **PC1** and **PC2** fields. The PC1 threshold field sets the low threshold limit. Values below the specified value in this field will be ignored. The PC2 threshold field sets the high limit. Values exceeding the specified value in this field will be ignored.

Values within the specified *threshold range* are traced and displayed in the rendered image. If the image is generally low in contrast, you should increase the threshold range. For a bright image where contours are pale or unclear, set PC1 to 0 and PC2 to a relatively low value, like 50 or 60. Then, the filter will disregard brighter values and concentrate on tracing darker areas. If the image is dark, set the threshold values in the opposite direction.

If you want more *detail* in the traced image, you must *lower* the **Standard deviation** value. However, a Standard deviation lower than the default value (which is 2.0) requires a higher PA (3.0 or 10.0) to work properly. *Raising* the Standard deviation results in larger, softer curves with less detail.

SOBEL

Sobel has the same effect as **Laplace**, but the edges are a bit broader and also a bit more blurred.

If you only apply it in one direction (you can apply it both vertically and horizontally) and check **Keep sign of result**, you will get something that looks a lot like an **Emboss** effect.

If you only apply it *horizontally*, you will get more contrast and color in your image. If you only apply it *vertically*, it will get a bit darker and there will be less contrast in the image.

Figure 31.5 *The right side of the image was altered with Sobel*

CHAPTER 32

Enhance Filters

Do you want to sell your old car? Here are the tools you'll need to enhance the advertisement image.

Adaptive Contrast

Adaptive Contrast is a very powerful contrast-enhancing filter. The effect is very strong, sometimes with an almost three-dimensional quality, so it's not suitable for all images.

Contrary to the other enhancing filters in this menu, Adaptive Contrast creates little change in the **Hue** and **Saturation** values, so if you use it in an image with faded colors, this filter will not retrieve lost color. It is, however, very effective in finding and accentuating hidden or faded **Brightness** values in an image.

Figure 32.1 *The two leaves to the left were enhanced with Adaptive Contrast*

Deinterlace

Deinterlace will help you adjust images captured by **video cards**. Sometimes, the even fields or odd fields don't get captured correctly. This filter can be used to correct that.

Despeckle

Despeckle is the filter to use if your image is noisy, if you scanned an image and there was some dust or fibers in the scanner, if you got a moiré pattern when you scanned a printed image from a magazine, or if your image has physical damage, like scratches.

- If your image is just **noisy**, or suffers from **moiré** effects, use Despeckle over the *whole image*.

- If **dust** or **scratches** are your problem, select the damaged area with the free selection tool and use Despeckle on that *selection.*

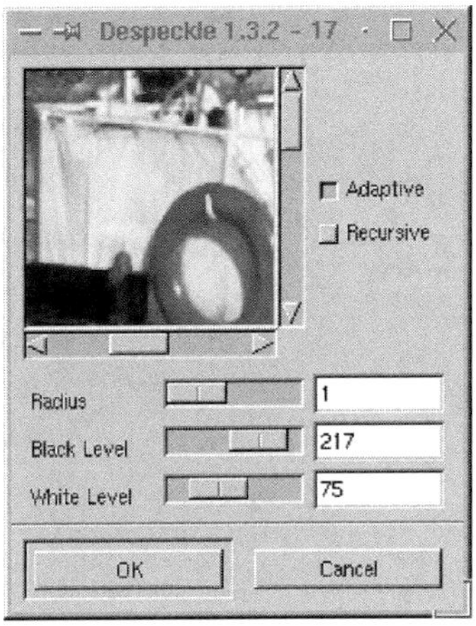

Figure 32.2 *The Despeckle dialog*

PARAMETERS

You have the following choices: **Radius** (if both **Adaptive** and **Recursive** are unchecked); **Radius** and **Recursive**; **Adaptive**; and **Adaptive** and **Recursive**.

Radius refers to the *window size*, which can be from 1 (3x3 pixels) to 20 (41x41). The image will be chopped up in several windows, with a specified size: for example, 3x3 pixels. In each of these windows, the filter will try to smooth the color range, and thereby remove unwanted defects like scratches or noisy pixels.

Adaptive will adapt the radius window size depending on the image (selection) content. It does it by using the **histogram** of the image. Adaptive despeckling gives a smoother result than only Radius, thereby producing a better output.

Recursive will *repeat* the Radius function, so that the smoothing effect gets stronger. It is, however, much slower than Radius.

You can also adjust the **Black Level** or **White Level** sliders to hide scratches. If the damage you want to repair is bright and the background is dark, raise the Black Level. If the scratch is dark against a white background, raise the White Level.

HOW TO USE DESPECKLE

If you use only **Radius**, a general algorithm is used to smooth the color range. If you set the radius high, the blur level will also be high.

If you use **Radius and Recursive**, you can use a smaller Radius to get the same effect as with a large Radius and no Recursive. Be careful, because Recursive can easily result in unwanted blurring.

If you use **Adaptive**, the filter will try to calculate the best window size, and will use a general algorithm to smooth the color range in each window.

If you use **Adaptive and Recursive**, an adaptive recursive algorithm will be used. This is very effective and you can use quite small radius values. It will, however, be even slower than Recursive.

General Advice

To remove a scratch or other defect, select the damaged area and use Recursive and Radius.

If you want to remove some noise, use Adaptive or perhaps a combination of Adaptive and Recursive. If you use Recursive and/or Radius on the whole image, it will often get too blurred (this is not a problem when you're only using it on a tiny selection).

Figure 32.3 *When you want to remove dust and scratches, just select the scratched area and apply Despeckle, as in the example provided here*

The scratch has been selected

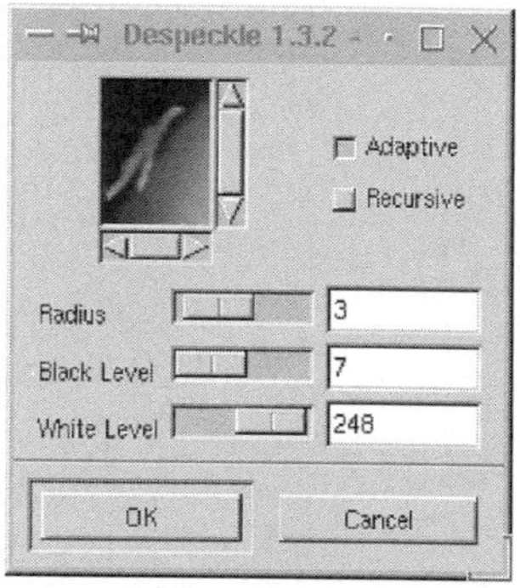

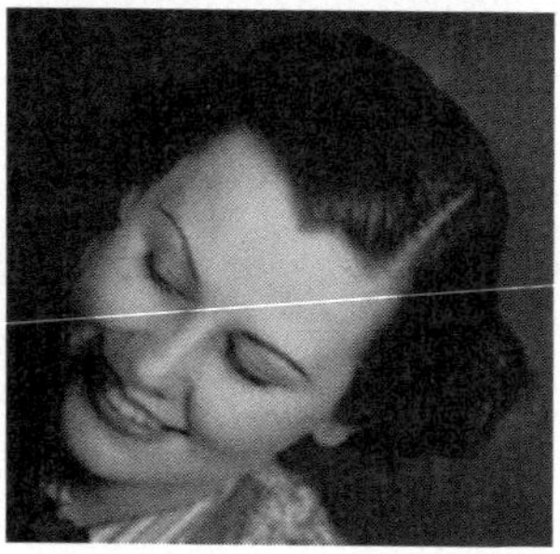

After applying Despeckle, the scratch is gone

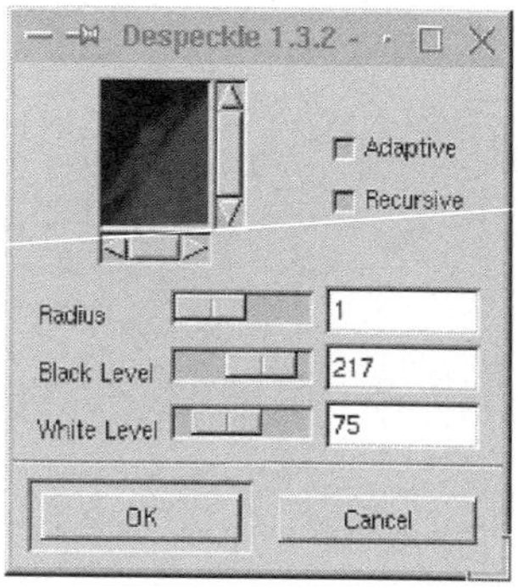

DESTRIPE

Destripe corrects images captured from video films, or poorly scanned images with stripes on them. This filter will add a striped interference pattern to the image.

You change the phase by dragging the **Width** slider, and if you can find the right setting, the two wave patterns will extinguish each other. Because the stripe pattern will be different for each image, you'll have to experiment to find the setting that will get rid of the stripes in your original. The **Histogram** checkbox will give you a better view of the current phase displacement.

NL FILTER

NL Filter is an efficient image enhancing filter (the "NL" stands for non-linear).

NL Filter uses a 7-hexagon pixel block that you can adjust with the radius slider (instead of using a fixed 3x3 pixel block for its filter algorithms).

Figure 32.4 *The NL Filter dialog*

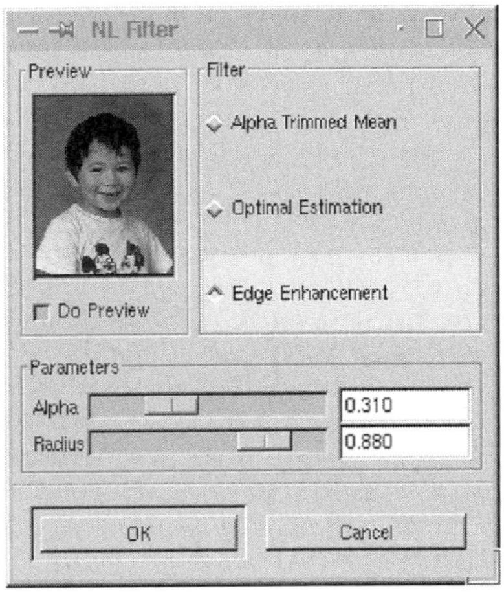

PARAMETERS

NL Filter provides three different filters: **Alpha Trimmed Mean**, **Optimal Estimation** and **Edge Enhancement**.

The **Radius** slider controls the strength of the filter. **Alpha** determines whether the filter will just smooth out, or reduce, noise. Recommended values for both Radius and Alpha are between 0.0 and 0.5. If you use values over 0.5, funny things will happen (but they can be quite artistic).

- Use **Alpha Trimmed Mean** and set the Alpha to 0.5 when removing single noise spots in the image.
- **Optimal Estimation** is very good for reducing dithering noise. Low Alpha values make the smoothing subtle and high values (around 1.0) smooth all parts of the image. Radius should be from 0.8 to 1.0 for this filter to work correctly.

- **Edge Enhancement** is the opposite of Optimal Estimation. Edge Enhancement sharpens edges instead of blurring them. Radius controls the effectiveness of the filter. Useful Radius values range between 0.5 and 0.9.

SHARPEN

Sharpen will sharpen unfocused images.

The interface is simple: The **Sharpness** slider controls the amount of sharpness, and you judge for yourself using the preview.

Sharpen is one of the more useful tools in Gimp for enhancing photographs. However, when you use Sharpen, you risk accentuating not only edges, but also noise or blemishes. If your image is very damaged or noisy, we recommend that you try the **NL Filter's** Edge Enhancement option, or the **Unsharp Mask** filter instead.

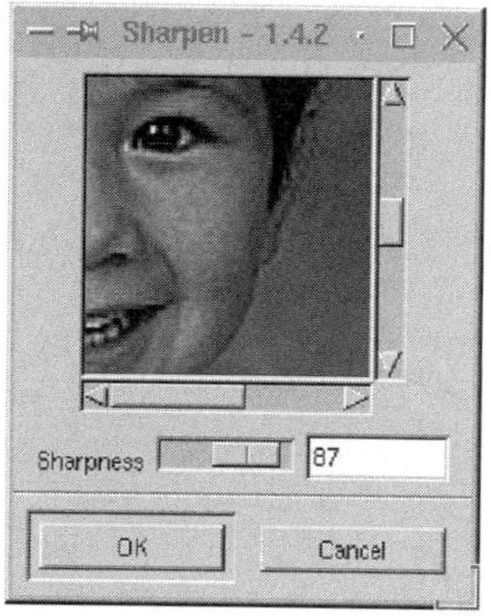

Figure 32.5 *The Sharpen dialog*

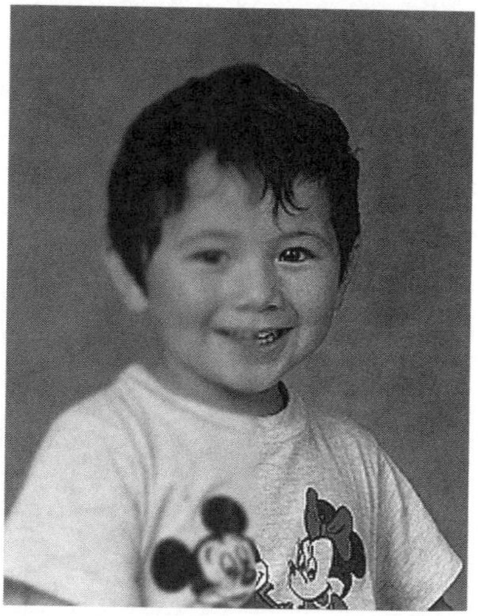

Figure 32.6 *The right part of the image was enhanced with Sharpen*

UNSHARP MASK

The **Unsharp Mask** filter will enhance your image by making it **sharper** without accentuating the small imperfections in the image. It's hard to tell by the name, but Unsharp Mask is based on a darkroom technique that was used before computer graphics arrived on the scene. Anyway, it's a very efficient filter for sharpening enhancements.

Why Should I Use Unsharp Mask Instead Of Sharpen?

Usually, it's much better to use **Unsharp Mask** than **Sharpen**. The reason for this is that Unsharp Mask will sharpen the edges in the image, and the human eye is very sensitive to unsharp edges. Actually, sharpening the edges in an image will make the whole image look sharp, because you will not easily detect the other parts that are less sharp. Also, because Unsharp Mask won't sharpen the entire image as much as the Sharpen filter does, the resulting image will look much more natural than the somewhat artificial look that Sharpen will produce.

Unsharp Mask can also be used to prepare images for Web and professional printing, because it allows you to control the thickness of the edges in an image.

Sharpening Without Distorting The Colors

When you enhance images, you often don't want the colors to be affected. Sharpening the colors in an image will usually just distort them and make them look unnatural, and that is no enhancement.

Tip: A useful piece of advice when you wish to sharpen up an unfocused image is to *decompose* the image to HSV, and only apply the enhancement filter to the **Value** part of the image. Afterward, you *compose* the image to RGB and you'll have a sharpened image where the colors have not been affected by the Sharpening process.

Parameter Settings

Instead of discussing exactly how this filter works in a mathematical way, we will try to tell you how to use it.

At the time of this writing (September 1999) there are only two parameters in this filter. **Blur Radius** and **Combine amount**. We will refer to these parameters as *Radius* and *Amount*.

- **Radius** refers to the thickness of the edges in the image. Higher values will produce thicker edges and more contrast in the image. Lower values will produce fine/crisp edges. You can set the radius to 0.1 and higher.
- **Amount** controls how much the image will be sharpened. This value is normally specified in percent, but we guess that you understand that 0.5 is the same as 50%. You can set the amount of sharpening to 1% (0.01) and higher.

Recommended Values

Amount

If we only had Amount to play with, there would be no problem figuring out how to use Unsharp Mask. Generally, we recommend starting out with low values, and repeating the filter several times instead of applying it once using a high value. Because Gimp has an excellent **undo/redo** function, you can easily find out what values you should use to get the best result by redoing/undoing your changes.

As a general guideline, values between 0.25 (25%) and 0.5 (50%) are appropriate for creating a gentle sharpening effect. Values between 0.5 (50%) and 2.50 (250%) will produce a stronger sharpening. If you want to create artificial-looking images, high values over 4.5 (450%) will do. The given values assume that you have a Radius of 1.0.

Radius

Radius determines how thick your edges will be after having applied Unsharp Mask. Low values such as 1.0 will produce very fine edges. Low values on lossy compressed images (JPEG) can sometimes produce unwanted grain and aliasing edges. If you encounter that problem when you use Unsharp Mask, try raising the Radius value to exceed 1.5.

A Radius from 1.0 to 2.0 will create thicker lines that may look unnatural on your computer monitor. They are, however, very useful when you want to **print** your image. It's not uncommon to use a low Amount with a Radius between 1.5 and 2.0 on all images that will be printed in a book, because imagesetters and printers don't show fine lines as well as a computer monitor.

A rule of thumb is to add 0.2 to the Radius value for each 30 ppi in your image. So, for example, a 300 ppi image will require a Radius of 2.0 and a 210 ppi image will require a Radius of 1.4. The algorithm is as follows:

Radius= (image ppi / 30) x 0.2

The values above are not fixed, and it's up to your common sense to experiment with different values. Naturally, you can use high values to create special effects in your image.

Figure 32.7 *These examples show the result of using different settings for the Unsharp Mask parameters. R is Radius and A is Amount.*

Original

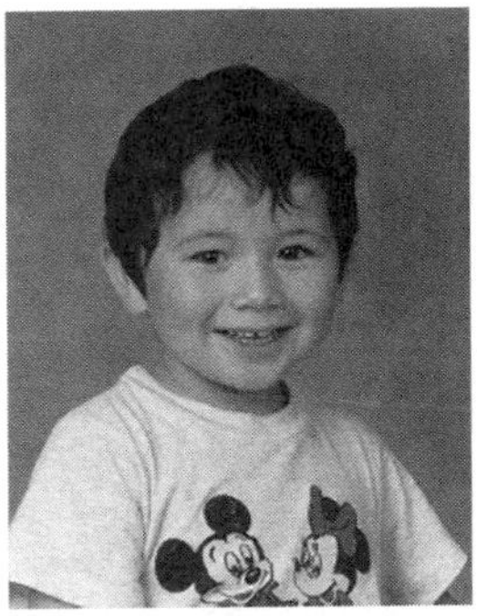

R=0.5 A=0.5

R=1 A=0.5

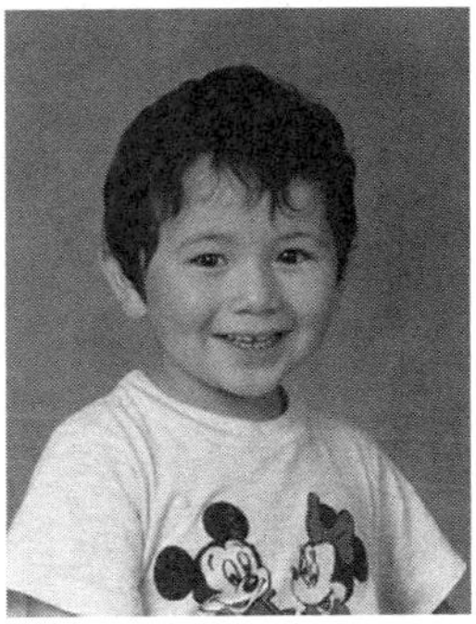

R=2 A=0.5

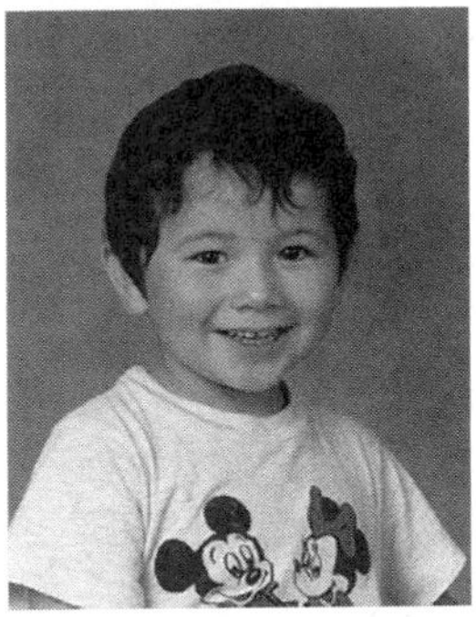

R=3 A=0.5

R=10 A=0.5

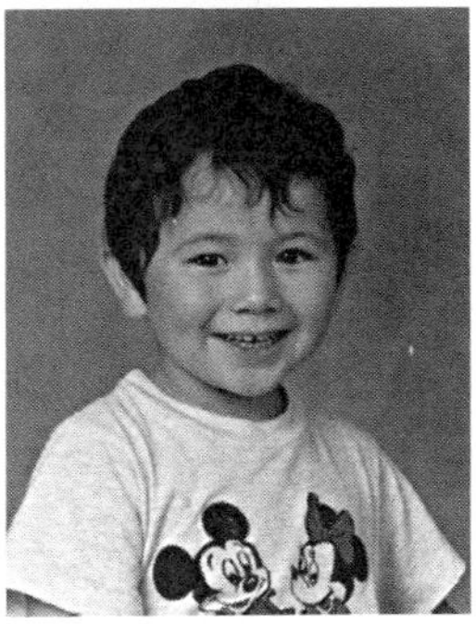

R=20 A=0.5

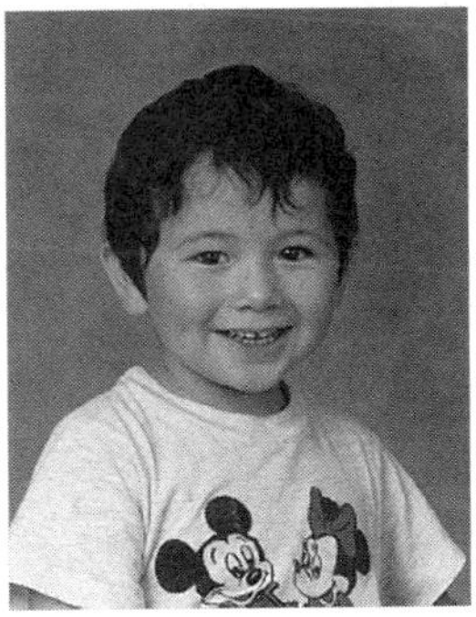

R=1 A=1.5

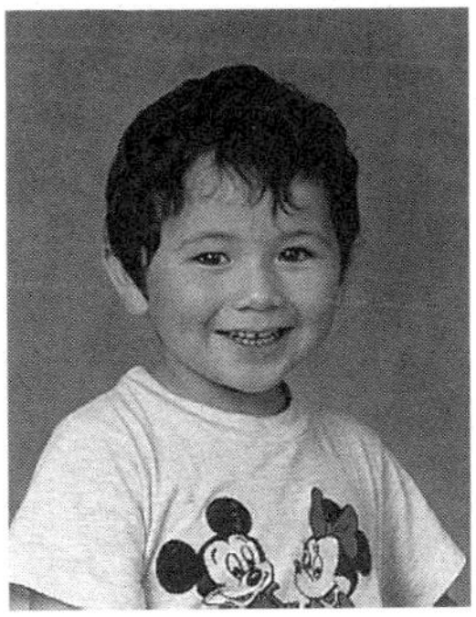

R=1 A=2.5

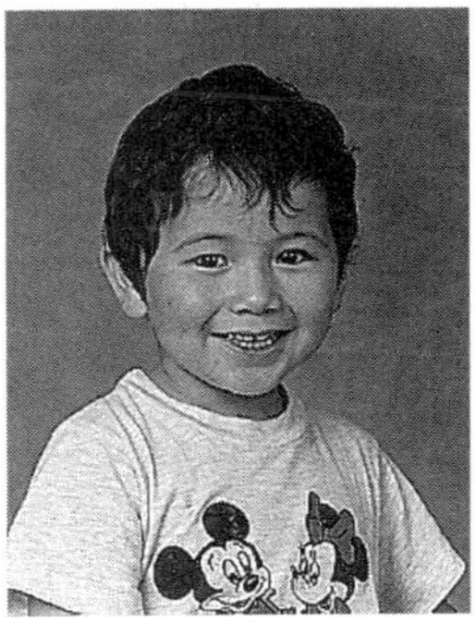

R=1 A=10

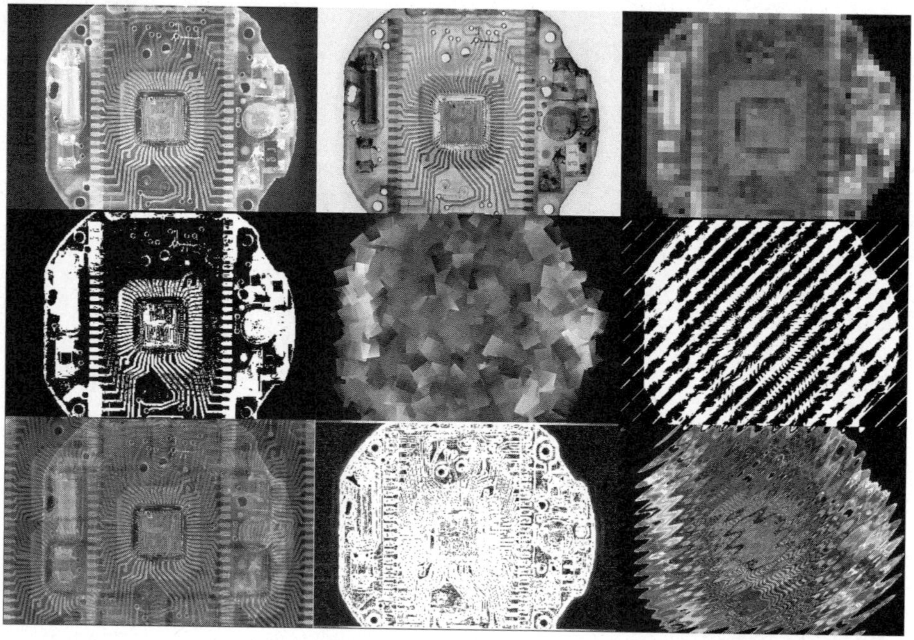

CHAPTER 33

Generic Filters

This is the math corner of Gimp. You will find different kinds of filters that apply mathematical formulas to your image, as well as Gimp's equivalent to Filter Factory.

Convolution Matrix

Convolution Matrix allows you to create simple custom filters. Convolution Matrix adds together the color values in the 5x5 pixel box around each pixel, multiplying each pixel in the box by the corresponding value from the matrix.

Examples

It works like this:

0	0	0	0	0
0	0	0	0	0
0	0	1	0	0
0	0	0	0	0
0	0	0	0	0

Divisor: 1 **Offset**: 0

The middle value represents the pixel to be modified. Here, the destination value is 1 (the source value and the surrounding pixels are multiplied by 0 so they don't count). The matrix can be used for offsetting. For example:

0	0	0	0	0
0	0	1	0	0
0	0	0	0	0
0	0	0	0	0
0	0	0	0	0

Divisor: 1 **Offset**: 1

The destination value for a pixel is the source value of the pixel above it, so this offsets the image one pixel downward. A simple blur works like this:

0	0	0	0	0
0	1	1	1	0
0	1	1	1	0
0	1	1	1	0
0	0	0	0	0

Divisor: 9 **Offset**: 0

Now, for each pixel, the value of that pixel and the eight surrounding pixels is taken, added together and divided by nine. Thus, the resulting pixel is the average of the 3x3 pixel region around it. Similarly, a very strong (and unsophisticated) sharpen filter works like this:

0	0	0	0	0
0	0	-1	0	0
0	-1	5	-1	0
0	0	-1	0	0
0	0	0	0	0

Divisor: 1 **Offset**: 0

This takes the center pixel, multiplies its value by five, then subtracts the values of the four immediately adjacent pixels from that. This kind of operation enhances the differences between colors.

The **Divisor** argument is just a number by which the result is divided, and the **Offset** is added to that. The Offset is useful in some cases, such as this:

0	0	0	0	0
0	1	1	0	0
0	1	0	-1	0
0	0	-1	-1	0
0	0	0	0	0

Divisor: 1 **Offset**: 128

In this case, the values on the lower right are subtracted from the values at the upper left. This produces a basic **embossing** effect.

Figure 33.1 *Embossing with the help of Convolution*

Since these values could easily be negative, and a picture can't have negative colors, we add 128 everywhere, making this in all likelihood something like a gray bump map.

The **Automatic** checkbox sets the **Divisor** so that it is the sum of the matrix values. If the sum is positive, the Offset is 0. If the sum is negative, the Offset is set to 255 (for inverting). If the Divisor is 0, the Offset is 128 (for embossing).

The **Channels** checkboxes control which channels the plug-in operates on. **Alpha** adds an additional factor to the calculations: the alpha channel. If Alpha is checked, the values of all pixels are weighted both by the matrix values and by its alpha value. Try this out by making an image with nearly transparent (low alpha) green and fully opaque red next to it. If you aren't using alpha weighting, and you blur the image, a brownish line will appear between the transparent and red regions, because the transparency (the "weakness," one might say) of the green wasn't taken into consideration. With alpha weighting on, the blurring won't create any unexpected artifacts.

UNIVERSAL FILTER

There are two different types of signal (image) processing: **linear** and **nonlinear**. A median algorithm is an example of a nonlinear filter. The **Universal Filter** is a linear filter, which means that you can describe a transfer function that describes the output in relation to the input.

In principle, a linear operation is reversible, but in practice a few nonlinear operations (like clipping and quantization) are involved, which limit the reversibility. As for any linear system, a frequency response can be calculated. This description is going to skip over the mathematics and theory and just describe the basic working algorithm.

At the moment, the Universal Filter uses a 3x3 **Matrix** and two other parameters (**Divider** and **Bias**). The extra parameters can be calculated from the Matrix in most cases, but you can set them if you want to.

For every pixel of the new image, the original pixel and the surrounding pixels are taken, multiplied with the values in the Matrix, added to the Bias value and divided by the Divider. If you change the Matrix values, different kinds of filters can be generated.

If you put the value 1 in every Matrix field (and leave the Divider and Bias values as calculated), you'll get a lowpass or blur effect, because you add all nine pixels to calculate the new one. If you want a smaller effect, you can increase the center value so the surrounding pixels will have less effect.

To get a highpass filter or sharpening effect, use a Matrix with -1 in all cells and a 9 in the center.

You can choose to run the filter in just one direction, by only using coefficients in the middle row or the middle column of the matrix. To invert the picture, put a -1 in the center field.

The values for Bias and the Divider are calculated so that the resulting image will be in the normal range of 0 to 255 for color or gray values. So the Divider is the absolute value of the sum of the Matrix. If the sum is 0, then the **Divider** is set to one. The Bias value is derived from the sign of the Matrix sum. If the sign is positive, the Bias is 0; if it is negative, the Bias will be 255. If the sum is 0, the Bias value will be 128.

All calculated values are rounded to integers and clipped to the range 0 to 255 after the computation.

User Filter (Adobe Filter Factory Emulator)

User Filter is a clone of Adobe Photoshop's **Filter Factory**. This is a real goldmine, because you can use all of the hundreds of available Filter Factory filters made for **Adobe Photoshop**.

An enormous amount of free filters are now available for Gimp. User Filter can handle all the different Filter Factor filter formats: .afs, .txt and .8bf plug-ins, as well as .ffl (Filter Factory libraries). Note that you can't use ordinary .8bf Adobe Photoshop plug-ins with the User Filter; they only work with Adobe Photoshop.

To understand Filter Factory, you'll need to read the pertinent sections of the Adobe Photoshop manual. There are too many Filter Factory filters for this manual to describe, but we plan to write some documentation about Filter Factory filters in the future.

To find Filter Factory filters and information about Filter Factory, start with the Filter Factory web page at `http://privat.schlund.de/f/filter-factory/` or search the web for "Filter Factory" with your favorite search engine.

Notice that you must add the line `(userfilter-path "${gimp_dir}/userfilter")` to your personal gimprc file (e.g., `vi ~/.gimp/gimprc`). You must also make a userfilter directory in your personal gimp directory (e.g., `mkdir ~/.gimp/userfilter`). You can now install your userfilters in the `~/.gimp/userfilter` directory. Of course you must also have the userfilter plug-in installed on your system. Please read "Compiling Plug-ins" starting on page 769 for how to compile plug-ins and "Web" on page 878 to find out where to download the latest version of User filter.

Operating The User Filter

The user interface is quite simple. First, you'll need to open the **Filter Manager** folder, where you can browse through the available filters. When you have decided which one to use, simply select it and press **Load**.

The preview will show how the result of the filter will appear. If you want to adjust any of the values, open the **Value** folder. The first time you open the **User Filter**, you won't find any values here, but after your first load/use you will find the values you used the last time, or the default values of the last filter.

If you have enabled **Update**, you will be able to see the preview change as you alter the values. If this isn't enough, you can open the **Edit** folder, where you will find the mathematical expression of the filter. If you understand how Filter Factory works, you can simply edit the function.

Tip: Sometimes, the User Filter can be quite slow when you scroll the preview. A solution to this problem is to disable Update, scroll and then try the preview again.

CHAPTER 34

Glass Effect Filters

Would you like to create a fish-eye lens or make your image look like it's behind a wall of glass? Then you'll find some interesting filters here.

Apply Lens

Apply Lens places a virtual **lens** (bulb) on top of your image. If you keep the original surroundings, it will look as if you had placed a crystal ball over your image. The **Lens reflection index** controls how *fish-eyed* or spherical the lens will be.

If you set the surroundings to **Background** color, you will get the background color from the toolbox. With **Transparent** surroundings you could create images such as nice surrealist buttons for web pages.

Figure 34.1 *The result of Apply Lens*

Before

After

Conical Anamorphose and Central Reflection

The **Conical Anamorphose** and **Central Reflection** plug-ins can best be described by making a parallel to funny mirrors in an amusement park.

If we assume that the image you're working on is a picture of you, it's like having a conical/tube mirror, which you are looking into from the bottom. What you see is a highly distorted image.

Parameter Settings

Naturally, since you are looking into the mirror-tube, you can't see yourself undistorted, but if you check **Keep original surroundings**, you will be able to see yourself in the center looking into the mirror. If you'd rather fill this area with a solid color, check the **Set surroundings to background color** button. Take a look at Figure 34.2 to get an idea of how the filters work.

Original *Conical Anamorphose* *Central Reflection*

Figure 34.2 *The result of Conical Anamorphose and Central Reflection*

Other Settings

The most important parameter settings are **Radius** and **Base angle**, which control the shape of the cone/tube (there is no base angle in Central Reflection because it is a tube).

Radius controls the size of the base or circular bottom of the reflecting cone/tube. **Base angle of cone** refers to the steepness of the reflecting cone. The Base Angle must be set to a value between 0 and 90 degrees.

The image is flipped vertically by default to make the image easier to understand. If you uncheck **Flip image vertically**, you will see what you would see if you were really looking into such a mirror, but this is probably not what you want — it looks *very* weird.

We recommend using **Antialias** to prevent the image from getting *jaggy*. Check this button, and you will get a much smoother image.

ELLIPSE

Ellipse is similar to **Apply Lens**. The effect simulates refracting through an elliptical lens.

You can set the quality of the rendering both horizontally (**X-Quality**) and vertically (**Y-Quality**). Setting high render quality will produce smooth edges, but it will also be slower. If the image is rectangular and the width is greater than the height, it will render well and relatively fast with a high Y-quality and a low X-quality.

If you check the **Make Circle** checkbox, the output image will always be square, and the distorted object will be circular. Also, the specified X and Y quality values will be averaged and both values will be set to the calculated mean.

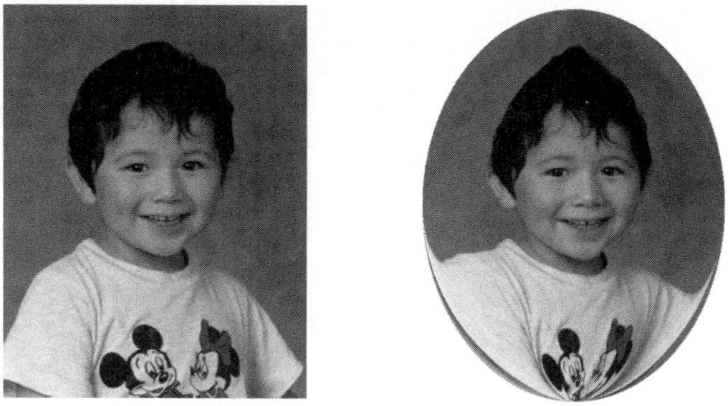

Before *After*

Figure 34.3 *The result of applying the Ellipse filter*

GLASS TILE

Glass Tile can make it look like your image is behind a *glass wall.*

You can set the **Height** and **Width** of the tiles to a value between 10 and 50 pixels. A perhaps more accurate explanation of what the filter does is that it splits your image in X*X pixel tiles, where each tile repeats a small part of the previous tile. This behavior will make it look like the object is behind a glass wall or shower curtain.

Figure 34.4 *The right side of the image was altered with Glass Tile*

RaX Structurizer

The **RaX** filter will create a *funny mirror* effect. It can also be compared to looking at a water reflection where the waves have no structure. You can control the behavior of this hallucinating effect filter by dragging the sliders.

Figure 34.5 *The right side of the image was altered with RaX*

REFRACT

The **Refract** filter will **distort** the image with an imaginary **lens**. The lens shape is determined by a second image (a map image). The side of the lens that faces the image is flat, and the side facing you is curved. The lens shape is determined by the map image. The map image should be a grayscale image. It will work with an RGB image but that will complicate things, so use a real grayscale image. There are a few parameters that you have to set to make your lens reflect the way you want.

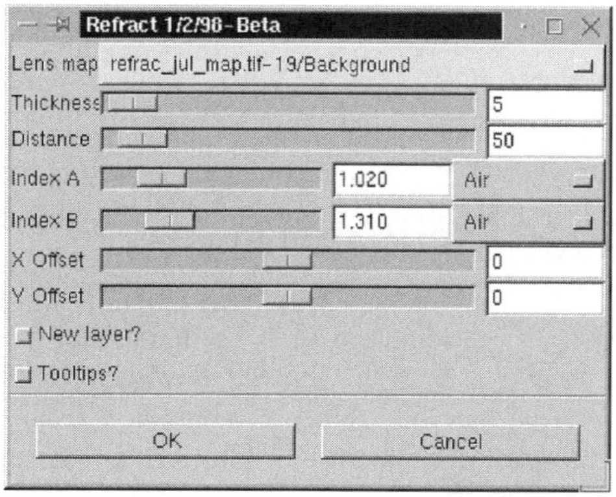

Figure 34.6 *The Refract dialog*

PARAMETERS

Depth (thickness): This slide controls the thickness of the lens. You can think of it as the thickness of a glass cylinder that we put the curved lens over. The actual lens is built up of a flat, solid cylinder that is X in thickness, and on top of that is a user-defined curved lens.

Distance: The distance between the bottom part of the lens and the image (you're holding the lens in the air and this is the distance from the image).

Index A and B: B refers to *the medium the lens is made of* (e.g., glass), and A is for *the medium you are looking through* (e.g., air). So, in order to make a lens of **ice**, set B to 1.309 and if you are looking though **air**, set A to 1.0003. If you don't want to set these figures manually, you can also pick it from the menu.

Offset: This is used to place the lens, but we think it's a lot simpler to make the map image the same size as the distort image, and make sure you place the map in the right place from the beginning.

Lens Map: You choose what map you should use as a lens in the drop-down menu. The map should be a grayscale image. **White** represents *maximal lens thickness*, and **black** represents *minimum or no thickness at all.* In order to make it appear like you're looking through a magnifying glass, create a black map image, and apply a radial black-and-white gradient to it. Figure 34.7 shows the map and the outcome after applying the filter.

Table 34.1 *Here are some values you can use to set a refraction index*

Type	Value	Type	Value
Air	1.0003	Ice	1.309
Flintglass	1.752	Zircon	1.923
Water	1.333	Ethyl alcohol	1.36
Fluorite	1.434	Rock Salt	1.544
Diamond	2.417	Crownglass	1.52
Turpentine	1.472	Glycerine	1.473

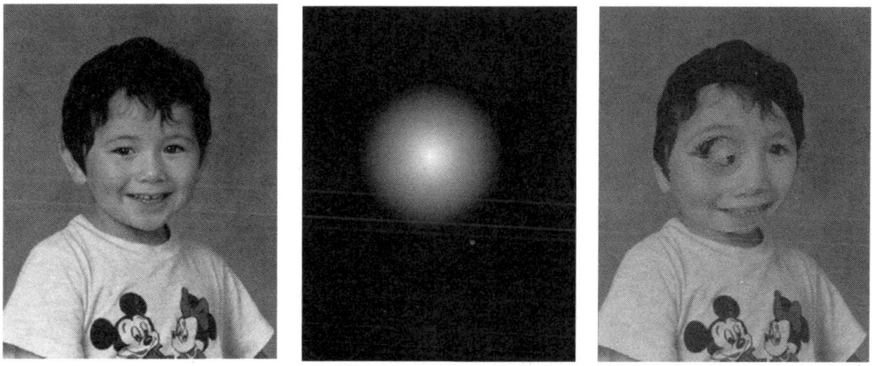

Original *Map* *Result*

Figure 34.7 *The outcome of Refract, with a circular gradient as a map image*

CHAPTER 35

Light Effect Filters

Light effects can add more than the usual flare to an image. The filters you find here are valuable accessories in your Gimp utensil kit.

FlareFX

FlareFX is a simple and well-made *lens flare* filter. It's easy to place the flare with the hair cross in the preview image, but if you need more precision, you can type the coordinates directly into the value fields.

Figure 35.1 *The FlareFX dialog*

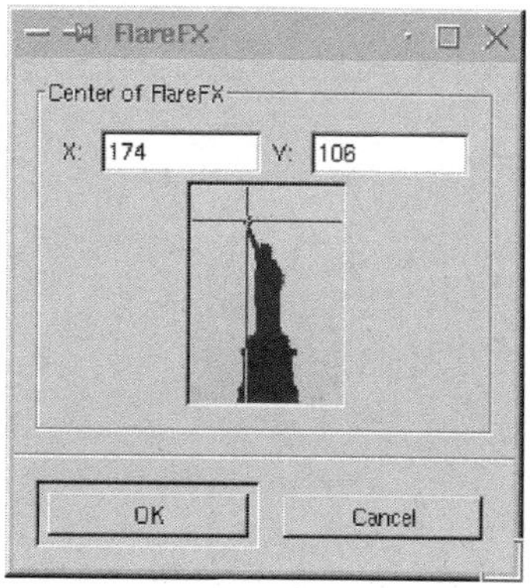

If, for example, you type 300/50, the position of the flare will be 300 pixels from the left and 50 pixels from the top of your image. (Note that you can't change the color or intensity of the flare, unless you change the parameters in the source code.)

Figure 35.2 *Before and after FlareFX was applied*

Before *After*

GFLARE

The **GFlare** filter may well be one of the most advanced flare-makers there is.

One of the best features in GFlare is that you can create different gflares for different situations, and **load** them in the **Selector** tab folder. This is also the right way to work with this plug-in.

When you need a different gflare-pattern, just copy one and edit the copy until you are satisfied. We think this is the best way to learn how to use GFlare. After that, you can learn how to use the **Settings** tab folder.

HOW TO USE GFLARE

Let's get started. Press the **Selector** tab, **copy** the default pattern and name it something appropriate in the name dialog. Then press **edit**, and a new dialog will pop up — the **GFlare Editor**.

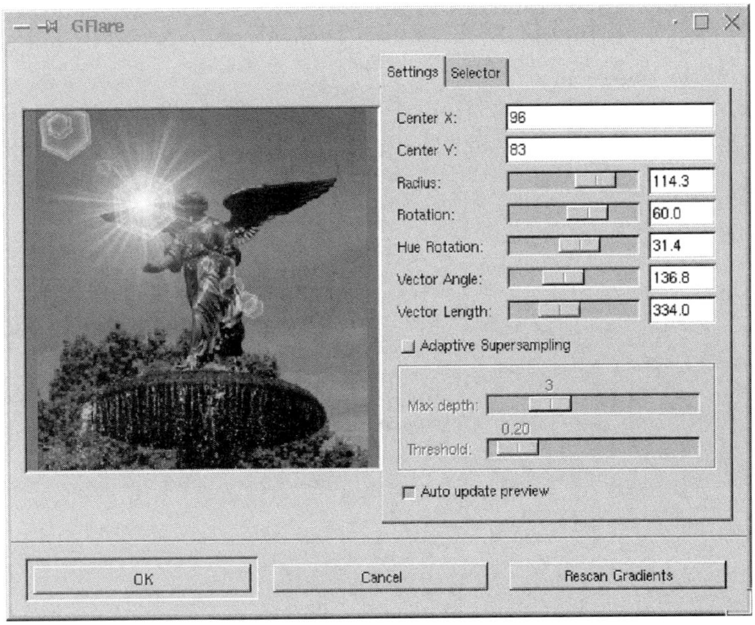

Figure 35.3 *The GFlare main window*

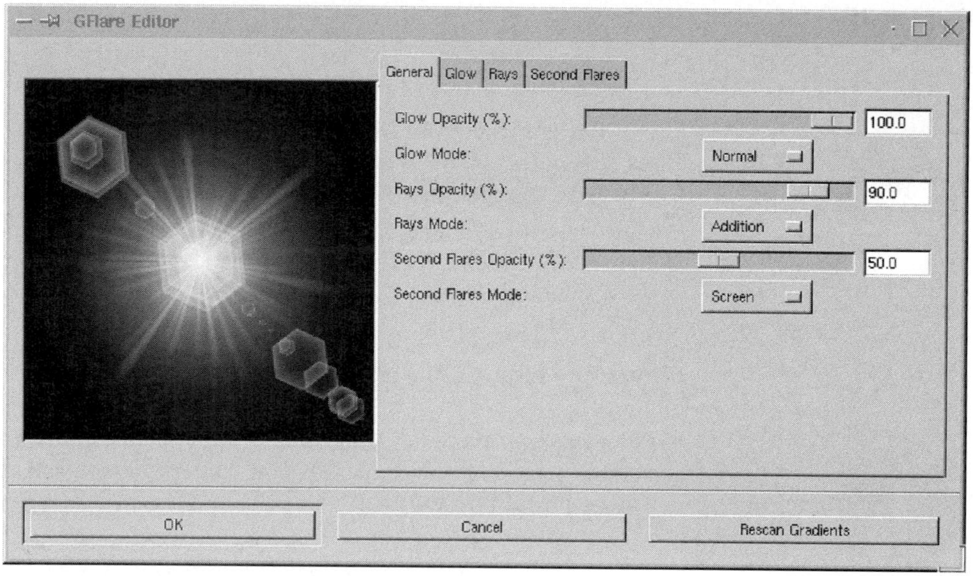

Figure 35.4 *The Main window in the GFlare*

THE GFLARE EDITOR

Here we have four tabs, where you can edit the three foundations that all gflares are based on, and a general view where you can set all possible combinations.

The three keystones of gflare are *Glow*, *Rays* and *Secondary Flares.*

Glow is the base foundation — the big fireball in the middle, **Rays** are the spikes that surround the glow, and **Secondary Flares** are the attached small novas in front and behind the central glow.

These three keystones make up the final gflare. You can see them as three separate layers, where Glow is on top, Rays is in the middle and Secondary Flares is at the bottom. In the **General** tab, you can set the **Opacity** and **Mode**, just like in ordinary layers (more information about Modes can be found in "Modes" starting on page 335).

Glow Settings

Glow has six different parameters:

- **Radial gradient:** Controls what color, shape and tone the glow will get from the center to the edge.
- **Angular Gradient:** Controls the circular color, shape and tone. If the **Rotation** option is set to 0, it will start at three o'clock and go counterclockwise. For example, if the Angular gradient fades out to transparency, the glow will also fade out (see Figure 35.6)
- The Radial and Angular Gradients are **multiplied** (see "Modes" starting on page 335) and the result is the final glow color.

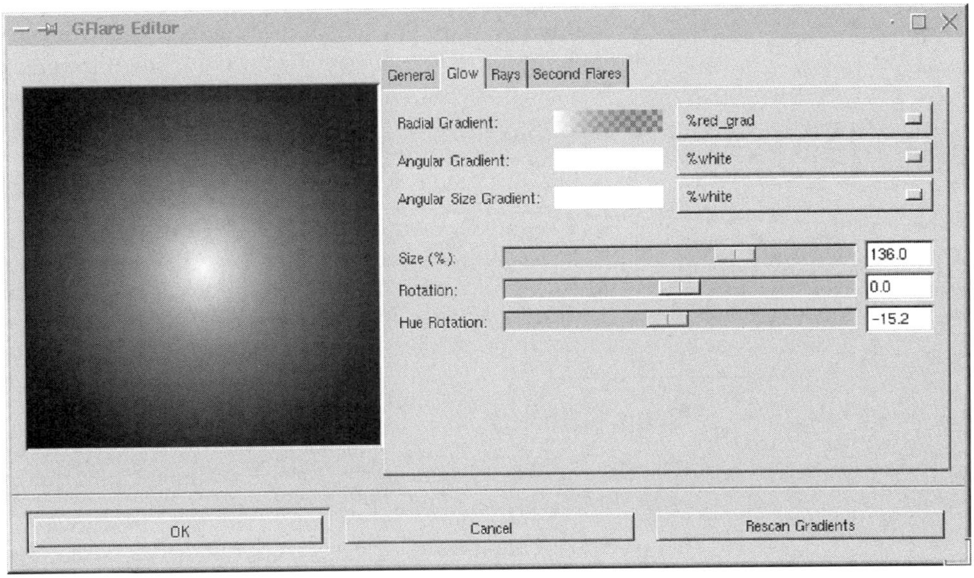

Figure 35.5 *Radial Gradient in the Glow tab*

Figure 35.6 *Angular Gradient in the Glow tab*

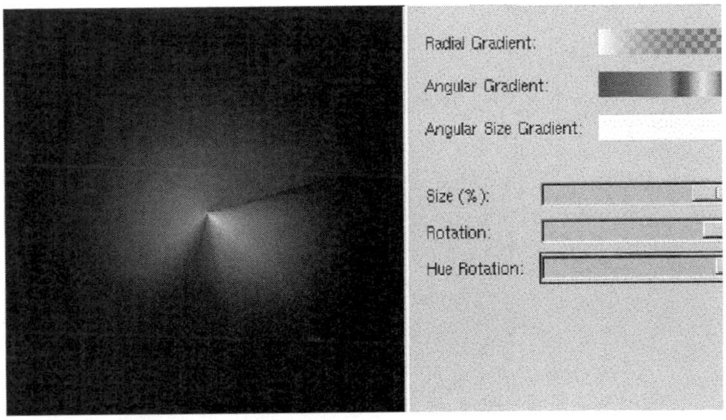

Figure 35.7 *The Angular Size Gradient*

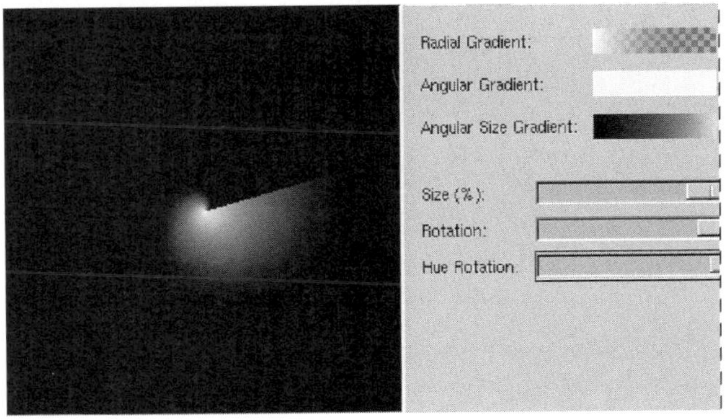

- **Angular Size Gradient:** Controls the size of the **radius**. It also starts at three o'clock, and goes counterclockwise.The radius depends on the **luminosity** of the gradient. If the "color" is black, the radius is 0%, and if the "color" is white, the radius is 100%. So, if the gradient goes from white to black, the radius will diminish as you move.
- **Size:** Controls the size in %.
- **Rotation:** Controls where the Angular Size Gradient starts in degrees.
- **Hue Rotation:** Controls the color of the whole glow. To understand the **HUE** color circle, read "HSV" on page 191. Note, the gradients starting with a "%" are internal gradients for the editor; the rest come from the gradient directories. You can add a gradient even when you're inside the editor. To do so, press **Rescan Gradients** to make it available.

Rays Settings

The Rays tab has the same controls as *Glow Settings*, plus two additional parameters: **# of Spikes** and **Spike Thickness**.

- **Spike Thickness:** Obviously controls the volume of the spikes.
- **# of Spikes:** Controls the amount of spikes, but this is not the whole truth. Technically, it determines how *dense* or *sparse* the "spikeflower" will be.

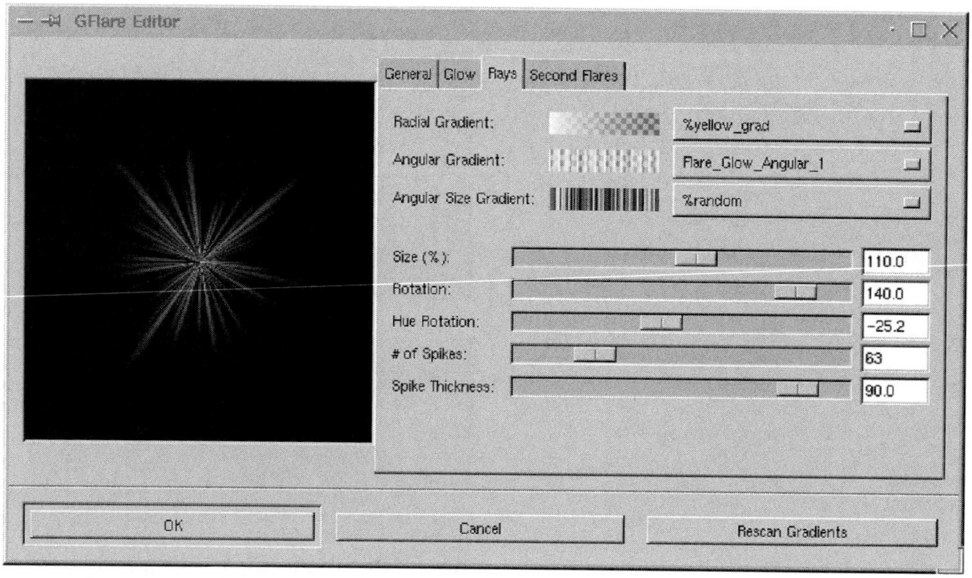

Figure 35.8 *The Rays tab in the GFlare Editor*

Second Flares Settings

The Second Flares tab has the same parameters as described in *Glow Settings*, plus two additional controls: **Shape of Second Flares** and **Random Seed**.

- **Shape of Second Flares:** Enables you to control the shape of the flares by choosing **circular** or **polygonal**. You can choose how many sides you want for your polygon, but if you choose a value of 30 or more, it will be the same as a circle.
- **Random Seed:** Controls how many flares there will be and where they'll be placed. If you set random seed to "1" you will use the current time as the seed value. This means that you will get a random number and location of flares each time you use the GFlare-pattern.

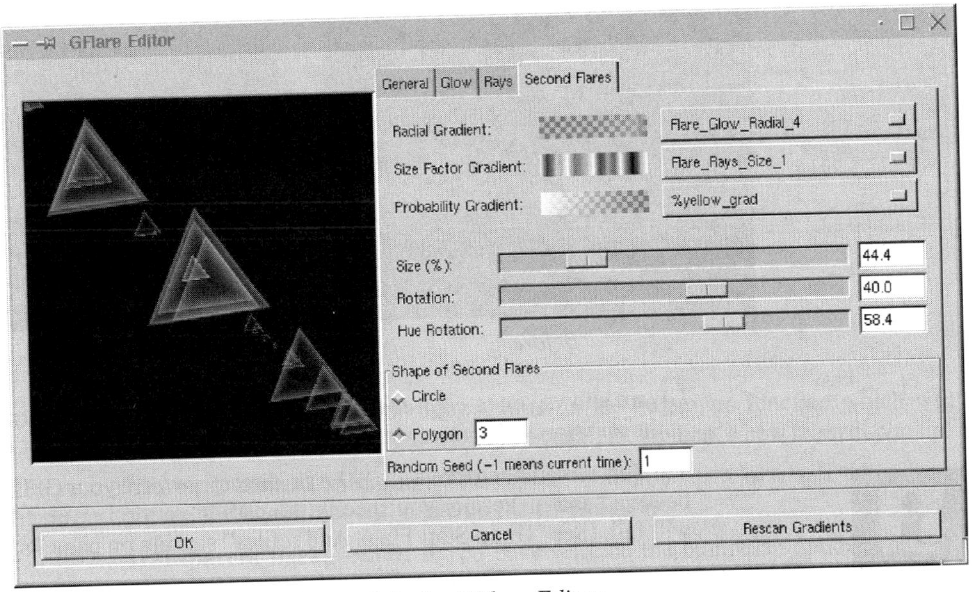

Figure 35.9 *The Second Flares tab in the GFlare Editor*

BACK TO THE MAIN WINDOW

Hopefully, you have now created a nice GFlare-pattern, so let's see what we can do with it in the Main dialog. Just press OK, and then click on the **Settings** tab.

To place a GFlare, just click at the place you want to put it in the preview window, and remember to have **Auto update preview** checked; otherwise, you won't see what you are doing. (You can also type the coordinates in the X and Y fields.)

- **Radius:** Controls the size of the GFlare.
- **Rotation:** The angle of the GFlare, and it corresponds to the angle of the Gflare keystones.

SUPER NOVA

The **Super Nova** plug-in creates a big shiny *super nova* in your image. The **R**,**G** and **B** slides determine the color of the super nova. You specify the color just like in the Color Selection dialog (which you access by clicking in one of the color swatches in the toolbox).

Figure 35.24 *The Super Nova dialog*

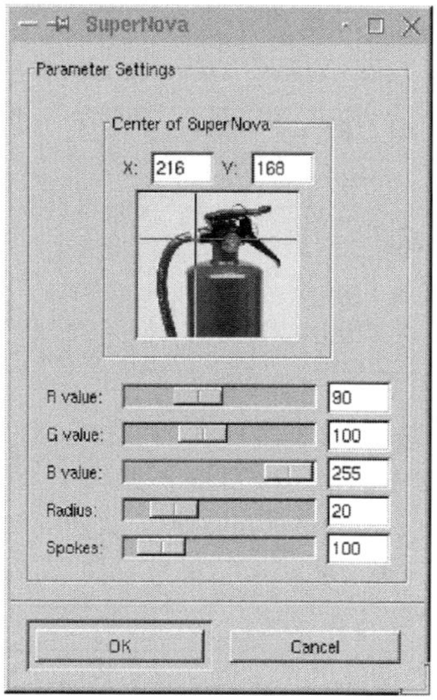

The problem is that you can't see what the color looks like until you apply the plug-in. We suggest that you open the color dialog and choose a color there. When you're happy with the color, type those RGB values in the Super Nova dialog. **Radius** is the radius of the inner part of the nova (the star part). **Spokes** determines how many spokes the nova will get. You place the nova with the cursor grid in the **preview** image (you can also type the coordinates in the X and Y input fields).

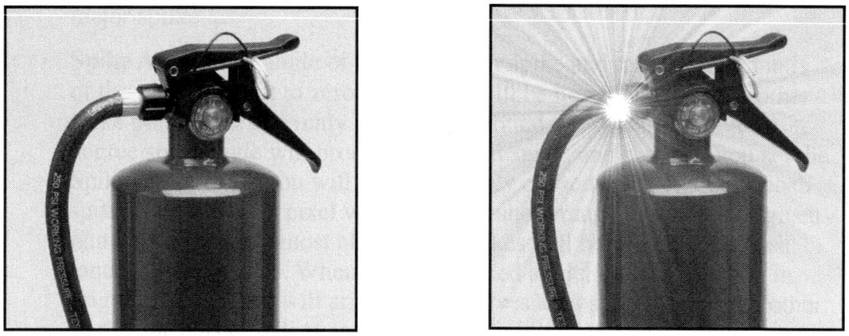

Figure 35.25 *Before and after Super Nova*

CHAPTER 36

Map Filters

There are many ways to use maps. If you want to bend text along a curve, you have to use a displacement map. To create 3-D effects you use a bumpmap. All of the Gimp map filters will be discussed in this chapter.

BUMP MAP

Bump Map works by *embossing* an image, and *mapping* this relief to another image. This will create a 3-D effect in the second image, just as if you had modeled it in clay.

BUMP MAP AND EMBOSS

First read about **Emboss** in "Distort Filters" starting on page 459 to understand the concepts of **Azimuth**, **Evaluation** and **Depth**.

There are many differences between Bump Map and the bumpmap option in the Emboss plug-in. First of all, in **Emboss bumpmap**, you can't specify a map image (see map image in Figure 36.2).

The Bump Map plug-in has more options than Emboss, and you can bumpmap any type of image. Emboss only works for RGB images without alpha.

Figure 36.1 *The Bump Map dialog*

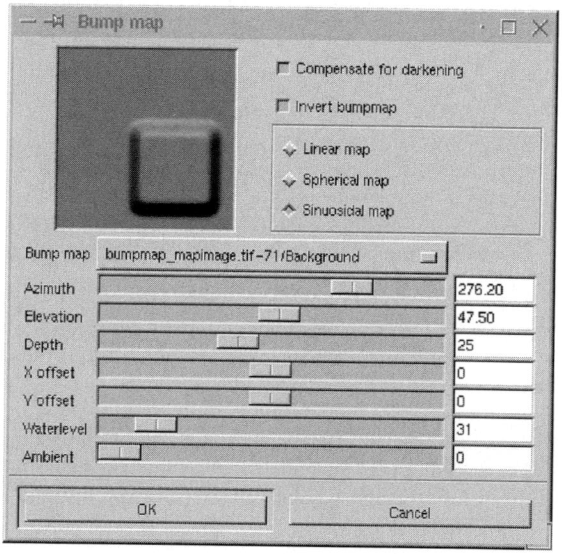

HOW TO USE BUMP MAP

Because you can bumpmap any image, you may have to adjust the position of the background bumpmap. To do so, use the **X** and **Y offset** slides. You may also want to compensate for the loss of luminance resulting from embossing by using the **Compensate for darkening** button. Because Emboss raises light pixels and carves dark pixels, it's quite simple to reverse so that otherwise dark and carved parts of your map will turn light and raised. To achieve this, check **Invert bumpmap**.

Figure 36.2 *An image and a map image are the two elements necessary to create a bumpmap*

Image to bumpmap

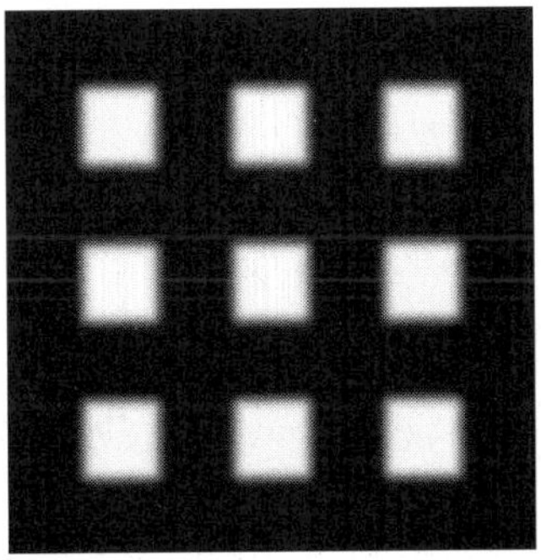

Map image

Result

The **Ambient** slide controls the amount of ambient light in your image. A high level of ambient light will make all shadows disappear, and the raised and carved parts will be less apparent.

Waterlevel only becomes relevant if there are **alpha values** or transparency in the map image. Transparent pixels in a map image will be treated as dark pixels, and therefore become carved. If you slide the Waterlevel up to 255, the transparent pixels will be flattened and turn invisible, just as if you had raised the water level in a pond.

If you check the **Invert bumpmap** radio button, they will be treated as light pixels and get raised, but Waterlevel will flatten that, too.

Linear map, **Spherical map** and **Sinusoidal map** are the three bumpmap types used to create a 3-D model. Figure 36.3 shows the relationship between different map modes, and how they raise/carve in relation to the luminance of the pixels.

Linear Map

Spherical Map

Sinusoidal Map

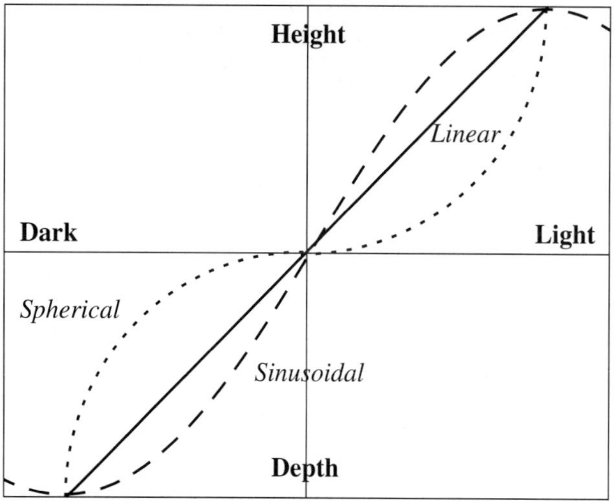

Figure 36.3 *These images illustrate the difference between the three map types*

Coordinate Map

The **Coordinate Map** filter does the same thing as the **Displace** filter (described in the next section). The creator of this filter writes that Coordinate Map is easier to use, and maybe he's right — you will have to try it for yourself. There is one limitation though, *it will only work with 256x256 pixel images.*

Here is how it works: The plug-in will map two images (one in the horizontal direction, and one in the vertical direction) on a **source** image. The source image will get the architecture from the **map** images. Read about the *Displace* filter and you will understand the Coordinate Map filter, too.

Displace

Displace is a general distort filter, which can be used for nearly all kinds of distortion. You can, for example, use it to *whirl*, *pinch*, *shift*, *spread* or *melt* your image. We will try to give you a short introduction to the hidden secrets of this filter.

Figure 36.4 *A text string was displaced along the roof line of the Chevelle*

How Does It Work?

It is clear that this filter will **displace** an image or part of an image; the question is how? To put it simply, the Displace filter needs a **displacement map** to tell it how to distort the image. The brightness or darkness values in this map control how Displace moves the image pixels. To make displacement easy, always use **grayscale** images as maps. It will work with colored images too, but as displacement depends on the brightness/darkness of the map, the color information is simply not used.

Summary

- Use grayscale images as displacement maps.
- The amount of displacement is based on the brightness/darkness of the map.

Calculations

As we know from earlier chapters, you can use 256 shades of gray in a grayscale image. How bright or dark a gray "color" is depends on the **Intensity** value, which goes from 1 (black) to 256 (white). In the middle of this range we find "medium gray," with a value of 128.

One of the fundamental parts of displacement is that the "dark values" 0 to 127 will be displaced in one direction, the "medium gray" value 128 will not be displaced at all, and the "light values" 129 to 256 will be displaced in the opposite direction of the dark values.

To make things easier we can put this range in a new perspective. If you think of -128 as total darkness, 0 as medium gray and +128 as total lightness, it becomes more clear that displacement will go in different directions, because we have negative and positive intensity in our map. The maximum displacement in either direction happens where the map has a value of either -128 or +128.

Summary

- Displacement is based on a brightness/darkness scale, ranging from -128 to +128.
- There will be no displacement where the value is 0.
- The displacement goes in two directions. Negative values displace in one direction, and positive values displace in the opposite direction.

The User Interface

Let's take a closer look at the user interface. As you can see, you can displace in both X and Y directions. You can also set how much you want to displace, and which map to use. To make it easy to understand, we will stick with only one direction (X in this case).

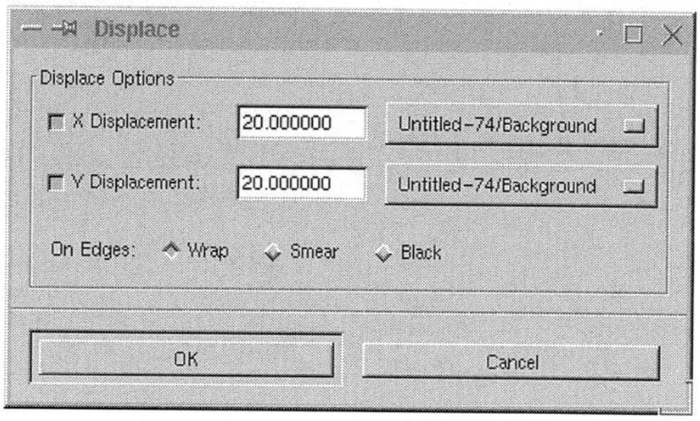

Figure 36.5 *The Displace dialog*

The first thing you have to do is create or open the image to be displaced. (We will render a grid system so you can see what's happening.)

The second thing you have to do is make a displacement map. The easiest way to do this is to duplicate your image (`right-click|Image|Channel Ops|Duplicate` or use the shortcut Ctrl+d), because the map must have the same size or proportions as the image you want to displace.

Convert the duplicate to grayscale (`right-click|Image|Grayscale`) and clear it (`right-click|Edit|Clear`).

Summary

- The map must have the same proportions as the image or selection that is going to be displaced.

Example 1: Basic Displacing

1. To make it easy, copy, grayscale and clear the image that is going to be displaced, and use that as the base for a map. Now, bring up the Displacement plug-in from the image that is going to be displaced.
2. Uncheck "Y", make sure that "X" is checked and check Black.
3. Set the X displacement to 50, and bring up the map image.
4. Fill the map with white (+128), choose the name of the map image in the displacement dialog and press OK. The image has now been displaced 50 pixels to the left, as shown in Figure 36.6.

Figure 36.6 *This image was displaced 50 pixels to the left*

5. Now press Ctrl+z and do it again, but this time with a map that is totally black (-128). The image has now been displaced 50 pixels to the right, as shown in Figure 36.7.

Figure 36.7 *This image was displaced 50 pixels to the right*

6. Let's do this with a map with a value of +64 (a gray with the Intensity value 191). This will displace the image 25 pixels to the left because (64 x 50)/128 is 25, which leads to the following algorithm: (value (of gray) x (displacement value))/128 equals the amount of displacement (Figure 36.8).

Figure 36.8 *This image was displaced 25 pixels to the left*

7. Positive values will displace to the left, and negative to the right. More examples: Gray value: -64 (dark) Displacement value: +50 -> (-64 x 50)/128 = -25 -> 25 pixels displacement to the right. Gray value: +64 and Displacement value: -50 -> (64 x -50)/128 = -25 -> 25 pixels displacement to the right.

Summary

- If you have positive "X" displacement values, a bright map will displace to the left and a dark to the right.
- The amount of displacement is based on this algorithm: (value x displacement)/128 = displacement in pixels, positive to the left and negative to the right.
- The above is also true for Y direction displacement, you just have to switch left to top and black to bottom.
- If you have positive "Y" displacement values, a bright map will displace to the top of the image and a dark to the bottom of the image.
- The amount of displacement is based on this algorithm: (value x displacement)/128 = displacement in pixels, positive to the top and negative to the bottom.

Example 2: Displacing In Two Directions

Now we move to more complex displacement. As you see in the dialog, you can displace in both **X** and **Y** directions. This means that you can, for example, displace the image towards the bottom-left corner. To achieve this, you have to make **two maps**, one white and one black. Map the black one to Y and the white one to X. Your image will now be displaced toward the bottom-left corner (Figure 36.9).

Figure 36.9 *This image was displaced both vertically and horizontally*

Examples 3 And 4: Spreading And Curving

We said earlier that you can achieve any kind of distortment with this plug-in, so we will give you two more examples:

Spread horizontal: Create a map made of horizontal black, white and gray stripes. The different intensities of the stripes will make the displaced image look as if you have spread it in horizontal ribbons. You have to experiment by yourself to figure out what you can do, but trust us — you can do a lot with this plug-in.

Curving Text: The obvious example is to bend text over something circular, such as a terrestrial globe. To achieve that, you'll have to create a suitable gradient (dark at both ends and light in the middle) with the **Gradient Editor**. In Figure 36.10 we have created a displacement map that will make the text flow around the shape of the car.

Figure 36.10 *How to make a text bend along a curve*

This practical example explains the theory of basic displacement pretty well

A two-layered image: the Chevelle in the background layer and the text in layer one

The Y displacement map

The final outcome after a few calculations

Using Transparency In Map Images

Sometimes, it's hard to create the kind of map you want, for example, when you only want to displace part of your image. When you experiment with different maps, you'll often want to darken/lighten them, but this will inevitably alter the medium gray value.

The perfect 0 will be transformed to something that will displace your image. The way to get around this problem is to make the static parts of your map **transparent**, because fully transparent pixels are treated as if they had a value of 0. Black pixels, which are (almost) transparent, are treated as having a value of a bit under 0, or somewhere around (-5). The same goes for semi-transparent white pixels, but they will get a positive value around (+5), so **alpha values** should play a very important part in your map making.

What Are Black, Smear And Wrap Good For?

Say that you're using a white map, a displace value of 50 and that you only want to displace in the X direction. When the image is displaced 50 pixels to the left, there will be 50 pixels *missing* at the right side of the image.

If you check **Black**, a black color will fill this part for you. If you check **Smear**, those 50 pixels will be stretched from the right part of the image. If you press **Wrap**, the 50 pixels you pushed out of the frame at the left side will appear at the right side of the image to cover for the missing pixels.

Figure 36.11 *The difference between Smear and Wrap*

Smear

Wrap

How To Calculate Where A Pixel Will End Up

Let's choose a pixel that is positioned at 50(x) and 50(y) in the image coordinate system.We go to our **maps** and check the **Intensity** value of the equivalent pixel in that position. In this case we presume that the Intensity value we got from map X (the horizontal displacement map) was 230, which means (230 - 128) = 102 in the displacement range. Map Y (the vertical displacement map) had an Intensity value of 55, which means (55 - 128) = -73 in the displacement range. We also choose a displacement value of 50 for X and 30 for Y. If we put these values in our algorithm.

- (102 x 50)/128 = 39.84, which is the displacement of map X (the pixel will displace 40 pixels to the left).
- (-73 x 30)/128 = -17.11, which is the displacement of map Y (the pixel will displace 17 pixels downwards).

These calculations tell us that our pixel will end up at x=10 and y=67, i.e., the pixel will be moved a bit closer to the bottom-left corner.

FRACTAL TRACE

Fractal Trace distorts your image using a **Mandelbrot** fractal. It does this by mapping your image to the fractal, as in Figure 36.12

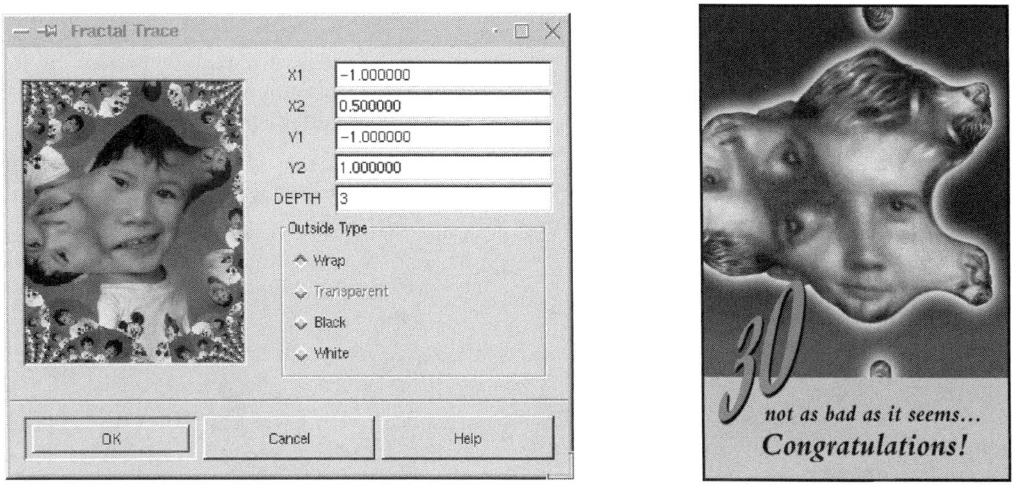

Figure 36.12 *The Fractal Trace dialog and an example of how the filter can be used*

FRACTAL TRACE AND FRACTAL EXPLORER

Five parameters control the Mandelbrot fractal; **X1**, **X2**, **Y1**, **Y2** and **DEPTH**. For a better understanding of these parameters, read about fractals in "Fractal Explorer" on page 595.

X(Y)1 and X(Y)2 correspond to the X(Y)min and X(Y)max parameters in the main Fractal Explorer dialog, and DEPTH is the same as the ITER(ations) parameter.

Note that the default value for DEPTH (3) is much lower in the Fractal Trace dialog than the default value for ITER in the Fractal Explorer dialog (50). If you increase the depth value, you'll map your image to a classic fractal shape, but this will yield less spectacular effects than using lower values (the opposite is true for Fractal Explorer).

OUTSIDE TYPE

This option lets you choose between four different backgrounds to cover up parts that were displaced by the fractal mapping. This works the same as the **On Edges** option in the **Displace** filter; read more about it in "What Are Black, Smear And Wrap Good For?" on page 548.

Note that to be able to use the **Transparent** option, you have to have an *alpha enabled* image. To make it so, select `right-click|Layers|Add Alpha Channel` before applying the Fractal Trace filter.

Illusion

Illusion duplicates your image (x) times, and puts them in a circle around the center of the original image. The surrounding images are superimposed on the original, so it looks a bit blurry or ghostlike.

The only option in this filter is how many (x) copies you want to apply to your image. Another word for this filter is **kaleidoscope,** which is a quite accurate description of what it does.

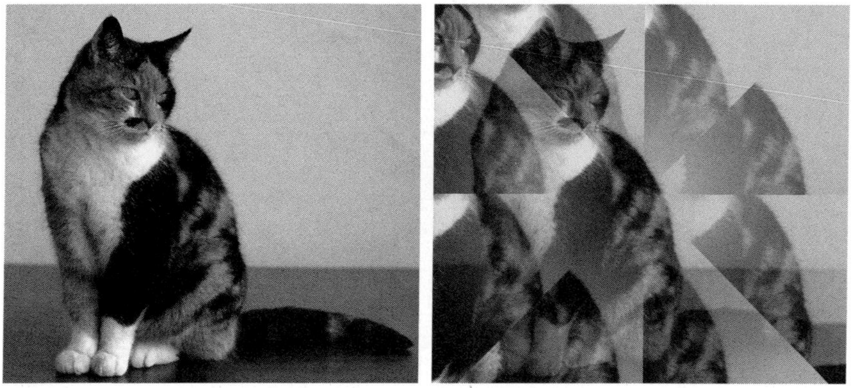

Before *After*

Figure 36.13 *The kaleidoscope effect that Illusion produces was used to illustrate the nine lives of this cat*

Make Seamless

The **Make Seamless** plug-in prepares an image for **tiling** by creating seamless edges. This filter does away with all those ugly edges, and it's an easy way to create good-looking patterns.

If you want to create a **seamless pattern** as a background for your desktop or in a web page, this is (often) the best tool to use. Note that the center of the original image will constitute the only focused part of the new image. Mirrors of the original image are placed in the center and in all four corners of the seamless image, and those mirrors blend together at the edges, causing it to look a bit blurred or double-exposed in those areas.

If an important part of your image (like a face) is somewhere other than in the middle, you may have to do some correction work by copying parts of the original image and pasting them into the seamless image. If you feel that the result of this filter is too soft or blurred, try to correct your image with the **Offset** command in the Image menu. Read more about it in "Offset" on page 294.

Figure 36.14 *These examples show the difference between tiling a pattern with and without Make Seamless*

MAP OBJECT

The **Map Object** filter will map your image to a **sphere**, a **plane**, a **box** or a **cylinder**. You can also apply different **lighting effects** to the mapped object to make it even more convincing.

You can even specify the properties of the "material" in the mapped object by changing the values for intensity and reflectivity. This is a very nice plug-in for creating 3-D-effects in Gimp. You can, for example, create a perfect soccer ball. There are, of course, many more applications for this excellent plug-in — the only limit is your imagination.

MAIN INTERFACE

In the main interface there is a **preview** window and tab for **Options**, **Light**, **Material** and **Orientation**. To be able to see what you're doing, you must first press the Preview button (there's no auto-preview because that would slow things down).

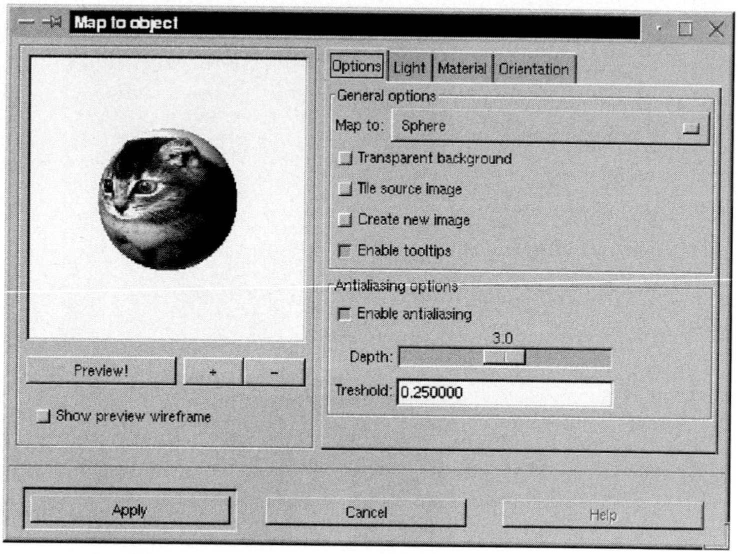

Figure 36.15 *Map Object's main dialog*

It is a good idea to use **Show preview wireframe**. Then, your object will be displayed as a wireframe, and you can see your actions take place in realtime. Whenever you need to take a good look, just press **Preview**. You can also **zoom** the preview by pressing **+** or **-**.

Options

You can choose to map to a **plane**, a **sphere**, a **box** or a **cylinder**. If you choose to map your image to a box or a cylinder, a new tab will appear called **Box and Cylinder**. See "Box And Cylinder" on page 557 for information on this folder.

- **Transparent background** results in a transparent surrounding (the drawable will turn transparent outside of the object).
- **Tile source image** means that the source image will be repeated or tiled to extend the map object (plane) into infinity. For example, if you map to a plane and this plane is tilted in some direction, there will be a lot of space around the output image. Instead of having this space filled by a background color or transparency, the plane will tile itself, filling the entire output image.
- **Create new image** preserves the original image, creating a duplicate image where the filter takes effect.
- **Enable tooltips** is a nice option. When you get to know the filter and already know what the tooltips are all about, you can disable the tooltip messages by unchecking this option.
- The **Enable Antialiasing** option enables you to turn antialiasing on or off, but we recommend you use it; otherwise, the images will look very jagged and ugly (there can of course be moments when a non-antialiased image can be useful). **Depth** refers to the amount of antialiasing — the

higher the value, the better the antialiasing, but it will also be slower. **Threshold** determines the limit of antialiasing, the process is interrupted when the difference between pixels is lower than the value in the input field.

Figure 36.16 *The Map Object filter offers a variety of 3-D objects for mapping your image. You only have to take a look at these examples to realize that you can create awesome images with this filter.*

Original

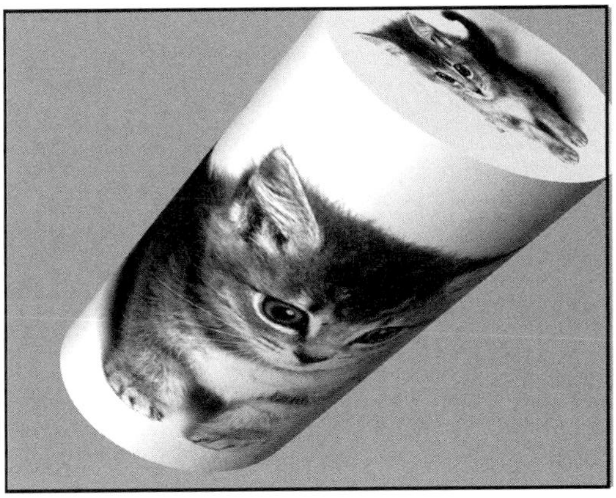

Cylinder

Box

Plane

Sphere

LIGHT

You can set the **type** of light, the light **color** and the **position** of the light source, and if you have chosen **Directional Light**, you can also set the **angle** of the light source.

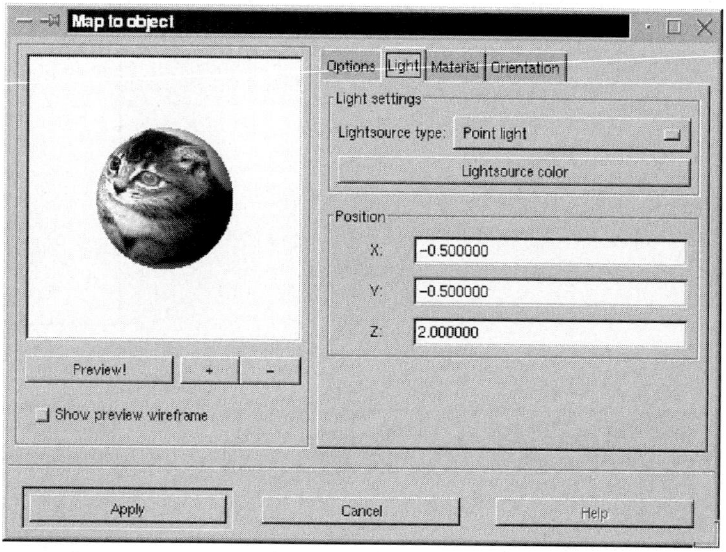

Figure 36.17 *The Light tab*

Light Settings

Point light is a sort of spotlight which shines straight onto your image. **Directional light** is a softer point light (more like a normal lamp in the ceiling). To set the color of the light, simply press **Lightsource Color**.

There are three coordinates for positioning point light: X,Y and Z. The X coordinate moves horizontally from -0.5 to 1.5, where -0.5 is the left-hand position, and 1.5 is the right-hand one. The same goes for Y; -0.5 is at the top and 1.5 is at the bottom. Z is the depth of the light, where 0 would be the flat surface of the computer monitor.

There is no upper limit for this coordinate, but if you exceed a value of 5, a little **blue dot** shows up on the image. You can grab this dot with the cursor and change the position of the light source by dragging (there are no limits for X and Y either — the values are only recommendations from our side).

MATERIAL

You can control different materials' **Intensity** and **Reflectivity**. The little spheres represent the *properties* of the material. Low values make the material look like the left sphere and high values make it look like the sphere to the right.

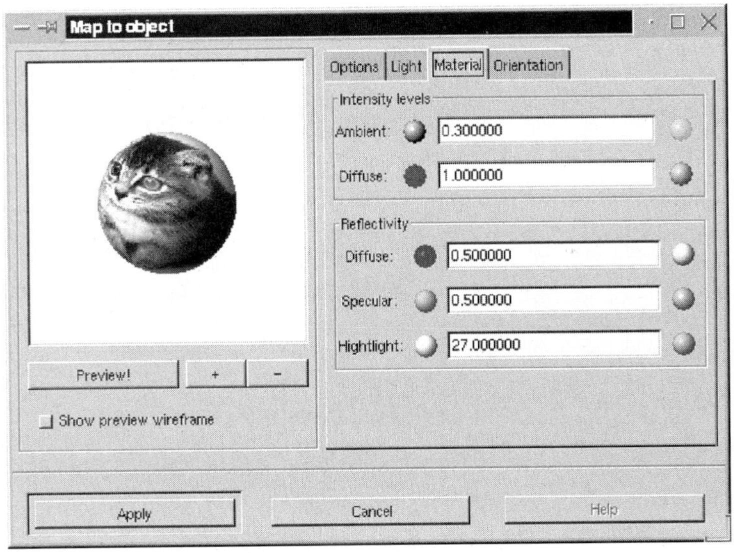

Figure 36.18 *The Material tab*

The values specified at the end of each of the following paragraphs are suggested max/min values.

Intensity Levels

- **Ambient** can be described as the intensity of the surrounding light that shines on the object. The brightest areas will not change intensity, but darker areas will get lighter as you increase this value. Think of your holiday snapshots, where very intense sunlight will produce bright and contourless features with very pale shadows *(0.1 -> 3.0)*.
- **Diffuse** can be described as the intensity of the directional light that shines on the object. The darkest (shadow) areas of the object never get darker, but brighter areas turn brighter as you increase the Diffuse value. This is like the difference between cloud shadow and sunlight, or between a dull and a shiny object *(0.5 -> 3.0)*.

Reflectivity

- **Diffuse** controls the contrast and distribution of light between the object and the reflection highlight. The mid-values are affected with this parameter. The glossier an object is, the darker the mid-values will be, because the contrast with the highlight spot will be greater. A dull/plastic object will have little highlight contrast in real life, so don't set this value high if that is the effect you want to achieve *(0.2 -> 0.9 with a nice value around 0.5)*.

- **Specular** controls the brightest values, or the sharpness/softness of the highlight, because a brighter highlight will have greater contrast to the mid-values. A glossy/metallic object will have bright highlights with sharper edges, and dull objects will have a dull, if any, highlight with soft, blurry edges *(0.4 -> 0.6).*
- **Highlight** controls the size of the highlight by changing the relation between the brightest/darkest areas and the mid-values. Higher values will make the highlight smaller, with a smoother mid-value distribution. Lower values will make it larger, and the darkest shadow areas will also be larger, which means that the transition from bright to dark will be more abrupt *(15 -> 50, but around 20 -> 30 is the best).*

ORIENTATION

The best way to understand this tab is to bring up the **wireframe preview** and play around. It will take you less than a minute to learn it.

X, Y and Z pos. move the drawable, just like **Offset** in the **Image menu**. The option name stands for the position of the center of the image.

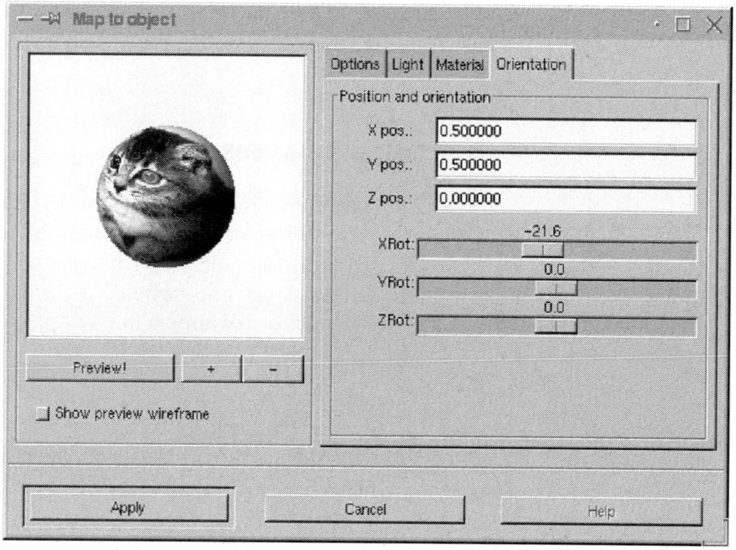

Figure 36.19 *The Orientation tab*

The default center value of the X and Y directions is 0.5.

For the Z direction, 0 is the center value (1 is maximal zoom, and negative values is "away from you") there is no limit for the negative scale (but for values under -60 you will probably not see anything).

XY controls the **Y** rotation around the **Z** axis, **YZ** controls the **Z** rotation around the **Y** axis and **XZ** controls the **Z** rotation around the **X** axis.

Box And Cylinder

This tab is only available if you choose to map against a **box** or **cylinder**. There are several drop-down menus where you can choose a different image for each side of the box, or top/bottom the cylinder. This makes it quite easy to design a very nice box that will look like a real package. For example, with a different end cap on the cylinder, you can create a telescope.

Figure 36.20 *The Box and Cylinder dialogs. It's very easy to design your own product package, because you can specify each side of the box or cylinder.*

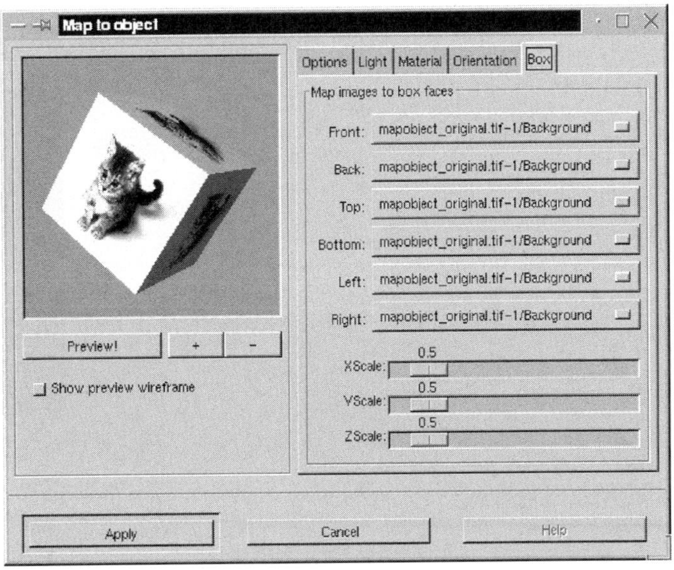

Box

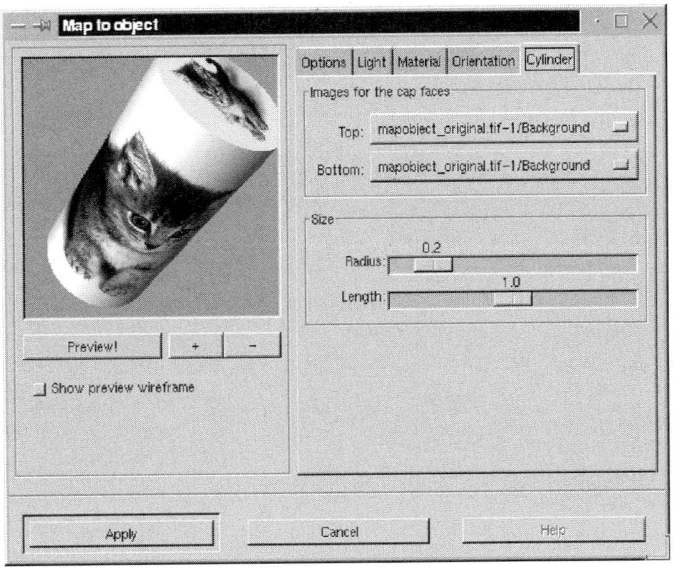

Cylinder

Paper Tile

Paper Tile makes your image look like it has been cut into small paper tiles, and then put together in a rather sloppy way, so that a variable gap is formed between each paper tile.

This filter is easy to use, and there are only a few options. You set the **size** and **shape** of the tiles (in pixels) with the width and height slide bars. **Slide** determines the size of the largest gap (also measured in pixels), and you can choose between a black or white background.

Figure 36.21 *The right part of the image was altered with Paper Tile*

Small Tiles

Small Tiles creates a tiled pattern, just as **Tile** does (see the next section), but it tiles the image within its original size, so the tiled pictures will get smaller.

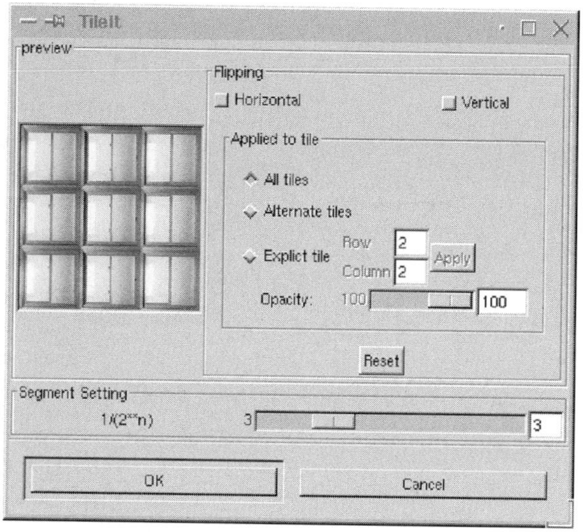

Figure 36.22 *The Small Tiles dialog*

Parameter Settings

The **Segment** setting slider controls how many segments/tiles that will be rendered. To create a more convincing pattern, you can also **flip** tiles both vertically and horizontally. You can flip a single tile with **Explicit tile**, but you have to press **Apply** to execute the flip. You can also flip every odd tile (counting from the left) with **Alternate tiles**. If you check **All tiles** the flip will affect all tiles.

If your image has an **alpha channel**, you can also set the opacity of your tile.

Before *After*

Figure 36.23 *Small Tiles will tile your image within the original image size. The tiles will thereby become smaller that the original image.*

TILE

Tile will tile your image according to the size you set *(but the new size must be larger than the old for this to work).* We recommend that you check the **New Image** checkbox, because this will leave the original image intact. **New Image** will create a new, tiled image.

An example may clarify how it works: Say that you have a 287x425 pixel image. If you set the new size to 574x850 you will get four original images in the new image. **Constrain Ratio** makes it easier to make "cleanly" tiled images.

Before

After

Figure 36.24 *You must enlarge the original image with Tile because the tiles have the same size as the source image*

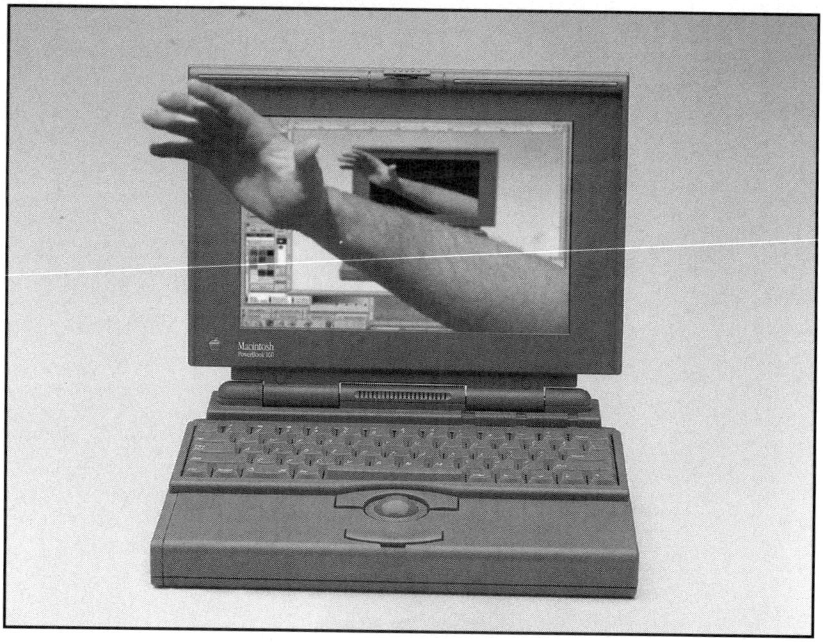
Macintosh
PowerBook 160

CHAPTER 37

Miscellaneous Filters

Assorted candy...here are all the filters that don't fit anywhere else. You can find filters for things like making stereographic images here. But most importantly, you'll find the ImageMap filter that targets web site creators.

DIFF

If you want to see the difference between the original image and the version that you are working on now, this is the filter to use. **Diff** is very simple to use. First, you specify the *before* and *after* images. Then, you specify how the difference should be displayed.

You can also select the **Output Type**; either New image, New layer in the present image or on the image that you invoked the filter from (but this will destroy the image).

Diff Methods

- **Subtract:** Shows the difference value of the pixels that have been altered, exactly like the Difference Mode does *(not the Subtract Mode).*
- **Paint unchanged:** Paints a mask over pixels that haven't been altered, so that only the changed parts are visible.
- **Paint changed:** Paints changed pixels, so that only the unchanged parts are displayed.
- **Two tone:** Paints changed pixels with the background color in the toolbox and unchanged pixels with the foreground color in the toolbox.

Figure 37.1 *These images clearly show the difference between the four Diff methods.*

They also seem to show that smoking makes you look older....

Original image

Manipulated image

Paint Changes

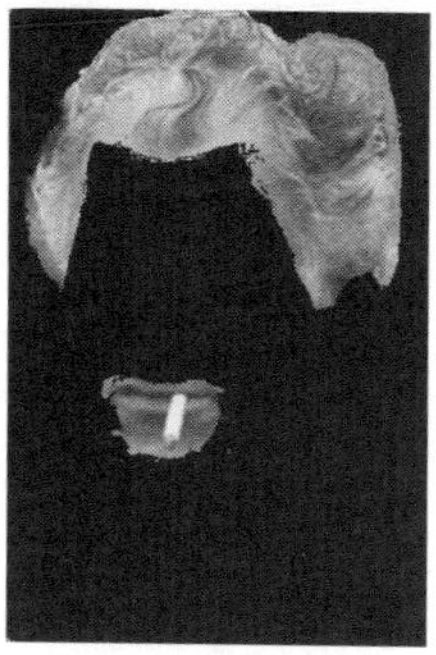

Paint Unchanged

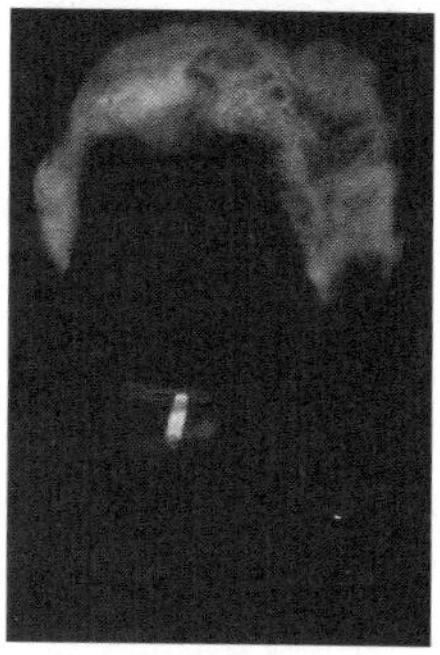

Subtract

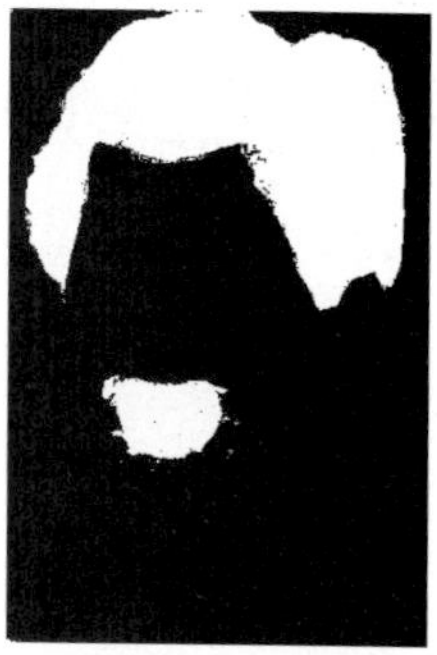

Two tone

ImageMap

Gimp's ultimate tool for **Imagemap** creation. Imagemaps are common items on web pages. You'll find them in navigation bars, where you click on different areas in the image to navigate with your browser.

The clickable areas in a navigation bar must be defined. This usually has to be done in a separate program like **MapEdit**, unless you do it manually. ImageMap integrates an imagemap editor into Gimp so you will never need to launch a different program.

How To Use ImageMap

Let's take a look at an example. This is a title bar for the "Fashion Clothing" company. The retro-styled navigation bar was created in Gimp with the help of **Gfig**, **Dynamic Text** in the `Filters|Render` menu and some photo stock images.

Figure 37.2 *We will use this image as a clickable imagemap in our web page*

The ImageMap Interface

Flatten (`right-click|Layers|Flatten Image`) and save your image in an appropriate graphic format (JPEG, PNG or GIF). If you save it as a GIF you must revert it to RGB mode before applying the filter. Invoke the filter **ImageMap** will now start.

The four blue buttons to the left are the main creation tools; they define *rectangular*, *circular* and *polygon* areas. The *arrow* is a marker tool. You use it to mark areas that you want to move or change. To create an area, press the appropriate button and click and drag it around the object you want to define as a clickable area. If you aren't satisfied with the shape of an area, you can remodel it with the arrow tool. We have created areas around the logo and the retro people, as you can see in Figure 37.3.

To remove a map area, select it and press the *delete* button (with the red X), and it will go away. To open the **Area Settings** dialog, select an area and press the magic wand button.

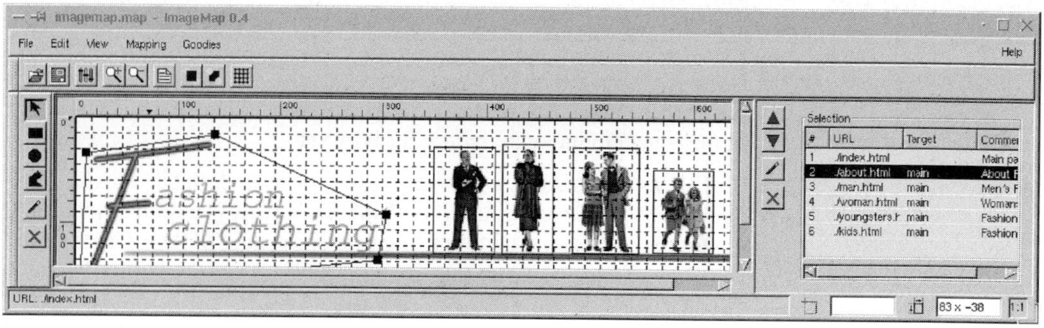

Figure 37.3 *ImageMap's main interface*

THE AREA SETTINGS DIALOG

Link

When you release the mouse after having created a clickable area, the **Area Settings** dialog will appear, displaying a link window where you specify the URL that the defined area should navigate to. In the **URL to activate when this area is clicked** input field you specify the URL of the link, but you can also open a file dialog to specify the file name/URL that should be the link.

If there are *frames* in your web page you can set the target ID in the target input field. (It's beyond the scope of this book to explain all HTML/web-specific words and we assume that you are somewhat familiar with web creation.)

You can also write a comment about the area, that will show up in places like Netscape's status window. We recommend that you use a comment that will inform the user where the link will take them.

Figure 37.4 *The Link tab*

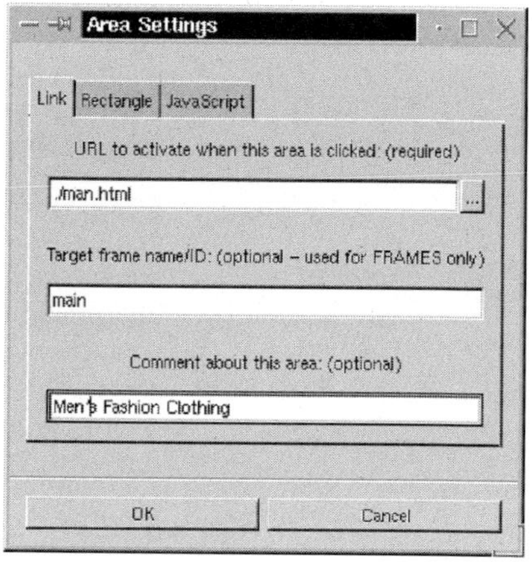

Rectangle, Circle And Polygon

If you want to edit a defined area, you can either use the **arrow/select** tool or the **Area Settings** dialog. Usually, mouse-clicking to define an area will suffice, but sometimes you need better precision. Because a polygon shape is built up of several nodes, you may want to add or remove nodes. You can't do that with your mouse, so this is where the Rectangle/Circle/Polygon tab comes in. To access the Area Settings window for a selected area, click on the **magic wand** tool.

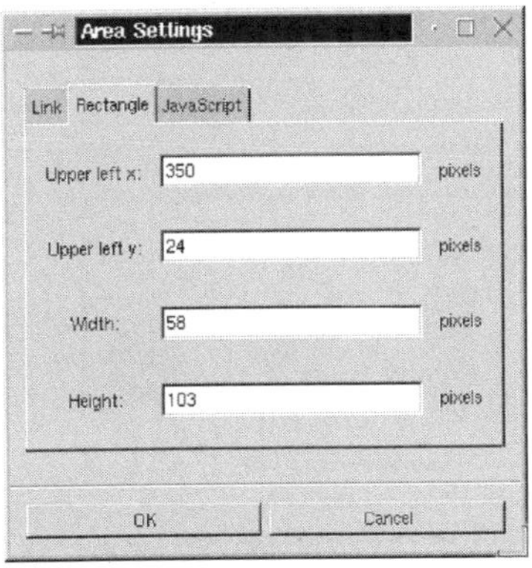

Rectangle

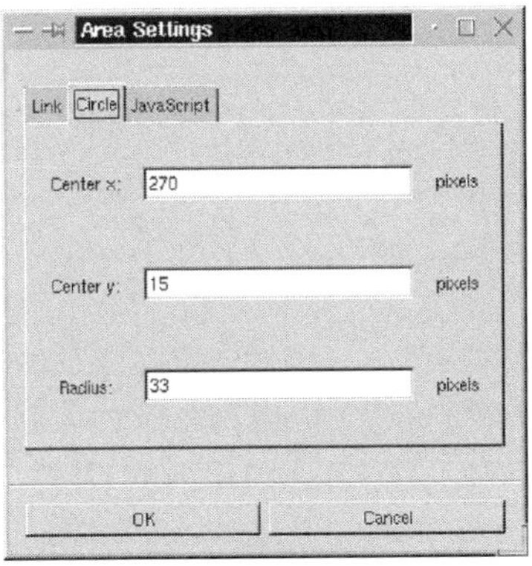

Circle

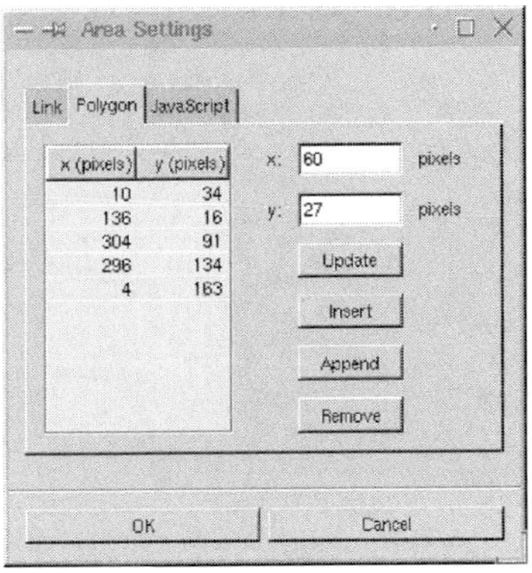

Polygon

Figure 37.5 *The different Area Settings tabs*

JavaScript

If you want to enable a JavaScript when you drag the mouse over and away from the area, you can do that in the **JavaScript** tab. You don't have to include the **onMouseover=** " and the ending " around the JavaScript function call, because those characters are added by ImageMap.

Figure 37.6 *The JavaScript dialog*

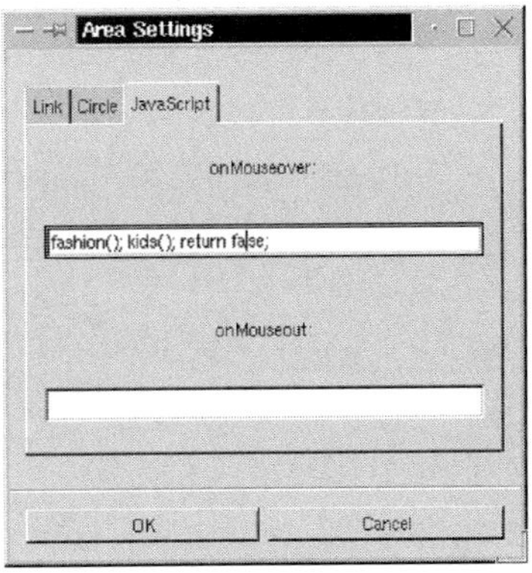

The Main Window

The Image Window

The main window is divided into two sections; the **image** window to the left, shown in Figure 37.7, and the **area** window to the right, shown in Figure 37.8.

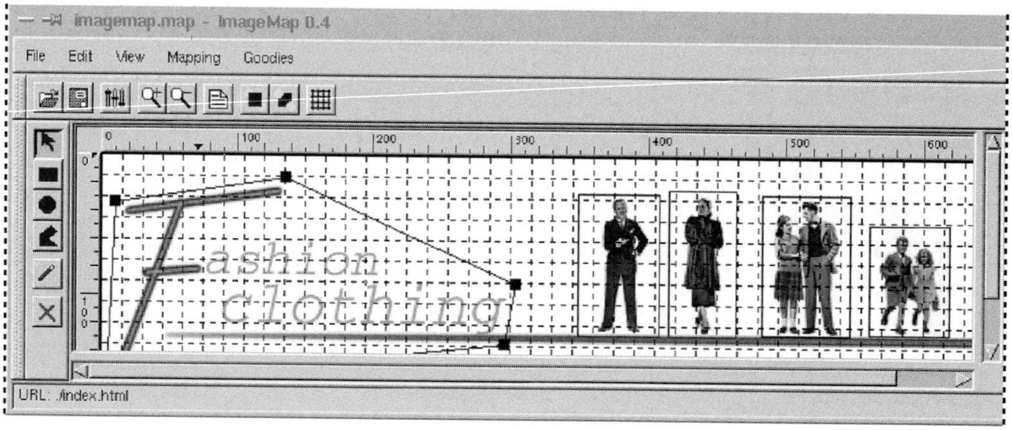

Figure 37.7 *The image part of the main window*

The image window displays your Gimp image, and it is here that you create imagemaps.

In the icon bar above the image window, you can **save** and **open** imagemap files, set **preferences** and **zoom** in and out. If two defined areas overlap each other, you can choose to send an area to front or to back using the **stack control** icons.

The Area Window

The area window displays a list with information of all created areas. Click one of the map areas in the list to select it. To change the specified order of overlapping areas, select the line and press the green arrows to move the line either up or down in the stack.

The left field below the area window describes the (absolute) current position of the mouse cursor in the image window. The right field describes the *width* and *height* of a dragged rectangular map, the *radius* of a circular map and the relative *cursor position* for polygon maps.

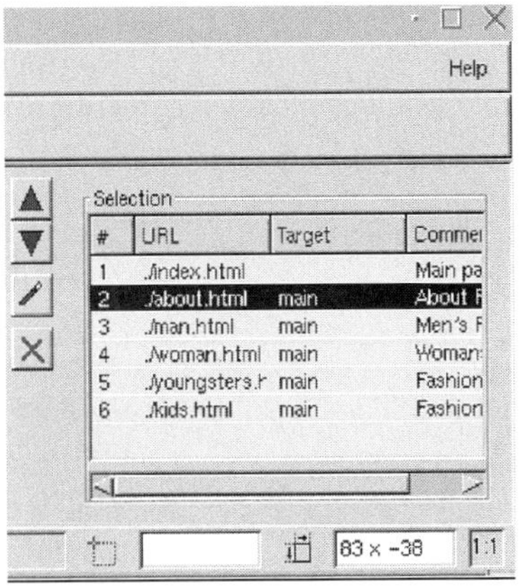

Figure 37.8 *The Area part of the main window*

Grid

A grid can be very helpful when you create definition areas. Click on the **grid** icon to add a grid system to the image window. If you aren't satisfied with the default grid size or shape, invoke `Goodies|Grid Settings` to bring up the **grid dialog**. Here, you can specify the type, proportions and position of the grid. To enable the new settings, press OK.

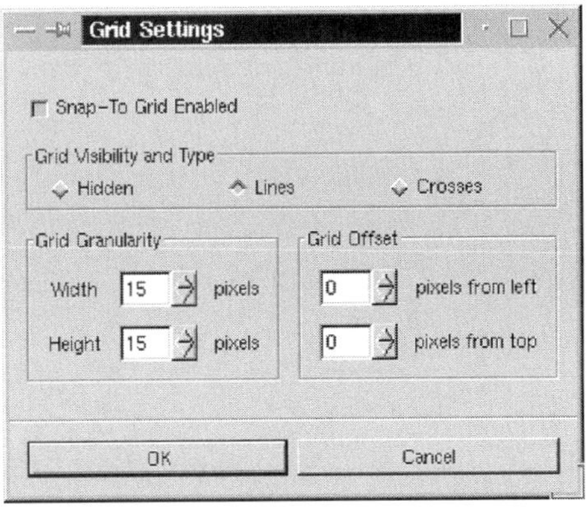

Figure 37.9 *The Grid dialog*

Mapinfo

When you have finished mapping, it's time to think of what type of imagemap to use. ImageMap supports three kinds of map file formats:

- **NSCA** is used by the NSCA web server and NSCA-related servers.
- **CERN** is used by the CERN web server.
- **CSIM** is used for *client side* imagemaps, i.e., imagemaps that are handled by the web browser instead of the web server.

We recommend that you use CSIM maps because they are so much easier to work with. To specify the map type, press the **Map Info** icon (the paper icon) and the **Settings for this Mapfile** dialog will appear. At the time of this writing (ImageMap 0.4), only the **Map file format** option is enabled. To set the map-info (type), check the appropriate button and press OK.

Creation Of The Map File

You have to save your map file to be able to paste the map information into your HTML document. Save your file with the `right-click|File|Save` command.

You will now have a map file containing all map information. All you have to do is open the map file in a **text editor** and open the **web page** that is going to include the imagemap in another text editor. Paste the map info to the appropriate place in your HTML code. (There are, of course, several editors and ways to do this, we only describe a generic way.)

Because you can open a map file for re-editing, don't delete the saved map file. The map file may come in very handy if you want to change your imagemap. So, remember to always copy/paste your map info into the HTML file.

Your Map Info May Look Like This:

```
<IMG SRC="/images/image_map-export.tif" WIDTH=680 HEIGHT=185
BORDER=0 USEMAP="#mapje">


<MAP NAME="mapje">
<AREA SHAPE="POLY" COORDS="10,34,136,16,304,91,296,
134,4,163,10,34,10,34" ALT="About Fashion Clothing"
TARGET="main" HREF="./about.html">
<AREA SHAPE="RECT" COORDS="349,26,408,127" ALT="Men's
Fashion Clothing" TARGET="main" HREF="./men.html">
<AREA SHAPE="RECT" COORDS="415,23,464,127" ALT="Women's
Fashion Clothing" TARGET="main" HREF="./women.html">
<AREA SHAPE="RECT" COORDS="483,26,547,126" ALT="Fashion
Clothing for teens" TARGET="main" HREF="./teens.html">
<AREA SHAPE="RECT" COORDS="561,47,619,125" ALT="Fashion
Clothing for kids" TARGET="main" HREF="./kids.html">
<AREA SHAPE="RECT" COORDS="0,0,680,185" ALT="Main page"
HREF="./index.html">
</MAP>
```

The HTML Code May Look Something Like This:

```
<HTML>
<HEAD>
<TITLE>
Imagemap creation in Gimp
</TITLE>
</HEAD>
<BODY>

<!-- Here the imagemap code begins-->

<IMG SRC="image_map-export.gif" WIDTH=680 HEIGHT=185
BORDER=0 USEMAP="#mapje">

<MAP NAME="mapje">
<AREA SHAPE="POLY"
COORDS="10,34,136,16,304,91,296,134,4,163,10,34" ALT="About
Fashion Clothing" TARGET="main" HREF="./about.html">
<AREA SHAPE="RECT" COORDS="349,26,408,127" ALT="Men's
Fashion Clothing" TARGET="main" HREF="./men.html">
<AREA SHAPE="RECT" COORDS="415,23,464,127" ALT="Women's
Fashion Clothing" TARGET="main" HREF="./women.html">
<AREA SHAPE="RECT" COORDS="483,26,547,126" ALT="Fashion
Clothing for teens" TARGET="main" HREF="./teens.html">
<AREA SHAPE="RECT" COORDS="561,47,619,125" ALT="Fashion
Clothing for kids" TARGET="main" HREF="./kids.html">
<AREA SHAPE="RECT" COORDS="0,0,680,185"
ALT="Main page" HREF="./index.html">
</MAP>

<!--And here the imagemap code ends-->
</BODY>
</HTML>
```

Magic Eye

Magic Eye lets you create 3-D stereo images in Gimp. I think everybody has seen 3-D images in magazines: a strange-looking image that you have to look at in a certain way, and up pops a flower or something. Now you can do the same thing in Gimp.

Figure 37.10 *The Magic Eye dialog*

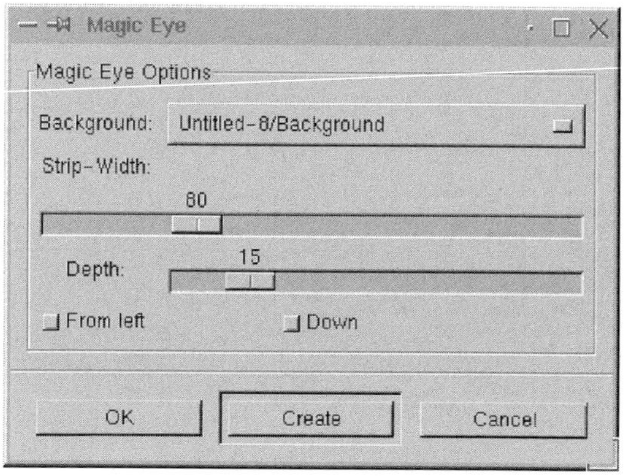

Example And Parameters

1. First create a **grayscale map image**, like the one shown in Figure 37.11. (This will be the image containing the 3-D thing that will pop up.) Remember that the brighter the object is in the map image, the higher it will pop up in the stereo image.

Figure 37.11 *The grayscale map image that will pop out in the stereogram image*

2. Create a **mask image**, like the one in Figure 37.12. (This is the image that will hide the map image.) The image must have several colors in it if this is going to work properly (a repeated texture is great) .

Figure 37.12 *The mask image that will build up the stereogram image.*

3. Bring up **Magic Eye** from the map image.
4. Select the mask image in the **Background** menu.
5. In the **Strip** slide bar, set how many columns (a column is one pixel wide) of the **mask** image you want to use for the background pattern clone strip (preferably between 50 and 100). The columns are counted from the left.
6. Remember that you must leave the first and last part of the **map image** black (about half the size of the background strip).
7. **Depth** is the amount of 3-D you want (or how much you want the thing to pop up).
8. **From left** will build your image from the left instead of from the middle of the image. (For some reason, a 3-D image is often easier to see if you create it from the left.)
9. **Down** *carves* the image instead of *raising* it.
10. You have now hopefully chosen **Depth**, **Mask** and **Strip**.
11. Press **OK** or **Create**, and the new 3-D image will appear (see Figure 37.13).

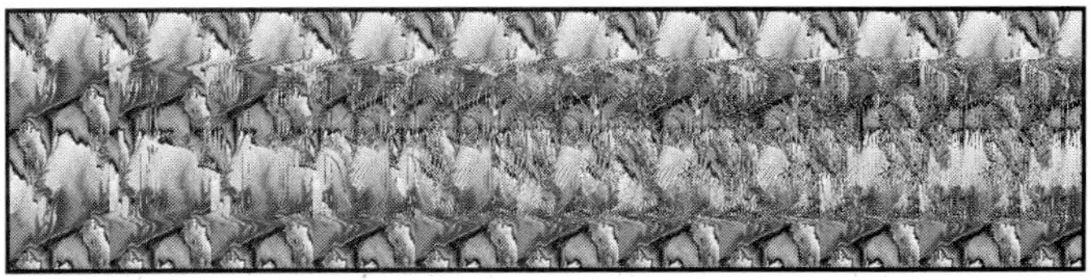

Figure 37.13 *The final stereogram*

STEREOGRAM

The **Stereogram** filter creates a 3-D stereogram of a **grayscale** image (similar to Magic Eye).

If you check **SIS** (Single Image Stereogram), the background will be used as a pattern. In **SIRDS** (Single Image Random Dot Stereogram), you'll only get stereo noise for background.

Figure 37.14 *The Stereogram dialog*

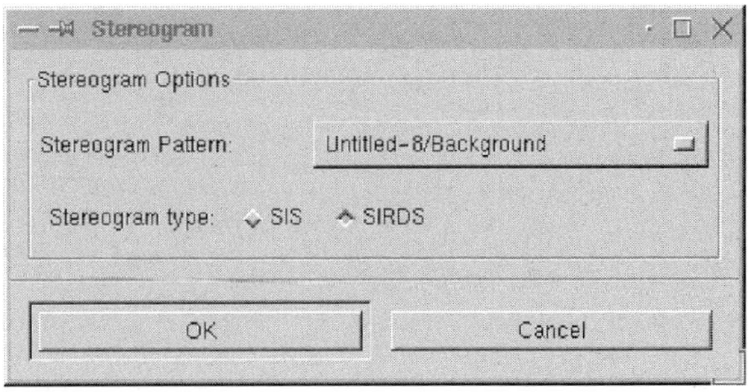

How To Use Stereogram

1. Create a simple **grayscale** image (the popup map).
2. Bring up the plug-in.
3. Choose a **background** (an RGB image of equal size).
4. Choose stereogram type: **SIS** or **SIRDS.**
5. Press **OK**.

Now you have a stereogram. Take a good look at it with the focus slightly behind the image, until the 3-D representation of your image appears in the stereo image.

Figure 37.15 *The map image, the background and the result after applying the Stereogram filter*

Popup map

RGB background

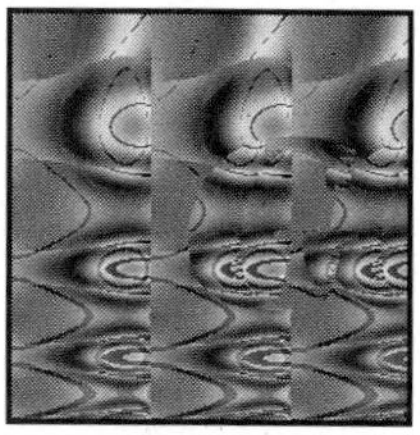

Result

Video

The **Video** plug-in creates the illusion that the image is an ordinary low-res/dot pitch **video monitor**. You can achieve this with different patterns, which means that you can create a whole lot of "bad monitors."

Figure 37.16 *The Video dialog*

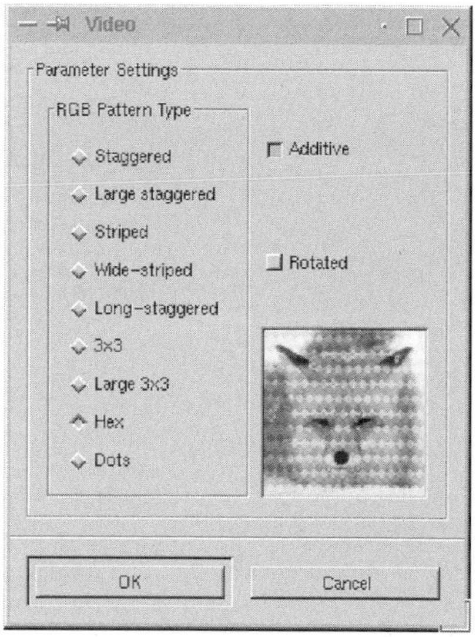

By default the pattern is horizontal, but you can check **Rotated** to make it vertical instead. Use **Additive** to get a more realistic look. For an explanation of Additive, see "Modes" starting on page 335. If you don't use Additive, the pattern will just get on top of the image and darken it a lot.

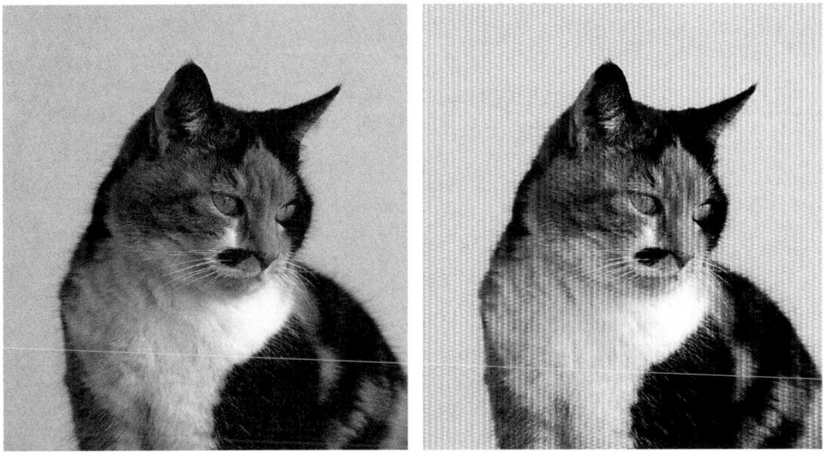

Figure 37.17 *The resemblance to a bad video display is quite remarkable; in this example the cat image is shown before and after Video has been invoked*

CHAPTER 38

Noise Filters

Noise filters will add noise effects to your image, such as monitor noise, film graininess or just pointillistic artistry. This is the place to find such a filter.

NOISIFY

Noisify adds random noise to the entire image. If you have used a lot of Sharpen to fix an unfocused photo, you can add a little noise to oversharp areas to make it look more natural.

Note: This filter will not work with indexed images.

PARAMETERS

You can add noise to all of the **RGB** channels, or to each RGB channel independently. The reference scale goes from 0.00 — no noise — to 1.00 — full noise level.

- Channel 0 is **red** (or gray in a grayscale image).
- Channel 1 is **green** (or alpha in a grayscale-alpha image).
- Channel 3 is **blue**
- Channel 4 is **alpha** (in an RGB-alpha image).

If the **Independent** button is checked, each channel will get the noise level you have specified with the sliders. If Independent is unchecked, the same relative noise pattern will be applied to all channels, so that the color balance from the original image is kept intact.

Figure 38.1 *Example of a high amount of noise in the right part of the image*

RANDOMIZE, HURL, PICK AND SLUR

These plug-ins cause **random displacement** of pixels in three different ways.

OPTIONS

The random displacement can be adjusted to affect 0% to 100% of the pixels. You can also specify if you want the filter to be repeated only once, or up to 100 times.

You can set the **randomization seed** to generate numbers from the current time so that there will be a new random operation every time you repeat the filter. If you set a value of your own choice in the input field, a given operation will be repeated each time. All three Randomize filters work for all image types. A warning is in place for **Hurling**, because a too high Randomization or Repeat value will produce solid noise with no trace of the original image.

Randomization Types

- **Hurling:** Changes a pixel to a random color, if it's within the given range of randomization.
- **Picking:** Applies the highest channel values picked from three random neighbor pixels to the channels in the chosen pixel.
- **Slurring:** This is similar to Picking, but this filter will distort your image downward. If a pixel is chosen to be slurred, there's an 80 percent chance that a channel value from the pixel directly above it will be applied; otherwise, a random neighbor above the chosen pixel will be used.

The color variation is usually less in Slurring and Picking than in Hurling because the channel value replacement often results in shades of gray.

Figure 38.2 *Because the Hurl effect is easy to overdo, you have to lower the values. The image to the right was Hurled with 20% randomization and 1 repeat. Pick and Slur were applied with 50% randomization and 3 repeats. Observe that only the right sides of the images have been altered.*

Hurl

Pick

Slur

SPREAD

The **Spread** plug-in **spreads** the pixels in your image. It will move a pixel to a random location. However, this location will be in the range of your setting in the slidebars. This makes it possible to spread the image *vertically*, *horizontally* or in *both directions*.

With this filter, the noise effect will not appear in the entire image as with the other noise filters. You will only see it in the border of contrasting areas. Also, because only the colors present in the image will be used, and there is no channel displacement, no new colors will be introduced.

Figure 38.3 *Spread was applied to the right side of the image*

CHAPTER 39

Render Filters

Would you like to create wonderful lifelike trees, or perhaps make an interesting texture? This is a real texture factory. You can create the most sophisticated images, drawings and textures here.

CML EXPLORER

Well, I suppose you might call **CML Explorer** the Swiss army texture maker. You can compose an abstract pattern based on 12 different mathematical functions, 14 different ways of composing those functions and 10 arrangement variations. As if that wasn't enough, you can also set 10 control parameters.

Now, if you think this is a lot...that's just the choice of settings for the Hue values of this plug-in. You also have those options for Saturation and Value, as well as a variety of additional options. Writing full documentation for this plug-in would be too extensive for this manual, but we'll give you a few guidelines.

Figure 39.1 *Example of a CML texture*

GENERAL SETTINGS

Functions

- The first function type is called **Keep Image's Value**. This means that the **Hue**, **Saturation** or **Value** of the image you opened this plug-in from will stay *unchanged*, so if you have chosen this function, there's no point in changing any of the other settings in that tab.
- **Keep First Value** doesn't have anything to do with your image — it just sets the initial colors to standard cyan "shower curtain" with a little spilloff from the surrounding colors in the HSV color circle (Saturation and Value also get a standard curtain).
- **Fill with parameter K**, sets a quite smooth surface, which is controlled by the **K** slide bar. The other functions that contain K are variations of the function, but they create very interesting brocade-like patterns when you raise the K-value (see the example to the top/right of Figure 39.2), though high values always end up with colored noise.
- **Delta** creates similar patterns. The **Sinus** function creates wavelike shapes (with the right setting), like northern light or curtain folds, as in Figure 39.1.

Composition And Arrangement

You can experiment with **Composition/Misc. Arrangement** as you like, but the effect varies so much with the other parameters that you can compare it to Forrest Gump's chocolates: You never know what you're gonna get....

Still, it is often the case that **Composition** functions starting with **Max** produce denser, darker patterns than **Min** functions.

Random Arrangement usually results in striped patterns, and **Gradient Arrangement** causes shifts or blends from one side of the pattern to the other, so you can't use a gradient arrangement for tileable patterns.

The Slide Bars

The slide bar settings are equally hard to predict, but this is generally true:

- **Moderation Rate** goes from vertical stripes to rounder shapes.
- **Environment Sensitivity** has a similar effect, but breaks up the pattern more.
- **Diffusion distance** changes the sense of size and direction.
- **Number of Subranges** increases complexity in the pattern.
- **Parameter K** and **Parameter P** affect functions containing those values.
- **Low Range and High Range** control the Value ranges of each HSV tab.

Figure 39.2 *A few more examples of CML textures. The multitude of options in the CML filter make it possible to create a very large number of different textures. The hard part is to control what texture you're going to get.*

Advanced Settings

The **Advanced settings** tab allows you to experiment with **Channel** sensitivity and **Mutations** for random seed. Use it with care, or you'll just end up with colored noise.

Other Options

This tab lets you set a **channel independent** initial value for the pattern you want to create. Note that this option often locks the pattern in a **horizontal** direction. You can also **Zoom** or **Offset** your pattern in this folder.

Miscellaneous Options

These options include the possibility to **copy** and **change** the settings from one channel to another. You have probably seen that you can save and load patterns you have created in CML explorer. Here's an option to just load the settings of a certain channel instead of the whole pattern.

Tip: You'll often get a better looking pattern by changing it to grayscale, and then back to RGB. After that, you can set any color you like with the Image/Color controls.

Checkerboard

The **Checkerboard** plug-in creates **Checkerboards** — what else?

The **Size** slide controls the size of the checkers in pixels (X x Y pixels). If you check **Psychobilly**, you'll get tiled 3-D "pouting" checkerboards (see Figure 39.5). Size now represents the biggest check in a tile.

Say that you set **Size** to 4 pixels, then the middle check (which is always the biggest one) will be 4x4, the next check will be one pixel thinner, until you get to the outer check which is always one pixel wide. The check size follows this algorithm: 1,2,3,... "check size"...,3,2,1. From this you can determine that each Psychobilly tile will be 16x16 (because 4x4=16).

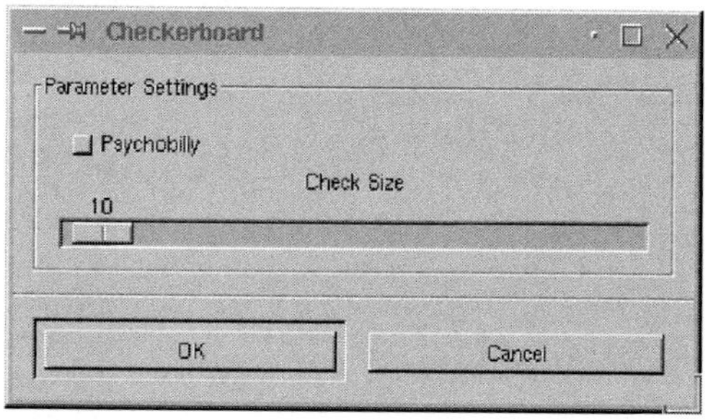

Figure 39.3 *The Checkerboard dialog*

If, for example, you choose 12 as check size, for an image that is 288x288, you will end up with four Psychobilly tiles, because 12x12 gives you tiles that are 144x144 pixels big, and there can only be four such tiles in a 288x288 image.

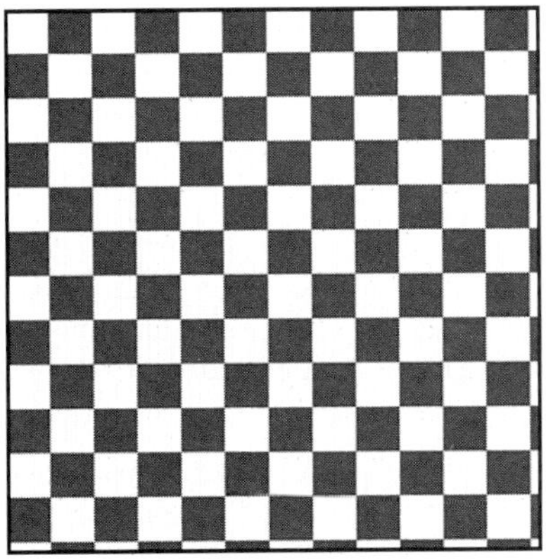

Figure 39.4 *Normal Checkerboard mode*

Figure 39.5 *Psychobilly Checkerboard mode*

DIFFRACTION PATTERNS

Diffraction Patterns lets you make **diffraction** or **wave interference** textures. You can change the **Frequency**, **Contours** and **Sharp Edges** for each of the RGB channels.

You can also set **Brightness**, **Scattering** and **Polarization** of the texture. There is no automatic preview, so you must press the preview button to update. This is a very useful filter if you want to create intricate patterns. It's perfect for making psychedelic, batik-like textures, or for imitating patterns in stained glass (as in a church window).

Figure 39.6 *The Diffraction patterns dialog*

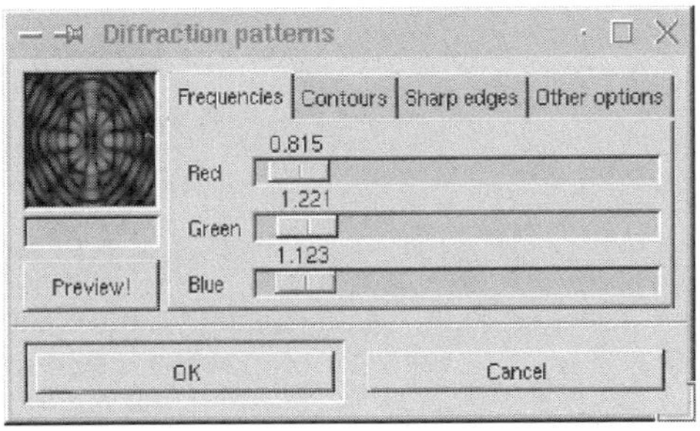

DYNAMIC TEXT

If you want to add a text string that consists of more than a few characters to your image, we recommend that you use the **Dynamic Text** plug-in. Dynamic Text is much more powerful than Gimp's ordinary text tool.

When you add text to an image with the Text tool in the toolbox, you can't edit it once you have applied the text to the image. For example, if you want to change "Hi" to "Hello" you have to erase the old floating text selection and reenter the new text.

With Dynamic Text, you don't have to worry about such things. It's easy to edit text; you can change "Hi" to "Hello" without any erasing or reentering operations. You can even write text in a separate text file, import it into Gimp and still be able to edit the text within Gimp. And of course, Dynamic Text has **multi-line** capability. The core Gimp text tool only handles single text lines.

When you first open Dynamic Text, it will create a special **GDyn** Text layer; otherwise, it will not be able to manage the text processing. Just press **Dismiss** and carry on.

THE MAIN WINDOW

The main **Dynamic Text** window will appear, showing a large **Text field**. This is where you type the text that you want to render into Gimp. You will also find several icon buttons and drop-down menus.

Let's quickly define the names of these options. Starting at the top-left corner you'll find the following icons:

- **Layer**
- **Load**
- **Color**
- **Antialias**
- **Left**
- **Center**
- **Right**,
- **Preview**
- **Special Character**

Directly above the Text field, there is an alphabetic **Font Preview** field. You can select a font in the drop-down menu, and view the new font in the Font Preview field (and in the Text field if you have written something there).

Style And Size

Above the Font Preview field, you'll find drop-down menus for Style and Size.

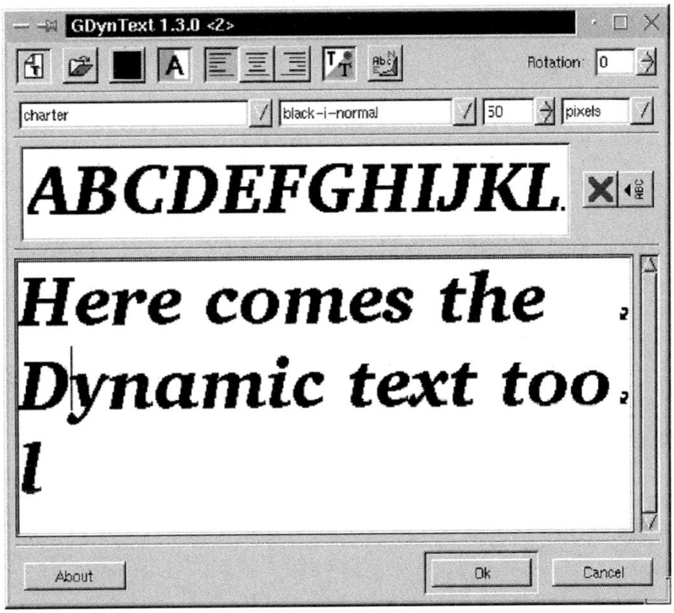

Figure 39.7 *The main Dynamic Text window; note the small arrows that indicate "non-linebreak"*

Style describes the three basic properties of the font variations. The first part of the style string describes the **weight** or thickness of the characters, such as *bold*, *demi* or *light*. The next part, which represents the **slant** or posture of the characters, is described by a single letter: i for *italics*, r for *roman* and o for *oblique*. The third and last part of the style string describes **spacing**, such as *normal* or *condensed*.

Size can be measured in either *points* or *pixels*. One point is always 1/72 of an inch (72 points per inch), and one pixel in Dynamic Text represents one pixel in your Gimp image. If you set this option to points instead of pixels, you will see a difference if you're using a high-resolution monitor.

For more information on fonts, read "How To Get Fonts To Gimp" starting on page 759, and "Text And Fonts" starting on page 165.

The Text Field

Type a sentence in the Text field. If the sentence is longer than the width of the window, Dynamic Text will display a small curved **arrow** in the right side of the window. The arrow means that there is *no line break*.

To create a real line break, press **Enter**, as you would in a normal text editor. If you select another font, the text will automatically be updated to show the new font. However, you can only use one style (font, size, justification, etc.) for text strings created with Dynamic Text.

Special Characters

If you want to include special characters, such as ©, Ò or †, you have to invoke the **Special Character** option by clicking on the "Abc" icon. This will bring up a window containing all characters and symbols present in the selected font. Choose a special character or symbol, and press **Insert**.

Don't get confused if you don't see any special characters right away when you open the dialog. Drag the slider down, and you will find the symbols a bit further down in the character list.

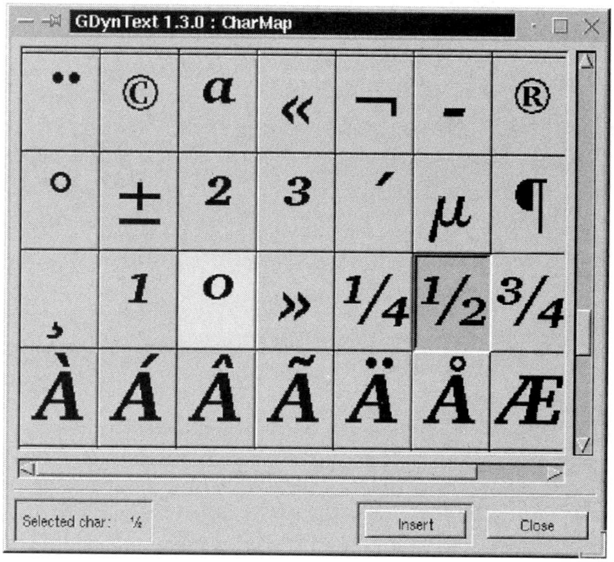

Figure 39.8 *The Special characters dialog. Just pick your character and click Insert. Notice that we have scrolled down a bit, in order to view the characters.*

Options

There are several advanced options in the Dynamic Text dialog.

If you are writing an entire text block, you may wish to set the **justification** of the text. The justification options allow you to set straight margins to the left or right or to align each line break to the center. This is done by enabling the **left**, **right** or **center icon**.

You can control antialiasing by enabling/disabling the **antialiasing icon** (the A icon). **Antialiasing** is enabled by default in Dynamic Text, and we recommend you always keep this button checked to prevent the letters from looking jaggy and ugly. (There is one exception to this rule, and that is when the font size is very small.)

You can also **rotate** the text by setting another rotation angle other than 0 in the **Rotation field**.

You can specify the **color** of the rendered text with the Dynamic Text tool. Pressing the **color icon** will bring up a color dialog where you can select a color. After you have pressed OK, the color icon will display the new color. Because you can only choose one color for your text, you may want to change the color later within the **dynamic text layer**. If you change the color in the layer, you can, for example, select a certain word and fill it with red, or you could use a gradient as fill "color." Still, keep in mind that any changes made within the layer will be erased the instant you open Dynamic Text again to re-edit the text.

Re-editing Dynamic Text

What's so great about Dynamic Text is that it allows you to re-edit rendered text. To change your text, make the dynamic text layer active and invoke the filter. Your text will now appear in the Text field (notice that this time, there is no message about layer creation). Edit the text as usual and/or set new text options. Press OK and the changed text will appear in the text layer.

If you'd like to keep the old text layer, then enable the **Layer icon**. With the Layer button checked, the modified text will be placed in a new layer, and the original text layer will be preserved. This procedure is very useful if you want to try out a variety of different text layouts or designs before deciding which one to use.

Loading Text From A Text File

If you want to render large amounts of text into Gimp, it may be convenient to edit the text in a normal text editor, such as Emacs or VI, and import it into Dynamic Text. To import text from a text file, press the **Load** button. A file browser will appear where you can specify which file to import. The imported text will be displayed in the Text field, and you can alter it just as you would text that you typed in the Text field.

Figures

The **Figures** plug-in adds a random number of **rectangles** of different size and color to your image. You can constrain the average rectangle size to **Min/Max Width** and **Height**.

Density controls the number of rectangles. A low density value results in a low number of rectangles, and a high value produces a whole lot of them. This plug-in can also be used as a *texture maker*.

Figure 39.9 *Figures was applied to the right side of this image*

FLAME

With the **Flame** filter, you can create stunning, randomly generated **fractal patterns**. You can't control the fractals as you can with the **Ifs Compose** filter, but you can steer the random generator in a certain direction, and choose from variations of a theme you like.

MAIN INTERFACE

In the main window, you can set **Rendering** and **Camera** parameters. The first three parameters in the Render display are **Brightness**, **Contrast** and **Gamma**. The result of these options is visible in the Preview window, but it's generally better to stick to the default values, and correct the rendered image later with Image/ Colors.

Figure 39.10 *Example of Flame*

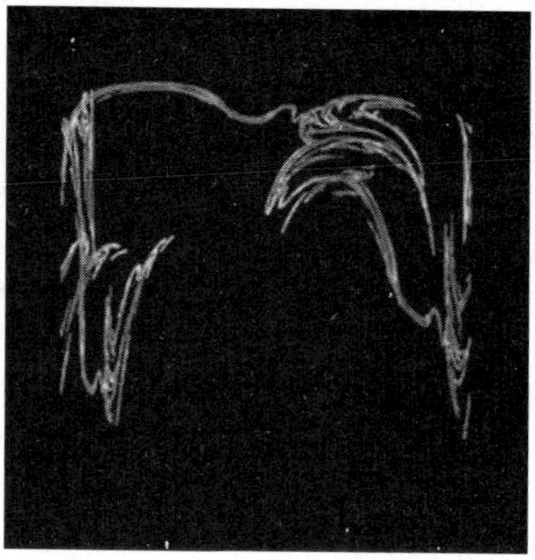

Figure 39.11 *The Flame dialog*

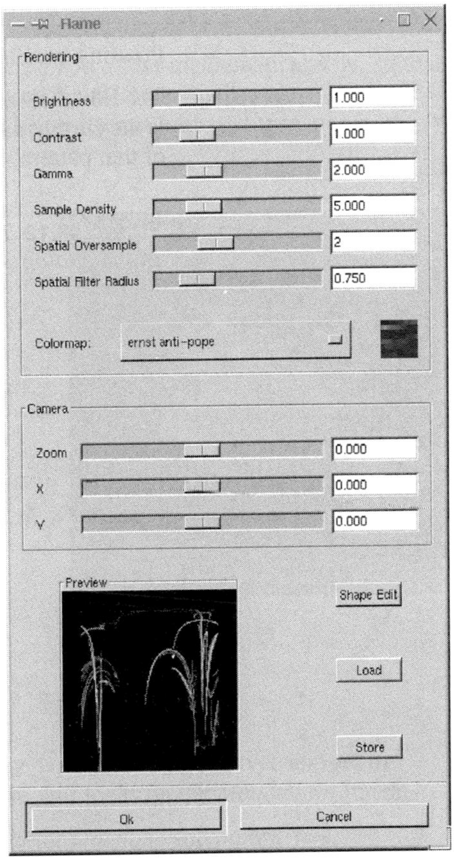

The other three parameters affect the rendering process and don't show in the preview window. **Sample Density**, which controls the resolution of the rendered pattern, is the most important of these. A high sample density results in soft and smooth rendering (like a spider's web), whereas low density rendering resembles spray or particle clouds. The **Camera** parameters allow you to **zoom** and **offset** the flame pattern, until you're happy with what you see in the preview window. Flame also offers the possibility to **store** and **load** your favorite patterns.

The **Colormap** controls the color **blend** in the flame pattern. You can set Colormap to:

- The current gradient from the **Gradient Editor**.
- A number of **preset** colormaps.
- The colors from images that are presently open in Gimp. You can use the **Smooth Palette** filter in the Filters/Colors menu to create suitable colormaps from your images.

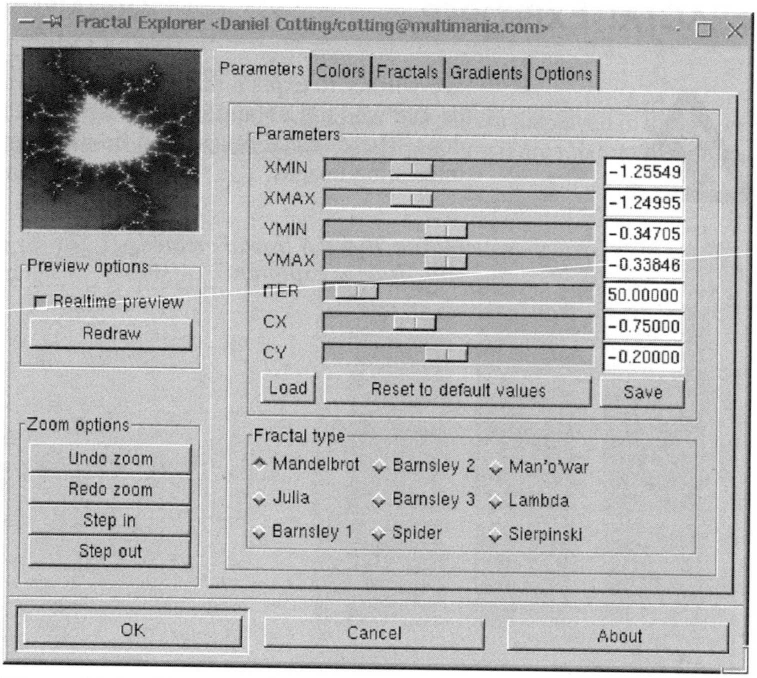

Figure 39.14 *The main view of Fractal Explorer*

PARAMETERS

XMIN And XMAX

XMIN controls how much the fractal will stretch to the left, and XMAX controls the stretch to the right.

YMIN And YMAX

YMIN controls how much the fractal will stretch *upward* (positive Y values in a coordinate system) and YMAX controls how much it will stretch *downward* (negative Y values).

ITER

ITER stands for *iterations,* which control the level of detail in the fractal. Many iterations will calculate more detail, which will take more time. It's not always best to have a high level of detail. Often a fractal will get more interesting when created with lower values. We have found that in the range between 16 and 70 you will find some very nice fractal patterns.

CX And CY

CX and CY have no impact on Mandelbrot and Sierpinski fractals. CX values between -5 and 0 control the *horizontal* distance of the two fractal parts. Low values (-5) take them apart totally, and high values (0) merge them totally. Values between 0 and +5 will do the same, but in a *vertical* direction. CY has a similar control mechanism, but not in a horizontal/vertical direction. CY works in a 45/225 and 135/315 degree direction.

Load, Reset And Save

These buttons let you load a specific setting from your personal fractal directory, or save a nice setting that you have made. **Reset** will reset the values to the default values.

Fractal Type

Here, you can choose between well-known fractal types like *Mandelbrot*, *Julia* or *Sierpinsky,* but you'll also find more exotic fractal types like *Man o' war* and *Spider*.

COLORS

A fractal consists of *three* parts. An **outer** part, an **inner** part and the *"fractal"* border between them.

Color Function

The **Sine** function controls the color of the inner and outer parts, while the **Cosine** function controls the fractal part. **None** means that you'll use linear instead of trigonometrical mapping for a certain color channel. By checking and unchecking the three color functions you can choose suitable colors for the different parts of your fractal.

The **Inversion** button will invert low color values to high color values and vice versa. For example, checking Inversion in the green channel will make areas that were previously low on green full of strong green color. To fully understand it, take a quick look at the **Channels** tab in the Layers & Channels dialog (`right-click|Layers|Layers & Channels`). Deselect all channels but the green channel, apply the `Image|Colors|Invert` command, and see what happens in the image and in the thumbnail channel representation.

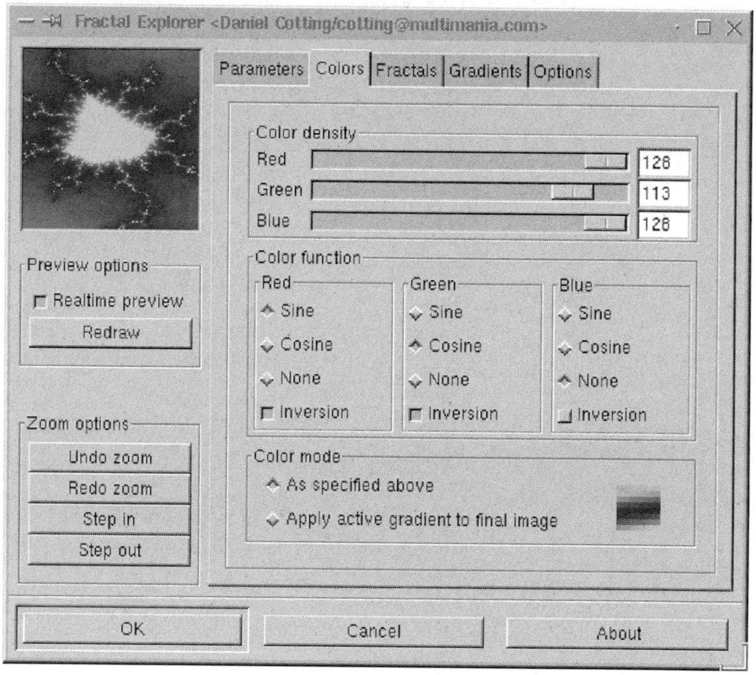

Figure 39.15 *The color view of the Fractal Explorer*

Color Density

You can also set the *intensity* of the color channels with the slides in **Color density**. This makes it possible to set any color you want to your fractal.

Color Mode

Either you use the color mode you have specified with the other Color options, which is what you see in the preview window, or you can use a **gradient** from the **gradient folder**. This option will map the gradient over your fractal. You can achieve quite fantastic-looking fractals this way.

Fractals

Here, you'll find some nice predefined fractals that you can use straight off, or use as a backbone or point of departure for your own experiments.

Gradients

Here, you specify the gradient to use in the **Colors** tab. A tip is to bring up the **gradient editor** so you can take a look at the gradients.

GENETIC

The **Genetic** filter generates **random textures**, much like the KPT Texture Explorer. The generated outcome of these filters is usually a geometrical pattern. If you want more variation in the random patterns, try the Qbist plug-in; see "Qbist" on page 631.

Figure 39.16 *A geometrical pattern created with Genetic*

The original texture is displayed in the middle square, and different variations surround it. If you like one of the alternative textures, click on it. The chosen texture now turns up in the middle, and variations on that specific theme are displayed around it. When you have found the texture you want, click on it and then click OK. The texture will now appear on your drawable.

Figure 39.17 *The Genetic dialog*

GFIG

This awesome plug-in adds basic drawing capabilities to Gimp. You can draw circles, lines, curves, ellipses, X-sided polygons (X >=3), stars, spirals and Bezier curves.

Figure 39.18 *Gfig is very handy for drawing uncomplicated drawings like this bike, or like the "F" in Figure 37.2 Naturally, Gfig is not limited to such simple tasks. In fact you can draw very complex images with Gfig, but that was never the purpose of this plug-in.*

The drawing can then be *rendered* into your image. The drawing objects have **control points** that can be moved/edited to adjust the shape of the object. There is also a **Selection** option in this plug-in, which transforms a Gfig drawing to a selection in your Gimp image, and a **Select+Fill** option, which enables you to fill a selection directly from Gfig.

USER INTERFACE

The user interface is divided into a **Preview** area with a *drawing* area and *user tools*, a **Settings** area with *object manipulation* options, **Grid settings** to control grids and a few **tabs** to control *paint* options.

PREVIEW AREA

In **Ops** you'll find all the drawing tools. You can *draw*, *delete*, *move*, *edit* and *copy* objects.

Lines

To draw a *straight line*, simply **click** on the spot where you want your line to begin, and **drag** and **release** the mouse button where you want it to end.

If you want a *crooked line* (built of several control points) hold Shift; this will make the control points attach to each other. For example, hold Shift, click on the first point, move, click on a second point, move, click on a third point, release Shift, move, and click to get the final point.

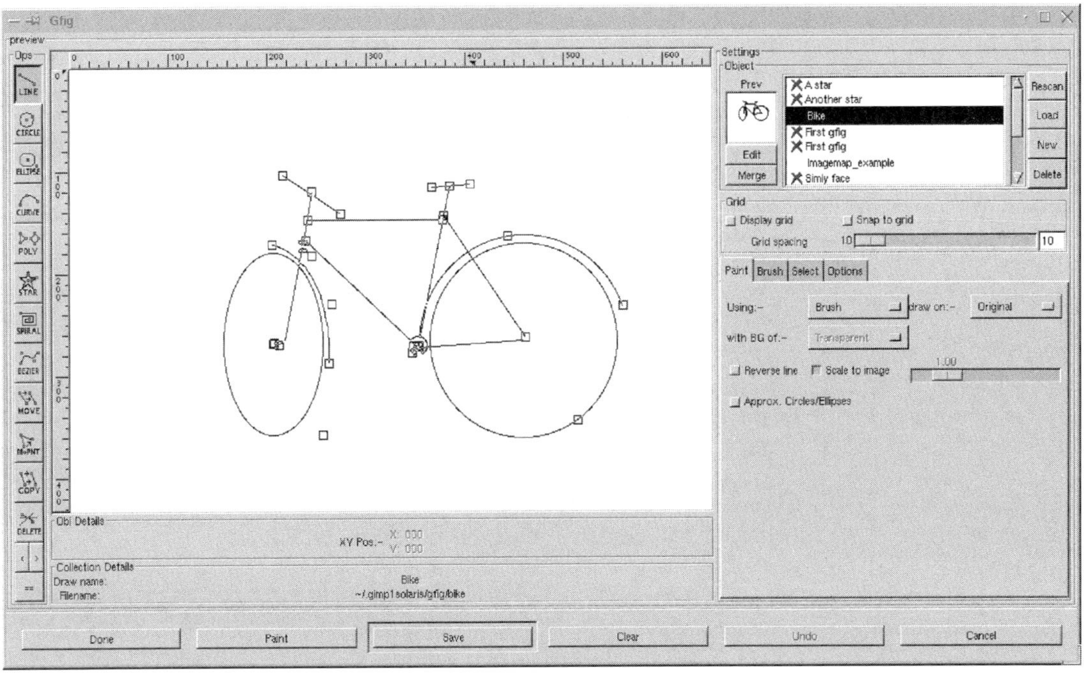

Figure 39.19 *The Gfig window; to view the result of the bike drawing, see Figure 39.18*

Figure 39.20 *Drawing lines in Gfig*

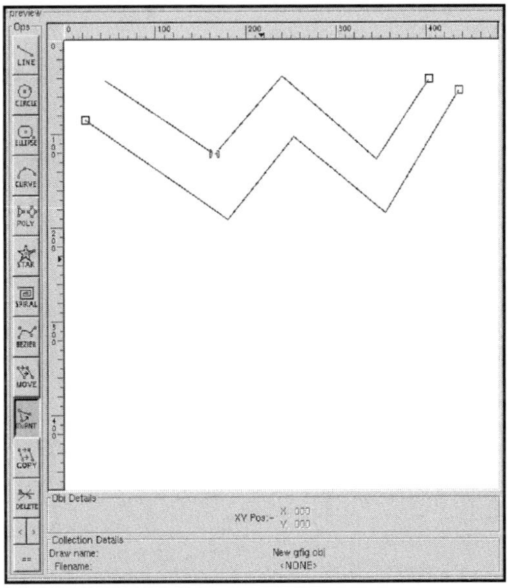

Circle

Draws a **circle**. The start click becomes the center of the new circle.

Ellipse

Draws an **ellipse**. The start click becomes the center of the new ellipse.

Curve

Draws an **arch** or a **semicircle**. The object has three points (two end points and a middle point).

To clear things up, follow this example: Start by drawing a curve where the curve points are placed in a horizontal row. This will result in a **straight line**; you can compare this to a tiny segment of a huge circle. Now, if you raise the middle point a bit, the curve will become a low **arch**. It now represents a larger part of the imaginary circle. Finally, reduce the distance between the two end points and you will find that the curve gets even more **circular**.

Figure 39.21 *Drawing curves in Gfig*

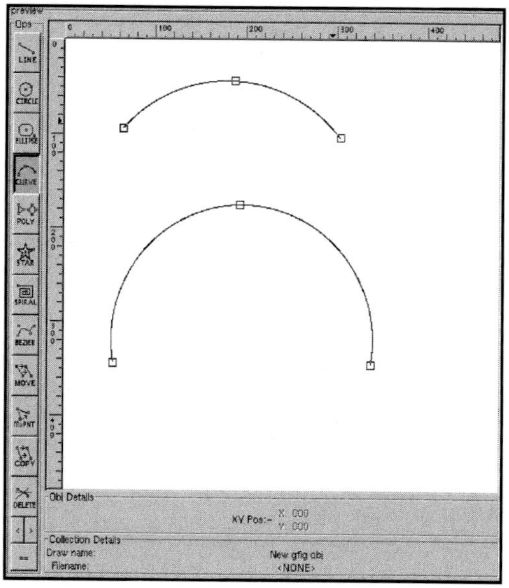

Poly(gon)

The default polygon is a **triangle**, but you can change this by double-clicking on the icon. This brings up a dialog where you can choose how many sides you want for your polygon.

Star

The default star has three spikes, but as with Poly, you can double-click to adjust the number of spikes. There are three controls points for further modification with **MvPnt**.

The **central** control point allows you to change the relative position of the star by rotating it around the outer control point. The **outer** control point controls the external radius of the star, and the **middle** control point controls the size of the core radius, which determine the relative length and sharpness of the spikes.

Spiral

This draws a spiral. You can set the number of **twists** by double-clicking on the spiral icon. This brings up a dialog where you can also set the direction to clockwise or counterclockwise.

Bezier

This lets you draw **bezier curves**. They're not as easy to modify as the Bezier curves in the toolbox because there are no handles to pull, but it works quite nicely for simple drawings. You'll have to practice a bit to learn how to control them. As usual, you end the curve with a Shift+click.

Move

This moves a single object or all objects in a drawing. To move a single object, just click at a control point and drag. To move all objects, hold Shift, click somewhere in the drawing area and drag. This will cause all objects in the drawing area to move.

MvPNT

MvPNT lets you move a single control point. This function lets you alter the shape of an object by **stretching** and **moving** the lines that it's made of. As you may have noticed, you can't change the shape of a circle — you can only make it smaller or move it. A way around this problem is to use polygons. If you use a polygon with a lot of sides, you will get something very close to a circle. If you simply choose the **MvPNT** tool, you'll only change it the usual way, but if you hold Shift and then click at a control point with the MvPNT tool active, you'll break up the polygon into a lot of lines. Now, you can drag at the "circle" control points any way you like.

Copy

This will copy an object. To use it, click and hold an object's control point, then drag the copy to where you want it.

Delete

This deletes an object (the entire object, not just a control point).

Miscellaneous

<, > and == let you **browse** your drawing as if every line of your drawing was a frame in a movie; < means backward, > means forward and == shows all lines in the drawing.

SETTINGS

Objects

One of the nicest things about **Gfig** is that you can save a whole bunch of drawings on disk. This makes it possible to create *standard figures* for your special needs.

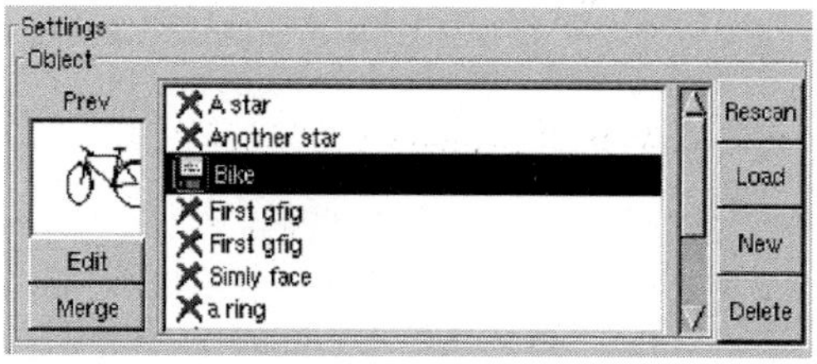

Figure 39.22 *The object part of Gfig*

To create a new drawing, just click **New** and name it in the **naming dialog**, and an empty drawing area will appear. The new drawing name is highlighted in blue, and there is a little floppy symbol at the left side of the name, indicating that the drawing hasn't been saved yet.

If you want to **rename** your drawing, just double-click its name. If you right-click at a name, you'll get a menu where you can **Save**, **Save as**, **Copy** and **Edit** the drawing.

To edit a drawing, choose the name and either right-click and select **edit** or press the Edit button. If you got some Gfig drawings from the Internet or from a friend, you can copy them to the gfig directory (`~/.gimp/gfig`), press **Re-scan** and they will appear in the name list. If you want to load a drawing outside of your Gfig directory, press **Load**. This brings up an ordinary open file dialog where you can choose a Gfig drawing. You can browse your drawings by highlighting them, and look at them in the **Prev** window. **Delete** pops up a dialog asking if you want to delete the drawing (both the file and the name in the browser).

The possibility to **merge** Gfig drawings is a very nice option. To do so, select a drawing and press **Edit**, then highlight the drawing that you want it to be merged with, and press **Merge**. The selected drawing will now merge with the highlighted drawing. Only the Edit drawing will be altered — the highlighted drawing will not be changed.

Command Bar

There's also a command bar at the bottom of Gfig. **Done** is for when you want to exit Gfig after you're finished with it. **Paint** executes your command, that is, it paints your Gfig drawing into a Gimp image according to your settings. **Save** saves a Gfig drawing. **Clear** will erase everything in the drawing area. **Undo** will undo your last operation. **Cancel** lets you exit Gfig, and drop all that you have done.

Grid

Grid controls the support grids in the Gfig drawing. If you have selected **Grid Type: Rectangle** in the **Options** tab, you can set the **grid size** in X*X pixels with the Grid spacing slide. You can also choose to *Display* the grid, and to make your objects *Snap to* the grid. **Snap to grid** is an excellent tool if you work with precision drawings. If you move objects with Snap, the anchor point you drag at will snap to the grid. If you move all your objects with Snap enabled, an invisible middle point will be calculated and that point will snap to the grid system.

THE TABS

Paint

The **Using** menu controls where paint is, or can be, applied. Use **Brush** to paint the outline of the drawing, **Selection** if you want to transform the drawing to a selection or **Selection+Fill** if you want to make a selection and then fill it with a color or pattern (see "Select" on page 608).

Figure 39.23 *The Paint tab*

Draw on determines where the drawing is placed. **Original** puts the drawing on the original image, **new** creates a new layer for the drawing and **Multiple** creates a new layer for each object in your drawing. If you select New or Multiple, you can also set what type of background you want for the new layer. There are four options: **Transparent**, **Background** (fills with the current background color in the toolbox), **White** and **Copy** (copies the original image to the new layer). If you choose Multiple, the previous layer will be copied to the new layer.

Example:

- Input image `julius.tif` and a Gfig drawing with three objects. **Draw on Multiple** with **Bg Transparent**. This setting results in:
  - **Background:** Julius
  - **Layer 0:** The first draw object
  - **Layer 1:** The second draw object
  - **Layer 2:** The third draw object.
- Input image `julius.tif` and a Gfig drawing with three objects. **Draw on Multiple** with **Bg Copy**. This setting results in:
  - **Background:** Julius
  - **Layer 0:** Julius plus object 1
  - **Layer 1:** Julius plus objects 1 and 2
  - **Layer 2:** Julius plus objects 1, 2 and 3.

This obviously fits like a glove when you want to make GIF animations (see "Animation Filters" starting on page 369).

With the **Reverse line** option, you can control the direction of brush strokes. Normally, the *rendering* of your stroke goes from the first control point to the last one. If you set **brush fade out** to 20 in the Brush tab, the stroke will fade out after 20 pixels (counted from the first control point). If you check Reverse line it will fade out from the last control point instead of the first. This option works with lines, curves and polygons. When it come to polygons, fading goes clockwise from the first control point if Reverse line is unchecked.

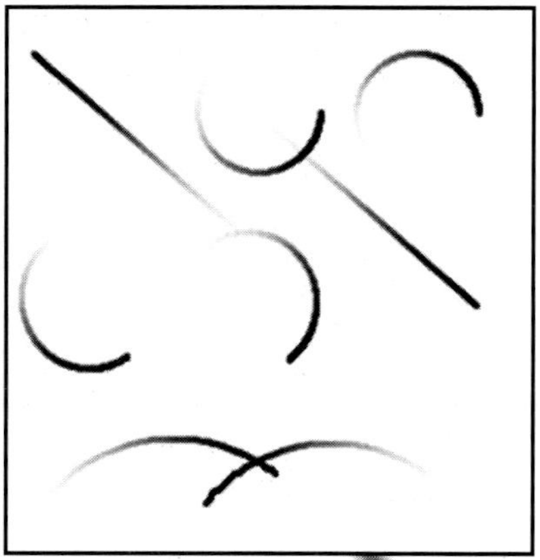

Figure 39.24 *The difference between having Reverse line unchecked and checked. If you check Approx Circles/Ellipse, fading will also apply to circles and ellipses.*

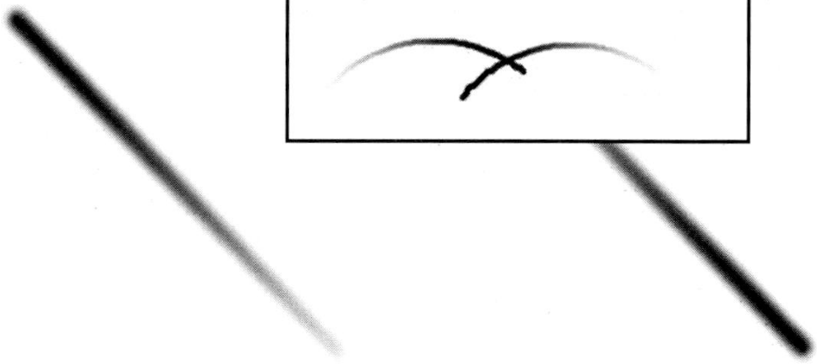

Figure 39.25 *Line in Gfig, which starts at 10,15 and ends at 220,220*

If you check **Approx. Circles/Ellipse**, fading also applies to circles and ellipses. The fading goes clockwise from the *first* control point. For example, if your first control point is at 5 o'clock, then the non-faded part will start at 5 o'clock and continue to fade so that your line fades out at 10 o'clock.

Using **Scale to image**, the drawings can be set to fit the image, or just get bigger or smaller. Just uncheck and drag the slider to *scale up/down*. This is a nice option that makes it easy to **magnify** your drawings and work with small details. When you're done, check Scale to image to *zoom out*.

Brush

In this tab you choose a suitable **paint brush**. A tip is to bring up the **Select brush** dialog so you can set the spacing and opacity of the brush; otherwise, Gfig will use the default values of the brush you select. To select a brush, highlight it, and it will be displayed in the preview.

You can choose from four different types of brushes. **Brush** is an ordinary brush, with a Fade Out control that controls where the stroke will start to fade out (If Fade Out is set to 0.0, there will be no fading). **Airbrush** is like a spray can with pressure control, **Pencil** is like a brush with hard edges, and **Pattern** allows you to paint with a pattern (much like the Clone tool does).

Figure 39.26 *The Brush tab, notice that fading is disabled if Fade Out is set to 0.0*

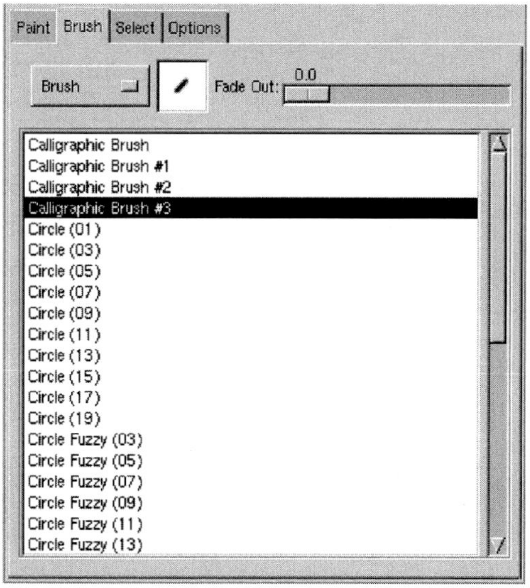

Select

This folder is only enabled when painting with **Select** or **Select+Fill**. In order to understand the different Selection types, you have to have a fairly good grasp of basic selection (see "Selection Tools" starting on page 109).

Figure 39.27 *The Select tab*

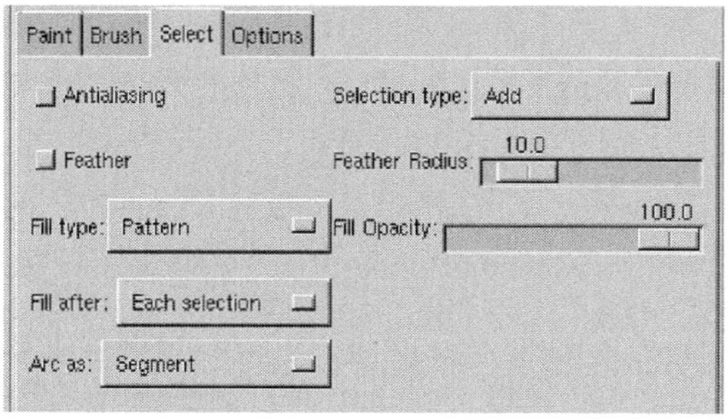

An Example

Suppose that you have made two (overlapping) star objects, and you have selected **Paint with Select** in the Paint folder. If you now choose **Add** as Selection type, you'll get a selection that is a *combination* of the two objects (a merged double star).

If you choose **Sub**, you'll get nothing (because there is no selection to subtract from), but if there had been a previous selection, the shape of the twin stars would be **cut** from this selection. If you choose **Replace**, the previous selection will be **replaced** with the star that you painted last in the drawing area. **Intersect** means that the intersection of the two star objects will become a selection.

You can fill the selection with a **pattern**, **foreground** or **background** color (Fill Opacity controls the transparency of the fill). You must bring up the **Pattern dialog** to set a pattern; otherwise, the last or default pattern will be used. The **Fill after** button controls the fill order; e.g., if you choose **All selections** and **Replace** as the selection type, only the last drawing object will be filled. If you had chosen **Each selection,** then all objects would get filled.

Feather controls the gradual transparency or edge softness of the selection. **Arc as** determines how curved objects will be treated. If you set this parameter to **Sector**, curves will be treated as circle sectors (pie slices), and if you set it to **Segment**, they are filled as circle segments (half-moons). The last option is Antialiasing, which is generally good to enable.

Options

This folder contains various options, like the possibility to make an image appear in the **preview** drawing area, or to **reload** it after applying a drawing. You can also **hide** the center points in drawing objects, get **tool tips**, set a different level of **undo**, or change the color and shape of the **grid** system. You can also choose to show the X/Y position of the mouse in the **Obj Details** window. If you want to achieve a high level of precision, this option is very useful.

Figure 39.28 *The Options*

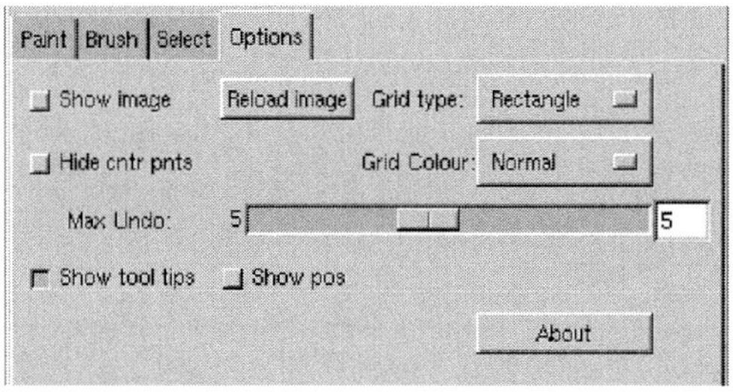

EXAMPLE

In order to understand this nice plug-in, we will give you a simple example: How to make a star with sparkles around it and a gradient fill.

1. Bring up a new (black) image, invoke Gfig and choose **New Object**.

Figure 39.29 *Click New in the Object part of Gfig*

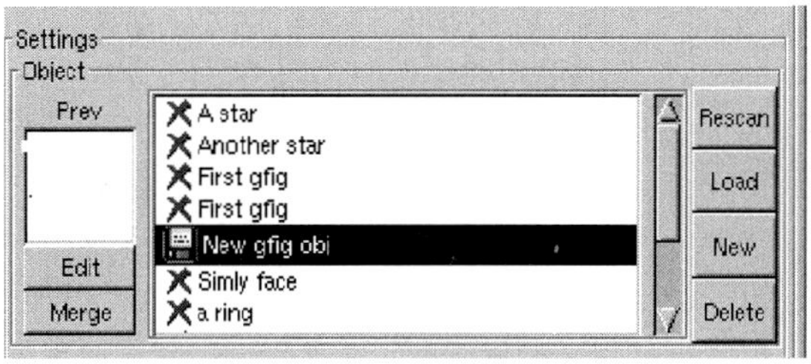

2. Choose the **star** object, set it to seven spikes and draw it.

Figure 39.30 *Double-click on the Star symbol in the Gfig drawing area*

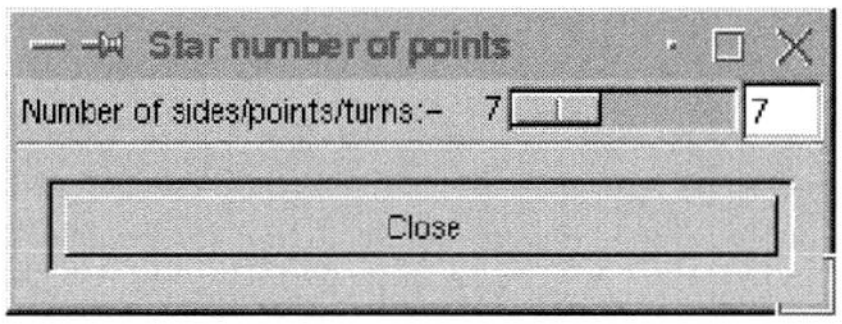

Figure 39.31 *Draw the star*

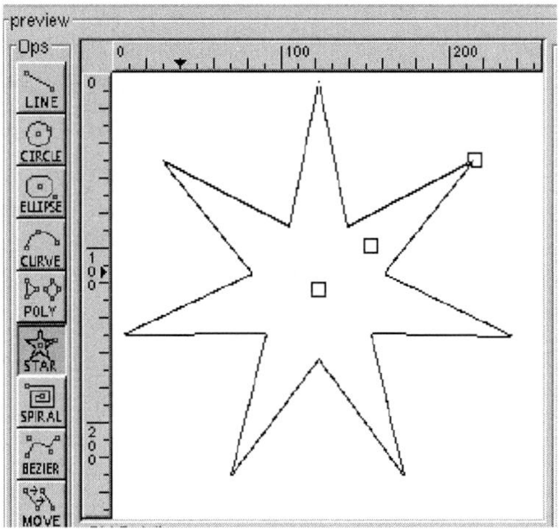

3. Choose **Paint with Brush** and a Brush/Small Galaxy brush.

Figure 39.32 *Click on the Brush tab to select the Galaxy brush*

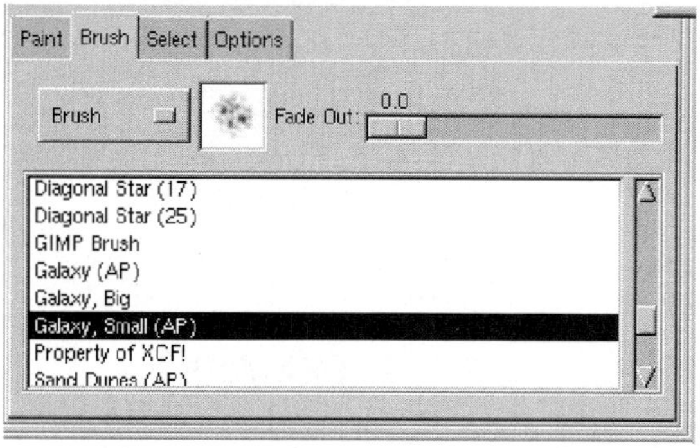

4. Press **Paint** to paint the sparkling outline of your star.

Figure 39.33 *The painted outline of the star*

5. Now switch to **Paint with Selection**.
6. Press **Paint**, which will produce a star-shaped **selection.**
7. Now, bring up the **Gradient Editor** and choose Cold_Steel as a gradient.
8. Double-click on the **Blend tool** (in the toolbox) and set Blend to Custom and Gradient to Conical (asymmetric) in the dialog.
9. Set the Blend tool in the center of the star and blend. You will now have a frosty star.
10. We have added a little extra glamour to the star by applying the `right-click|Filters|Light Effects|Sparkle` plug-in.

Figure 39.34 *The final frosty star*

Figure 39.35 *The star will look more frosty if you add some Sparkle to it*

GRID

With the **Grid** filter you can easily create a grid system. The Size parameter controls the size and proportions of the grid squares, measured in pixels. **Offset** controls where (in pixels) the first unbroken square will be drawn.

Figure 39.36 *The Grid filter is both useful and versatile.*

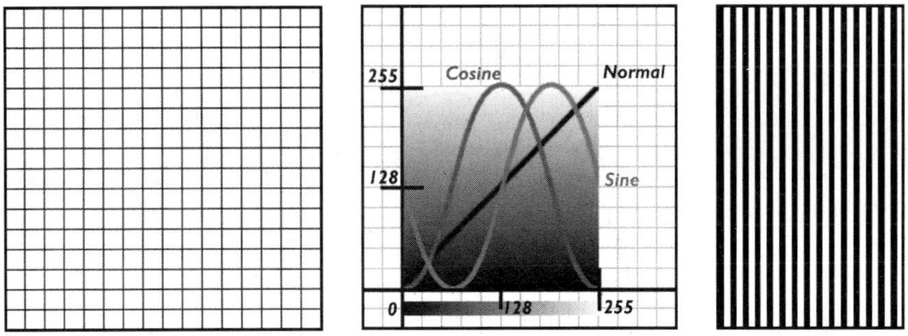

Simple Grid *Grid as base in a curve diagram* *Grid used to make stripes*

HFG

HFG creates **height fields** just like in a map, except that a map is real and HFG generates its height fields randomly.

HFG can produce very interesting results if it's used together with the BumpMap filter. If you use an HFG, generated image as a map with the `right-click|`

`Filters|Map|Bump Map` plug-in, you will actually see the hills and valleys in the bumpmapped image.

A warning is needed here. If the Color button is not checked, the rendered image may turn out black.

The HFG Interface

- The **Points** value sets the number of major hills.
- **Area of Effect** controls the "rockiness" of the landscape. Values can be set to between 0.01 and 0.99. Low values will produce a very rocky landscape. Useful values tend to lie around 0.5.
- **Mass Displacement** controls how many small hills, or peaks, will be rendered. It's a relative value and should be between 1 and the specified number of Points. A low value tends to give you a large number of small hills.
- **Seed** controls the randomization value. It can either be a fixed value or it can be set to the current time by checking the time button.

HFG image, used as map in the bumpmap

Solid image to bumpmap

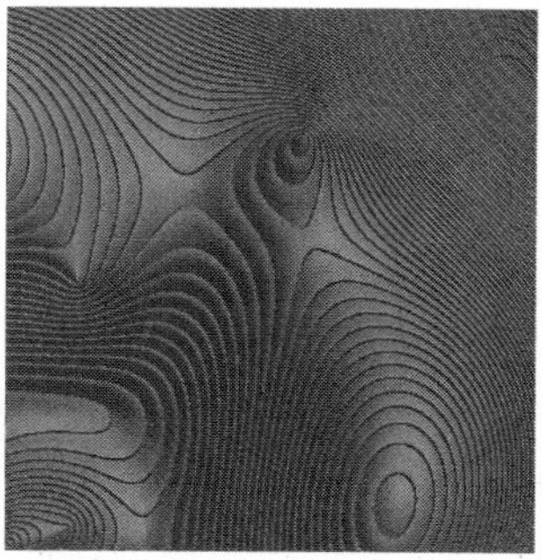

Bumpmapped result

Figure 39.37 *Example of how HFG can be used to create a bumpmapped 3-D landscape*

Harmonic Colors

The **Harmonic Colors** filter creates softly blurred diamond-shaped *color clouds*. A sine function controls the color distribution. Changing the **phase** values in a certain color channel means that the amount of that color and its complimentary (inverted) color will be adjusted.

As you might expect, **Y phase** values affect the horizontal scale and **X** the vertical scale. Low or high values produce weaker colors and middle values produce the strongest colors. You can set negative values or values exceeding 1.00, but that is not recommendable. To avoid strange banding, stick to the value range from 0 to 0.99.

Figure 39.38 *Example of Harmonic Colors*

IFS Compose

This **fractal**-based plug-in is truly wonderful! With this versatile instrument, you can create amazingly naturalistic organic shapes, like leaves, flowers, branches, or even whole trees.

Figure 39.39 *Landscape, flowers, trees...it was all created in IFS Compose.*

How To Use IFS Compose

The key to using this plug-in lies in making very *small* and *precise* movements in fractal space. The outcome is always hard to predict, and you have to be extremely gentle when you change the pattern. If you make a fractal triangle too big, or if you move it too far (even ever so slightly), the preview screen will black out, or more commonly, you'll get stuck with a big shapeless particle cloud.

A word of advice: When you have found a pattern you want to work with, make only small changes, and stick to variations of that pattern. It's all too easy to lose a good thing. Contrary to what you might believe, it's really much easier to create a leaf or a tree with IFS Compose than to make a defined geometrical pattern (where you actually know what you're doing, and end up with the pattern you had in mind).

The Main Interface

The plug-in interface consists of the **compose area** to the left, a **preview** screen to the right, and some tabs and option buttons at the bottom of the dialog.

The *Default* setting (in the preview window) is three equilateral triangles. To create a new pattern, you **Move**, **Rotate/Scale** and **Stretch** these triangles. You either use the three buttons under the compose area, or press the right mouse button to access a popup menu.

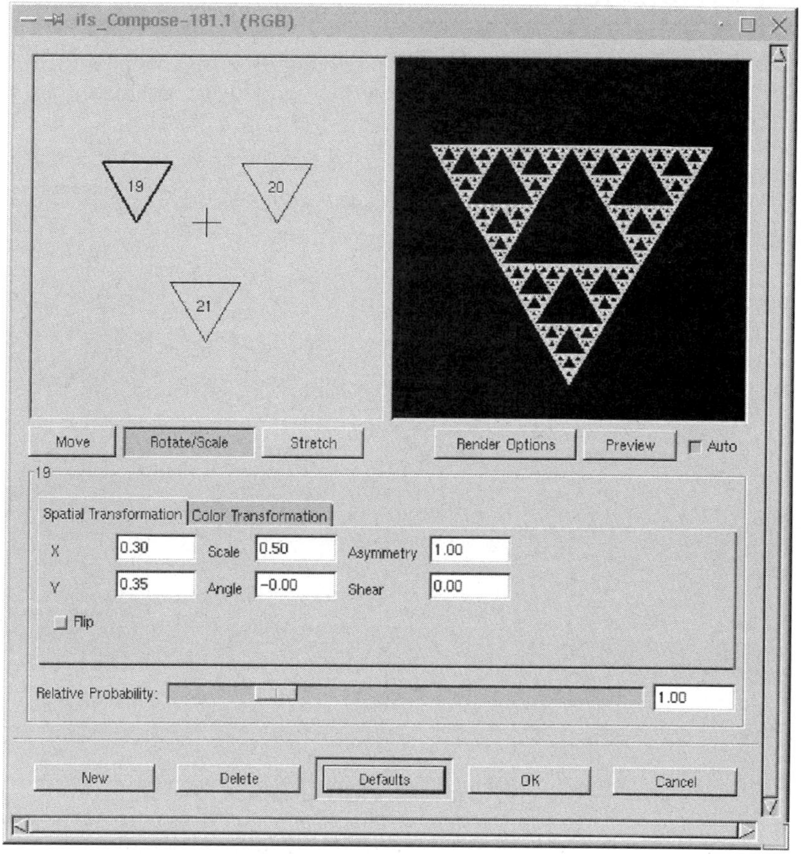

Figure 39.40 *The main IFS Compose dialog*

EXAMPLE

This is a rather complex plug-in, so to help you understand it, we'll guide you through an example where you'll create a leaf or branch.

Figure 39.41 *Leaf created with IFS Compose*

Many forms of life, and especially plants, are built like mathematical fractals, i.e., a shape that reproduces or repeats itself indefinitely into the smallest detail. You can easily reproduce the shape of a leaf or a branch by using four (or more) fractals. Three fractals make up the tip and sides of the leaf, and the fourth represents the stem.

1. Before invoking the filter: Select `File|New Image`. Add a transparent layer with `Layers|Layers & Channels|New Layer`. Set the foreground color in the toolbox to green, and set the background to white.
2. Open IFS Compose. Start by **rotating** the right and bottom triangles, so that they point *upward*. You'll now be able to see the outline of what's going to be the *tip* and *sides* of the leaf.

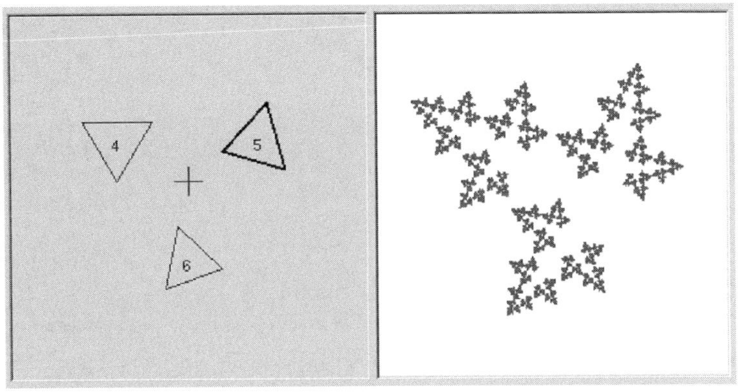

Figure 39.42 *The first stage of our leaf*

3. To make the leaf symmetrical, adjust the *bottom* triangle to point slightly to the *left*, and the *right* triangle to point slightly to the right.

4. Press **New** to *add* a fractal to the composition. This is going to be the stem of the leaf, so we need to make it long and thin. Press **Stretch**, and *drag* to stretch the new triangle. Don't be alarmed if this messes up the image, just use **Scale** to adjust the size of the overlong triangle. You'll probably also have to move and rotate the new fractal to make it look convincing.

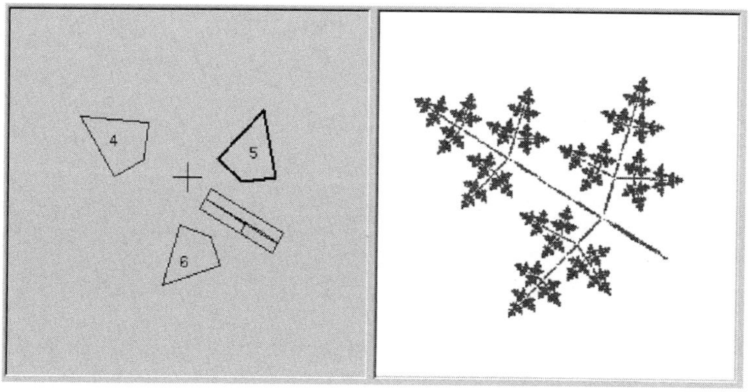

Figure 39.43 *The second stage of our leaf*

5. You still have to make it look more leaf-like. Increase the **size** of the top triangle, until you think it's thick and leafy enough. Adjust all fractals until you're happy with the shape. Right-click to get the popup menu, and choose **Select all**. Now all fractals are selected, and you can scale and rotate the entire leaf.

Figure 39.44 *The third stage of our leaf*

6. The final step is to adjust **color**. Click on the **Color Transformation** tab, and choose a different color for each fractal. To do this, check **Simple** and press the *right* color square. A color circle appears, where you can click or select to choose a color.

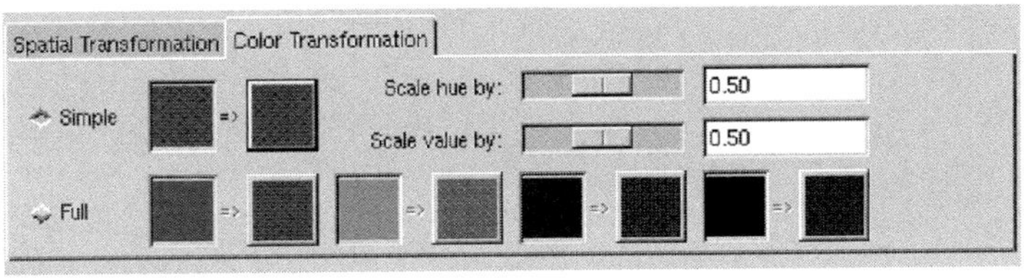

Figure 39.45 *Final stage, adding the right*

7. Press **OK** to apply the image, and voilà, you've just made a perfect fractal leaf! Now, when you've got the hang of it, you'll just have to experiment and make your own designs. All plant-imitating fractals (be they oak trees, ferns or straws) are more or less made in this fashion, which is leaves around a stem (or several stems). You just have to twist another way, stretch and turn a little or add a few more fractals to get a totally different plant.

Figure 39.46 *We have just created this delicate fern leaf with amazing detail, just by a few simple operations in the IFS Compose filter*

Main Options

- **Relative Probability:** Determines influence or total impact of a certain fractal.
- **Spatial Transformation:** Gives you information on the active fractal, and allows you to type a value instead of changing it manually. Changing parameters with the mouse isn't very accurate, so this is a useful option when you need to be exact.
- **Simple color transformation:** Changes the current fractal color (which is the foreground color in the toolbox) to a color of your choice.

- **Scale Hue/Value:** When you have many fractals with different colors, the colors *bleed* into each other. So even if you set "pure red" for a fractal, it might actually be quite blue in some places, while another "red" fractal might have a lot of yellow in it. Scale Hue/Value changes the color strength of the active fractal, or how influential that fractal's color should be.
- **Full color transformation:** Changes color influence from the other (inactive) fractals. You can, for example, in the red fractal, set Full color transformation to red in all of the swatches, and you won't get any influence at all in that part of the fractal composition.

Render Options

- **Spot Radius:** Determines the density of the "brushstrokes" in the rendered image. A low spot radius is good for thin particle clouds or spray, while a high spot radius produces thick, solid color strokes much like watercolor painting (see Figure 39.47 at the bottom right). Be careful not to use too much spot radius — it takes a lot of time to render.
- **Subdivide:** Controls the level of detail.
- **Iterations:** Determines how many times the fractal will repeat itself. (A high value for Subdivide and Iterations is for obvious reasons a waste of process time unless your image is very large.)
- **Max. Memory:** Enables you to speed up rendering time. This is especially useful when working with a large spot radius; just remember to use even multiples of the default value: 4,096, 8,192, 16,384....

Figure 39.47 *Ther e is no end to what you can create with IFS Compose and a little imagination*

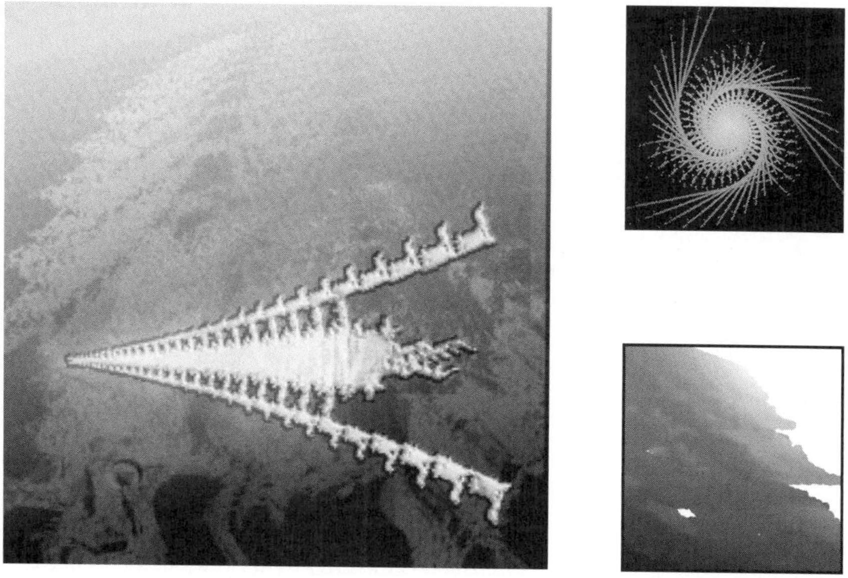

JIGSAW

The **Jigsaw** filter will create a jigsaw puzzle of your image. Jigsaw puzzles and puzzle pieces can be nice gadgets for web pages.

EXAMPLE

In the following example we will make a half-finished jigsaw puzzle.

1. Start by opening an image that will make a nice puzzle. Open the Layers & Channel dialog (`right-click|Layers|Layers & Channels`) and **duplicate** the background layer. Name this layer *Puzzle*.
2. **Bucket Fill** the original image layer (Background) with an appropriate background color (we used a plain white background).
3. Make the *Puzzle* layer active. Apply the Jigsaw filter and press **OK** (we will explain the parameters later on).
4. Create a **new layer** with a white fill type (the width and height must be the same as in the background layer). Name this layer *White Puzzle* and make sure that it is the top layer. Select this layer and run the Jigsaw filter once again with the same values (`right-click|Filters|Repeat Last`).
5. Apply `right-click|Image|Colors|Brightness-Contrast` to the *White Puzzle* layer. Adjust the contrast to the highest value and press `OK`. You will now have a white puzzle without highlights and shadows.
6. In the *White Puzzle* layer, select the pieces that should be missing from the puzzle with the **Fuzzy Selection** tool. Select the first piece, then hold down Ctrl and select the next piece, and so on, until you have selected all pieces.
7. Select the *Puzzle* layer and toggle off the eye icon from the *White Puzzle* layer.
8. Move the selection (still with the Fuzzy selection tool enabled) and you will get a **floating selection**. Double-click on the Floating Selection bar in the Layers & Channels dialog, and name the layer *Missing Pieces*.
9. Select the *Puzzle* layer and run `right-click|Script-Fu|Shadow|Drop Shadow`. Use the following parameter values in the Drop Shadow dialog: **Xoffset = 4**, **Y offset = 4**, **Blur Radius = 10**, **Color = Black**, **Opacity = 80** and check **Allow Resizing**. You will now see a shadow under your puzzle.
10. Select the *Missing Pieces* layer. Select a puzzle piece with the **Bezier** tool. Carefully adjust the Bezier curve so that you'll only select one piece. When you have turned the Bezier curve into a selection, run `right-click|Select|Float`.
11. Double-click on the Floating selection bar in the Layers & Channels dialog, and name the layer *Single Piece*. Now, you can move your piece to an appropriate place and maybe rotate it a bit. Run the **Drop Shadow** script on this piece, and use the same values as before.

12. Toggle on the eye icon for all layers except the *White Puzzle* layer and the *Missing Pieces* layer, and you will have a nice jigsaw puzzle image.

Figure 39.48 *The final result of our Jigsaw example*

Parameter Settings

The Jigsaw filter has a few parameters.

- The **Number of Tiles** sliders control the number of tiles rendered vertically and horizontally.
- The **Bevel width** slider controls the slope of the edges of the puzzle pieces (a hard wooden puzzle would require a low Bevel width value, and a soft cardboard puzzle would require a higher value).
- The **Highlight** slider controls the strength of the highlight that will appear on the edges of each piece. You may compare it to the "glossiness" of the material the puzzle is made of. Highlight width is relative to the Bevel width. As a rule of thumb, the more pieces you add to the puzzle, the lower Bevel and Highlight values you should use, and vice versa. The default values are suitable for a 500x500 pixel image.
- The **Jigsaw Style** radio buttons control the shape of the puzzle pieces. We used **Curved** pieces for the example image.

L-Systems

Lindenmayer Systems, called L-Systems, is a mathematical formalism designed primarily for concise description of natural shapes of plants. You can find out more about the history of L-Systems in the publications mentioned at the end of this description.

Figure 39.49 *L-Systems*

The whole concept of L-Systems consists of two main parts:

- Preparing the L-Systems description.
- Applying this formula to render a graphic representation.

During the preparation stage, the program iteratively applies a set of rewriting rules onto a string. The process starts with an initial string (called *axiom*) and for every iteration this string grows longer. The preparation is finished when the given number of iterations have been completed.

A Simple Example

To clarify this description, let's take a look at a simple example:

```
Axiom = A
Rules = A -> BA and
        B -> A
```

What does it mean?

It means that we start with a **string** of **length 1** that contains the letter **A**. For each iteration, we replace every **A** with a string **BA** and every **B** with string **A**. This is how it goes:

```
Iteration 0   A
Iteration 1   BA
Iteration 2   ABA
Iteration 3   BAABA
Iteration 4   ABABAABA
```

Note that we can use many different letters in both the axiom and the rules. If a string should contain a letter for which no rule has been defined, it will be ignored and passed to the resulting string. For example:

```
Axiom = A
Rules = A -> BA
        B -> AC
```

```
Iteration 0   A
Iteration 1   BA
Iteration 2   ACBA
Iteration 3   BACACBA
```

As you can see, by using a small and concise description we can obtain quite complex and long character strings. This is the first important lesson about L-Systems. You need only define the **seed** and **rules** that govern growth to generate large and complicated, yet interesting, data.

Graphic Representation

To **convert** the string generated during the *first phase* of the process into its **graphical representation**, we must come to an agreement on some assumptions. You can compare the **rendering** process to an imaginary *turtle* that draws a line while wandering over our image. What the turtle does is to "*eat*" consecutive characters, and then it decides what to do next based on that information. Any character that has no meaning for the turtle is simply ignored. The following three characters have **fixed meanings**:

- The **F** character means **go forward** one step, drawing a line.
- The **f** character means **jump forward** one step.
- The (and) characters will cause our turtle to save its state (position, heading, parameters of its drawing tool), decrease the step length by a given factor and to draw a subsystem until it encounters a matching closing brace.
- Traditionally, the characters **+** and **-** mean turn left and turn right, but in this plug-in they are defined as so-called **special rules**. Users are encouraged to keep the original meaning of these two signs for the sake of readability.

As an illustration for the render process, walk through the following example:

String to be rendered: **F+fFf+AFAF**. Let's assume that the initial position of the turtle is (0,0), initial heading is 0 degrees (the turtle is "looking" to the right), step length is 1 and the turn angle associated with the **+** and **-** characters is equal to 90 degrees.

Interpreted character	Position (x,y)	Heading	Result
	0,0	0	
F	1,0	0	a line from (0,0) to (1,1)
+	1,0	90	
f	1,1	90	
F	1,2	90	a line from (1,1) to (1,2)
f	1,3	90	
+	1,3	180	
A	1,3	180	(character ignored)
F	0,3	180	a line from (1,3) to (0,3)
A	0,3	180	(character ignored)
F	-1,3	180	a line from (0,3) to (1,3)

It's when you combine the possibilities offered by a concise description of long strings, by rewriting the rules with a drawing turtle that lets the characters describe its way, that you get a really powerful tool.

This idea is called L-Systems.

Take a look at the final example before we move on to some implementation details. This is **Koch's curve**. Below, you have its definition as an L-System; first three iterations, and a picture drawn on the basis of the third string.

```
Axiom = F
Rules = F -> F-F++F-F

Iteration 0   F
Iteration 1   F-F++F-F
Iteration 2   F-F++F-F-F-F++F-F++F-F++F-F-F-
F++F-F
...
```

As you can tell from the picture, the angle added to the current turtle heading by **+** and **-** characters equals 60 degrees.

Figure 39.50 *L-System*

Using The L-Systems Plug-in

What can you do with the L-Systems Plug-in?

- You can create a new L-System and give it a unique name and a unique file name in which the definition will be stored. You can also use an existing L-System as a base of a newly defined one, but be sure not to forget to change the file name or you will lose either the new or the old one! All this is done within the top-left part of the plug-in's GUI. There is a list with all defined L-Systems and a set of buttons to perform various operations on them.
- You can define your L-System by entering an **axiom**, a set of **rules** and the number of **iterations** that should be performed before rendering. Use the first page of the notebook at the bottom of the GUI. Adding rules is as simple as pressing the **Add** button and filling in the pop-up dialog window. The same goes for editing and removing rules.
- You can define a set of additional rules applied once only after the last iteration. You'll learn more about such rules later. To manipulate the set of last rules you should switch to the second page of the notebook widget.
- Once you've defined the L-System, you have to move on to the *third page of the notebook* at the bottom of the GUI, and specify the correct information about at least two *special symbols*: **+** and **-**. This is because the special rules for these characters are always included in the set of special rules. The only thing you will probably have to do is to provide correct information about the turn angles.
- Here I should explain something. What does these *magic* special rules entries mean? That's quite simple, the rule:

  ```
  + -> 60.00:    <<CURRENT>>:    -1: -1%:(NO CHANGE)
  ```

  means exactly the following: The **plus** character will cause the turtle to increase its heading angle by 60 degrees, to keep the current brush, not to change brush spacing (the first **-1**), not to change the opacity (the second **-1**) and not to change the drawing color.
- In the end you can change various rendering parameters like **initial position** and **heading**, **step length**, **turn** and **step** randomness and others.

Advanced Features

Using Braces

As I explained before, you can introduce **matched braces** in both the **axiom** and in all **rules**. They are significant during the rendering process because they cause the turtle to draw part of the L-System in a separate context. The most common use of braced L-Systems is to draw plant-like shapes. You use braces to denote that after the turtle draws *a branch*, it should return to the position where the branch started and continue drawing the *main trunk*. You can change **brush shapes**, **colors**, **spacing** and so on while drawing the branch, but all of these changes will have no effect on the visualization of the trunk and, possibly, the consecutive branches.

As an example, look carefully at the definition of L-Systems with names that start with "Plant/".

The Purpose Of Last Rules

An additional set of rules applied once, just before rendering, serves several purposes. First, it can be used to translate abstract objects (with no turtle meaning) used in main rules into something visible. You often do this when designing plants or flowers. In this case, every character in main rules and the axiom would have a specific meaning, like root, trunk, leaf and so on. Every such abstract symbol should be transformed into something visible with a given color, brush shape and length.

Secondly, you can use last rules to modify the generated shape to make it look more interesting. This is quite common when the L-System looks like a kind of grid. It would be more interesting if you could see the way the turtle has drawn the shape but that's impossible because many lines are connected in a single point.

To avoid that, one should define a set of three simple last rules, which will make turns less sharp:

```
+ -> +F+

- -> -F-

F -> FF
```

Be sure to adjust the definition of + and - in the special rules section. They must use half the angle they had before the introduction of the last rules. Probably, the length of a single step will also have to be cut in half.

Effective Use Of Special Rules

Last rules are not only turns! You can use them quite extensively to make your L-Systems look more lively and realistic.

- First comes **brushes**, which will provide you with various textures and line styles.
- Second is **color**. The purpose of using color in the image you are painting is something you probably know better than me!
- Third is **opacity**. It works great in plants, where, for example leaves can be made somewhat translucent to make the picture more interesting. Painting with a semi-opaque paint can also produce nice effects when

drawing patterns with intersecting lines. The final color of various parts of the image will then depend on how many times the pixel has been painted — and with what color!

- Fourth and last is **spacing**, which probably has only one use: to make the program draw just a single *print* of a brush instead of an awful *line* painted with a brush that was not designed for it.

Where To Look For More Information

If you are interested in the concept of L-Systems look for the following books/articles. For more references, look in Prusinkiewicz's book.

- P. Prusinkiewicz, J. Hanan Lindenmayer Systems, Fractals and Plants in series *"Lecture Notes in Biomathematics,"* Springer Verlag, 1989.
- A. R. Smith *"Plants, Fractals and Formal Languages"* in ACM Computer Graphics, vol. 18, no 3, July 1984.

Figure 39.51 *Examples of L-Systems creations. As you can see, they are quite a bit like the IFS Compose outputs. The main difference, from a user perspective, is that you can save L-Systems figures. On the other hand L-Systems are much more abstract, and it is much harder to create and control the organic shapes.*

Maze

The **Maze** filter will generate a **maze**. If you want to use it in a pattern, you can make the maze *tileable* by checking the **Tileable?** checkbutton.

The **Width** and **Height** sliders control how many pathways the maze should have. The *lower* the values for width and height, the *more* paths you will get. The same happens if you *increase* the number of pieces in the Width and Height **Pieces** fields.

You can specify random **Seed** or use the current **Time** as randomizer. Using random seed means that the maze pattern will be different each time you invoke the filter.

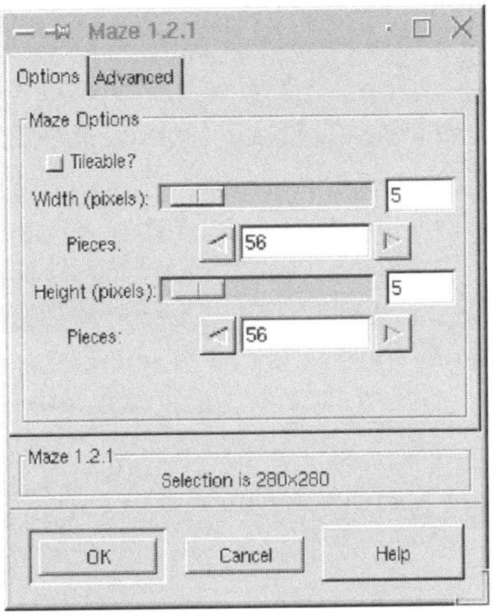

Figure 39.52 *The Maze dialog*

NCP

NCP generates random cloud formations. The rendered image is *tileable*, so you can use it as a seamless **pattern**.

The amount of major clouds is controlled by the **Point** parameter. A high value will produce more major clouds. The number of minor clouds is controlled by the **foo-point** parameter. This is a value between 1 and the specified number of major clouds.

You can control the randomization with the **Seed** value or check **Time** to use the current time as a randomization value. If you are interested in biology, you might like to run `right-click|Image|Colors|Autostretch Contrast` on the generated image. The outcome may look like molecule chains, intestinal organs, neural fibers or skin tissue, depending on the values you have specified. Also try `right-click|Image|Colors|Adaptive Contrast`, which will produce a more chemical or crystalline effect.

Figure 39.54 *NCP*

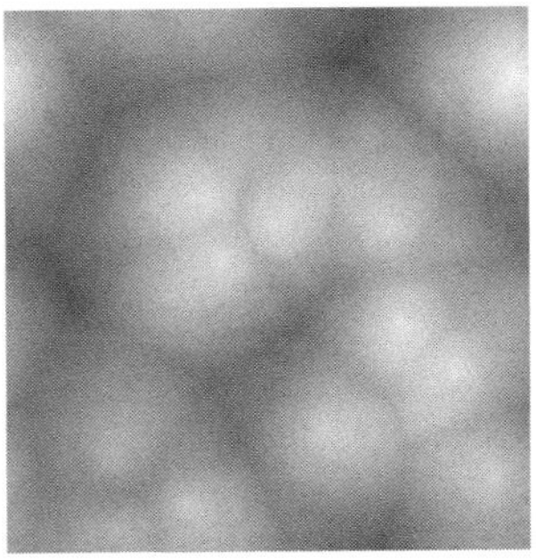

PLASMA

Plasma generates colorful *clouds*, which can be used for **textures**. However, the rendered plasma image is not tileable like the NCP filter.

You control the turbulence in the plasma cloud with the **Turbulence** slide. High values give a hard feeling to the cloud (like an abstract oil painting or mineral grains), low values produce a softer cloud (like steam, mist or smoke). You can also generate **Seed** for random variations in the plasma cloud.

Sometimes the strong colors may be distracting, and a more interesting surface will appear when you desaturate the image using `right-click|Image|Colors|Desaturate`.

Figure 39.55 *Example of plasma*

PHOTO MOSAIC

Photo Mosaic creates a **mosaic** of a target image, where the mosaic stones consists of a lot of small source images. This is not an unknown image manipulation technique. Last time I saw it was in the poster for the film *The Truman Show* with Jim Carrey. The poster cleverly built-up a portrait of Jim Carrey from of a lot of small pictures of TV-sets showing the actor in different situations.

IMAGE LIBRARIES

To make this filter produce a realistic photo mosaic, you'll need a huge image library. We are not talking about several hundred images. We mean several thousand images! Our image library comprises around 7,000 images. Luckily, the images don't have to be big.

Photo Mosaic doesn't use the CD-ROM image library as it is. It creates a special Photo Mosaic **library** containing downscaled images of the real image library so the actual image library will be smaller. What you have to remember about the source images for the Photo Mosaic image library is that they must be of *equal size*. The exact size is not important, but they should all have the same height and width.

When you invoke this filter, start by pressing the **Help** button. There you will find all the information that you need to create a Photo Mosaic image.

The Photo Mosaic image in Figure 39.56 was created from 1,000 tiles, or source images. Notice that to view the portrait in the image, you must look at it from a distance.

Figure 39.56 *You must view the Photo Mosaic from a distance in order to get the picture*

IMAGE SIZE

When we created this image, it was essential to make it rather large: 1122x1234 pixels (the original was later downscaled to save print space). Using a small target image with lots of detail makes little sense, because you will never be able to see the source images; the tiles will be too small.

The tiles used to render a small image will be downscaled to perhaps just one or two pixels in height and width. This will obviously make it impossible to see what kind of image it was originally. Images with too many small details will also not render well as Photo Mosaic images.

RANDOM PATH

With the default settings, **Random Path** creates multi-colored splotches similar to mold or vegetation. If you change the preferences, the path shapes will turn into long fiber or vein-like formations. The density of the Random Path pattern is controlled by the **Steps** and **Repeats** slide bars, and the color can be set to foreground, background or randomly picked colors.

Figure 39.57 *The Random Path dialog*

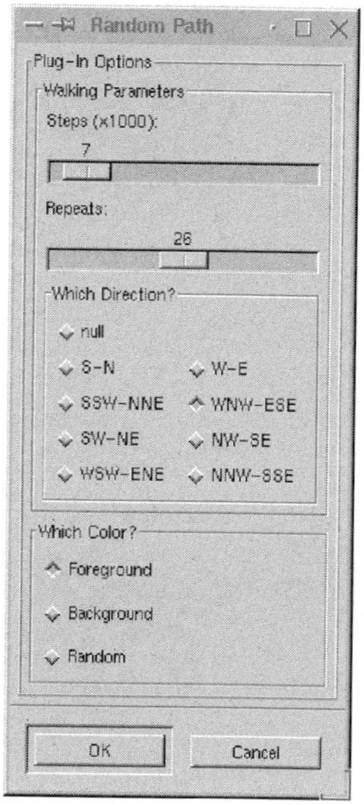

This filter is especially effective for creating mineral surfaces like stone, raw metal or marble-like patterns.

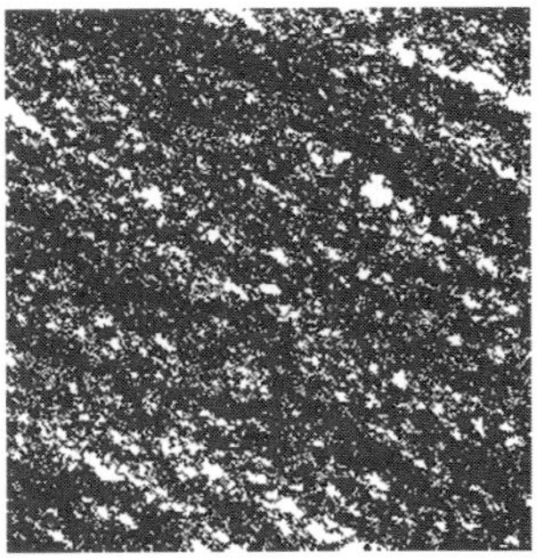

Figure 39.58 *Random Path creates rock-like*

QBIST

The **Qbist** filter generates *random* textures, much like KPT Texture Explorer.

The original texture is displayed in the middle square, and different variations surround it. If you like one of the alternative textures, click on it.

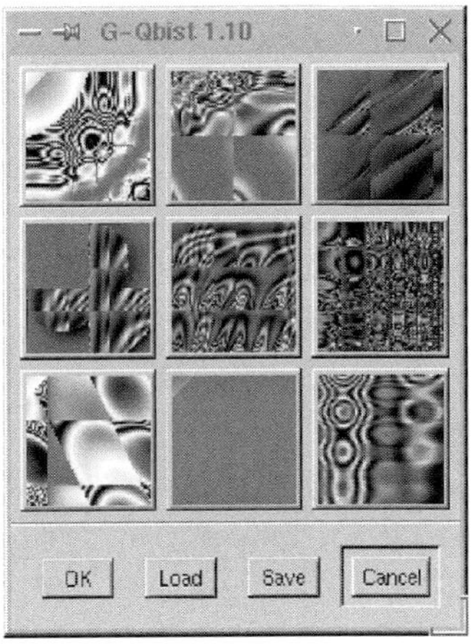

Figure 39.59 *The Qbist*

The chosen texture now turns up in the middle, and variations on that specific theme are displayed around it. When you have found the texture you want, click on it and then click OK. The texture will now appear on your drawable.

You can save and load your textures. This is quite handy because it's almost impossible to re-create a good pattern by just clicking around. You may also want to check out "Genetic" on page 599, which creates more geometrical patterns, or see "GAG" on page 377, which is another pattern generator of the same type.

Figure 39.60 *Qbist example*

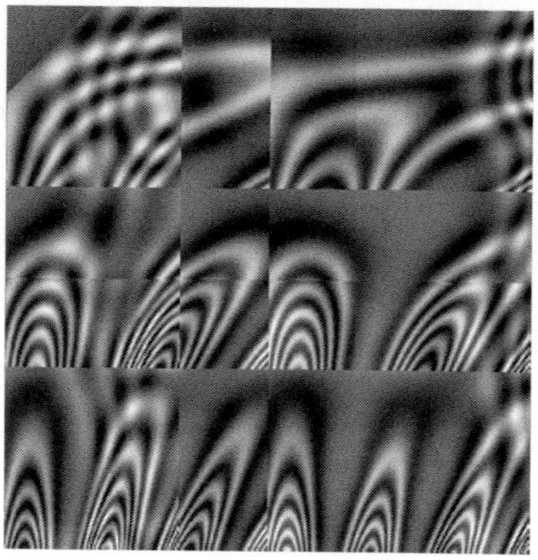

SINUS

The **Sinus** filter lets you make **sinusoidally** based *textures*, which looks rather like watered silk or plywood. This plug-in works by using two different colors that you can define in the **Colors** tab. These two colors then create wave patterns based on a sine function.

You can set the **X** and **Y scales**, which determine how *stretched* or *packed* the texture will be. You can also set the **Complexity** of the function; a high value creates more interference or repetition in the pattern. **Random seed** can be used to increase variation in the rendered patterns.

Figure 39.62 *The Sinus dialog*

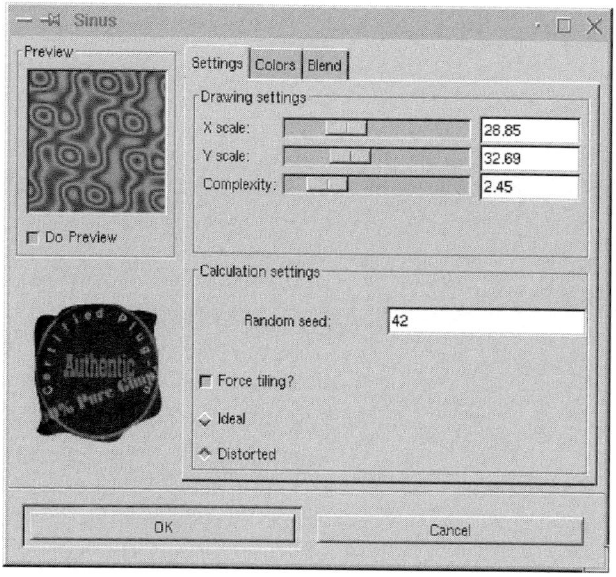

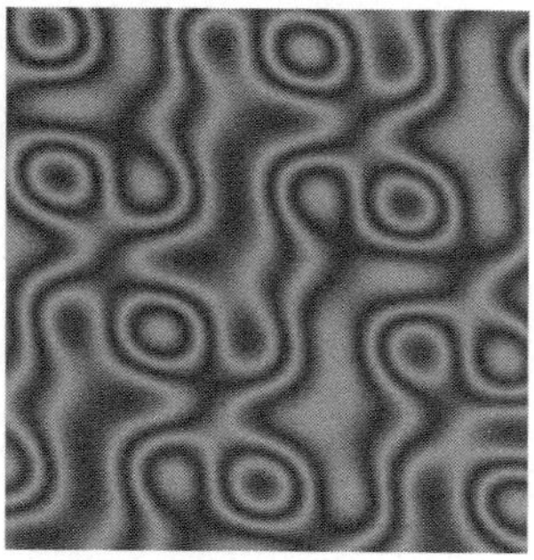

Figure 39.61 *Making a plywood-like pattern in Sinus is fairly easy.*

FUNCTIONS

X/Y Scale

A low **X/Y** value will maximize the horizontal/vertical stretch of the texture, whereas a high value will compress it.

Complexity And Random Seed

Complexity controls how the two colors interact with each other (the amount of interplay or repetition). **Random seed** increases variation in the pattern.

Force Tiling

If you want to use the texture as a *tiled* background in a web page, this option creates better looking tiles (though not quite seamless).

Tip: To get a perfect result, flip the tiles in the **Make Seamless** plug-in in the **Filters/Map** menu so that they mirror each other.

Ideal/Distorted

This option gives additional control of the interaction between the two colors. **Distorted** creates a more distorted interference between the two colors than **Ideal**.

THE COLOR TAB

Here, you set the two colors that make up your texture. You can use **Black and white** or the **foreground/background** colors in the toolbox, or you can choose a color with the **color icons**.

The **Alpha channel** controls the transparency of your texture; just remember that you need an alpha-enabled background or a layer.

THE BLEND TAB

In this folder you control the blend of the two colors. You can choose between three functions to set the blend: **Linear**, **Bilinear** and **Sinusoidal**.

The **Exponent** controls which color is dominant. If you set the exponent to -7.5, the *left* color will dominate totally, and if you set it to +7.5 it will be the other way around. A zero value is neutral.

Solid Noise

Solid Noise is a great texture maker. Note that this noise is always gray, even if you applied it to a very colorful image (it doesn't matter what the original image looks like — this filter doesn't use background information). This is also the filter you use for creating displacement maps for the Warp plug-in (see "Warp" on page 396.)

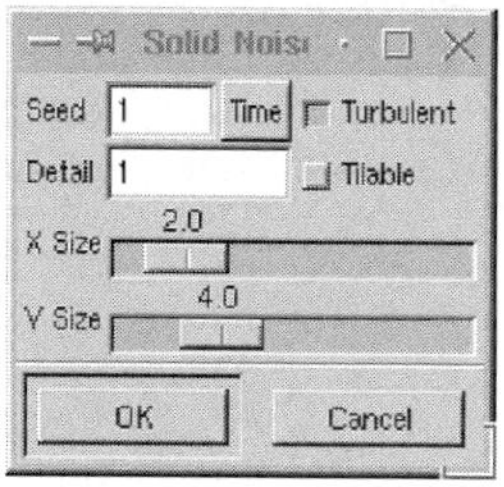

Figure 39.63 *The Solid Noise dialog*

Figure 39.64 *Exampl e of Solid Noise*

Parameter Settings

- **X** and **Y Size** control size and proportion of the noise shapes in X and Y directions.
- **Seed** generates a random variation in your texture.
- **Detail** controls the amount of detail in the noise texture. Higher values give a higher level of detail, and the noise seems to be made of spray or small particles, which makes it feel *hard.* A low value makes it more *soft* and *cloudy.*
- If you check **Turbulent**, you'll get very interesting effects, often something that looks much like oil on water (or living tissue).
- If you check **Tileable**, you'll get a noise which can be used as tiles. For example, you can use it as a background in an HTML page, and the tile edges will be invisible (seamless).

PART VIII

Miscellaneous Gimp Functions

- *How To Use AnimFrames*
- *Xinput And Tablets*

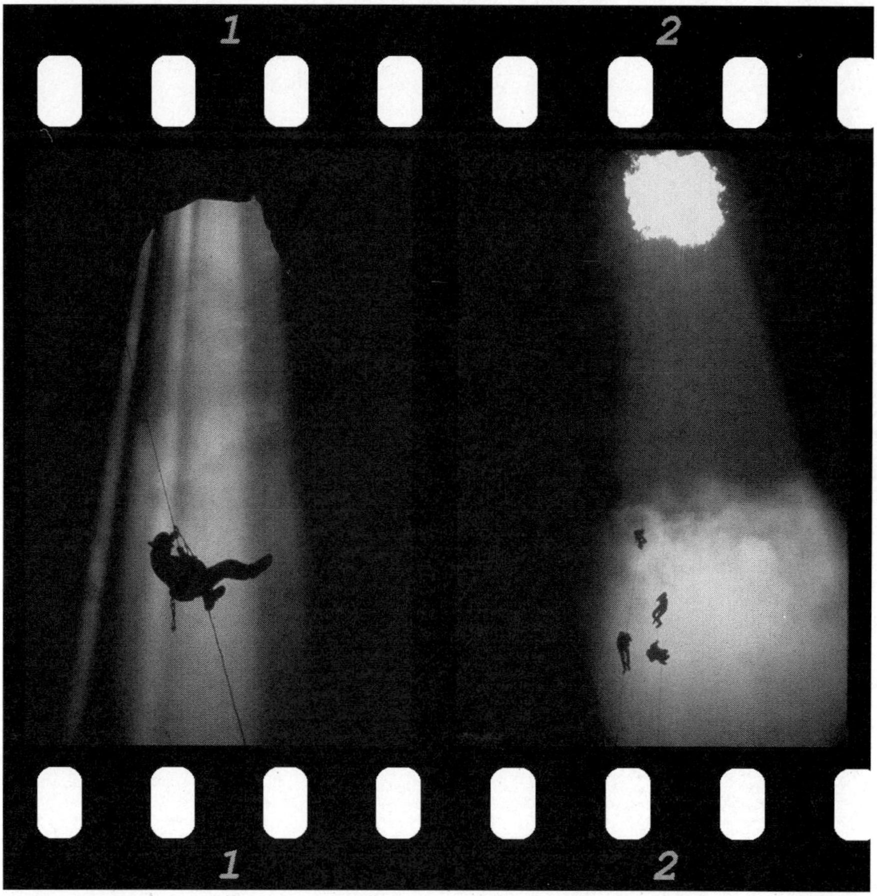
1
2

CHAPTER 40

Advanced Animation With Gimp Or How To Use AnimFrames

Gimp has many excellent tools for making animations. The far most advanced of these tools is AnimFrames. We will unleash the power of it in this chapter.

BASIC CONCEPTS

You will find the AnimFrames tool under `right-click|AnimFrames`. As the name indicates, AnimFrames works with image frames. A frame is an ordinary Gimp image saved with a special extension.

When you make an ordinary **GIF** animation you create a *multi-layered* image, where the object that you want to animate moves a little bit for every new layer. If you want to use more than one animation object, you have to put all of the objects in the same layer. This makes it hard to create advanced animations.

If you want to work with several objects that can move *independently* of each other, the ordinary Gimp animation filters do not suffice. To find out more about the Gimp animation filters, read "Animation Filters" starting on page 369.

AnimFrames overcomes this problem in a wonderful way. Instead of using a single multi-layered image, AnimFrames works with several images, where each image can have several layers with different objects in them. This makes every object independent of the other animation objects, just like in a cartoon frame where several people move around independently, because each character has been painted on a separate plastic sheet.

HOW TO CREATE AN ANIMATION WITH ANIMFRAMES

MAKING A FRAME

1. The first thing you have to determine when you create an animation is the *size* of the background image. When you've made up your mind, select `right-click|File|New`, and specify the desired size in the dialog box.
2. AnimFrames is built up of *frames*, and to turn your image into a frame, you must first **save** it. Choose `right-click|File|Save as` and save the new image as `animationname_0001.xcf` (the special extension for AnimFrames is `_0001.xcf`).
3. Now, it's time to create the frames. Choose `right-click|AnimFrames|Duplicate Frame`. This brings up a dialog asking you to specify how many duplicates you want, or in other words, how many frames you want for your animation (the slide only goes as far as to 50 frames, but you can easily change that by typing a number of frames in the field.)

Format And Save Functions

The format must be **XCF** (Gimp's native file format), but if you are low on disk space, you can choose a *compressed* XCF by adding `.gz` or `.bz` to the end of the frame name. To make this work, you must of course have either **gzip** or **bzip2** installed on your system.

Don't worry about saving; all frames are stored on disk immediately without explicit save. The same happens when you work with other tools in AnimFrames, so you only have to save when you *exit* AnimFrames.

How To Navigate Frames

We assume that you have now created a few basic frames, for example, 10 frames. We are in frame number 1 (`name_0001.xcf`).

> Before we start discussing this topic in depth, we must make something very clear; *you must never open two frames in Gimp at the same time!*
>
> If your animation is called **My_anim**, always make sure that you don't open `My_anim_0001.xcf` and `My_anim_0002.xcf` at the same time.
>
> *If you let this happen, things can get really bad, and in the worst scenario, destroy your animation and crash Gimp!*

This is certainly something that we want to avoid, so we suggest you use the special **AnimFrames** menu commands for navigating the frames instead. You can navigate in the following ways:

- `Goto First` will bring you to frame My_anim_0001.xcf
- `Goto Next` -> My_anim_0002.xcf
- `Goto Prev` -> My_anim_0001.xcf
- `Goto Last` -> My_anim_0010.xcf
- `Goto Any` will bring up a dialog asking you which frame to go to

The author of the plug-in suggests that you assign hotkeys to the `Goto` commands, because you will move around a lot in your frames.

Read more about hotkeys in "Default Shortcuts And Dynamic Key Bindings" starting on page 9. You can choose any key bindings you like, but here are a few suggestions:

`Goto First`	`Ctrl+Alt+1`
`Goto Prev`	`Alt+1`
`Goto Next`	`Alt+2`
`Goto Any`	`Alt+3`
`Goto Last`	`Ctrl+Alt+2`

YOUR FIRST ANIMATION

HOW TO MAKE A MOVE PATH

The main tool in AnimFrames is the **Move Path** tool. This tool allows you to move your animation object along a specified *path*. You need at least two things to make an animation:

- A set of frames, i.e., your 10 `My_anim` images
- An object to animate

1. To make an **animation object**, start by creating a new transparent image (`right-click|File|New`) and paint a simple object in the center of the image — a big, red do, for example.
2. Open the first frame (`My_anim_0001.xcf`) and select the **Move Path** option in the **AnimFrames** menu, and the Move Path window will appear. This window is where you control the animation sequence. This simple example will help you get a basic understanding of how Move Path works. Later in this chapter, we'll return for a more in-depth description of the *Move Path* window.
3. In the Source Select field, set **SourceImage/Layer** to your animation object. Set **Handle** to *Center,* **Stepmode** to *Loop* and **Mode** to *Normal.*
4. Mouse-click somewhere in the **preview** window, press the **Add Point** button and click somewhere else in the preview window.
5. Now, set the **Start Frame** slider to your *first* frame and the **End Frame** slider to your *last* frame. Leave the Layerstack and Preview Frame as they are and press **OK**.

You have now created your first animation. The red dot will move from the first click-point to the second, and it will use ten frames to complete the movement. In order to view the animation, you must select `AnimFrames|Frames Flatten` and include all of your frames in the **Select Frame Range** input field in the Frames Flatten dialog.

The second step is to make your frames turn into a *multi-layered* image. Do this by selecting `AnimFrames|Frames to Image` and choosing all your frames. Now, you can watch the animation with the **Animation Playback** filter in the `Filters/Animation` menu.

If you want to save it as a GIF animation, you will have to *index* your image first. We suggest that you stick to **RGB** during the whole animation process, and don't convert to **Indexed** until you're done. Presently, you can only save your animations as GIF, but it's probably only a matter of time before other animation formats will be supported by Gimp.

Note that the animation object must be of the *same type* as the frame. You can't mix indexed images with RGB images, but an RGB and an RGB alpha will work just fine. The frame and the object layer don't need to be of the same size.

Move Beyond The Basics With The Move Path Tool

How Far Can AnimFrames Take Me?

There are nearly no limits to what you can achieve with AnimFrame, but certain kinds of animations are harder to create than others. To create some effects, you may have to edit frames by hand.

We've made an animation demo (see "Animation Gallery/Tutorial" on page 651), where we show a few examples of what AnimFrames is capable of; like *panning* the background, making an aftertext that *rolls* over the frame, a *perspective* intro text, moving objects *away* from you and *towards* you, setting different *speeds* to objects, etc.

The Animation Studio

The **Move Path** window is the heart of AnimFrame, so let's have a closer look at what it can do and what the parameter settings signify.

The dialog is divided into three different parts: **Source Select**, **Move Path Preview** and a bottom part where you set some slides and buttons.

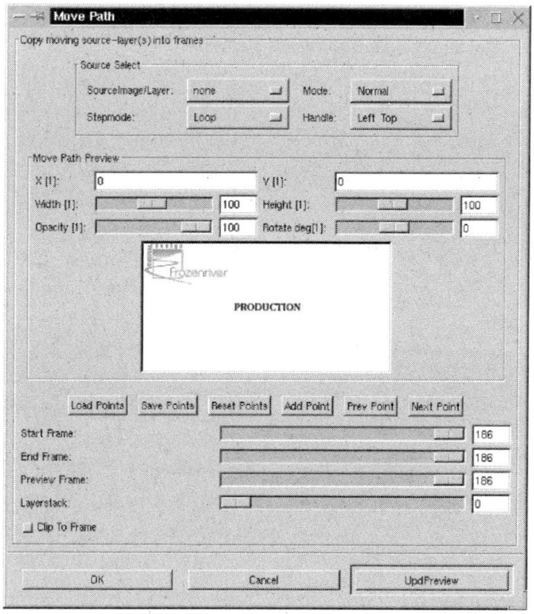

Figure 40.1 *The Move Path dialog*

SOURCE SELECT

SourceImage/Layer

This menu is where you select the **animation object**, i.e., the layer or image where your animation object is. You can only open AnimFrames/Move Path from a frame image, so you must keep a frame image (just one!) open, as well as one or more object images.

Mode

Here, you define how to combine the color/brightness values of the imported layer/image and the rest of the layers in the frame. You can read more about modes in "Modes" starting on page 335.

Handle

The Handle determines which part of the imported image/layer should be used as a point of departure for the move path. Handle is used for locking a certain corner of the source layer/image to the move path. If you select top-left handle, the control point will stick to the top-left corner of the source layer, forcing the layer's position to the bottom-right side of the control point.

Stepmode

Stepmode determines the sequence of the animation. **Loop** creates a continuous animation from the first control point to the last. **Loop reverse** does the same but goes the other way around — from the end point to the first control point. (**Once** and **Once reverse** are currently the same as Loop, but that will change with the development of this plug-in). **Ping Pong** makes your animation go from the first point to the last point, back to the position after the first point, to the position before the last point and so on. **None** cancels the animation. We recommend that you stick to Loop and Loop reverse, and control the output by animating different sequences separately, or by exchanging frames.

THE PREVIEW WINDOW

Here's where the actual setting of the animation takes place. By placing a number of **control points** along a track, you create a linear moving **path** for the object. Note that the path and the points are *invisible*. You can only see them by stepping your way forward or backward with the **Next Point/Prev Point** buttons.

Tip: If you find it hard to visualize a path created with the mouse in the preview window, make a freehand drawing of the track to guide you when you place the control points. When you have finished the path, you can erase the pencil lines.

Move Path Preview And Control Points

The animation object will move from the first to the last control point over the frames you set using the slides **Start Frame** and **End Frame**.

By default, the *first* control point is placed in the top-left corner. If you want to start from here, continue the path by pressing the **Add Point** button to add a *second* point to the path. Then, *click* in the preview window to set the **position** of the second control point.

If you don't want the path to begin from the top-left corner, **change** the position of the first control point by clicking in the preview window to set the new position. To continue the move path, press **Add Point**, click on a new position to set the *second* control point, and so on.

If you want to *adjust* the position of a control point, press **Prev Point** or **Next Point** to navigate the path. The status of the point controls will now change from X[2] to X[1], for example, so you know what control point you are dealing with. Adjust the position of the chosen control point by clicking at the spot in the preview window where you want it, and the move path will automatically conform to the new position.

Note: You can't add a control point to adjust the path between two existing points. You can only add to *prolong* the path, so always make sure that you stand at the *last* control point when you add a new point; otherwise, it will be quite hard to follow the path you're creating.

If you want to prolong the path by adding another control point, press the **Next Point** button until you arrive at the last control point, then press **Add Point** and click at the place where you want to put it.

Because the animation object's *move path* is determined by the control points, you will have to use a lot of control points to create a circular path. The maximum number of control points are 256, but that is quite sufficient for most GIF animations.

Options

A very nice option is the possibility to **save** and **import** control points. This makes it possible to let different objects use the same move path (you can also save your favorite move path for later use).

You can create a very exact moving path by inserting a value in the control point *position* fields **X** and **Y**. The values here give you the necessary numerical information about every point's position.

Note: The position cross is not restricted to the area inside the preview. Dragging it outside of the preview window will, for example, enable you to pane the background.

The **Width** and **Height** controls allow you to resize the layer/image at a certain control point. This is, of course, ideal for zooming.

Opacity controls transparency of the object image. You can, for example, use this control to fade in and out of images. As you see, these controls allow you to create many of the common effects you've seen in ordinary movies.

A really nice feature is the **Rotate deg** option, which enables you to rotate the animation layer. With this option it's very easy to *spin* an object around.

A Short Example

1. Create 50 frames.
2. Create a simple cross in a new image (let the image be 25x25 pixels).
3. Open **Move Path** and make 12 control points.
4. Set control point 1 to 0°, point 2 to 90°, point 3 to 180° and so on.
5. Set **Source Image/Layer** to the cross image you made.
6. Set **Handle** to center.
7. Set every control point to be in the center of the preview area.
8. Press **OK**.

Now you have 50 film frames of a spinning cross. OK, it's a fairly simple example, but the function is very versatile. You can easily create a spinning plane, a car moving in a circle, etc. It's just up to your imagination.

Control Slides

The Frame Slidebars

These slidebars control where and how the import layer should be placed in your frame. The **Start Frame** and **End Frame** sliders determine which frames the image/layer (with the current move path) should be imported to. The **Preview Frame** slider controls which frame you'll see when you press the update preview button. Note that this only works for the first and last control points. This tool is for viewing the beginning and end of an animation sequence

The Layerstack

The **Layerstack** slidebar controls in which position the imported layer/image will be placed in relation to the other layers in the frame. In order to understand this you must think of the layers as a stack of cards. If the layerstack is set to zero, then the layer will end up on top of all other layers (cards). If the layerstack is set to 1, then the layer card will be inserted between the first and second layer cards, etc.

The AnimFrame Menu

Undo And Preview

Other than the preview in the Move Path tool, there is no preview that lets you see your animation while it's under production (it would be too slow to load and unload images from disk, especially if there are a lot of layers). If you want a preview, you can either step forward with the **GotoNext** command (use the assigned shortcut command), or create a multi-layered image with **Flatten Frames** followed by **Frames to Image**, and view it with `right-click|Filters|Animation|Animation Playback`.

There is no **Undo** in AnimFrames, because all frames are saved immediately. A way around this is to always keep your layers in the frames. If you aren't satisfied with a certain frame layer sequence, then you can easily delete it with the **Frames Layer Delete** command.

Frames LayerDel And Delete Frames

The **Frames LayerDel** command will bring up a dialog asking you to specify what Frame Range should be affected, and the position of the unwanted layer sequence in the Layerstack. Be careful here, because when you press OK, there's no return.

The **Delete Frames** command will delete the frame that you opened the Delete Frames dialog from. It can also delete the following frames in the range you specify.

Frames Convert

If you want to *export* your frames to different image formats, you can use the **Frames Convert** command.

The drop-down menu lets you select whether you want to keep the image type (RGB) or convert it to a different format (Gray, Indexed or RGB). This is essential if you want to save your frames in GIF format, because GIF images by definition are indexed. The field above the menu is for specifying image format by typing the suffix (such as .gif, .tiff or .jpeg) To verify what frames to convert, use the **From Frame** and **To Frame** slidebars.

If you want to, you can also set a new base name for the frames in the **Basename** field. Just remember that the basename is the whole path plus the name of the image without the number extension. For example, don't use `/home/me/gap/test_0001.gif`, use `/home/me/gap/test` which is the correct basename, because the *_0001.gif* extension is added automatically.

The **Flatten** checkbox flattens the frames before you save them. If you save them as GIF's, flattening is not necessary, because GIF can handle layers. However, if you want to save them as TIF images (or any other image format that does not handle layers), you have to flatten the images first, because TIF doesn't support layers.

When you save the frames as an indexed image, you can specify the desired number of colors with the **Color** slide. You can also let the indexed image be dithered by checking the **Dither** checkbox.

Exchange Frame

Exchange Frame is used for *rearranging* your frames. In the dialog, set what frame you want to swap the current frame with. For example, if you invoke the command from frame 3 and set the slide to 5, then frame 3 will end up as frame 5, and frame 5 will end up as frame 3.

Frames Flatten And Frames To Image

Invoke the Frames Flatten command when you want to preview your animation, and the Frames to Image command when your animation is finished and you want to save it as a GIF animation.

Frames Flatten will flatten the layers in each frame. The result of applying this command is a sequence of merged (AnimFrames) frames, which can be viewed step-by-step with `AnimFrames|Goto Next`. All frames must be flattened before you can preview your animation using this command.

To create a **GIF** animation, you can't use the frames as they are, flattened or not; you'll need an image composed of several layers to do that.To convert your set of flattened *frames* to a multi-layered *image*, you must use the **Frames to Image** command.

When you use **Frames Flatten**, we recommend that you do this on a copy, and not the original frames (`cd "your frame directory" && mkdir framecopy && cp * framecopy` in a terminal window). If you flatten the original frames, you'd better make sure that everything's OK, because once the frames are flattened there is no way to edit the frame layers.

Frames to Image is a bit more friendly; it creates a new image and won't destroy the original.

Frames To Image Options

In the **Layer Mergemode** parameter area, you'll find the most important parameter settings in the Frames to Image dialog box.

- **Clipped to image** is generally the most efficient option. Clipped to image will create a multi-layered image from multi-layered frames. Each frame will be flattened on the fly and merged into a single layer in the resulting multi-layered image. The resulting image will be of the same size as the frame.

- **Flattened image** is nearly the same as *Clipped to image*. The main difference is that if your animation has transparent parts, they will be filled with the background color in the toolbox.
- **Expand as necessary** will enlarge the resulting image if any of the frame layers are outside of the frame canvas.
- **Clipped to bottom layer**, used with an unchecked **Exclude BG-Layer** checkbox, can be quite useful. In order to set the size of the animation, you often start working with an empty bottom layer. As you create the animation, you add a lot of layers. When you are finished, you'll want to keep the *size* of the bottom layer, but not the actual bottom layer. If this is the case, *Clipped to bottom layer* is the perfect tool.

In the **Select Layer(s)** parameter area you can select which frame layers should be included in the image conversion.

- With the check buttons, pick the layers by **Pattern** or by **Layerstack** position. There are *tooltips* for each selection type, so just point, and you will get an explanation.
- When you have decided how to search for/select the layers, insert the search pattern name or layerstack position numbers in the **Select Pattern** input field.

Frame Duplicate

As we've mentioned before in "Making A Frame" on page 640, this tool is used for creating **base frames** in an animation. Note that if you are in the middle of an animation and want to duplicate a frame, the duplicate frames will be inserted after the original frame.

Frames Crop, Resize And Scale

All of these tools work exactly as they would on an ordinary image, but they take effect on *all* of your frames. So, think carefully before you press OK, because these actions have *no undo*!

Resize and **Scale** will bring up the old familiar dialogs, just as they would have if you had invoked them on an ordinary image.

Crop is a bit different because you'll only get a parameters settings dialog. In order to use Crop effectively, use a few *guides* to set up your cropmarks in the frame. When you have set those marks, you'll know what parameters to set in the Crop dialog:

- **Offset X** is the distance from the left side to the first vertical cropmark and **Y offset** is the distance from the top of the image to the first horizontal cropmark.
- **New height** is the distance from the top cropmark to the bottom cropmark, and **New width** is the distance from the left to the right cropmark.

Split Img To Frames

This is a very versatile tool. You can use it to convert MPEG and GIF animations to frames and thereby edit animations more easily. There aren't many options here, the main thing is to set the *extension* (image type), but the default extension (which is XCF) is often the best choice.

Parameter Settings

- **Inverse order** means that the top layer will be frame 1 and the background layer will be the last frame. You will have to check how your animation is stored to determine what type of order you need.
- **Flatten** doesn't really flatten. If any of the layers that will become a frame contain transparent areas, those areas will be filled with the background color from the toolbox.

Frames Modify

If you want to *modify* several frames at once, this is the command to use.

Parameter Settings

1. First, use the sliders to specify the **range**; that is, which frames should be affected by the operation.
2. Then, with the **Select Layer(s)** check buttons, pick the layers by **Pattern** or by **Layerstack** position. There are *tooltips* for each selection type, so just point, and you will get an explanation.
3. When you have decided how to search for/select the layers, insert the search pattern name or layerstack position numbers in the **Select Pattern** field.
4. Check the **Case sensitive** checkbox if you want to differentiate layer names with or without capital letters.
5. If you want to perform the operation on frames that you *haven't* selected, check **Invert Selection**.
6. When you have set all of these parameters, it's time to choose what to do in the **Function** drop-down menu. If you choose the *rename Layer(s)* option, you also have to specify the new name in the **New Layername** field. If you choose the *apply filter on Layer(s)* option, then the `right-click|Filters|Animation|Filter All Layers` dialog will appear (see "Filter All Layers" on page 371).

Framesequence Shift

This filter will *shift* your frames just like you shift cards in a deck of cards.

Suppose that you have 9 frames and you want to shift the frame sequence starting from frame 2 and ending in frame 7. You want to move this sequence 2 steps (**N = 2** in the dialog).

Then, frame 2 will be the new frame 4, frame 3 will become frame 5, etc. until you reach frame 8 which will be frame 2 and frame 9 which will now be frame 3.

FILTER LAYERS

USING A SCRIPT OR FILTER

There is a **Script-Fu** that can be very useful when dealing with animations. It's the `right-click|Script-Fu|Animators|Sel To AnimImage` script, which lets you apply any filter (plug-in) on all layers in an image.

You may think this is equal to `right-click|Animation|Filter All Layers` (see "Filter All Layers" on page 371), but that isn't completely true. If you want to apply a filter smoothly in each layer, the *Selection to AnimImage* script is the better choice.

Example

You have ten layers and you want to apply `right-click|Filters|Distort|Whirl` with slightly different values to each layer. If you use *Filter all Layers*, you have to do this by hand, but if you use *Sel To AnimImage*, you only have to set the start and end values. The script will calculate the values between the start and end layers, and create a smooth transition.

These operations can only be performed on an image, not on frames, so you must first convert your frames with the **Frames to Image** command. When you are finished, you can easily transform it back to frames with the **Split Image to Frames** command.

ANIMATION GALLERY/TUTORIAL

We have made a little animation to show you some of the things you can do with AnimFrame. The animation is 186 frames long.

Zooming

The animation begins with a logo that moves toward you before it *bounces* back, *stretches* out and finally *fades* away. Those effects were quite easy to achieve:

We started by specifying a low value for **Width** and **Height** in the first point in the logo's **Move Path**, so that the logo would appear to move toward the camera.

The fade away/stretch effect was created by setting the **opacity** in the final point to 0%, the **X scale** to 200 and the **Y scale** to 0.

Figure 40.2 *The object seems to be moving towards the camera*

Figure 40.3 *To make the object fade away, you will have to use a variable amount of opacity*

Fading

The next phase in the animation was to *fade over* from the background in the bouncing logo scene to the space background in the next scene. This was done by placing the space background in the lowest layer in a series of 10 frames, then we made a **Move Path** with the blue logo background with 100% opacity in the first control point and 0% opacity in the final control point.

Figure 40.4 *Blending scenes is very easy; you just adjust the opacity of the top layer*

StarWars Text

Then, we amused ourselves by creating a paraphrase of the rolling perspective text in a movie we assume you've never heard of. (Don't bother reading the text; it's quite meaningless).

For the *perspective* effect we used an image that was higher than the frame, and then we skewed the text with the **Transform/Perspective** tool. The *Move Path* (center handle) begins a bit below the actual frame, and the second and final points, were placed a bit below the center of the image.

The final point also scaled down the import image to about a third of its original size. This made the text float away, just like in the movie. Afterward, we adjusted the time each frame was shown to keep the text from accelerating as it moves away.

Figure 40.5 *The StarWars text was a bit harder to achieve. The main problem was that the speed of the flying text accelerates as it moves deeper into space. To slow down the text acceleration, we increased the number of frames per control point as the text moves farther away.*

Paning And Accelerating

The space scene displays an orbiting spacecraft or satellite. The spacecraft *accelerates* as it moves away from you and around the Earth. As background setting we used a large image of the Earth seen from space.

The space part of the background was *paned* with the **Move tool**, and the last stage in the scene was a pane and zoom down toward the Earth.

Then we added the spacecraft image with a move path from the right side of the "screen" to the left. At the same time as the spacecraft was moving along the path, it was *scaled down*. This created the acceleration effect, and the feeling that the beholder is moving away from the spacecraft as it disappears beyond the horizon.

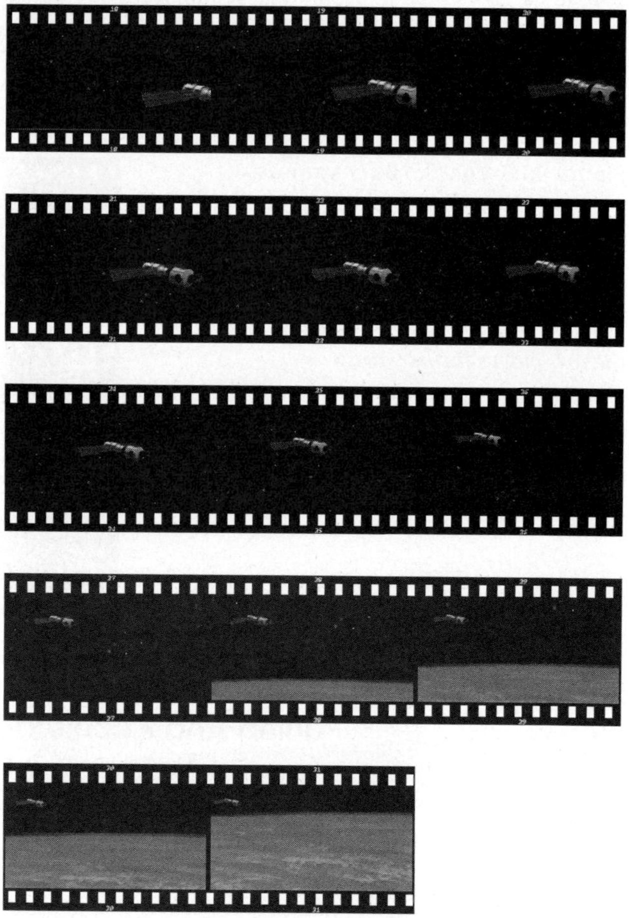

Figure 40.6 *To make the spacecraft accelerate in its orbit, we had to use a combination of two layers. The background layer displaying the Earth, and another layer showing the spacecraft.*

The spacecraft was made to move from one side to the other while it was zoomed out. At the same time, the Earth was paned in the background layer.

Fading Again

Now, it's time for some propaganda in the *Help Us Fight the Evil Empire* fade-out scene. This text was faded in the same fashion as the bouncing logo background, only in reverse direction.

Figure 40.7 *The Evil Empire sequence was made using the same technique as in Figure 40.4*

Moving Around

The final scene displays the production team behind this animation, and this book. The Frozenriver logo was made to circulate around the word "Production" and fade away at the same time. This was done by using *"Production"* as a background. The logo was then made to move around the text in a five-point move path, where the opacity was lowered for each control point.

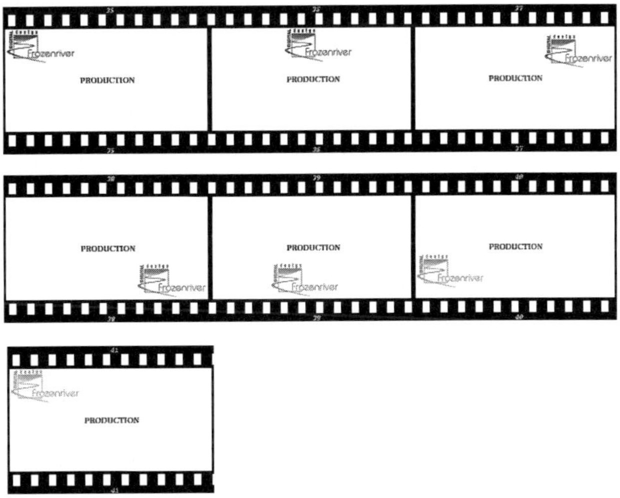

Figure 40.8 *This effect is very simple to achieve. The control points were placed around the center, and the transparency was increased while the object moves.*

Note: This animation demo comes both in GIF and AnimFrame format, and can be downloaded from `ftp://manual.gimp.org/pub/manual`.

WACOM

CHAPTER 41

Drawing Tablets And Gimp

In this chapter, we will show you how to use a digitized drawing tablet in Gimp. The X extension that let us use tablets in Gimp is called Xinput. We will show you how to enable and configure Xinput and tablets in Linux with XFree86 as Xserver.

INTRODUCTION

WHAT IS A DRAWING TABLET?

When we speak about a tablet, we refer to a digitized *drawing tablet* in combination with a *digital pen*. This pen can be **pressure sensitive**, which means that if you press harder, the pencil stroke will get thicker.

There are other kinds of tablets that operate without pens, such as tablets for CAD. However, for working in Gimp, you'll need a pen-enabled tablet, because Gimp is a program for graphic artists.

Platforms And Brands

We will review *Wacom* tablets in this chapter. There are naturally other brands, such as *SummaSketch*, but due to hardware limits we will focus on Wacom tablets. We will cover all types of Wacom tablets from *ArtPad* to the latest *Intuos* tablet.

Secondly, we will only discuss configuration and installation under **Linux XFree86**; it will, however, most likely be the same for all other versions of UNIX that can use XFree86.

There is support for Xinput in most major Unix/X11 implementations, such as *Solaris*, *OSF/1*, *HP-UX* and *AIX*, but the main problem is that there are no drivers that enable you to use Wacom tablets. Wacom makes drivers for IRIX, but since we have no access to SGI machines, we are unable to continue the discussion in that direction.

What About USB Tablets?

Linux support of **USB** (**Universal Serial Bus**) is very limited at the time of writing. There are, to our knowledge, no supported USB tablets, so we strongly recommend that you buy a **Serialport tablet** instead.

INSTALLING AND CONFIGURING

First of all, Gimp 1.0.x doesn't support tablets *(even though the current developer version has tablet support, and the next Gimp release will include this feature).* This limits the usage, but does not prevent it. There are two ways of using a tablet in Gimp 1.0.x. The simplest way is to use the pen as a complement to the mouse, but then you will not be able to bring the pressure sensitivity into play.

If you want to make full use of the pen's capabilities, you will have to *patch* and *compile* Gimp yourself. However, this is no trivial task. It can get very complicated if you have an old version of X11 (XFree86), because then you will also have to *recompile* X11.

Using The Pen As A Mouse Replacement

Without pressure sensitivity the pen is an incomplete instrument, but it will still improve the precision and ease of freehand drawing immensely compared to drawing with your mouse. This section provides you with information on how to use a digitized pen as a replacement or complement to the mouse with all Wacom tablets, except the *Intuos* tablet, which will be discussed in "The Wacom Intuos Tablet" on page 671.

The Right XFree86 Version

Xinput and Wacom tablets have been supported by XFree86 since the 3.1.2D release. However, we always recommend getting the latest and greatest version (which at the time of writing is 3.3.3.1), because many new features have been added and bugs resolved.

One of the most notable new features is the **Switch/AlwaysCore** function, which makes it possible to use the pen and the mouse at the same time. You can switch between the mouse and the pen without having to specify which one is your pointing device.

If you don't have XFree86 3.3.3, or never installed it, we strongly recommend that you upgrade. Otherwise, you'll find that working with your tablet will be slow and cumbersome.

In relatively new Linux distributions, most major Linux distributors include upgrade packages that will make it relatively easy to upgrade to XFree86 version 3.3.3 or newer.

We will cover the basic configuration of tablets within the XF86Config file. This section is required for all tablets, including the Intuos tablet and/or when pressure sensitivity is enabled.

Without Auto Switch Between Mouse And Pen

If you didn't upgrade to 3.3.3., you can't use the **auto switch** when changing from mouse to pen and vice versa. The XFree86 config file will in this case be very easy to configure.

The XF86Config file can be found in the following locations:

`/etc/XF86Config`

`/usr/X11R6/lib/X11/XF86Config`
(most of the time this file is symlinked to `/etc/X11/XF86Config`).

The **Xserver** will search for the file in the same order, so be sure to edit the right file (i.e., if you have a `/etc/XF86Config` file, don't edit the `/usr/X11R6/lib/X11/XF86Config` file).

Most of the time the config data for Xinput and Wacom tablets are already present in the XF86Config file, and are just being commented out. We will describe how to edit the file to add the Xinput support, and if you already have the data, you can naturally just remove the comment hash mark.

The three sections to edit are the **Files**, **Module** and **Xinput** sections.

The Files Section

Start by making a backup copy of your XF86Config file (in a shell `cp /etc/X11/XF86Config ~/XF86Config.old`). Then, invoke your favorite text editor.

Note: You must edit the file as the root user; otherwise, you will not be able to save your changes.

If you are in a **KDE** environment, type: `kedit /etc/X11/XF86Config` or in a **GNOME** environment, type: `gedit /etc/X11/XF86Config`.

Scroll down until you see the following section:

```
Section "Files"
   RgbPath        "/usr/X11R6/lib/X11/rgb"
   FontPath       "/usr/X11R6/lib/X11/fonts/Type1/"
   FontPath       "/usr/X11R6/lib/X11/fonts/Speedo/"
   FontPath       "/usr/X11R6/lib/X11/fonts/misc/"
   FontPath       "/usr/X11R6/lib/X11/fonts/75dpi/:unscaled"
   FontPath       "/usr/X11R6/lib/X11/fonts/100dpi/:unscaled"
   FontPath       "/usr/X11R6/lib/X11/fonts/75dpi/"
   FontPath       "/usr/X11R6/lib/X11/fonts/100dpi/"
EndSection
```

Notice that the **RgbPath** and **FontPath** may not be the same in your installation. All you have do here is add the **ModulePath** (i.e., where the Wacom driver is located). The most common location for all drivers (modules) available for XFree86 is `/usr/X11R6/lib/modules`, but that may not be the case in your installation.

To check it out, execute `ls -l /usr/X11R6/lib/modules/` in a shell. This will probably render the following output:

```
[olof@whopp olof]$ ls -l /usr/X11R6/lib/modules/
total 1157
-rwxr-xr-x   1 root    root        552962 Oct 10  1998 pex5.so
-rwxr-xr-x   1 root    root        14192  Oct 10  1998 xf86Elo.so
-rwxr-xr-x   1 root    root        13634  Oct 10  1998 xf86Summa.so
-rwxr-xr-x   1 root    root        24411  May 12 14:22 xf86Wacom.so
-rwxr-xr-x   1 root    root        565762 Oct 10  1998 xie.so
[olof@whopp olof]$
```

If you don't get this output, your drivers (modules) are located elsewhere and you will have to find them by executing something like:

```
find /usr/X11R6/ -name xf86* -print
```

in a shell. The file list above may not be exactly the same on your system, but you must have a file named `xf86Wacom.so`, since it's the Wacom **tablet driver**.

Add the following entry to the files section **ModulePath**:

```
"/usr/X11R6/lib/modules/"
```

The path, i.e., `"/usr/X11R6/lib/modules/"`, should naturally reflect the directory where you have your drivers (modules). The XF86Config file will now look like this:

```
Section "Files"
   RgbPath       "/usr/X11R6/lib/X11/rgb"
   FontPath      "/usr/X11R6/lib/X11/fonts/Type1/"
   FontPath      "/usr/X11R6/lib/X11/fonts/Speedo/"
   FontPath      "/usr/X11R6/lib/X11/fonts/misc/"
   FontPath      "/usr/X11R6/lib/X11/fonts/75dpi/:unscaled"
   FontPath      "/usr/X11R6/lib/X11/fonts/100dpi/:unscaled"
   FontPath      "/usr/X11R6/lib/X11/fonts/75dpi/"
   FontPath      "/usr/X11R6/lib/X11/fonts/100dpi/"
#Setting the ModulePath
   ModulePath    "/usr/X11R6/lib/modules/"
EndSection
```

The Module Section

The next step is to load/enable the driver/module for use within XFree86 (X11). The section in the XF86Config file that takes care of that, is the *Module section*. In a standard XF86Config file, this section is not present or commented out with a #. We have our **Module** section above the **Pointer** section.

Here is an example that you can copy into your XF86Config file *(don't copy the Pointer section).*

```
#Copy from here
Section "Module"
        Load "xf86Wacom.so"
EndSection
#to here -- don't include the "Pointer" section

Section "Pointer"
   Protocol         "Mouseman"
   Device           "/dev/mouse"
EndSection
```

The Xinput Section

Now, you have to enable the *pen/tablet* as an extension to X11 (as an Xinput device). You do that in the *Xinput section*. This section is not present or commented out in the standard XF86Config file.

We have added the **Xinput** section right after the **Pointer** section. As in the Module section, we provide an example for you to copy into your config file. We will talk about options and settings later, but we guess that you are eager to get started and use your pen:

Here is an example that you can copy into your XF86Config file *(don't copy the Pointer section).*

```
Section "Pointer"
   Protocol        "Mouseman"
   Device          "/dev/mouse"
EndSection


#Copy from here
Section "Xinput"
    SubSection "WacomStylus"
        Port "/dev/ttyS1"
        DeviceName "Wacom"
        Mode Absolute
        Suppress 6
    EndSubSection
    SubSection "WacomCursor"
        Port "/dev/ttyS1"
        Mode Absolute
        Suppress 6
    EndSubSection
    SubSection "WacomEraser"
        Port "/dev/ttyS1"
        Mode Absolute
        Suppress 6
    EndSubSection
EndSection
#to here i.e don't include the "Pointer" section
```

Actually, you don't need all of it, but it's better to be prepared to enable pressure sensitivity, isn't it?

You're still not quite ready to start using your pen. First, you have to connect your Wacom tablet to the right **serial port** of your computer. According to our config file it will be the `ttyS0` serial port (`COM1` under **DOS/Windows**). If you have connected your Wacom tablet to `ttyS1` (`COM2` under DOS/Windows), you have to replace `ttyS0` with `ttyS1` in the config file.

If you are all done now, *restart* your **Xserver** in order to load the driver and enable your tablet. You must, of course, save the config file before you restart the Xserver.

The simplest way to restart the Xserver, and the whole Linux computer, is to press Ctrl+Alt+F2 and Ctrl+Alt+Delete. This will restart the whole computer, so before you do it, make sure to save all current work. There are more elegant ways to do this in a Unix/Linux environment, but this is an easy solution for a beginner.

Using The Pen In Gimp

You don't have to configure or rebuild Gimp. All you have to do now is empower the pen. This is done with **xsetpointer**. If you have heeded our configuration example, you will be able to use the pen by entering the command `xsetpointer Wacom` in a shell, while you run X.

The digitized pen will now be your pointing device. You can set the buttons on the pen to emulate the mouse buttons; for example, enter `xmodmap -e "pointer = 1 4 3 2"` to reset the pen buttons. To switch back to your mouse, enter `xsetpointer Pointer`. This sets the pen tip to button 1, the eraser to button 2, and the pen button to button 3.

As you may realize, this way of working is a real pain. The right way is to enable **auto switch** between the mouse and the pen.

Enabling Auto Switch Between Mouse And Pen

If you haven't read "Without Auto Switch Between Mouse And Pen" on page 659, do so now, because we will only cover the differences here.

First of all, you must have **XFree86 3.3.3** or newer installed on your Linux system. An easy way to find out what version you have is to read the man page; execute `man XFree86`, scroll down to the end of the page and read what version the man page was written for. Most Linux distributors provide upgrade packages for enabling a smooth and easy upgrade to XFree86 3.3.3 or newer. See "Xinput" on page 881 to find out where to pick up your upgrade.

Because you will already have enabled tablet support in your XF86Config file, and we assume that you have tested it, all you have to do now is add some new entries in the config file. The only thing you need to edit is the **Xinput** section.

Next, you'll find an example of an Xinput section that you can copy and use as a template for your own entries.

As you can see, we have added several subsections containing a Core device that is in **AlwaysCore** *"mode."* This device and setting is what causes XFree86 to auto switch from the mouse to the pen when you let go of the mouse and touch the pen instead (and vice versa). Now *restart* your Xserver, and you will be able to test it out.

XFree86 will now automatically switch and enable you to use the selected pointing device instantly — no need to execute `xsetpointer` anymore.

Auto Switch In Gimp

Auto switch between mouse and pen makes everything so much easier, doesn't it? You can instantly shift between the advantage of having fast and easy access to the menus (using the mouse) and being able to use the pen's superior painting qualities.

There is no configuration that you must perform and no commands to execute. However, you can still only use the pen as an ordinary pointing device; there is no *pressure sensitivity*. Although this is undeniably better than when you had to

```
Section "Xinput"
    SubSection "WacomStylus"
        Port "/dev/ttyS1"
        DeviceName "Wacom"
        Mode Absolute
        Suppress 6
    EndSubSection
    SubSection  "WacomStylus"
        Port "/dev/ttyS1"
        DeviceName "WacomCore"
        Mode Absolute
        AlwaysCore
        Suppress 6
    EndSubSection
    SubSection "WacomCursor"
        Port "/dev/ttyS1"
        Mode Absolute
        Suppress 6
    EndSubSection
    SubSection "WacomCursor"
        Port "/dev/ttyS1"
        DeviceName "CursorCore"
        AlwaysCore
        Mode Absolute
        Suppress 6
    EndSubSection
    SubSection "WacomEraser"
        Port "/dev/ttyS1"
        Mode Absolute
        Suppress 6
    EndSubSection
```

switch between mouse and pen manually, there is still room for improvements. You can get pressure sensitivity in Gimp, and the next passage will tell you how.

Pressure Sensitivity And Auto Switch Between Tools

Before you start reading here, you should first read and comply with the passages "Without Auto Switch Between Mouse And Pen" on page 659 and "Enabling Auto Switch Between Mouse And Pen" on page 664.

Having followed these instructions, you will have the **Xinput** support that Gimp needs to enable pressure sensitivity and auto switch between tools. The auto switch function will also enable you to assign the pen to a certain tool in the Gimp toolbox. You can, for example, easily map the eraser part of your pen to the eraser tool.

This section will cover all Wacom tablets except the new Intuos tablet. As before, you will still need the XFree86 3.3.3 or newer, but this time you will also need to enable **Xinput** in **Gtk** and *patch* **Gimp**. See "FTP" on page 880 for where to download Gimp and Gtk. You will also need a special Gimp patch. See "Xinput" on page 881 to learn where, find the most up-to-date version of this patch.

Xinput Support In Gtk

Gtk already has support for **Xinput**, so all you have to do is enable it, i.e., configure it using `--with-xinput=xfree` and *recompile* it. We recommend that you make a special Gimp install directory where you install both Xinput- enabled Gtk and Gimp. Furthermore, it is a good idea to have another personal Gimp directory than the usual `.gimp` in your home directory. Here is an example of how to uncompress, extract, configure, compile and install Gtk with Xinput support (all of this is done in a terminal window such as xterm). Your commands may of course be slightly different, but basically it will be the same procedure.

```
[olof@whopp olof]$ gunzip gtk+-1.0.6.tar.gz
[olof@whopp olof]$ tar xvf gtk+-1.0.6.tar
[olof@whopp olof]$ cd gtk+-1.0.6
[olof@whopp gtk+-1.0.6]$ ./configure --prefix=/opt/gimpinput \
--with-xinput=xfree
[olof@whopp gtk+-1.0.6]$ make
[olof@whopp gtk+-1.0.6]$ su root -c "make install"
Note: You must provide the root password
[olof@whopp gtk+-1.0.6]$
```

Compilation Problems

If your compilation failed, it could be for a number of reasons. First of all, check that you have all of the X11 development files available for your Gimp distribution. There are variations between the different distributions, so we can't give you an exact instruction on how to check this. However, if you have used `rpm` as an installation tool, you can try `rpm -q -a | grep X`.

In our Linux distribution this command would result in a line like this:

```
XFree86-devel-3.3.3
```

Your result may differ slightly, but the string to look for is `XFree86-devel`.

We also recommend that you read "Installing A Source Distribution" on page 48. Here, you will find a lot of useful information concerning compilation and common compilation problems.

XINPUT SUPPORT IN GIMP

We need to enable **Xinput** support in Gimp in order to obtain auto switching tools and pressure sensitivity. You will have to *patch* Gimp and rebuild it from scratch. This is not a trivial task, but we hope that by guiding you through this procedure, we will make it as easy as possible for you.

Patching Gimp

Start by downloading **Gimp 1.0.2** and the special **Gimp Xinput patch**. We suggest that you to read "Installing A Source Distribution" on page 48 before making any attempt to patch, configure and make Gimp.

Okay, ready to give it a try? We will, as usual, give you an example to follow. We assume that you have both Gimp and the patch in your home directory.

```
[olof@whopp olof]$ gunzip gimp-1.0.2.tar.gz
[olof@whopp olof]$ tar xvf gimp-1.0.2.tar
[olof@whopp olof]$ gunzip patch-gimp-xinput.10.gz
[olof@whopp gimp-1.0.2]$ cd gimp-1.0.2
[olof@whopp gimp-1.0.2]$ patch -p1 < ../patch-gimp-xinput.10
patching file `app/Makefile.am'
patching file `app/app_procs.c'
Hunk #1 succeeded at 32 (offset 4 lines).
Hunk #2 succeeded at 510 (offset 16 lines).
patching file `app/brushes.c'
[snip]
patching file `app/tools.h'
Hunk #1 succeeded at 135 (offset 4 lines).
patching file `app/undo.c'
[olof@whopp gimp-1.0.2]$ ./configure --prefix=/opt/gimpinput \
--with-gtk-prefix=/opt/gimpinput --disable-gtktest \
--enable-gimpdir=.gimpinput
[olof@whopp gimp-1.0.2]$
```

After this you have to edit the **Makefile** in the **app** directory. Just run `gedit` or `kedit app/Makefile`. Scroll down until you find:

```
desaturate.h                \
```

Now, you have to *insert* two lines after the `desaturate.h` line. Following is an example of what it will look like. Did you notice the backslash "\" sign? When you insert this sign it tells **make** that it should *skip* the next character (which in this case is the *newline* character or enter). The important thing to remember is that you must insert an enter directly after the "\"sign. If there is a space or other character than the newline character (enter), **make** will fail to compile Gimp.

```
desaturate.c            \
desaturate.h            \
devices.c               \
devices.h               \
dialog_types.h          \
disp_callbacks.c        \
```

As you see, we have inserted two new lines: `devices.c` and `devices.h`. Now, continue to scroll down until you find `desaturate.o`. Now, insert `devices.o` after `desaturate.o`. See the example below:

```
colormaps.o commands.o convert.o convolve.o crop.o cursorutil.o \
curves.o datafiles.o desaturate.o devices.o disp_callbacks.o\
draw_core.o drawable.o drawable_cmds.o edit_cmds.o  \
```

All you have to do now is compile and install Gimp:

```
[olof@whopp gimp-1.0.2]$ make
[olof@whopp gimp-1.0.2]$ su root -c "make install"
Note: You must provide the root password
[olof@whopp gimp-1.0.2]$
```

Running The New Gimp

Before you can run Gimp with Xinput support, you have to create a **start-up** file or set your `LD_LIBRARY_PATH` every time you want to start Gimp. We recommend creating a start-up file, because it will make your Gimp life so much easier. Create this file called `Gimp` in `/opt/gimpinput/bin` (open `gedit` or `kedit`, copy the example provided by us, and save it as `Gimp` in your home directory):

```
#!/bin/sh
LD_LIBRARY_PATH=/opt/gimpinput/lib export LD_LIBRARY_PATH
exec /opt/gimpinput/bin/gimp "$@"
```

Before you use the start script, you must make it *executable* and move it to your `gimpinput bin` directory. This is how you do it:

```
[olof@whopp olof]$ chmod 755 Gimp
[olof@whopp olof]$ su root -c "cp -p /home/olof/Gimp \
/opt/gimpinput/bin"
```

Note: You must provide the root password. Also note that the lines above consist of one single line. The "\" indicates that you should continue without hitting enter.

```
[olof@whopp olof]$ /opt/gimpinput/bin/Gimp
```

The last line (above) will start up the new Xinput-enabled Gimp. If you run into any sort of problems during the installation and configuration of Gimp, read "Obtaining Gimp" on page 48 and "Compiling Plug-ins" starting on page 769.

Assigning Gimp Tools To The Pressure Sensitive Pen

To be able to use the new features in Gimp you have to make some configurations. Gimp provides you with a nice GUI to do that. Invoke `Dialogs|Input Devices`, and the device dialog will appear where you can set the necessary values.

All you have to do is set the **Wacom** in the **Device** drop-down menu to *Screen Mode*. Then, set **Eraser** in the **Device** drop-down menu to *Screen Mode.* Take a look at Figure 41.1 to see how the settings should look.

Figure 41.1 *Settings for the pen (Wacom) and the eraser (Eraser). These settings are used to enable Gimp tool auto switch for different parts of the pen.*

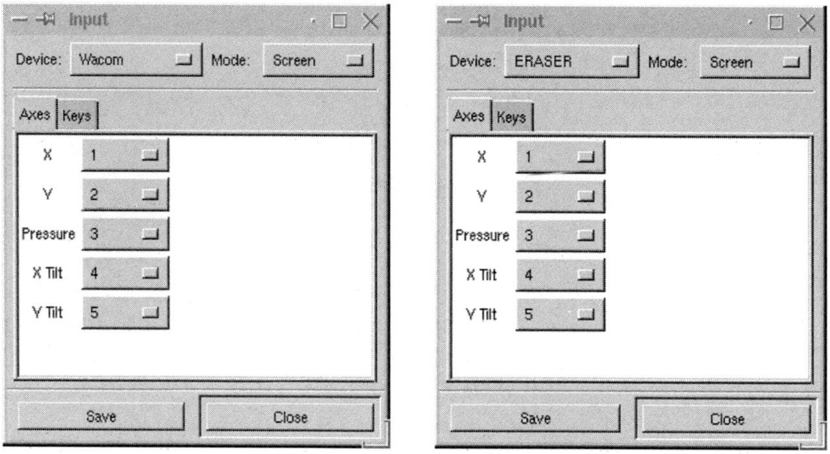

Wacom (pen) *Eraser (eraser)*

When you are done, press Save and then Close. Now, we will assign a Gimp tool to the end part of the pen (where there is an eraser on a real pencil).

Bring up the Device Status dialog using `Dialogs|Device Status`. Bring up a new image in Gimp using `File|New`, move the pen over the tablet and navigate so that the cursor points to the new image. The *Wacom* button will now be enabled in the Device Status dialog box.

Select the brush tool in the toolbox. Turn the pen around (point with the eraser), repeat the same steps as before, but this time enable the eraser tool instead of the brush tool. Grab the mouse and press **Save** in the Device Status dialog.

Figure 41.2 *Gimp's Device Status dialog*

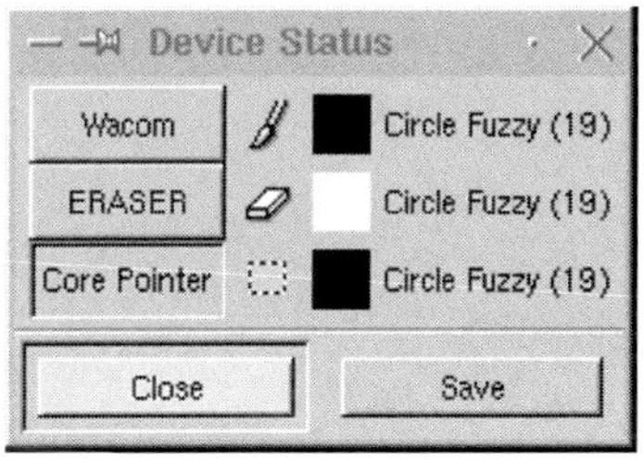

You are now ready to use your tablet, but remember that this is a patched Gimp and that the pressure sensitivity can be a bit crude. There may also be bugs. A known bug is that the Device Status dialog doesn't get updated as it should. However, this bug does not affect the functionality. The only tool that is pressure sensitive is the brush; the other tools (such as the eraser) will just benefit from the convenient auto switching feature.

The Wacom Intuos Tablet

What Is Intuos?

Intuos is Wacom's latest tablet. It includes several new tools and features such as **tool-ID** (auto recognition of which pen you are using), **Airbrush**, a special **4Dmouse**, and of course, the digital **pen**. There are also more buttons integrated with the pen, which makes it easier to work in an X11 environment that demands three buttons.

All of those features are not supported in Gimp or XFree86. Naturally, you can still use the pressure-sensitive pen, the eraser and the 4Dmouse as you would with an ordinary Wacom tablet.

The development version of Gimp, **Gimp 1.1.x**, which is still not ready for everyday use, has a much better support for Wacom tablets and especially the *Intuos* tablet (see "A Sneak Preview Of Gimp 1.1.x" on page 674).

Enabling Intuos Support In XFree86

Before you enable Intuos support, read and comply with the sections "Using The Pen As A Mouse Replacement" on page 659 and "Pressure Sensitivity And Auto Switch Between Tools" on page 666.

Don't restart X11 until we tell you to in the following example. As far as Intuos is concerned, you don't need to worry if you don't have XFree86 3.3.3 or newer, as long as you have (at least) XFree86 3.3.2.

In XFree86 3.3.3.1 there is an early beta driver for Intuos, but we recommend that you get the latest development version of the driver (which works just like a charm for us). See "Xinput" on page 881 to find out where to download it from.

On A Glibc-Based System

If you are on a **Glibc**-based system, there are precompiled drivers for both XFree86 3.3.2 and 3.3.3; otherwise, you will have to recompile XFree86. If you are on a Glibc-based system, just download the precompiled driver for your XFree86 version and copy it to your **module** directory:

```
[olof@whopp olof]$ chmod 755 xf86Wacom.so
[olof@whopp olof]$ cp -p /usr/X11R6/lib/modules/xf86Wacom.so \
xf86Wacom.so.old
[olof@whopp olof]$ su root -c "xf86Wacom.so \
/usr/X11R6/lib/modules/"
Note: You must provide the root password. Also note that the lines
above consist of a single line. The "\" indicates that you should
continue without hitting enter.
[olof@whopp olof]$
```

Now, you can restart your Xserver and/or computer to empower the Intuos support.

Finding Out If Your System Is A Glibc System

What if you don't have a Glibc Linux system, and how do you find out if you have one? To check if you have a Glibc system, you only have to enter an `ls` command, like this:

```
[olof@whopp olof]$ ls -l /lib/libc.*
lrwxrwxrwx   1 root     root           13 Jan  8 20:43 \
/lib/libc.so.6 -> libc-2.0.7.so
[olof@whopp olof]$ ls -l /lib/ld-2*
-rwxr-xr-x   1 root     root       160241 Oct 13  1998 \
/lib/ld-2.0.7.so
[olof@whopp olof]$
```

Note: The "\" is just an indicator that the line didn't fit inside the page margins of this book, and that it really is a single unbroken line.

If your commands inform you that you have `libc-2.0.x.so` and `ld-2.0.x.so` (where x is a number), then you do have a Glibc-based system.

On A Non-Glibc System

If you don't have those files, then you have to get the source code of the driver, i.e., the `xf86Wacom.c` file. You also have to get source code distribution of XFree86. See "Xinput" on page 881 for where to download both the driver and the XFree86 source code distribution from.

First *uncompress* and *extract* your XFree86 3.3.3.1 source code distribution (or newer; we assume you didn't download an old one). Then, copy `xf86Wacom.c` to the `xc/programs/Xserver/hw/xfree86/common/` directory.

If you already have XFree86 3.3.2 or 3.3.3, 3.3.3.1, but not a Glibc system, then it may be wise to download the XFree86 source distribution that matches your system. This will save a lot of time, because you'll only need to rebuild the Wacom driver.

If you have downloaded a source distribution of XFree86 that matches your XFree86 version and copied `xf86Wacom.c` to the right directory, all you have to do is:

```
[olof@whopp olof]$ cd xc
[olof@whopp olof]$ make wacom
[olof@whopp olof]$ cp programs/Xserver/hw/xfree86/common/ \
xf86Wacom.so .
```

Now, **copy** the driver to the right directory, as we did before in this section.

If you have a non-Glibc system as well as an old XFree86 version, then you have to *recompile* and *install* the whole XFree86 distribution, and that is really beyond the scope of this book.

A Sneak Preview Of Gimp 1.1.x

Gimp 1.1.x is the development version of Gimp that will be released as **Gimp 1.2** when it's finished. Remember that it's still under development and may contain bugs that make it unstable to use. Furthermore, it may not even compile for you.

Nevertheless, we think it would be nice to know what you can do in Gimp 1.1.x, since it provides advance information of what is to come in the next Gimp release. For Gimp artists who are thinking of investing in a digitized tablet, this information may help you decide which tablet to buy.

Pressure Sensitivity

Gimp 1.1.x has support for *pressure sensitivity* in all of the paint tools that make use of brushes, such as the paintbrush, eraser, airbrush and ink tools. This will, for example, make it possible to use the eraser with more precision than before.

The pressure sensitivity is also very much improved, so it's not as crude as in the patched version of Gimp 1.0.x. You will be able to draw extremely fine lines, and the pen can be set to react to very small changes in pressure and tilt.

The Ink Tool

But perhaps the biggest news is a new item in the toolbox called **Ink**. The Ink tool was created with tablets in mind. It supports **tilting** and **pressure sensitivity**, and you can easily regulate the shape of the tip. Using this tool with a digital pen is just like drawing with a calligraphic ink pen, where the stroke depends on both the pressure and the tilt of the pen. In fact, this tool is so good that you would have to buy a really expensive ink pen to match the precision you'll find in Gimp's Ink tool.

To get the best out of the Ink tool we recommend the *Intuos* tablet. You can use an older Wacom tablet or a PenPartner as long as the **ROM** version is 1.4 and above. However, it's harder to configure and we haven't tested it with our ArtPad II, because it has an older ROM version.

Using Tablets With Gimp

Getting Started

Note: This section does not apply to Gimp 1.0. We will, however, cover the usage of tablets in Gimp 1.1.x (which will become 1.2).

Pen/Monitor Coordination

When you use a digitized tablet, a common misconception is that you can make instant sketches, as you would on ordinary paper. This is wrong. Drawing with a digital pen is quite different, and to control it, you need to practice.

Coordination is the single most important training moment. On ordinary paper, you can see what you draw at a glance. When you draw on a tablet, you'll have to move your focus from the pen to the monitor to see what you're doing, which is totally different. You need to practice pen/monitor coordination.

Try this simple, but effective training method:

Create a new Gimp image, and with your mouse (and the `right-click|Filters|Render|Gfig` plug-in) draw a few circles and crosses. Now, you can start drawing with the tablet. Draw circles around the crosses, and crosses within the circles. After a little while you will be able to master the necessary pen/monitor coordination. (This exercise is mentioned in the Intuos manual.)

USING PRESSURE SENSITIVITY

Using Gimp's ordinary pressure-sensitive tools, the *brush*, *eraser* and *airbrush,* is no problem at all. The pressure you exercise will control the amount of paint; if you press harder you will get more paint, and vice versa.

Note that the Device Status dialog is a bit different in Gimp 1.1.x. It will display the current brush (and pattern) assigned to the Ink tool (pen tip), Core tool (mouse) and Eraser (the eraser part of the pen), and the 4-D mouse if you have one. Obviously, patterns can't be applied by the Eraser tool, and brushes can't be used by the Ink tool, but you can of course choose to assign, for example, the clone tool to the eraser part of the pen, in which case the pattern swatch becomes relevant.

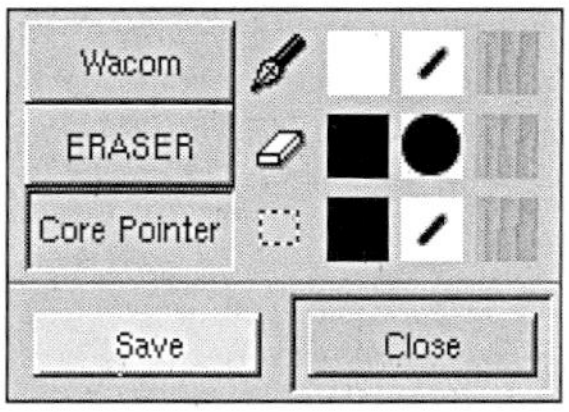

Figure 41.3 *The Device Status dialog in Gimp 1.1.x*

USING THE INK TOOL

Gimp's best tablet tool is the **Ink** tool. Sketch with this tool, and you will get a genuine *WOW* feeling. The tool is so good that it will surpass all traditional ink pens that you have ever used before.

Ink Options

If it's not already up, open the Ink tool's **Option** dialog by double-clicking with the digital pen on the Ink tool in the toolbox.

- The first parameter sliders are **Size** and **Sensitivity**. These options refer to the general pixel size of the pen tip you're using and the general pressure sensitivity of the Ink tool.
- **Tilt Sensitivity** is one of the more interesting Ink tool parameters, because without tilt sensitivity, the Ink tool would act like any ordinary calligraphic brush. *Tilt sensitivity* means that the magnetic field in the tablet will react to the angle of the pen, so that you can change the inclination of the pen tip by leaning the pen in different angles against the tablet.

Because a tilt-sensitive pen behaves more like a real ink pen, it may be harder to master for an inexperienced hand, but it gives you an incomparable artistic freedom and always produces a more sophisticated pen stroke. In fact, there are certain calligraphic fonts that can't be drawn without changing the tilt.

We recommend setting both Pressure and Tilt sensitivity to a rather high value in order to create a superb ink pen. If you set the values low, the ink pen will just feel sluggish.

- **Speed Sensitivity** is the parameter that controls how the pen reacts to the speed of your hand as you move the pen over the tablet. When you make fast sketches, the pen stroke will turn thicker where you slow down, and get thinner the faster you move the pen, just the way an ordinary ink pen works. If you draw pencil-like sketches with a lot of lines, this parameter should be set to a high value.
- **Angle Adjust** is dependent on the Tilt Sensitivity. Angle Adjust allows you to *deviate* from the inclination of the calligraphic pen tip shape. The higher the tilt sensitivity, the more change in the designated pen tip angle. This option is particularly interesting if you're an experienced calligraphic artist, and are used to holding traditional ink pens in a certain fixed angle as you draw (and sometimes need to tilt the pen in another angle to achieve a certain effect).

Pen Tip Types And Shape Adjustment

Gimp's Ink tool lets you choose between three basic pen types: **Round**, **Square** or **Diamond-shaped**.When you have chosen a pen type, you can adjust the shape and tilt angle manually in the **Shape** preview window.

If you have worked with traditional calligraphic pens before, you'll know that you have to use many different pen tips to achieve different effects, most notably when you draw calligraphic text. Also, if you like to work with thick and large pen strokes, it is very important to choose an appropriate pen tip shape, because this will have a strong impact on the appearance of the start and finish of your pen strokes.

Figure 41.4 *The Ink tool's Options dialog*

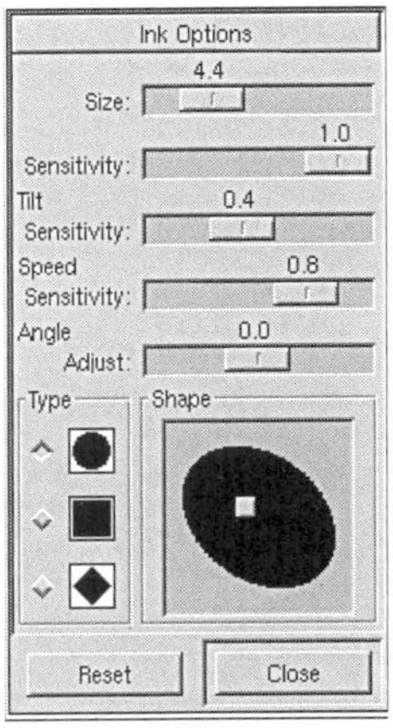

Methods And Tips

Perhaps you've seen your art teacher draw sketches on the blackboard? The drawing is ready in a blink of an eye, and it looks so perfect. This is naturally very impressive, but what you don't know is that the teacher cheats.

Before class, he made some nearly invisible help lines and small dots. He will see the lines, but you will not because you view it from a distance.

The same goes for computer graphics. Very realistic drawings are usually made with a photograph as a template. With a digitized tablet, this is a piece of cake. Just put your photo on the tablet and draw. It's an easy way to trace the image.

Even if you want to paint imaginary things, one or several photos can be used as templates or models.

If you are used to making sketches on paper, then a tablet will help. You can make you sketches as you are used to, and then put the sketch on top of the tablet and trace it. When you are more used to your new tablet you may want to skip the paper stage and sketch straight away on your Linux workstation.

A Simple Tutorial

There are, of course, as many ways to use a Wacom tablet as there are artists, and most traditional drawing techniques apply just as well to the digitized ink pen and tablet as for real paper and ink pens.

We hope that this tutorial will give you some ideas on how you can use Gimp and a tablet when you create your own paintings and drawings.

Figure 41.5 *This image was sketched with a pressure and tilt sensitive pen, using the Ink tool in Gimp. It feels like sketching with a $100 pen, and looks even better!*

Creating A Template And A Palette

1. We started off with an old color photo. The photo was scanned and imported to Gimp, where it was converted to indexed color mode (`right-click|Image|`**`Indexed`**). In the Indexed Option dialog, we chose to generate an optimal palette of 256 colors.

2. Because the photo was too small to act as a template, we also made a letter-sized printout from our black-and-white laser printer.

3. The next step was to create a palette from the indexed image with the `right-click|Image|Save Palette` command. We named the new palette, and applied the `Ops|Refresh Palettes` command in the Color Palettes dialog, so that the new palette would be available.

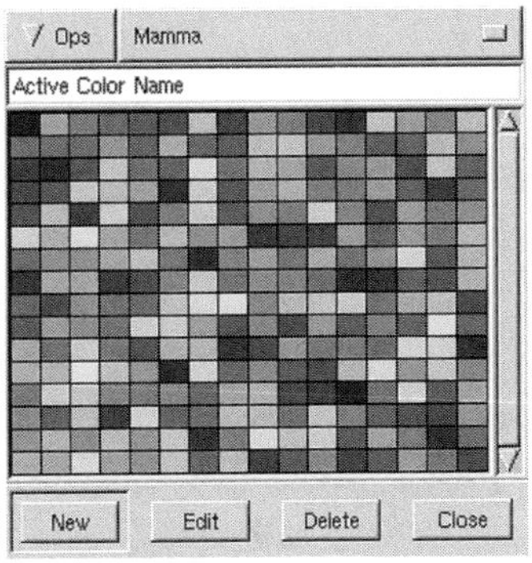

Figure 41.6 *The template photo and the extracted color palette*

Making The Sketch

Now, we can start using our Wacom pen.

4. First, we created a new 500x1000 pixel Gimp image with a white background. Then, we opened up the **Layers & Channels** dialog and created a new transparent layer.

5. It is in this layer that we will draw the first sketch. We placed the printed copy of the photo under the tablet's transparent plastic sheet so that we could use the printed image as a template.

6. We activated the **Ink tool** in the toolbox, and "double-tapped" with the pencil tip on the Ink tool symbol to access the Ink Options dialog.

7. In the Ink Options dialog, we used the default values, except for **Tilt Sensitivity**, which we raised to 0.8. We used a **diamond** shaped pen type, and tilted it manually, as you can see in the Shape preview window in Figure 41.7.

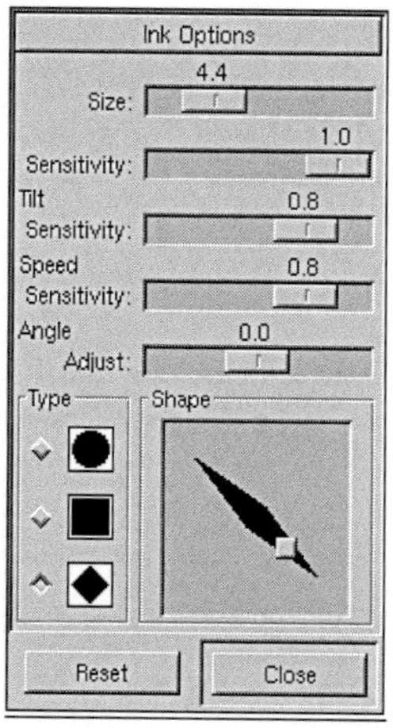

Figure 41.7 *We used these settings in the Ink Options dialog*

8. Following the outline of the template, we made a simple drawing, in which we varied the pressure so that the ink drawing would have thinner lines in brighter, or more detailed parts, and thicker lines where we wanted to put emphasis on shadow areas.

Figure 41.8 *Different pen pressure creates thicker or thinner lines*

Painting The Sketch

9. The next step was to open the palette we made from the indexed image. We assigned the pen to the **Free-hand** select tool (lasso) and selected the face, arms and legs (using Shift+lasso to select several disconnected areas). Then, we chose one of the skin-colored swatches in the indexed palette, and filled the selected areas using the **Bucket Fill** tool. The Fill tool was set to **Behind** mode, so that the contours would remain intact.

Figure 41.9 *A solid skin tone was painted in the transparent sketch layer using Behind mode*

10. After applying the base color, we made a new transparent layer and continued to draw using colors from the color palette. For the purpose of demonstrating, we used a couple of different techniques. To build volume in the face area, we switched to the **Brush tool**, where we used a large, soft brush with low opacity. With the brush we painted soft shadows and color blend in the skin tone. For the arms and legs, we used the **Ink** tool again. With short, determined strokes and a fine pencil tip, we worked to achieve a crayon-like effect.

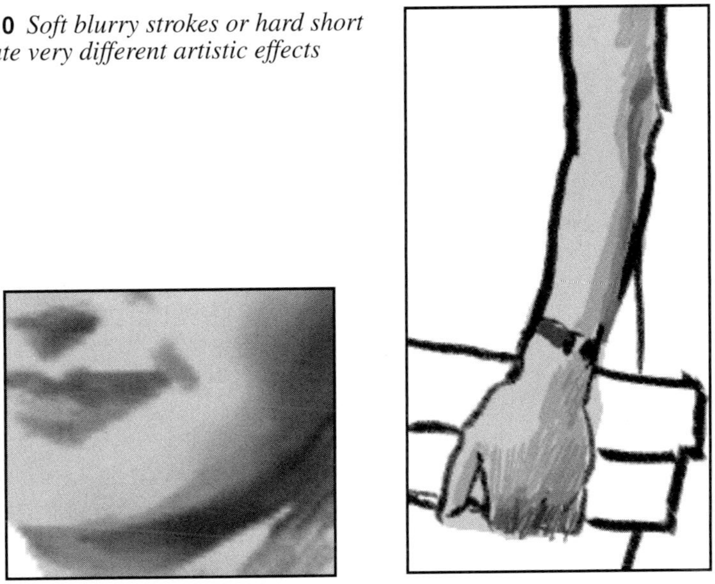

Figure 41.10 *Soft blurry strokes or hard short strokes create very different artistic effects*

Making The Dress

11. For the dress, purse and hair, we used some of the default patterns in the **Patterns** dialog, and added a little 3-D effect by using a large, soft brush with low opacity in *Overlay* or *Multiply* mode.

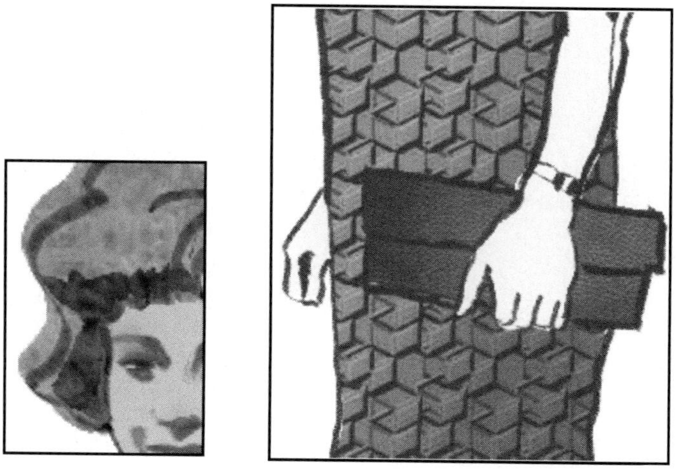

Figure 41.11 *The Red Cubes pattern was applied to the dress, Leather to the purse and Burlwood to*

Drawing The Background

For a background, we used a black-and-white photo of a busy street. To create the drawing, we used the same method that is described in "Transforming A Photograph To A Drawing" on page 28.

12. We copied the scanned image into the white background layer, and placed a new white layer on top of it. This layer was set to **Screen** mode, so that the black paint strokes would be transparent.

13. We momentarily set the screen layer to half the normal opacity, so that we could see the underlying image. The drawing was made with the **Ink** tool, where *Tilt* and *Speed* sensitivity were set to maximum values.

14. The sketch was made using many fast pen strokes, where we tried to follow the contours or the general direction of the dimensional planes in the image. The combination of the two layers made the drawing much more detailed without losing its sketch-like quality.

15. We also added some `right-click|Filters|Blur|Gaussian Blur` and `right-click|Filters|Distort|Value Propagate` to smooth out some of the roughness. The last touch was to add some texture with `right-click|Filters|Artistic|Canvas`.

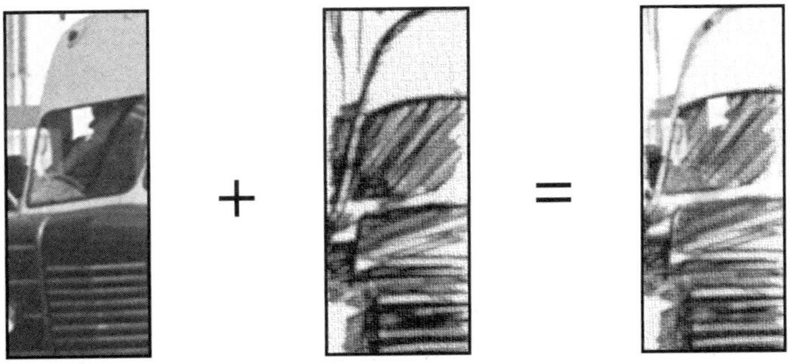

Figure 41.12 *Drawing black lines in a Screen mode layer will make the underlying image show through just enough to improve the drawing without spoiling the illusion*

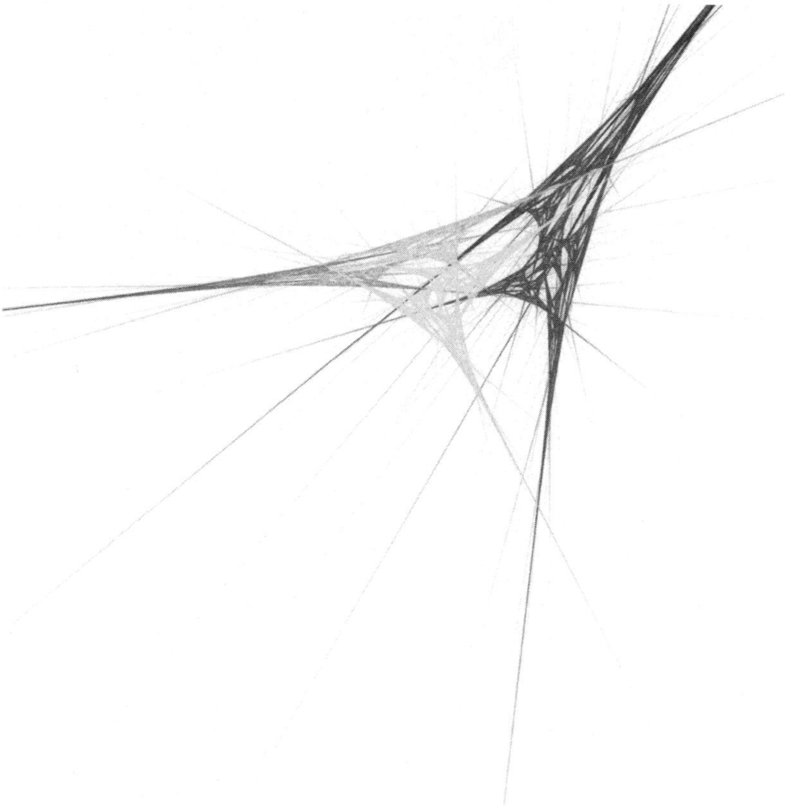

PART VIII

Script-Fu

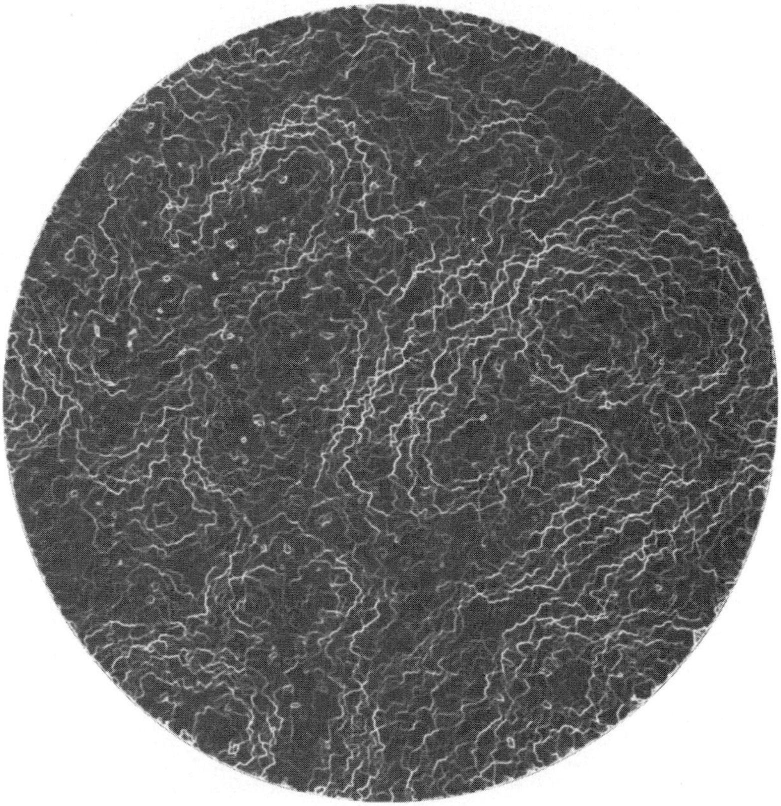

CHAPTER 42

Script-Fu: Description And Function

In this chapter, we will take a look at what's under the Xtns/Script-Fu menu in the toolbox and the right-click menu.

Script-Fu?

Script-Fu is what the Windoze world would call a "macro." But Script-Fu is more powerful than that. Script-Fu is based on an interpreting language called **Scheme**, and works by using querying functions to the Gimp *database*. You can do all kinds of things with Script-Fu, but an ordinary Gimp user will probably use it for automating things that:

- He/she wants to do frequently.
- Are really complicated to do, and hard to remember.

Remember that you can do a whole lot with a Script-Fu. The scripts that come with Gimp can be quite useful, but they can also serve as models for learning Script-Fu, or at least as a framework and source of modification when you make your own script. Read "Mike Terry's Black Belt School Of Script-Fu" starting on page 697 if you want to learn how to make scripts.

We will describe some of the most useful scripts in this chapter, but we won't cover them all. There are simply too many scripts. Some of the scripts are also very simple and you will probably not need any documentation to be able to use them.

Script-Fu (Scheme) isn't the only scripting language available for Gimp. But Script-Fu is the only scripting language that is installed by default. Other available scripting extensions are **Perl** and **Tcl**. You can download and install both extensions at `http://registry.gimp.org`.

Installing Script-Fus

The great thing about Script-Fus is that you can share your script with all your Gimp friends. There are several scripts that come with Gimp by default, but there are also scripts that are available for download all around the Internet.

If you have downloaded a script, copy or move your new script to your `.gimp/scripts` directory and do a **refresh**.

The script will now appear in one of your menus. If you don't find it, look for it under the **root file** menu filters. If it doesn't appear at all, something was wrong with the script.

Note that you can't use more than one Script-Fu dialog at a time, so don't open a script and one more after that. The last one will never be opened and displayed.

Do's and Don'ts

A common error when you are dealing with Script-Fus is that you simply bring them up and press the OK button. When nothing happens, you probably think that the script is broken or buggy, but there is most likely nothing wrong with it.

Think again. Did you really read the information in the dialog, or did you just press the button? If you forgot an input the script needs, or if you gave it the wrong input, the script will fail. One of the most common errors is that the **font** specified in the script dialog hasn't been installed on your system. So please check the information in the dialog before blaming the script.

DIFFERENT KINDS OF SCRIPT-FUS

There are two kinds of Script-Fus — **standalone** scripts and **image-dependent** scripts. You will find the standalone variants under `Xtns`|`Script-Fu`|Type of Script, and the image-dependent scripts are placed under `right-click`|`Script-Fu`|Type of Script.

STANDALONE SCRIPTS

We will not try to describe every script in depth, as we did with the filters. Most Script-Fus are very easy to understand and use. At the time of this writing, the following types are installed by default:

- Patterns
- Web page themes
- Logos
- Buttons
- Utils
- Make Brush
- Misc.

Patterns

You will find all kinds of pattern-generating scripts here. Generally, they are quite useful because you can add many arguments to your own patterns.

We'll take a look at the **Land** script. In this script you have to set the image/pattern *size*, and specify what levels of *random* to use for your land creation. The colors used to generate the land map are taken from the currently selected gradient in the gradient editor. You must also supply values for the level of *detail*, land and sea *height/depth* and the *scale*. Scale refers to the scale of your map, just as in an ordinary road map, 1:10 will be typed as 10.

Figure 42.1 *The Land script*

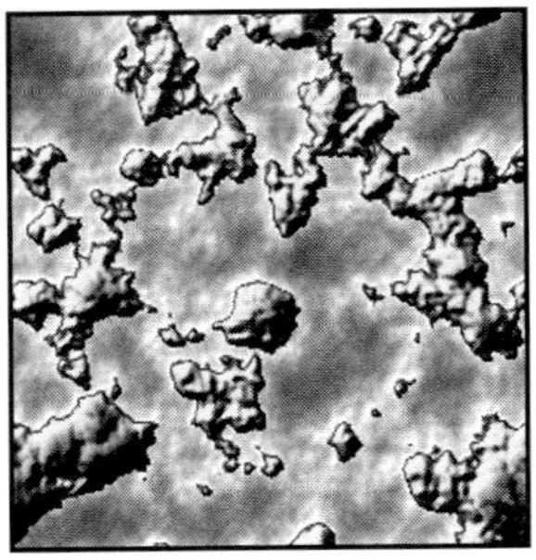

Web Page Themes

Here is clearly a practical use for scripts. By creating a script for making custom text, logos, buttons arrows, etc., for your web site, you will give them all the same style and shape. You will also be saving a lot of time, because you don't have to create every logo, text or button by hand.

You will find the Gimp.org theme under the Web page theme submenu. If you want to create your own theme, this script will serve as an excellent template that you can modify to create a theme for your web site.

Figure 42.2 *Have you ever seen this logo before :-) When the Gimp folks created* `www.gimp.org`*, they made things a bit easier by creating scripts for text, logos, buttons and headings.*

Most of the scripts are quite self-explanatory, but here are some hints:

- Leave all strange characters like ' and " intact.
- Make sure that the pattern specified in the script exists.
- *Padding* refers to the amount of space around your text.
- A high value for **bevel width** gives the illusion of a *higher* button.
- If you type `TRUE` for "Press", the button will look pushed down.
- Choose **transparency** if you don't want a solid background. If you choose a solid background, make sure it is the same color as the web page background.

Logos

Here you will find all kinds of logo-generating scrips. This is nice, but use it with care, as people might recognize your logo as being made by a known Gimp script. You should rather regard it as a base that you can modify to fit your needs. The dialog for making a logo is more or less the same for all such scripts:

1. In the **Text String** field, type your logo name, like *Frozenriver.*
2. In the **Font Size** text field, type the size of your logo in pixels.
3. In the **Font** text field, type the name of the font that you want to use for your logo.
4. To choose the color of your logo, just click on the **color** button. This brings up a color dialog.
5. If you look at the current **command field**, you can watch the script run.

Figure 42.3 *Gimp has a large collection of logo scripts, but you should be aware that a lot of people may recognize your web page logo as generated by a script and not by you*

Make Buttons

Under this headline you'll find a script that makes beveled buttons. The script has a dozen parameters or so, and most of them are similar to those in the logo scripts. You can experiment with different settings to come up with a button you like.

Utils

Under Utils you will find a small but nice script: the **Fontmap** script, which makes an image of your fonts. You will have to type the names of the fonts you want displayed in the **Fonts** text field. A tip is to use **xfontsel** to see what fonts are installed (see "How To Get Fonts To Gimp" starting on page 759).

The **Custom gradient** script creates an image of the current custom gradient in the gradient editor. This can be useful if you want to pick colors from a gradient as in a palette.

Misc.

Under **Misc**. you'll find scripts that can be quite useful, but aren't suitable for the other submenus. An example is the **Sphere** script. You will have to set the **radius** in pixels to determine the sphere size. The **lighting** angle is where at the sphere you point the spotlight. This value also has an impact on the sphere shadow. If you don't want a shadow, you will have to type `FALSE`. The last thing you have to select is background color, and the color of your sphere.

Figure 42.4 *A Gimp Script-Fu generated 3-D sphere*

Make Brush

This script lets you make your own custom rectangular/circular brushes, with or without feathered (blurred) edges. To ensure full control over the parameters, you will have to look in "Brushes, Gradients, Palettes And Patterns" starting on page 171. The script will automatically store your brush in your personal brush directory. You just have to press refresh in the Brush Selection dialog to use your newly created brush.

IMAGE-DEPENDENT SCRIPTS

The image-dependent script is a script that will perform operations on an existing image. These scripts are more like the plug-ins in the Filters submenu. At the time of this writing, the following script groups are installed by default:

- Decor
- Modify
- Animators
- Stencil Ops
- Alchemy
- Shadow
- Render
- Utils
- Selection

STENCIL OPS

Here, you'll find two scripts: *Carve-It* and *Chrome-It*, which can render some truly nice artistic effects on grayscale images.

Carve-It

Chrome-It

Figure 42.5 *Carve-It and Chrome-It are popular special-effect*

Alchemy

Unsharp Mask

One of the most useful Script-Fus is **Unsharp Mask**, which *sharpens* an unfocused or blurred image. Unsharp Mask is often a better alternative than `right-click|Filters|Enhance|Sharpen`.

Sharpen will accentuate all of your image, including scratches, noise and other imperfections that you don't want in your image. Unsharp Mask works by increasing the contrast of edges and nearby pixels, while leaving other areas pretty much untouched. This makes Unsharp Mask ideal for enhancing scanned images. The *mask value* controls the amount of sharpening, or more accurately, how wide the edge areas should be.

Figure 42.6 *Unsharp mask is a very useful image-enhancing tool*

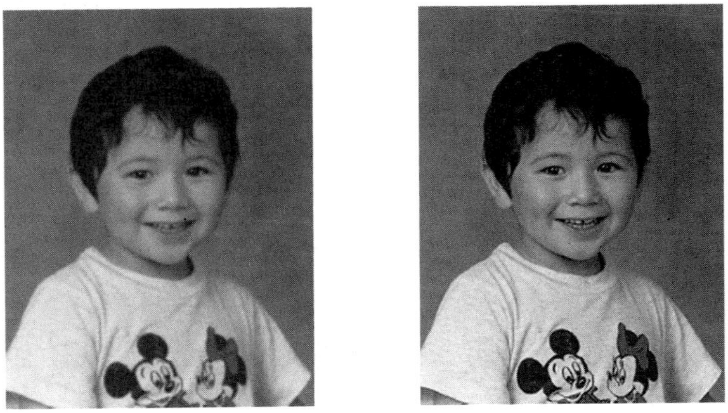

Before Unsharp Mask *After Unsharp Mask*

If you apply image-effect functions like Scale, Rotate and Perspective, try using Unsharp Mask afterward, as those types of filters use *interpolation* and thereby soften or blur your image. If you just want to enhance a small part of your image, then the ordinary Sharpen filter is an adequate tool (you can't use Unsharp Mask on selections).

Note: There is now also an Unsharp Mask plug-in available (not a script) that has the same functionality, but has even better precision; see "Unsharp Mask" on page 498.

Tip: It's a good idea to run Unsharp Mask twice, with half the mask value instead of just once with the whole value. This will sharpen more smoothly (don't forget to flatten the image).

SHADOW

Here are two really useful scripts that you will probably use quite frequently: **Drop Shadow** and **Perspective Shadow**.

Drop Shadow

Drop Shadow will cast a shadow behind your selected object. It has three important parameters. **X** and **Y offset** determine where the shadow will be placed in relation to the selected object. Offset is measured in pixels. High values make the shadow look like it's far away, and low values will make it look closer to the object. The **blur** value is also important, because a shadow that is cast far from the object has a higher blur level.

Figure 42.7 *The Drop Shadow script could well be one of the most useful scripts in Gimp, unless you count day-to-day automation scripts*

Perspective Shadow

Perspective Shadow has a very important parameter: the **perspective angle**. If this angle is set to 0 or 180, there will be no shadow, because the script assumes that the object has no thickness. This also means that this script looks fine in certain angles, but unnatural in others.

The other parameters are quite self-explanatory. You'll get more blur if the horizon is far away, and the **shadow length** is the length in relation to the selected object.

Figure 42.8 *Perspective Shadow is a very useful script. Make sure you remember where it's located. The Shadow scripts are often left unused, just because they are located under the Script-Fu submenu*

SCRIPT-FU
EVERLAST
EVERLAST

CHAPTER 43

Mike Terry's Black Belt School Of Script-Fu

Author Mike Terry

The Road To Script-Fu Mastery

So, little grasshopper, you have found Gimp, and you want to learn of its secrets?

More specifically, you wish to learn of its fantastic scripting abilities, no? You are perhaps tantalized at the prospect of automating image-editing drudgery, or maybe you seek the kind of precision in your work that only a well-written script can achieve....

Well, you have come to the right place, my friend, as Mike Terry's Black Belt School of Script-Fu can train you in the not-so-ancient art of Script-Fu.

Course Outline

In this training course, we'll introduce you to the fundamentals of **Scheme** necessary to use Script-Fu, and then build a handy script that you can add to your toolbox of scripts. The script prompts the user for some text, then creates a new image sized perfectly to the text. We will then enhance the script to allow for a *buffer* of space around the text.

Meet Your Instructor

Let me first confess that I am currently only a yellow-belt of this art, and as such, can only take you so far. However, together, we can press on and reach new heights. If I err, omit some important detail in this training or am just plain wrong about something, please email me so I may correct it. Similarly, if you have tips or suggestions on how to improve your training, please forward them to me.

I hope you benefit from this training, and may you soon become a Master of **Script-Fu**!

Audience

These training sessions are intended for the beginning Script-Fu'er. When I heard that Gimp was scriptable, I got very excited, and wanted to dive right in. Unfortunately, the tutorials were scant and incomplete, especially if you knew no Scheme (like I didn't). After about two days of trying to force my square peg of C/C++ knowledge into the round hole of Scheme, I reckoned a tutorial from the ground-up, chock-full of demos, would do the new Script-Fu'er a lot of good.

Currently, then, the tutorial is really aimed at the beginner, but as I learn more, I will expand it so we can all be Script-Fu Masters! Your suggestions and complaints are welcome:

`Michael Terry`

`mterry@soulfry.com`

Lesson 1: Getting Acquainted With Scheme

Before We Begin...

Before we begin, we have to make sure we're all at the same training hall. That is, you must have Gimp installed and fully functional. To get the latest version of Gimp, or for pointers on installing it and getting it running, we refer you to Gimp's central home page. (This tutorial was written using Gimp 1.0.0.)

Let's Start Scheme'ing

The first thing to learn is that:

- *Every statement in Scheme is surrounded by parentheses ().*

The second thing you need to know is that:

- *The function name/operator is always the first item in the parentheses, and the rest of the items are parameters to the function.*

However, not everything enclosed in parentheses is a function — they can also be items in a list — but we'll get to that later. This notation is referred to as **prefix** notation, because the function prefixes everything else. If you're familiar with **postfix** notation, or own a calculator that uses *Reverse Polish Notation* (such as most HP calculators), you should have no problem adapting to formulating expressions in Scheme.

The third thing to understand is that:

- *Mathematical operators are also considered functions, and thus are listed first when writing mathematical expressions.*

This follows logically from the prefix notation that we just mentioned.

Examples Of Prefix, Infix, And Postfix Notations

Here are some quick examples illustrating the differences between *prefix*, *infix*, and *postfix* notations. We'll add a 1 and 3 together:

- Prefix notation: + 1 3 (the way Scheme will want it)
- Infix notation: 1 + 3 (the way we "normally" write it)
- Postfix notation: 1 3 + (the way many HP calculators will want it)

Practicing In Scheme

Now, grasshopper, let's practice what we have just learned. Start up Gimp, if you have not already done so, and choose `Xtns/Script-Fu/Console`. This will start up the **Script-Fu Console** window, which allows us to work interactively in Scheme. In a matter of moments, the Script-Fu Console will appear:

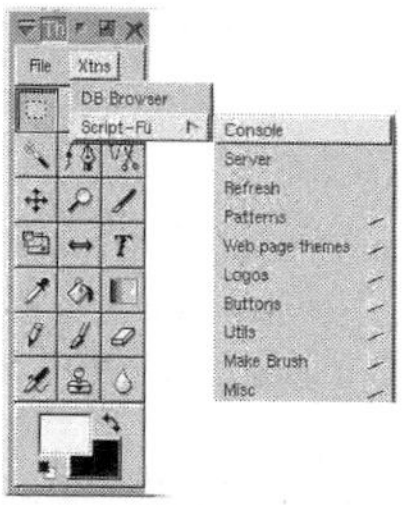

Figure 43.1 *Starting up the Script-Fu console*

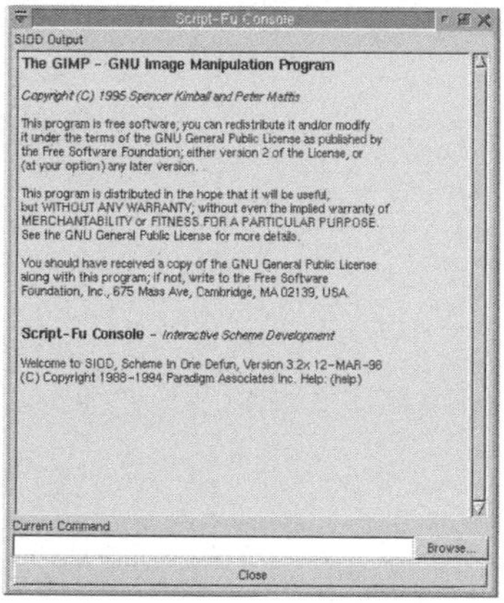

Figure 43.2 *The Script-Fu console*

THE SCRIPT-FU CONSOLE WINDOW

At the bottom of this window is an entry-field entitled **Current Command**. Here, we can test out simple Scheme commands interactively. Let's start out easy, and add some numbers:

```
(+ 3 5)
```

Typing this in and hitting Return yields the expected answer of `8` in the center window.

Now, what if we wanted to add more than one number? The "+" function can take two or more arguments, so this is not a problem:

```
(+ 3 5 6)
```

This also yields the expected answer of `14`.

So far, so good — we type in a Scheme statement and it's executed immediately in the Script-Fu Console window. Now for a word of caution....

WATCH OUT FOR EXTRA PARENS

If you're like me, you're used to being able to use extra parentheses whenever you want to — like when you're typing a complex mathematical equation and you want to separate the parts by parentheses to make it clearer when you read it. In Scheme, you have to be careful and *not insert* these extra parentheses incorrectly. For example, say we wanted to add 3 to the result of adding 5 and 6 together:

```
3 + (5 + 6) + 7= ?
```

Knowing that the + operator can take a list of numbers to add, you might be tempted to convert the above to the following:

```
(+ 3 (5 6) 7)
```

However, this is incorrect — remember, every statement in Scheme starts and ends with parens, so the Scheme interpreter will think that you're trying to call a function named "5" in the second group of parens, rather than summing those numbers before adding them to 3.

The correct way to write the above statement would be:

```
(+ 3 (+ 5 6) 7)
```

Make Sure You Have The Proper Spacing, Too

If you are familiar with other programming languages, like C/C++, Perl or Java, you know that you don't need white space around mathematical operators to properly form an expression:

```
3+5, 3 +5, 3+ 5
```

These are all accepted by C/C++, Perl and Java compilers. However, the same is not true for Scheme. You must have a space after a mathematical operator (or any other function name or operator) in Scheme for it to be correctly interpreted by the Scheme interpreter.

Practice a bit with simple mathematical equations in the Script-Fu Console until you're totally comfortable with these initial concepts.

Lesson 2: Of Variables And Functions

So, my student, you are curious and want to know about variables and functions? Such vigor in your training — I like it.

Variables

Now that we know that every Scheme statement is enclosed in *parentheses*, and that the function name/operator is *listed first*, we need to know how to create and use **variables**, and how to create and use **functions**. We'll start with the variables.

Declaring Variables

Although there are a couple of different methods for declaring variables, the preferred method is to use the `let*` construct. If you're familiar with other programming languages, this construct is equivalent to defining a list of local variables and a scope in which they're active. As an example, to declare two variables, a and b, initialized to 1 and 2, respectively, you'd write:

```
(let*        (
                    (a 1)
                    (b 2)
             )
             (+ a b)
)
```

or, as one line:

```
(let* ( (a 1) (b 2) ) (+ a b) )
```

Note: You'll have to put all of this on one line if you're using the console window. In general, however, you'll want to adopt a similar practice of indentation to help make your scripts more readable. We'll talk a bit more about this in the section "White Space" on page 702.

This declares two local variables, `a` and `b`, initializes them, then prints the sum of the two variables.

What Is A Local Variable?

You'll notice that we wrote the summation `(+ a b)` within the parens of the `let*` expression, not after it.

This is because the `let*` statement defines an area in your script in which the declared variables are usable; if you type the `(+ a b)` statement after the `(let* ...)` statement, you'll get an error, because the declared variables are only valid within the context of the `let*` statement; they are what programmers call *local variables*.

The General Syntax Of let*

The general form of a `let*` statement is:

```
(let* ( variables ) expressions )
```

where **variables** are declared within parens, e.g., `(a 2)`, and **expressions** are any valid Scheme expressions. Remember that the variables declared here are only valid within the `let*` statement — they're **local variables**.

White Space

Previously, we mentioned the fact that you'll probably want to use **indentation** to help clarify and organize your scripts. This is a good policy to adopt, and is not a problem in Scheme — **white space** is ignored by the Scheme interpreter, and can thus be liberally applied to help clarify and organize the code within a script. However, if you're working in Script-Fu's Console window, you'll have to enter an entire expression on one line; that is, everything between the opening and closing parens of an expression must come on one line in the Script-Fu Console window.

Assigning A New Value To A Variable

Once you've initialized a variable, you might need to change its value later on in the script. Use the `set!` statement to change the variable's value:

```
(let* ( (theNum 10) ) (set! theNum (+ theNum \
theNum)) )
```

Try to guess what the above statement will do, then go ahead and enter it in the Script-Fu Console window.

Note: The "\" indicates that there is no line break. Ignore it (don't type it in your Script-Fu console and don't hit Enter), just continue with the next line.

FUNCTIONS

Now that you've got the hang of variables, let's get to work with some *functions*. You declare a function with the following syntax:

```
(define (name param-list) expressions )
```

where `name` is the name assigned to this function, `param-list` is a space-delimited list of parameter names, and expressions is a series of *expressions* that the function executes when it's called. For example:

```
(define (AddXY inX inY) (+ inX inY) )
```

`AddXY` is the function's name and `inX` and `inY` are the variables. This function takes its two parameters and adds them together.

If you've programmed in other imperative languages (like C/C++, Java, Pascal, etc.), you might notice that a couple of things are absent in this function definition when compared to other programming languages.

- First, notice that the parameters don't have any "types" (that is, we didn't declare them as strings, or integers, etc.). Scheme is a type-less language. This is handy and allows for quicker script writing.
- Second, notice that we don't need to worry about how to "return" the result of our function — the last statement is the value "returned" when calling this function. Type the function into the console, then try something like:

```
(AddXY (AddXY 5 6) 4)
```

LESSON 3: LISTS, LISTS AND MORE LISTS

We've trained you in variables and functions, young Script-Fu'er, and now we must enter the murky swamps of Scheme's lists. Are you ready for the challenge?

DEFINING A LIST

Before we talk more about lists, it is necessary that you know the difference between **atomic values** and **lists**.

You've already seen atomic values when we initialized variables in the previous lesson. An atomic value is a single value. So, for example, we can assign the variable "x" the single value of 8 in the following statement:

```
(let* ( (x 8) ) x)
```

(We added the expression `x` at the end to print out the value assigned to `x`—normally you won't need to do this. Notice how `let*` operates just like a function: The value of the last statement is the value returned.)

A variable may also refer to a list of values, rather than a single value. To assign the variable `x` the list of values `1`, `3`, `5`, we'd type:

```
(let* ( (x '(1 3 5))) x)
```

Try typing both statements into the Script-Fu Console and notice how it replies. When you type the first statement in, it simply replies with the result:

```
8
```

However, when you type in the other statement, it replies with the following result:

```
(1 3 5)
```

When it replies with the value `8` it is informing you that `x` contains the atomic value 8. However, when it replies with `(1 3 5)`, it is then informing you that `x` contains not a single value, but a list of values. Notice that there are no *commas* in our declaration or assignment of the list, nor in the printed result.

The syntax to define a list is:

```
'(a b c)
```

where `a`, `b`, and `c` are *literals*. We use the *apostrophe* (`'`) to indicate that what follows in the parentheses is a **list** of literal values, rather than a function or expression.

An empty list can be defined as such:

```
'()
```

or simply:

```
()
```

Lists can contain atomic values, as well as other lists:

```
(let*
   (
            (x '("The Gimp" (1 2 3) ("is" \
("great" ()) ) ) )
   )
   x
)
```

Notice that after the first apostrophe, you no longer need to use an apostrophe when defining the inner lists. Go ahead and copy the statement into the Script-Fu Console and see what it returns.

You should notice that the result returned is not a list of single, atomic values; rather, it is a list of a literal ("`The Gimp`"), the list `(1 2 3)`, etc.

How To Think Of Lists

It's useful to think of lists as composed of a "**head**" and a "**tail**." The head is the first element of the list, the tail the rest of the list. You'll see why this is important when we discuss how to add to lists and how to access elements in the list.

Creating Lists Through Concatenation (The Cons Function)

One of the more common functions you'll encounter is the `cons` function. It takes a value and prepends it to its second argument, a list. From the previous section, I suggested that you think of a list as being composed of an element (the head) and the remainder of the list (the tail). This is exactly how `cons` functions — it adds an element to the head of a list. Thus, you could create a list as follows:

```
(cons 1 '(2 3 4) )
```

The result is the list `(1 2 3 4)`.

You could also create a list with one element:

```
(cons 1 () )
```

You can use previously declared variables in place of any literals, as you would expect.

Defining A List Using The list Function

To define a list composed of literals or previously declared variables, use the `list` function:

```
(list 5 4 3 a b c)
```

This will compose and return a list containing the values held by the variables `a`, `b` and `c`. For example:

```
(let*        (
                    (a 1)
                    (b 2)
                    (c 3)
             )
             (list 5 4 3 a b c)
)
```

This code creates the list `(5 4 3 1 2 3)`.

Accessing Values In A List

To access the values in a list, use the functions `car` and `cdr`, which return the first element of the list and the rest of the list, respectively. These functions break the list down into the head::tail construct I mentioned earlier.

The car Function

`car` returns the first element of the list (the head of the list). The list needs to be non-null. Thus, the following returns the first element of the list:

```
(car '("first" 2 "third"))
```

which is:

```
"first"
```

The cdr function

`cdr` returns the rest of the list after the first element (the tail of the list). If there is only one element in the list, it returns an empty list.

```
(cdr '("first" 2 "third"))
```

returns:

```
(2 "third")
```

whereas the following:

```
(cdr '("one and only"))
```

returns:

```
()
```

Accessing Other Elements In A List

OK, great, we can get the first element in a list, as well as the rest of the list, but how do we access the second, third or other elements of a list? There exist several "convenience" functions to access, for example, the head of the head of the tail of a list (`caadr`), the tail of the tail of a list (`cddr`), etc.

The basic naming convention is easy: The a's and d's represent the heads and tails of lists, so

```
(car (cdr (car x) ) )
```

could be written as:

```
(cadar x)
```

To view a full list of the list functions, refer to Appendix C, which lists the available functions for the version of Scheme used by Script-Fu.

To get some practice with list-accessing functions, try typing in the following (except all on one line if you're using the console); use different variations of `car` and `cdr` to access the different elements of the list:

```
(let*
   (
            (x '       (
                       (1 2 (3 4 5) 6)
                       7 8
                       (9 10)
                  )
            )
   )
   ; place your car/cdr code here
)
```

Try accessing the number 3 in the list using only two function calls. If you can do that, you're on your way to becoming a Script-Fu Master!

LESSON 4: YOUR FIRST SCRIPT-FU SCRIPT

Do you not need to stop and catch your breath, little grasshopper? No? Well then, let's proceed with your fourth lesson — your first Script-Fu Script.

CREATING A TEXT BOX SCRIPT

One of the most common operations I perform in Gimp is creating a box with some text in it for a web page, a logo or whatever. However, you never quite know how big to make the initial image when you start out. You don't know how much space the text will fill with the font and font size you want.

The Script-Fu Master (and student) will quickly realize that this problem can easily be solved and automated with Script-Fu.

We will, therefore, create a script, called **Text Box**, which creates an image correctly sized to fit snugly around a line of text the user inputs. We'll also let the user choose the **font**, **font size** and **text color**.

GETTING STARTED

Editing And Storing Your Scripts

Up until now, we've been working in the Script-Fu Console. Now, however, we're going to switch to editing **script text files**.

Where you place your scripts is a matter of preference — if you have access to Gimp's default script directory, you can place your scripts there. However, I prefer keeping my personal scripts in my own script directory, to keep them separate from the *factory-installed* scripts.

In the `.gimp` directory that Gimp made off of your home directory, you should find a directory called `scripts`. Gimp will automatically look in your `.gimp` directory for a `scripts` directory, and add the scripts in this directory to the Script-Fu database. You should place your personal scripts here.

The Bare Essentials

Every Script-Fu script defines at least one **function**, which is the script's main function. This is where you do the work.

Every script must also *register* with the **procedural database**, so you can access it within Gimp.

We'll define the main function first:

```
(define (script-fu-text-box inText inFont inFontSize
inTextColor))
```

Here, we've defined a new function called `script-fu-text-box` that takes four parameters, which will later correspond to some text, a **font**, the font

size, and the text's **color**. The function is currently empty and thus does nothing. So far, so good — nothing new, nothing fancy.

Naming Conventions

Scheme's naming conventions seem to prefer lowercase letters with hyphens, which I've followed in the naming of the function. However, I've departed from the convention with the parameters. I like more descriptive names for my parameters and variables, and thus add the "`in`" prefix to the parameters so I can quickly see that they're values passed into the script, rather than created within it. I use the prefix "`the`" for variables defined within the script.

It's Gimp convention to name your script functions `script-fu-abc`, because then when they're listed in the procedural database, they'll all show up under `script-fu` when you're listing the functions. This also helps distinguish them from plug-ins.

Registering The Function

Now, let's register the function with Gimp. This is done by calling the function `script-fu-register`. When Gimp reads in a script, it will execute this function, which registers the script with the procedural database. You can place this function call wherever you wish in your script, but I usually place it at the end, after all my other code.

Here's the listing for registering this function (I will explain all its parameters in a minute):

```
(script-fu-register
   "script-fu-text-box"                ;func name
   "<Toolbox>/Xtns/Script-Fu/Text/Text Box";menu pos
   "Creates a simple text box, sized to fit around the user's \
    choice of text,font, font size, and color."
   "Michael Terry"                     ;author
   "copyright 1997, Michael Terry"     ;copyright notice
   "October 27, 1997"                  ;date created
   ""                      ;Image type that the script works on
   SF-VALUE "Text:"        "\"Text Box\"";a text variable
   SF-VALUE "Font:"        "\"Charter\"";a text variable
   SF-VALUE "Font size:"   "45"        ;a text variable
   SF-COLOR "Color:"       '(0 0 0)    ;color variable
)
```

If you save these functions in a text file with a `.scm` suffix in your script directory, then choose `Xtns|Script-Fu|Refresh`, this new script will appear as `Xtns|Script-Fu|Text|Text Box`.

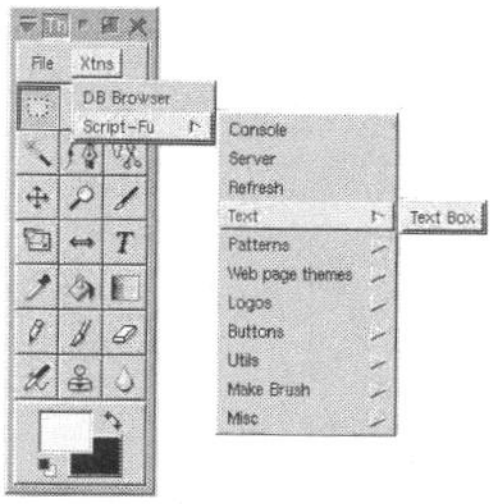

Figure 43.3 *The new script will appear in the menu after you have refreshed your Script-Fu directory*

If you invoke this new script, it won't do anything, of course, but you can view the **prompts** you created when registering the script (more information about what we did is covered next).

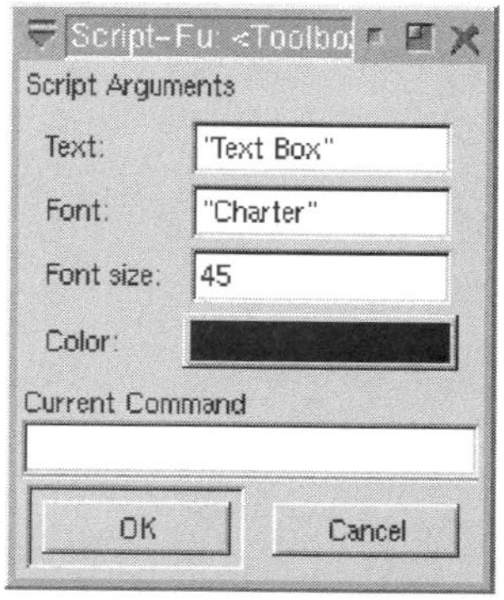

Figure 43.4 *The new script dialog*

Finally, if you invoke the **DB Browser** (the procedural database browser — `Xtns|DB Browser`), you'll notice that our script now appears in the database.

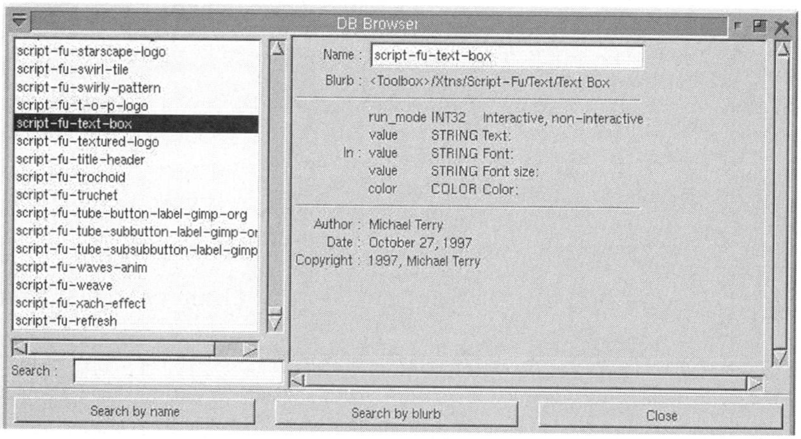

Figure 43.5 *The DB Browser*

Steps For Registering The Script

To register our script with Gimp, we call the function `script-fu-register`, fill in the seven required parameters and add our script's own parameters, along with a description and default value for each parameter.

The Required Parameters

- The **name** of the function we defined. This is the function called when our script is invoked (the entry-point into our script). This is necessary because we may define additional functions within the same file, and Gimp needs to know which of these functions to call. In our example, we only defined one function, `text-box`, which we registered.
- The **location** in the menu where the script will be inserted. The exact location of the script is specified like a path in Unix, with the root of the path being either `toolbox` or `right-click`.

If your script does not operate on an existing image (and thus creates a *new* image, like our Text Box script will), you'll want to insert it in the **toolbox** menu — this is the menu in Gimp's main window (where all the tools are located: the selection tools, magnifying glass, etc.).

If your script is intended to work on an image being *edited*, you'll want to insert it in the menu that appears when you right-click on an open image. The rest of the path points to the menu lists, menus and sub-menus. Thus, we registered our Text Box script in the Text menu of the Script-Fu menu of the Xtns menu of the toolbox (`Xtns|Script-Fu|Text|Text Box`).

If you notice, the **Text** sub-menu in the **Script-Fu** menu wasn't there when we began — Gimp automatically creates any menus not already existing.

- A **description** of your script. I'm not quite sure where this is displayed.
- Your **name** (the author of the script).
- **Copyright** information.
- The **date** the script was made, or the last **revision** of the script.
- The **types** of images the script works on. This may be any of the following: RGB, RGBA, GRAY, GRAYA, INDEXED, INDEXEDA. Or it may be none at all — in our case, we're creating an image, and thus don't need to define the type of image on which we work.

Registering The Script's Parameters

Once we have listed the required parameters, we then need to list the parameters that correspond to the parameters our script needs. When we list these params, we give *hints* as to what their types are. This is for the dialog which pops up when the user selects our script. We also provide a **default** value.

This section of the registration process has the following format:

```
Param-type "Prompt text" "default value"
```

The different parameter types, plus examples, are listed in *Table 43.1*.

Table 43.1 *Parameter list*

Param Type	Description	Examples
SF-VALUE	Accepts numbers and strings. Note that quotes must be escaped for default text.	SF-VALUE "Text:" "\"Some text\"" SF-VALUE "A number:" "34"
SF-COLOR	Indicates that a color is requested in this parameter.	SF-COLOR "Color:" '(0 0 0)
SF-TOGGLE	A checkbox is displayed, to get boolean value.	SF-TOGGLE "Resize?" TRUE
SF-IMAGE	If your script operates on an open image, this should be the first parameter after the required parameters. Gimp will pass in a reference to the image in this parameter.	SF-IMAGE "The image" 0
SF-DRAWABLE	If your script operates on an open image, this should be the second parameter after the SF-IMAGE param. It refers to the active layer. Gimp will pass in a reference to the active layer in this parameter.	SF-DRAWABLE "The layer" 0

Now, young student, this was a lot of information, so take a break.

LESSON 5: GIVING OUR SCRIPT SOME GUTS

You show great dedication to your studies, my student. Let us thus continue with your training and add some functionality to our script.

CREATING A NEW IMAGE

In the previous lesson, we created an empty function and registered it with Gimp. In this lesson, we want to provide *functionality* to our script — we want to create a new image, add the user's text to it and resize the image to fit the text exactly.

Once you know how to set **variables**, define **functions** and access **list** members, the rest is all downhill — all you need to do is familiarize yourself with the functions available in Gimp's procedural database and call those functions directly. So fire up the DB Browser and let's get cookin'!

Let's begin by making a new image. We'll create a new variable, `theImage`, set to the result of calling Gimp's built-in function `gimp-image-new`.

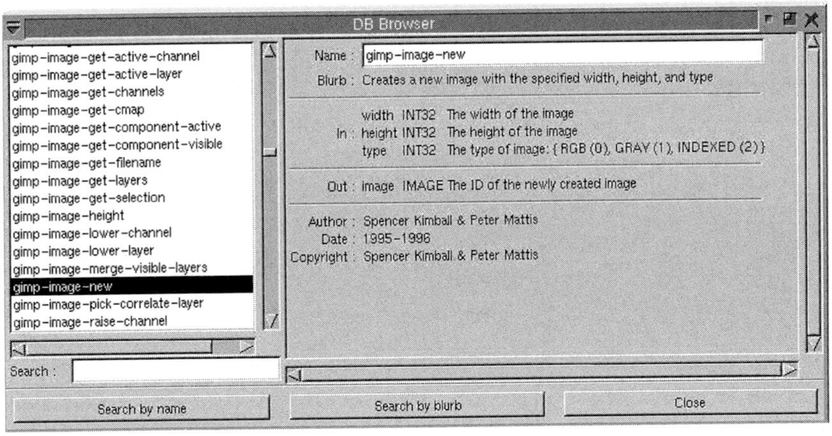

Figure 43.6 *The DB Browser*

As you can see from the **DB Browser**, the function `gimp-image-new` takes three parameters — the image's **width**, **height** and the **type** of image. Because we'll later **resize** the image to fit the text, we'll make a 10x10 RGB image. We'll store the image's width and sizes in some variables, too, as we'll refer to and manipulate them later in the script.

```
(define (script-fu-text-box inText inFont inFontSize inTextColor)
(let*
(
   ; define our local variables
   ; create a new image:
   (theImageWidth  10)
   (theImageHeight 10)
   (theImage (car (gimp-image-new theImageWidth theImageHeight RGB) )
   ; theText is a declaration for the text we create later
   (theText)
```

Note: We used the value RGB to specify that the image is an RGB image. We could have also used 0, but RGB is more descriptive when we glance at the code.

You should also notice that we took the **head** of the result of the function call. This may seem strange, because the database explicitly tells us that it returns only one value — the ID of the newly created image. However, all Gimp functions return a list, even if there is only one element in the list, so we need to get the head of the list.

Adding A New Layer To The Image

Now that we have an image, we need to add a layer to it. We'll call the `gimp-layer-new` function to create the layer, passing in the ID of the image we just created. (From now on, instead of listing the complete function, we'll only list the lines we're adding to it. You can see the complete script here.) Because we've declared all of the local variables we'll use, we'll also close the parentheses marking the end of our variable declarations:

```
   ; create a new layer for the image:
   (theLayer (car (gimp-layer-new theImage theImageWidth \
   theImageHeight RGB_IMAGE "layer 1" 100 NORMAL) ))
   ; end of our local variables
```

Once we have the new layer, we need to add it to the image:

```
(gimp-image-add-layer theImage theLayer 0)
```

Now, just for fun, let's see the fruits of our labors up until this point, and add this line to show the new, empty image:

```
(gimp-display-new theImage)
```

Save your work, select `Xtns/Script-Fu/Refresh`, run the script and a new image should pop up. It will probably contain garbage (random colors), because we haven't erased it. We'll get to that in a second.

Adding The Text

Go ahead and **remove** the line to display the image (or comment it out with a **;** as the first character of the line).

Before we add text to the image, we need to set the **background** and **foreground** colors so that the text appears in the color the user specified. We'll use the `gimp-palette-set-back/foreground` functions:

```
(gimp-palette-set-background '(255 255 255) )
(gimp-palette-set-foreground inTextColor)
```

With the colors properly set, let's now clean out the garbage currently in the image. We'll select everything in the image, and call **clear**:

```
(gimp-selection-all theImage)
(gimp-edit-clear theImage theLayer)
(gimp-selection-none theImage)
```

With the image cleared, we're ready to add some **text**:

```
(set! theText (car (gimp-text theImage theLayer 0 0 inText 0 \
TRUE inFontSize PIXELS "*" inFont "*" "*" "*" "*")))
```

Although a long function call, it's fairly straightforward if you go over the parameters while looking at the function's entry in the DB Browser. Basically, we're creating a new text layer and assigning it to the variable `theText`.

Now that we have the text, we can grab its **width** and **height** and resize the image and the image's layer to the text's size:

```
(set! theImageWidth  (car (gimp-drawable-width theText) ) )
(set! theImageHeight (car (gimp-drawable-height theText) ) )
(gimp-image-resize theImage theImageWidth theImageHeight 0 0)
(gimp-layer-resize theLayer theImageWidth theImageHeight 0 0)
```

If you're like me, you're probably wondering what a **drawable** is when compared to a layer. The difference between the two is that a drawable is anything that can be drawn into; a layer is a more specific version of a drawable. In most cases, the distinction is not important.

With the image ready to go, we can now re-add our display line:

```
(gimp-display-new theImage)
```

Save your work, refresh the database and give your first script a run! You should get something like Figure 43.7.

Figure 43.7 *Our text box*

Clearing The Dirty Flag

If you try to close the image created without first **saving** the file, Gimp will ask you if you want to save your work before you close the image. It asks this because the image is marked as *dirty*, or unsaved. In the case of our script, this is a nuisance for the times when we simply give it a test run and don't add or change anything in the resulting image — that is, our work is easily reproducible in such a simple script, so it makes sense to get rid of this *dirty* flag.

To do this, we can clear the dirty flag after displaying the image:

```
(gimp-image-clean-all theImage)
```

This will dirty count to 0, making it appear to be a "clean" image.

Whether to add this line or not is a matter of personal taste. I use it in scripts that produce new images, where the results are trivial, as in this case. If your script is very complicated, or if it works on an existing image, you will probably not want to use this function.

Lesson 6: Extending The Text Box Script

Your will and determination are unstoppable, my eager student. So let us continue your training.

Handling Undo Correctly

When creating a script, you want to give your users the ability to **undo** their actions, should they make a mistake. This is easily accomplished by calling the functions `gimp-undo-push-group-start` and `gimp-undo-push-group-end` around the code that manipulates the image. You can think of them as matched statements that let Gimp know when to start and stop recording manipulations on the image, so that those manipulations can later be undone.

If you are creating a new image entirely, it doesn't make sense to use these functions because you're not changing an existing image. However, when you are changing an existing image, you most surely want to use these functions.

As of this writing, undoing a script works nearly flawlessly when using these functions. However, it does seem to have some trouble undoing everything, now and then, and it seems to have the hardest time when calling another script that doesn't itself call these functions.

Extending The Script A Little More

Now that we have a very handy-dandy script to create text boxes, let's add two features to it:

- Currently, the image is resized to fit exactly around the text — there's no room for anything, like drop shadows or special effects (even though many scripts will automatically resize the image as necessary). Let's add a **buffer** around the text, and even let the user specify how much buffer to add as a percentage of the size of the resultant text.
- This script could easily be used in other scripts that work with text. Let's **extend** it so that it returns the image and the layers, so other scripts can call this script and use the image and layers we create.

Modifying The Parameters And The Registration Function

To let the user specify the amount of buffer, we'll add a parameter to our function and the registration function:

```
(define (script-fu-text-box inText inFont inFontSize inTextColor inBufferAmount)
(let*
(
    ; define our local vars

    ; create a new image:
    (theImageWidth  10)
    (theImageHeight 10)
    (theImage   (car (gimp-image-new theImageWidth theImageHeight RGB) ) )
    (theText)
    (theBuffer)
    ; create a new layer for the image:
(theLayer (car (gimp-layer-new theImage theImageWidth theImageHeight RGB_IMAGE \
"layer 1"  100 NORMAL) ))
)
...
)
(script-fu-register
"script-fu-text-box"
"<Toolbox>/Xtns/Script-Fu/Text/Text Box"
"Creates a simple text box, sized to fit around the user's choice of text,\
 font, font size, and color."
"Michael Terry"
"copyright 1997, Michael Terry"
"October 27, 1997"
""
SF-VALUE "Text:" "\"Text Box\""
SF-VALUE "Font:" "\"Charter\""
SF-VALUE "Font size:" "45"
SF-COLOR "Color:" '(0 0 0)
SF-VALUE "Buffer amount (0 - 100% height of text):" "35"
)
```

Adding The New Code

We're going to add **code** in two places: right before we **resize** the image, and at the **end** of the script (to return the new image, the layer and the text).

After we get the text's height and width, we need to **resize** these values based on the buffer amount specified by the user. We won't do any error checking to make sure it's in the range of 0-100% because it's not life-threatening, and because there's no reason why the user can't enter a value like "200" as the percent of buffer to add.

```
(set! theBuffer (* theImageHeight ( inBufferAmount 100) ) )
(set! theImageHeight (+ theImageHeight theBuffer theBuffer) )
(set! theImageWidth  (+ theImageWidth theBuffer theBuffer) )
```

All we're doing here is setting the buffer based on the height of the text, and adding it twice to both the height and width of our new image. (We add it twice to both dimensions because the buffer needs to be added to both sides of the text.)

Now that we have resized the image to allow for a buffer, we need to **center** the text within the image. This is done by moving it to the (**x, y**) coordinates of (`theBuffer, theBuffer`). I added this line after resizing the layer and the image:

```
(gimp-layer-set-offsets theText theBuffer theBuffer)
```

Go ahead and save your script, and try it out after refreshing the database. You should now get a window like Figure 43.8.

Figure 43.8 *The finished text box*

All that is left to do is return our image, the layer, and the text layer. After displaying the image, we add this line:

```
(list theImage theLayer theText)
```

This is the last line of the function, making this list available to other scripts that want to use it.

To use our new text box script in another script, we could write something like the following:

```
(set! theResult (script-fu-text-box "Some text" "Charter" "30" '\
(0 0 0) "35") )
(gimp-image-flatten (car theResult) )
```

Congratulations, my student, you are on your way to your Black Belt of Script-Fu!

PART IX

Perl-Fu

- *Perl Introduction*
- *Dov Grobgeld's Perl-Fu Tutorial*

CHAPTER 44

A Perl Introduction

This chapter is a brief introduction to Perl for users who are not familiar with Perl, or aren't experienced programmers. We can't teach you how to program in Perl, but we will try to demonstrate some of Perl's utility and power.

INTRODUCTION

Perl-Fu is not a part of the core Gimp 1.0.x distribution. However, the next version of Gimp (1.2) will include Perl-Fu as a standard part of Gimp. There's no need to grumble over the fact that you run Gimp 1.0.x. Perl-Fu is available as a plug-in to Gimp 1.0.x, and Perl-Fu is also included in the development version of Gimp.

Perl-Fu is a plug-in that makes it possible to write Gimp scripts in **Perl**, just like the *Script-Fu* plug-in makes it possible to write Gimp scripts based on **Scheme**. Yes, both Perl-Fu and Script-Fu are plug-ins.

In our opinion, Perl is considerably more straightforward and easy to use than Scheme. Furthermore, there are a lot more publicly available Perl scripts (and experienced Perl programmers), than there are scripts based on Scheme. Note that we are not referring to specific Gimp scripts, but to scripts in general.

Perl is also *the major* scripting language used by **CGI** scripts. If you are somewhat familiar with UNIX shell scripts, then Perl will be very easy to learn. In fact, you will probably find Perl scripts more uncomplicated to write than shell scripts. Just about every **awk**, **sed** and other tweaks that you usually execute in a shell script can be done natively in Perl without the help of other UNIX shell programs.

In "A Tutorial For Perl Gimp Users" starting on page 735, you will find *Dov Grobgelb's* Perl-Fu tutorial. It's a very good tutorial, and if you are familiar with Perl, you will probably be able to use Perl-Fu right away. However, the tutorial doesn't cover "learning Perl." That is a vast topic, and it's simply beyond the scope of this book; but we will give you a crash course in Perl.

HOW EXPERIENCED DO YOU HAVE TO BE?

For total script newbies, the crash course will make it easier to read and understand Dov's tutorial. After reading the crash course, you can make the decision of whether Perl-Fu is something that you want to use or not. If you want to learn more about Perl-Fu, then the best advice we can give you is to go and buy a Perl book and learn the basics of Perl programming. If you are familiar with shell scripting, for example, then you can probably (with some help from Perl's on-line documentation) start to use Perl-Fu after reading the crash course and Dov's tutorial. The *Perl-Fu man pages* covers every command in the Perl-Fu plug-in, and you'll find them in the "Perl-Fu Man Pages" appendix starting on page 835. Those pages are an excellent source of information when you write Perl-Fu scripts.

Just to make it clear: You will need to understand Perl if you want to use Perl-Fu, but Perl is a very extensive language, and you don't need to learn all of it. It's often sufficient to learn elementary Perl-Fu for basic Gimp scripting. When you are a more experienced Perl programmer, you can learn more about advanced Perl scripting. In this chapter, we will discuss how you install and configure the Perl-Fu plug-in. This is generally a simple procedure, but if you don't have Perl installed, then it can be a bit more troublesome.

Perl-Fu Installation And Configuration

If you have read the previous chapters about installing miscellaneous accessories to Gimp (see "Drawing Tablets And Gimp" starting on page 657 and "Scanning And Scanners" starting on page 219), then you'll probably expect to find 10 or more pages about how to install Perl-Fu.

Well, we will not do it this time. If you have read this far, you should have gathered enough experience by now and only need some hints. There are also a lot hints about compiling in "Compiling Plug-ins" starting on page 769.

Hints

It's always a good idea to get the latest source code of the Perl-Fu plug-in and the **Gtk Perl** extension that Perl-Fu needs. Check out "Perl-Fu" on page 881 to find out where to download Perl-Fu and the Perl Gtk module.

First of all, make sure that your Gimp and Gtk libraries are in your library search path. This is controlled in Linux by the `/etc/ld.so.conf` file. Solaris (and most other Unix dialects) uses the `LD_LIBRARY_PATH` environment variable to control the library search path.

Second, you must have your Gimp and Gtk binary directory in your path (controlled by the `PATH` environment variable). The **configure** programs that are used to prepare both Perl-Fu's and Gtk's Perl Module are dependent on finding `gimp-tool` and `gtk-config`.

If you have multiple installations of Gimp and/or Gtk, it is very important to set both `PATH` and `LD_LIBRARY_PATH` to search in the right directories first.

Suppose that you have Gimp 1.0.x and Gtk 1.0.x installed under `/opt/gimp` and Gimp 1.1.x and GA 1.2.x installed under `/opt/gimp1.1` and you want to enable Perl-Fu within Gimp 1.1.x.

Then you have to set the `PATH` to:

```
PATH=/opt/gimp1.1/bin:$PATH
```

and your `LD_LIBRARY_PATH` to:

```
LD_LIBRARY_PATH=/opt/gimp1.1/
lib:$LD_LIBRARY_PATH.
```

This procedure will ensure that you compile and install Perl-Fu and the Perl Gtk module for usage in Gimp 1.1.x.

If you don't set your environment correctly, it is more or less certain that you will fail to compile and install Perl-Fu. Naturally, you will also need to have Perl installed on your system. Either Perl 5.004_04 or Perl 5.005 or higher.

Our last tip is that you must read the **README** and **INSTALL** files that come with Perl-Fu and the Perl Gtk module. If you think you can manage without them, then you're either suffering from a severe case of hubris, or (which is more unlikely) you really are an expert on UNIX, Gimp and Perl with associated configuration, compilation, installation, etc.

CRASH COURSE

We can't cover all basic Perl functions here, but we will try to explain the fundamental functions that you'll need to understand before taking on Dov's Perl tutorial. This section is for absolute beginners, so don't expect to understand other Perl scripts after you have read this crash course and Dov's tutorial.

DEFINING A PERL SCRIPT

Normally, when you execute a program the program file is a **binary** file built up of ones and zeros. However, a Perl program file is different, because Perl is an *interpreting language*. Perl uses *ordinary text files that humans can read* and not binary 0 and 1 files.

It's therefore necessary to tell the operating system that it should use the Perl interpreter (i.e., execute the file with the help of Perl) when the operating system launches the file. This is done by "chmod:ing" the file:

```
chmod 755 perl_fu_script.pl
```

and with a special line in the top of the Perl file:

```
#!/usr/local/bin/perl
```

This special line tells the OS that it should use Perl to execute the file. (Naturally the location of Perl is site specific, but in this case it was `/usr/bin/perl`.)

You have probably heard of **shell scripts**. Shell scripts make use of readable files, just like Perl does. A shell script's first line is:

```
#!/bin/sh
```

(or `#!/bin/bash` most of the time on a Linux system).

As you see, there are several types of scripting languages, and the first line in the text files tells us which type of interpreter to use. *The rest of the file contains the script code.*

The `-w` switch that comes after `#!/usr/local/bin/perl` orders Perl to warn you if there are *potential errors* in your script. We strongly recommend always using the `-w` flag in your Perl scripts.

PERL FUNCTIONALITY MODULES

A core Perl installation has a lot of **functions** available for the programmer, and it is also possible to install extra Perl **modules** to add more functions to Perl if needed.

Loading all Perl functions all the time will make a Perl program slow (that definition is not totally correct, but it's good enough for now). A better way is to load functionality into Perl only when you need it.

For example, say you are writing a network application that is supposed to copy a remote file (a file present on another computer) to your computer. Then you may need the `Net:remotecopy` (this command is purely fictitious) functionality in

Perl. This functionality is not present by default in Perl, so you must tell Perl to load the functionality. This is done by the `use` command in Perl:

```
use Net:remotecopy;
```

This line will tell Perl to load the "remotecopy" functionality. After you have loaded `Net:remotecopy`, you can use all the remote copy commands in a Perl program. It is similar to a Perl-Fu script (which is just a name of a Perl script using Gimp functionality)

```
use Gimp;

use Gimp::Fu;
```

This tells Perl to load the `Gimp` functionality and the `Gimp::Fu` functionality. So, why do you have to load two modules? Well, the **Gimp** module provides you with basic Gimp functionality in Perl. The **Gimp::Fu** module (that is dependent on the Gimp module) loads a set of more *Gimp* functions that make it easy to write Perl-Fu scripts.

Perl Variables

Variables are things that can store things. For example, the variable `A` can store the value `10`. In Perl you define a variable like this:

```
$variable = 10;
```

Notice the ending "**;**" which tells Perl that it has reached the end of the command (this is mandatory for all Perl commands). We could also write:

```
$variable

=

10

;
```

But that is not as elegant, is it?

Perl Functions

A **function** in Perl is a **routine** that *does things for you.* Most of the time, functions are used to help the programmer in different ways.

Instead of writing the same thing in the code a number of times, the programmer can do this once in a single function. He will then *call on that function when he needs it*. This means that you don't need to type all those lines of code, but also that you get a code that is simpler to understand.

In fact, when you import a functionality module (such as the Gimp module), then you import a lot of functions that you can use in your code, such as the `gimp_displays_flush` function that will flush Gimp's display. In order to flush Gimp's display, enter:

```
gimp_displays_flush();
```

and the display will be flushed. This is obviously much easier than writing the "flush display" code every time you need it (you would also have to know how to implement the function; now, you just have to know how to use it).

To create your own functions, also called **subroutines**, you have to declare the function by the special name: `sub` followed by the name of the function that you want to implement:

```
sub karins_flush_display {
                    gimp_displays_flush();
}
```

This is naturally a quite meaningless function. Nevertheless, you can now use `karins_flush_display();` instead of the `gimp_displays_flush();` function call.

A Perl-Fu script has one or several self-defined subroutines that you use to manipulate or create Gimp images.

Variables And Functions

In Perl-Fu scripts you will frequently see:

```
sub some_function {
            my($variable1, $variable2) = @_;
#The subroutine code
#Hash marks are comment marks in a Perl script
}
```

The keyword `my` makes the variables (`$variable1` and `$variable2`) *local variables* within the subroutine. This means that you *can't access them or the values they carry outside the subroutine.*

The @_ is a special variable carrying the arguments that the subroutine was called with (well, that's not the whole truth but it's good enough for now; and we don't want to get too complicated here). Let's say that you have this code:

```
sub some_function {
        my($variable1, $variable2) = @_;
        print $variable1 + $variable2;
            #(print will simply print the sum \
 of $variable1 and $variable2)
}

some_function(1,2);
```

Then, `some_function` is called with `1` and `2` as arguments. Perl reads the whole file and stores the subroutine. Then, Perl will execute the first command, which in this case is `some_function(1,2);`.

The line `my($variable1, $variable2) = @_;` lets us assign 1 to `$variable1`, and 2 to `$variable2`, because they are stored in the special `@_` variable in that order. The next line will simply print 3, because that is the sum of 1 and 2.

Perl-Fu Specials

What's special about Perl-Fu scripts is the `\&function_name` that is used in the **registry** part of Perl-Fu (don't worry, Dov will cover the registry part of Perl-Fu). Anyway, this is a very special way of including the subroutines to call in Perl scripts. *You must use that kind of reference when you call your first and only subroutine in the registry part of Perl-Fu.*

Loops

Do you want to repeat the same thing over and over again? Then, you should use Perl's **loop** functionality. There are several ways of doing this in Perl, but we will only explain the **for** loop because it is used in Dov's tutorial.

Dov uses a **for** loop as in this tutorial:

```
$number_of_loops = 10;
for ($i=0; $i<$number_of_loops; $i++) {
   #(The code)
}
```

The `$i=0; $i<$number_of_loops; $i++` tells us that the loop start value is 0 (`$i=0`) and that each time the loop is done we will add 1 to `$i` (`$i++`). Before starting a loop we will check if `$i` is less than 10 (`$i<$number_of_loops`). If it is, we will continue to loop, and if it isn't, we will exit the loop:

```
$number_of_loops = 10;

for ($i=0; $i<$number_of_loops; ++$i) {
        print $i;
}
```

This is a simple example loop that will print `0123456789` when you run the code. This line shows that we have made 10 loops, and that we started on 0 and ended on 9.

Some Final Notes

We haven't really learned much about Perl — we have barely showed some of the Perl functions that you'll need to understand Dov's tutorial. If you find Perl-Fu interesting, we suggest that you buy a "Learn Perl" book.

Such a book along with the *example Perl-Fu scripts* that you'll find in the Perl-Fu distribution, and of course the *Perl-Fu manpages* (that you will find in the "Perl-Fu Man Pages" appendix starting on page 835) will be a very good start to explore Perl-Fu. ***Also, don't forget to read Dov's excellent Perl-Fu tutorial—consider it mandatory!***

new($width, $height, 0);
new($img, $width, $height, 1,
($img, $layer, 0);
_layer($img, $layer);
_active_drawable($img);
palette_get_foreground();
foreground([0,0,0]);
0,0,100,0,0,0,0);

CHAPTER 45

A Tutorial For Perl Gimp Users

Author Dov Grobgeld

Background

One of the wonderful features of Gimp is that all its functionality may be accessed through scripting. So far, most of the script programming for Gimp has been done through **Scheme** through **Script-Fu**. Unfortunately, the Scheme environment Gimp provides is very primitive, e.g., it doesn't provide any reasonable error handling. Furthermore, most users are not familiar with Scheme as a language. Some users may, therefore, prefer to write scripts for Gimp in **Perl**.

Perl, as a language, is probably more familiar to the web-literate users, because it is the preferred language for writing **CGI** scripts. Now, Gimp scripts may also be written with Perl. This tutorial will describe how to write such plug-ins and scripts for Gimp.

As there are several excellent tutorial texts describing the Perl language, this tutorial assumes that the reader has a *working knowledge of Perl* and will concentrate on using Gimp with the Perl modules Gimp and Gimp::Fu written by Marc Lehmann, `pcg@goof.com`.

What You Need

The Perl::Gimp tutorial scripts have been tested with the following versions:

- Gimp version 1.04 or later, with all its prerequisites
- Perl version 5.005 or later
- The perl module Gtk, version 0.5121 or later
- The Gimp module, version 1.083 or later

Perl and all its associated modules are available in source form from the Perl Comprehensive Archive network, **CPAN**. It is also possible to download them in RPM format from the `ftp.gimp.org` web site.

The Gimp Module

Most scripts make use of the simplified interface **Gimp::Fu** provides with the Gimp module. Gimp::Fu provides a framework for entering parameters to the script in a frame-like interface, just like Script-Fu, but also allows the script to be run in batch mode from the command line. This tutorial details the construction of a Gimp::Fu script, but first, we want to show you the general framework of a Perl-Fu script

A basic Perl-Fu script

```
#!/usr/local/bin/perl

use Gimp;
use Gimp::Fu;

# Register extension to gimp
register ... ;
```

The interesting items to note in the script are the use of the two modules Gimp and Gimp::Fu, the register function and the way control is handed over to the Gimp module on line 9.

THE GIMP PDB

All functions known to Gimp are available through the **procedural database** (PDB). All the **PDB** functions may be called from Perl. These PDB functions are either internal to Gimp, or have been made available through a plug-in or a script extension. As far as the caller is concerned, there is no difference. When a Perl function is registered through the register function, it will appear in the PDB as well.

Gimp provides a PDB browser available in `Xtns|DB BROWSER`. This browser provides a way to view all of the functions in the PDB, as well as their input and output parameters. The DB Browser entry for `gimp_image_new`, looks like Table 45.1.

Table 45.1 *The Gimp_image_new's PDB entry*

Name	gimp-image-new		
Blurb	Creates a new Image with the specified width, height and type		
In	width	INT32	The width of the image
	height	INT32	The height of the image
	type	INT32	The type of image { RGB (0), GRAY (1), INDEXED (2)}

The entries in the PDB browser are given in Scheme style with dash characters. *The perl programmer must use underline characters instead.* A call to create a new image of size 100x150 of type RGB looks like the following:

```
$img = gimp_image_new(100, 150, RGB)
```

The PDB entry earlier shows that `gimp_image_new` is called with three parameters (`width`, `height` and `type`). These are all of type `INT32`.

An exception to this rule are Script-Fu scripts that are registered in the database with a dash instead of an underline character. To call these, the following syntax must be used:

```
gimp_call_procedure("script-fu-basic1-logo", \
 1, "Hello", 10, "Helvetica", [0,0,0],[1,1,1]);
```

Note: When calling a PDB function from Perl::Gimp that has an image and a drawable as the first two arguments, only the drawable should be given as argument in the calling sequence.

GIMP::FU AND THE REGISTER FUNCTION

Gimp-Fu is Perl's answer to Script-Fu. It provides a simplified method for accepting parameters for a script through a Gtk interface, just like Script-Fu, but it has some additional bells and whistles.

The main function for a Gimp-Fu script is the **register** function. This function declares the interface of the script to Gimp. The register function takes the following 10 parameters that must all be provided:

1. The name of the function — A string. This is the name of the function as it will be known in the PDB.
2. A brief description — A string.
3. A help text — A string.
4. The authors name — A string.
5. The copyright of the script — A string.
6. Creation date — A string.
7. Menu path — A string. The path has one of the following two forms:

   ```
   Xtns|Perl-Fu|Script Name
   right-click|Perl-Fu|Script Name
   ```

   If first form is given, then the script is a standalone script that appears in the menu hierarchy under `Xtns|Perl-Fu` and takes all of its inputs through the Gimp::Fu interface frame. If the second form is given, then the script is tied to the image menu popped up through the right button over any image. In this case, Gimp::Fu will add, as the first two parameters to the script, the **image** and the **drawable** active when the script was invoked.

8. The acceptable image types — A string. This is a list, of acceptable image types. This field is only used for scripts that are in the `right-click` menu hierarchy. Possible values are listed in Table Table 45.2.

Table 45.2 *Possible values of image*

Value	Meaning
*	Any images are accepted
RGB	RGB images

Table 45.2 *Possible values of image(continued)*

Value	Meaning
RGBA	RGB images with alpha channels
GREY	Grey level images

1. Parameters — A reference to an **array** of parameters. (A reference to an array in Perl is simply an array written within square brackets.) Each parameter in turn is a reference to an array containing the following five values:
   - The type of parameter. The types recognized by Gimp::Fu and Perl are given in Table 45.3.
   - The name of the parameter — a string
   - A help text for the parameter
   - Default value for the parameter. This should be given in the form listed in Table Table 45.3.
   - An array defining allowed range for the value. This is only possible for `PF_SLIDER` and `PF_SPINNER`

Table 45.3 *PF values*

Type	Possible Forms	Comment
PF_INT PF_INT32 PF_INT16 PF_INT8	42	A number. PF_INT is a synonym to PF_INT32.
PF_VALUE PF_FLOAT	3.141	A floating point number.
PF_TOGGLE PF_BOOLEAN	0 1	A boolean value.
PF_SLIDER PF_SPINNER	An integer value through a slider and a spinner interface. The range parameter should be specified and is interpreted as minimum, maximum, and step, e.g., [0,100,1].	
PF_FONT	-*-blippo-*-*-*-*-24-*-*-*-*-*-*-*	A font in X11 font format. This interface launches a font browser.
PF_STRING	“A string”	A string.
PF_COLOR PF_COLOUR	[255,127,0] #ff7f00	A color may either be expressed as a reference to an array of three components, or as a hexadecimal triple, proceeded by the hash sign.
PF_TOGGLE	0 1	A boolean toggle.

Table 45.3 *PF values (continued)*

Type	Possible Forms	Comment
PF_IMAGE	-	An image.
PF_DRAWABLE	-	A drawable.
PF_BRUSH		A brush.
PF_GRADIENT		A gradient.
PF_PATTERN		A pattern.

10. A reference to an array of return types of the sub in the 11th parameter.
11. The **sub** to be called — A reference to a sub. This **subroutine** will be called when the associated menu entry is declared through the menu path described in Step 9. When the sub is called, it is passed as arguments to the list of parameters declared in field 9, declared in the above table, and in the case of a `right-click` script, the active image and layer as first and second parameters.

    A reference to a sub in Perl may be declared in two ways: by declaring a subroutine at a different place in the source file (e.g., *sub run* and reference it by writing `\&run`), or by writing it inline:

    ```
    sub { ($text, $color) = @_ ; ... }
    ```

    The sub is expected not to need to display a new image after it has created it. Instead, it is expected to return the new image or images that were created in accordance with the return types declared in parameter 10 of the register call described in Step 10. This behavior has been added in order to be able to call the sub **noninteractively**.

A Commented Script

The following Gimp::Fu script example shows the steps described in the previous section. It registers a script that takes the **size** of the image and a **color** and then produces an image of the requested size with the requested color. Quite useless, but it shows the important steps of how to register a script, how to create a new image, and how to access some PDB functions.

Uni Perl-Fu script

```
#!/usr/local/bin/perl -w
use Gimp;
use Gimp::Fu;

sub img_uni {
    my ($size, $color) = @_;
    # Create a new image
    $img = gimp_image_new($size, $size, RGB);
    # Create a new layer
    $layer = gimp_layer_new($img, $size, $size, RGB,
                      "Layer 1", 100, NORMAL_MODE);
    # add the layer to the image
    gimp_image_add_layer($img, $layer, -1);
    # Set the background to the required color
    gimp_palette_set_background($color);
    # Paint the layer
    gimp_edit_fill($layer);
    # Return the image
    return $img;
}

register
    "img_uni",                  # fill in name
    "Create a uniform image",   # a small description
    "A tutorial script",        # a help text
    "Dov Grobgeld",             # Your name
    "Dov Grobgeld (c)",         # Your copyright
    "1999-05-14",               # Date
```

Most of these commands are directly copied from the PDB.

This script shows the essential steps of producing a standalone script:

- Creating a new image (line 8).
- Creating one or more layers (lines 10 through 11).
- Attaching the layer to the image (line 13).

- Do some painting operations in the layers (lines 15 through 17).
- Return the image to the caller (line 19).
- Register the extension (lines 22 through 35).

To test the script, save it in the directory `$HOME/.gimp/plug-ins` and then start Gimp. It is generally a good idea to test the syntax of the script with `perl -c` before starting Gimp. (A more official way to add scripts is to use the `gimptool --install-bin` command).

Note: Due to a bug in Gimp (verified for version 1.0), it is not possible to add scripts when Gimp is running. It is possible, however, to change a script that has already been registered, as long as the parameters don't change.

Figure 45.1 *The script is now accessible through the menu system through the Xtns top menu*

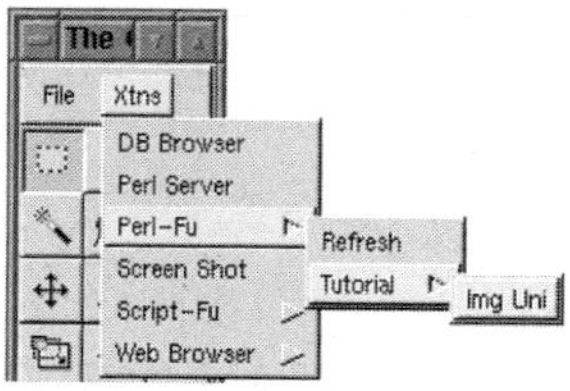

Figure 45.2 *When choosing this menu entry, the following screen is popped up*

Figure 45.3 *Choosing the default values results in this image*

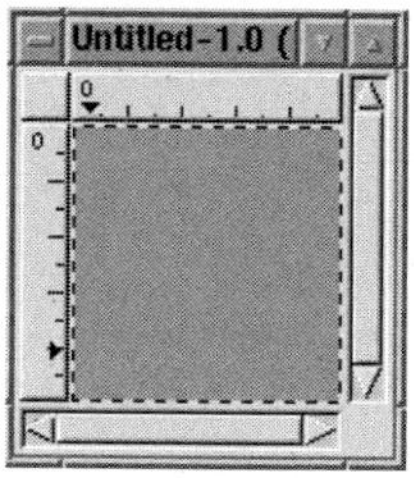

OBJECT-ORIENTED SYNTAX

Gimp::Fu provides an alternative **object-oriented** syntax for the image and the drawable commands. The following table shows the **procedural** versus the **object-oriented** syntax for a few commands:

Table 45.4 *OO syntax*

Procedural Syntax	Object-Oriented Syntax
gimp_image_add_layer($drw,-1);	$img->add_layer($drw, -1);
gimp_drawable_width($drw);	$drw->width();

The substitution rule for converting a PDB turning into a method is as simple as erasing `gimp_image_` from the beginning of the function call and calling this method through the image object. Similarly, for the `gimp_drawable_` functions.

Note: The object-oriented syntax is only syntactic sugar that makes the calling syntax cleaner in some cases. The error messages are still given in the procedural format.

PAINTING AREAS WITH SELECTIONS

In the *uni* script the function `gimp_edit_fill` was called to fill the whole image. Looking at the information for `gimp_edit_fill` in the DB browser, we find the following (see Table 45.5)

Table 45.5 *The PDB entry of* `gimp_edit_fill`

Name	gimp-edit-fill		
Blurb	Fill selected area of drawable		
In	drawable	DRAWABLE	The drawable to fill from

In Perl::Fu, the image parameter should not be given because it is automatically calculated from the drawable parameter.

If a selection is active when `gimp_edit_fill` is called, only the selection is painted. There are lots of ways to choose a selection as can be seen when searching for a `select` in the PDB. The example below uses `gimp_rect_select`, whose entry in the PDB looks as follows (see Table 45.6).

Table 45.6 *The PDB entry of* `gimp_rect_select`

Name	gimp-rect-select		
Blurb	Create a rectangular selection over the specified image		
In	image	IMAGE	image
	x	FLOAT	x coordinate of upper-left corner of rectangle
	y	FLOAT	y coordinate of upper-left corner of rectangle
	width	FLOAT	the width of the rectangle: width > 0
	height	FLOAT	the height of the rectangle: width > 0
	operation	INT32	the selection operation: {ADD (0), SUB(1), REPLACE (2), INTERSECT (3) }
	feather	INT32	feather option for selections
	feather_radius	FLOAT	radius for feather operation

Paint Area Selection Script

A simple use of this function is to select a rectangle in the middle of an image and paint that rectangle with a user-defined color. This example also introduces a couple of new features:

- The script is associated with an image because its menu path starts with `right-click`. As a result, the callback sub on line 13 receives two additional parameters: the active image and the selected drawable.
- The use of a subroutine without a name as a parameter to register.
- The use of the PDB functions `gimp_undo_push_group_start` and `gimp_undo_push_group_end`. These functions declare an **undo** group. When an undo is applied to the image, instead of having the individual operators undo, all of the actions between the undo start and the undo group calls are undone at once.
- The return type of the register function defines what new images should be displayed by Gimp. In this case, we don't want to display any new images and, therefore, return an empty array.

Figure 45.4 *The result when the paint-select script is used on Figure 45.3*

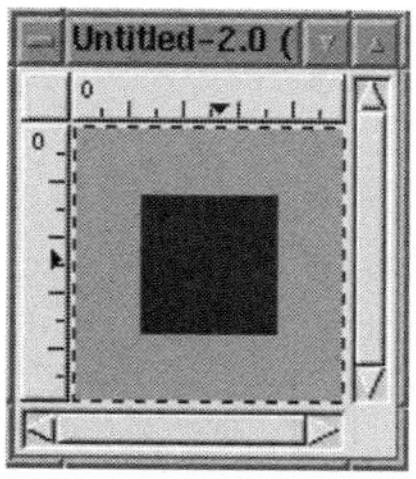

Paint-select Perl-Fu script

```
#!/usr/local/bin/perl -w

use Gimp;
use Gimp::Fu;

register
    "img_paint_select",
    "Paints the selection", "Paints the selection",
    "Dov Grobgeld", "Dov Grobgeld", "1999-05-14",
    "<Image>/Perl-Fu/Tutorial/Paint Select",
    "*",
    [
     [PF_COLOR, "color", "Rectangle color", [0,0,255]] ],
    sub {
        my($img, $layer, $color) = @_;
        my($width, $height) = (gimp_image_width($img),
                               gimp_image_height($img));

        print "img width heigh = $img ($$img) $width $height\n";
      #Select a rectangle inside the image and paint it with color
        gimp_undo_push_group_start($img);
        gimp_rect_select($img,
                         $width/4, $height/4, $width/2, $height/2,
                         SELECTION_REPLACE, 0,0);
        gimp_palette_set_background($color);
        gimp_edit_fill($layer);
```

LOOPS

In Perl, it is simple to write loops that, together with the various selection tools, gives powerful creative possibilities. Here is an example that mixes colors in circles. There is nothing really new here, but it shows the power of what we described previously.

Circles Perl-Fu script

```
#!/usr/local/bin/perl
use Gimp;
use Gimp::Fu;

sub circles {
    my ($size, $bgcolor, $radius) = @_;
    # Create the background
    $img = gimp_image_new($size, $size, RGB);
    $layer = gimp_layer_new($img, $size, $size, RGB,
                        "Layer 1", 100, NORMAL_MODE);
    gimp_image_add_layer($layer, -1);
    gimp_palette_set_background($bgcolor);
    gimp_edit_fill($layer);
    my $ncircles = int($size/$radius/2);
    for ($i=0; $i<$ncircles; $i++) {
        for ($j=0; $j<$ncircles; $j++) {
            # Be creative and mix colors
            $color = [$i*30, ($ncircles-$j)*25, ($i+$j)*15];
            # Select a circle
            gimp_ellipse_select($img,
                        $i*$radius*2, $j*$radius*2,
                        $radius*2, $radius*2,
                        SELECTION_REPLACE, 1, 0, 0);
            # Paint the color in the circle
            gimp_palette_set_background($color);
            gimp_edit_fill($layer);
            gimp_selection_none($img);
        }
    }
    return $img;
}
# register the script
register "circles", "a loop", "a loop", "Dov", "Dov", "1999-05-
```

CREATING TEXT

HELLO WORLD — WRITING TEXT IN AN IMAGE

To create text, the `gimp_text_fontname` function may be used. In this function, the font is specified in the X11 font conventions. (There are also some older functions, `gimp_text` and `gimp_text_ext`, in which the different X11 fields are specified explicitly.)

The Hello-world1 Perl-Fu script shows an example of a script that creates an image containing "Hello world".

Figure 45.5 *Result of the Hello-world1 Perl-Fu script*

The Hello-world1 Perl-Fu script makes use of the function `xlfd_size` which extracts the size of the font from the X11 font name. This is necessary because the authors of `gimp_text_fontname` decided that the font size within the font name is ignored.

The text created on line 20 is a floating layer that needs to be anchored to its parent layer. This is done on line 23 through the call to `gimp_floating_sel_anchor()`.

In the Hello-world1 Perl-Fu script, the image size is unrelated to the text size (see Figure 45.5). This is taken care of in the Basic-logo Perl-Fu script, which is a more complex example showing the basic steps for a logo-generating script:

- Extraction of the string size.
- Creation of an image with the size of the string and borders.
- Creation of a drawable with the same size.
- Creation of text and anchoring it.

Figure 45.6 *The result of the Basic-logo Perl-Fu script is much more satisfying*

Hello-world1 Perl-Fu script

```
#!/usr/local/bin/perl

use Gimp;
use Gimp::Fu;

sub text1 {
    my($font, $text) = @_;
    # Create a new image
    $img = gimp_image_new(350, 100, RGB);
    # Create a new layer and draw it to the image at the top
    $drw = gimp_layer_new($img, $img->width, $img->height,
                    RGB, "BG", 100, NORMAL_MODE);
    $drw->add_layer(-1);
    gimp_palette_set_background("black");
    gimp_edit_fill($drw);
    # Choose color of text
    gimp_palette_set_foreground([255,255,0]);
    # Create the text
    my $border = 10;
    my $text_layer = gimp_text_fontname($drw,  0, 0, $text,
                                $border, 1,
                                xlfd_size($font), $font);
    gimp_floating_sel_anchor($text_layer);
    return $img;
}


# register the script
register "hello_world1", "basic text", "basic text", "Dov",
"Dov",
    "1999-05-14",
    "<Toolbox>/Xtns/Perl-Fu/Tutorial/Basic text 1",
    "*",
```

Basic-logo Perl-Fu script

```
#!/usr/local/bin/perl
use Gimp;
use Gimp::Fu;

sub basic_logo {
    my($font, $border, $text, $bgcolor, $fgcolor) = @_;
    # Get the string size
    my($width, $height)
   = gimp_text_get_extents_fontname($text, xlfd_size($font),
$font);
    # Add border
    $width+= 2*$border;
    $height+= 2*$border;
    # Create a new image of this size with the border added
    $img = gimp_image_new($width, $height, RGB);
    # Create a new layer for the background, fill it, and add it
to the
    #image
    my $background = gimp_layer_new($img, $width, $height,
                            RGB, "Background", 100,
                            NORMAL_MODE);
    gimp_palette_set_background($bgcolor);
    gimp_edit_fill($background);
    gimp_image_add_layer($background, 1);
    # Choose color of text
    gimp_palette_set_foreground($fgcolor);
    # Create the text
    my $text_layer = gimp_text_fontname($background, 0, 0, $text,
                              $border, 1,
                              xlfd_size($font), $font);
    gimp_floatinµg_sel_anchor($text_layer);
    return $img;
}

# register the script
register "basic_logo", "basic logo", "basic logo",
 "Dov Grobgeld", "Dov Grobgeld",
 "1998-05-19",
```

FLOATING SELECTIONS

When a region has been selected through one of the selection routines, the area outlined by the selection may be copied to the **cut-buffer** through the `gimp_edit_copy` command. The cut-buffer may subsequently be pasted into a different layer through the `gimp_edit_paste` command. When a layer is pasted, it becomes a **floating selection**. This floating selection may be moved to its required position by the `gimp_layer_set_offsets` command, and is pasted by the `gimp_floating_sel_anchor` command. Another way of determining the position of a pasted layer is to create a selection in the target image before the cut-buffer is pasted.

This is illustrated in the Horiz-cat Perl-Fu script, which works on one image and takes another image as a parameter, which it concatenates to the right of the first image. Lines 13 through 28 show how the second image is copied and glued into the first image.

Horiz-cat Perl-Fu script

```
#!/usr/local/bin/perl
use Gimp qw( :auto );
use Gimp::Fu;

sub horiz_cat {
    my($img1, $drw1, $drw2) = @_;
    # Get image 2
    $img1 = $drw1->image();
    my $img2 = gimp_drawable_image($drw2);
    # Get sizes through OO syntax
    my($w1, $h1) = ($drw1->width, $drw1->width);
    my($w2, $h2) = ($drw2->width, $drw2->height);
    # The new height is the maximum height of the images
    my $hmax = $h1 > $h2 ? $h1 : $h2;
    # Create an undo group
    gimp_undo_push_group_start($img1);
    # Resize the drawable layer to make room for the img
    gimp_image_resize($img1, $w1+$w2, $hmax, 0, ($hmax-$h1)/2);
    gimp_layer_resize($drw1, $w1+$w2, $hmax, 0, ($hmax-$h1)/2);
    # Copy $drawable2 and paste it into the new space of
 $drawable1
    # select all of img2
    gimp_selection_all($img2);
    # copy it to the clipboard
    gimp_edit_copy($drw2);
    # make a selection in img 1 in the position where it is to be
 pasted
    gimp_rect_select($img1, $w1, ($hmax-$h2)/2, $w2, $h2, 0,0,0);
    # paste and then anchor it
    my $floating_layer = gimp_edit_paste($drw1, 0);
    gimp_floating_sel_anchor($floating_layer);
    # Close the undo group
    gimp_undo_push_group_start($img1);
    # Update the display
 gimp_displays_flush();
    return undef;
 }
```

THE PERL SERVER AND STANDALONE SCRIPTS

So far the scripts have all been started from the menu structure within menu. The scripts can, however, be from the command line as a normal Perl program. When run this way, the script tries to connect to the **Perl-Server**, and if it fails, it launches Gimp on its own. If you plan to run several scripts this way, it is obviously much faster to run the Perl-Server; launching Gimp takes quite a bit of time. The Perl-Server may be started from the Xtns menu.

When a Perl-Fu script is run from the command line, the result is the same as when it is run through the menus, except that it may be run with the `--output` parameter. This is in case the script saves the result to a file instead of displaying it within Gimp.

The file name for the `--output` allows special image-saving parameters, such as interlace, quality factor, and so forth, to be set. See the Gimp::Fu man page for details. The normal rules about image and file types are still valid, so, to save an image as a GIF file, it must be converted from RGB to an indexed script. Currently, this functionality must be included in each script, but it is possible that a future version of Gimp::Fu will include this conversion as an option.

Here are two invocations of the scripts declared above, but with output written to a JPG file and a PNG file. They can't be saved as GIF because the scripts do not index the images.

```
uni -o /tmp/uni.png -size 100 -color "#5050ff"
basic-logo -o /tmp/bl.jpg -text "Perl rules"
```

This interface also enables running the **perl debugger** on the Perl-Fu scripts.

Note: The image is saved to the directory where Gimp was started from and not to the directory in which the scripts were invoked.

A SHELL FOR GIMP-PERL

When using the Perl-server, it is not necessary to use Gimp::Fu and the register function. Instead, **Gimp::Net** and a sub named *net* may be declared. For a simple but powerful example of the use of Gimp without Fu, here is a an interactive Gimp-Perl shell that may be run from the command line:

```
#!/usr/local/bin/perl

use Gimp;
use Term::ReadLine;

sub net {
    $term = new Term::ReadLine;
    while( defined ($_ = $term->readline("Gimp> "))) {
        $res = eval($_) . "\n";
        print("Error: $@"), next if $@;
        print "\n";
```

Here is an example of an interactive session with this shell:

```
Gimp> $img = gimp_image_new(100,100,RGB)
Gimp> $drw = $img->layer_new(100,100,RGB_IMAGE, "bg", 100,\
NORMAL_MODE)
Gimp> $img->add_layer($drw,-1)
Gimp> $img->display_new
Gimp> $drw->edit_fill
Gimp> gimp_displays_flush()
```

End Notes, Links And References

Notes

This tutorial has covered only a small part of the possibilities available to a script writer. In particular, the following issues available to Gimp::Perl scripts have not been covered:

- The possibility of writing customized Gtk interfaces.
- Writing full-fledged plug-ins that manipulate the tile data through the Perl Data Language (PDL) module.
- Using Perl::Gimp in a CGI environment.
- How to fill with gradients in a plug-in.

- How to do "free selections."

Links And References

Marc Lehmanns Gimp page, `http://gimp.pages.de`

The online version of this tutorial,
`http://imagic.weizmann.ac.il/~dov/gimp/perl-tut.html`

The Scheme tutorial this tutorial is based on,
`http://imagic.weizmann.ac.il/~dov/gimp/scheme-tut.html`

The Gimp home page, `http://www.gimp.org`

Gimp Registry with Perl plug-ins, `http://registry.gimp.org/`

PART X

Advanced Installations

- *How To Provide Fonts To Gimp*
- *To Make Or Not To Make, Plug-ins With Gimp*

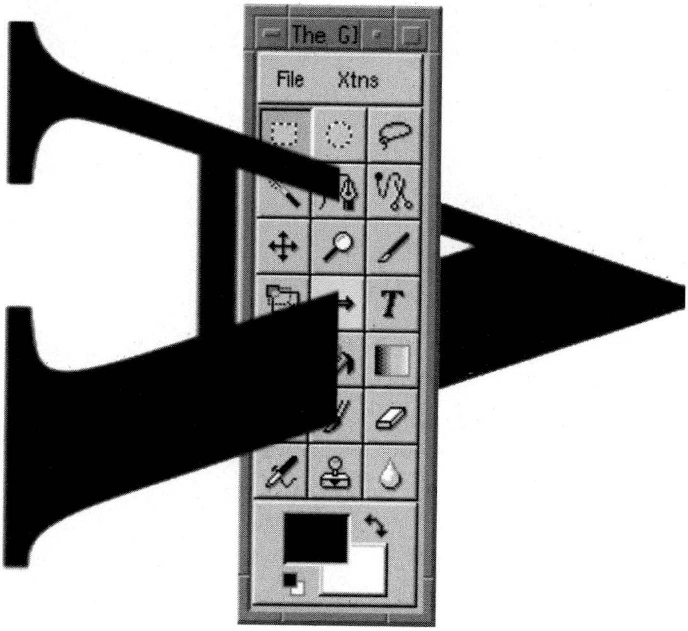
The GI
File Xtns

CHAPTER 46

How To Get Fonts To Gimp

In this chapter, you'll find some basic information about how to make fonts available to Gimp in X-window.

How Fonts Work In Gimp

All of the fonts you use in Gimp come from the **X-Server**. There is no internal font render in Gimp, so Gimp needs X to render the fonts. This is also why the text tool dialog looks a bit like the **xfontsel** program in X.

Scalable Fonts

First of all, use scalable fonts (Type 1 or Speedo) in Gimp. As you can tell from the name, these fonts can be scaled up and down without losing quality. There are also bitmapped fonts in X. When you scale a bitmap font, it will lose its shape and get very jaggy and ugly.

Where Are The Fonts And Font Path

To find out where X keeps its fonts, type `xset -q <enter>` in a shell. The last line in the output indicates your **font path**. If you are an XFree86 user and use the default XF86 configuration, you have to perform some editing to make sure that the **Type 1** and **Speedo** fonts, are the first to come up when X is looking for a certain font. To do so, place the Speedo and Type 1 directories first in your `Fontpath`.

Another way is to add the string `:unscaled` after your bitmap fonts. If you add this string, the scalable (i.e., the Type 1 fonts) will be used if you need to scale your fonts up or down. The font path in the `XF86Config` file may look like the following (this may only work with XFree 86):

```
Section "Files"
   RgbPath     "/usr/X11R6/lib/X11/rgb"
   FontPath    "/usr/X11R6/lib/X11/fonts/misc:unscaled"
   FontPath    "/usr/X11R6/lib/X11/fonts/75dpi:unscaled"
   FontPath    "/usr/X11R6/lib/X11/fonts/100dpi:unscaled"
   FontPath    "/usr/X11R6/lib/X11/fonts/MY_NEW_FONTS"
   FontPath    "/usr/X11R6/lib/X11/fonts/Type1"
   FontPath    "/usr/X11R6/lib/X11/fonts/Speedo"
   FontPath    "/usr/X11R6/lib/X11/fonts/misc"
   FontPath    "/usr/X11R6/lib/X11/fonts/75dpi"
   FontPath    "/usr/X11R6/lib/X11/fonts/100dpi"
EndSection
```

This fragment of the XF86Config file will set up all scalable Type 1 fonts before the bitmap fonts, thus ensuring that Xwindow will (if available) use a nice, smooth T1 Helvetica instead of the jaggy bitmap version of the same font.

To find out what kind of **Type 1** fonts you have, change the directory to the Type 1 dir, and read the `fonts.dir` file (e.g., `cd /usr/X11/lib/X11/fonts/Type1 && more fonts.dir`) in a terminal window. All of your available Type 1 fonts will be displayed. One of the most common reasons for a Script-Fu to fail is that the specified Script-Fu font isn't available. This makes the script *bug*, and there will be no output.

INSTALLING FONTS

TYPE 1 FONTS INSTALLATION AND THE TYPE1INST PROGRAM

We will only cover **Type 1** fonts *(postscript fonts)*, other font types are beyond the scope of this chapter.

Download a program called type1inst (written by James Macnicol) from `ftp://sunsite.unc.edu/pub/Linux/X11/xutils` or one of its mirrors.

Preparing For Installation

At the time of this writing, the file is called `type1inst-0.6.tar.gz.` Unpack the program like you did with the Gimp archive (see "Obtaining And Installing Gimp" starting on page 43). Copy the files `type1inst` and `t1embed` to a directory in your PATH (for example, `/usr/local/bin).`

To see your PATH, execute `echo $PATH` in a shell. If you aren't the system administrator, then you probably can't install files in system directories. To overcome this problem, create a **bin** directory in your home directory and install the `type1inst` program there. To include the program in your PATH, do the following if you run **Bash**, **Sh** or **Ksh** as your shell:

```
export PATH=$PATH:$HOME/bin
```

Copying The Fonts To The Fonts dir

Copy the Type 1 fonts that you want to install in a directory of your own choice. If you have a large font collection and you want easy font management in Gimp, install an **xfontserver** or install the fonts in different directories with 20 fonts in each.

Font Management

Here's how we manage fonts at Frozenriver: Karin needs a lot of fonts, but if you load all fonts into X and Gimp, it becomes hard to choose and find the right font. We have solved this by making different directories for each type of font, e.g we have one directory for artistic fonts, one for strictly business fonts, and so on. This makes it easy for Karin to load and unload the fonts depending on what she wants to do.

Running type1inst

When you have copied the fonts, `cd` to the directory where you installed the fonts.Run `type1inst`, and then `mkfontdir`. This will create the necessary `font.dir`, `font.scale` and `font.alias` files in this directory, respectively.

Loading The Fonts Into X

Load the fonts into X by applying xset +fp full path to the font directory. The fonts are now installed, and you can use them in Gimp. If you installed the fonts while you had Gimp running, you must **restart** Gimp.

Notice that the + is placed in front of `fp`. If you put the plus sign in the wrong place, all of the default font directories will be queried for the font name first. If there is a font with the same name as yours, this font will be used instead of your own.

The *Helvetica* font is a good example. The standard Helvetica font that comes with X is of poor quality, but if you download Acrobat Reader from Adobe, a very nice Helvetica font is included.

If you install these fonts with `xset fp+`, you will never see them because the standard Helvetica font that comes with X is placed in front of the font you installed when X is looking for its font directories.

INSTALLING TYPE 1 FONTS BY HAND

It's not always possible to use the `type1inst` program. If you can't, you'll have to install the `fonts.*` files manually.

The Font File

Generally, you have to load the font file in a text editor and look in the **file header** for name, type and so forth. The header of the file ends with the `eexec` command. Everything after that is binary font data and of little interest. You can only do this with PS font files. Such files normally end with `.pfb` and have `%!PS-Adobe-Font` typed in the first line of the file.

THE FONT FIELD IN THE FONT FILE

The first thing you need to understand is how to code the **font field** in the `font.scale` file. Here is an example line:

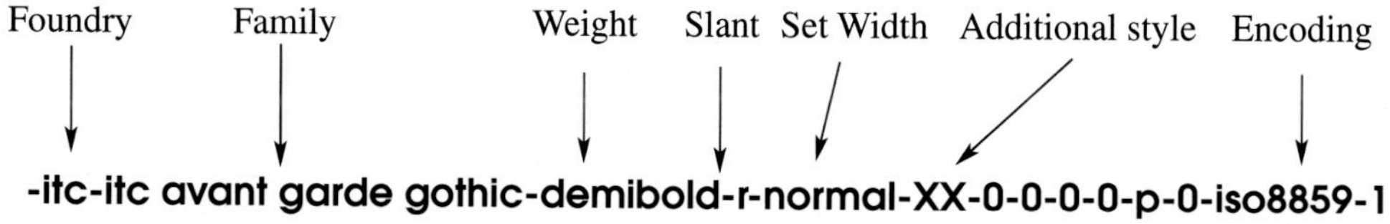

Extracting Data

Load the `pfb` in a file editor (like `vi file.pfb`) in a terminal such as xterm, and search for data. Here's what to look for:

- **Foundry:** The registered name of the font foundry, usually a company name. This was written in the PS font file: `usage: 24954 31846%% ITC Avant Garde Gothic is a registered trademark of International Typeface`. This means that the font will use ITC as Foundry.
- **Family:** The font family to which the font belongs. There are usually a lot of font files in a font family, all with different characteristics (such as *bold*, *thin*, *condensed* and so forth). Contents of the font file's read-only is `def/FamilyName (ITC Avant Garde Gothic)`, which will display as **itc avant garde gothic** in the family field.
- **Weight:** The weight of the font (for example, *medium*, *bold*, *thin* and so forth). This is the information in the PS file `readonly def/Weight (Demi)`, which will put **demibold** in the weight field.
- **Slant:** The *posture* of the font. If there is no slant information for the font, it will display as Roman or *upright* posture, and there will be an **r** in the slant field. If there is slant information (such as *Gothic Demi Oblique*) the slant is Oblique, and there will be an **o** in the slant field.
- **Set Width:** This is the horizontal width. Here, you have to search the font name. *Condensed* is an example of a width type.
- **Additional Style:** This is a rarely used option for additional styles; it's hardly ever used in PS fonts.
- **Encoding:** This is what type of languages the font supports. This example from the PS file `def/Encoding StandardEncoding` will end up as **iso8859-1**; for example, *isolatin1* in the encoding field
- The rest is the same as in the example line. It's the standard PS font line.

The following section provides some tables that can help you with your decoding. They are taken from the source of the `type1inst` program.

Generally, `type1inst` will make the job for you. If the Foundry information isn't right, then you can look in the **font** file or the **log** file which `type1inst` creates. Most of the time, it's quite easy to figure out what's missing.

TABLES

Table 46.1 *The Foundry table*

Company	Foundry
Adobe	adobe
Publishers Paradise	paradise
Bigelow & Holmes	b&h
Bitstream	bitstream
International Typeface Corporation	itc
IBM	ibm
LETRASET	letraset
Monotype Corporation	monotype
SoftMaker	softmaker
URW	urw
Jonathan Brecher	brecher
Brendel Informatik	brendel
A. Carr	carr
FontBank	fontbank
Hershey	hershey
A.S.Meit	meit
Andrew s. Meit	meit
S.G. Moye	moye
D. Rakowski	rakowski
David Rakowski	rakowski
Reasonable Solutions	reasonable
Southern Software	southern
Title Wave	titlewave
ZSoft	zsoft

Table 46.2 *The Weight table*

Weights	Weight
book	book
demibold	demibold
semibold	demibold
demi	demibold
semi	demibold
extrabold	extrabold
boldface	bold
bold	bold
heavyface	heavyface
heavy	heavy
ultrablack	ultrablack
extrablack	extrablack
ultra	ultra
black	black
extralight	extralight
light	light
thin	thin
super	super
normal	medium
regular	regular
roman	regular

Table 46.3 *The Slant table*

Slants	Slant
italic	i
roman	r
regular	r
cursive	i
kursiv	i
oblique	o
obl	o
slanted	o
upright	r
inclined	i

Table 46.4 *The Set Width table*

Widths	Set Width
extracondensed	extracondensed
condensed	condensed
cond	condensed
sans	sans
wide	wide
cn	condensed
narrow	narrow
extracompresse	extracompresse
compressed	compressed
extraextended	extraextended
extended	extended
expanded	expanded
normal	normal

Table 46.5 *The Additional style table*

Styles	Style
alt	alternate
beginning	beginning
display	display
dfr	dfr
ending	ending
ep	expert
exp	expert
ornaments	ornaments
osf	oldstylefigures
outline	outline
sc	smallcaps
shaded	shaded
shadowed	shadowed
stencil	stencil
swash	swash
sw	swash
one	one
two	two
three	three
four	four
a	alternate

CHAPTER 47

Compiling Plug-ins

In this chapter, we will explain how to compile plug-ins so they can be used in Gimp.

The following example shows what appeared when we compiled the `waterse-lect.c` file in the way we just described:

```
/tmp/cca017741.o(.text+0xc):undefined reference to `gimp_main'
/tmp/cca017741.o(.text+0x87):undefined reference to `gdk_input_list_devices'
/tmp/cca017741.o(.text+0xc5):undefined reference to `g_strcasecmp'
/tmp/cca017741.o(.text+0x626):undefined reference to `gtk_preview_get_type'
/tmp/cca017741.o(.text+0x632):undefined reference to `gtk_object_check_cast'
/tmp/cca017741.o(.text+0x63d):undefined reference to `gtk_preview_draw_row'
/tmp/cca017741.o:In function `update_buckets':
/tmp/cca017741.o(.text+0x682):undefined reference to `gtk_widget_draw'
/tmp/cca017741.o:In function `update_gimp_color':
/tmp/cca017741.o(.text+0x6e2):undefined reference to \
`gimp_palette_set_foreground
```

Libraries

This happens when the necessary libraries aren't linked to the executable that you are trying to build. A **library** is a set of **functions**, for example, a function that creates a *window* or a *scrollbar*. The compiler checks that the functions are available for the plug-in to use when it is executed.

Another Try

Now, let's try to compile it with:

```
gcc -o plug-in plugin.c -L/usr/local/lib -lgtk
-lgimp
```

Now the plug-in compiles cleanly on the system. If you work on Sun Solaris system, add the following before even starting to think about libraries:

```
-I/usr/local/include
```

Include File

The error messages telling you that an **include** (header file) is missing looks like this:

```
waterselect.c:39: gtk/gtk.h: No such file or
directory
```

Although this message tells us that a file named `gtk.h` is missing, this is not always the case. A more correct answer is that the compiler (more accurately the *preprocessor* compiler) can't find it in the directories it was configured to search.

To tell the compiler where to search for the file, add the following:

```
-I/where/to/search
```

Because the file is located in `/usr/local/include/gtk`, and the error was "can't find `gtk/gth.h`," this tells us that the compile line will be:

```
gcc -o plug-in plugin.c -L/usr/local/lib \
 -lgimp -lgtk -I/usr/local/include
```

`-I/usr/local/include` that was added tells the compiler to search that directory for **include** files (in our case, `gtk/gtk.h`). The compiler will find the file because it will add:

```
gtk/gtk.h
```

to:

```
/usr/local/include
```

resulting in:

```
/usr/local/include/gtk/gtk.h
```

which is where the file is located.

The -L Flag And How To Find Out Which Libs To Link

The **-L** flag works the same way. It tells the compiler where to search for libraries (in this case, the libraries `libgimp.so` and `libgtk.so`). The `-lgimp` is a shortcut, so we don't have to write `libgimp.so`.

To determine which libraries to add and which directories to include, look inside the code (generally located in the beginning of the file). Here's an example from the `waterselect.c` file:

```
#include <stdlib.h>
#include <stdio.h>
#include <math.h>
#include <gtk/gtk.h>
#include "libgimp/gimp.h"
```

This code tells us that the compiler will include five files when it compiles the code. The first three are ordinary standard C **include** files and the other ones are special Gimp and GTK files.

The -I Flag

The standard C header files are located in a standard include directory, which the compiler will search. However, the `gtk.h` and `gimp.h` files aren't in a standard directory, so tell the compiler (`-I flag`).

If the `-I flag` is /`usr/local/include`, the compiler will try to get the `gtk.h` files in:

```
/usr/local/include/gtk/gtk.h.
```

The source code lines can also give us a hint about which libraries to link with (in this case, `libgimp` and `libgtk`). The standard C library and Math library are linked by default on most systems.

How To Use Gimptool To Get Lib And Include Flags

If you invoke Gimptool with the command `gimptool --libs`, it will reply with the following (site dependent):

```
-L/usr/local/lib -lgimpui -lgimp \
-L/usr/local/lib -L/usr/openwin/lib \
-R/usr/openwin/lib -lgtk -lgdk -lglib -lXext \
-lX11 -lsocket -lnsl -lm
```

It will give you all of the libraries and -L flags that were used to compile Gimp. This can be very useful if you compile a plug-in that needs the TIFF library and the Gimptool libraries. Then, you can invoke gcc like this:

```
gcc -o plug-in 'gimptool --libs' -ltiff plugin.c
```

Gcc will now compile and link your plug-in with all Gimp libraries, in addition to the TIFF library. If you want to include all **include** flags, invoke Gimptool like this:

```
gimptool --cflags
```

It will reply with a list of the `CFLAGS` used to compile Gimp.

What To Do When There Are Several Source Files

A plug-in can contain more that one C source code file. If the extra file is a **header file** (named `plugin.h`), then we can compile the plug-in just as we did before. The header file is a file that specifies functions and how to call these functions. Look at the files (or just the header file) to find out what **include** directories to include and which libraries to link.

If the plug-in is built up of several files (such as: `pluginmain.c`, `pluginpart1.c`, `pluginpart2.c`, etc.), compile each part separately and then link them to an executable plug-in.

Object files must be made out of each part. These object files will then be **linked**, thus creating the final executable plug-in. For example:

```
gcc -c pluginmain.c -I/usr/local/include
gcc -c pluginpart1.c -I/usr/local/include
gcc -c pluginpart2.c -I/usr/local/include
gcc -o plug-in pluginmain.o pluginpart1.o \
pluginpart2.o -L/usr/local/lib -lgtk -lgimp \
 -lgimpui -lmpeg
```

On the first three lines, the object files are made. The compiler is instructed to make object files by adding the `-c` flag. When object files are made, we don't need to worry about libraries, we only have to make sure that the compiler finds the **include** files which is why only the `-I` flag is used when the object files are created.

On the last line, the final plug-in is made. Here, we don't need to worry about **include** files, we only have to make sure that we **link** the libraries needed by the plug-in. When the object files are made, descriptions of library function calls are included by including header files. The plug-in object file happily uses them because it assumes that it will be linked to these libraries later on. You can also use the `gimptool --cflags` and `gimptool --libs` commands to include libraries and directories. We recommend using Gimptool to avoid errors, and a lot of typing.

On the last line, the compiler is told that the final outcome will be a plug-in by adding `-o plug-in`, then the object files made in the first three lines. Because a lot of library functions have been used in the object files, add the libraries to provide these functions to the plug-in by adding `-lgimp`, `-lgimpui`. Tell the compiler where to search for the libraries by adding `-L/usr/local/lib`. The directory `/usr/lib` and `/lib` are also searched by default.

When building a plug-in that consists of several parts, compiling the different parts manually is often the wrong method to use. If something goes wrong, you will have to type all your commands again. The solution is to create a **Makefile**. A Makefile is a specification that the Make command uses as an input to compile the entire plug-in with the help of the compiler.

How To Create A Makefile And How To Use It

Now, we'll take a look at how to create a simple Makefile. This will help us understand the structure of a Makefile, so that we'll know how to edit a Makefile which comes with a plug-in. The following is an example of a generic Makefile:

```
CC = gcc
INCDIR = -I/usr/local/include -I/usr/local/tiff/include
CFLAGS = -O2
LIBDIR = -L/usr/X11/lib -L/usr/local/lib
LFLAGS = -lgimp -lgtk -lX11 -ltiff -lgimpui
HEDERS = plugin.h plugin2.h
SOURCES = pluginmain.c pluginpart1.c pluginpart2.c
OBJECTS = pluginmain.o pluginpart1.o pluginpart2.o

plug-in: $(OBJECTS) $(HEADERS)
    $(CC) $(CFLAGS) -o $@ $(OBJECTS) $(INCDIR) $(LIBDIR) $(LFLAGS)
```

This Makefile builds the object files first, and then links the plug-in. To use it, replace the **header**, **object** and **source** files with the correct ones. You can also change what libraries to link and what directories to search for **libs** and **includes**. The `CFLAG -O2` represents optimization of the executable. Notice the tab at the last line. If you forgot the tab you will get this error message:

```
Makefile:11: *** missing separator. Stop.
```

A Makefile Example

Here's how the Makefile looked when we built the **Guash** plug-in at our Linux system (there is a Makefile included in the distribution of Guash; this example is only for training):

```
CC = gcc
INCDIR = -I/usr/local/include
CFLAGS = -O2
LIBDIR = -L/usr/local/lib
LFLAGS = -lglib -lgdk -lgtk -lgimp
HEADERS = guash-directory.h guash-banner.h
SOURCES = guash.c
OBJECTS = guash.o

guash: $(OBJECTS) $(HEADERS)
       $(CC) $(CFLAGS) -o $@ $(OBJECTS) $(INCDIR) $(LIBDIR)
$(LFLAGS)
```

The important thing is to *change* and maybe *add* **include** and **library** directories so it will fit your system. Remember that you can write a Make-file in several different ways, this is only one of many.

Variables

When you edit your Makefile, it may not look like this, but with the basic instruction and knowledge about how to compile, you should be able to edit it anyway. The first eight lines are variables that are called later on lines 10 and 11 with `$(VARIABLE)`. The special `$@` variable is an internal variable that expands to the first word in the line above it (i.e., Guash, in this example).

To build the plug-in, invoke Make by entering `make` or:

```
make -f WhatYouCallYourMakefile.
```

Make will invoke **gcc** to build your object files and to link your executable.

A common error that occurs when you use a Makefile to compile a plug-in that comes as an archive is that the Make-program complains about **dependencies**. If so, remove the `.deps` directory (`rm -rf .deps`) in the building directory. Dependencies can also be included in the Makefile. You will find them at the end of the file. Remove them, and everything should work fine.

How To Use Gimptool In A Makefile

This is the way to change the previous Makefile using Gimptool instead of specifying all of the libraries and include directories.

```
CC = gcc
INCDIR = `gimptool --cflags`
CFLAGS = -O2
LIBDIR = `gimptool --libs'
HEADERS = guash-directory.h guash-banner.h
SOURCES = guash.c
OBJECTS = guash.o

guash: $(OBJECTS) $(HEADERS)
       $(CC) $(CFLAGS) -o $@ $(OBJECTS) $(INCDIR) $(LIBDIR)
```

There is a lot less typing involved, and you may also be sure of getting all of the necessary Gimp-related libraries and includes into the Makefile. If the plug-in needs more libraries or include directories, you can add it after the `gimptool` command:

```
INCDIR = `gimptool --cflags` -I/usr/opt/include
```

or like this:

```
LIBDIR = `gimptool --libs' -L/opt/lib -ltiff
```

CONFIGURE TO AUTOMATE THE BUILDING PROCESS

The **configure** script that comes with the plug-in is a way to *automate* the process of making a Makefile. The configure script will try to find the **include** files and libraries that the plug-in needs.

If you are on a common UNIX platform like Solaris or Linux, then it's simple to use a configure script. To build your plug-in, enter the following in the directory where you unpacked the plug-in:

```
./configure && make
```

Now, the plug-in will be compiled and ready to use. Make sure that you are in the directory where the configure script is located; otherwise, you will get this error message:

```
bash: ./configure: No such file or directory.
```

If you don't have a certain file or library, or the script can't find it, then you will have to install it or tell the script where to find it.

To find out how to tell the script where to find **include** files and libraries, invoke the script like this:

```
./configure --help
```

This will result in several lines of flags that you can supply the script with. Here's an extract of the most important flags that you can include in your script:

```
--libdir=DIR
```

```
--includedir=DIR
```

With these two flags you can add an **include/library** directory like this:

```
--includedir=/your/includedir.
```

If you want to add more than one **include** directory, you have to do it this way if you work in an ordinary shell:

```
export CFLAGS="-I/one/includedir -I/another/includedir"
```

If you are working in a **C shell**, then you have to do it like this:

```
setenv CFLAGS "-I/one/includedir -I/another/includedir"
```

If you want to add more than one **libdir**, enter the same commands as for the `CFLAGS`, but type: `LDFLAGS` instead.

You may run into several problems, especially if you are using a UNIX dialect that is different from what the authors of the configure script were working on. If you run into a problem, first try to add all of the libraries and **include** directories to the script with the `FLAGS` or manually in the generated Makefile. If this still doesn't solve the problem, try writing to the Gimp mailing list.

PART XII

Appendixes

- Initiation Files And Command Line Switches
- Man Pages
- Siod Reference
- Perl-Fu Man Pages
- Links And References

Appendix A

Gimp Start Flags And rcfiles

Ordinarily, Gimp is launched by an icon or a menu in your favorite window manager, but you can also start it manually. There are several initiation files that control the behavior of Gimp.

GIMP COMMAND LINE SWITCHES AKA FLAGS (OPTIONS)

An excellent source of information about the **command line switches** and **environments** that Gimp supports can be found in the Gimp **man page**. It's located in the `doc dir` in your Gimp source distribution, and normally you only have to enter the command `man gimp` after you have installed Gimp to open the man page.

All of this is done in a shell, such as in an **xterm** or **rxvt** window. As we mentioned earlier, you have probably hidden all this in your Window Manager so you only have to click on an icon or open a menu. If you want to test **flags** and different **environments** or even run Gimp without Xwindow, you must do this in a shell.

Typing `gimp --help` or `gimp -h` and pressing Enter will result in a short description of available flags that you can give Gimp:

```
[olof@olof olof]$ gimp --help
Usage: gimp [option ...] [files ...]
Valid options are:
  -h --help Output this help.
  -v --versionOutput version info.
  -b --batch <commands>Run in batch mode.
  -n --no-interfaceRun without a user interface.
  --no-data Do not load patterns, gradients, palettes, brushes.
  --verbose Show startup messages.
  --no-splashDo not show the startup window.
  --no-splash-imageDo not add an image to the startup window.
  --no-shm  Do not use shared memory between Gimp and its plug-
                      ins.
  --no-xshm Do not use the X Shared Memory extension.
  --display <display>Use the designated X display.
[olof@olof olof]$
```

The -h and --help flags obviously printed out the above message. The -v and --version flags show what version of Gimp you are running (this information is also available in the About dialog and the splash screen that shows up when you start Gimp). It will typically look like this:

```
[olof@olof olof]$ gimp -v

GIMP version 1.0
```

Always visit www.gimp.org, ftp.gimp.org or one of its mirrors to get the newest stable version of Gimp.

Batch Mode And No-Interface

The -b and --batch options allow you to execute Gimp with arguments to run. This is ideal if you want to execute a lot of commands to a lot of files. Otherwise, it would be quite annoying to have a GUI do all these actions (**open** image, **apply** commands, **save** image, **open** another image, apply command etc.). The <commands> shown earlier is a Script-Fu that will do the actual work for you (even if you can execute ordinary gimp pdb commands directly).

-n and --no-interface are suitable if you run Gimp in batch mode because most of the time you don't want to have a user interface if you are running a batch. This will also save some memory and system resources. Here is an example of two batch commands:

```
gimp -n -b '(gimp-procedural-db-dump "pdb_dump.tmp")' '(gimp-quit
0)'
```

These will dump Gimp's pdb database to a file called pdb_dump.tmp in your working directory. Here is an example of a custom script that is invoked by Gimp (my-script is your own personal custom script):

```
gimp -n -b '(my-script 1 "\"Sample text.\"")' '(gimp-quit 0)'
```

The (gimp-quit 0) is so Gimp quits gracefully and returns the command prompt to you.

If you don't have X-window up and running (i.e., you are running your UNIX session in a console that has no graphic capabilities or you have a modem connection to your UNIX host with a vt100 terminal only), then you still can run Gimp in batch mode; just do it like this:

```
Xvfb :1 -screen 0 10x10x8 -pixdepths 1 &

gimp --display :1.0 -n -b '<commandos> ' '(gimp-quit 0)'
```

This will fire up an invisible X-server, in which you run Gimp.

More Options

As you saw above, we introduced a new flag, --display. Because X lets you run Gimp on one host and display it on another, you have to specify on which display to run Gimp's user interface.

Normally you run and display Gimp on the same host, and you don't have to barter about display settings. Here's an example of how to use the display option in Gimp. Say that you have a "supercomputer" at your campus running UNIX, and this computer has Gimp installed. Then, it would be more than efficient to edit huge Gimp images at this computer while displaying them at your local workstation or X-terminal. Here is a quick how to. At your workstation, you will execute a command allowing the supercomputer to display Gimp on your workstation:

```
[olof@olof olof]$ xhost niceriver.frozenriver.com (my local
supercomputer ;)

niceriver.frozenriver.com being added to access control list
```

The second line enabled the supercomputer to access our X-server at our workstation. All we have to do now is to `telnet`, or `rlogin` or `rsh` to the supercomputer:

```
[olof@olof olof]$ rlogin niceriver.frozenriver.com

[olof@niceriver olof]$
```

Now, we are logged in to the supercomputer. All we have to is open Gimp and tell it where to display (at `olof.frozenriver.com`), and which display to use at olof.frozenriver.com. Because we only have one display at `olof`, we will use display number 0:

```
gimp --no-xshm --display olof.frozenriver.com:0.0
```

Now, Gimp will display at your workstation and you can work with it just as if you had run Gimp at your workstation. When you are finished with Gimp you just have to log out from the supercomputer and tell your workstation that you don't want the supercomputer accessing your X-server:

```
[olof@olof olof]$ xhost - niceriver.frozenriver.com

niceriver.frozenriver.com being removed from access control list
```

The last line tells us that the supercomputer no longer can access our X-server. There are, of course, better ways to handle remote display, that have better security, automatic transfer of the display environment, etc., but that is beyond the scope of this book.

We introduced another new option earlier,`--no-xshm`, which tells Gimp not to try to use X-shared memory. We have to do this because we ran Gimp on a different host. If we run Gimp on the same host that we displayed Gimp at, we can use X-shared memory to speed things up a little bit, and also to save system resources. There is another shared memory flag, `--no-shm`, which tells Gimp not to share memory with its plug-ins. It's generally good to let Gimp do this, but if you encounter problems it can be wise to turn it off.

`--no-splash` tells Gimp not to show the splash when it starts. If you just tell Gimp `--no-splash-image`, then the splash will be shown, but without the image.

`--verbose` will start up Gimp a little more verbosely and you will see in the shell how it's phrasing the different initialization files..

```
[olof@olof olof]$ gimp --verbose

parsing "/home/olof/.gimp/gtkrc"

parsing "/usr/local/share/gimp/gimprc"

parsing "/home/olof/.gimp/gimprc"

parsing "/home/olof/.gimp/pluginrc"

writing "/home/olof/.gimp/pluginrc"

parsing "/home/olof/.gimp/menurc"

Starting extensions: extension_script_fu
```

The last option is `--no-data`, which you can use if you run Gimp in batch mode and don't need brushes, gradients, palettes or patterns. The start-up time for Gimp will then be minimized.

Installing A New Version Of Gimp

If you are installing a new version of Gimp, please remember to remove your personal `rc` files, by renaming the `.gimp` directory to `.gimp.old`. Then, you can open your old files and cut and copy special file modifications.

Initialization Files AKA RC-FILES

Gimp has a lot of initializations files that control the behavior of Gimp. Most of the options that you set in different rc files are done using the **Preference** dialog (see Chapter 5). We will only take a look at the options that you can't set from the dialog.

GIMPRC And ~/.GIMP/GIMPRC

The **system-wide** `gimprc` and the **personal** `gimprc` located in your gimp directory (usually `~/.gimp/gimprc`) control nearly all of Gimp's options. To make changes in your **personal** `gimprc` file (`~/.gimp/gimprc`) you have to bring it up in an editor and edit the file:

```
[olof@olof olof]$ xemacs ~/.gimp/gimprc
```

There won't be much in it, because most of the options are written in the system-wide `gimprc` file (usually `/usr/local/share/gimp/gimprc`). If you want to change a system-wide setting, then copy it from the system-wide `rc` file, paste it into your personal `rc` and then change the setting. Because the system-wide `rc` file is phrased before the personal `rc` file, everything written in the personal file will override what's written in the system-wide file. It's a good idea to open the system-wide `rc` file to get a glimpse of what you can change. If you are a system administrator, it's wise to change the system-wide `rc` file to fit your site's needs.

As you can see, the file is more or less self-explanatory, and we will only comment on things that you can't set in the **Preference** dialog.

```
# This is the system-wide gimprc file. Any change made in this file
# will affect all users of this system, provided that they are not
# overriding the default values in their personal gimprc file.
#
# Lines that start with a '#' are comments.
# Blank lines are ignored.

# The variable gimp_dir is set to either the interned value
# .gimp or the environment variable GIMP_DIRECTORY. If
# the path in GIMP_DIRECTORY is relative, it is considered
# relative to your home directory.

(prefix "/usr/local")
```

```
(exec_prefix "${prefix}")
(gimp_data_dir "${prefix}/share/gimp")
(gimp_plugin_dir "${exec_prefix}/lib/gimp/0.99")
```

You ***shouldn't change*** these preferences, but if you feel you must, you can only do it in an **editor**.

```
# Set the temporary storage directory...files will appear here
# during the course of running the gimp. Most files will disappear
# when the gimp exits, but some files are likely to remain,
# such as working palette files, so it is best if this directory
# not be one that is shared by other users or is cleared on machine
# reboot such as /tmp.
(temp-path "${gimp_dir}/tmp")

# Set the swap file location. The gimp uses a tile-based memory
# allocation scheme. The swap file is used to quickly and easily
# swap files out to disk and back in. Be aware that the swap file
# can easily get very large if the gimp is used with large images.
# Also, things can get horribly slow if the swap file is created on
# a directory that is mounted over NFS.  For these reasons, it may
# be desirable to put your swap file in "/tmp".
(swap-path "${gimp_dir}")

# Set the brush search path...this path will be searched for valid
#  brushes at startup.
(brush-path "${gimp_dir}/brushes:${gimp_data_dir}/brushes")

# Specify a default brush. If none is specified it Defaults to the
#  "1circle.gbr" brush which is just a single pixel-sized brush.
#  The brush is searched for in the brush path.
(default-brush "19fcircle.gbr")
```

Not adjustable in the Preferences dialog.

```
# Set the pattern search path...this path will be searched for
# valid patterns at startup.
(pattern-path "${gimp_dir}/patterns:${gimp_data_dir}/patterns")

# Specify a default pattern.
#  The pattern is searched for in the specified pattern paths.
(default-pattern "wood2.pat")
```

Not adjustable in the Preferences dialog.

```
# Set the palette search path...this path will be searched for
# valid palettes at startup.
(palette-path "${gimp_dir}/palettes:${gimp_data_dir}/palettes")

# Specify a default palette.
#  The pattern is searched for in the specified pattern paths.
(default-palette "Default")
```

Not adjustable in the Preferences dialog.

```
# Set the gradient search path...this path will be searched for
# valid gradients at startup.
(gradient-path "${gimp_dir}/gradients:${gimp_data_dir}/gradients")

# Specify a default gradient.
#  The gradient is searched for in the specified gradient paths.
(default-gradient "German_flag_smooth")
```

Not adjustable in the Preferences dialog.

```
# Set the plug-in search path...this path will be searched for
# plug-ins when the plug-in is run.
(plug-in-path "${gimp_dir}/plug-ins:${gimp_dir}/plug-ins/script-
fu:${gimp_plugin_dir}/plug-ins")


# Set the path for the script-fu plug-in.  This value is ignored by
#  the GIMP if the script-fu plug-in is never run.
(script-fu-path "${gimp_dir}/scripts:${gimp_data_dir}/scripts")
```

Not adjustable in the Preferences dialog.

```
# The tile cache is used to make sure the gimp doesn't thrash
# tiles between memory and disk. Setting this value higher will
# cause the gimp to use less swap space, but will also cause
# the gimp to use more memory. Conversely, a smaller cache size
# causes the gimp to use more swap space and less memory.
# Note: the gimp will still run even if 'tile-cache-size' is
# set to 0. The actual size can contain a suffix of 'm', 'M',
# 'k', 'K', 'b' or 'B', which makes the gimp interpret the
# size as being specified in megabytes, kilobytes and bytes
# respectively. If no suffix is specified the size defaults to
# being specified in kilobytes.
(tile-cache-size 10m)


# Speed of marching ants in the selection outline
#  this value is in milliseconds
#  (less time indicates faster marching)
(marching-ants-speed 300)


# Set the number of operations kept on the undo stack
(undo-levels 5)


# Set the color-cube resource for dithering on 8-bit displays
#  The 4 values stand for Shades of red, green, blue and grays
#  Multiplying the # of shades of each primary color yields
```

```
#  the total number of colors that will be allocated from the
#  gimp colormap.  This number should not exceed 256.  Most of the
#  colors remaining after the allocation of the colorcube
#  will be left to the system palette in an effort to reduce
#  colormap "flashing".
(color-cube 6 6 4 24)
```

Not adjustable in the Preferences dialog.

```
# Install a GIMP colormap by default -- only for 8-bit displays
# (install-colormap)

# Specify that marching ants for selected regions will be drawn
#  with colormap cycling as opposed to redrawing with different
# stipple masks. This color cycling option works only with 8-bit
# displays (colormap-cycling)

# Tools such as fuzzy-select and bucket fill find regions based on
#  a seed-fill algorithm.  The seed fill starts at the initially
# selected pixel and progresses in all directions until the
# difference of pixel intensity from the original is greater than a
# specified threshold ==> This value represents the default
# threshold
(default-threshold 15)
```

Not adjustable in the Preferences dialog.

```
# There is always a tradeoff between memory usage and speed.  In
# most cases, the GIMP opts for speed over memory.  However, if
# memory is a big issue, set stingy-memory-use
# (stingy-memory-use)

# When zooming into and out of images, this option enables the
#  automatic resizing of windows
# (allow-resize-windows)

# Context-dependent cursors are cool.  They are enabled by
```

```
# default. However, they require overhead that you may want to do
# without. Uncomment this line to disable them.
# (no-cursor-updating)

# Layer preview sizes:
#  none:    no previews in layers dialog/layer selector
#  small:   32x32
#  medium:  64x64
#  large:   128x128
#  #:       #x#
(preview-size small)

# Tooltips
#  Comment this out to disable the tooltips in the toolbox
# (dont-show-tool-tips)

# Controlling ruler visibility
#  The default behavior is for rulers to be ON
#  This can also be toggled with the View->Show Rulers command or
# shift+control+r (dont-show-rulers)
```

Not adjustable in the Preferences dialog.

```
# Ruler units
#  The units of rulers can be one of: (pixels inches centimeters)
#  The default is pixels
(ruler-units pixels)
```

Not adjustable in the Preferences dialog. Don't change this unless you know what you are doing.

```
# Disable auto saving
#  Just uncomment the line below...
# (dont-auto-save)
```

Not adjustable in the Preferences dialog. It doesn't do anything at the moment.

```
# Disable confirmation before closing an image without saving
#  Just uncomment the next line
# (dont-confirm-on-close)
```

Not adjustable in the Preferences dialog.

```
# Setting the level of interpolation
#  Uncommenting this line will enable cubic interpolation.
#  By default, GIMP uses linear interpolation, which is faster, but
#  has poorer quality
# (cubic-interpolation)

# Set the gamma correction values for the display
#  1.0 corresponds to no gamma correction.  For most displays,
#  gamma correction should be set to between 2.0 and 2.6
#  Run the utility "gamma_correct" to determine appropriate values
#  for your display.
#
# One important item to keep in mind:  Many images that you might
#  get from outside sources will in all likelihood already be
#  gamma-corrected.  In these cases, the image will look washed-out
#  if the gimp has gamma-correction turned on.  If you are going
#  to work with images of this sort, turn gamma correction off
#  by removing this line, or setting the values to 1.0.
#  gamma-correction 1.0
#  gamma-correction 2.0
#                ___
(gamma-correction 1.0)
```

Not adjustable in the Preferences dialog. See Chapter 13 on how to make a gamma correction.

```
# Set the manner in which transparency is displayed in images
#  Transparency type can be one of:
#    0: Light Checks
#    1: Mid-Tone Checks
#    2: Dark Checks
#    3: White Only
#    4: Gray Only
#    5: Black Only
#  Check size can be one of:
```

```
#     0: Small
#     1: Medium
#     2: Large
(transparency-type 1)
(transparency-size 2)
```

The rest of the file contains paths for different plug-ins. Quite often you have to add a line like this to specify the path to auxiliary files for some new plug-ins. These lines are ***not adjustable*** in the Preferences dialog.

```
(fractalexplorer-path "${gimp_data_dir}/
fractalexplorer:${gimp_dir}/fractalexplorer")


(gfig-path "${gimp_data_dir}/gfig:${gimp_dir}/gfig")


(gflare-path "${gimp_dir}/gflares:${gimp_data_dir}/gflares")
```

MENURC

This is a **personal-only** file located in your `.gimp` directory. This is where all of your dynamically changed **key bindings** end up. The easiest way to edit this file is to do the key binding in Gimp. The altered shortcuts will be written to this file as soon as you quit Gimp. If your key bindings are beyond repair, then remove the file:

```
[olof@olof olof]$ rm ~/.gimp/menurc
```

There is also a key binding file that will make Gimp use Photoshop's key bindings. It's located in the **system-wide** directory, and it's called `ps-menurc`. If you want to use it, just copy it to your `.gimp` directory:

```
[olof@olof olof]$ cp /usr/local/share/gimp/ps-menurc ~/.gimp/
```

But why use Photoshop key bindings when there are Gimp key bindings?

PLUGINRC

This file holds information about all the plug-ins available to Gimp. ***Do not edit this file!*** If Gimp starts having problems with plug-ins, then you can delete this file and Gimp will write a new one for you:

```
[olof@olof olof]$ rm ~/.gimp/pluginrc
```

GTKRC

This file is also a **personal-only** file. It controls the behavior of the **GTK tool kit** that Gimp uses for its menus, tabs, etc. One of the few reasons to edit this file is to change the font or font size that Gimp uses in the menus. Here is an extract:

```
# style <name> [= <name>]
```

```
# {
#   <option>
# }
#
# widget <widget_set> style <style_name>
# widget_class <widget_class_set> style <style_name>

style "ruler"
{
  font = "-adobe-helvetica-medium-r-normal--*-80-*-*-*-*-*-*"
}

style "default"
{
  font = "-adobe-helvetica-medium-r-normal--*-100-*-*-*-*-*-*"
}

#style "lsystem_rules"
#{
#  font = "-*-courier-medium-r-normal--*-100-100-100-m-*-*-*"
#}


widget_class "*Ruler*" style "ruler"
widget_class "*" style "default"
```

To understand how to change the font line, please read "Text And Fonts" starting on page 165 and "How To Get Fonts To Gimp" starting on page 759. This file is otherwise quite self-explanatory.

Appendix B

Gimp Man Pages

There are two Gimp man pages: one for Gimp and one for a utility called Gimp-tool.

THE GIMP MAN PAGE

NAME

Gimp — an image manipulation and paint program.

SYNOPSIS

Gimp [–h] [—help] [-v] [—version] [–b] [—batch <*commands*>] [–n] [—no–interface] [—no–data] [—verbose] [—no–shm] [—no–xshm] [—display *display*] [—no–splash] [—no–splash–image] [—debug–handlers]

DESCRIPTION

Gimp is the GNU Image Manipulation Program. It is used to edit and manipulate images. It can load and save a variety of image formats and can be used to convert between formats.

Gimp can also be used as a paint program. It features a set of drawing and painting tools such as airbrush, clone, pencil and paint brush. Painting and drawing tools can be applied to an image with a variety of paint modes. It also offers an extensive array of selection tools like rectangle, ellipse, fuzzy select, bezier select, intelligent scissors and select by color.

Gimp offers a variety of plug-ins that perform a variety of image manipulations. Examples include bump-map, edge detect, gaussian blur and many others.

In addition, Gimp has several scripting extensions which allow for advanced non-interactive processing and creation of images.

OPTIONS

The *Gimp* accepts the following options:

–h, —help
Display a list of all commandline options.

–v,—version
Output the version info.

–b,—batch <*commands*>
Execute the set of <*commands*> non-interactively. The set of <*commands*> is typically in the form of a script that can be executed by one of the Gimp scripting extensions.

–n, —no-interface
Run without a user interface.

—no–data
Do not load patterns, gradients, palettes or brushes. Often useful in non-interactive situations where startup time is to be minimized.

—verbose
Show startup messages.

—no–shm
Do not use shared memory between Gimp and its plug-ins. Instead of using shared memory, Gimp will send the data via pipe. This will result in slower performance than using shared memory.

—no–xshm
Do not use the X Shared Memory extension. If Gimp is being displayed on a remote X server, this probably needs to be enabled. Also useful for any X server that doesn't properly support the X shared memory extension. This will result in slower performance than with X shared memory enabled.

—display *display*
Use the designated X display.

—no–splash
Do not show the splash screen.

—no–splash–image
Do not show the splash screen image as part of the splash screen.

—debug–handlers
Enable debugging signal handlers.

Environment

DISPLAY
to get the default host and display number.

XENVIRONMENT
to get the name of a resource file that overrides the global resources stored in the RESOURCE_MANAGER property.

Files

Most Gimp configuration is read in from the users init file, **$HOME**/.Gimp/Gimprc. The system-wide equivalent is in **$PREFIX**/share/Gimp/Gimprc. The system-wide file is parsed first and the user Gimprc can override the system settings. **$PREFIX**/share/Gimp/Gimprc_user is the default Gimprc placed in users home directories the first time Gimp is ran.

$HOME/.Gimp/gtkrc — users set of GTK config settings. Options such as widget color and fonts sizes can be set here.

$PREFIX/share/gtkrc — system-wide default set of GTK config settings.

$HOME/.Gimp/menurc — user's set of key bindings.

$PREFIX/share/menurc — system-wide set of key bindings.

$HOME/.Gimp/plug-ins — location of user installed plug-ins.

$HOME/.Gimp/pluginrc — plug-in initialization values are stored here. This file is parsed on startup and regenerated if need be.

$HOME/.Gimp/tmp — default location that Gimp uses as temporary space.

Gimp's data files are stored in **$PREFIX**/share/Gimp where **$PREFIX** is set on install, but is typically /usr/local.

$PREFIX/share/Gimp/brushes — system wide brush files.

$HOME/.Gimp/brushes — user created and installed brush files. This files are in the .gbr (Gimp brush) format.

$PREFIX/share/Gimp/palettes — the system wide palette files. The files are copied to the user palettes directory when Gimp is first ran to allow the user to modify the palettes. This directory is not searched for palettes by default.

$HOME/.Gimp/palettes — copies of the system palette files as well as user-created and -modified palette files.

$PREFIX/share/Gimp/patterns — basic set of patterns for use in Gimp.

$HOME/.Gimp/patterns — user-created and -installed Gimp pattern files. This files are in the .pat format.

$PREFIX/share/Gimp/gradients — standard system wide set of gradient files.

$HOME/.Gimp/gradients — user-created and -installed gradient files.

$PREFIX/share/Gimp/palettes — system wide palette files.

$HOME/.Gimp/palettes — user-created and -installed palette files.

$PREFIX/share/Gimp/scripts — system-wide directory of scripts used in Script-Fu and other scripting extensions.

$HOME/.Gimp/scripts — user-created and -installed scripts.

$PREFIX/share/Gimp/gflares — system-wide directory used by the gflare plug-in.

$HOME/.Gimp/gflares — user-created and -installed gflare files.

$PREFIX/share/Gimp/gfig — system-wide directory used by the gfig plug-in.

$HOME/.Gimp/gfig — user-created and -installed gfig files.

$PREFIX/share/Gimp/Gimp_splash.ppm — graphic file used for the Gimp splash screen.

$PREFIX/share/Gimp/Gimp_logo.ppm — graphic file used in the Gimp about dialog.

$PREFIX/share/Gimp/Gimp_tips.txt — list of tips displayed in the "Tip of the Day" dialog box.

See Also

The X man page available on your Unix workstation

COPYRIGHT

Copyright © 1995 Spencer Kimball and Peter Mattis

Permission to use, copy, modify and distribute this software and its documentation for any purpose and without fee is hereby granted, provided that the above copyright notice appear in all copies and that both that copyright notice and this permission notice appear in supporting documentation.

Suggestions And Bug Reports

Any bugs found should be reported to the Gimp Developer mailing list at Gimp-developer@scam.xcf.berkeley.edu or you may want to make use of the online bug-tracking system available on the Web at http://www.wilberworks.com/bugs.html.

Before reporting bugs, please check to see if the bug is mentioned in the FAQs or the mailing list archive. See the section on Other Info for locations of these.

When reporting Gimp bugs, it is important to include a reliable way to reproduce the bug, version number of Gimp (and probably GTK), OS name and version and any relevant hardware specs. It is also very important to include as much info as possible about the X-server the problem was found on including at least server name, the visual and the bit depth.

If a bug is causing a crash, it is very useful if a stack trace can be provided. And of course, patches to rectify the bug are even better.

Other Info

The canonical place to find GIMP info is at http://www.Gimp.org. Here you can find links to just about every other Gimp site, tutorials, data sets, mailing list archives and more.

There is also a Gimp User Manual available at http://manual.gimp.org that goes into much more detail about the interactive use of Gimp. (Check www.Gimp.org for an up-to-date location; this location is not permanent)

The latest version of Gimp and the gtk libraries is always available at ftp://ftp.Gimp.org.

AUTHORS

Spencer Kimball and Peter Mattis.

With patches, fixes, plug-ins, extensions, scripts and more, from lots and lots of people including but not limited to Lauri Alanko, Shawn Amundson, John Beale, Zach Beane, Tom Bech, Marc Bless, Edward Blevins, Roberto Boyd, Seth Burgess, Brent Burton, Ed Connel, Andreas Dilger, Larry Ewing, David Forsyth, Jim Geuther, Scott Goehring, Heiko Goller, Michael Hammel, Christoph Hoegl, Jan Hubicka, Simon Janes, Ben Jackson, Tim Janik, Tuomas Kuosmanen, Peter Kirchgessner, Karl LaRocca, Jens Lautenbacher, Laramie Leavitt, Raph Levien, Adrian Likins, Ingo Luetkebohle, Josh MacDonald, Ed Mackey, Marcelo Malheiros, Ian Main, Torsten Martinsen, Federico Mena, Adam D. Moss, Shuji Narazaki, Sven Neumann, Stephen Robert Norris, Erik Nygren, Miles O'Neal, Jay Painter, Mike Phillips, Raphael Quinet, James Robinson, Mike Schaeffer, Tracy Scott, Manish Singh, Nathan Summers, Mike Sweet, Eiichi Takamori, Tristan Tarrant, Owen Taylor, Ian Tester, James Wang and Kris Wehner.

THE GIMP-TOOL MAN PAGE

Name

gimp-tool — script to perform various Gimpy functions

SYNOPSIS

gimp-tool [—prefix*[=DIR]*] [—exec–prefix*[=DIR]*] [—version] [—libs] [—cflags] [—build *plug-in.c*] [—install *plug-in.c*] [—install-admin plug-in.c]

DESCRIPTION

gimp-tool is a tool that can, among other things, build plug-ins and install them if they are distributed in one .c file.

Gimp-tool is also used by programs that need to know what libraries and include-paths *Gimp* was compiled with .m4 macros for use with GNU autoconf are also included, to make detection of these libraries etc., easy for the upstream maintainer.

OPTIONS

Gimp-tool accepts the following options:

—build *plug-in.c*
Compile and link *plug-in.c* into a Gimp plug-in.

—install *plug-in.c*
Compile, link, and install *plug-in.c* into the user's personal Gimp configuration directory (for example, /home/che/.Gimp/plug-ins/)

—install–admin *plug-in.c*
Compile, link, and install *plug-in.c* into the system-wide Gimp plug-ins directory (for example, /usr/lib/Gimp/0.99/plug-ins/)

—version
Display the currently installed version of Gimp.

—libs
Display the libraries Gimp was compiled with.

—cflags
Display the flags that were passed to the compiler when Gimp was compiled.

ENVIRONMENT

GTK_CONFIG to get the location of the gtk-config program.

CC to get the name of the desired C compiler.

CFLAGS to get the preferred flags to pass to the C compiler.

SEE ALSO

The gimp man page and the gtk-config(1) man page available on your UNIX workstation.

COPYRIGHT

Copyright © 1995 Spencer Kimball and Peter Mattis

Permission to use, copy, modify and distribute this software and its documentation for any purpose and without fee is hereby granted, provided that the above copyright notice appear in all copies and that both that copyright notice and this permission notice appear in supporting documentation.

Appendix C

SIOD: Scheme In One Defune, Reference Appendix

Not all of the functions in this appendix have been implemented in Gimp. This is the complete list of SIOD functions for your reference.

Reference Section For Built-in Procedures

Note that the arguments to built-in procedures are always optional and default to ( ). Many of these procedures call a C library function of the same or similar name, in the obvious way. Therefore, you can refer to the UNIX manual page for more detailed information about function behavior. Such procedures are indicated with a bold **U**.

`(%%%memref address)`

This is a low level routine which should not be invoked in normal code. References a byte of memory at address. Used mostly to cause a core dump for debugging purposes by referencing address 0 or -1.

`(%%closure env code)`

This is a low-level routine which should not be invoked in normal code. If code is a cons of the form (arlist . body), then env is a list of frames, and the application of the closure will invoke the interpreter. Otherwise, code should be of type tc_subr_X and the application of the closure will pass the env as the first argument to the C procedure implementing the subr.

`(%%closure-code closure)`

This is a low-level routine which should not be invoked in normal code. Returns the code passed to %%closure.

`(%%closure-env closure)`

This is a low-level routine which should not be invoked in normal code. Returns the env passed to %%closure.

`(%%stack-limit amount silent)`

If amount is non-null, it sets the runtime stack check pointer to allow for that number of bytes. If silent is non-null, the resulting (or current) stack size is returned; otherwise, a message is printed.

`(* x1 x2 ...)`

Returns the product of all its arguments, or 1 if no arguments.

`*after-gc*`

A variable, the value is an express evaluated after the gc has done its work. For example:

```
(set! *after-gc* '(if (< (gc-info 4) 5000) (allocate-heap)))
```

`*args*`

A variable, bound to the list of arguments passed to the main program siod.

`(*catch tag body ...)`

A special form. Tag is evaluated and kept in a special location while all the forms in the body are evaluated. Normally returns the value of the last form except if a *throw is encountered within the dynamic scope of the evaluations. Errors may be caught by using a tag of 'errorobj.

`*env*`

A variable, bound to the list of environment values passed to the main program siod.

`*eval-history-ptr*`

A variable, default ( ), but if set to a list (possibly circular), then each call to eval will cause the car of the list to receive a pointer to the form being evaluated, and then the variable will be set to the cdr of the list. Useful for writing a retrospective trace debugging capability.

`*pi*`

A variable, value 3.1416.

`*plists*`

A variable, internal to the implementation of get and putprop.

`(*throw tag value)`

Locates an active *catch for which the tag is identical and then forces the *catch form to return the value.

`*traced*`

A variable, value is a list of procedures that have been traced.

`(+ x1 x2 ...)`

Returns the sum of its arguments.

`(- x1 x2 ...)`

With one argument returns the negation; returns the difference of the first argument and the sum of the rest.

`(/ x1 x2 ...)`

With one argument returns the inverse; otherwise, returns the quotient of the first argument and the product of the rest.

`(< x y)`

Returns true if x is numerically less than y.

`(<= x y)`

Returns true if x is numerically less than or equal to y.

`(= x y)`

Returns true if x is numerically equal to y.

`(> x y)`

Returns true if x is numerically greater than y.

`(>= x y)`

Returns true if x is numerically greater than or equal to y.

`(F_GETLK fd ltype whence start len)`

The fd may be an integer or file. The function fcntl (**U**) is called on the file descriptor and an appropriate struct flock constructed from the ltype, whence, start and len arguments, and the lock operation F_GETLK. The ltype may be F_RDLCK,F_UNLCK, or F_WRLCK. Whence may be SEEK_CUR, SEEK_END or SEEK_SET.

`(F_SETLK fd ltype whence start len)`

Same as F_GETLCK but with lock operation F_SETLK. **U**.

`(F_SETLKW fd ltype whence start len)`

Same as F_GETLCK but with lock operation F_SETLKW. **U**. For a good example see the command script cp-build.

`(abs x)`

Returns the absolute numerical value of x.

`(access-problem? filename method)`

Invokes the access function (**U**) on the filename and flags created from the method string which should contain one or more of the characters "rwxf"returning non-null if there is a problem with accessing the file in that way. For example:

```
(if (access-problem? "x.y" "r") (error "can't read x.y"))
```

`(acos x)`

Returns the inverse cosine of x.

`(alarm seconds flag)`

Invokes the alarm function (**U**). The handling of which will cause an error to be signaled in so many seconds. But if flag is false, then the error will not be signaled if the alarm took place inside a system call or other critical code section.

`(allocate-heap)`

Attempts to allocate (call the C library malloc procedure) to obtain an additional heap. The size of the heap and the maximum number of heaps are determined at startup time. Returns non-null if successful.

`(and form1 form2 form3 ...)`

A special form which causes the evaluation of its subforms in order, from left to right, continuing if and only if the subform returns a non-null value.

`(append l1 l2 l3 l4 ...)`

Returns a list which is the result of appending all of its arguments. Example:

```
(append '(a b) '(c d)) => (a b c d)
```

`(apply function arglist)`

Applies the function to the argument list arglist.

`(apropos substring)`

Returns a list of all symbols containing the given substring.

`(aref array index)`

Returns the element of the array at the given index.

`(array->hexstr string)`

Takes a string or byte array and returns a string in representing the values of the elements in hex.

`(aset array index value)`

Stores the value at the given index in the array.

`(ash value bits)`

Arithmetic shift of value a given number of bits to the left (positive) or right (negative).

`(asin x)`

Returns the inverse sine of x.

`(ass key alist function)`

Returns the first element of the alist such that the function applied to car of the element and the key returns a non-null value. For example:

```
(define (assq x alist) (ass x alist eq?))
```

`(assoc key alist)`

Same as (ass key alist equal?).

`(assq key alist)`

Same as (ass key alist eq?).

`(assv key alist)`

Same as (ass key alist eql?).

`(atan x)`

Returns the inverse tangent of x.

```
(atan2 x y)
```

Returns the inverse tangent of x/y.

```
(base64decode x)
```

Given a string X in base64 representation returns a string with bytes computed using the base64 decoding algorithm. See rfc1521.txt.

```
(base64encode x)
```

Returns a string computed using the base64 encoding algorithm.

```
(begin form1 form2 ...)
```

A special form which evaluates each of its subforms one after another, returning the value of the last subform.

```
(benchmark-eval nloops exp env)
```

A zero-overhead way of evaluating the exp *n* times.

```
(benchmark-funcall1 nloops f arg1)
```

A zero-overhead way of calling the function f *n* times on arg1.

```
(benchmark-funcall2 nloops f arg1 arg2)
```

A zero-overhead way of calling the function f *n* times on arg1 and arg2.

```
(bit-and x y)
```

Returns the bitwise logical "and" (C language & operator) of numerical arguments x and y.

```
(bit-not x)
```

Returns the bitwise logical complement (C language ~ operator) of numerical argument x.

```
(bit-or x y)
```

Returns the bitwise logical "or" (C language | operator) of numerical arguments x and y.

```
(bit-xor x y)
```

Returns the bitwise logical "xor" (C language ^ operator) of numerical arguments x and y.

```
(butlast x)
```

Returns a new list which has all the elements of the argument x except for the last element.

```
(bytes-append x1 x2 ...)
```

Returns a new byte array by appending its arguments which may be strings or byte arrays.

`(caaar x)`

Same as (car (car (car x))).

`(caadr x)`

Same as (car (car (cdr x))).

`(caar x)`

Same as (car (car x)).

`(cadar x)`

Same as (car (cdr (car x))).

`(caddr x)`

Same as (car (cdr (cdr x))).

`(cadr x)`

Same as (car (cdr x)).

`(car x)`

If x is the result of (cons a b), then (car x) is the same as a.

`(cdaar x)`

Same as (cdr (car (car x))).

`(cdadr x)`

Same as (cdr (car (cdr x))).

`(cdar x)`

Same as (cdr (car x)).

`(cddar x)`

Same as (cdr (cdr (car x))).

`(cdddr x)`

Same as (cdr (cdr (cdr x))).

`(cddr x)`

Same as (cdr (cdr x)).

`(cdr x)`

If x is the result of (cons a b), then (cdr x) is the same as b.

`(chdir path)`

Changes default directory to path. **U**.

`(chmod path mode)`

Changes the file mode of path. **U**. For example, to add execute access permission to the file f:

```
(chmod f
   (encode-file-mode (append '(XUSR XGRP XOTH)
            (cdr (assq 'mode (stat f))))))
```

`(chown path uid gid)`

Changes file ownership. **U**.

`(closedir stream)`

Closes a directory stream. **U**.

`(cond clause1 clause2 ...)`

A special form where each clause is processed until the predicate expression of the clause evaluates true. Then, each subform in the predicate is evaluated with the value of the last one becoming the value of the cond form:

```
(predicate-expression form1 form2 ...)
```

`(cons x y)`

Allocates a list object with x as the car and y as the cdr. For example:

```
(cons 1 (cons 2 (cons 3 ())))
```

evaluates to

```
(1 2 3)
```

`(cons-array dimension kind)`

Allocates an array (currently limited to one dimension). The kind may be string, byte, double or lisp (default).

`(copy-list x)`

The top level cons objects of x are copied, returning a new list.

`(cos x)`

Returns the cosine where x is in units of radians.

`(cpu-usage-limits soft-limit hard-limit)`

Invokes getrlimit if the arguments are null or otherwise setrlimit. **U**.

`(crypt key salt)`

A form of string hash. **U**.

`(current-resource-usage kind)`

Kind is the symbol SELF or CHILDREN, calls getrusage, **U**.

`(datlength data ctype)`

Returns the dimension of the data as if viewed as an array by the datref function.

`(datref data ctype index)`

References the data as if it were an array of C data type ctype, at the given index. The ctype may be CTYPE_CHAR, CTYPE_DOUBLE, CTYPE_FLOAT, CTYPE_LONG, CTYPE_SHORT, CTYPE_UCHAR, CTYPE_ULONG, or CTYPE_USHORT. The data may be a string or byte array.

`(decode-file-mode x)`

Returns a list of symbols given a numerical file mode.

`(define subform1 subform2)`

A special form used to assign a value to a variable in one of two ways:

```
(define variable value)
```

or to create a procedure

```
(define (procedure-name arg1 arg2 ...)
            form1
            form2
            ...)
```

`(delete-file path)`

Deletes the file specified by path.

`(delq element list)`

Deletes the elements of the list which are eq to its first argument. Possibly modifying the list using the set-cdr! operation.

`(encode-file-mode list)`

Takes a list of file mode symbols and returns the numerical value. SUID, SGID, RUSR, WUSR, XUSR, RGRP, WGRP, XGRP, ROTH, WOTH, XOTH.

`(encode-open-flags list)`

Takes a list of open (**U**) flag symbols and returns a numerical value. NONBLOCK, APPEND, RDONLY, WRONLY, RDWR, CREAT, TRUNC, EXCL.

`(endpwent)`

See **U**.

`(env-lookup indentifier environment)`

Returns an object such that the car is the location where the value of dentifier is stored.

`(eof-val)`

Returns the object returned by read upon encountering an end of file condition.

`(eq? x y)`

Returns true if x and y are the same object.

`(equal? x y)`

Returns true if x and y are equal objects.

`(eqv? x y)`

Returns true if x and y are the same object or numerically equal.

`errobj`

This variable is assigned to the offending object when the error procedure has been invoked. Useful mainly during interactive debugging.

`(error message object)`

Prints the error message, then aborts the current execution by invoking *throw using the symbol errobj as the tag and the cons of the message and the object as the value. Equivalent to:

```
(define (error message object)
   (if (> (verbose 0))
           (writes nil "ERROR: " message "\n"))
   (set! errobj object)
   (*throw 'errobj (cons message object)))
```

`(eval expression environment)`

Evaluates the expression in the context of the environment. This is not a special form. For example:

```
(eval (read-from-string "(+ 1 2)"))
```

evaluates to 3.

`(exec path args env)`

Calls execv or execve **U**.

`(exit status)`

Calls exit. **U**.

`(exp x)`

Computes the exponential function of x.

`(fast-load path noeval-flag)`

Loads a file of binary format expressions; if noeval-flag is true returns a list of the forms instead of evaluating them.

`(fast-print object state)`

Outputs a fast (binary) format representation of object, where the state is a list of (file hash-array index).

`(fast-read state)`

Inputs a form which had been output in fast (binary) format.

`(fast-save filename forms nohash-flag comment-string)`

Creates a file by using fast-print to output each of the forms. A true value for the nohash-flag will cause symbol names to be output each time they are encountered. Otherwise, a more optimal index representation is used. The comment-string is used as the first line of data in the file.

`(fchmod filedes mode)`

The filedes may be a number or an open file object. **U**.

`(fclose stream)`

Closes the open file stream. **U**.

`(fflush stream)`

See **U**.

`(file-times path)`

Returns a list of the st_ctime and the st_mtime returned by the stat function. **U**.

`(first x)`

Returns the first element (car) of the list x.

`(fmod x y)`

Floating point mod. **U**.

`(fnmatch pattern string flags)`

Returns true if the string matches the pattern. **U**.

`(fopen path mode)`

Opens the file and returns a file stream. **U**.

`(fork)`

Creates a child process. Returning a numerical pid in the parent, ( ) in the child, or call error if the child cannot be created. **U**.

`(fread size-or-buffer stream)`

Returns a new string of size bytes by calling fread (**U**). Or uses the buffer (a string or a byte array) instead and returns the number of bytes read. Returns ( ) on end of file.

`(fseek file offset direction)`

The direction is SEEK_CUR, SEEK_END or SEEK_SET. **U**.

`(fstat stream)`

Calls fstat (**U**) and returns an alist with elements dev, ino, mode, nlink, uid, gid, rdev, size, atime, mtime, ctime, blksize, blocks, flags and gen.

`(ftell stream)`

Calls ftell (**U**) to return the current offset into a file.

`(fwrite data stream)`

Write the data, a string or byte-array to the stream. Or, data can also be a list of a string or byte-array and a numerical length.

`(gc)`

Invokes the garbage collector.

`(gc-info item)`

ITEM	VALUE
0	true if copying gc, false if mark and sweek
1	number of active heaps
2	maximum number of heaps
3	number of objects per heap
4	amount of consing of objects before next gc

`(gc-status [flag])`

If flag is not specified, prints information about the gc. Otherwise, flag can be used to turn on or off gc messages or turn on or off the gc itself when in stop and copy mode.

`(get object key)`

Returns the key property of the object.

`(getc stream)`

Reads a character from the stream, returns ( ) for end of file. **U**.

`(getcwd)`

Returns the current working directory. **U**.

`(getenv name)`

Returns the value of the environment variable named, or ( ). **U**.

`(getgid)`

Returns the group id of the process. **U**.

`(getgrgid gid)`

Returns a list of members of the specified numerical group. **U**.

`(getpass prompt)`

Prompts the user and reads a line with echoing turned off. **U**.

`(getpgrp)`

Returns the process group ID of the calling process. **U**.

`(getpid)`

Returns the process ID of the calling process. **U**.

`(getppid)`

Returns the parent process ID of the calling process. **U**.

`(getpwent)`

Returns an alist representing the next item in the /etc/passwd file. **U**.

`(getpwnam username)`

Returns the /etc/passwd file entry for the given username. **U**.

`(getpwuid)`

Returns the /etc/passwd file entry for the given user id. **U**.

`(gets stream)`

Reads a line from the stream, ( ) on end of file.

```
(getuid)
```

Returns the uid of the current process. **U**.

```
(gmtime value)
```

Decodes the value into an alist. The value defaults to the current time. **U**.

```
(hexstr->bytes str)
```

Decodes the hex representation into a byte array.

```
(href table key)
```

The hash table is a one-dimensional array of association lists.

```
      (define (href table key)
         (cdr (assoc key
                    (aref table (sxhash key (length table))))))
```

```
(hset table key value)
```

Stores the value into the hash table slot indicated by key.

```
(html-encode str)
```

If str contains any special html characters (<>&), a new string is returned with these replaced by their corresponding representations < > &.

```
(if predicate-form true-form false-form)
```

A special form that evaluates the true-form or the false-form depending on the result of evaluating the predicate form.

```
(intern str)
```

Looks up a string in the symbol table or enters a new symbol.

```
(kill pid sig)
```

Calls the kill function **U**, with sig defaulting to SIGKILL.

```
(lambda (arg1 arg2 ...) form1 form2 ...)
```

Returns an applicable procedure object (CLOSURE) with the given argument list and expression subforms. For example:

```
      (mapcar (lambda (x) (* x x)) '(1 2 3))
```

evaluates to:

```
      (1 4 9)
```

Also used by the define special form.

`(larg-default list index default-value)`

References the list according to index, but skipping over strings that begin with a colon or a dash. If the list is not long enough, it returns the default-value instead. Most useful when used with the *args* variable inside a main program.

`(last list)`

Returns the last cons in a list.

`(last-c-error)`

Returns the value of the C library strerror(errno) (**U**) interned as a symbol.

`(lchown path owner group)`

Changes the ownership of a symbolic link. **U**.

`(length object)`

Returns the length of an object which may be a string (acts like strlen) or a list or an array.

`(let (binding1 binding2 ...) form1 form2 ...)`

A special form where each binding is a (variable value) pair. It works by computing the values, establishing the bindings, and then evaluating the forms, returning the value of the last one. For example, the following evaluates to 30:

```
(let ((x 10)
   (y 20))
   (+ x y))
```

`(let* (binding1 binding2 ...) form1 form2 ...)`

A special form where each binding is a (variable value) pair. It works by sequentially computing each value and then establishing a binding. For example, the following evaluates to 30:

```
(let* ((x 10)
   (y (+ x 10)))
   (+ x y))
```

`(letrec (binding1 binding2 ...) form1 form2 ...)`

Useful when the value forms of the bindings are lambda expressions with which you desire to program mutually recursive calls.

`(link existing-file entry-to-create)`

Creates a hard link. **U**.

`(list item1 item2 ...)`

Conses up its arguments into a list.

`(lkey-default list index default-value)`

Returns the substring on the right-hand size of the equal sign of the first element of the list of the form index=value, or the default-value if none are found. Useful when processing the *args* value inside a main program.

`(load fname noeval-flag search-flag)`

If search-flag is true it looks for fname in the current directory and then in the SIOD_LIB directory. The forms from the file are parsed according to the "parser:xxx" directive at the beginning of the file (default "parser:read"). If the neval-flag is true, then a list of the forms is returned; otherwise, the forms are evaluated.

`(load-so fname init_fcn)`

Loads the dynamic library specified by fname, invoking the init_fcn if specified (default init_fname).

`(localtime value)`

Returns an alist representing the value as a localtime. **U**. Value defaults to the current time.

`(log x)`

Computes the natural logarithm of x.

`(lref-default list index default-fcn)`

Returns the index element of the list or the result of calling the default-fcn if the list is not long enough.

`(lstat path)`

Returns the stat information of a logical link. **U**.

`(make-list length element)`

Creates a list of the given length filled with the element specified.

`(mapcar fcn list1 list2 ...)`

Returns a list which is the result of applying the fcn to the elements of each of the lists specified.

`(max x1 x2 ...)`

Returns the maximum of x1, x2, etc.

`(md5-final state)`

Returns a byte array computed from the state, derived from the RSA Data Security, Inc. MD5 Message-Digest Algorithm. See rfc1321.txt. Example:

```
(define (md5 str)
   (let ((s (md5-init)))
        (md5-update s str)
        (array->hexstr (md5-final s))))
```

`(md5-init)`

Returns an md5 algoritm state as a byte array.

`(md5-update state string length)`

Performs the update step of the md5 algorithm using data from the string up to length, or length can be an open file object, in which case the data from the file is used to perform the update.

`(member key list)`

Returns the portion of the list where the car is equal to the key, or ( ) if none found.

`(memq key list)`

Returns the portion of the list where the car is eq to the key, or ( ) if none found.

`(memv key list)`

Returns the portion of the list where the car is eqv? to the key, or ( ) if none found.

`(min x1 x2 ...)`

Returns the numerical minimum of its arguments.

`(mkdatref ctype ind)`

Creates a closure functionally equivalent to (lambda (x) (datref x ctype ind)).

`(mkdir path mode)`

Creates a directory with the specified numerical access mode. **U**.

`(mktime alist)`

Returns the numerical time value corresponding to the alist in the same format as returned by the localtime function. **U**.

`(nconc l1 l2)`

Makes the cdr of the last cons of l1 point to l2.

`(nice increment)`

Changes the priority of the current process by the increment. **U**.

`nil`

Do not change the value of this variable, which is bound to the empty list.

`(not x)`

Returns the reverse truth sense of x.

`(nreverse list)`

Destructive reversal of the elements of a list using set-cdr!.

`(nth index list)`

References the list using index, with the first element being index 0.

`(null? x)`

Returns true if x is the empty list.

`(number->string x base width precision)`

Formats the number according to the base, which may be 8, 10, 16 or the symbol e or f. The width and precision are both optional.

`(number? x)`

Returns true if x is a number.

`(opendir path)`

Returns a directory stream. Note that in UNIX, path is the name of a directory, but in WIN32 path is a wildcard pattern. **U**.

`(or form1 form2 ...)`

A special form which causes the evaluation of its subforms in order, from left to right until a form evaluates to a non-null value.

`(os-classification)`

Returns UNIX, win32, vms.

`(pair? x)`

Returns true if x is a pair (created by cons).

`(parse-number str)`

Convers a string to a number.

`(pclose stream)`

Used to close a stream opened using popen. Makes sure the associated process is killed. **U**.

`(popen command type)`

Executes the command in a child process and opens a stream connected to the process standard output if type is r, or the standard input if type is w. **U**.

`(pow x y)`

Computes the result of x raised to the y power.

`(prin1 object stream)`

Outputs the standard readable representation of the object to the stream, which defaults to the standard output.

`(print object stream)`

Same as prin1 followed by output of a newline.

`(print-to-string object string no-trunc-flag)`

Puts the readable representation of the object into the string, starting at the first character unless the no-trunc-flag is true, in which case the representation starts at the current length of the string.

`(prog1 form1 form2 form3 ...)`

A special form which evaluates all its subforms but returns the value of the first one. A useful shorthand to employ instead of using a let.

`(putc char stream)`

Outputs the character to the stream. **U**.

`(putenv setting)`

With setting of the form “key=value”, this makes a new environment binding available to the getenv function of the current and subsequent child processes, or updates an old one. **U**.

`(putprop object value key)`

Not implemented.

`(puts string stream)`

Outputs the string to the stream. **U**.

`(qsort list predicate-fcn access-fcn)`

Implements the recursive quicksort algorithm on elements of the list compared by using the predicate-fcn on the results of invoking the access-fcn.

Example	Result
(qsort '(3 1 5 4 2) <)	(1 2 3 4 5)
(qsort '((3 a) (2 b)) < car)	((2 b) (3 a))

`(quit)`

Causes the read-eval-print loop to return, usually resulting in an exit from the main program of siod, but may not when other C programs are utilizing the libsiod functionality.

`(quote x)`

A special form that returns x without evaluating it. Commonly written in abbreviated format as 'x.

`(rand modulus)`

Computes a random number from 0 to modulus-1. Uses C library rand.

`(random modulus)`

Computes a random number from 0 to modulus-1. Uses C library random.

`(read stream)`

Inputs characters from the stream; returns the parsed standard expression, or (eof-val).

`(read-from-string string)`

Performs a read operation on the characters in the string.

`(readdir directory-stream)`

Returns the name of the next entry in the directory stream or ( ) of none left.

`(readline stream)`

Reads a line of characters from the stream, returning ( ) on end of file. The terminating newline is not included in the string, which is usually more convenient. For example, this procedure for loading a tab-delimited spreadsheet file:

```
(define (load-spread-sheet filename)
   (if (>= (verbose) 2)
           (writes nil ";; loading spread sheet " filename "\n"))
   (let ((result nil)
           (line nil)
           (f (and (not (equal? filename "-")) (fopen filename "r"))))
   (while (set! line (readline f))
           (set! result (cons (strbreakup line "\t") result)))
   (and f (fclose f))
   (nreverse result)))
```

`(readlink path)`

Returns the contents of the symbolic link at path. **U**.

`(realtime)`

Returns a double precision floating point value representation of the current realtime number of seconds. Usually precise to about a thousandth of a second.

`(rename from-path to-path)`

Renames a directory or file within a file system. **U**.

`(require path)`

Computes a variable name by concatenating "*" + path + "-loaded*" and then calling (load path nil t) if and only if the variable is not bound to true. After the file is loaded the variable is set to true. This is the correct way of making sure a file is only loaded once.

`(require-so path)`

Computes a variable name by concatenating "init_" + path, and calling (load-so path) if and only if the variable is not bound to true. After the shared library has been loaded the variable is set to true. The correct way of making sure a shared library is only loaded once is:

```
(require-so (so-ext 'name))
```

`(rest x)`

Returns the rest of the list x, in other words, the cdr.

`(reverse x)`

Returns a new list which has elements in the reverse order of the list x.

`(rld-pathnames)`

Returns a list of the pathnames which represent shared libraries that have been loaded by the current process.

`(rmdir path)`

Removes the directory entry specified by path. **U**.

`(runtime)`

Returns a list containing the current cpu usage in seconds and the subset amount of cpu time that was spent performing garbage collection during the currently extant read-eval-print loop cycle.

`(save-forms filename forms how)`

Prints the forms to the file, where how can be "w" (default) or "a" to append to the file.

`(sdatref spec data)`

Used as the %%closure-code by mkdatref.

`(set! variable value)`

A special form that evaluates the value subform to get a value, and then assigns the variable to the value.

`(set-car! cons-cell value)`

Changes the car of the cons-cell object to point to the value.

`(set-cdr! cons-cell value)`

Changes the cdr of the cons-cell object to point to the value.

`(set-eval-history length circular-flag)`

Creates a list of the specified length and establishes bindings for *eval-history-ptr* and *eval-history*. The list is circular if the flag is specified true. Try the following:

```
(define (fib x) (if (< x 2) x (+ (fib (- x 1)) (fib (- x 2)))))
(set-eval-history 200)
(fib 10)
(mapcar (lambda (x) (if (pair? x) (car x) x)) *eval-history*)
```

`(set-symbol-value! symbol value env)`

Finds the location of the value cell for the specified symbol in the environment env and sets the value.

`(setprop obj key value)`

Not implemented.

`(setpwent)`

Resets the pointer into the /etc/passwd file. **U**.

`(setuid x)`

Sets the userid of the process. **U**.

`(sin x)`

Computes the sine function of the angle x in radians.

`(siod-lib)`

Return the setting of the siod library directory.

`(sleep n)`

Sleeps for *n* seconds, where n may be fractional on some systems.

`(so-ext path)`

Appends the path with the file extension for shared libraries.

`(sqrt x)`

Computes the square root of x.

`(srand seed)`

Resets the algorithm seed for the rand function. **U**.

`(srandom seed)`

Resets the algorithm seed for the random function. **U**.

`(stat path)`

Returns an alist describing file status information, or ( ) if the path cannot be accessed (last-c-error), may be used to return the reason.

`(strbreakup string sep)`

Returns a list of the portions of string indicated by the separator.

```
(strbreakup "x=y&z=3" "&") => ("x=y" "z=3")
```

`(strcat str1 str2)`

Copies the string str2 into str1 starting at the current active end of str1, which is determined by the location of a 0 byte, calling error if there is not enough room left in str1. **U**.

`(strcmp str1 str2)`

Returns 0 if str1 and str2 are equal, or -1 if str1 is alphabetically less than str2 or 1 otherwise. **U**.

`(strcpy str1 str2)`

Copies str1 into str1 or calling error if there is not enough room. **U**.

`(strcspn str indicators)`

Returns the location of the first character in str which is found in the indicators set; returns the length of the string if none found. **U**.

`(strftime format-string alist)`

Uses the format-string to compute a string using broken-up time/data information from the alist (defaults to the current time) **U**, for example:

```
(strftime "%B" '((mon . 3))) => "April"
```

`(string->number str radix)`

Converts the string to a number assuming the specified radix.

`(string-append str1 str2 str3 ...)`

Returns a new string which contains the concatenation of all its string arguments.

`(string-dimension str)`

Returns the maximum possible length of a string array.

`(string-downcase str)`

Returns a new string converting all the characters of str to lowercase.

`(string-length str)`

Returns the active string length of str.

`(string-lessp str1 str2)`

Returns true if str1 is alphabetically less than str2.

`(string-search key str)`

Locates the index of the key in the specified string. Returns ( ) if not found.

`(string-trim str)`

Returns a new string made by trimming whitespace from the left and right of the specified string.

`(string-trim-left str)`

Like string-trim, but only the left-hand side.

`(string-trim-right str)`

Like string-trim, but only the right-hand side.

`(string-upcase str)`

Returns a new string with all the lowercase characters converted to uppercase.

`(string? x)`

Returns true if x is a string.

`(strptime str format alist)`

Parses str according to format and merges the values with the alist. **U**.

```
(cdr (assq 'mon (strptime "March" "%B"))) => 2
```

`(strspn str indicators)`

Returns the location of the first character in str which is not found in the indicators set; returns the length of the str if none found. **U**. For example:

```
(define (string-trim-left x)
   (substring x (strspn x " \t")))
```

`(subset pred-fcn list)`

Returns the subset of the list such that the elements satisfy the pred-fcn. For example:

```
(subset number? '(1 b 2 c)) => (1 2)
```

`(substring str start end)`

Returns a new string made up of the part of str beginning at start and terminating at end. In other words, the new string has a length of end - start.

`(substring-equal? str str2 start end)`

An efficient way to determine if the substring of str2 specified by start and end is equal to str1.

`(swrite stream table form)`

This is the same as the write-smart-html procedure described in ftp://ftp.std.com/pub/gjc/www95-paper.html.

`(sxhash data modulus)`

Computes a recursive hash of the data with respect to the specified modulus.

`(symbol-bound? symbol env)`

Returns true if the symbol is bound in the environment.

`(symbol-value symbol env)`

Returns the value of the symbol in the environment.

`(symbol? x)`

Returns true if x is a symbol.

`(symbolconc arg1 arg2 ...)`

Slightly more efficient than calling intern on the result of using string-append on the arguments. This procedure actually predates the availability of the string data type in SIOD.

`(symlink contents-path link-path)`

Creates a directory entry link-path pointing to the contents-path. **U**.

`(system arg1 arg2 ...)`

Appends the string arguments to form a command to be executed by the operating system. **U**.

`t`

Please do not change the global value of this variable, bound to a true value.

`(tan x)`

Computes the tangent of the angle x specified in radians.

`(the-environment)`

A special form which returns the interpreter environment structure for the current lexical scope.

`(trace fcn1 fcn2 ...)`

Traces the specified interpreted procedures by modifying the closure objects.

`(trunc x)`

Returns the integer portion of x.

`(typeof x)`

Returns a symbol describing the type of the object x, or the integer type code.

`(unbreakupstr list sep)`

The reverse of strbreakup. The following example saves a list of lists as a tab delimited spreadsheet:

```
(define (save-spread-sheet filename data)
   (if (>= (verbose) 2)
            (writes nil ";; saving spread sheet " filename "\n"))
   (let ((result data)
            (f (and (not (equal? filename "-")) (fopen filename
"w"))))
   (while result
            (writes f (unbreakupstr (car result) "\t") "\n")
            (set! result (cdr result)))
   (and f (fclose f))))
```

`(ungetc char stream)`

Puts the char back into the stream for the next call to getc.

`(unix-ctime x)`

Converts the integer time x into a string. **U**

`(unix-time)`

Returns the current number of seconds since 1-JAN-1970 GMT. **U**

`(unix-time->strtime x)`

Returns a string of the form "YYYYMMDDHHmmSSdd" which is useful in some contexts. This predates the availability of the strftime procedure.

`(unlink path)`

Deletes the specified entry from the directory structure. **U**

`(untrace fcn1 fcn2 ...)`

Untraces the specified procedures.

`(url-decode str)`

Performs the url decode operation on the str. See people.delphi.com/gjc/chtml.html for example usage.

`(url-encode str)`

Locates characters in the str which should not appear in a url, and returns a new string where they have been converted to the %NN hex representation. Spaces are converted to "+" signs.

`(utime path modification-time access-time)`

Sets the file modification and access times. **U**

`(verbose arg)`

Sets the verbosity level of SIOD to the specified level or returns the current level if not specified.

Table C.1 *Verbose arguments*

Verbose Level	Effect on System
0	No messages.
1	Error messages only.
2	Startup messages, prompts, and evaluation timing.
3	File loading and saving messages.
4 (default)	Garbage collection messages.
5	display of data loaded from files and fetched from databases.

`(wait pid options)`

Waits on a child process by calling the waitpid function, where options may be a list containing (WCONTINUED WNOWAIT WNOHANG WUNTRACED). Returns a list of the process pid and final exit status. The fork-test.scm and http-stress.scm modules provide example usage. **U**

`(while pred-form form1 form2 ...)`

If pred-form evaluates true, it will evaluate all the other forms and then loop.

`(writes stream data1 data2 data3 ...)`

Outputs the data arguments to the stream without quoting strings or special characters.

Appendix D

Perl-Fu Man Pages

Gimp Man Page

Name

Gimp/Perl extension for writing Gimp Extensions/Plug-ins/Load & Save–Handlers.

This is mostly a reference manual. For a quick introduction, look at the *Gimp::Fu* man page. For more information, including tutorials, look at the Gimp–Perl pages at http://gimp.pages.de.

Synopsis

```
use Gimp;
```

Other modules of interest:

```
use Gimp::Fu;      # easy scripting environment
use Gimp::PDL;     # interface to the Perl Data Language
```

these have their own man page.

Import Tags

If you don't specify import tags, Gimp assumes qw/:consts main xlfd_size/ which is usually what you want.

:auto

Import useful constants, like RGB, RUN_NONINTERACTIVE... as well as all libgimp and pdb functions automagically into the caller's namespace. BEWARE! This will overwrite your AUTOLOAD function, if you have one!

:param

Import PARAM_* constants (PARAM_INT32, PARAM_STRING, etc.) only.

:consts

All constants from gimpenums.h:

> BG_IMAGE_FILL, RUN_NONINTERACTIVE, NORMAL_MODE, PARAM_INT32, etc.

spawn_options=*options*

Set default spawn options to *options*; see the *Gimp::Net* man page.

default

The default (unless '' is specified) is main xlfd_size :consts.

Getting Started

You should first read the *Gimp::Fu* man page and then come back. This man page is mainly intended for reference purposes.

Also, Dov Grobgeld has written an excellent tutorial for Gimp–Perl. You can find it at http://imagic.weizmann.ac.il/~dov/gimp/perl–tut.html.

Description

I think you already know what this is about: writing Gimp plug-ins/extensions/scripts/file–handlers/standalone scripts, just about everything you can imagine in Perl. If you are missing functionality (look into TODO first), please feel free to contact the author.

Some highlights:

- Networked plug-ins and plug-ins using the libgimpinterfaces (i.e., to be started from within Gimp) look almost the same (if you use the Gimp::Fu interface, there will be no visible differences at all); you can easily create hybrid (networked & libgimp) scripts as well.
- Use either a plain pdb (scheme–like) interface or nice object– oriented syntax, i.e.

  ```
  gimp_image_new(600,300,RGB)
  ```

  is the same as

  ```
  new Image(600,300,RGB)
  ```

- Gimp::Fu will start Gimp for you, if it cannot connect to an existing Gimp process.
- You can optionally overwrite the pixel–data functions by versions using piddles (see the *Gimp::PDL* man page).

Noteworthy Limitation (Subject To Change):

- Callback procedures do not pass return values to Gimp.

Outline Of A Gimp Plug-in

All plug-ins (and extensions) **must** contain a call to Gimp::main. The return code should be immediately handed out to exit:

```
exit main;   # Gimp::main is exported by default.
```

Before the call to Gimp::main, *no* other PDB function must be called.

In a Gimp::Fu–script, you should call Gimp::Fu::main instead:

```
exit main;   # Gimp::Fu::main is exported by default as well.
```

This is similar to Gtk, Tk or similar modules, where you have to call the main eventloop. Attention: Although you call exit with the result of main, the main function might not actually return. This depends on both the version of Gimp and the version of the Gimp/Perl module that is in use. Do not depend on main to return at all, but still call exit immediately.

If you need to do cleanups before exiting you should use the quit callback (which is not yet available if you use Gimp::Fu).

CALLBACKS

If you use the plain Gimp module (as opposed to Gimp::Fu), your program should only call one function: main. Everything else is going to be **called** from Gimp at a later stage. For this to work, you should define certain call-backs in the same module you called Gimp::main.

init (), query (), quit ()

The standard libgimp callback functions. run( ) is missing, because this module will directly call the function you registered with gimp_install_procedure. Some only make sense for extensions, some only for normal plug-ins.

<installed_procedure>()

The callback for a registered function (gimp_install_procedure and friends). The arguments from Gimp are passed as normal arguments (with the exception of arrays being passed without a preceding count).

The return values from <installed_procedure>( ) are checked against the specification, with the exception that a single undef is treated like no arguments. You can return less, but not more results than specified.

If you die within the callback, the error will be reported to Gimp (as soon as Gimp implements such a functionality) as an execution error.

net ()

This is called when the plug-in is not started directly from within Gimp, but instead from the **Net-Server** (the Perl network server extension you hopefully have installed and started).

CALLING GIMP FUNCTIONS

There are two different flavors of gimp-functions. Functions from the **PDB** (the Procedural DataBase), and functions from **libgimp** (the C-language interface library).

You can get a listing and description of every PDB function by starting the **DB Browser** extension in the Gimp**Xtns** menu (but remember that **DB Browser** is buggy and displays "_" (underscores) as "–" (dashes), so you can't see the difference between gimp_quit and gimp–quit. As a rule of thumb, **Script-Fu** registers scripts with dashes, and everything else uses underscores).

libgimp functions can't be traced (and won't be traceable in the foreseeable future).

To call pdb functions (or equivalent libgimp functions), just treat them like normal Perl (this requires the use of the :auto import tag, but see below for another possibility):

```
gimp_palette_set_foreground([20,5,7]);
                        gimp_palette_set_background("cornsilk");
```

If you don't use the :auto import tag, you can call all Gimp functions using OO-Syntax:

```
Gimp->gimp_palette_set_foreground([20,5,7]);
```

```
Gimp->palette_set_background("cornsilk");
Palette->set_foreground('#1230f0');
```

As you can see, you can also drop part of the name prefixes with this syntax, so its actually shorter to write.

"But how do I call functions containing dashes?" Well, get your favorite Perl book and learn Perl! Anyway, newer Perls understand a nice syntax (see also the description for gimp_call_procedure):

```
"plug-in-the-egg"->(RUN_INTERACTIVE,$image,$drawable);
```

Very old Perls may need:

```
&{"plug-in-the-egg"}(RUN_INTERACTIVE,$image,$drawable);
```

(Unfortunately, the plug-in in this example is actually called "plug_in_the_egg" *sigh*. Formatters note: take a look in the plug-in source code, and you will be 100% sure about the name.)

Special Functions

In this section, you can find descriptions of special functions, functions having different calling conventions/ semantics than I would expect (I cannot speak for you), or just plain interesting functions. All of these functions must either be imported explicitly or called using a namespace override (Gimp::), not as Methods (Gimp->).

main(), Gimp::main()

Should be called immediately when Perl is initialized. Arguments are not yet supported. Initializations can later be done in the init function.

xlfd_size(fontname)

This auxiliary functions parse the XLFD (usually obtained from a PF_FONT parameter) and return its size and unit (e.g., (20,POINTS)). This can conveniently be used in the gimp_text_..._fontname functions, which ignore the size (no joke ;). Example:

```
$drawable->text_fontname (50, 50,"The quick", 5, 1, xlfd_size \
                    $font, $font;
```

Gimp::init_gtk()

Initialize Gtk in a similar way the Gimp itself did it. This automatically parses Gimp's gtkrc and sets a variety of default settings (visual, colormap, gamma, shared memory...).

Gimp::init([connection-argument]), Gimp::end()

This is an alternative and experimental interface that replaces the call to Gimp::main and the net callback. At the moment it only works for the Net interface (the *Gimp::Net* man page), and not as a native plug-in. Here's an example:

```
use Gimp;
Gimp::init;
<do something with the gimp>
```

The optional argument to init has the same format as the GIMP_HOST variable described in the *Gimp::Net* man page. Calling Gimp::end is optional.

Gimp::lock(), Gimp::unlock()

These functions can be used to gain exclusive access to the Gimp. After calling lock, all accesses by other clients will be blocked and executed after the call to unlock. Calls to lock and unlock can be nested.

Currently, these functions only lock the current Perl Server instance against exclusive access; they are nops when used via the Gimp::Lib interface.

Gimp::set_rgb_db(filespec)

Use the given rgb database instead of the default one. The format is the same as the one used by the X11 Consortium's rgb database (you might have a copy in /usr/lib/X11/rgb.txt). You can view the default database with Perldoc -m Gimp, at the end of the file (the default database is similar, but not identical to the X11 default rgb.txt)

Gimp::initialized()

This function returns true whenever it is safe to call gimp functions. This is usually only the case after gimp_main or gimp_init have been called.

Gimp::register_callback (gimp_function_name,perl_function)

Using this function you can overwrite the standard Gimp behavior of calling a Perl subroutine of the same name as the gimp function.

The first argument is the name of a registered Gimp function that you want to overwrite ('perl_fu_make_something'), and the second argument can be either a name of the corresponding perl sub ('Elsewhere::make_something') or a code reference (\&my_make).

SPECIAL METHODS

This section describes methods that behave differently than you might expect, or methods uniquely implemented in Perl (that is, not in the PDB). All of these must be invoked using the method syntax (Gimp–> or $object–>).

gimp_install_procedure(name, blurb, help, author, copyright, date, menu_path, image_types, type, (params), (return_vals))

Mostly same as gimp_install_procedure. The parameters and return values for the functions are specified as an array ref containing either integers or array–refs with three elements, [PARAM_TYPE, "NAME", "DESCRIPTION"].

gimp_progress_init(message,())

Initializes a progress bar. In networked modules this is a no-op.

gimp_progress_update(percentage)

Updates the progress bar. No–op in networked modules.

gimp_tile_*, gimp_pixel_rgn_*, gimp_drawable_get

With these functions you can access the raw pixel data of drawables. They are documented in the *Gimp::Pixel* man page, to keep this manual page short.

gimp_call_procedure(procname, arguments...)

This function is actually used to implement the fancy stuff. It's your basic interface to the PDB. Every function call is eventually done through his function, i.e.:

```
gimp_image_new(args...);
```

is replaced by

```
gimp_call_procedure "gimp_image_new",args...;
```

at runtime.

gimp_list_images, gimp_image_get_layers, gimp_image_get_channels

These functions return what you would expect: an array of images, layers or channels. The reason why this is documented is that the usual way to return PARAM_INT32ARRAY's would be to return a **reference** to an **array of integers**, rather than blessed objects.

server_eval(string)

Evaluates the given string in array context and returns the results. It's similar to eval, but with two important differences: The evaluating always takes place on the server side/server machine (which might be the same as the local one) and compilation/runtime errors are reported as runtime errors (i.e., throwing an exception).

Object-Oriented Syntax

In this manual, only the plain syntax (that languages like C use) is described. Actually, the recommended way to write Gimp scripts is to use the fancy OO-like syntax you are used to in Perl (version 5 at least). As a matter of fact, OO-syntax saves soooo much typing as well. See the *Gimp::OO* man page for details.

Debugging Aids

No, I can't tell you how to cure immune deficiencies (which might well be incurable, as AIDS might be able to survive in brain cells, among other unreachable (for medication) parts of your body), but I *can* tell you how Gimp can help you debugging your scripts:

Gimp::set_trace (tracemask)

Tracking down bugs in Gimp scripts is difficult: no sensible error messages. If anything goes wrong, you only get an execution failure. Switch on tracing to see which parameters are used to call pdb functions. This function is never exported, so you have to qualify it when calling.

tracemask is any number of the following flags or'ed together:

TRACE_NONE nothing is printed.

TRACE_CALL all pdb calls (and only pdb calls!) are printed with arguments and return values.

TRACE_TYPE the parameter types are printed additionally.

TRACE_NAME the parameter names are printed.

TRACE_DESC the parameter descriptions.

TRACE_ALL all of the above. set_trace returns the old tracemask.

Gimp::set_trace(\$tracevar)

Write trace into $tracevar instead of printing it to STDERR. $tracevar only contains the last command traces, i.e., it's cleared on every PDB invocation.

Gimp::set_trace(*FILEHANDLE)

Write trace to FILEHANDLE instead of STDERR.

Supported Gimp Data Types

Gimp supports different data types like colors, regions, strings. In Perl, these are represented as:

INT32, INT16, INT8, FLOAT, STRING

Normal Perl scalars. Anything except STRING will be mapped to a Perl-double.

INT32ARRAY, INT16ARRAY, INT8ARRAY, FLOATARRAY, STRINGARRAY

Array refs containing scalars of the same type, i.e., [1, 2, 3, 4]. Gimp implicitly swallows or generates a proceeding integer argument because the preceding argument usually (this is a de-facto standard) contains the number of elements.

COLOR

On input, either an array ref with 3 elements (i.e., [233,40,40]), a X11-like string ("#rrggbb") or a color name ("papayawhip") (see set_rgb_db).

DISPLAY, IMAGE, LAYER, CHANNEL, DRAWABLE, SELECTION

These will be mapped to corresponding objects (IMAGE => Gimp::Image). In trace output you will see small integers (the image/layer/etc..-ID)

PARASITE

Represented as an array ref [name, flags, data], where name and data should be Perl strings and flags is the numerical flag value.

REGION, BOUNDARY, PATH, STATUS

Not yet supported (and might never be).

AUTHOR

Marc Lehmann <pcg@goof.com>

SEE ALSO

perl(1), gimp(1), the *Gimp::OO* man page, the *Gimp::Data* man page, the *Gimp::Pixel* man page, the *Gimp::PDL* man page, the *Gimp::Util* man page, the *Gimp::UI* man page, the *Gimp::Feature* man page, the *Gimp::Net* man page, the *Gimp::Compat* man page, the *Gimp::Config* man page, the *Gimp::Lib* man page, the *Gimp::Module* man page, the *scm2perl* man page and the *scm2scm* man page.

GIMP::FU MAN PAGE

NAME

Gimp::Fu – "easy to use" framework for Gimp scripts

SYNOPSIS

```
    use Gimp;
                        use Gimp::Fu;
```

(this module uses Gtk, so make sure it's correctly installed)

DESCRIPTION

Currently, there are only three functions in this module. This fully suffices to provide a professional interface and the ability to run this script from within Gimp and standalone from the commandline.

Dov Grobgeld has written an excellent tutorial for Perl-Fu, see "A Tutorial For Perl Gimp Users" starting on page 735. While not finished, it's definitely worth a look! You can find it at http://imagic.weizmann.ac.il/~dov/gimp/perl-tut.html.

INTRODUCTION

In general, a Gimp::Fu script looks like this:

```
#!/path/to/your/perl
use Gimp;
                    use Gimp::Fu;
register <many arguments>, sub {
                    your code;
                    }
exit main;
```

(This distribution comes with example scripts. One is examples/example-fu.pl, which is a small Gimp::Fu-script you can take as a starting point for your experiments).

Attention: At the moment it's necessary to always import the Gimp::Fu module after the Gimp module.

THE REGISTER FUNCTION

```
register
  "function_name",
  "blurb", "help",
  "author", "copyright",
  "date",
  "menu path",
  "image types",
  [
   [PF_TYPE,name,desc,optional-default,optional-extra-args],
   [PF_TYPE,name,desc,optional-default,optional-extra-args],
   # etc...
  ],
  [
   # like above, but for return values (optional)
  ],
  ['feature1', 'feature2'...], # optionally check for features
  sub { code };
```

function name

The pdb name of the function, i.e. the name under which it will be registered in the Gimp database. If it doesn't start with "perl_fu_", "plug_in_" or "extension_", it will be prepended. If you don't want this, prefix your function name with a single "+". The idea here is that every Gimp::Fu plug-in will be found under the common perl_fu_–prefix.

blurb

A small description of this script/plug-in.

help

A help text describing this script. Should be longer and more verbose than blurb.

copyright

The copyright designation for this script. Important! Save your intellectual rights!

date

The "last modified" time of this script. There is no strict syntax here, but I recommend ISO format (yyyymmdd or yyyy-mm-dd).

menu path

The menu entry Gimp should create. It should start either with <Image>, if you want an entry in the image menu (the one that opens when clicking into an image), <Xtns>, for the Xtns menu or <None> for none.

image types

The types of images your script will accept. Examples are "RGB", "RGB*", "GRAY, RGB" etc... Most scripts will want to use "*", meaning "any type."

The Parameter Array

An array ref containing parameter definitions. These are similar to the parameter definitions used for gimp_install_procedure, but include an additional **default** value used when the caller doesn't supply one, and optional extra arguments describing some types like PF_SLIDER.

Each array element has the form [type, name, description, default_value, extra_args].

<Image>-type plug-ins get two additional parameters, image (PF_IMAGE) and drawable (PF_DRAWABLE). Do not specify these yourself. Also, the run_mode argument is never given to the script, but its value can be accessed in the package-global $run_mode. The name is used in the dialog box as a hint, the description will be used as a tooltip.

See the section Parameter Types for the supported types.

The Return Values

This is just like the parameter array, just that it describes the return values. Of course, default values don't make much sense here. (Even if they did, it's not implemented anyway.) This argument is optional.

The Features Requirements

See the *Gimp::Features* man page for a description of which features can be checked for. This argument is optional (but remember to specify an empty return value array, [], if you want to specify it).

The Code

This is either an anonymous sub declaration (sub { your code here; }, or a coderef, which is called when the script is run. Arguments (including the image and drawable for <Image> plug-ins) are supplied automatically.

It is good practice to return an image, if the script creates one, or undef, since the return value is interpreted by Gimp::Fu (like displaying the image or writing it to disk). If your script creates multiple pictures, return an array.

PARAMETER TYPES

PF_INT8, PF_INT16, PF_INT32, PF_INT, PF_FLOAT, PF_STRING, PF_VALUE

Are all mapped to a string entry, since Perl doesn't really distinguish between all these datatypes. The reason they exist is to help other scripts (possibly written in other languages! really!). It's nice to be able to specify a float as 13.45 instead of "13.45" in C! PF_VALUE is synonymous to PF_STRING, and <PF_INT> is synonymous to <PF_INT32>.

PF_COLOR, PF_COLOUR

Will accept a color argument. In dialogs, a color preview will be created which will open a color selection box when clicked.

PF_IMAGE

A Gimp image.

PF_DRAWABLE

A Gimp drawable (image, channel or layer).

PF_TOGGLE, PF_BOOL

A boolean value (anything Perl would accept as true or false). The description will be used for the togglebutton label!

PF_SLIDER

Uses a horizontal scale. To set the range and stepsize, append an array ref (see Gtk::Adjustment for an explanation) [range_min, range_max, step_size, page_increment, page_size] as "extra argument" to the description array. Default values will be substitued for missing entries, like in:

```
[PF_SLIDER, "alpha value", "the alpha value", 100, [0, 255, 1] ]
```

PF_SPINNER

The same as PF_SLIDER, except that it uses a spinbutton instead of a scale.

PF_RADIO

In addition to a default value, an extra argument describing the various options *must* be provided. That extra argument must be a reference to an array filled with Option-Name = Option-Value> pairs. Gimp::Fu will then generate a horizontal frame with radio buttons, one for each alternative. For example:

```
[PF_RADIO, "direction", "the direction to move to", 5,\
                    [Left => 5, Right => 7]]]
```

draws two buttons, when the first (the default, "Left") is activated, 5 will be returned. If the second is activated, 7 is returned.

PF_FONT

Lets the user select a font and returns an X Logical Font Descriptor (XLFD). The default argument, if specified, must be a full XLFD specification, or a warning will be printed. Please note that the Gimp text functions using these fontnames (gimp_text_..._fontname) ignore the size. You can extract the size and dimension by using the xlfd_size function.

In older Gimp-Versions a user-supplied string is returned.

PF_BRUSH, PF_PATTERN, PF_GRADIENT

Lets the user select a brush/pattern/gradient whose name is returned as a string. The default brush/pattern/gradient–name can be preset.

PF_CUSTOM

PF_CUSTOM is for those of you requiring some nonstandard-widget. You have to supply a code reference returning three values as the extra argument:

```
(widget, settor, gettor)
```

widget is Gtk widget that should be used.

settor is a function that takes a single argument, the new value for the widget (the widget should be updated accordingly).

gettor is a function that should return the current value of the widget.

While the values can be of any type (as long as it fits into a scalar), be prepared to get a string when the script is started from the commandline or the PDB.

PF_FILE

This represents a file system object. It usually is a file, but can be anything (directory, link). It might not even exist at all.

MISCELLANEOUS FUNCTIONS

save_image(img,options_and_path)

This is the internal function used to save images. As it does more than just gimp_file_save, I thought it would be handy in other circumstances as well.

The img is the image you want to save (which might get changed during the operation!), options_and_path denotes the filename and optinal options. If there are no options, save_image tries to deduce the filetype from the extension. The syntax for options is

```
[IMAGETYPE[OPTIONS...]:]filespec
```

IMAGETYPE is one of GIF, JPG, JPEG, PNM or PNG options include

options valid for all images

+F	flatten the image (default depends on the image)
–F	do not flatten the image

options for GIF and PNG images

+I	do save as interlaced (GIF only)
–I	do not save as interlaced (default)

options for PNG images

–Cn	use compression level n

options for JPEG images

–Qn	use quality "n" to save file (JPEG only)
–S	do not smooth (default)
+S	smooth before saving

some examples:

`test.jpg`	save the image as a simple jpeg
`JPG:test.jpg`	same
`JPG-Q70:test.jpg`	the same but force a quality of 70 "
`GIF-I-F:test.jpg`	save a gif image(!) named test.jpg non-inerlaced and without flattening

AUTHOR

Marc Lehmann <pcg@goof.com>

SEE ALSO

perl(1), the *Gimp* manpage.

Gimp::OO Man Page

Name

Gimp::OO — Pseudo-OO for Gimp functions.

Synopsis

```
use Gimp;   # Gimp::OO is now part of Gimp.
```

Description

As you might have noticed, you can sort most Gimp functions into three groups, depending on the nameprefix: gimp_, plug_in_, extension_ etc.

What's more, there are functions groups like gimp_image_ or gimp_selection_, operating on a common object, **Images** and **Selection** in this case.

If you only had the plain syntax, your scripts would quickly acquire the "vertical Gimp syndrome":

```
gimp_palette_set_foreground(...)
                  gimp_layer_new(...)
                  gimp_palette_set_background(...)
                  gimp_image_add_layer(...)
```

Of course, your fingers will suffer from severe injuries as well.

A solution to this situation is to use OO-syntax. Gimp plays some (very) dirty tricks and provides a number of classes, like Gimp::Image and Gimp::Palette that allow shorter identifiers to be used (all these appear with the Gimp:: prefix as well as without, i.e., Gimp::Palette is the same class as Palette).

If you call a method, Gimp tries to find a Gimp function by prepending a number of prefixes until it finds a valid function:

```
$image = Gimp->image_new(...);
              # calls gimp_image_new(...)

$image = Image->new(...);
              # calls gimp_image_new as well

$image = new Image(...);
              # the same in green

Palette->set_foreground(...)
              #calls
              #gimp_palette_set_foreground(..)
```

Return values from functions are automatically blessed (through The Magic Autobless feature ;) to their corresponding classes, i.e.:

```
$image = new Image(...);
              # $image is now blessed to
              # Gimp::Image
```

```
$image->height;
             # calls gimp_image_height($image)
$image->flatten;
             # likewise gimp_flatten($image)
$image->histogram(...);
             # calls gimp_histogram($image,...),
             # since gimp_image_histogram
             # does not exist
```

The class argument ($image in the above examples) is prepended to the argument list.

Another shortcut: Many functions want a (redundant) image argument, like:

```
$image->shear ($layer, ...)
```

Because all you want is to shear the $layer, not the $image, this is confusing as well. In cases like this, Gimp allows you to write:

```
$layer->shear (...)
```

and automatically infers the additional IMAGE-type argument.

As the (currently) last goodie, if the first argument is of type INT32, its name is "run_mode" and there are no other ambiguties, you can omit it, i.e. these three calls are equivalent:

```
plug_in_gauss_rle (RUN_NONINTERACTIVE, $image, $layer, 8, 1, 1);
plug_in_gauss_rle ($image, $layer, 8, 1, 1);
plug_in_gauss_rle ($layer, 8, 1, 1);
```

You can call all sorts of sensible and not-so-sensible functions, so this feature can be abused:

```
patterns_list Image;     # will call gimp_patterns_list
quit Plugin;             # will quit the Gimp, not an Plugin.
```

There is no image involved here whatsoever.

AVAILABLE CLASSES

The following classes (with and without Gimp::) are available. The prefixes that are checked are shown as well (the null prefix "" is implicit).

Gimp (there is no Gimp::Gimp, only Gimp::)

```
gimp_
```

Layer

```
gimp_layer_
                  gimp_drawable_
                  gimp_floating_sel_
                  gimp_image_
```

```
                gimp_
                plug_in_
```

Image

```
gimp_image_
                gimp_drawable_
                gimp_
                plug_in_
```

Drawable

```
gimp_drawable_
                gimp_layer_
                gimp_image_
                gimp_
                plug_in_
```

Selection

```
gimp_selection_
```

Channel

```
gimp_channel_
                gimp_drawable_
                gimp_selection_
                gimp_image_
                gimp_
                plug_in_
```

Display

```
gimp_display_
                gimp_
```

Palette

```
gimp_palette_
```

Plugin

```
plug_in_
```

Gradients

```
gimp_gradients_
```

Edit

```
gimp_edit_
```

Progress

```
gimp_progress_
```

Region

(none except the implicit null prefix)

Tile

```
gimp_tile_
```

PixelRgn

```
gimp_pixel_rgn_
```

GDrawable

```
gimp_gdrawable_
```

Brushes

```
gimp_brushes_
```

Parasite

```
parasite_
                              gimp_
```

AUTHOR

Marc Lehmann <pcg@goof.com>

SEE ALSO

perl(1), the *Gimp* manpage.

Gimp::Data Man Page

Name

Gimp::Data — Set and get state data.

Synopsis

```
use Gimp::Data;
$Gimp::Data{'value1'} = "Hello";
                  print $Gimp::Data{'value1'},", World!!\n";
```

Description

With this module, you can access plug-in-specific (or global) data in Gimp, i.e., you can store and retrieve values that are stored in the main Gimp application.

An example would be to save parameter values in Gimp, so that on subsequent invocations of your plug-in, the user does not have to set all parameter values again (the *Gimp::Fu* man page does this already).

%Gimp::Data

You can store and retrieve anything you like in this hash. Its contents will automatically be stored in Gimp, and can be accessed in later invocations of your plug-in. Be aware that other plug-ins store data in the same "hash", so better prefix your key with something unique, like your plug-in's name. As an example, the Gimp::Fu module uses "function_name/_fu_data" to store its data.

This module might use a persistent implementation, i.e., your data might survive a restart of the Gimp application, but you cannot count on this.

Limitations

You cannot store references, and you cannot (yet) iterate through the keys (with keys, values or each).

Author

Marc Lehmann <pcg@goof.com>

See Also

perl(1), the *Gimp* manpage.

GIMP::UTIL MAN PAGE

NAME

Gimp::Util — some handy routines for Gimp-Perl users

SYNOPSIS

```
      use Gimp;
                              use Gimp::Util;
```

DESCRIPTION

Gimp-Perl is nice, but when you have to write 10 lines every time just to get some simple functions done, it very quickly becomes tedious :-/

This module tries to define some functions that aim to automate frequently used tasks, i.e. it's a sort of catchall–bag for (possibly) useful macro functions. If you want to add a function just mail the author of the GimpPerl extension (see below).

In Gimp–Perl (but not in Gimp as seen by the end user) it is possible to have layers that are NOT attached to an image. This is, IMHO a bad idea, you end up with them and the user cannot see them or delete them. So we always attach our created layers to an image here, to avoid memory leaks and debugging times.

These functions try to preserve the current settings like colors, but not all do.

Also: These functions are handled in exactly the same way as PDB-Functions, i.e., the (hypothetical) function gimp_image_xyzzy can be called as $image–>xyzzy, if the module is available.

The need to explicitly use Gimp::Util will go away in the future.

FUNCTIONS

get_state (), set_state state

get_state returns a scalar representing most of Gimp's global state (at the moment foreground color, background color, active gradient, pattern and brush). The state can later be restored by a call to set_state. This is ideal for library functions such as the ones used here, at least when it includes more state in the future.

layer_create image, name, color, pos

Creates a colored layer, insert into image and return layer.

text_draw imag, layer, text, font, size, fgcolor

Creates a colored text, draw over a background, add to img, ret img.

image_create_text text, font, size, fgcolor, bgcolor

Creates an image, add colored text layer on a background layer, return img.

layer_add_layer_as_mask image, layer, layermask

Takes a layer and add it as a mask to another layer, return mask.

gimp_text_wh $text, $fontname

Returns the width and height of the "$text" of the given font (XLFD format)

gimp_drawable_mask $drawable

Returns an array (x,y,w,h) containing the upper-left corner and the size of the current mask, just as needed by pixelrgn and similar functions.

gimp_image_layertype $alpha

Returns the corresponding layer type for an image, alpha controls whether the layer type is with alpha or not. Example: imagetype: RGB -> RGB_IMAGE (or RGBA_IMAGE).

gimp_image_add_new_layer $image, $index, $fill_type, $alpha

Creates a new layer and adds it at position $index (default 0) to the image, after filling it with gimp_drawable_fill $fill_type (default BG_IMAGE_FILL). If $alpha is non-zero (default 1), the new layer has alpha.

gimp_image_set_visible $image, @layers,

gimp_image_set_invisible $image,@layers mark the given layers visible (invisible) and all others invisible (visible).

gimp_layer_get_position $layer

Returns the position the layer has in the image layer stack.

gimp_layer_set_position $layer, $new_index

Moves the layer to a new position in the layer stack.

AUTHOR

Various, version 1.000 written mainly by Tels (http://bloodgate.com/). The author of the Gimp–Perl extension (contact him to include new functions) is Marc Lehmann <pcg@goof.com>

GIMP::PIXEL MAN PAGE

NAME

Gimp::Pixel — how to operate on raw pixels

SYNOPSIS

```
use Gimp;
use Gimp::PDL;     # you need Gimp::PDL for pixel access
use PDL;           # to make sensible things with the pixels

# Gimp::GDrawable - The GDrawable structure
# Gimp::Tile      - The Tile family of functions.
# Gimp::PixelRgn  - The PixelRgn family of functions.
```

DESCRIPTION

You can access the pixels in a drawable through tiles or pixel regions. This man page explains how this is done in Perl. All classes (Gimp::GDrawable, Gimp::Tile, Gimp::PixelRgn) are available with and without the Gimp:: prefix.

GDRAWABLES

Well, you know drawables (also known as PARAM_DRAWABLE or Gimp::Drawable)? In Gimp, drawables are things you can draw on: layers, channels or whole images. While most functions named gimp_drawable_something operate on drawable_IDs, some functions (notably the ones operating on raw pixel data!) need a GDrawable instead. Every drawable has a corresponding GDrawable; you can get it with the gimp_drawable_get function:

```
my $gdrawable = $drawable->get;
```

When the $gdrawable is destroyed, it is automatically flushed and detached, so you don't need to do this yourself.

TILES

Tiles are the basic building blocks of all drawables. Each drawable consists of a "grid" of tiles, each tile having the same size. The size of a tile is always the same (it's hardcoded in your Gimp program).

The gimp_tile_width and gimp_tile_height functions return the current width/height of a tile (at the moment, this is 64x64).

How do I get a tile? First, you have to grab a GDrawable structure. You can get one from any drawable, by calling the get function:

```
my $gdrawable = $drawable->get;
```

In a sense, <$gdrawable> contains all tiles. Changes you make to them might not be reflected in the image until you destroy this variable. (Thats the reason I used "my" in the above example. Once $gdrawable gets out of scope, the drawable in the Gimp automatically gets updated).

To get access to a tile, you have to call get_tile or get_tile2. get_tile expects row/column numbers of the tile, while get_tile2 expects pixel coordinates and will return the tile that pixel is in:

```
my $tile = $gdrawable->get_tile2(1,75,60);
```

The data method returns and sets the raw pixel data.

```
$piddle = $tile->data; # get the tile data as a piddle
$piddle *= 0.5;        # do sth. with the pixels
$tile->data($piddle); # and modify the tile
```

PixelRegions

PixelRegions are rectangular parts of a drawable. You can access single pixels, rows, columns and rectangles within these regions. Don't expect me to explain everything now, I don't understand the mechanism too well myself.

How do I create a pixel region? First, you have to grab a GDrawable structure. You can get one from any drawable, by calling the get function:

```
my $gdrawable = $drawable->get;
```

Now, you can create as many PixelRgn structures as you want from the GDrawable:

```
my $region = new PixelRgn($gdrawable,0,0,50,30,1,0); # with "new"
my $region = $gdrawable->pixel_rgn(0,0,50,30,1,0);#or from a \
                                                   #drawable
```

Which method you choose is purely a question of style...

The following functions return packed pixel data (see the *Gimp::PDL* man page for an easier way to manipulate on image data):

```
$piddle = $region->get_pixel(45,60);
                  #return the pixel at (45|60)
$piddle = $region->get_row(45,60,10);
                  #return ten horizontal pixels
$piddle = $region->get_col(45,60,10);
                  #same but vertically
$piddle = $region->get_rect(45,60,10,12);
                  #a 10x12 rectangle
```

To modify pixels, the dirty bit of the region must be set (I believe, but I don't see what the dirty bit in a region is for, so I might be wrong), and you can write pixel data to the region with the following functions, each one corresponding to a get-function:

```
$region->set_pixel($piddle,45,60);
                  # set pixel at (45|60)
$region->set_row($piddle,45,60);
                  # set a row "
```

```
$region->set_col($piddle,45,60);
                        # set a column
$region->set_rect($piddle,45,60);
                        # set a whole rectangle
```

Please note that (unlike the C functions they call), the size arguments (width and/or height) are missing; they can be calculated from the piddle.

AUTHOR

Marc Lehmann <pcg@goof.com>

SEE ALSO

perl(1), Gimp(1).

GIMP::COMPAT MAN PAGE

NAME

Gimp::Compat — compatibility functions for older versions of Gimp.

SYNOPSIS

<loaded automatically on demand>

DESCRIPTION

Older versions of Gimp (version 1.0 at the time of this writing) lack some very important or useful functions.

This module is providing the most needed replacement functions. If you happen to miss a function, then please create a replacement function and send it to me ;)

These functions are handled in exactly the same way as PDB-Functions, i.e., the (hypothetical) function gimp_image_xyzzy can be called as $image->xyzzy, if the module is available.

FUNCTIONS

gimp_text_fontname, gimp_get_extents_fontname

These are emulated in 1.0.

gimp_paintbrush

The last two arguments only available in 1.1 are simply dropped.

AUTHOR

Various, Dov Grobgeld <dov@imagic.weizmann.ac.il>. The author of the Gimp-Perl extension (contact him to include new functions) is Marc Lehmann <pcg@goof.com>

GIMP::FEATURE MAN PAGE

NAME

Gimp::Features — check for specific features to be present before registering the script.

SYNOPSIS

```
use Gimp::Features;
```

or

```
use Gimp::Features qw(feature1 feature2 ...);
```

DESCRIPTION

This module can be used to check for specific features to be present. This can be used to deny running the script when neccessary features are not present. While some features can be checked for at any time, the Gimp::Fu module offers a nicer way to check for them.

gtk

Checks for the presence of the gtk interface module.

gtk-1.1, gtk-1.2

Checks for the presence of gtk–1.1 (1.2) or higher.

perl-5.005

Checks for Perl version 5.005 or higher.

pdl

Checks for the presence of a suitable version of PDL (>=1.9906).

gnome

Checks for the presence of the Gnome-Perl module.

gtkxmhtl

Checks for the presence of the Gtk::XmHTML module.

unix

Checks whether the script runs on a unix-like operating system. At the moment, this is every system except windows, macos, os2 and vms.

gimp-1.1, gimp-1.2

Checks for the presense of Gimp in at least version 1.1 (1.2).

This feature can only be checked **after** Gimpmain> has been called (usually found in the form exit main). See the *Gimp::Fu* man page on how to check for these.

FUNCTIONS

present(feature)

Checks for the presense of the single feature given as the argument. Returns true if the feature is present, false otherwise.

need(feature,(function-name))

Requires a specific feature. If the required feature is not present, the program will exit gracefully, logging an appropriate message. You can optionally supply a function name to further specify the place where this feature was missing.

This is the function used when importing symbols from the module.

missing(feature-description,(function-name))

Indicates that a generic feature (described by the first argument) is missing. A function name can further be specified. This function will log the given message and exit gracefully.

describe(feature)

Returns a string describing the given feature in more detail, or undef if there is no description for this feature.

list()

Returns a list of features that can be checked for. This list might not be complete.

Author

Marc Lehmann <pcg@goof.com>

See Also

perl(1), Gimp(1).

Gimp::Config Man Page

Name

Gimp::Config — config options found during configure time.

Description

The Gimp::Config module creates a tied hash %Gimp::Config which contains all the definitions the configure script and Perl deduced from the system configuration at configure time. You can access these values just like you access any other values, i.e., $Gimp::Config{KEY}. Some important keys are:

IN_GIMP	=> true when Gimp-Perl was part of the Gimp distribution.
GIMP	=> the path of the Gimp executable
prefix	=> the installation prefix
libdir	=> the Gimp system-wide libdir
bindir	=> paths where Gimp binaries are installed
gimpplugindir	=> the Gimp plug-in directory (without the /plug-ins–suffix)

See Also

The *Gimp* man page.

Gimp::Pod Man Page

Name

Gimp::Pod — Evaluate pod documentation embedded in scripts.

Synopsis

```
use Gimp::Pod;

$pod = new Gimp::Pod;
```

```
$text = $pod->format ();
$html = $pod->format ('html');
$synopsis = $pod->section ('SYNOPSIS');
$author = $pod->author;
@sections = $pod->sections;
```

DESCRIPTION

Gimp::Pod can be used to find and parse embedded pod documentation in Gimp-Perl scripts. At the moment, only the formatted text can be fetched; future versions might have more interesting features.

METHODS

new

Returns a new Gimp::Pod object representing the current script or undef, if an error occurred.

format(($format))

Returns the embedded pod documentation in the given format, or undef if no documentation can be found. Format can be one of 'text', 'html', 'man' or 'latex'. If none is specified, 'text' is assumed.

section($header)

Tries to retrieve the section with the header $header. There is no trailing newline on the returned string, which may be undef in case the section can't be found.

copyright

Tries to retrieve fields suitable for calls to the register function.

sections

Returns a list of paragraphs found in the pod.

AUTHOR

Marc Lehmann <pcg@goof.com>

SEE ALSO

perl(1), Gimp(1),

GIMP::NET MAN PAGE

NAME

Gimp::Net — Communication module for the Gimp–Perl server.

SYNOPSIS

```
use Gimp;
```

DESCRIPTION

For Gimp::Net (and thus commandline and remote scripts) to work, you first have to install the "Perl-Server" extension somewhere where Gimp can find it (e.g.,, in your .gimp/plug-ins/ directory). Usually, this is done automatically while installing the Gimp extension. If you have a menu entry C<<Xtns>/Perl-Server> then it is probably installed.

The Perl Server can either be started from the C<<Xtns>> menu in Gimp, or automatically when a Perl script can't find a running Perl Server.

When started from within Gimp, the Perl-Server will create a unix domain socket to which local clients can connect. If an authorization password is given to the Perl Server (by defining the environment variable GIMP_HOST before starting Gimp), it will also listen on a tcp port (default 10009). Since the password is transmitted in cleartext, using the Perl-Server over tcp effectively **lowers the security of your network to the level of telnet**. Even worse: The current Gimp::Netprotocol can be used for denial of service attacks, i.e., crashing the Perl Server. There also *might* be buffer overflows.

ENVIRONMENT

The environment variable GIMP_HOST specifies the default server to contact and/or the password to use. The syntax is [auth@][tcp/]hostname[:port] for tcp, [auth@]unix/local/socket/path for unix and spawn/ for a private gimp instance. Examples are:

```
www.yahoo.com                    # just kidding ;)"
yahoo.com:11100                  # non-standard port "
tcp/yahoo.com                    # make sure it uses tcp
authorize@tcp/yahoo.com:123      # full-fledged specification "
unix/tmp/unx                     # use unix domain socket "
password@unix/tmp/test           # additionally use a password "
authorize@                       # specify authorization only "
spawn/                           # use a private gimp instance "
spawn/nodata                     # pass --no-data switch "
spawn/gui                        # don't pass -n switch
```

CALLBACKS

net()

Is called after you have succesfully connected to the server. Do your dirty work in this function, or see the *Gimp::Fu* man page for a better solution.

FUNCTIONS

server_quit()

Sends the Perl Server a quit command.

get_connection()

Return a connection id which uniquely identifies the current connection.

set_connection(conn_id)

Set the connection to use on subsequent commands. conn_id is the connection id as returned by *get_connection( )*.

BUGS

(Ver 0.04) This module is much faster than it was thought to be... Silly that I wondered whether I should implement it in Perl or C, since Perl is so fast.

AUTHOR

Marc Lehmann <pcg@goof.com>

SEE ALSO

perl(1), the *Gimp* manpage.

21/May/99 Perl 5.004, patch 04 1

GIMP::LIB MAN PAGE

NAME

Gimp::Lib — Interface to libgimp (as opposed to Gimp::Net)

Synopsis

```
use Gimp; # internal use only
```

Description

This is the package that interfaces to Gimp via the libgimp interface, i.e., the normal interface to use with Gimp. You don't normally use this module directly, look at the documentation for the package "Gimp".

Author

Marc Lehmann <pcg@goof.com>

See Also

perl(1), the *Gimp* man page.

Gimp::PDL Man Page

Name

Gimp::PDL — Overwrite Tile/Region functions to work with piddles. This module is obsolete, please remove any references to it.

Synopsis

```
use Gimp;
                  use Gimp::PDL;
                  use PDL;
```

Description

This module overwrites some methods of Gimp::Tile and Gimp::PixelRgn. The new functions return and accept piddles. The last argument (height) of gimp_pixel_rgn_set_rect is calculated from the piddle. There is no other way to access the raw pixeldata in Gimp.

Some examples:

```
$region = $drawable->get->pixel_rgn (0,0, 100,100, 1,0);

$pixel = $region->get_pixel (5,7);
                  # fetches the pixel from (5|7)

print $pixel; " "
                  # outputs something like
```

```
                     # [255, 127, 0], i.e. in
                     # RGB format ;)
$region->set_pixel ($pixel * 0.5, 5, 7);
                     # darken the pixel
$rect = $region->get_rect (3,3,70,20);
                     # get a horizontal stripe "
$rect = $rect->hclip(255/5)*5;
                     # clip and multiply by 5
$region->set_rect($rect); " "
                     # and draw it! "
undef $region; " "
                     # and update it!
```

Author

Marc Lehmann <pcg@goof.com>

See Also

The *Gimp::Pixel* man page, perl(1), Gimp(1).

This module is obsolete, please remove any references to it.

Gimp::UI Man Page

Name

Gimp::UI — "simulation of libgimpui", and more!

Synopsis

```
use Gimp::UI;
```

Description

Due to the brain-damaged (read: "unusable") libgimpui API, I had to reimplement all of it in Perl.

```
$option_menu = new Gimp::UI::ImageMenu
$option_menu = new Gimp::UI::LayerMenu
$option_menu = new Gimp::UI::ChannelMenu
```

```
$option_menu = new Gimp::UI::DrawableMenu \
                (constraint_func, active_element, \var);

$button = new Gimp::UI::PatternSelect;

$button = new Gimp::UI::BrushSelect;

$button = new Gimp::UI::GradientSelect;

$button = new Gimp::UI::ColorSelectButton;
```

AUTHOR

Marc Lehmann <pcg@goof.com>. The ColorSelectButton code is written by Dov Grobgeld <dov@imagic.weizmann.ac.il>, with modifications by Kenneth Albanowski <kjahds@kjahds.com>.

SEE ALSO

perl(1), the *Gimp* man page.

APPENDIX E

Sane-Supported Scanners

This appendix provides a list of scanners supported by Sane 1.0.1.

LEGEND

You need to enable this backend in Sanes `dll.conf` (in the `sane config` directory). Otherwise, Sane will not enable your scanner.

There are four types of status:

- Stable: This is proven and works well if it's supported.
- Beta: Usually works just fine but it can sometimes hit a bug.
- Alpha: This may work but it needs more development and debugging.
- New: This package is so new that it doesn't have a qualified status.

The comments column often indicates how well the backend works. (It can be wise to run `find-scanner` to find out more about the notes.)

Manufacturer	Model	Backend	Status	Comment
Abaton	Scan 300/GS	abaton	alpha	All known modes and functions supported
	Scan 300/S	abaton	alpha	Untested, use with caution
AGFA	Focus GS	agfafocus	alpha	6 bit gray
	Focus Lineart	agfafocus	alpha	Lineart only? Untested
	Focus II	agfafocus	alpha	Gray only
	Focus Color	agfafocus	alpha	
	Focus Color Plus	agfafocus	alpha	3-pass
	Arcus II	microtek	beta	Arcus *II*, not Arcus!
	StudioScan II	microtek	beta	Not quite functional yet
	StudioScan IIsi	microtek	beta	Not quite functional yet
	SnapScan 300	SnapScan	alpha	Only 8 bits/sample
	SnapScan 310	SnapScan	alpha	Only 8 bits/sample
	SnapScan 600	SnapScan	alpha	Only 8 bits/sample
	SnapScan 1236s	SnapScan	alpha	Only 8 bits/sample
Apple	Apple Scanner	apple	alpha	4 bit, 16 shades of gray
	OneScanner	apple	alpha	8 bit, 256 shades of gray; backend needs more work
	ColorOneScanner	apple	alpha	Only non-color modes
Artec/Ultima	AT3	artec	alpha	Works (developer's own model)
	A6000C	artec	alpha	Very alpha
	A6000C PLUS	artec	alpha	Testing in progress
	AT6	artec	alpha	Testing in progress
	AT12	artec	alpha	Testing in progress
BlackWidow	BW4800SP	artec	alpha	Rebadged Artec AT3
Canon	CanoScan 300	canon	alpha	1 pass; flatbed scanner
	CanoScan 600	canon	alpha	1 pass; flatbed scanner
	CanoScan 2700F	canon	alpha	1 pass; film scanner
Escom	Image Scanner 256	umax	stable	SCSI-ID=UMAX UG 80

Manufacturer	Model	Backend	Status	Comment
Epson	GT-5500	epson	?	OK
	GT-7000	epson	?	OK
HP	HP ScanJet Plus	hp	alpha	
	HP ScanJet IIc	hp	alpha	
	HP ScanJet IIp	hp	alpha	
	HP ScanJet IIcx	hp	alpha	
	HP ScanJet 3c	hp	alpha	
	HP ScanJet 4c	hp	alpha	
	HP ScanJet 6100C	hp	alpha	
	HP ScanJet 3p	hp	alpha	
	HP ScanJet 4p	hp	alpha	
	HP ScanJet 5p	hp	alpha	
	HP ScanJet 6200C	hp	alpha	
	HP ScanJet 6250C	hp	alpha	
	HP PhotoSmart PhotoScanner	hp	alpha	
Kodak	DC20	dc25	alpha	DC-20 is untested!
	DC25	dc25	alpha	
	DC210	dc210	alpha	
Linotype Hell	Jade	umax	stable	SCSI-ID=LinoHell Office
	Jade2	umax	stable	SCSI-ID=LinoHell Office2
	Saphir	umax	stable	Not tested
	Saphir2	umax	stable	SCSI-ID=LinoHell SAPHIR2
	Saphir Ultra	umax	stable	Not tested
	Saphir Ultra II	umax	stable	Not tested
	Saphir HiRes	umax	stable	Not tested
	Opal	umax	stable	Not tested
	Opal Ultra	umax	stable	Not tested
Microtek	ScanMaker E6	microtek	beta	
	ScanMaker E3	microtek	beta	
	ScanMaker E2	microtek	beta	3-pass
	ScanMaker 35t+	microtek	beta	Slide-scanner
	ScanMaker III	microtek	beta	
	ScanMaker IISP	microtek	beta	
	ScanMaker IIHR	microtek	beta	3-pass
	ScanMaker IIG	microtek	beta	Gray only
	ScanMaker II	microtek	beta	3-pass
	ScanMaker 600Z(S)	microtek	beta	Untested
	ScanMaker 600G(S)	microtek	beta	Gray only

Manufacturer	Model	Backend	Status	Comment
	ScanMaker V300	microtek2	alpha	
	ScanMaker V310	microtek2	alpha	
	ScanMaker V600	microtek2	alpha	
	ScanMaker E3plus	microtek2	alpha	
	ScanMaker X6	microtek2	alpha	
	ScanMaker X6EL	microtek2	alpha	
	ScanMaker 330	microtek2	alpha	
	ScanMaker 630	microtek2	alpha	
	ScanMaker 636	microtek2	alpha	
	ScanMaker 9600XL	microtek2	alpha	Only flatbed mode (?)
	Phantom 636	microtek2	alpha	
Mustek	MFC-600S	mustek	beta	1 pass; (f/w >= 1.01; scsi id MFC-06000CZ)
	MFC-600CD	mustek	beta	1 pass; (f/w >= 2.03; scsi id MFC-06000CZ)
	MFS-6000CX	mustek	beta	3 pass; (f/w >= 2.71; scsi id MSF-06000CX
	MSF-6000SP	mustek	beta	1 pass; (f/w >= 3.12; scsi id MSF-06000SP)
	MFS-8000SP	mustek	beta	1 pass; (f/w >= 2.05; scsi id MSF-08000SP) lineart drops lines?
	MFC-800S	mustek	beta	1 pass; (f/w == 1.06; scsi id MFC-08000CZ) color fails?
	MFS-1200SP	mustek	beta	1 pass; (f/w == 1.00; scsi id MSF-12000SP)
	MFS-1200SP	mustek	beta	1 pass; (f/w == 1.07; scsi id MFS-12000SP)
	MFS-1200SP	mustek	beta	1 pass; (f/w == 1.02; scsi id MFS-12000SP) color fails?
	MFS-12000CX	mustek	beta	3 pass; (f/w == 2.71; scsi id MFS-12000CX)
	SE-6000SP		beta	1 pass; (f/w == ? ; scsi id C03 S10IDW)
	SE-12000SP		beta	1 pass; (f/w == 1.01; scsi id C06 S12IDW)
Nikon	LS-20	coolscan	beta	LS-30 is not supported
	LS-1000	coolscan	beta	Doesn't support gamma correction
	AX-210	umax	stable	
Polaroid	DMC	dmc	stable	
Plustek	Plustek 4830	plustek	beta	
Qtronix	Sagitta Gray	sagitta	alpha	No monocrome-mode at the moment

Manufacturer	Model	Backend	Status	Comment
SHARP	JX-610	sharp	new	Preview/Color Lineart/Lineart/ Threshold does not work
	JX-250	sharp	new	Color Lineart does not give useful output
	JX-330	sharp	new	Not tested
Siemens	S9036	agfafocus	alpha	Gray only
	ST400	st400	alpha	6 bit gray
Tamarack	Artiscan 6000C	tamarack	beta	3 pass, 300 DPI; please report success to **R.E.Wolff@BitWizard.nl**
	Artiscan 8000C	tamarack	beta	3 pass, 400 DPI; please report success to **R.E.Wolff@BitWizard.nl**
	Artiscan 12000C	tamarack	beta	3 pass, 600 DPI
UMAX	Vista S6	umax	stable	
	Vista S6E	umax	stable	
	UMAX S-6E	umax	stable	
	UMAX S-6EG	umax	stable	
	Vista-S8	umax	stable	Not tested
	Supervista S-1	umax	stable	
	UMAX S-12	umax	stable	
	UMAX S-12G	umax	stable	
	Astra 600S	umax	stable	
	Astra 610S	umax	stable	
	Astra 1200S	umax	stable	
	Astra 1220S	umax	stable	
	UC 630	umax	stable	Version 1.6 OK, others only lineart OK
	UG 630	umax	stable	
	UG 80	umax	stable	
	UC 840	umax	stable	Version 1.6 OK, others only lineart OK
	UC 1260	umax	stable	Version 1.6 OK, others unknown
	Mirage	umax	stable	Not tested
	Mirage II	umax	stable	Not tested
	Mirage IIse	umax	stable	Not tested
	Vista-T630	umax	stable	OK for some firmware versions; on others only lineart
	PSD	umax	stable	
	PowerLook	umax	stable	Not tested
	PL-III	umax	stable	Only works with some scanners (unknown why)
	PowerLook III	umax	stable	Not tested
	PowerLook 2000	umax	stable	Not tested
	PowerLook 3000	umax	stable	Not tested
	Gemini D-16	umax	stable	

Manufacturer	Model	Backend	Status	Comment
Vobis	HighScan	microtek2	alpha	Only E3plus-based models
Vobis/Highscree	Scanboostar Premium	umax	stable	OK, SCSI-ID=LinoHell Office2
Vuego	310S	SnapScan	alpha	Close SnapScan 310-compatible

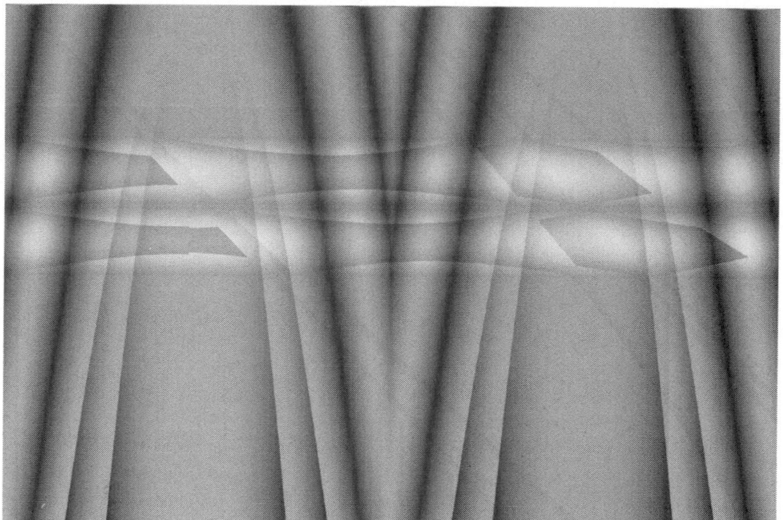

Appendix F

Links And References

In this appendix, you will find all kinds of Gimp-related links. You will also find some bibliographic links to useful books, or books that we use at Frozen-river.

LINKS

Web

Resource	URL
The one and only Gimp.org	`http://www.gimp.org`
Latest Gimp news	`http://xach.dorknet.com/gimp/news/index.html`
Plug-in registry to the latest plug-ins available for Gimp; you can also upload your own plug-ins here	`http://registry.gimp.org`
Gimp FAQs	`http://www.rru.com/~meo/gimp`
GUM	`http://manual.gimp.org`
Scripts	`http://www.gimp.org/scripts.html`

IRC (dev chat) channel #Gimp

Server	Port	Location
irc.mint.net / irc.gimp.org	6666	Maine, USA
irc.canweb.net	6667	Toronto, Canada
irc.canberra.edu.au	6666	Canberra, Australia
irc.giblets.com	6667	Texas, USA
dazed.nol.net	6667	Texas, USA
irc.eanut.org	6667	Texas, USA
pandora.hrz.uni-bielefeld.de	6667	Germany
irc.chillin.org	6666	Florida, USA
irc.coherent.net	6667	Chicago, USA
irc.olg.com	6667	Maryland, USA

Books

Title	ISBN
Photoshop Web Techniques	1-56205-733-2
Preparing Digital Images for Print	0-07-882146-0
Photoshop WOW Book	0-201-88370-8
Desktop Scanners	0-13-080904-7
Looking Good in Print	1-56604-856-7

Mail

List	Address
gimp-developer	information at: `www.gimp.org/mailing_list.html` to subscribe or send mail to: `"majordomo@scam.xcf.berkeley.edu"` and put "subscribe gimp-developer yourname@your.domain" in the body
gimp-user	info at: `www.gimp.org/mailing_list.html` to subscribe send mail to: `"majordomo@scam.xcf.berkeley.edu"` and put "subscribe gimp-user yourname@your.domain" in the body
gimp-announce	info at: `www.gimp.org/mailing_list.html` to subscribe send mail to: `"majordomo@scam.xcf.berkeley.edu"` and put "subscribe gimp-announce you name@your.domain" in the body
Japanese Gimp mailing list	info at: `www.gimp.org/mailing_list.html` to subscribe send mail to: `"gimp@hypercore.co.jp"`
Hungarian Gimp mailing list	info at: `www.gimp.org/mailing_list.html` to subscribe send mail to: `listproc@kva.hu` with "SUBSCRIBE GIMP YOURNAME" as the subject where your name is yourname@your.domain

FTP

The main FTP site is ftp.gimp.org, but try to use a mirror near you.

Location	URL
Africa	ftp://ftp.is.co.za/applications/gimp/
Australia	ftp://gimp.zeta.org.au/
	ftp://ftp.au.gimp.org/pub/gimp/
	ftp://ftp.progsoc.uts.edu.au/pub/
Austria	ftp://gd.tuwien.ac.at/graphics/gimp/
Belgium	ftp://gimp.rug.ac.be/pub/gimp/
Croatia	ftp://ftp.linux.hr/pub/gnome/
Finland	ftp://ftp.funet.fi/pub/sci/graphics /packages/gimp
France	ftp://stef.u-picardie.fr/mirror/ftp.gimp.org/
	ftp://ftp.minet.net/pub/gimp/
Germany	ftp://infosoc.uni-koeln.de/pub/ftp.gimp.org/
	ftp://ftp.tuts.net/mirror/gimp.org/
	ftp://ftp.fh-heilbronn.de/mirrors/ftp.gimp.org/
Greece	ftp://sunsite.ics.forth.gr/sunsite/pub/gimp/
Japan	ftp://SunSITE.sut.ac.jp/pub/archives/packages/gimp/
	ftp://ftp.u-aizu.ac.jp/pub/graphics/tools/gimp/
	ftp://ring.nacsis.ac.jp/pub/graphics/gimp/
	ftp://ring.aist.go.jp/pub/graphics/gimp/
	ftp://ring.asahi-net.or.jp/pub/graphics/gimp/
	ftp://ring.so-net.ne.jp/pub/graphics/gimp/
	ftp://mirror.nucba.ac.jp/mirror/gimp
Korea	ftp://ftp.kreonet.re.kr/pub/tools/X11/ftp.gimp.org/
Poland	ftp://ftp.tuniv.szczecin.pl/pub/Linux/gimp
	ftp://sunsite.icm.edu.pl/pub/graphics/gimp
Romania	ftp://ftp.kappa.ro/pub/mirrors/mirrors-2/ftp.gimp.org/
Sweden	ftp://ftp.acc.umu.se/pub/gimp
	ftp://ftp.sunet.se/pub/gnu/gimp/
Taiwan	ftp://linux.cis.nctu.edu.tw/pub/packages/X/gimp/
Turkey	ftp://ftp.hun.edu.tr/pub/linux/gimp
United Kingdom	ftp://ftp.flirble.org/pub/X/gimp/
	ftp://ftp.lmh.ox.ac.uk/pub/linux/

Location	URL
	ftp://unix.hensa.ac.uk/mirrors/ftp.gimp.org/pub/gimp/
United States	ftp://ftp.insync.net/pub/mirrors/ftp.gimp.org/
	ftp://ftp.cs.umn.edu/pub/gimp/
	ftp://froody.res.cmu.edu/pub/gimp/
	ftp://gimp.cs.stevens-tech.edu/mirrors/gimp/
	ftp://ftp.ameth.org/pub/mirrors/ftp.gimp.org/

Perl-Fu

What	URL
Perl-Fu Home Page	http://gimp.pages.de
GTK Perl Module	ftp://ftp.gtk.org/pub/gtk/perl/
Perl	http://www.perl.com

Sane

Program	URL
Sane home page	http://www.mostng.com/sane
Sane program download	ftp://ftp.mostang.com/pub/sane
Xsane home page	http://www.wolfsburg.de/~rauch/sane/sane-xsane.html
Xsane download	See Xsane home page
Solaris SCSI drivers	ftp://ftp.fokus.gmd.de/pub/unix/kernel/scg/
Linux SCSI How-to	http://metalab.unc.edu/LDP/HOWTO/HOWTO-INDEX-3.html#ss3.1

Xinput

What	URL
XFree86 home page	http://www.xfree86.org
Xinput home page	http://lepied.com/xfree86/
Percompiled/Linux Xinput Intous drivers	http://www.levien.com/free/linux_intuos.html
Xinput how-to	http://www.gtk.org/~otaylor/xinput/howto/index.html
Gimp Xinput patch	http://www.gtk.org/~otaylor/xinput/patches.html

INDEX

G

M

N

O

P

U

V

W

X

Z